Śaivism
in
Philosophical Perspective

Śaivism in Philosophical Perspective

A Study of the Formative Concepts, Problems and Methods of Śaiva Siddhānta

K. SIVARAMAN

MOTILAL BANARSIDASS PUBLISHERS
PRIVATE LIMITED • DELHI

Reprint Edition: Delhi, 2001
First Edition : Varanasi, 1973

ISBN: 81-208-1771-0

Also available at:

MOTILAL BANARSIDASS

236, 9th Main III Block, Jayanagar, Bangalore 560 011
41 U.A. Bungalow Road, Jawahar Nagar, Delhi 110 007
8 Mahalaxmi Chamber, Warden Road, Mumbai 400 026
120 Royapettah High Road, Mylapore, Chennai 600 004
Sanas Plaza, 1302 Baji Rao Road, Pune 411 002
8 Camac Street, Calcutta 700 017
Ashok Rajpath, Patna 800 004
Chowk, Varanasi 221 001

Printed in India
BY JAINENDRA PRAKASH JAIN AT SHRI JAINENDRA PRESS,
A-45 NARAINA, PHASE-I, NEW DELHI 110 028
AND PUBLISHED BY NARENDRA PRAKASH JAIN FOR
MOTILAL BANARSIDASS PUBLISHERS PRIVATE LIMITED,
BUNGALOW ROAD, DELHI 110 007

To

My Father

PREFACE

Little need be said by way of apology for writing a book on Śaiva Siddhānta. There is always a scope for saying something new and something different especially in the field of religion where study cannot be separated from interpretation. Religious facts are meanings which need to be set every time they are approached in a new horizon of understanding. Like religious discourses which have to be given anew books on religion will have to be written anew.

The book is inspired by the personal conviction that a careful and patient study of Śaiva Siddhānta, which is a typical, though not the only formulation of Śaivism, should prove useful for a more balanced appraisal of Indian religiosity. Śaiva Siddhānta marks a distinct shift in the religio-philosophical consciousness of India and represents a unique reaction, culturally and existentially against the ascendency of positivism over the Indian mind. Through its long and rich history it represents a constructive reaction to the theological, ethical and aesthetic aspects of Vedānta. It provides a corrective to the view, entertained not without some justification, that Indian religious thought does not affirm freedom, love and personality. The importance of these values with reference to Christian situation has been the subject of discussion in the writings of contemporary religious thinkers like Tillich, Marcel, Berdyaev and Buber. In the light of my acquaintance with their writings, I restudied Śaiva Siddhānta and came to realise the deeper significance of these concepts not only for Śaiva Siddhānta but also for religion as such.

The book was originally submitted as a thesis for the degree of Doctor of Philosophy at the Department of Philosophy, Banaras Hindu University, some ten years ago. Only minor stylistic changes have been made. A systematic analysis of the chief concepts of Śaiva Siddhānta, less as a textual exposition than as free problematic construction within the framework of textual interpretation is what has been attempted. In making an analytical study of the philosophy of Śaiva Siddhānta traditionally accepted as normative, I have not felt it necessary to depart also from the traditional method of developing the sense of the formative ideas through a series of interrogations and answers. This seems to me still the best form of elicitting the meaning of a concept by means of sustained internal criticism. The views of the texts and commentaries are freely utilised wherever found adequate and relevant. No attempt has been made to trace the historical evolution of ideas or enter into a comparative study undertaken for the sake of comparison. The latter can be useful but they presuppose an earnest study of the ideas themselves. In analysing the religious dimension of Indian philosphical culture the analytical tools of contemporary philosophical thinking of Phenomenology and Existentialism are far more helpful than the traditional western concepts. The concept of Philosophy that is implied by the generality of Indian religious thought involves cognitive analyses but made avowedly in the service of explicating religious experience.

I must ask the readers to bear with the style of writing. The rendering of difficult and intricate texts into English has been anything but easy. I have concentrated on exactitude which has rather been at the cost of simplicity in construction. I have endeavoured to describe what the Śaiva philosopher believes in and practices rather than what he should believe, arguing as it were in the first person and interiorising all external criticisms.

I had the inestimable advantage of discussing Sanskrit texts with eminent Sanskrit scholars of Banaras. Mīmāṁsāratna A. Subrahmanya Shastri helped me to construe difficult passages from Sanskrit commentaries. To the memory of Panditarāja T. V. Ramachandra Dikshitar I can only pay my homage. He introduced me to the world of traditional scholarship in letter and spirit which made it possible for me to study Śivāgra Bhāṣya, the principal Sanskrit text utilised in the writing of the book. I have great pleasure in acknowledging with gratitude my debt to Professor T. R. V. Murti to whom I owe my general orientation to Indian Philosophy. I am grateful to my colleagues in the Department of Philosophy, Banaras Hindu University, specially to Drs. R. K. Tripathi and A. K. Chatterjee for their frank criticisms.

Dr. A. K. Chatterjee shouldered the most wearisome burden of correcting the proofs. To Dr. Miss Bithika Mukherji I am in special debt for her helpful suggestions regarding the reorganisation of chapters. My thanks are also due in no small measure to Dr. Miss Padma Misra and Dr. Miss K. Bokil who made valuable suggestions. Dr Padma Misra's was also the most arduous task of editorial assistance and supervision at a critical time during the printing of the book. I also greatly appreciate the help rendered at different stages of the writing of the book by my young friends Mr. T. Shivamurthy, Miss V. K. Annakutty, Miss Krishná Banerjee, and Fr. Chacko Valiaveetil. I also express my appreciation of the expeditiousness with which Messrs. Motilal Banarsidass could publish the book.

I pay my homage to the memory of the late Kāśīvāsī Arunandi Tambiran of Kāśī mutt, Tiruppanandal who was responsible for my coming to Banaras Hindu University to teach myself Śaiva Siddhānta.

Banaras Hindu University
11 Sept. 1972

K. SIVARAMAN

SCHEME OF TRANSLITERATION.

(TAMIL)

Vowels		Consonants	
அ	a	க	k
ஆ	ā	ச	c
இ	i	ட	ṭ, ḍ
ஈ	ī	த	t, d
உ	u	ப	p, b
ஊ	ū	ற	ṛ, tṛ, dṛ
எ	e	ர	r
ஏ	ē	ங	ṅ
ஐ	ai	ஞ	ñ
ஒ	o	ண	ṇ
ஓ	ō	ன	n
ஔ	au	ந	n
ஃ	ah	ம	m
		ய	y
		ல	l
		ள	ḷ
		ழ	z
		வ	v

SCHEME OF TRANSLITERATION

(SANSKRIT)

VOWELS :

अ	—	a	ऋ	—	ṛ	औ	—	au
आ	—	ā	ॠ	—	ṝ	*Anusvāra* (ं)	—	ṁ
इ	—	i	ऌ	—	ḷ	*Visarga* (:)	—	ḥ
ई	—	ī	ए	—	e			
उ	—	u	ऐ	—	ai			
ऊ	—	ū	ओ	—	o			

CONSONANTS :

Gutturals			*Palatals*			*Cerebrals*		
क्	—	k	च्	—	c	ट्	—	ṭ
ख्	—	kh	छ्	—	ch	ठ्	—	ṭh
ग्	—	g	ज्	—	j	ड्	—	ḍ
घ्	—	gh	झ्	—	jh	ढ्	—	ḍh
ङ्	—	ṅ	ञ्	—	ñ	ण्	—	ṇ

Dentals			*Labials*			*Semi-Vowels*		
त्	—	t	प्	—	p	य्	—	y
थ्	—	th	फ्	—	ph	र्	—	r
द्	—	d	ब्	—	b	ल्	—	l
ध्	—	dh	भ्	—	bh	व्	—	v
न्	—	n	म्	—	m			

Sibilants			*Aspirate*		
श्	—	ś	ह्	—	h
ष्	—	ṣ			
स्	—	s			

ABBREVIATIONS

BK	—	Bhoga-Kārikā
BS	—	Brahma-Sūtras
CVTS	—	Caturveda-Tātparya-Saṁgraha
IPV	—	Īśvara-Pratyabhijñā-Vimarśiṇī
MA	—	Mṛgendra-Āgama
MK	—	Mokṣa-Kārikā
MNP	—	Mukti-Niścaya-Perurai
NK	—	Nāda-Kārikā
Ñ	—	Ñānāmirtham (Tamil)
ÑVM	—	Ñānāvaraṇa Vilakka Māpāḍiam (Tamil)
PA	—	Pauṣkara-Āgama
PB	—	Pauṣkara-Bhāṣya
PMNK	—	Paramokṣa-Nirāsa-Kārikā
PP	—	Potri-p-pahrodai (Tamil)
RT	—	Ratna-Traya
SB	—	Śivāgra-Bhāṣya
SDS	—	Sarva-Darśana-Saṁgraha
SJB	—	Śivajñāna-Bodham (Sanskrit)
SÑP	—	Śivañāna-Potam (Tamil)
SKB	—	Śrikaṇṭha-Bhāṣya
SMD	—	Śivārkamaṇi-Dīpikā
SMKK	—	Śivasamavāda Maruppuk Kandanakandanam (Tamil)
SN	—	Saṁkalpa-Nirākaraṇam (Tamil)
SNP	—	Śivaneriprakāśam (Tamil)
SP	—	Śaiva-Paribhāṣā
SRS	—	Śataratna-Saṁgraha
SSM	—	Śruti-Sūkti-Mālā
SSP	—	Śaiva-Siddhānta-Paribhāṣā
SSUM	—	Śivasamavāda Urai Maruppu (Tamil)
STV	—	Śiva-Tattva-Viveka
SVP	—	Śiva-Prakāśam (Tamil)
TAP	—	Tiruvarutpayan (Tamil)
TKP	—	Tirukkalitruppadiyar (Tamil)
TM	—	Tiru Mandiram (Tamil)

TP	—	Tattva-Prakāśa
TTN	—	Tattva-Traya-Nirṇaya
TU	—	Tiru undiār
Māpāḍiam	—	Śivajñāna-Māpāḍiam (Tamil)
Supakkam	—	Śivajñāna-Siddhi-Supakkam (Tamil)
Parapakkam	—	Śivajñāna-Siddhi-Parapakkam (Tamil)
Sambandar	—	Sambandar-Tēvāram (Tamil)
Appar	—	Appar-Tēvāram (Tamil)
Sundarar	—	Sundarar-Tēvāram (Tamil)
Schomerus	—	Der Śaiva Siddhānta, eine Mystik Indiens
Ingalls	—	Material for the study of Navya-Nyāya

Table of Contents

BOOK THREE

ON BOND : PĀŚA

BOOK FOUR

ON SELF : PAŚU

I

INTRODUCTION TO THE PHILOSOPHY OF ŚAIVA SIDDHĀNTA

The Point of View

The 'philosophy' in the Philosophy of Śaiva Siddhānta requires an understanding of the nature of the general ethos of philosophical thinking in the Indian setting. The original source out of which systematic thinking developed in India is an attitude to life describable as 'religious' in the broadest sense of the term. Philosophical reflection was confronted from the very outset with a world of meaning which is religious. By religion we refer to an element in the structure of consciousness itself, not an item or enterprise of culture which arrives at some stage in its history under certain favourable conditions. Religion stands for the basic dispositional attitude, containing an under standing of life and the world in terms of their dimension of depth, which may be described as holy or sacred. As a basic structural characteristic of human existence itself, religion is indifferent to culture and epoch even though exercising a profound impact on them.[1]

Understanding philosophical reflection as a function of religion and religious life whose meaning is grasped in terms of structure rather than history and culture, precludes approaching the issue of the beginning of philosophy as any but a philosophical issue. The rise or beginning of philosophy is other than the simple chronological rise and development of a belief or theory. All reductive explanations in terms of circumstances of time, place and individual influences appear quite incpt in the case of Indian philosophical thinking. A concept of philosophy is implied in the generality of Indian philosophy requiring to be understood and appreciated in contradistinction to science and even culture, civilization and the life of the people, race or nation. Philosophy in so far as it is a human enterprise is surely affected by these climates; in abstracting it from the general cultural life of a nation and especially from the matrix of pre-philosophy from which it has emerged, one may truly run the risk of obscuring the significance of its problems and ideals.[2] Still, a philosophical doctrine has a timeless quality about it, a fundamental unalterableness of its quest coinciding with the unaltering core of human nature itself.[3]

The importance of the temporal flux for understanding a philosophical system in the Indian context should not however be underrated. What a philosophic doctrine contains may be true *a priori* and therefore timeless but when the 'interpreter' — philosophical systems are only systems of interpretations — claims that a philosophic doctrine expresses such and such an *a priori* claim, the interpreter's claim is pre-eminently a product of time and history. Rival philosophical systems of Indian religious thought are only seemingly static, existing side by side as it were, from without beginning. They are, equally, structures in time influencing each other in their different stages of development and at the same time retaining a discernible self-identity.[4] It is not therefore suggested that modifications or changes in the doctrinal growth of a philosophical system are unimportant. The system, even as it is viewed in terms of its logical inter-connectedness, must also be placed in a historical sequence. What is here suggested is that it is also equally necessary that a philosophical or theo-philosophical system like Śaiva Siddhānta[5] be placed on the map of the subject of which the system is a systematic interpretation.

In our inquiry concerning the beginning of Śaiva Siddhānta at any rate we shall not deal with it as a mere system of belief and faith of great antiquity but rather as a 'living' philosophical system. The philosophy of Śaiva Siddhānta is living in the sense that the issues it raises and answers are still live issues of great consequence for the thought and life of those who are grasped by it. It is therefore as much contemporary in its relevance as it indeed is old and traditional.[6] In so far as its problems are not merely of particular and local interest it belongs to the contexts of life as such rather than merely to the contexts of history. An inquiry into the beginning of Śaiva Siddhānta should not be an archaeological search for the origin of a cult or belief.[7] It should rather be an inquiry into that primordial situation out of which philosophy in its characteristic form as a view and a way of life as Śaiva Siddhānta could arise.

Indian philosophy approaches the question of the nature of philosophy in terms of the proper object of philosophical thought. It embodies in a picturesque way a genuine phenomenology of religious quest. The quest here implies paradoxically the conviction of possessing an adequate notion of the object of the quest, of thought having already reached its goal. Indian philosophy is not in this respect 'a free adventure' without any idea of the destination to be reached. The goal of the philosophical quest is in a sense present from the very beginning of the quest. It is present and yet does not render the quest superfluous. It guides the quest. To be able to ask for something one must have that partially. It cannot otherwise be the object of a quest. The quest for meaning already betrays in some measure being imbued with meaning. The philosopher has and has not that which he seeks.[8]

The quest of the Indian philosopher, broadly speaking, is the search for the transcendent, call it by any spatial image of height or depth. Experience is analysed with the sole object of discriminating the 'real' from the apparent, the true from the false.[9] Philosophic consciousness may be identified with this disposition to pierce the surface, to penetrate appearances and realize the real. It is the quest for and achieving of transcendence. The quest for transcendence constitutes the governing motive of reflection but the initial impulse to this activity may come, as it may be shown presently, from a source deeper than a mere philosophic disposition. The discrimination between the true and the false may itself be in the service of providing urgency to a more basic urge or mode of consciousness.

A characteristic basis of metaphysical idealization seems to be instanced in what may be called the mystical or religious consciousness. Reality encounters the saint as it were as a present fact of consciousness. "How could I deny him who has thrust himself into the orbit of my consciousness ?" exclaims a saint.[10] 'Discovery' of the real, if this language is at all apt in the context of religious consciousness, is marked by an immediate spontaneity. The feeling of reality is a primary immediate datum. The saint is already in communion with the source of life and value. He does not come upon it or fumble into it through appraisal born of reflection. Faith[11] in the presence of a supreme will, the intuitive awareness with which one apprehends the ground of all positivity, is not a question of intellectual inference or speculative reasoning. Reflection or idealization is only in the service of enlivening, deepening and in one word, 'realising' this experience of 'co-presence' or 'communion'. Philosophy is the dynamics by means of which this peculiar sensitiveness being already there is accelerated and sustained into an abiding, ever-growing experience.[12] Philosophy helps bring about what is alone both necessary and sufficient for it, namely, integration and self-surrender. The source of knowledge here is almost analogous to contact or union and the measure of a true 'philosophy' consists in the extent to which it succeeds in transforming this experience of contact into one of conscious unity which is the precondition of the experience of Bliss.

The numinous 'other', in the impressive words of Otto, is a primary immediate consciousness.[13] The 'other' is not, however, 'wholly' other. Intuition of it entails one's issuing from one's isolated selfhood, and a free surrender of subjectivity as such.[14] It is intuition of reality with which the self spontaneously affirms its akinness, continuity and union. The intuition of continuity, of being continuous with the reality which is also other than oneself, is primary.[15] It is the perception of an other which is yet along with oneself, the Beyond which nevertheless is within, the Absolute which yet is related. In the same moment of awareness I become alive to or awakened to something in me that is other than and alien to myself and also simultaneously to something that is closer to me than my own-self.[16] By means of what is close and continuous with myself I seek to overcome the other. Philosophy is a self-interpretation of this experience and its twin moments of otherness and continuity in their existential separation and essential unity.

A philosophy adequate with regard to this apprehension, interpreting and illumining it cannot be pure monism.[17] Baron von Hugel is perhaps right when he says that religion has no subtler and deadlier enemy than every and all kinds of monism.[18] Aside from the element of transcendence which monism ultimately denies,[19] religious consciousness demands in a peculiar sense of the term, a conservation of the self that is conscious of the Given.[20] The 'givenness' of God as no object is ever given, the reality of the 'conscious' self and above all the consciousness itself which constitutes the 'ever-growing' experience of Bliss—all are to find a place in a 'metaphysic' or 'theology' of religious consciousness.[21] God the supreme reality is not the unknowable and the Indeterminate to be denoted barely as That.[22] It is Being which is Given (*jñeya*) which means that it is also at once, and without equivocation, a personality admitting of personal communion with it. This again means that the self also ineffably is, which intuits (*jñātṛ*) and communes with the real and whose sense of communion with it is as real as the Given itself.[23] At the same time the sense of oneness or continuity between the *jñeya* and the *jñātṛ* in religious insight should also be accounted for. The Given is also 'one' with the knower's knowledge so that it can be said that in the insight the apprehending consciousness is identical with the apprehended.[24]

A philosophical appreciation of the real surely involves 'negation' of appearance, a going beyond phenomena. But this negation ultimately finds a fixed limit; it leaves untouched the centre of religious relationship in which one is intuitively aware of the transcendent as an immediate Presence. The centre of relationship is the bedrock on which stands the philosophic apprehension of the real and which is not subject to the negation which the appreciation involves. It is as it were the 'sacramental' foundation of the negation of appearance and the implied affirmation of Being. As the world of appearance, of division and dissociation recedes a new mode of formation comes more immediately to the fore. There is an immediate apprehension of creative action or Will in its most subtle and mysterious operation working in intimate union with one's own. The Transcendent is perceived in the form of action of spirit upon spirit mediated through all our physical and psychological experiences. It is the unvariant, inalienable With of man's being, one With without being reduced to the reality of the latter. Man in his being and will is penetrated by the transcendent, yet inward action of the being and will of God.[25]

Philosophy thus becomes a function of life illumining it in terms of its depth and reality. It becomes a study of the hidden links of the macrocosm (*aṇḍa*) with the microcosm (*piṇḍa*).[26] It is intuitive assurance of the absence of a transcendental limit isolating man from God and the world. The categories and concepts analysed, the fundamental principles of existence (*tattva*) enumerated—these are not dry metaphysical abstractions but are conceptualized modes of expression and symbolic images of spiritual life and experience, expressive of their hidden linkage.[27] Philosophy thus ceases to be a mere analysis of concepts for its own sake, but is underneath its overt analytical form, a hidden phenomenology of spiritual life.[28]

The method of approach which Śaiva Siddhānta adopts in its philosophy is apparently similar to the methods employed in any classical

Indian philosophical system. *Pramāṇa*, the acknowledged means of valid knowledge, provides a common universe of logically weighty discourse for the Indian philosopher. The methodology implied by the concept of *pramāṇa* is one of supplying evidence.[29] The form that is adopted expressly as the method of philosophising is in the classical style.[30] First, an assertion or statement is made. The assertion is potentially an argument, being not a mere statement but a conclusion along with supporting evidence. That it is so becomes obvious in the context of one's not being ready to accept the statement or what is the same, preferring a counter-statement as a more plausible alternative thereby implicitly rejecting the original one. In such a context of disagreement or dispute the statement or assertion is transformed into a supported conclusion. It is not so much interest in polemics that hastens the Śaiva Siddhānta philosopher to encourage and counter with disagreements, as the clear methodological awareness that disagreement provides an occasion for summoning evidence. This is with a view to achieving an intelligent resolution of the problem. The statement or assertion remains unsupported and therefore without cognitive assimilation till evidence is actually given in its support. And evidence is called for only when there is scope for actual disagreement whether someone really disagrees in that manner or not.[31] This explains why the *siddhāntin* hardly makes an assertion without also countering with ever so many forms or types of contradicting the assertion.[32]

But this is only one side of the question of method. There is also an existential side to the inquiry which exhibits concern for meaning and lends concreteness to the philosopher's method of approach. Underneath the overt formal manner of arguing and discoursing is at work a method of intuitive description and characterisation in tune with the deepest notes of personal experience (*anubhava*).[33] Intuitional method is the means to the philosopher's apodictic certitude (*siddhānta*) with its implicit claim to universality and necessity. This is expressly acknowledged in the demand for accepting the authority of Revelation which only points to the necessity of raising ourselves to the authority's standpoint and experience the truth as it is unveiled therein.

The system of Śaiva Siddhānta must be understood in keeping with this concrete method of approach. A system unfolds starting with its initial parts. The principal parts of Śaiva Siddhānta are not indeed initial parts but rather central parts, each one of which is already virtually the whole.[34] The Bond or Fetter, and what is subject to bondage or fetter and the Lord that redeems from Bondage—these are the three principals embracing the whole of Śaiva Siddhānta. But the whole of Śaiva Siddhānta is needed to understand the principals. Their interconnection are more like the vital ties of an organism where each part exists by the existence of the whole.

We can speak of the 'system' of Śaiva Siddhānta in more senses than one : coherence of its scheme within itself.[35] The coherence between concepts which Śaiva Siddhānta strives to preserve is at bottom the coherence of a single passionate thought and experience. It is idle to look for a logic in the abstract as a clue for its systematic structure as the logic itself is dictated by the guiding clue of a hidden experience. The 'system' is nothing but a continual application of this thought or experience. Just as music gives meaning to the rhythm of a dance, a hidden thread underlies the systematic character of philosophy giving it its inward coherence.

The fundamental ideas in terms of which the system is developed presuppose each other, and in isolation or abstraction from mutual relevance they are meaningless. Śaiva Siddhānta fights the demand to conceive one of them absolutely in complete abstraction from the total scheme. It is exercised self-consciously to exhibit this truth as may be seen from its treatment of the concepts of God, self and the world.[36]

Hostile criticisms of the system of Śaiva Siddhānta inspired by considerations of a *priori* logic, and attempts to treat it as an untenable half-way house to absolutism[37] or alternately as falling short of the ideal of a thorough theism are misguided.[38] They derive from inattention to the true analysis of its concepts and also from a graver fault of interpretation, namely a false expectation with regard to the nature of a system. This engenders a wilful blindness to the distinctive elements of its philosophy.

Formative Concepts of Śaiva Siddhānta

Śaiva Siddhānta is a sustained philosophical formulation of the central aim and insight of religious consciousness. In so far as it is not monistic it is also not an absolutism. Absolutism in the precise sense of the term as applicable to the context of Indian Philosophy involves *inter alia*, negation of the many as such, while monism merely asserts oneness. But a negation of the many is implicit assertion of the one. All absolutisms are monistic though all monisms are not absolutistic. Śaiva Siddhānta in so far as it is non-absolutistic, is non-monistic or pluralistic. Pluralistic as it is, it is not however a pluralism in the sense that it is a 'non-dualism' which also denies difference. Denial of difference is not the same as negation of the many with its implicit assertion of the one, and therefore in not being a pluralism it does not also become either monistic or absolutistic.[1]

As pluralistic in the sense of being non-absolutistic Śaiva Sidhānta conceives reality in three ultimate, irreducible modes—*pati*, *paśu* and *pāśa*.[2] The three are not mere appearances, distinctions set up and held apart in the whole that is reality. They are modes of reality distinct and primordial. It is not possible to derive one from another and much less all the three from a whole or unity. The alternative to a philosophy of one real seems to be a philosophy of three reals. While more reals than three are reducible to three,[3] the three cannot be further reduced without accepting the alternative of one. A 'dualism' of two ultimates is inherently unstable.[4] Without a third category interposing, the two cannot remain two. The implied logic here may be understood by reference to the place of relation in a metaphysic of realism. Admission of relation as a third real over and above the two relata is a necessary condition for their co-existence and connection. Deny the ultimacy of relation, realism ceases to be a plausible standpoint.[5]

Pati, *paśu* and *pāśa*—roughly, God, self and the world, are therefore logically distinct, though distinction may not also imply difference (*bheda*). Distinction is not necessarily difference just as non-distinction is not necessarily identity.[6] The presence of a third distinct conserves, logically speaking, the co-existence of the three. If there were only God and self, and no world how would the two be distinguished ? What is the logical basis for speaking of God and self as two ? There cannot be *pati* and *paśu* without *pāśa*. Nor can there be only God and the world and no self. *Pati* and *pāśa* imply necessarily *paśu*, the bound self. The latter is the ground of the distinction between *pati* and *pāśa*. Nor again can there be *paśu* and *pāśa* only and no *pati*. If there were only *paśu* and *pāśa*, being always in a state of bondage *paśu* cannot distinguish itself from *pāśa*. Indeed in the absence of a state different from that of being bound it cannot even know itself as bound.

Śaiva Siddhānta thinking therefore remains to the end faithful to the pattern of the three as ultimate.[7] *Pati*, *paśu* and *pāśa* as such, implying respectively lordship, being bound and being bond in terms of which they are differentiated, surely are not ultimate but their ontologial distinction is ultimate.[8] It is this inherent resistance to monism that gives the system the appearance of pluralism.

The label of pluralism applied to Śaiva Siddhānta nevertheless is misleading.[9] Śaiva Siddhānta in positing a 'plurality' of distincts does not hold along with pluralism or monadism that the distincts are unrelated or exist prior to relation and are externally related. If the distincts are related, it follows that they are not independent distincts. Relation presupposes dependence of one term upon another, though dependence does not have to be mutual and relation need not be symmetrical. But dependence again is impossible between terms which are possessed of existence in their own right. Therefore Śaiva Siddhānta holds that *paśu* and *pāśa* are dependent or finite existences and *pati* is independent infinite Being. *Paśu* and *pāśa* do not first exist in their own right and then become dependent.

It is true that to distinguish between *pati*, *paśu* and *pāśa* is, in a sense, to separate them. It is to think of them as *distinct* entities. But does this also entail thinking of them as *separately existing* entities? Śaiva Siddhānta admits not a factual separateness but only a cognisable difference between the things 'separated' as connoted by the three terms. The pluralisticts' fundamental assumption is that real involves reciprocal otherness. Śaiva Siddhānta without denying an ontological basis for an otherness of existence, denies however what it is supposed to imply, namely, unrelatedness.[10] It denies otherness in any sense but as existential, and affirms essential relatedness. Factual otherness is not denied any more than a *de facto* existent as such is denied.

It follows from this that though God is mentioned as if one of several reals or ultimates, God is by definition infinite or unlimited being, just as the other 'ultimates' are, by definition again, finite and dependent beings.[11] The reality to which God refers is not merely one among others, not even the first or the highest, but rather the very source and ground of being. In this sense, the three ultimates of the system may not be considered ultimate 'existents' in the same sense of the term existence.[12] Śaiva Siddhānta has recourse to a duality of expression while speaking of God, one co-ordinately and super-ordinately in relation to *paśu* and *pāśa* and the other incommensurable with them. The two expressions are respectively *pati* and *śivam*.[13]

Now, how are the three ultimate modes of reality derived? As explained before Reality is not approached in terms of what is not appearance. The presence of the transcendent is a primary datum; that it is a presence means that it is known simply and not as the solution of a problem. Though it is encountered immediately and not negatively in contrast to the world,[14] the encounter in its turn entails a contrast. The primary intuition of God is an awareness in contrast to which the world's 'alien' nature, its intrinsic meaninglessness becomes apparent. What was uncritically taken for reality and value suddenly becomes luminously meaningless and 'unreal' (*asat*), in contradistinction to the numinous reality (*sat*).[15] The reflexive sense of contrast serves to sustain the original encounter of the numinous and transforms the encounter into an experience of union and eventually into a trans-experiential unity.

The philosophical edifice of Śaiva Siddhānta is reared on the consciousness of this contrast—the contrast between the sacred apprehended as Being and the profane perceived as Non-being.[16] The contrast, more distinctively in Śaiva Siddhānta, takes the form of an appreciation of Divine Grace which shows by its very Reality and Freedom the hollowness of the reality of the world and its 'enslaving' nature. In our every day world we are not in contact with ourselves. We are supremely self-oblivious in our empirical life. The world therefore symbolises servitude, the enchainment of existence.[17] The contrast is between freedom which is implied by awareness of and life in. Grace and bondage of deprivation from God, which is entailed by the awareness of and life in the world. One is the source of our liberation, our light and life and the other of our servility, bondage, darkness and death. The contrast in sum, is between the possibility of authentic existence and freedom in which one finds one's true being and an inauthentic existence in which one is lost in the concern with what is alien and consequently is in a state of unfreedom.

Now, this contrast itself may be seen to entail yet another contrast.[18] As *pati* is distinguished from *pāśa*, the contrasting self is also distinguished from either of them in the same act, *as different alike from the two differents*. This is *paśu*. The reality of *paśu* is coeval with the reality of the distinction between *pati* and *pāśa*. The reality of the distinction between bondage and liberation implies the reality of a bound self, on bid to being liberated from its 'connate' condition of bondage or unfreedom.

The three ultimate modes of reality of Śaiva Siddhānta may thus be derived from a sense of contrast which is basic to religious consciousness.[19] Contrast implying distinction contradicts distinctionless unity. The sense of contrast implicit in numinous consciousness in its completeness is as it were the measure of the numinous reality and therefore it may not be taken to signify a mere distinction of levels involving self-transcendence. The contrast is certainly not proof of ontological difference between the elements contrasted; the reality of either does not guarantee the reality of the other *qua* the other. But the opposite is also not true. The contrast is not also mere negation, as it has been argued in absolutisms. Knowledge of contrast is *sui generis*, not reducible to mere knowledge with its twin-edges of affirmation and negation. The contrast is ultimately in the service of contributing to a fullness of our awareness of the ultimate Reality. Śaiva Siddhānta has the distinction of enunciating triple categories of *pati*, *paśu* and *pāśa* as a means to evoke an 'existential' awareness of Śiva—the Numinous.[20]

If 'abstract' monism is a heresy against the numinous character of Being, 'abstract' dualism implying a transcendental gulf between man and God is a heresy against Being's absoluteness. An extreme form of dualism, it is not surprising, tends by an inherent logic to develop into an extreme form of monism.[21] Only God is everything. Human reality is, like darkness in relation to light, nothing. But the paradox is, that though man is nothing before God, he is also what conquers nothingness by virtue of His presence. Being can be understood in terms only of conquest of nothingness. Without the standpoint of non-being, Being cannot be the numinous reality.

It is because of these considerations that Śaiva Sidhānta finds itself in a position of scrupulous non-alignment with classical absolutisms and pluralisms, dualisms and non-dualisms. The distinction between dualism and non-dualism is a typical instance of the inexhaustive divisions characteristic of Indian philosophy. The positive and the negative in this instance are not mutually exclusive and therefore do not represent a formal logical distinction. The negative case of non-dualism conceals distinctions which are quite as relevant as the distinction between it and the positive case. Śaiva Siddhānta shows unusual sensitiveness to these distinctions and distinguishes its point of view in sharp outlines from these philosophical perspectives.[22]

Meaning of Śaiva Siddhānta

The formulation of Śaiva Siddhānta and a determination of the scope or range of its meaning from the very outset seems to have hinged round a grouping of philosophical faiths under an 'ingroup-outgroup' structure.[1] Under this form Śaiva Siddhānta encounters the faith of the 'other'. This needs a careful analysis as it is decisive both historically and doctrinally, for the self-interpretation of the meaning of Śaiva Siddhānta.

Superficially viewed, this looks like erecting a conceptual and even an emotional wall between those who belong and those who do not belong. Śaiva Siddhānta, says Umāpati, is dark to the Outer schools of faith but light to the Inner ones.[2] Are some faiths in the dark and others only in the light ? The 'light and darkness' model and the implied rejection of rival systems as false and meaningless may suggest that Śaiva Siddhānta accomplishes nothing more than a dogmatic re-affirmation of its own principles. The term 'Siddhānta' itself which is appropriated as a proper and not a mere generic name by the system lends support to the view that in its own self-understanding it is a Dogmatics in the sense of being regarded as 'final' in the problem-sense of the term, and as public property open for rational conviction. The manner in which rival philosophical systems are hierarchically arranged and refuted suggest that they are treated as the rungs of a ladder, moments in an evolutionary process and they progress toward a logically tenable and satisfactory position or standpoint each linked to the moments preceding and following it but in which the 'lower stands refuted by the 'higher' and the 'highest' refutes all of the rest.[3]

Rationalism apart, the case is simply not true. Firstly, the issues involved are not logical even if one were to assume that there is available a logic, a kind of natural norm by which one can adjudicate between the rival claims to ultimacy and finality by religious-philosophical systems. What is more, the spirit of Śaiva Siddhānta is not one of rejection but inclusion. No system of faith including atheism, is as such in darkness. Error there is, and it is endemic to the human, 'receptive' factor, but untruth none. This is a distinction which needs a careful phenomenological analysis in the light of the Śaiva Siddhānta understanding of Revelation.[4] The 'darkness-light' imagery is in fact suggestive of the insight that the 'outer' or 'alien' faiths are not so much to be refuted as that they must be displaced by an overwhelming disclosure of the light of the true. Light symbolises divine Grace as the principle of positivity and as the very apotheosis of unveilment.

Every philosophical faith, it is a commonplace of Indian thought, is freedom-oriented. It is avowedly a way of thought and life toward accomplishing unconditional freedom.[5] One's earthly existence comes to acquire a certain authenticity in the light of the prospect of entering into a 'new' existence. Each system of faith may therefore be viewed as a sphere of existence having a binding power. In each, one is as it were grasped by a certain view of life as Reality itself and is determined to shape existence in accordance with it. Phenomenologically considered each is an exclusive and enclosed world representing as it were an independent sphere of life, isolated and therefore a kind of infinity. It is impossible to reach the next stage from one to another by mere development from within in the name of adequacy or completeness. Each philosophical faith consistent with its claim to be philosophical, claims to be adequate and complete and indeed the only such picture of Reality.

Nevertheless, isolated though they stand, they have a positive relation to each other. Here again one must not abandon the phenomenological perspective. Though in one sense each faith is an enclosed sphere there is also a sense in which each strives to integrate the other may be on its own terms. The alternate suppositions of belief and unbelief appear essentially incommensurable. And yet the believer's perspective in relation to that of the unbeliever is one of inclusion. It overflows and integrates it. The world of a man of light overflows in all directions and integrates the world of blind men. Such is the lesson of the story of the blind men and the elephant.[6]

Rival philosophical faiths thus considered in a vertical dimension, can also be viewed positively as successive 'steps' on the way towards a life that is perfected and enriched. From the perspective of life's ascent or upward climb these faiths may be viewed as halting places. Passage from one to the other involves a leap. Humanly speaking, it is not a continuation of the preceding state but a *negation* of it. Spiritual ascent is a *non-mediatized* progress and a relentless application in cognitive life of the rubric of a 'first view' (*pūrvapakṣa*) superseded by the 'final view' (*siddhānta*).

A grasping of the very Grace-structure present unconditionally in this process of ascent or advance, an understanding of all faiths atheistic, agnostic and heretical alike in terms of their translucence, viewed in the light of Revelation, marks the truly accomplished end of Siddhānta. Śaiva Siddhānta in claiming its lebel as a proper name is in accord with its original usage of referring to Revelation (*śaivāgama*) theologically understood, as a self-manifestation of Grace itself. It may thus be seen that Śaiva Siddhānta is not itself one more faith or standpoint not even the 'highest' but rather an awareness of the condition under which all schools of faith and standpoints could as it were find their anchorage.[7] It is a 'religion above religion' which situates every religion including itself considered as a mere religion, by going beyond or rather beneath its concrete immediacy in the direction of its even more concrete experiential depths which are in a primordial noetic contact with the real.

In order to argue for his principles what the *siddhāntin* does in effect is to show that each of the other systems ostensibly at variance with his position, is actually a part of his own system.[8] It is a part of it though mistakenly viewed as presenting the truth as such in all its dimensions. Consequently it is not rejected but 'included' as a partial illustration of itself. Śaiva Siddhānta's criticism of rival philosophical schools consequently amounts to an immanent criticism, an understanding from within. It is neither acceptance of them as they stand nor an *a priori* rejection of them as half-way houses. Śaiva Siddhānta's classificatory scheme of them is designed to show that its own 'system' includes and is illustrated rather than refuted by the other schools. While a distinction is made between those which are 'close' and those that are 'outside' its concern, nothing in effect Śaiva Siddhānta shows, can be wholly outside it, wholly wrong or lacking in meaning. Śaiva Siddhānta even implies that the *pūrvapakṣas* are in a way inevitable as a consequence of an overinsistence on itself as a unity. Their very contentions in apparent rejection of what Śaiva Siddhānta system stands for are in a sense illustrative of the system. Śaiva Siddhānta is Siddhānta in showing that any *siddhānta* rejecting a *pūrvapakṣa* is Siddhānta but in a poor way and therefore not deserving of the title as a proper name.[9]

In the various grouping of the *pūrvapakṣas* what comes in for a most relentless de-valuation judged from the criterion of absolute truth are scepticism, relativism, agnosticism and pessimisms of all kinds. Philosophies of life which flounder in darkness unaware of Divine Presence are those which espouse a positivistic theory of knowledge and reality or an empiricism which merely 'drifts' with no immanent teleology, uphold naturalism and materialism in answer to the question of what is real or advocate a hedonistic ethics or alternately an austere ethic of righteous self-effort and self-denial—all these belong to the 'outgroup'. Such, are the philosophical points of view which are blind to the factor of Grace though they may be negatively aware of it in the sense that they also strive for realisation of freedom. But really speaking, there is no negative apprehension of Grace; Grace is a living reality to be known dynamically through the exercise and experience of it. It is a Presence and Presence is always to be understood in terms of will, as *active* presence,[10] so that it cannot be ignored but only *resisted.*[11] To be unaware of Grace is to deny it implicitly. We may distinguish again two attitudes in this connection, the attitude of an overt denial of Grace which may take the form of aggressive anti-theism, agnosticism and atheism; and an attitude involving implicit denial of Grace which may take the forms of metaphysical dualisms, pluralisms, monisms and pantheisms all of which are curiously agreed upon not according a 'metaphysical' recognition to Grace.

The 'ingroup' on the other hand, recognises the factor of Grace. It is sharply distinguished from the outgroup in its general acceptance of a basis which is beyond the metaphysical reason of man but not beyond man. Grace is beyond my thought and speech but not beyond me in so far as I am in relation therewith and am in consequence ineffably one with it in my deepest essence and destined beyond the limitation of finite existence. With this recognition philosophical function becomes existentially one with religion, not only at its periphery but in its core. The goal of religion is the goal of philosophy. To know God is to know the real. Philosophy becomes both a concern and a quest. Dialectic is subordinated to theological concern. Doctrines assume the shape of symbolic dogmas.

While in this group there is an intuitive appreciation of the transcendent reference, the appreciation is still only of the transcendent as transcending the immediate conditions of bondage, as *different* from finite man (*paśu*). It is not appreciation of the Transcendent which is also immanent in man and his finite conditions articulating them by its supporting Presence. The Transcendent becomes merely another plane of existence, another mode of being, a state of freedom and perfection into which man shall be lifted or transformed. While there is emphasis on the transformation of man there is absence of a true apprehension of the transcendent from beyond man, as Presence which is not merely the goal but also the *source* of man's fulfilment. In this respect this 'ingroup' too shares with the two kinds of 'outgroup' considered above the character of being outside the circle of the immediate concern of Śaiva Siddhānta. The 'ingroup' is still only the fringe of the 'outgroup'.

The three broad groupings that have been considered—the Outermost, the Outer and the Inner-outer[12] may be historically identified in their respective order with (i) the Heterodox (*nāstika*) systems comprising of Lokāyata-materialism, Buddhism and Jainism, (ii) the Orthodox Hindu systems of philosophy (*āstika*) consisting of roughly of the six systems of thought, and (iii) the Tāntric group and its varieties which differ in outlook and orientation from the Orthodox group while also sharing with them a similar ideal of freedom from finitude. These are the three-fold *pūrvapakṣas* in relation to which Śaivism in its generality claims to be an 'accomplished end', a 'philosophy of these philosophies', implicit in them and yet transcending them in scope and meaning.

The 'heterodox' systems—the Lokāyata materialism, Buddhism and its metaphysical schools, and Jainism are at the outer periphery.[13] From the standpoint of Śaivism, their quest amounts to viewing reality under the exclusive mode of *pāśa*. The point of agreement between these systems seems to be a concerted repudiation of the category of self distinguished from not-self. The underlying argument in its plausible form seems to be : consciousness can be thought of only in the measure in which it is given in an immediate relationship either to itself or to another. This seems to inspire the 'bodily' self of the materialist,. the 'psychic' self of the Buddhist, and the 'mutable' self of the Jaina. In what may be described as the grossest form of consciousness, body is taken to be the point of reference undistinguished from self. The point of reference, gross as it is, still marks a shift from the grosser forms of not-self such as one's house, kith and clan with which too one is initially identified.[14]

'I am my body' is a dramatic focus on the act of self-manifestation in rejection of an earlier 'I am my kith and kin, my estate', 'I am my home and garden'. It replaces the earlier identification by the awareness of a new dimension of self-identity: I *as* body am not my kith and kin and environment but one that shows forth sentience.

But does this not demand a similar shift of the point of reference from the corporeal to something more inward and inalienable ? 'I am my senses', 'I am my mind', 'I am my life'—these in answer represent the successive points of reference toward recovering self-identity. The decisive element in the experience of selfhood, namely its severe me-ness with its refusal to be 'mine' to itself, disqualifies the candidacy of not-self to be self.[15] With regard to every case of not-self body, sense, vital air, psyche and intellection we can say 'my body', 'my sense' etc. What can also be mine cannot be me or I. The semantic superfluity of 'mine' in addition to 'me' as when we say 'my body' is evidence of the unplausibility of equating 'self' with embodied existence. The semantic situation also after all reflects a kind of presumptive evidence, at least in a negative way.

Similarly, consciousness and cognitions—the psychical series are not distinguished on the ground that they are absolutely indivisible in experience by the Buddhist. If subjective existence is but a series only of a cognition, that is, 'self-less', how is recognition possible ? Memory requires more than mere dating of a fact in the past. It must be dated in *my* past. *I* must think that I directly experienced its occurrence. Recognition of this is an important stage in the understanding of the inner dynamics of the law of *karma*. Similarly, is not *self's* resistance to mutability a condition of its selfhood ? How can there be a changing self ?[16]

The negativism of the heterodox systems expresses itself in its characteristic denial of a revelatory source of knowledge. The denial may rest either on a narrow reliance on perception as the only legitimate evidence of reality (materialism) or more flexibly on human reason and its self-sufficiency. Either way it amounts to a denial of the presence of revelation in man's knowledge. Insensitiveness to the presence of revelation in reason, which is present without figuring as a premise in the process of reasoning, is part of non-acceptance of the basis through which Grace is experienced, namely, self.

To recognise self may not be also to accord recognition to the factor of Grace, but not to recognise self is certainly also not to recognise Grace. Non-intuition of the true nature of 'I' takes away the very basis for the need for Grace. If acquiescence is unthinkable, refutation also becomes difficult. Grace can be significantly denied by taking one's stand on one's self. But when self is not adequately distinguished from the not-self, the element of Grace which is inseparable with self also cannot be distinguished. Grace is a function of being and if being were denied even against one's intuitive experience of it in oneself there is no middle ground left to demonstrate the reality of Grace.

In the history of Śaivism in its characteristic form as Śaiva Siddhānta during its earlier phase, we come across the interesting phenomenon of its encounter with these 'heterodoxies'.[17] Significantly, refutation is not done in the scholastic manner but takes the form of 'miracles'. But what is demonstrated through miracles is not a show of one's power, but the reality of the power accessible within man and transcending 'human' conditions of knowledge and existence. The method of demonstration through miracles is the method of witness. Witness to the mystery of being which gives itself to an attitude of surrender of subjectivity. It is by such genuine manifestation of the mystery of being a philosophy of 'no-being' can be refuted.[18] Śaiva Siddhānta has its root in the demonstration and vindication of the reality of Grace by the Śaiva saints who are significantly termed the Founders of Śaivism (*samayācārya*).

In terms of the principle that the 'lower' should be understood in terms of the 'higher', *pāśa* must be understood in relation to finite self (*paśu*). Not to recognise *paśu* is also not to know the true nature of *pāśa*. The principles constitutive of nature and mind (*pāśa*) must be sought in man (*paśu*). The elements of the structure of being are immediately experienced by man within himself so that the structure may not be dissolved into its elements.[19] It is against the bed-rock reality of self that the true nature of existence (*tattva*) as objective and therefore inert becomes intelligible.[20]

The 'orthodox' group marks a true advance over the heterodox in this respect. They distinguish the two ultimate modes of *pāśa* and *paśu* in effect by recognising the priority of the latter. The group is identified with the historical systems of (i) Nyāya-Vaiśeṣika, (ii) Pūrva-Mīmāṃsā, (iii) Ekātmavāda and its varieties, (iv) Sāṅkhya, (v) Yoga, and (vi) Pañcarātra.[21] The 'Brahminical' systems of philosophy conceive reality on the pattern of an 'inner core', namely, the self, permanent amidst the impermanent; they include pluralisms, dualisms and realisms on the one side, and absolutisms on the other, all of which conceive reality on the pattern of substance.[22]

These doctrines are indiscriminately grouped irrespective of their metaphysical differences for their common 'exotericism'. The hypostatization of the knowing self misses the reality of grace as does the hypostatization of the known object. The pattern or norm of self is deceptive. The self to be a self has to be self-transcending.[23] The real I is encountered in the transition from or transcendence beyond the me. Its true frontier is known not in the 'profane' context of me-mine but in being 'purified' of the me. One grows in true self-awareness as one leaves behind the 'me' which is alien to the nature of one's self and comes by a knowledge of spirit which is akin to, and 'one' with it.

It is not that God is not recognised in these systems. God is not recognised as spirit or freedom. The reality of spirit is made to resemble the reality of 'soul' or 'self'.[24] Spirit is dynamic will and self must be understood in the light of spirit.[25] With all their advance over the earlier point of view the 'orthodox' group is not an effective reaction against the ascendency of positivism over thought.

The 'secular' character of their approach is reflected in their attitude to scriptural authority. With their true insight into the problem of the need for an extra-philosophical source of knowledge, they do not look upon the evidence of scripture as evidence of grace. The doctrine of eternal, unoriginated scripture is implicitly a denial of the eternal source of revelation in man. This is exhibited by their 'empirical' approach to scripture which is an extra-empirical source of knowledge.[26] The Nyāya-Vaiśeṣika deny self-validity to knowledge[27] and approach the problem of being in the spirit of rational cosmology and rational theology. Pūrva-Mīmāṁsā accepts the *karma-kāṇḍa* but rejects the *jñāna-kāṇḍa* of the Veda as *arthavāda*.[28] The Uttara-Mīmāṃsā like-wise pays exclusive attention to *jñāna-kāṇḍa* and denies any sequence between *jñāna-kāṇḍa* and *karma-kāṇḍa*,[29] and again exegetically subjects the Veda to criticism.[30]

The third group of philosophical systems stand in refreshing contrast to the exotericism of the orthodox approach. This comprises the

Tāntric schools of Pāśupata, Mahāvrata, Kāpāla, Vāma, Bhairava and Aikya-vāda. The systems exhibit the attempt to conceive spirit not on the pattern of an adamantine self but of something involving transcendence of self. This shows itself in the form of their enumeration of more principles than those traditionally accepted in the orthodox group.[31] The true self, not the *paśu*, must be the ideal and the ideal involves overcoming of inner bonds and the attainment of pure and perfect spirithood.[32] The freedom that these systems proclaim and the only one that they acknowledge is exemption from the slavery of mental and sub-mental attitudes. Positively it is the freedom of self-realization or attainment of the nature of pure spirit, thus marking an advance over the 'freedom' of self-perfection of the earlier group.

God, understood not speculatively but 'religiously' as the transcendent source of 'grace', emerges clearly in the third phase. The question of man implies the question of God. Indeed it is identical with it. The term God acquires meaning only in the context of a quest for Grace.[33] All other terms of philosophy corresponding to *paśu* and *pāśa* also find their place in the same context. The question of God is raised by the very structure of our 'bounded' existence which provides the orientation for theism.

These differences in the approach to the question of God also reflect their need to accept special revelations in the light of which they can build their systems as paths of spiritual realization.[34] Barring the last mentioned, namely the Aikya-vāda Śaiva, who is more typical of the Śaiva group yet to be considered, but is ranked with these Tāntric systems for a significant reason,[35] all of them have their own exclusive *tantras* as norms of interpretation; the *tantras* do not involve a repudiation of the general Vedic authority but are certainly not inspired in their philosophic contents by the Veda. This has called forth a condemnation of them by the Vedic group.[36]

The demand for a true understanding of the interrelatedness of God, self and the world is in evidence from these attempts. A radical difference of approach to those categories is called for. A correct approach to the concept of *pāśa*, not merely as the phenomenal world or as beyond it but as connected dialectically with man's freedom, seems to be the key. The problem of bondage, and freedom from bondage demands a precise interpretation of freedom. What does freedom from finitude mean ?[37]

A man who is free or has attained freedom is free from some impediment or constraint. Indian philosophy interprets attainment of freedom, in a general sense to mean freedom from the erstwhile yoke of bondage. A more specific meaning of freedom from the standpoint of existential awareness of the transcendent, will be the 'freedom to'. The free man according to it is he who is free to enjoy union with God. But this again means that one is free from anything that would prevent one from enjoying union with God. Freedom to enjoy is another way of saying freedom from any sort of engagement or impediment that stands in the way of fulfilling one's will to enjoy. It is freedom from impediments of both commission and omission which have been thwarting one's desire for 'freedom to enjoy'; freedom both from preoccupation with phenomenal existence—'body, sense, world and worldly life' and from a more primordial privation of the knowledge and will of which the former seems a consequence. Both the causal and the consequential are felt impediments—Bonds (*pāśa*) that enslave man from whose constrictions he seeks freedom.

Again the expression 'free from', as it has been pointed out[38], suggests that one is *happy* and *relieved* to be without those things one is freed from. A set of circumstances become constraining only when one wants to do something which these circumstances prevent. The world is a bondage to the extent that the circumstances of one's worldly existence hinder the accomplishment of the desire for freedom to enjoy. Without the implication of will to enjoy we should hardly know the meaning of freedom. Bondage is a thwarting of one's will and freedom is a thwarting of bondage. The freeing agent merely arrests the arresting of the constraint or opposes the opposing of the constraint.[39]

The real meaning of *pāśa* gets defined in this analysis. *Pāśa* is not only the unwelcome burden of the 'world' of our appropriation and enjoyment which deflects our will under its weight but is what *constrains* or *impedes* our will. Real freedom will be freedom from such constraint. Freedom or deliverance is not in other words pre-eminently freedom from the 'constitutive condition of actuality', from the world and from the will to live,[40] but rather from egoism which is the hampering impediment to freedom. Overcoming of this impediment coincides with the transformation, not abandonment of actuality.

The freedom espoused in other systems, those of the last mentioned group included, is therefore not the end but indeed the beginning. It is freedom from one or more of the conditions of bondage but not from unconditioned condition of bondage, namely, the primal blind self-assertion of will which is also metaphysically the evil of its Privation. The 'freed' according to these systems indeed are bound selves, no more free from *pāśa* and therefore no less in need of inculcation from the higher reaches of knowledge. This reorientation of the concepts of God, man and the world distinguishes the genera of philosophical Śaivism which accepts the category of *mala* from the aforementioned groups of philosophy. The latter are, in a true sense, though certainly in different degrees, 'outer' to the philcsophical framework of Śaivism determined by this distinction between bondage and liberation.[41]

On the philosophical side this expresses itself in a clear-cut distinction between *pati*, *paśu* and *pāśa*. *Paśu* has its destiny in realising *patī* which it accomplishes by conquering *pāśa*.[42] *Pati* is the Transcendent Spirit that is at the same time immanent in the conditions of finite life and existence constitutive of man's bondage. As immanent in them *pati* is the redeemer of man from the limiting conditions of bondage. Indeed, through them man is eventually redeemed from the primordial cause of these conditions which constitute the core of man's bondage. *Pāśa*, in other words, comprises (i) the phenomenal realm of existence inclusive of the objective and the subjective spheres—the'impure' matter subject to the law of time, (ii) the realm of moral causation involving the sequence between action and its result which sustains phenomenal existence through a succession of rebirth, (iii) a superphenomenal realm of existence — Pure Matter above the scope of (i) and (ii), which while partaking of the nature of phenomena serves also to mediate between spirit and the finite man,[43] and lastly, and most importantly (iv) a primordial, positive condition of Impurity which being beginninglessly present has been beginninglessly 'clouding' the spirit of man and thereby in a beginningless sense again, occasioning the phenomenal life of man. The four 'species' of bonds (*pāśa*), namely *mala*, *karma* and the two *māyā-śuddha* and *aśuddha*, together with self (*paśu*) and God (*pati*) constitute the six 'eternals' of philosophical Śaivism.[44]

The Śaiva philosophical schools constitute the real 'ingroup' of Śaiva Siddhānta. The approach to the questions of freedom and bondage entails identical analysis both in thought and in discourse. This also involves an identical attitude towards the question of scriptural authority—the acceptance of the Śaiva Āgama which expressly presuppose and indeed claim to trans-create the Veda, as independent revelations.[45] The schools with which Śaiva Siddhānta has closest affinity are six in number—*Pāṣāṇavāda*, *Bhedavāda*, *Śivasamavāda*, *Śivasaṅkrāntavāda*, *Avikāravāda* and *Nimittakāraṇa-Pariṇāmavāda* (*Śivādvaita*).[46]

We find here again all the varieties ranging from pluralism to monism, though, unlike those of the 'orthodox' variety, their metaphysical character is subordinated to an existential concern reflected in their exclusive pre-occupation with the issues of bondage and liberation. It is their conception of the relation of the three modes under which Reality is conceived that determines the pluralistic or the non-pluralistic character of these philosophies. More specifically, differences in the conception of the nature of relation between *pāśa* and *paśu* involve differences in the conception of the relation between *paśu* and *pati*. The movement is from radical dualism through qualified dualisms to non-dualism. Relation between self and God in the state of liberation is the deciding point. *Pāṣāṇavāda* and *Bhedavāda* at one end conceive it to be one of otherness, interpreting freedom as consisting of *being* freed from *pāśa*.[47] The middle three conceive it as one of similarity or parity implying dualism and also a supervening unity in the form of equality in natures.[48] The last one conceives of the relation as one of mergence, union and identity.[49]

There is thus a progressive approach to the ideal of '*advaita*'. The advaitism of the philosophy of Śaiva Siddhānta is determined by its relative affinity to these six schools. Nevertheless Śaiva Siddhānta considers all of them, *Śivādvaita* not excepted, *pūrvapakṣa*, in relation to its character as 'Siddhānta'.[50] The Transcendent Spirit is as such beyond the moments of difference (*adhikāra*), non-difference (*bhoga*) and identity (*laya*). It is no more realised in terms of *paśu's* bare freedom from *pāśa* than in terms of *pāśu*, freed from *pāśa* becoming merged in the reality of *pati*.[51] Spirit must be realised in non-dual Experience and a differenceless coincidence of the three is the *implicans* of such experience. Advaitic Experience should involve freedom from the 'I'; utter self-surrender in being as well as in will is the essential prerequisite for the manifestation (*abhivyakti*) of Freedom. But Freedom is not mere self-dissolving dispersal. It is also the integrative Experience of Bliss (*ānanda*).[52] Freedom *from* the I must also signify Freedom *for* the I. The I is not here reaffirmed but restored. Freedom is Experience of Inheritance.

The 'accomplished' character of Śaiva Siddhānta, therefore, follows from acceptance of the criterion of experience—Value Experience. The reliable testimony embodying this Experience is Siddhānta *par excellence*. No other authority can lay claim to our credence than the value of Truth itself (*siddhānta*) and its self-revelation in intuitive Experience.

Formative Factors of Śaiva Siddhānta[1]

Śaiva Siddhānta's claim to universality and absoluteness for itself rests upon a conception of knowing which underlies its approach to the question of revelation. It reminds one of a famous passage in Plato's Republic about the parallel between the 'good' and the sun.[2] Just as the perception of colour requires something more than the presence of a coloured surface to be seen, and an eye to see it, so the simplest act of knowledge demands something more than a knowable object and a knowing mind. There must also be that which answers to the presence of the light of day. The sun is neither the colours that we see nor the eyes which see them. It has a transcendent being. The word serves as that transcendent condition of intelligibility in phenomenal life. Knowledge of every kind depends on a 'natural' illumination by him who is the truth. Intuition or insight higher than knowledge similarly depends on a further 'supernatural' illumination from the same source. All knowledge is therefore illumination and is continuous.

Just as a scene looks different in all its different details according to the degree of illumination under which it is beheld, so also the actual meaning of statements are variously intelligible. Minds illuminated in unequal degrees apprehend their objects diversely. A better illumined mind does not simply apprehend what the less illumined apprehends *plus* something more. It apprehends what we call common to him and the other one, in a 'new light'. Systems of thinking represent the apprehensions of a mind at successive stages of its pilgrimage towards God and therefore at different levels of illumination.[3]

The Śaiva Siddhānta concept of Revelation and its types rests on this philosophy of 'Illuminism'. Śiva is the source of all knowledge and is the author of all *Vidyās*.[4] All systems of philosophy from that of the materialist onwards are Śiva's illumination and determined by the exigency of the selves in different degrees of spiritual maturity and therefore in need of *different* inculcations from above. *Śāstras* of *different* truth value are revealed by Him in free association with agents (*paśu*) like Brahmā, Viṣṇu etc., and the result is the vogue of Hiraṇya-garbha-Āgama, Pāñcarātra-Āgama etc. The non-absolute nature of these *śāstras* is to be traced to the variable associative agents admittedly of different spiritual worth, while the element of illumination is to be traced to the one spiritual Sun, namely, Śiva.[5]

From this it follows that the unmediated revelation from the invariable source of illumination, namely, Śiva must be true absolutely, unconditionally and impersonally. Such are the Revelations of the Veda. Intuitions of the Transcendent Reality are already revealed to man 'generally' which provide the norm for all spiritual endeavour. There is no spiritual aspiration which is not inspired or illumined by the Veda.[6] *A priori* it can be said that no departure or deviation from the Veda is possible in so far as the Veda is the repository of truth for all grades of minds. It is the general revelatory source of knowledge for all spiritual philosophies. For Śaiva Siddhānta too, the Veda is the source of authority.[7]

The hymns of the Veda are the fountainhead of wisdom by which is kept open a perennial access to the primordial saving knowledge. The one presence within and beyond the many serves as the 'archetypal' mystery revealed by the Veda which it is the job of reason (*yukti*) to plumb and confirm from individual experience (*anubhava*).[8] According to the Śaiva Siddhānta theological way of understanding, it, the Vedic tradition in its entirety is one continuous Revelation.[9] The Saṁhitās and the Brāhmaṇas, the Āraṇyakas and the Upaniṣads, the Itihāsa and the Purāṇa — all represent one homogeneous tradition. Now within this Revelation, knowledge of the Highest is revealed in two characteristically distinct and complementary ways. The unity of God-head is indicated *vis-a-vis* deities like Agni, Vāyu etc., which are the intelligent 'essence' of phenomena whose inmost essence in turn is the Highest Deity.[10] In becoming aware of the deities, one becomes also aware of the Deity of the deities, whose operative aspects only are personified in and as these deities. The universal has to be known through the particulars as their inmost reality and not as the particulars themselves are known.

One Śaiva saint, St. Appar has described[11] the 'hero' of the Vedas (*veda-nāyaka*), the Infinite Śiva Himself, the truth underlying all the divinities which are spoken of in the Veda. The saint says : 'People tend fire in worship but they know not that fire is a form of the light of the Lord. The feet of the setting sun they worship in their twilight prayers; but who is the sun but a form of Hara ? All the Vedas pray but to the Lord alone even when they invoke other deities.' An intuitive appreciation of the one and only God though variously described as Indra, Varuṇa etc., was implicit from the very inception though it is possible for one to be unaware of it.[12] The saint refers to the story of a tortoise of the well challenging the tortoise of the sea: 'can your ocean compare with our well ?'

Side by side with this 'general' orientation we find also a more direct and specific reference to the Highest, as for example in the section of the Śatarudrīya, which is the theophany of the God above gods—Rudra.[13] The former, that is, the general approach without the latter would be lacking in definiteness and conclusiveness even as the latter without the former would be dogmatic. Similarly, in the Upaniṣads too this dual approach to the nature of the unconditioned is evident. One is the general 'cosmic-acosmic', negation-affirmation approach to the *ātman* characteristic of the major Upaniṣads.[14] The other is the more direct method of identifying it with the personalised aspect such as the 'three-eyed, blue-necked and tranquil' as we have in the Śaiva Upaniṣads.[15] For Śaiva Siddhānta the latter is more revealing as containing the real key for the understanding of the *brahman-ātman* equation of the 'earlier' Upaniṣads.[16]

In the same way coming to the Purāṇas which expound the Vedic theogony with imagination, the 'general' way of extolling the supremacy of God-head is through praising gods like Brahmā, Viṣṇu, Agni and others and indicating the unity of the underlying Divine Power which manifests itself through them.[17] The more specific and unequivocal method seen in the light of which alone the apparently conflicting accounts of the supremacy of gods make sense, is that of expounding the glories of Śiva and his unmistakable supremacy over other gods. Thus while all the Purāṇas are equally important as conveying the same truth, those Purāṇas with the help of which we are able to appreciate their unity are from the point of view of the seeker more significant.[18] It is in this sense that the Śaiva Purāṇas come to merit greater attention.

A clue to the *second* type of revelation which Śaiva Siddhānta admits in a distinctive manner is implicit in the foregoing account. The distinction between the 'general' approach and the ultimate of direct approach is significant. It is in the light of the latter that the former is illumined. The former without the latter is unspecific and equivocal. It is like the cryptic, laconic *sūtra* without the aid of the commentary which alone gives one the discerning eye to see the meaning of the *sūtra.*[19] It is not that the commentaries represent a higher truth than that of the originals but from the point of view of the learner are more important as giving greater urgency to his quest. The commentaries make the inner meaning of the original accessible.

The above consideration emphasises the need for an 'exegetical' access to the Veda. The unaided free-lance exegeses developed through the refractory media of 'human' agencies will not do.[20] The 'human' approaches even though illumined by the invariable source of illumination can approximate in different degrees to the truth. The competence to reveal the truth in the case of the human preceptors is only with respect to things intelligible to their understanding and does not extend beyond their scope.[21] An authentic representation of the Vedic Revelation accomplished and final in character like the Vedas themselves of which they are 'expansions' is required. This technically, is Śaiva Siddhānta[22]—the final truth relating to Śiva, the only legitimate, valid complement to the Veda which is traceable to that very source to which the Vedas themselves are traced. The *āgama* may be taken to represent an attempt to rediscover the eternal message *within* the Veda and its tradition over against a distorted and 'humanly' misused Veda.

A general revelation was needed against a natural revelation of 'human' attempts to know Reality. It is the latter that provides the basis of communication for the general revelation which has necessarily to be adapted to the requirements of the human intellect. General revelation comes as the *corrective* to knowledge due to a natural revelation while also presupposing it. The specific revelation, however, arises against a general revelation not as corrective but as *supplement.* The Veda is indeed revelation of Truth itself, eternal and inerrant. It cannot be superseded by another revelation while also not ceasing to reveal truth. But it can be supplemented, the supplementation answering to the requirement of the seeker who is prepared for more specific and exclusive inculcation of knowledge. The Vedic texts themselves *inter se* admit of supplementation without the implication of supersession.[23] The logic is merely stretched. In the true sense, supplementation bears on human interpretations of Revelation. It is in the light of a possible misinterpretation which by its misplaced emphasis tends to obscure the Divine provenience of the Veda that supplementation becomes necessary. The supplement merely removes the veil and reveals what it supplements in its true colour.

The significance underlying the 'duality' of approach—the general and the specific is ultimately linked up with the concepts of bondage and liberation.[24] There are degrees of bondage and therefore also degrees of liberation.

The perspectives of the seeker accordingly can never be the same. The distinction between a present sense of *realisation* against the previous moment of a mere *quest* is intrinsic to spiritual life. Revelation is necessarily hierarchical and perpetually self-supplementing. Nor does this detract from the categorical nature of truth which it reveals. Truth is always absolutistic though there may be degrees of realising it. Siddhānta is not *anekānta.*

Śaiva Siddhānta terms the 'specific', also the 'true',[25] to distinguish it from its earlier, unsupplemented phase which relatively has only the semblance of truth but is not true. The perspective of the free (which is a relative term) is the perspective of truth, and this again only implies that it has a claim to be considered the norm in the light of which the other perspectives must be interpreted. The distinction between the true and the untrue is not a distinction between two co-ordinates. Nor is their difference merely qualitative as between red and blue. Such difference warrants only distinction but in the true and false distinction, there is something more than mere distinction. The distinction is made a ground for 'outgrowing' the one and accepting the other. The one is intelligible only as dependent on the other for its existence.[26] The general and the specific are not alternative standpoints, neither are they opposed. The one is interpretative of the other. The general is illumined by the specific.

Tirumūlar, a great authority on Tamil Śaivism, distinguishes the Veda from the *āgama*:[27] The *āgama along with the Veda* is true; Divine Revelation is two-fold, the general and the specific. The *āgama* and the Veda which are Divine Revelation also are thus distinguished *for the seeker.* For the great, however, they are non-distinguishable.

Śrīkaṇṭha's oft quoted view on this subject also must be understood in this light. 'The Veda and the *āgama* are of equal authority as Divine Revelation. The only difference is that the latter may be studied by persons of all castes while the study of the former is restricted to the first three classes'.[28] This distinction apparently made in sociological terms conceals a deeper truth. From the angle of the truly spiritual who is imbued with the divine eros the *āgama* is surely the Revelation. For those others who are spiritual in the general, 'lay' way Veda is Revelation. It is for the average and not for the initiate that the state, the family, the law and other social organisations have been created. For him alone exists educational institutions involving a progressive approach through privileges of class and learning. Recitation of the Veda, performance of the scripturally ordained duties etc. and the functional differentiation in terms of class which they presuppose are all for the non-initiate. But for the 'spiritual' whose life is directed towards the higher value disclosed to it in a 'descent' these do not exist.[29] It carries with it a new insight into a kind of holiness which is above social morality.[30] This also explains the plausibility of the existence of Śaivāgama and Śāstra literature in languages other than the officially recognised medium of Sanskrit.[31]

This brings us to a third type of revelation recognised in Śaiva Siddhānta which is intrinsically the most important and is in the spirit of the earlier distinction between general and special revelations. This is personal revelation through direct experience, a personal discovery of the reality and mystery of the 'Thou'.[32] Existence of this type of revelation is indeed the presupposition underlying the two earlier types which are impersonal.[33] Here revelation is in its pure form as immediate intuition. Even the other types of revelation are timeless embodiments of intuitions but they are mediated by word (*vāc*). *Śruti* is objective truth, impersonal and universal 'knowledge'. But personal revelation is intuitive experience. *Śruti* is what is heard but *anubhava* is direct insight. The latter is a kind of seeing. *Śruti* — the Veda and the *āgama* — is not strictly knowledge but the method of knowledge. It initiates knowledge but personal revelation is knowledge itself. Personal revelation as historically understood is a demonstration that bestowal of revelation is received only in the context of *mokṣa*, and also conversely that *mokṣa* occurs only within the context of a correlation of revelation.

Personal revelation is concrete life. Its proof is its manifestation in the life of Spirit. The experience of the mystic saints is the only demonstration of spiritual truths. Śaiva Siddhānta in the form in which it is formulated and systematised as *śuddhādvaita* by Meykandār and his successors is chiefly inspired by this type of revelation. It is in the light of this evidence a co-ordination of the truths within the Veda itself, of the Veda and the *āgama* and again within the *āgama* of the divergent accounts of their knowledge-section becomes possible.

The 'God' of the Śaiva hymns of the mystic saints is not different from the 'God' of Śaiva-siddhānta-śāstra, even as it is sometimes argued that the God of the Bible is not the same as the God of Anselm, Augustine or Aquinas. The latter speak as philosophers in the terminology of 'secular' philosophies of Aristotle and others. The Vedāntic terminology interpreted and re-interpreted by Śaiva Siddhānta is itself implicitly 'religious'.[34] The implicit element is brought out on the criterion of personal revelation and its embodiment in the hymns of the saints.

Personal revelation defies all categorisations. There is no assignable limit or number to the modes of personal revelation. Sambandar, the child-saint of Śaivism says: 'the *modus operandi* of bestowal of Grace for those who shall be its recipients, and its glorious nature is truly beyond the limits of saying. One has only to submit before my Lord, surrendering oneself and hear the truth.'[35] It can only be discerned through an intuitive awareness of its manifestation. Authentic accounts of lives of saints and their awakening to the reality of Divine Revelation alone can be our evidence. Tense moments of crises in such lives are also moments of self-revelation of Grace. *Periyapurāṇam* the book on saints and saintly life by a saint is therefore, intrinsically the most valuable document for Śaiva Siddhānta, being a record of the original witness of those who participated in the 'revealing' acts of divine Grace. Their participation in the happenings of the revelatory character of the acts of the bestowal of Grace was manifest through their creative responses: potentially revelatory facts become actual revelation through the creative responses of saints. The act of reception is part of Revelation.[36]

Śaiva Siddhānta Literature

Śaiva canonical literature in Tamil forms the fountain-head of Śaiva Siddhānta philosophy. It is in the form of mystical outpourings of the saints of different periods arranged and redacted at about the tenth century A. D. According to the account by one of the later Śaiva preceptors (Umāpati), Nambi Āndār Nambi redacted the Śaiva canons in ten books; the first three of Tirujñāna-sambandar (7th century), books four to six of Tirunāvuk-karasar (7th century), Sundarar's (9th century) hymns forming the seventh book, the *Tiruvācakam* and *Tirukkovai* of Māṇikkavācagar (3rd or 9th century) being the eighth, *Tiruvisaippā* and *Tiruppallāndu* by nine different saints (between 900-1100 A. D.) being the ninth and Tirumular's *Tirumandiram* (circa 6th century) the tenth. To these ten an eleventh was added by Nambi himself, a miscellany of poems by saints like Pattinattār, Karaikkāl Ammaiyar and others. The twelfth in the list later on added was *Periyapurāṇam* of Sekkilār (12th century).

The place of Tirumular in the canonical literature of Śaiva Siddhānta deserves special notice. Tirumular's *Tirumandiram* is the earliest exposition of Śaiva Siddhānta in its metaphysical, moral and mystical aspects, and the work describes itself as an *āgama*. Tirumular also was aware of the affinities and differences between Vedānta and Siddhānta as may be seen from his interpretation of *mahāvākyas*. *Periyapurāṇam* relates the tradition of how Tirumular originally came from Kailāsa to South and composed *Tirumandiram*, a work of 3,000 verses, in the course of some three thousand years. The work is very abstruse and defies systematic understanding. Scholars suspect a possible influence of Pratyabhijñā-Darśana on Śaiva Siddhānta through the aforementioned legend, but there is no supporting evidence available from the text itself. Tirumular shows acquaintance with Tāntricism of different shades and also with innumerable sects and schools of Śaivism but there is no evidence of an attempt to incorporate them into Śaiva Siddhānta. Śaiva Siddhānta does not emerge in clearly demarcated lines in relation to the Tantra and the Śaiva schools of faith.

The rise of Meykanda Śāstra in the 13th and the 14th centuries owes its main inspiration to the canonical literature but its emergence as a philosophical theology and scriptural evaluation must be understood against a foreground and a background. The background was the tradition of the Śaivāgama which was kept alive through the vogue of Upāgama and its commentaries and also of independent manuals recapturing the philosophical contents of the knowledge-section of the major *āgamas*. Of the first variety, three deserve special mention—(i) *Pauṣkara-Āgama,* (ii) *Mṛgendra-Āgama*, and (iii) *Mātanga-Āgama*. All three have been extensively commented upon by renowned men in the field. *Matanga-Vṛtti* is by Bhaṭṭa Rāmakaṇṭha (11th century). *Mṛgendra-Vṛtti* is by Nārāyaṇakaṇṭha (11th century) and *Mṛgendra-Vṛtti-Dīpikā* is by Aghora Śiva (12th century). *Pauṣkara-Bhāṣya* is by Umāpati (14th century). The fundamental differences of Śaiva philosophy from the Vaiśeṣika, the Nyāya, the Sāṅkhya and the Vedānta, and the Śabda-Brahma-vāda on the one side and Buddhism and also Jainism on the other are brought out in different philosophical manuals grouped as *Aṣṭa-Prakaraṇa*. *Tattva-Prakāśikā* by king Bhoja of Dhāra (11th century) is a lucid presentation of Śaiva Siddhānta and its thirty-six *tattvas*. There are two commentaries on the work, one by Śrīkumāra and the other by Aghora Śiva. The first seems the earlier as may be seen from Aghora Śiva's reference to it in the beginning of his commentary. Its contents are in consonance with the spirit of *Śivādvaita* of Śrīkaṇṭha and comes in for refutation by Aghora Śiva. *Tattva-Saṅgraha* and *Tattva-Traya-Nirṇaya* are by Sadyojyoti (10th century) and are, according to Aghora Śiva, digests respectively of the vidyāpāda of (i) *Raurava,* and (ii) *Svāyambhuva*-Āgamas. Śrīkaṇṭha (11th century), not the same as the commentator on Brahma-Sūtra, wrote *Ratna-Traya*, a critical exposition of the meaning and inter-relation of the three principal concepts of the *āgama*, namely, *bindu*, *śakti* and *śiva*. *Bhoga-Kārikā* and *Mokṣa-Kārikā* are by Sadyojyoti again and are detailed analyses of the concepts of (i) *bhoga*, and (ii) *mokṣa* in the light of their treatment in *Raurava*. The former is commented on by Aghora Śiva and the latter by Bhaṭṭa Rāmakaṇṭha. *Paramokṣa-Nirāsa-Kārikā* of Sadyojyoti is based on two and half aphorisms of *Raurava* relating to the different theories of *mokṣa* and is again commented on by Bhaṭṭa Rāmakaṇṭha. Nārāyaṇakaṇṭha (11th century), the author of *Mṛgendra-Vṛtti* also belongs to this group. Bhaṭṭa Rāmakaṇṭha's *Nāda-Kārikā* with Aghora Śiva's commentary on it deserves special mention as the single work on the Saiva philosophy of language. Aghora Śiva, the most prolific writer of this group, gave a definite turn to the philosophy of Śaiva Siddhānta towards dualism. Through his *vṛtti* on *Sarvajñānottara-Āgama* (not available now) he becomes the target for criticism in the hands of Śivāgra yogin, and Śiva-jñāna yogin,. commentators of *Śiva-jñāna-Bodham,* in Sanskrit and Tamil, respectively.

The conflict with Vedānta which this early phase of Śaiva speculation with its rigid framework of dualism and its concept of God as *kevala nimitta* (only efficient cause) and again as only personal had, was soon to be overcome in the next phase of development. From the point of view of Śaiva Siddhānta, in a true sense there can be no antagonism between the philosophical ontology of Vedānta and the personalism of the Śaivāgama with its integrated spectrum comprising sections of devotion (*caryā-pāda*), ritual (*kriyā-pāda*), meditation (*yoga-pāda*) and gnosis (*jñāna-pāda*). Śaivāgamas do not put forward a purely theistic doctrine of the externality of the world to God. The latter concept finds its great critic in Bādarāyaṇa who points out the contradictions inherent in such a position. The world cannot be a co-ordinate of God external to Him. Instead of viewing phenomena as a necessary qualification of the actuality of Being, Śaiva Siddhānta views it as a free manifestation, freely retracted and therefore freely created.

The rise of Śaiva Siddhānta philosophy as Non-dualism represented in the Meykanda literature was preceded by another phase of development which marked an anti-thesis to the earlier phase of dualism. This was *Śivādvaita* represented in the commentary of Śrīkaṇṭha (12th century) on *Brahma-Sūtras*. *Śivādvaita*, indeed, has a long and continuous history and is traceable to *Vāyavīya-Saṁhitā* of the *Śiva-Mahāpurāṇa* and also to *Sūta-Saṁhitā* of *Skanda-Purāṇa*. Śrīkaṇṭha presents in his commentary the quintessence of Upaniṣadic philosophy consisting in the teaching of *saguṇa-brahman* who is none other than Śiva. Śrīkaṇṭha advocates a theory of Non-dualism which he distinguishes from (i) *atyanta-bheda-vāda*—absolute difference as between pot and cloth, (ii) *atyantābheda-vāda*—absolute non-difference as between rope and 'snake', and (iii) *abheda-bheda-vāda*—difference and non-difference. He maintains a Non-dualism of the distinct, such as may be illustrated by the body-soul analogy. The *Śivādvaita* is of significance for the formulation of Śaiva Siddhānta philosophy. Appaya's (16th century) *Śivārkamaṇi-Dīpikā* on Śrīkaṇṭha's commentary is a monument of learning and rare spiritual discernment and shows an exceptional understanding of the issues involved in reconciling the Vedānta with Siddhānta (*āgama*). Its influence on at least one outstanding commentator on *Śivajñāna-Bodham*, namely, Śivajñāna Yogin is quite unmistakable.

Meykandār's (13th century) *Śivajñāna-Bodham* and the new phase of development that it initiated in Śaiva thought must be understood against these earlier developments. The revolutionary advent of *Śiva-jñāna-Bodham* seems to have been immediately preceded by two kinds of works in Tamil; one is in continuation of the *āgama* approach, namely, *Ñānāmirdam* by Vagisa (12th century). This work is, however, said to be part of Jñānāvaraṇa-Siddhānta. Śivajñāna Yogin thinks that *Ñānāmirdam* is only part of the 'general' phase of development within the Śaivāgama represented by the Pauṣkara, Mṛgendra, Matanga and other *āgamas*. The other works that preceded *Śivajñāna-Bodham* are *Tiruvundiār* and *Tirukkaḷitruppadiār*, two complementary works by teacher and pupil. The tradition of a pupil writing treatises elucidating the teacher's work is typical of the Meykanda-Śāstra under which group are included the aforementioned two works. These works are, in contrast with the 'general' approach of the *āgama* speculations, unsystematic, mystical-theological and esoteric. One prefatory verse of *Tirukkalitruppadiār* says : "As I came to know in utter surrender of self surrendering even the sense of 'I know', similarly shall others through such self-surrender learn from me, so said one, said one, and I am communicating that truth to you".

It is this inherent difference of methods of approach — the general and the existential, the method of demonstration and definition and the method of intuitive witness, and inculcation through a line of preceptors, that divides the corpus of *āgama* philosophies into water-tight groups in mutual conflict giving rise to the phenomenon of divergent 'schools' of Śaiva philosophy, although based on the same scriptural authority. What united the Śaiva group against the bewildering welter of 'secular' metaphysical systems 'groping' in the night of a mere general revelation of truth, itself in its turn becomes a source of conflict. This is incompatible with the spirit of accepting a special revelation. What is therefore needed to restore the harmony of the *āgama* speculation is to subordinate the claims of special revelation to those of personal revelation and illumine it in the light of the latter.

Meykandār's *Śivajñāna-Bodham* initiates a new phase of development in Śaiva thought by co-ordinating the 'two' approaches inherent in Śaiva Siddhānta. The 'two'— the general and the ultimate, are not two different or alternate standpoints. One is the presupposition of the other. It is a difference of perspective in which there is also the demand that one be subordinated to the other so that there is really no difference.

Śivajñāna-Bodham, literally an exegetic evaluation (*bodha*) of the philosophic contents of the Śaivāgamas and by implication all philosophic contents (*Śiva-jñāna*), therefore marks a true renaissance in the development of Śaiva doctrine and practice and the inauguration of a new syncretist phase of *advaita* in which the differences of 'difference' (*bheda*) and 'non-difference' (*abheda*) become mere distinctions. The evaluation is based on the authority of personal revelation, the inner thread linking all revelations and therefore it also came to be distinguished as the tradition of Knowledge (*Jñānāvaraṇa*); *Jñānāvaraṇa* complements without contradicting the *karmāvaraṇa* phase of the earlier Śaiva Siddhānta.

The basis on which co-ordination of truths becomes possible is the basis of Experience. It is the concept of the real as utterly beyond man's thought (*pāśa*) and beyond man too so long as he is self-assertive and therefore 'enslaved' (*paśu*). The *jñānāvaraṇa* phase is, in other words, a movement towards *advaita* and away from *dvaita*, implicit as well as overt. What could have helped *Śivajñāna-Bodham* formulate its *śuddhādvaita* are (i) the *advaita* taught in the Śaiva hymns—*Tevāram* and *Tiruvācakam*, (ii) the tradition of certain *āgamas* which are unlike those merely expounding the three concepts of *pati*, *paśu* and *pāśa* in their mutual exclusion as for example, the *Sarvajñānottara* (said to belong to Yoga-Sāṅkhya, as distinct from the Jñāna-Sāṅkhya group) which taught *advaita* in categorical terms, and also (iii) the tradition of *Śivādvaita*. *Śivādvaita* was admittedly the nearest approach to Śaiva Siddhānta ideal of Non-duality. Umāpati, the fourth successor in the line of Meykandār's tradition, recognises the closest affinity between *Śivādvaita* and Śaiva Siddhānta.

Śivajñāna-Bodham is a work of twelve *sūtras*, the first six 'general' and the second, special or 'ultimate'. The general again consists of two subdivisions of three *sūtras* each, the first three evidencing through the aid of metaphysical reason the reality of *pati*, *paśu* and *pāśa*, and the second three 'defining' them. The special also consists of three *sūtras* on Spiritual Means (*sādhana*) and three on Spiritual Fruit (*phala*). The structure of the work thus bears resemblance to *Brahma-Sūtras* of Bādarāyaṇa with its four *adhyāyas* or *pādas*.

A comparison of *Śivajñāna-Bodham* with *Brahma-Sūtra* will be significant. The latter despite its purport to be systematic is heterogeneous in its contents and diffuse in structure inspiring partisan spirit in the commentators each claiming support for his own point of view. *Śivajñāna-Bodham* is homogeneous in its teachings by intent being a treatise of inculcation (*upadeśa śāstra*). *Brahma-Sūtra* merely records the different views of Vedāntic thought in a loose, systematic way but without adjudication and evaluation. *Śivajñāna-Bodham* is a unitary composition evaluative in a personal way traceable to one spiritual genius and is avowedly conclusive (*siddhānta*). The former is related directly to the Upaniṣads while the latter is more immediately connected with the ethos of Śaivāgamas of which it may be said to be a free evaluative exegesis (Āgama-Mīmāṁsā). It must, however,be remembered that Meykandār attempts as much to synthesize the Āgama and the Veda as to synthesize the 'divergent' trends of Āgamic philosophy. This is quite evident from his interpretation of concepts like *advaita, ānanda, sat, asat* etc.

While the task of systematization was completed by Meykandār, further elaborations of the system on the metaphysical (theological) and epistemological sides were made by Aruṇandi the immediate disciple and erstwhile preceptor of Meykandār. *Śivajñāna-Siddhi*, written by Aruṇandi on *Śivajñāna-Bodham* consists of two parts—*parapakkam* and *supakkam*, the former refuting other schools of philosophy, and the latter setting forth the fundamentals of Siddhānta. The second may be considered a commentary in verse form on *Śivajñāna-Bodham*. '*Irupāvirupabtu*' is also by Aruṇandi, in the form of a dialogue between teacher and pupil, and the central theme of the dialogue is *mala*.

Umāpati (14th century), a pupil's pupil of Aruṇandi, completes the work of his predecessors in three directions : (i) to define the standpoint of *śuddhādvaita* Śaiva Siddhānta of Meykandār by distinguishing it from the different internal schools of Śaivism; Umāpati's *Saṅkalpa-Nirākaraṇam* is logically a continuation of Aruṇandi's *parapakkam*. (ii) Restatement of the contents of *Śivajñāna-Bodham* and *Śivajñāna-Siddhi* in a crisp and unambiguous form but rearranged under the two headings of General and Special; Umāpati's *Śivaprakāśam* is a complete exposition of the two earlier works and provides a useful basis for all subsequent philosophical literature in Tamil for approaching the truths of *Śivajñāna-Bodham*. The masterly commentary of Śivajñāna Yogin on the latter owes its form and structure to *Śivaprakāśam*. (iii) Elaboration of the doctrine of Grace which is the inner theme of the metaphysics and mysticism of Śaiva Siddhānta. The bearing of Divine Grace on the life and destiny of man is brought out in four works: (a) *Pōtrippahrodai* which traces the career of the individual soul from its birth and through all its series of births up to the time it attains its destined end, namely, '*mukti*,' and shows that every event that befalls its life is conducive to its well-being and is embodiment of Grace; (b) *Kodik Kavi*, which extols the triumph of Grace over the principle of evil and the uplifting of the soul fighting its way through doubt and despair; (c) *Nenju Vidu Thūthu*, a poem of a message of devotion sent to his guru, having for its theme God's Grace and compassion towards souls, which regulates all events of the world for the benefit of the souls; (d) *Tiruvarutpayan*, a systematic presentation of the theme of Divine Grace and its Fruits, which is also equally a presentation of Śaiva Siddhānta from a key angle. *Unmai Neri Viḷakkam* (Umāpati's authorship of which is disputed) is a clear formulation of the doctrine of *Daśakāryas*; the cue for this doctrine was to be found in Umāpati's *Śivaprakāśam* where he distinguishes three distinct stages in spiritual Realisation, namely, abandoning association of *pāśa*, realizing or achieving of Knowledge and becoming identified in Advaitic union with the God of Knowledge (*Jñeya*). This is elaborated into ten sequences in *Unmai Neṛi Viḷakkam*. *Daśakāryas* become the theme for discussion and elaboration in post-Umāpati literature. *Tuhaḷaru-Bodham* elaborates the ten under thirty-three. The Śāstra literature that developed during this period under the inspiration of the last mentioned work is grouped as Pandāra-Śāstra and the literature is spread over a period of four hundred years. One omission in our list of fourteen *śāstras* is *Unmai viḷakkam* by Manavācagam Kadandār, in the form of a dialogue between guru Meykandār and his disciple, who is the author himself.

Our literary history of Śaiva Siddhānta will be incomplete without reference to the principal commentaries in Sanskrit and Tamil that came to be written between 14th to 18th centuries. The most outstanding of them and the one that seems to have exercised a decisive influence on subsequent commentaries is that of Umāpati on *Pauṣkara-Āgama*. Umāpati's *Pauṣkara-Bhāṣya* like another of his Sanskrit works, namely, *Śata-Ratna-Saṁgraha*, an anthology of Śaivāgama texts with his own lucid commentary, admits of having been written by Umāpati in the introductory verses as well as in the colophon. Tradition identifies this Umāpati with the Santānācārya, and we have no reason to set aside the tradition. Doctrinal affinities between

Śivaprakāśam and *Pauṣkara-Bhāṣya* are beyond dispute. That the latter is polemical in tone and does not contain the main contents of *Śivaprakāśam* should not be baffling; one is written as a commentary of an *āgama* that belongs according to our classification to the 'General' group; the other is written expressly in line with *Śivajñāna-Bodham*. It is also possible to discern two stages in the life of Umāpati from this, namely ,the period before his advent in the tradition of Meykandār and the period following it.

The philosophical contents of this commentary and the two other commentaries must be appraised in relation to Śrīkaṇṭha's commentary on *Brahma-Sūtra*. Umāpati quotes Śrīkaṇṭha's remarks under *patyadhikaraṇa* and expresses himself in favour of the view that the *kevala-nimitta* view of God's causality impugned in the *adhikaraṇa* is not the view of Śaiva Siddhānta, but does not feel committed to defend the concept of *abhinna-nimittopādāna-kāraṇa* on lines of Śrīkaṇṭha. Umāpati is aware of the closeness of *Śivādvaita* to his position and even says that the distinction between the two is only terminological not conceptual. Still he distinguishes the standpoint of Śaiva Siddhānta from *Śivādvaita*, and seeks to reinterpret passages from *Vāyavīya* and *Sūta Saṁhitās* of *Śivādvaita* import.

Śivāgra Yogin's commentary on the Sanskrit version of *Śivajñāna-Bodham*, however, inclines to accept Śrīkaṇṭha's view of Śiva as not only the *nimitta-kāraṇa* but also the *upādāna-karaṇa* and gives a detailed exposition of the rival point of view, namely, that of *Pauṣkara-Bhāṣya* followed by detailed criticism. It is of interest to note that Śivāgra Yogin follows very closely *Pauṣkara-Bhāṣya*. The same objections in the same language are raised at innumerable places; one can even profitably consult *Śivāgra-Bhāṣya* to correct the readings of the text of *Pauṣkara-Bhāṣya*. And yet Śivāgra Yogin departs from Umāpati's point of view on important matters. Where he so departs he is in agreement with Śrīkaṇṭha.

The third commentary in our list is that of Śivajñāna Yogin (18th century) in Tamil on *Śivajñāna-Bodham*. Coming last it has the advantage of reinterpreting and reconciling the rival points of view. *Drāviḍa Māpāḍiam* (Skt. *mahābhāṣyam*) as this work is called, bears evidence of influence from three quarters—(i) *Pauṣkara-Bhāṣya* of Umāpati, (ii) *Śivāgra-Bhāṣya*, and (iii) *Śivārkamaṇi-Dīpikā* of Appaya. Appaya's insightful solution to problems, his manner of reconciling the Āgama with Veda in terms of its implicit Śaiva content make an undeniable appeal. The main lead for *Drāviḍa Māpāḍiam* however comes from Umāpati, the Sanskrit commentator as well as the one of Meykandār's line. On every vital issue Umāpati is followed and Śivāgra Yogin criticised. Śivajñāna Yogin brings to bear on his work the stamp of his own spiritual genius, and the manner in which he reconciles differences of viewpoints without compromising the central insight gives his commentary a distinction seldom to be matched by other works of its kind.

BOOK TWO

ON GOD : PATI

II

THE EXISTENCE OF GOD

God as the Ground of Cosmic-Dissolution

A plausible way of demonstrating the reality of the supreme Being to ourselves who are part of the world-process is to understand it in terms of the world as being its *terminus* or ground of *resolution*. A 'cause' becomes intelligible when viewed as that in which the effect *terminates*. The causal control of an effect demands primarily, *retraction* of the effect into non-existence and consequently a manifestation and conservation of its own existence. The cause, whatever else be its nature, must first be the 'abysmal' ground of the resolution of the effect. Indeed, in the case of God viewed as 'cause' of the world, the divine characteristics, such as eternity, ubiquity, being spirit, being Being itself—derive from that in virtue of which he is indeed cause, namely, his being the ground of the resolution of the effect. The cause is defined by its being the 'whither'[1] and the 'whence' of its effect.

If the entire phenomenal world were, then, to imply a causal ground as its whither and whence, it follows that such a ground be intrinsically transcendent to the world and to the processes to which the world seems subject. The cause of the world-process must be what is both implied by it and also at once *transcends* it. It must be a super-cosmic principle at once of the nature of being, the resolving ground of all becoming, and also of the nature of personal will that creates and sustains as well as retracts the processes of becoming.[2] Everything that is, has the fact of its being through being and from being—the Being and the Will of God.

Viewed in this light it should be obvious that of the cosmic functions -Creation, Conservation and Dissolution attributed to God conceived as the cause of the world, Creation and Conservation of the world are not of the same significance for the transcendence of God as Dissolution or Retraction which is therefore cosmic operation *par excellence*. He alone is the causal ground of phenomena who can retract the phenomena wholly without residue unto himself. The world should be retractable in entirety before, and as a condition of, re-creation. Dissolution 'precedes' Creation.[3] What cannot be dissolved or disposed of cannot be created. What resists retraction will resist also creation.[4] The same cannot be urged on behalf of creation. Though it is accepted as a truism that what has no beginning has no end, spiritual philosophies espousing *mokṣa* as the supreme value seem to imply one exception, namely in the case of bondage. Man becomes free from his condition of bondage, which itself has no true beginning.[5] Admission of uncreated beginningless situations which are not without termination is acceptance of the priority of dissolution or of destruction over creation.

To say that destruction is *prior* to creation does not, of course, imply that *first* comes destruction and *then* creation in order of time. The temporal order of what comes earlier and what later inverts the logical relation. Dissolution is logically, objectively prior to creation as it conditions, and is not conditioned by creation. It is comparable to the objective priority of time to change.[6]

Even the temporal priority of creation to destruction seems to be grossly exaggerated. It would be exaggeration, and therefore untrue to think that a period of creative function is followed by a period of destruction. In fact creation itself seldom can get under way without destruction intervening at every conceivable step. The world cannot be conceived to undergo creation and conservation unmediated by destruction. The seed has to *change* its form before it can sprout; further, unless each day *passes* it cannot grow into a sapling and then into a tree. Conservation too is likewise unintelligible without the intervention of destruction. To persist is to persist through change. To endure is not conceivable without the moments of perishing. To be, indeed, is dissolution in the making. To live in fact is to die slowly and imperceptibly.[7]

The processes of creation and conservation *occur* and terminate, while termination itself seems to endure interminably.[8] It is not necessarily consummated in another process unlike creation and conservation which have their destiny in destruction. Destruction may, therefore, be said to include and transcend the other two processes. While it is legitimate to speak logically of commencement and end of the offices of creation and conservation it is not legitimate to speak so with regard to the supreme office of dissolution. The latter is typical of the interminable Being itself.[9]

What spells out the nature of being the effect of a cause, is not therefore so much the circumstances of the effect coming into being as that in which is entailed the circumstance of its coming and stay, namely its terminability. The terminable is the effect and the terminus or the terminator, itself non-terminable, is the cause.[10] A cause as different from a mere condition is the non-terminable terminus or the resolving ground of the effect. The conditions that may be necessary for bringing the effect into being must be distinguished from a cause which is a necessary and also a sufficient condition to produce it is in its own turn not likewise conditioned by other causes.

The belief underlying the conception of God as the universal Destroyer (*sarva-saṁhāra-kartā*) rests on the insight that all things of the universe, the inert objects, classes or species of lives, the life of the individual, the history of the group and the nation, the course of the cosmos with its immense conglomerations of stars and nebulae and galaxies—all alike are subject unexceptionally to the general process of termination and re-emanation. Everything of the natural and the cultural world, of the corporeal and the non-corporeal world, of the spoken and the speech-world is involved in inexhorable change. Not only the visible spheres of the universe but all conceivable spheres of being even those of the highest world become resolved into their cause. Even gods as part of the corporeal world are subject to the general rule of absorption and re-emanation.[11] A hundred million creator-gods have perished and so have as many a million conserving gods.' Time too paradoxically is involved in that process: it passes or lapses and re-emerges.

In a state of total, residueless absorption the ground of the absorption, as there must be one, outlives such absorption.[12] This alone implies the possibility of a new creation, that the End is not final. A Vedic text[13] says: when there is no darkness when there is neither day nor night, neither being nor non-being, Śiva alone (is). When Śiva remains alone, having absorbed into Himself the entire universe everything other than Himself, moving and unmoving, sentient or insentient, all the luminaries like the sun and the moon being absent, all divisions of time being no longer there, all forms and names being absent, '*tamas*' or darkness alone reigning everywhere, then endures Spirit in its undimmed light as the Witness of all.[14] What is spoken of here as '*tamas*' is the state of serene sleep (*suṣupti*) where there is no cognising whatever of created existence in any particular aspect of its manifestation.[15] The Destroyer is the 'Lonely Witness' left to witness the drama of universal Dissolution—'the Witness of all, transcending the darkness of destruction'.[16] Dissolution of the moving and the non-moving universe is indeed typical of the nature of Spirit conceived as the world ground.[17] It is the *eater* (*attṛ*) of the movable and the immovable.[18] The Upaniṣad says that the *brāhmaṇa* and the *kṣatriya* are the food (*odana*) of *brahman* to which is added Death as such, as the condiment or sauce (*upaśecana*).[19] Consuming Death itself as sauce is suggestive of universal Dissolution. The Destroyer is also the Great Devourer (*mahāgrāsa*).[20] All this universe and its worlds He offers as oblations in the fire of His own light.[21] One Upaniṣad raises in a significant way the question : 'why is Rudra known as the One Rudra (*eko rudraḥ*) ?' and replies that it is 'for the reason that Rudra is one alone, all things apart from him having never stood at any time whatever, as his peer or as his second for the reason that they stood merged in him.'[22]

The notion of God as the whole and sole cause is the most initial notion that one can form about God in relation to the given world. Śaiva Siddhānta expresses this truth in a manner which is indicative of God's reality in a general and also in a unique sense. It does this by reference to that feature of God which entails the truth of the assertion that He is the creative cause of the entire universe. The Destroyer is, and alone is the creative God.[23] He that ends, also begins.[24]

The world-ground, to which all the cosmic operations, creation and conservation as well as dissolution are to be ultimately referred, is therefore, labelled significantly by one of the functions, as the Destroyer. If the ultimate plenum may be known in terms of any special function it is Dissolution, it being alone capable of representing the transcendent as encompassing and therefore, truly transcending all cosmic functions. The sole ground and agent of cosmic functions is also, pre-eminently, the Destroyer.[25]

The ground and agent of world-dissolution is alone the ground and agent of world-creation and world-preservation.[26] *Saṁhāra-kartṛ* is the real *sṛṣṭi-kartṛ* and *sthiti-kartṛ*, not *vice versa*.[27] Śaiva Siddhānta is emphatic in repudiating the suggestion that Śiva the supreme Reality is but one of the 'trinities' to whom are respectively assigned the three cosmic functions. The Destroyer-God is not the mere deity of destruction who has a co-ordinate function and existence along with the deities of creation and preservation. The term *hara* denotes the Supreme Being in a general as well as in a unique sense.[28] Literally, of course, *hara* is one that destroys, and yet its application extends not to any destroyer nor again to a mere destroyer but only to a specific one to whom it belongs uniquely. Śiva, the Supreme, who is indicated suggestively by the name of *Hara* is not to be identified with '*rudra*' to whom belongs the office of *limited* dissolution. Śiva is *mahā-rudra*, not *guṇi-rudra*.[29] He is the universal Destroyer of whom *rudra* and other deities are only the operative aspects.[30]

The Śaivāgamas make this crucial distinction in univocal terms.[31] They say that *Śrīkaṇṭha-rudra*, the agent of periodic dissolution (*avāntara-pralaya*) is but a mature soul belonging to that group or class of *paśus* which, though bound are not bound as we the earthly souls are, but whose bonds are snapped at the time of final Dissolution.[32] About Śiva Himself it is said that He is *pati*, the Lord of the bound (*paśupati*) who freely descends and assumes the states of *laya*, *bhoga* and *adhikāra*[33] and takes on the respective forms of *śiva*, *sadāśiva* and *maheśvara* and performs the respective functions of dissolution, governance and creation of all the realms of existence including the realm of speech. As referred to *Śiva* the Agent *par excellence*, differences of the functions of *sṛṣṭi*, *sthiti*, and *saṁhāra* do not imply a difference in the cause of the functions : *śiva*, *sadāśiva* and *maheśvara* are functional differences belonging to the same unity behind them, whereas, with reference to the intermediary agencies, their differences involve differences of agents also.

In the Śaiva hymns too the same distinction is drawn at innumerable places.[34] Śiva's 'office' of Dissolution is not co-ordinate with the offices of the trinity, including that of *rudra*. The entire universe with its creators, conservers and destroyers is under Śiva's control 'even as dried leaves whirl under the control of a stormy wind.'[35] He is the Creator of the creator. He is the God that sustains the sustainer of creation. He remains hidden from what He sustains. Confounding Śiva with one of the trinities is, therefore, a species of theological heresy,[36] of confounding God with creature, the transcendent with the non-transcendent, the Ever Free with the Bound, and comes in for a vehement condemnation at the hands of the Śaiva hymnists.

That *Śiva* is not one of the trinities is expressed in the fore-mentioned citations from the Śaiva hymns in two characteristic ways. He is above them and behind them, and the latter therefore know Him not.[37] Secondly, though Śiva is of the very essence of them He remains distinct from them. The latter, in so far as they are different *inter se*, (that is to say that creator is not the sustainer and sustainer is not the destroyer), are also different from what is commonly present in all of them as the indwelling spirit. Śiva alone is transcendent[38] and His inalienable presence, by which is meant His pervasive will, is the condition for the cosmic operations of creation, conservation as well as resolution at all levels.[39]

The Destroyer is the only transcendent Being (*tattvātīta*) transcending all *tattvas*, who freely phenomenalises and performs the cosmic functions and controls the performance through intermediary agencies like *rudras*. The latter reside with *brahmā* and *viṣṇu* in the *guṇa-tattva* and their sphere of action consequently does not extend even beyond the sphere of *prakṛti-tattva*, the twentyfifth in the scheme of thirty-six *tattvas* which span the entire universe of the spoken and the speech world. *Hara* (Destroyer) is the causal ground of the trinity (*trimūrti*) beyond the three *guṇas* which is their sphere,[40] beyond the categorisation of gross, subtle and the unmanifest through which all forms pass and re-pass,[41] beyond even all names, forms and activities.[42] Even though there is no one proper name to denote Him, all names like *brahmā*, *viṣṇu*,[43] *rudra* indeed connote that Supreme, nameless principle[44] which may be named if at all as the great Lord (*parameśvara*).[45]

The Supreme Reality disclosed in religious experience is of the nature of a presence *behind* and *beyond* the phenomena. It is essentially different from the contingent nature of the world from whose reality it stands contrasted.[46] It manifests itself not only as a presence but as the presupposition of all that there is. It is the mysterious and its mystery is the mystery of Being.[47] The designation of the Supreme Reality as Destroyer is metaphysical as it is also mythological. The concept of Destroyer represents God as the universal Being. Everything is 'nought' (*śūnya*) before Being.[48] God is not some*thing* or some*one* which exists *along with* the totality of beings. He is Being itself. The universal represents a level of consciousness where in the particular is totally 'dissolved'.[49] Otherwise if the latter were to persist, the universal would lose itself in the particularities and become indistinguishable from the particular. It would itself become a particular. The true universal, however, is neither a species of the particular, not even the most exalted of its kind, nor a sum-total of particulars but something unique belonging to a level of being from which level indeed there *are* no particulars.[50] Thus again it may be seen that reference to God in terms of the function of Destruction contained in the expression *Hara* involves a conception of Godhead which is assimilable to the philosophical notion of the Absolute. Destroyer is not only the Supreme Being. It is the Absolute itself. *Hara* implies not only the unity and supremacy of deity; it indicates its absoluteness as that *other than* which there is nothing.[51]

Paradoxically the creative Cause of the world can only be a 'God' for whom the created world shall be just as 'nought'. It cannot be one whom the world confronts as one's creation, an evolute or embodiment or even an exteriorisation as theisms and pantheisms would have it. Such notions do not evidence a disjunction of phenomena from "that profoundly hidden essential yet forgotten" transcendent ground, namely, the Absolute.

The Absolute is described in Śaiva Siddhānta as absolute Destroyer. A thing existing absolutely (that is not in a necessary relation to any other) and a thing existing absolutely as Destroyer, are compatible.[52] The notions of Creator and Conserver as applied to the Absolute Being define by relations and conditions that which is conceived as exclusive of both. The notion of Destroyer, on the other hand, indicates it by 'dissolving' relations and conditions and by making it 'free' from the phenomenal. Designation of the Absolute by the term Destroyer is indeed recognition of the impossibility of defining in the strict sense, the absolute by the notion of a mere cause. A cause is a relation and what exists absolutely as a cause exists absolutely under relation. What exists *merely* as cause exists merely for the sake of something else. It cannot be final in itself. It cannot have 'aseity' as truly distinguished from the effect of which it is cause.[53] An 'absolute' cause indeed depends on its effect for its reality. To the extent it exists *necessarily* as cause, it is not self-sufficient; it depends on the effect as on the condition through which alone it realises its existence *qua* cause. Destroyer, therefore, implies *free* causality. The God that exists in and as His Creation exists so through His own freedom. His 'existence *in actu*' is not through and in His Creation.

The Destroyer stands for eternity which truly transcends temporality. Eternity is not mere simultaneity which is suggested by the functions of creations and conservations unaccompanied by dissolution. The God who is merely 'simultaneous' with his creation would himself be subject to the anxiety of the future, being subject to a process that is open to the future. He cannot be the foundation of courage. He cannot be the inspiration to conquer death. Only the Destroyer is the Death of Death (*kāla-kāla*),[54] the 'realm beyond the realm destroyed', and is the ultimate foundation of ontological courage in the face of the anxiety of transitoriness.[55]

The Knowledge of God's Existence

Śaiva Siddhānta does not pretend to be rationalistic in its theology. It does not purport to be an empirically grounded theism though it adduces *a posteriori* proofs, and undertakes to argue from the known to the unknown.[1] The term *Śaiva Siddhānta* itself primarily stands for Śaivāgamas,[2] the body of revealed scripture which forms the original source of the knowledge of the transcendent Reality.[3] The system of Śaiva Siddhānta is only an exegetical interpretation of the intuitions embodied in scriptural revelation. In this respect it is similar to Vedānta; the *Vedānta-Sūtra* of Bādarāyaṇa, unlike the Sūtras of Gautama or Kaṇāda, merely 'threads together'[4] in an intelligible arrangement the different statements of the Vedānta, namely, the Upaniṣads, and unfolds a coherent system within this framework. Likewise one may say that it is the intuitions of the Śaivāgamas that set the philosophy of Śaiva Siddhānta on its feet.

To admit revelation as the source of our knowledge (*pramāṇa*) of God implies two things. God is not a 'wholly other', utterly unlike anything known and experienced, because in that case revelation cannot intelligibly 'reveal' Him. To reveal is indeed to communicate in the idiom intelligible to a person and in a manner assimilable by human reason.[5] At the same time God cannot be also like any given object or fact knowable in the ordinary way by perception and reason, as in that case God does not also have to be 'revealed'. Revelation as a significant means of knowledge does not duplicate the functions of other means of knowing. Admission of revelation as the means of our knowledge of God, therefore, demands both that God is not a remote being totally removed from the realm of experience and also that He is nevertheless beyond the evidences of sense and reason.

Indeed in an ultimate sense God is knowable only by spiritual intuition, not through any of the modes of cognition. The latter belong to the sphere of demonstrative, discursive knowing, the scope of the validity of which is conditioned to a reality that binds (*pāśa*) and is inapplicable in the case of God who liberates (*pati*). Even the revealed word as such cannot give us the intuition of God.[6] The luminous word-form and its concatenations belong to the sphere of 'mediate' knowledge (*apara-jñāna*, *bindu-jñāna*). Even the 'silence' of the transcendental speech (*parā vāc*) cannot take the place of intuition of God[7] which is immediate (*aparokṣa*) and ultimate (*para-jñāna*). God is the import beyond the comprehension of the word, the Light that stands outreaching all light.[8]

Revelation presupposes a philosophical attitude the framework of which is grounded in an existential awareness of God's presence. This awareness which is always presupposed should grow into a full cognitive reflection with the help of reason aided by revelation before it can ripen into an intuition in spiritual life. Adducing reason in support of affirmation of God's reality is not to reduce God to rational necessity, but is a free personal and inter-personal way of appropriating the truth and certitude which of course derives from the authority of the revealed word. This is so in so far as in man as a person is included, pre-eminently, his rational nature. God's reality is 'sown' initially in a mind prepared for it, by means of revelation and this grows into reflection by the metaphysical use of reason and culminates in the advent of spiritual intuition mediated by a life of self-surrender and union. So both for a 'metaphysical' knowledge of the 'general' reality of God and also for the mystical intuition of His ultimate nature for which this knowledge is a preparation, revelation alone provides the initial cue.[9] With the help of revelation alone we are able to approach God both with regard to his 'that' and 'what'.[10]

However, the question whether knowledge of God has to be revealed, whether an approach to the problem cannot be made through independent reasoning still remains to be considered. God is supersensuous and all that is needed to evidence its reality is some acceptable means of knowledge which is adequate for cognising what is beyond the reach of the sense. Inference is expressly such a means accepted by the generality of Indian philosophers.

Independent reasoning as employed in Rational Theology and Rational Cosmology takes either of two forms : direct reasoning or demonstration, that is, the method of reason—through a conclusion derived from a general rule and a particular subsumed under it, and indirect reasoning through postulation. Speculative theology in the west as well as in the east makes a free use of these methods in proving the existence of God. The question before us is whether these methods can be *pramāṇa* in the strict sense of the term with regard to evidencing God's reality. Can reasoning in other words have independent logical value in the matter of 'proving' the reality of God ?

Two types of direct, inferential reasoning are recognised in Indian logic[11] : one, the ordinary syllogistic reasoning like inferring the presence of fire from observing smoke and the other, reasoning by analogical argument which may be illustrated by way of examples : as particular objects like jars are effects of a cause, the world too is the effect of a cause. Reasoning in the latter case is not based on actual perception but on 'conceiving from likeness'. It involves an extension of a principle verified in experience to something beyond experience,[12] while ordinary syllogistic inference expressly purports to apply to cases falling within common experience. It is only the 'analogical' inference (*sāmānyato-dṛṣṭānumāna*) that can apply in the case of God who is supersensuous reality and transcends the sphere of common experience.

But even analogical inference can only indicate the probability of the conclusion already known or available through some other means. It cannot independently establish the existence of something which *ex-hypothesi* falls outside sensuous experience. If God also could be perceived as the potter is perceived we might discover whether the predicate of 'being the cause of the world' belongs, or does not belong to God. But in fact it is only the predicate that may be said to be 'perceived' if at all. The subject is never perceived. Whether the predicate is factually connected with the subject as its predicate or not cannot therefore be asserted.[13]

But this is to exaggerate. In principle analogical inference does not differ from ordinary inference, and is no less or more defensible. Both involve a leap from one particular to another, and if in one case it is justified because we pass through a general truth based on observation, in the case of analogical reasoning also, there is mediation by a general truth based on the extension of observation. From the observation of how the sequence of action relates to the causal agent as in the case of the pitcher it is meet to infer unerringly from any product of action to a causal agent responsible for its production.[14] The latter need not be actually perceived. It is more a perception of the universal (*sāmānya*). In the mediate syllogistic reasoning also it is the perception of the universal that legitimates the leap from the 'fire in the hearth' to the unseen fire on the hill.

It seems nevertheless true that inference based on the observation of an universal (*sāmānyato-dṛṣṭānumāna*) cannot have *independent* logical value for proving God's existence. One can at best infer agency (*dharma*) from the fact of the world considered as effect. This cannot amount to a source of one's knowledge of God's existence. The latter will have to be initially 'revealed' by another source of knowledge; reason can be ancillary to the testimony of that source. The proof for the existence of God may be valid in form but formal validity of an argument is no guarantee of the material truth of its conclusion.

Śaiva Siddhānta in fact admits of a scope for as many as four varieties of inference,[15] all alike mediate forms of knowledge, which proceed from the perceived to the unperceived. To take them in reverse order, we have one variety of inference which is expressly called scriptural inference (*āgamānumāna*) which is applicable to cases which do not fall within the purview of any of the known modes of inference and relates strictly to scripturally revealed materials. Such are the arguments given in the scriptures, for example, about gods etc. There is then the argument from the perceived cause to the unperceived effect (*kāraṇa-liṅgānumāna*). Perceiving dark heavy clouds in the sky we infer about the impending rain.[16] Similarly from our knowledge that we enjoy and suffer now as a consequence of what we did in previous births we analogously infer that what we do here in this life will bear a similar consequence hereafter. There is thirdly the argument from the perceived effect to the unperceived cause (*kārya-liṅgānumāna*)[17] where the middle term is related to the major term as effect to a cause. Such are the cosmological or the causal arguments which infer from the gross, physical elements, the existence of subtle elements and a still subtler source of those elements.[18]

Lastly comes the variety in which the middle term is related to the major term neither as a cause nor as an effect (*anubhayātmaka*) but is found uniformly related to the other in experience. We do not indeed perceive the relation between the two terms but find one to be similar to the objects which are related to the other.[19] This may be illustrated by the argument that a thing must have attributes because it is like a substance. From the character of smell which is perceived (*ādheya*) we infer an unperceived 'ground' (*ādhāra*) of this character, namely the earth-element (*pṛthvī*). Such are again the metaphysical arguments from *śakti* to a possessor of *śakti* (*śakta or śaktipati*), from the function of knowledge and will to an owner of the function, namely self.

Two forms of this argument from analogy are recognised, one pertaining to the seen or the seeable (*dṛṣṭa-sādhana*) and the other pertaining to what is unseen and yet may be conceived on similarity (*sāmānyato-dṛṣṭa-sādhana*) based on what is seen in the generality of particular cases.[20] The former is based on an observed concomitance of the middle and major terms, as of pot and the potter and inferring the potter on seeing the pot. The second one is based on similarity of the relation to be established to another which is known through perception, as in the case of inferring the 'existence' of ghosts.[21]

The argument for the existence of agent—God conceived on the analogy of the agency of potter is avowedly of the second type. Even where the argument takes the form of inference from the effect to a cause, the 'cause' to which the effect points is only a conceivable predicate (*dharma*); a subject (*dharmin*) of that predicate is posited on the analogy of known subjects having predicates. The evidence for the reality of the subject of the predicate must in the last resort come from direct intuition (*svarūpa-jñapti*) which is transcendentally embodied in scriptures.

Analogical reasoning in short is formally at least as valid as any inference which employs the category of the universal. Though valid it is no *pramāṇa* of God's reality except when it is taken as ancillary to a more basic source of knowledge, namely Revelation.

God as Reality : The Central Argument

The metaphysical argument by which the reality of God, viewed as the Destroyer-Creator of the world, is sought to be vindicated must be understood in its proper perspective. It is not a vindication of 'the system's faith in inference rather than its faith in a living God'.[1] The argument does not seek to prove a metaphysical as different from a religious God, some principle logically required to account for the existence of motion or change in the world. *Hara*, the ultimate whither and whence of the world, is the God of religion related to the problem of ultimate meaning and fulfilment of human existence, of death and immortal life.[2] The God whom the argument seeks to 'prove' is to be understood in terms of the experience that evokes Him.

The metaphysical argument seeks to support the truth of the Ground and Designer of the universe intimated in scriptures as the Destroyer who is the source of the dissolution and re-creation of the universe. Accordingly, that from whose existence we seek as it were to read off the reality of God as the necessary condition of the world must be of the nature of effect like any known effect of a cause. The world in its implication of a causal Agent-Ground is comparable to a pitcher or a cart or any product[3] *which in its characteristic form as effect*, owes its being to the will and knowledge of some human agent.

Now, in what sense do we say that the world is the effect of a cause ? To analyse the world as effect, to indicate its being contingent or conditional upon a causal agent seems to say nothing of significance. If only somehow we could see the world as effect, then the cosmological argument would be a tautology; 'the world is effect' would be another way of saying that it had a cause.

Therefore, this part of the argument, namely the premise from which the Destroyer is sought to be inferred deserves a deeper analysis and supplementation in more specific ways. The formulation of the metaphysical argument for God seems to be in answer to these requirements. The premise stated in its generality is as follows : the aggregate that is the world is indeed a produced something,[4] being subject to the three significant operations of origin, duration and termination — something which in its entirety 'comes stays and goes'.[5] The world exists but as effect, that is as subject to evolution and resolution.

Two things are suggested here about the world which deserve attention. The world is, firstly, something and not nothing, that is, non-existent.[6] And secondly it is something of a determinate nature, namely its existence is temporal.[7] It exists in time and ceases to exist in time. Temporality is not a feature merely *in* the world but also *of* the world. The second feature about the world, in some sense admitted in all theistic proofs, refers to the 'contingency' of the world's existence the admission of which serves to label the argument. The world is something which exists and ceases to exist in so far as everything in the world is observed to be likewise contingent. The world of everything is not different from everything of the world. It is legitimate to presume from the seen contingency of the world of things to a time or state when nothing of it could exist.[8] But in that case where everything would cease to exist, nothing could be conceived to come into existence, in the absence of something to produce it. Something there must be which is capable of not ceasing to exist, something involving eventual destruction of everything and is not itself destroyed, namely, God.

The world exists

But before showing the significant truth about the world's existence in time, it has to be acknowledged initially that the world *is*. The world must exist. The most formal statement we seem capable of making about the 'world' involving a minimum of theory is that the world intelligible to our understanding is *qua* intelligible an existent, in whatever sense the term 'world' is understood.[9] Experience to which we always rightly appeal for a basis of our beliefs certainly allows us to contemplate the world given to it as *existing*. This commonplace verdict of experience constitutes the empirical element in the metaphysical argument from the known world to its unknown Creator-Maintainer-Destroyer.

The proposition implied in the assertion of the contingency of the world namely that the world 'exists' is relatively innocuous compared to the logical complexity of a statement like ' God exists'. Śaiva Siddhānta expresses the theological truth that *God does not exist*, that is to say, does not exist merely in fact as with all other beings, by accident or by sufferance as cause, condition or favourable environment, by saying that God coincides with Being as such. God is the 'I am'. He self-exists rather than happens to exist.[10] By his power of existence all other things exist.

In the case of the world its existence is asserted under the same conditions under which we assert the existence of any particular object of the world; and precisely in the sense in which 'existence' is asserted here, existence is indeed denied of God. By existence of a table we mean the table's possessing a determinate position in the scheme of space-time-causality. In the metaphysically significant but naive words of popular saying it is what 'comes and goes',exists and ceases to exist. Things are experienced in the world as existing, and so may the world also be experienced. The 'cause' of the world cannot be said to exist in the same sense. The 'cause' of the object of experience cannot also be an object of experience. It must if at all be conceived to exist outside the conditions under which we affirm the world's existence. The 'cause' of what exists cannot exist because by cause we mean that which cannot cease to be, and what cannot cease to be does not 'exist'. The being of God therefore can be affirmed by analogy only.

But it may be asked whether the *siddhāntin's* existential premise is any less complex logically speaking. Is it self-evident that 'the world' exists ? Is it possible to demonstrate the existence of any particular entity[11] let alone the world or God ? True, demonstrative arguments can only issue in equation, not in existence-statements. What is claimed in the statement 'the world exists' must be carefully analysed. The 'world' is a possible object of experience, a presentation. What is given to our knowledge individually in our sense-experience is called, in the collective the world, and either way no attempt at demonstration is made in support, it being considered a scandal to have to demonstrate it. The world is not non-existent, no less or no more than an object given to my normal experience. If the non-existent cannot be presented — Śaiva Siddhānta joins hands with the generality of Hindu philosophical thought in rejecting the heresy that there can be perception of the non-real (*asatkhyāti*), neither can the presented world be non-existent. When this is admitted it may be seen that one is not far from admitting the 'contingency' of the world's existence.

The world exists in time

A thing 'existing' in the present span of time has necessarily a 'before' and an 'after'. A thing 'is' is inconceivable without the circumstances of its origination and destruction which are the factors which determine its history. Origination and termination are the factors contributing towards the 'enduring' of a thing.[12] The belief in a positive effect is inconsistent with the repudiation of a condition under which it ceases to be. An unconditioned event, an 'endless' incidence is a contradiction. An event in the world cannot be thought of without a 'prior' and a 'posterior'. It is an event as taking place at a particular moment and not later or earlier.

Perception, it is argued, is evidence only in favour of the truth that something is, and therefore, presumably, the world is; but to go further and say that the world has origin and end is to indulge in speculation. This objection however presents no serious difficulty in the light of what has been said before; once one is able to wrest the admission that there is the world—on which the commonsense verdict of perception seems unanimous, it is not difficult to show that this belief in a 'positive' world is incompatible with the repudiation of production and termination for the same. If from the perceived fact thata thing is it can be asserted that the 'world' also is, is it not plausible to understand 'the world is' exactly in terms of our understanding of 'a thing is' ?

In all natural phenomena it is a commonplace that a state of arrest is perceived to break up into a state of motion. Having been brought to that state of arrest the object tends towards a break-up of the arrest. Perception on which the naturalist lays great credence evidences the state of 'arrest' in nature, in the collective as well as in the individual sphere. And 'arrest' obtains between the two poles of complete inhibition and complete emergence. Perception is evidence not only with regard to isolated particulars 'coming and going' but also of a class of things existing and perishing as such; the world itself is only a 'class' of multiple things. The seasonal sprouting of seeds as a class and their seasonal decay is a commonplace instance.[13] It may be perceived that seasonally every species becomes extinct as a whole. Therefore it is conceivable that in time the 'world' as a whole may also come to an end.[14]

But the entire argument proceeds on the assumption, it may be thought, that the world is a world in time. It may well be that the world in the collective, unlike the particular things and events that we observe, is a world only in space and not in time pointing to a before and an after.[15] An event in the world occurring at a determinate time is determined by factors which we describe as the cause of the event. The occurrence of these factors, individually and collectively, must have in turn been determined by a prior event or set of events; the latter is the 'cause' of the earlier event accepted as the cause of the original. This only means that every cause is effect in its turn; there is no such thing as the first cause of the world.

The 'world' in whichever sense taken, is, in other words, eternal;

change characterising the physical reality corresponding to what is called 'dissolution' (*pralaya*), is *in* the world in perpetual process, and not *of* the world as such.[16] There is no reason to suppose that the world has had a beginning or will have an end.

The substance of this objection seems to be that while each item in the world considered separately is 'contingent' these items may together constitute a whole which itself may not be contingent.[17] It may be shown in reply that the world as a whole has conceivably no existence other than as the assemblage of its parts. The 'world' itself is conceived as a unique object and this unique object is not different from each of the objects on the basis of whose similarity to their totality the latter is called object.[18] This is at any rate, a more innocuous assumption than to hold to the contrary, namely, that the world as a whole is necessarily different from its parts.

To say that the world as a whole may not be an object in time while things in the world are temporal is to introduce a necessary distinction and even heterogeneity between the two natures. This is certainly unwarranted. The question is : is the 'world' one more entity over and above the entities constitutive of it or is the world only a name for the totality of things ? To take it in the second sense is certainly less presumptive. The 'world' is but an extension of an event, having a longer span of duration.

The argument, nevertheless, is only negative, it may be said. The 'world' and the things of the world are not different and what may be asserted of the one is not unassertible of the other. But what are the positive grounds on which it may be asserted that the world is only effect, subject to the processes of origin and end as well as duration ?

Some Arguments to show that the world is only effect

Śaiva Siddhānta suggests certain arguments for showing that the world is temporal and a becoming. These characteristics are constitutive of its nature as effect. The arguments, each in a unique manner it may be seen, suggest by implication the non-becoming nature of the *cause* of the world, which is Being or *sat*.

The world is a composite whole composed of the forms of 'male, female, and the neuter.'[19] A whole of parts is, necessarily, liable to destruction. A composite is conditioned by a cause or causes. It is impermanent in the sense of being brought into being, even as the incomposite as that which is never composed, is eternal.

The part-whole analysis in philosophy is open to equivocation. There are instances where we refer to the 'part' of a thing and its function without the implication that the whole of which it is part is a composite (*avayavin*). We distinguish, for example, aspects of an indiscernible whole like ether (*ākāśa*) without dividing in the sense of separating its parts as discrete units. We likewise speak of a 'part' of original matter (*māyā*) as undergoing evolution, and of a 'partial' manifestation of knowledge. When we speak of 'part' in the context of the world, we mean by it not the partial (*ekadeśa*) but the part (*avayava*) that goes with other parts to constitute the whole (*avayavin*), and imply thereby that the 'whole' exists but as made up of the parts, and does not exist prior to it.[20]

The description of the composite character of the world in terms of 'male, female, and the neuter' is significant. It suggests that compositeness permeates the entire corporeal kingdom, and more, it extends to the incorporeal too, which also is 'made up of' the elements and the elementals. The 'neuter' refers to the inorganic while 'male' and 'female' typify the organic world of which it is the most pervasive feature.[21]

Compositeness is a unitary feature which characterises the entire world, corporeal and incorporeal. The question of the possibility of a 'break' in the world taken as a whole as far as this feature of compositeness is concerned does not arise; by world, we do not refer to a new entity different from what it is composed of; compositeness and a consequent impermanence are the necessary features of all things of the world.

Another argument of a metaphysical nature is also suggested for considering the world as only the effect of a cause. By world we mean a plurality of insentient things. Two features are significantly conjoined here : materiality or being not spirit (*jaḍatva*) and plurality or not being an unity (*anekatva*). Their *conjunction* is indicative of the non-eternal nature of the world.[22] What is characterised by manifoldness *and* materiality cannot be conceived as containing the ground of its own existence. A manifold of material objects cannot have self-existence. In passing from effect to cause we pass from the sphere where both these features (*jaḍatva, nānātva*) are present together, to a sphere where either can be present but not both. It is not merely an ascent from the many to the one but also simultaneously from the inert to the intelligent.

The applicability of the epithet inert or non-intelligent (*jaḍa*) to classes of objects indicated by 'male' and 'female' may not be questioned. That in virtue of which this distinction of gender is made pertains to corporeal body which is part of matter. Embodied life is in no way an exception to material existence; it rises, stays and perishes just as any other inert object. Man's death is proof of his organic relation to the world of nature.[23] 'All go unto one place, all are dust and all turn to dust again.'[24]

These two arguments taken together suggest by implication that the 'cause' of the world must in one important respect at least be different from the world. It cannot also share the characteristics of the world in virtue of which the world is said to be effect. Not only must it be different from the composite, manifold *cum* material world of phenomena; it must be different from all the alleged causes from which the world may be thought to have arisen, because the so-called causes also share in the character of compositeness and inertia. The *cause* of the world in the true sense of the word cause cannot, in other words, be *pāśa* or its species.[25]

The need for this kind of a stipulation about the cause of the world arises because some Indian cosmologies trace the world's existence to a 'cause' which is not different from the world as far as those peculiar characteristics are concerned whose presence serves to mark off the world as effect. The theory of Primal Atoms (*paramāṇus*) forming the ultimate constituents of the material world, is an instance in point. Even the atoms have a limited size and shape as well as spatial positions and therefore are really composite in constitution.[26] There is no conclusive evidence in favour of more ultimate entities in which is to be found the utmost limit of diminishing magnitude other than a molecule (*tryaṇuka*) which possesses a minimal gross magnitude. One sure evidence for the composite character of atoms is admission of conjunction (*saṁyoga*) between two *paramāṇus* which is inconceivable except on the admission of parts for them.[27]

Even granting that the *paramāṇus* are in some mysterious sense incomposite, we can show by the application of the second test that they cannot surely be the ground of their own existence. *Paramāṇus* are many and material, and are, therefore, only derived effects producible and terminable.[28] Such is also the case with *prakṛti* of the Sāṅkhya system, another suggested causal principle of the world. *Prakṛti* is really not one but a homogeneous state. It is nothing apart from the three constituents (*guṇa*) in mutual equilibrium, a hypothetical state produced by their tensions. It therefore can be labelled 'inert and multiple' and is no different from the world as an assemblage of heterogeneous inert things.[29]

Does not Śaiva Siddhānta, to anticipate one of its own doctrines, admit *māyā* as the causal principle of the universe ? *Māyā*, which is admittedly not one, material cause of the world that it is, is not 'intelligent' either. How can it be cause judged by the present test ? To answer that each *māyā* taken by itself is one and that, therefore, while it is inert (*jaḍa*), it is not multiple (*aneka*) is a quibble.[30] The same defence can be made on behalf of all things, many and material in nature. It is true that Śaiva Siddhānta admits two *māyās*; whether they are numerically two remains, however, to be seen. Another argument is surely needed to show that the 'ground' of the world truly transcends the world even more truly than in the case of a barely material cause transcending its effect.[31]

What is unique about the existence of the world which makes it only the effect of a cause is that it is denotable as 'this'. The world is ostensively definable as a 'he, she and it'.[32] The expressions 'he, she, and it' are verbal equivalences of pointing at particular things; they are demonstratives in the use of which what is constant is the relation of something being *presented*. Their uniqueness of designation derives from their use from a particular point in space and time. When, for example, we stand in front of a particular object at a particular moment and say 'he', 'she', or 'it', we mean a given object of our attention; and to generalize this we think of 'he' and other demonstratives as standing for direct presentation.

These demonstratives have indeed greater generality than ordinary descriptive expressions. While the latter can describe only certain objects, every object can from some point of view or other be correctly referred to as 'he' 'she' or 'it'. Anything and everything is 'he', 'she' or 'it'. If they are universals they are also in one respect different from other universals, in as much as they cannot be used as symbols. What assures uniqueness to an object presented is just the fact that it is presented; its uniqueness lies in its being 'he', 'she' , or 'it'. It is unique because it is given.

Nothing brings out the fact that the world is 'becoming' and not 'being' so tellingly as its mode of cognisability. The world besides being complex (*viśiṣṭa-kārya*), manifold and inert, is also object, objectively known. It is presented as object. That it is presented as object indeed suggests that it is not non-existent;[33] we cannot refer demonstratively unless what is thus referred to is actually presented. At the same time it also suggests that what is known as object has no transcendent being. What is known as object to a subject suffers by comparison with the subject; the latter is *conscious* of change thus overreaching the sphere of change. The object depends for its intelligibility on the subject, while the subject does not depend so on the object.

The subject too, nevertheless, fares no better. A subject *to which* something is presented as object of knowledge, 'he' , 'she' and 'it', shares the same status as the object; the transcendent ground of the objective world cannot be sought from the subject either.[34] The world-cause must be transcendent to the objectifying knowledge as well as to the objectified world. It cannot be an object to a subject or even a subject confronting the object. It must be Being itself (*sat*); the subject-object world as one of becoming is, relatively, non-being (*asat*).[35]

The realist objectifies everything in thought and hypostatises them into categories of the real, thus vindicating the objectivity of knowledge and its adequacy for knowing reality. For Śaiva Siddhānta, while valid knowledge is adequate for knowing that something exists, what is thus validly known to exist is for that very reason '*asat*' in character;[36] it exists but precariously, as existence in time.

The realist may argue : Non-being refers to those objective things which form the basis of knowledge of negation, the negative facts which are the 'given' of negative knowledge. If, however, the positive world objective and validly knowable as 'this' were itself non-being (*asat*), then the very distinction between *sat* and *asat* would be in the melting pot.[37]

Śaiva Siddhānta uses the term *asat* in referring to the world in a different sense. The world is 'non-being' not in the sense of non-existence (*abhāva*). Existence (*bhāva*) and non-existence (*abhāva*) are in fact understood as determinations of the 'given'. What is positively known to exist (*upalabdhi*) will by its very nature, due to a distribution of the constituent qualities of matter, become the object of negation (*anupalabdhi*) and *vice versa*.[38] Why do we observe by the method of difference that sometimes a thing is present and sometimes not to our observation ? The metaphysical interpretation is consistent with commonsense. When present it is noticed and surely not when it is not present. Being present, like not being present, is the predicament of material evolution due to a distribution of its manifest (*rajas*) and non-manifest (*tamas*) qualities (conditioned in each case of knowledge by the moral deserts of the knower). The status of the empirical world from the point of view of knowledge is, therefore, precarious in the sense that at one time it may be unknown and at another time known. The alternation between 'is' and 'is not', between manifestation and non-manifestation[39] which infests the very order of material existence is the characteristic feature indicated by the term *asat*; if the 'world' exists in this sense, the cause of the world also cannot 'exist'.[40] The 'cause' has to be precisely what is constitutionally immune from this disability.

In other words, if to denote as 'this' is the unique characteristic of the world, it follows what we mean by 'cause' of the world cannot be 'denoted' as 'this'; it cannot be the 'given' of knowledge. All references to it as '*that*' (*tat*) are, therefore, only symbolic; indicating the world as 'he', 'she' and 'it' on the other hand is non-symbolic; these are experientially certified demonstratives. Hence it is said paradoxically that the world as the given of valid 'experiential' knowledge is not Being (*asat*).

This point brings out the slant of sense Śaiva Siddhānta gives to the term *asat*. The world as *veridically* known is not on a par with an illusory content like that of rope-snake.[41] The 'given' is not Being but it is not also non-existent. What is presented is not Being, but what never really exists is never presented. A category which is neither absolute existence nor absolute non-existence like the 'illusory' being (*mithyā*) is not admissible. To the extent we distinguish valid knowledge from error within the vantage ground of experience itself we cannot equate the given as such with illusory being.

The rejection of the given world as illusory rests on the epistemological assumption that an illusory 'being' whose nature and being are exhausted in the illusory context itself (*prātibhāsika*) is given in a perceptual illusion.[42] This has to be first accepted before 'givenness' as such may be contemplated as possibly equivalent to 'illusoriness'. But on the view pertaining to the status of the content of illusion such as the one Śaiva Siddhānta will advocate, it is legitimate to mean by the 'given' precisely that which is not illusory. The illusory content is not a unique unrecognisable presentation. It is also like any known content of knowledge; only in this case it is mis-related.[43] Error is a mistaken relation of two terms. That they can be mis-related implies they can be rightly related also. To deny the very distinction between true and the false within the given, will be in effect to deny the distinction between the given as false and what is not given as real. Even to argue that the cognised (*dṛśya*) is false and the not-cognised (*adṛśya*) is real, a distinction between the real and the false will have to be initially accepted with reference to the world of the cognised.

What is said to be common between illusory knowledge and valid knowledge is that the content is known in a particular form with a determinate characteristic and is expressed through words and concepts. This is, in other words, knowledge through essence. The essence is the essence of things and forms no part of them. Therefore, knownness — knowledge through essence, is equivalent to the false.[44]

But on the view according to which 'essence' (*dharma*) and thing (*dharmin*) are identical[45] it can be argued that knownness is equivalent, and necessarily equivalent to the real. To know a thing in a determinate form and as speakable *is* to know the real.[46] How else can the distinction between illusory knowledge and valid knowledge be maintained ? Śaiva Siddhānta will admit differences of dimension within the real and even grade them in an heirarchy. The 'speakable' over-reaches the category of the presentable and is the guarantee of its own reality. The 'ungiven' *sat* however, eventually transcends even the speakable.[47] What is to be noted here is that these distinctions are alike ontological.

There is a difference between the *advaitin's* approach from the world to its cause and the approach of Śaiva Siddhānta. For the one it involves a transition from 'appearance' to reality. The relation of appearance to reality, to be sure, is more intimate than the relation of effect to cause and involves no such temporal succession as is involved in causal relation. Moreover it is also true that the world and the world-cause are not merely different; the difference is made the ground for the rejection of the one as false and the assertion of the reality of the other. If they are merely different, and not different as real and unreal how can one pass from the knowledge of the world to a knowledge of its 'cause' ? There is no other way of knowing the real except through a rejection of the false.

Śaiva Siddhānta approaches the reality of God in a different spirit. The theory of the 'illusoriness' of the world is not a necessary formulation of religious consciousness, which is alive to the reality of God more as the 'Absolute Thou' than as being in general negatively implied by the phenomena. The philosopher starts his quest with a feeling of the vanity of life. A consciousness of this feeling is only negatively a search for absolute certitude, a demand for an unconditioned state of self-existence and meaning. The saint or the mystic on the other hand, does not start with life's vanity. He is sensitive to it only negatively, his primary intuition being that of a self-existent Free Will which is the ground as well as the conserver of being and meaning. It is more directly an appreciation of that in contrast to which the world's evanescence and meaninglessness become apparent. It is the appreciation of Divine Grace more so as the latter makes its presence felt and shows by its very reality the hollowness of the 'reality' of the world from which it stands contrasted. The measure of its reality is in proportion to the completeness of the contrast.[48]

Śaiva Siddhānta also pleads for rising above dualism, where all givenness as such vanish.[49] In the ecstatic intuition of God there can be no givenness. For *Śiva-jñāna* there is no 'given' world.[50] But this does not imply 'negation' of the world in respect of its existentiality. It rather signifies the world ceasing to be opaque and regaining its translucence in the light of divine knowledge.[51]

Parity of speech-world with the spoken[52]

Thus the world is shown to be effect in terms of its compositeness, heterogeneity, inertness and, above all, its experiential character. The objection of the Mīmāṁsaka to the argument of the theist is that the middle term (*hetu*) being effect of a cause, can not be established in regard to the subject (*pakṣa*) of the inference, namely the world, and that, therefore, the argument is open to the fallacy of unestablished ground (*hetvasiddhi*).[53] In anticipation of this objection it is pointed out that the composition of the world itself, its plurality and materiality and its empirical mode of cognisability, eloquently establish its character as effect.

Now what about the realm of *śabda*? Just as it is legitimate to assume a parity between events of the world and the world itself considered as one big event, Śaiva Siddhānta sees a parity between the spoken world (*artha-prapañca*) and the world of speech (*śabda-prapañca*). In holding that the perceived world is effect, what disappears and appears, exception cannot be made in the case of the world of word-essences or Ideas which partake of phenomena. The latter, although the ground of our phenomenal knowledge and even inclusive of Revelation, is also effect, producible and terminable.

The Mīmāṁsaka's argument for the eternity of word (*śabda*) is based on the following considerations: The word and its sense go together and it is impossible to conceive of them as beginning in time. The eternity of their relation actually follows from the eternity of the 'word' and sense.[54] A word is a collocation of two or more letters (*varṇa*) which are articulate sounds. The latter are partless, universal and therefore eternal as against the 'sound' (*dhvani*) which is a manifestor of word or word-parts and is transient and limited. The *siddhāntin's* objection is to the effect that a word-part (*varṇa*) is perishable because it is only a product although of a different order of production.[55] The reasons (*hetu*) adduced are the same as used in support of the non-eternity of the world of sense (*artha-prapañca*). The *śabda* is a whole of parts as is evident from the division of words into those signifying one class of gender indicated by the expressions 'he' and 'she', and those signifying another class indicated by 'it'. Again, it is many and material.[56] The *varṇas* which compose a *śabda* are really many as may be seen from the following illustration. The word 'a'[57] is a noun when it denotes a cow, is a participle when it suggests sorrow, is a verb when taken as a command and is an adverb when it means motion. Although because of the similarity of the letter it is superficially taken as a case of one word with a plurality of meanings, in fact each word is different as it has a different signification. It is *jaḍa* as well because of its mutability. The Mīmāṁsakas themselves regard both *śabda* and *artha* as non-intelligent (*acetana*). Both these characteristics, namely *anekatva* and *acetanatva* of *śabda*, cryptically suggested by the expression he-she-it, together constitute its non-eternality. Lastly, *śabda* is known discursively through auditory perception. It is true that the articulate sound of *varṇa* becomes the object of our experience through adjuncts (*upādhi*) but even then what is experienced is the *varṇas* themselves of the form of the manifest *vāk* (*vaikharī*).[58] Consistently, Śaiva Siddhānta deems even the *āgama-pramāṇa* as a species of *pāśa-jñāna*[59] and, therefore, *pati* cannot be known even through this means, lest *pati* become *asat* in character.[60]

III

GOD AS CAUSE

From the World to the World-Cause

The earlier phase of the metaphysical argument consisted of the assertion of an existential premise, namely, the world exists, and exists necessarily as effect. It is effect in the sense that it is not the ground of its own existence but depends metaphysically on something *beyond* itself. The second phase of the argument to be considered presently is the argument proper, an inference by complementary relation that there must be a cause of the world which must, in the ultimate analysis, be the ground of world-resolution — the Destroyer-God. From the Transcendent spirit in whom has 'dissolved' the world and from nowhere else can the world evolve again into existence[1]. This sums up the conclusion of the argument about the reality of agent-God taken in a general sense, and also in the unique sense in which He may be conceived as the 'cause' of the world.

The 'general' part of the conclusion about God's causality again consists of (i) a vindication of the 'existent' nature of the world; the world is not non-being, such that its 'evolution' may be conceived as pure becoming, sheer emergence. The world is not a flux but being and only as such does it evolve and resolve; the 'non-being' cannot be a term in a causal relation;[2] and (ii) an argumentation to the effect that the world, an existent reality which undergoes the processes of evolution and resolution points necessarily to an intelligent agent that initiates and sustains the processes; for that which exists there is no coming into being without will-causality (*nimitta kāraṇatva*).[3]

The 'special' sense in which God's causality is understood in Śaiva Siddhānta will now become intelligible. From that into which it was resolved, from that alone, the resolved can re-emerge for the excellent reason that it had resolved therein. What is produced must be that which had dissolved. The 'first cause' of the world derives its plausibility from the circumstance that it is the ground of world-resolution (*layādhiṣṭhāna*)[4].

From the foregoing account it is evident that the metaphysical 'cause' of the world-process as conceived in Śaiva Siddhānta is not mere

Being which is the inoperative ground of phenomena, devoid of character (*nirviśeṣa*) unlike the objective phenomena of which it is cause. The cause is conceived as both Being and Will, transcendent and yet immanently present in the world as cause is present in the effect. It is cause, not in the negative sense that because of it the effect is and that it is therefore indispensable even for the appearance of the effect. It is cause more positively in the sense that it positively wills the world into existence and sustains it by its immanence; and this itself is intelligible because it is what can freely will the world into non-existence; being free, the will freely abstains from creating; being free to abstain, it abstains from abstaining, that is, it creates.

The cause in other words is transcendent spirit, the efficient cause[5] (*nimitta kāraṇa*). The transcendent spirit is also identical with transcendent will, the indispensable 'means' (*karaṇa, sahakāri-kāraṇa*) for the operation of these cosmic functions. As transcendent ground (*paramādhāra*) whence arises and whither tends all world-process, it is also in the deep sense of the term the material cause (*upādāna kāraṇa*). Intrinsically transcendent as spirit, the cause is also immanent in the world as being and will. It is therefore not only the *sole* cause in a profound way, but it is also in some sense, identical with the effect that is the world. The metaphysical argument does not seek for a cause that is removed from the world. The God approached 'cosmologically' is the God *immanent* in the cosmos; the world indicates an agent who functions without ever ceasing to be related to the world.[6] The cause is continuous with the effect. God is continuous with the world as the perennial ground of its resolution and evolution.

The finite and contingent character of the world one may admit. But is this admitted significance of the world a sufficient ground for positing a transcendent cause and its unity and 'identity' with the effect ? Is it not plausible to agree with the premise of the metaphysical argument without necessarily agreeing with its conclusion? In other words, is not the argument unsound ?

The various points of view which are in disagreement with the thesis of Śaiva Siddhānta about the Destroyer being the cause of the world may be reviewed in a progressive order so that by an immanent criticism of them we may arrive at the *siddhāntin's* conclusion. Logically arranged, these positions employing the category of cause in a metaphysical sense range from Accidentalism (*animitta-vāda*) at one end of the scale to the[7] Transcendentalism (*nimittakāraṇa-vāda*) of Śaiva Siddhānta at the other.

Accidental creation

Accidentalism which ascribes the changing characteristics of the world to sheer accidence or chance (*yadṛcchā*) amounts to an unquestioning repudiation of causality and therefore of the very possibility of systematic knowledge. Accidentalism either does not assert anything and by implication denies the possibility of metaphysical knowledge, or it asserts something. What exactly the theory of accidental production asserts is not however clear. Does it hold that the effect is absolutely uncaused (*animitta*) or only that it is produced out of what is not a cause ? Either alternative seems unintelligible. In the one case it is a contradiction to speak of an effect which does not admit of a cause. In the other, if it is produced out of something that is not a cause, then that something, at least, may be held to be cause. The position is thus inherently unstable and deserves mention as an extreme case denying causal explanation outright[8] as against all other positions including that of the naturalist (*svabhāva-vādin*) which accept causality in some form or other.

Spontaneous creation

The naturalist ascribes whatever is characteristic of the world not to accidents but to things themselves[9]. If the world is not determined by chance neither is it determined by some external principle. The processes of origination and termination to which the world is subject is neither fortuitous nor imposed from without; they are inherent in the very nature of things.

If the world were not by nature disposed to dissolution and creation, even an all-powerful Destroyer could do nothing with it.[10] Why should one posit a Destroyer-agent for the world and also admit, as one must, a natural predisposition on his part to bring about destruction? Why not only the latter?[11]

In answer it may be asked: is the alleged 'agent', namely, the material stuff of the world naturally disposed to 'dissolve' and re-structure again, a determinate cause or not? That is to say, is it cause by virtue of some condition or adjunct qualifying it or is it cause unconditionally ? If latter, the why and wherefore of the effect would remain unexplained. If former, does its agency consist in being controlled from without, or is it itself of the nature of a causative agent? The second alternative is not admissible because there is no evidence to show that an inert, material cause can independently have agency in relation to its effect.[12] Inertness (*jaḍatva*) which is synonymous with *object* (*asat*) and agency (*kartṛtva*) which belongs to the subject work contrariwise. As for the other alternative it is only another way of stating that the material cause of the world is grounded in the creative power (*kriyā-śakti*) of an intelligent agent.

Again, the naturalist admits that the world is subject to modification (*vikāra*) but maintains that these modifications are 'natural' (*svabhāva*) to the world. How can alteration (*vikāra*) be compatible with the persisting nature (*svabhāva*) of a thing?[13] If to evolve is natural to the world the world must *always* be evolving. How can it also resolve? If luminosity is a natural property of light, how can it also possess darkness?[14]

A real must be a uniform unvariant mode of existence. It cannot comprise two heterogeneous functions like coming to be and decease. In reply, it may be held that to act uniformly is not necessarily to act exactly in the same way but to follow consistently the same law or order of varying succession (as for example, in a certain series of numbers). Dissolution following Creation and being in turn followed by it, this order may be uniform.[15] What is natural to the world is evolution-dissolution as such and not evolution and dissolution as two different and opposed states. They are the facets of one and the same changing process, and not as for example for the Buddhists, two mutually excluding point-instants in time. This leads to a curious paradox. If alteration (*vikāra*) is the persisting nature (*svabhāva*) of the world, it amounts to saying that the world has no unalterable nature of its own. The naturalist is forced to the predicament of disowning anything in the name of nature.[16]

The naturalist conceding some scope for 'causation' in the *siddhāntin's* sense may argue that the world of elements themselves may be conceived of at once as the effect and the cause; as effect there is alteration (*vikāra*), namely, origination and dissolution, and as cause there are the natural elements, earth, water and so on. In reply it may be observed that as the realm of elements is admittedly the 'accusative' of some action the agent of such action cannot also be the world but something different.[17] To act is to be active and to be acted upon is not to be active, so that how can one and the same thing be both at once?.

Causal efficiency consists in the power to *initiate* change. If we rigorously apply this norm, cause has to be transcendent. A causal agent like the elements of earth is said to move and also be moved; it does not really initiate change because as moved, it becomes a patient also. Instead of initiating an impulse it merely communicates what it has received from outside.

The naturalist accepting this condition can still argue on following lines: the four primary elements which are perceptible can *inter se* act as causative agents in relation to themselves. Each of them, by turn, can be 'different' in relation to the rest and 'cause' them; air sustains the other elements and in doing that sustains itself; fire destroys the remaining three and also itself through them; water creates the rest and through them is self-created. Here it may be noted that the nominative (*kartṛ*) and the accusative (*karman*) are kept apart and still a naturalist theory of causation is not given up.

But a cause should not merely be different from the effect but also be 'transcendent'.[18] What is cause cannot also become effect but should always be cause. The naturalist's elements are disqualified as causes because each of them alike is, admittedly, created, sustained and destroyed.

A permanent transcendent agent for the world is what seems to be demanded in the name of cause : a permanent conserving 'ground' from which the world, having resolved therein, re-emerges, which is also intelligent, unlike the world's-seed (*jagad-bīja*) of the naturalist. The processes of resolution and evolution are not spontaneous but spontaneously willed by an intelligent cause.

Spontaneous destruction

The Buddhist however finds this notion of something resolving into a cause and evolving thence meaningless. If the cause continues to be then there is no causation as the effect does not have to be produced; the continuant cannot be supposed to *originate* what has already come into existence. If what exists can again be brought into existence there will be no end to this duplication process.[19] Again destruction is only negation and is not effected. Destruction, in other words, refers to the fluxional nature of reality; the fluxional nature is not distinct from the real entity itself; 'destruction of a thing' is a misnomer;

destruction is not an event in the history of the thing, there being nothing like a thing apart from its history. Destruction may however be conceived as a subsequent event in regard to the immediately preceding event.[20]

Destruction is a necessary characteristic of productibility. The very causes that lead to the production of an entity, lead also to its destruction *in the very next moment*. Existence is therefore momentary; it is definable by the character of dying immediately after being produced. Things are necessarily different every moment. Indeed 'difference of time is difference of thing'.[21] Whatever exists exists in that particular form, in that particular mode, then and there and no-where and 'no-when' else.

Origination is not the production of the effect with the cause remaining permanent, but *replacement* of one event by another event. Destruction or decease similarly must be inherent in things and must mean absolute cessation of existence. If a thing is not perishable constitutionally it must be imperishable; no external 'destroyer' can make it cease to exist. But if it is perishable by its consititution, it will perish in the very next moment of its birth without having to await destruction at the hands of an agent.

So it is the uncritical popular notion of a thing having a 'before' and an 'after' and a temporal span which is at the back of the view that the world as effect points to a transcendent cause. But on the view that existence is momentary, the world is a continual coming and going, a producing and a being produced. In the place of a causal agent of the world what we really have is the initial instant of existence itself which has its causal efficiency in relation to the succeeding instant of existence. As against the view that God is the cause of the world, according to the fluxionist, what is actual at any moment, if at all, is as such and altogether the cause of what succeeds that instant.[22] The emergence of the effect is facilitated by the immediately precedent cessation of the cause.

Let us examine this doctrine of impermanence or momentariness.[23] Of what is impermanence predicated ? Is it of an existent or non-existent or of both ? It can be of none of these if predication of impermanence were not to amount to a tautology or contradiction. The existent will always be existent and cannot become impermanent. The non-existent is always non-existent and it is meaningless to say it is impermanent. Nor can the existent and non-existent be said to be impermanent. If something were existent it cannot also be at the same time non-existent and if non-existent it cannot also be existent, and either way it cannot be impermanent. The momentary particular which emerges anew into existence refuses to be brought under the categories of being (*sat*) and non-being (*asat*) or a combination of the two;[24] to say it is *sat* is to deny its momentariness; to say it is *asat* is to reduce the world to non-existence; to say it is both is to join the camp of the relativist (*anekānta-pakṣa*). How then are we to understand it ?

The Buddhist theory of causation underlying the doctrine of momentariness is untenable. There is only a sequence of particulars and there is no question of one thing causing another. A cause is a mere occasion for the emergence of the effect. The effect is non-existent before coming into existence. When it comes into existence the cause ceases to exist. This is pure succession and no causation. How can what belong to two different point instants, that is, two different occurrents be related to each other as cause and effect ? Causal relation presupposes that the relata must be continuous.[25] To assert to the contrary is to assert that the non-existent (*asat*) is the cause. If effect originates from nothing the effect itself will be of the nature of nothing. If no cause be required that there may be an effect then anything may come into being at any time. There can be nothing like causal determination.

The Buddhist argues that destruction dependent on an agent is not conceivable either in respect of the series as a whole or in respect of each member of the series. But the very presupposition of a philosophy of spiritual life which Buddhism too must share is that destruction does not take place without a cause. Something is destroyed and destroyed as a result of knowledge or discipline. The pursuit of ethical discipline, the knowledge that everything is momentary and painful, admitted as the means of bringing about destruction of ignorance is a vindication that destruction does not take place of its own accord but is caused.[26]

Therefore, as against the Buddhist's objection that what exists cannot again come into existence, it may be replied that it is really a case of the resolved evolving from whence it has resolved.[27] It may be argued that what is resolved must be resolved for ever and that if it should evolve again it will have but two natures, different and even opposite. To anticipate later elucidation it may be said here that the process of resolution and evolution are not unconditioned,[28] natural phenomena;

resolution and re-evolution are occasioned by a two-fold need, the need for a 'ripening' of the cosmic *sañcita* and the need for a 'ripening' of the pre-cosmic impurity of spirit (*mala*l. The sequence of the processes is not therefore an inherent and uncaused phenomenon, but is conditioned by the circumstances that these cosmic processes are for the sake of redeeming the selves from a condition of connate Impurity and Ignorance. When this condition is not present, the processes of resolution and evolution also will cease to obtain as mutually distinct processes.

That things are subject to destruction one may accept; that 'total' destruction indeed goes on constantly is also the Buddhist doctrine. But what is the evidence for the assertion that 'destruction' is only resolution and not absolute termination, and that the resolved re-emerges again from its condition of resolution? How can it be demonstrated that the product exists prior to its production and that it does not cease to exist after its decease or destruction?

Pre-existence of effect (*satkārya-vāda*)[29]

The answer to this question is, that the prior existence of the effect and the continued existence of the cause in the effect are absolutely necessary for causation[30] in so far as cause cannot be a mere occasion for the coming into existence of the effect. From the ground of resolution the effect re-evolves as before because the effect in its essence is identical with the cause from which it comes forth.[31] Production is differentiation and dissolution is reintegration.[32] The process of becoming implies change, and change consists not of replacement of one particular by another with discontinuity between the two, but of transition of a form (*dharma*) from an unmanifest to a manifest state and from the manifest back to the unmanifest. The substrate of becoming is being; becoming is really self-becoming.

The theory of 'pre-existent effect' implies that the cause and effect are alike existent in so far as the non-existent cannot be a term in a causal relation and that the existent effect is only a transformation of the cause and hence the same in substance with it. The word transformation itself, one may see, is suggestive of a change of form and the implied changelessness or sameness of the substance when the form changes. Denial of this would mean contradiction.

For bringing about an effect an appropriate material is resorted to; every material is not by nature capable of producing every effect.

Fitness of the material is a condition of production as otherwise every effect could result from any cause. As effect is non-different from cause, the existent cause cannot imply the non-existence of the effect—such are the classical arguments[33] advanced in support of the thesis that existence issues but from existence and not in any conceivable manner from non-existence.

It may be asked: the fact that the activity of a causal agent is required is itself evidence that the effect cannot exist in the material cause before its production. If the effect were already implicit in the cause what is the need of the causal operation of an agent like the potter? The double-edged nature of this objection is obvious : if the effect were non-existent in the cause then also causal operation is required; and the agent must be able to produce any effect that he wants from a material cause. If he is not able to do so the presumption can only be that from a determinate cause a determinate effect is produced. The admission of a determinate capacity of the cause to produce a determinate effect is but a tacit acceptance of the theory of the pre-existent effect.[34]

The objection that if effect were pre-existent causal operation would serve to accomplish nothing is futile. What is accomplished is manifestation of the effect from its previously resolved condition; the implicit becomes the explicit. The operation of digging of a tank serves to bring to light water underneath the earth. It may be argued that while a pot is produced anew from the clay material, in the other case water which is merely hidden under the surface of the earth is brought out.

There are indeed two kinds of causal evolution; one where it involves a transition from a previously resolved unmanifest condition to manifestation, and the other where the transition consists in the removal of obstruction, so that a previously veiled object becomes now unveiled by the causal operation.[35] The two are indeed identical: in the one case there is an express removal of obstruction—unveiling; the other case of the unmanifest becoming manifest, the unmanifest merged condition is itself the obstruction on the 'removal' of which we say the effect is produced.[36]

The theory of pre-existent effect can be restated in the terminology of form and substance. Every instance of change being an exemplification of causation involves the coincidence of (i) variable forms, and (ii) non-variable substance. The clay in relation to the forms of pots, say jars and pitchers, into which it 'becomes' is non-variable, permanent material substance. The latter, namely, jars and pitchers on the other hand are what come and go. The substance in so far as it conserves with its unity unbroken through all change of forms is the 'substrate' (*dharmin* or *guṇin*) while the fleeting form is the attribute (*dharma* or *guṇa*). Clay has determinate form as lump which as it 'becomes' jar is left behind in favour of a new determinate form; the destruction of the jar again is but the mergence of 'jar' form and the emergence of another determinate form. In universal Dissolution all determinate forms are absorbed and the material cause regains its indeterminate formless blank character.[37] In Creation again it stands as the back-ground of the emergence of forms.[38]

True, causal relation according to *satkārya-vāda* is a relation of form and substance, of *guṇa* and *guṇin*; it is not as it is held by the *asatkārya-vādin* a relation of one form with another form ((that is contrary to the first).[39] A mere sequence of *guṇas*, a succession of particulars is no causation. Two *guṇas* may be related but only through the mediation of *guṇin*. Continuity of cause and effect involves the twin relations of identity-in-difference (*bhedābheda*) and identity (*abheda*), one with reference to forms and the other with reference to permanent matter. From the point of view of the changing forms which consist in leaving behind one determinate form and acquiring another new one (*pariṇāma*) there is identity in difference, and from the point of view of the ever-conserving pre-existent matter (*satkārya*) there is identity.[40]

Modifications of *asatkārya-vāda*

The *Śūnya-vāda* school of Buddhism does not take its stand on *asatkāryavāda*, not because it favours the theory of pre-existent effect that a school of Buddhism can never accept, but because causation itself is a mark of the unreal.[41] The dilemma about the cause is: is 'becoming' of the non-existent or of the existent ? The non-existent cannot become; the existent does not have to become.[42] Neither, what cannot be conceived as identical nor what is different from each other, is established as real.[43] The real as cause, being no more determinable as existent (*sat*) than as non-existent (*asat*) is *śūnya* the Indescribable. The world can be traced but to *śūnya* if at all, as its cause.

The true meaning of *Śūnya-vāda* is that there is no 'essence' in phenomena.[44] Having no essence of its own the world is neither produced nor destroyed. That alone may be deemed the essence of anything which does not depend on something else. Can we point to any such essence which stands independently by itself so that we can say it is real? If 'to exist' cannot be the essence of things, a *fortiori*, 'non-existence' too cannot be their essence. We cannot therefore affirm positively about a thing; neither can we deny anything of it. To say that something *is not* is as much to invest it with an essence as to say that it *is*.

Similarly about the process of change we cannot talk intelligibly of a process either with reference to the permanent or to the momentary. The permanent cannot be cause without abandoning its character and taking up another at the same moment which is impossible. The momentary too is incompatible with process. What appears comes from nowhere and goes nowhere and so there is no process.[45] There being no relation between two moments even the temporal relation of prior and later, strictly, is unwarranted.

There is thus only *śūnya* which again is neither eternal nor destructible. There is no process, no cycle of worldly existence and, therefore, no cause immanent or transcendent. Causation is a mark of the unreal.

In criticism, we may ask: what is this *śūnya* or nullity? What precisely is its ontological status? *Is* there *śūnya* identical with the real or is there *not*? In either case its being indeterminate is untrue. If the *śūnyavādin* denies it the character of being the subject of 'neither real nor unreal' he contradicts himself because the characteristic of the absence of be the subject of real or unreal is predicated of it. If he affirms the character of being subject of 'neither real nor unreal' again he contradicts himself because neither characteristic can be predicated of it. The very statement that 'neither real nor unreal' can be the subject of a predicate presupposes the subjecthood of 'neither real nor unreal' and therefore implies either it is real or unreal and, either way, cannot be 'neither real nor unreal', that is, *śūnya*.[46] The *śūnya* of the *śūnyavādin*, in other words, is non-distinguishable from *asat*, and his dialectical flourish against both *satkārya-vāda* and *asatkārya-vāda* notwithstanding his position is reducible to but one of the two, namely, the second.

The Jaina characteristically attempts to combine the two views of causation and in effect dispenses with a transcendent cause.[47] The Jaina view is that effect is neither an origination absolutely nor is it pre-existent absolutely. The effect is pre-existent in its cause from the point of view of substance (*dravya*) but from the point of view of modification (*paryāya*) it is an origination. If the effect is taken to be absolutely pre-existent, the cause causes nothing; again if the effect is absolutely non-existent then too it cannot be brought about. That which does not retain its preceding form like the one which does not shed its preceding form—the momentary and the permanent, cannot be cause.[48] Effectuation is therefore possible of only that which exists but relatively, or, in other words, both exists and does not exist. The effect is pre-existent in the form of a substance though not pre-existent in the form of modification. The world, argues the Jaina, points neither to *asat-śūnya* of the Buddhist nor to *sat-śiva* of the Śaivite. The world is self-subsistent as at once the cause and the effect. If the atoms of which the world is made are looked at from the point of view of change (*paryāya*) and the emergent qualities they are liable to destruction, but if looked at from the point of view of the underlying substance (*dravya*) they are eternal.

The position that the world is its own cause as well as effect *qua* existent and non-existent, is reminiscent of the naturalist's theory which predicates the two conflicting predicates of alteration and unchanging nature at once to the world. If something exists it cannot also not exist and *vice versa*.[49]

The Jaina of course does not imply by his *astināsti-vāda* the predication of two contradictory states of 'is' (*asti*) and 'is not' (*nāsti*) simultaneously to the same reality. The law of manifoldness or diversity of the nature of reality (*anekānta*) affirms the possibility of diverse attributes in a unitary entity. The cause is both non-identical and identical, non-synchronous and synchronous with the effect, the former before the origination of the effect and the latter at the time of the origination.

But if it be admitted that the cause exists, the effect too must exist although in a latent form. The Jaina says that it is only after the clay substance has undergone modification that the effect, 'jar' comes to be, and that so far as this modification is concerned the effect is a new origination. But this is not tenable. Existence cannot come from non-existence and *vice versa*. The jar (*dharma*) is nothing but clay (*dharmin*) modified in a particular manner, so that with the cause existing the effect too exists, and exists categorically.[50] And, the latent becoming manifest, involves the intelligent agency of a cause which is also the ground of becoming.[51]

The theory of pre-existent effect or the self-becoming of the cause thus derives its further plausibility when examined in the light of some of the dialectical modifications of *asatkārya-vāda*. The cause must be of the nature of being (*sat*) if it is neither non-being (*asatkārya-vāda*) nor being *and* non-being (*anekānta-vāda*) nor neither (*śūnya-vāda*).[52] From being comes being; and self-becoming and will-causality are the obverse and reverse of the same truth. Finally will-causality is not compatible with anything other than the agency of the Destroyer.

The World-Cause as Agent

It may not be thought that the plea for the existential continuity of cause and effect which Śaiva Siddhānta affirms against the heterodox systems of Buddhism and Jainism is at variance with its earlier contention that cause should be the transcendent factor in a causal operation. The latter thesis was defended against the naturalist who would accept a material cause for the world (*jagad-bīja*)[1] but no efficient cause. Against the naturalist it was argued that causation was inconceivable without admission of an efficient cause that transcended the processes of change. The heterodox systems, however, by a radical revision of the concept of change making it total and 'uncaused' in the sense of not implying a permanent intelligent cause, advocate a novel theory of causation. According to them the very distinction between the efficient and material becomes questionable. Against such systems Śaiva Siddhānta pleads for the admission of cause which is continuous with its effect, in so far as something cannot come from nothing. It is necessary to recognise a permanent material cause (*upādāna kāraṇa*) which conserves and does not cease in the effect which it produces. To recognise such cause is a necessary first step for raising the question of an efficient cause for the world.[2]

The thesis of Siddhānta is in sum : belief in a material cause implies and is implied by belief in the theory of pre-existent effect (*satkārya-vāda*) and belief in either entails in turn belief in a transcendent cause—an agent for the world. In making these assertions Śaiva Siddhānta finds itself in opposition to several of the 'orthodox' standpoints as well. The Nyāya-Vaiśeṣika admits an abiding material cause in which the effect inheres (*samavāyi-kāraṇa*) but rejects a theory of pre-existent effect. The Sāṅkhya admits *satkārya-vāda*, but rejects a transcendent God, as in some sense *prakṛti* which it admits as the material cause of the world-process includes the *nimitta kāraṇa* as well.

Theory of new creation (*ārambha-vāda*)

The Vaiśeṣika maintains an absolute difference between cause and effect like the Buddhist whom he resembles in advocating a theory of pre-non-existent effect.[3] The cause is not the stuff or the material which is transformed or fashioned into the effect.[4] The effect is non-existent before and is a newly *created* whole, *different* from its causal constituents or even their conjunction.

But the difference between the *asatkārya-vāda* of the Buddhist and that of the Vaiśeṣika must not be ignored. For the Buddhist when the effect is produced the cause ceases to be; cause and effect cannot exist together. For the Vaiśeṣika the cause in which the effect inheres is the abiding ground of the effect; the effect cannot exist apart from it. The Vaiśeṣika only denies the pre-existence of the effect but does not deny the continued existence of the cause. The jar-halves are there when the jar is produced; the latter as effect subsists in the jar-halves which are its constituents and is sustained by them. The cause originates the effect as intimately connected with it and persists as the ground (*ādhāra*) of the effect. Even when the effect ceases to exist, its 'non-existence' is predicable of its cause alone. The cause is that which 'precedes, originates, underlies, sustains and even survives the effect'.[5] Some mysterious bond of affinity holds the two together but the affinity is not of course of identity.

A previously non-figuring effect is still not an 'other' to the cause; it abides *in* it by relation of inherence (*samavāya*) even as quality (*guṇa*) abides *in* the qualified (*guṇin*), organs (*avayava*) *in* an organism (*avayavin*) and so on. The difference between the Buddhist theory of causation and this one is: existence for the Vaiśeṣika is not momentary. In consonance with the spirit of the 'orthodox' schools it is maintained here that nothing is for less than at least two instants, those of origination and stay; nor can a thing disappear earlier than the third instant after it is made.[6]

Still the Vaiśeṣika is an *asatkāryavādin*. Causation involves emergence of a new entity. All production is mere rearrangement and rearrangement induces the emergence of a 'new' effect. The effect produced is a new thing altogether and is distinct from the substance from which it arises. A theory of pre-non-existent effect (*asatkārya-vāda*) logically slides into the theory of 'origination' or new creation (*ārambha-vāda*).

Every effect produced is a case of a fresh combination of parts forming a new whole. The constituent parts will have to *combine* together in order to participate in the whole. This means that even as a material cause is necessary in which the whole, namely, the effect subsists by inherence, a 'non-material' cause is also equally necessary to explain the emergence of heterogeneous bodies from homogeneous constituents — a cause which produces the effect with its distinctive form and character, by being intimately connected with the material cause of the effect. There can be no inhering cause without a non-inhering cause and also *vice versa*. Causation as it were requires a putting together of things as well as things which are put together.

The *ārambhavādin's* objections to *satkārya-vāda* are based on this very ground: how can a *unitary* material cause for the world be conceived of when it is possible only with multiple material causes, mediation by the other necessary factor in the process of causation, namely the non-material cause.[7] The cause has necessarily to be multiple in order to be able to combine to give rise to a determinate effect.

Likewise, again, the *nimitta kāraṇa* has necessarily to be a *third* category of cause in the Vaiśeṣika scheme, identical neither with the supporting ground (*ādhāra*) of the effect nor with what is bound up with the existence of the effect through the medium of that ground. By the same logic by which the effect is conceived to be different from its cause the efficient cause also is different necessarily from the material cause. The emergence of the effect into existence from prior non-existence requires also separate location of that in which the effect inheres (*samavāyi-kāraṇa*) and that by whose agency the effect is produced (*nimitta kāraṇa*).[8]

The argument in favour of the theory of *ārambha-vāda* and all that the theory implies is furnished from its Atomism which postulates the existence of an infinite number of eternal material particles as the ultimate constituents of all produced substances. Every product is ultimately composed of atoms, ultimate indivisible units, homogeneous and eternal and these atoms combine in various arrangements creating bodies of various forms.

The hypothesis of primal atoms is based on certain ingenious arguments. An entity like the mote in the sunbeam which is of least visible magnitude we infer to be in turn created or made by entities of still finer magnitude. The mote in the sunbeam points backwards to a 'finer' constituent from which it has emerged just as it points forward to objects of grosser magnitude that may emerge into existence. The nether limit where this process of producing and being produced terminates, whence all effects originate in succession and which itself is not originated as there must be one lest there be contradiction, is the atom.

Another argument is: differences in the configuration of minuteness (*parimāṇa-tāratamya*) must find its limit in something to rest. It is impossible to conceive of an infinite scale of diminishing configuration as in that case the observed differences in the configuration of minute objects cannot be accounted for. If there is limitless divisibility into parts all effects produced from a combination of parts would be products of an infinity of component parts. The observable differences in the dimensions of different effects would remain unaccounted.[9]

The arguments adduced in favour of the Atom theory cannot be sustained. The first argument indeed expresses a general principle acceptable to Śaiva Siddhānta too, namely that gross things are produced from finer stuff. But this principle, if rigorously applied, should lead to the postulate of an infra-atomic stuff, or matter which is of the nature of pure potentiality.[10] But to reach this and reach the intelligent spirit which underlies it as its ground the notion of cause as creation or fresh construction (*ārambha*) has to be given up. Causation implies the manifestation of what is unmanifest, the actualisation of the potential.

The atomist however understands increase or decrease in the grossness of matter externally in terms of arrangements and dispositions of parts; difference of size is the cause of difference of substance. The resultant whole changes as a result of changes in the part. Every material effect, *qua* effect, is reducible to parts finer in comparison, and the lowest limit of this process of reduction constitutes atoms, the fine particles *par excellence*. What is needed to show that the conclusion does not follow is to demonstrate the unsoundness of the reason (*hetu*) that is adduced; does change in parts entail change in the size of the resultant whole ? As an example where the effect does not increase in size relatively to the size of its constituent cause, may be cited the instance of milk changing into curd. Change in the constituent parts is not accompanied by change in the size of the whole.[11]

The second argument too is inconclusive. It is assumed that when the whole is broken up into parts a limit is reached beyond which the breaking up cannot go and that 'atoms' constitute such a nether limit. The error here lies in the assumption that atoms are partless. From a division of wholes into parts and of parts conceived as wholes again to *their* parts we cannot reach the part-less. All that the argument warrants is the acceptance of the smallest visible particles (*trasareṇu*). The supposed partless atoms are not established by the argument; what it establishes, namely partible atoms, is not what the atomist has in mind.[12]

The hypothesis of atoms is inherently untenable. The atoms being many and material can only be derived effect, producible and terminable.[13] We call something 'gross' when the effect is 'manifest' and is perceived as many and finite (*ekadeśa*) and something 'subtle' when the effect is resolved and becomes imperceptible, one and infinite (*vyāpaka*). The atomists cannot therefore justifiably conceive of the material cause of the world as the infinitesimal, unextended atoms just because of the term '*aṇu*' connotes the 'subtle'.[14] That the atoms are themselves derived effect and terminable is further evident from the admission of conjunction between two *paramāṇus* at the time of creation;[15] conjunction is inconceivable except on the admission of parts for the conjunctives, namely, atoms. When two atoms are conjoined, is the conjunction partial or total ? It cannot be the latter because a total conjunction between two *paramāṇus* is incompatible with the Vaiśeṣika belief that an atom possessing magnitude (*mūrtatva*) and tactility (*sparśatva*) excludes another atom and resists absorption. Therefore, conjunction will have to be admitted only as partial (*avyāpya-vṛtti-saṁyoga*) and not as pervading the whole of its substratum. This means that atoms have parts, and distinguishable parts as one admitting conjunction and another not admitting conjunction.[16]

Again, the contention that the effect is a whole over and above its constituent causes invites all the criticisms urged on an earlier occasion against those maintaining discontinuity between cause and effect. The *ārambhavādin* assumes that mere numerical addition of the parts conjoined accounts for the *difference* of the whole from its parts. It is argued that the whole is produced *after* the parts are brought in a particular order of conjunction and is again destroyed when conjunction of the parts and not the parts themselves are destroyed. Strictly, this amounts to deriving the non-existent from the existent; this is as little warranted as deriving the existent from the non-existent.

A single material cause demanded by the theory of pre-existent effect cannot account for 'conjoining' of the constituent causes, and without conjoining of parts the effect does not come into existence. So it is argued. But this argument is not acceptable. In all the instances of a positive effect (*bhāva-kārya*) the mediation of a non-material cause for the production of the effect is not necessary. On the contrary its absence in the case of the world is quite evident from the scriptural declaration about the world originating from one unitary source. In such instances of effects as sound, the question of a non-material cause becomes inapplicable; the originating source of sound is *ākāśa* which is unitary. Nor may it be held that a conjunction of a sound-producing medium like drum with *ākāśa* is the non-material cause. There is no agreement in absence in the case of the relation between the alleged non-material cause and its effect; when the drum-ether conjunction disappears, certainly sound does not disappear.[17]

When two atoms are conjoined so as to form a dyad and a dyad into a triad, the conjoining is determined by a moral purpose, namely to produce *bhoga* for the souls and the cause which occasions this motion is the cumulative moral deserts,[18] time and so on; the agent's will is but one such occasioning factor. The atoms themselves are said to have no spontaneity of their own but they seem to be at the same time quite predisposed to conjoin and disjoin and only await the touch of the occasioning cause. Creation and Dissolution are explained in terms of composition and decomposition of the atoms; a *nimitta kāraṇa* is required merely to bring order and co-ordination of the material cause and give direction towards definite results. God conceived as the 'cause' of the world is not also the 'ground' of the world.

The shortcomings of the atom theory evidence the demand for the recognition of a Destroyer-Creator; if the atoms dissolve whence can they emerge again and regroup[19]? The *nimitta kāraṇa* must not merely will the causal operation transcendentally but sustain it in its very being. There is a demand in other words to conceive of the *nimitta kāraṇa* not merely as a cause in a causal series but as the 'cause' of the entire series of cause and effect — the *prima causa* as well as the *ultima substantia*.[20]

Theory of self-becoming (*pariṇāma-vāda*)

The Sāṅkhya-Yoga advocates *satkārya-vāda* and even admits a 'cause' which combines both *upādāna kāraṇa* and *nimitta kāraṇa* but would not identify that with intelligent agent. The function of *nimitta kāraṇa* is not to serve as an extrinsic principle of movement, to occasion from without the creation of the effect. *Prakṛti*, which the Sāṅkhya advocates as the First Cause of all becoming, is self-moved; movement is but an aspect of its being. *Prakṛti* is not inert matter in need of a Prime Mover. It is inherently dynamic and has a spontaneity of action towards a manifestation of its infinite forms. The manifestation in so far as it serves the moral purpose of experience (*bhoga*) of the self is held in check by the merit and demerit of the experient self (*bhoktṛ*) till it is counteracted by an opposite force. The obstruction to manifestation must be removed; the effect already existing becomes manifest on its removal. This then is the function of *nimitta kāraṇa*;[21] the *nimitta kāraṇa* does not communicate any impulse to the material cause. It merely facilitates its manifestation.

Now whence comes this *nimitta kāraṇa*? *Prakṛti* does not have to seek for this principle of facilitation outside its own nature. At the level of *prakṛti* there is no scope for distinction between *upādāna* and *nimitta*; when *prakṛti* evolves into *mahat* the distinction sets in.[22] The constituents (*guṇas*) themselves occasion the movement (*pravṛtti*); according to the Sāṅkhya the *karma* counteracts the obstruction or arrest (*āvaraṇa*) which is a *dharma* opposed to itself, while according to Yoga it is God's will which overcomes all obstructions right from the commencement of the state of equilibrium which itself is the greatest obstruction to the manifestation of the effect. What is conspicuous in this account is the denial of any role to *nimitta kāraṇa* as a direct cause in the production of the effect.

The evolved world is caused wholly and solely by the unevolved.[23] This logically excludes the supposition of an intelligent agent conceived as cause. Causation is a case of self-becoming; the intelligent agent cannot 'become' the world any more than the world can resolve into it. If, therefore, a non-intelligent material cause capable of self-becoming could be admitted, to assume a *nimitta kāraṇa* again is prolix.

The notion of a *nimitta kāraṇa* as other than the *upādāna kāraṇa* is not only redundant but is riddled with difficulties.[24] What is the aim of all manifestation? With an intelligent Agent, the question of 'why creation' cannot be satisfactorily answered. The 'final' cause cannot be included under the category of *nimitta kāraṇa* if the latter were conceived as different from the *upādāna*. An intelligent will cannot be conceived to have created the world unless it be out of self-interest or compassion. Self-interest would mean a lack of accomplishment of something desired and impotence for the will. A benevolent will would have removed the element of misery from the face of its own creation. If misery in creation were due to *karma* then it comes to admitting some role for the non-intelligent in effectuation. Why not accept it in the case of *prakṛti*, which is the formal, material, first as well as the final cause of creation ?

The burden of the Sāṅkhya theory of causation is that the non-intelligent can have causal efficiency. The flow of milk from the cow's teats in itself non-intelligent serves to nourish the calf. The non-conscious magnet exercises causal efficiency in relation to iron-filings. The postulate of *prakṛti* as the cause of the world, its evolution and dissolution is not only plausible but has also the merit of encompassing teleology satisfactorily which the assumption of intelligent creatorship fails to explain.[25]

Nor may it be objected that if the non-intelligent *prakṛti* were the cause of the world, evolution should mean always evolution or dissolution always dissolution as it was urged earlier against the naturalist. Evolution and involution are continuous processes; evolution is self-becoming and involution is self-becoming in the reverse. Moreover, though evolution of *prakṛti* is self-evolution it is for the sake of the selves in so far as evolution serves a moral purpose.[26] Experience of pleasure and pain following in the wake of a life of affirmation, and a renunciation of experience following a discrimination of *prakṛti* and *puruṣa* (or, more simply, as with the Yoga, pleasure and avoidance of pain) are the ends which the evolution of *prakṛti* subserves. The self-becoming process is immanently conditioned by the two ends of enjoyment (*bhoga*) and emancipation (*kaivalya*) of the *jīvas*. Controlled by the interest of the *jīvas* evolution proceeds as if controlled by self-interest.

The premise of the metaphysical argument, namely, the composite character of the material world which the *siddhāntin* uses in support of an intelligent agent for the world in the hands of the Sāṅkhyaite serves to argue for the existence of *puruṣas*, *for whom* there is evolution.[27] The spiritual element is admitted but it does not figure as cause. The argument, that all change points to an agent invested with the powers of intelligence (*jñāna-śakti*) and action (*kriyā-śakti*) equal to effect becoming, is met with the concept of the non-intelligent *pradhāna* itself which possesses in virtue of its constituents *sattva* and *rajas* what corresponds to the powers of *jñāna* and *kriyā*.[28] 'Unborn, one, red, white and black giving birth to manifold progeny similarly formed.'[28a] The Being (*sat*) spoken of in the Chāndogya Upaniṣad should be understood in accordance with this passage which explicitly states that *prakṛti* composed of *rajas*, *sattva* and *tamas*, indicated by the three colours, is the cause of the manifold progeny.

In criticism we may begin with the last. *Prakṛti* is made up of three qualities in equipoise; it does not possess *sattva* and *rajas* to the exclusion of *tamas* so that it may be said to have parity with the conscious and willing spirit.[29] This reference to the *guṇas* raises another important issue. *Guṇa* for the Sāṅkhyaite means a constituent and not an 'attribute' as it is for Śaiva Siddhānta. The *prakṛti* of the Sāṅkhya is nothing but three *constituents* in equipoise.[30] Being many and material it can be the unevolved material cause of the world but only in a relative sense. In relation to its evolutes *prakṛti* is material cause but in relation to more subtle principles, it is effect. Śaiva Siddhānta calls *that* the material cause, whence alone everything is derived and wherein everything resolves,[31] and not the one which is so but in a relative sense. The indestructible *māyā-śakti* of God is alone the material cause of the world.[32]

The necessary relation obtaining between dissolution and evolution is not intelligible without reference to a *nimitta kāraṇa*. Threads etc. although a self-contained material cause cannot be transformed into a piece of cloth without the agency of a weaver endowed with knowledge and action equal to weaving it.[33] All effects are pervaded necessarily (*avinābhāva*) by material cause but in necessary association with a will; clay material 'becomes' a pot but only when animated and sustained by the will of the potter.[34] So *māyā* cannot evolve the world unless the intelligent agent in whose being it is rooted wills the evolution any more than a seed can send up its shoot without the element of moisture present in the earth which supports it.[35]

The *sat* of the Upaniṣads described as the cause of the world cannot be non-intelligent for volition is predicated of it as shown by Bādarāyaṇa. 'It reflected, may I become many'. The *prakṛti* spoken of as the cause of the universe in the cited passage refers only to the ultimate material cause which has an intelligent agent as its ground (*adhiṣṭhāna*). So admission of a *nimitta kāraṇa* far from being prolix is a necessity even to make material causation intelligible. The question of a final cause presents greater difficulty to the advocate of *prakṛti* than it does to the advocate of an intelligent *nimitta kāraṇa*. The causal efficiency of non-intelligent beings is not demonstrated by the Sāṅkhya illustrations.[36] The milk from the teats of the cow does not itself feed the calf; neither does magnet itself attract the iron filings. The varied nature of the created world is due to differences in the contributory factors[37] and does not detract from the compassionate nature of the agent.

The real crux of the problem relates to the notion of change. The Sāṅkhyaite's adherence to an ultimate dualism rests upon a dichotomy between the changing and the intelligent. *Prakṛti* and *puruṣa* are polar concepts. The changing is the non-intelligent and the intelligent is the non-changing; the two thoroughly exclude each other and yet *prakṛti* is made to subserve the interest of the unchanging *puruṣa*. This entails admission of material and efficient causality for *prakṛti*, *puruṣa* being rendered incompetent for the role because of his non-active nature.

Material and efficient causes distinguished

Intelligence and agency on the one hand and non-intelligence and material causality on the other, however, go together. There can be no promiscuity in their relation. The non-intelligent clay is the material cause and the pot-maker with adequate knowledge and action for making the pot, is the efficient cause. It may be seen here that clay *per se* can never be conceived as cause of the pitcher without involving the notion of the potter the efficient cause, so that even to cite clay as an instance of material cause involves some abstraction. The efficient cause while generically distinct from the material cause is at the same time the ground and condition of the latter.

Such are the implications of admitting *māyā* as the material cause to which sphere belongs all change. But change does not pertain to material cause considered independent of efficient cause. All change is willed change, so that it is equally true to say that all change *originates* from the spontaneity of will.[38] There are two distinguishable sides to every case of pervasion of cause in the effect, one in the form of will (*saṁkalpa*) and the other in the form of a modal transformation of material. The potter's will may be conceived to 'pervade' his creation, namely, the pot in so far as he comprehends every part of the pot as he fashions it.[39] If he does not, the pot shall be made by him as little as, say, a mountain.[40] According to *satkārya-vāda*, which is admitted in the system, the cause is continuous in the effect in the sense that the material cause pervaded by *the intelligent efficient cause immanent* in it as will evolves into effect. The clay material 'becomes' pot etc. but as permeated by the intelligence and will of the potter.[41] The material cause evolves its effects from the presence of Śiva.[42] It is the *nimitta kāraṇa*, then, that has a direct causality in the production of the effect. When *māyā* is admitted technically, as the material cause of the world, it is always to be understood as a moment, a necessary moment of will causality.[43]

The World-Cause As the Will

The conception of *cit* as the eternal world-ground has not as yet been shown to provide a principle of change. *Māyā* is the material cause and is what becomes according to the theory of self-becoming. It is not also the dynamic source of becoming. The real dynamic principle of causality presupposed in the theory of pre-existent effect is intelligent will (*cit-śakti*) inherent in spirit (*cit*). It is this principle which makes it possible to conceive the 'cause' of the world as spirit instead of merely as substance. A 'substance' implies isolation from what is not itself, being a transcendent reality set over against and removed from the other. But God is not separated from the world or man. If he were separate spiritual life involving 'partaking' of Spirit will become inconceivable[1].

It is the power inherent in Being that officiates as instrumental cause (*karaṇa*) in the performance of cosmic functions. Instrument (*karaṇa*) and agent (*kartṛ*) are correlatives distinguishable but inseparable. That, by virtue of which, amongst others, God is conceived to be agent of cosmic function is identical with the differentia of the agent, namely, intelligence (*cit*). Cosmic agency presupposes possession of knowledge and freedom not as an extraneous assumption but as integral to the role.

In the case of self-becoming with regard to material cause we distinguished between a non-manifest aspect of the cause and an aspect that is manifest through the act of becoming. In the case of the agent in relation to the effect too we may likewise distinguish between a non-manifest aspect of the agent considered in himself and an active aspect in relation to the effect of which he is causative agent. The term *nimitta kāraṇa* refers to the agent in the former respect—the intelligent being because of whose presence or rather because of which presence is occasioned the effect. In the aspect oriented in relation to the effect the agent is the instrumental cause (*sahakāri-kāraṇa*, *karaṇa*). This is actually the causal meaning *par excellence* (*sādhakatama*). The volition of the agent, his will to create which is brought into play in relation to the created world, is the *sahakāri-kāraṇa*, while the agent considered as a being whose function is will is the efficient cause. It is the distinction between the agent (nominative) and the means (instrumental) by which the agent brings to pass something (accusative) analogous to the potter and his flywheel which as it were concretise the potter's will to create pots.[2]

Permanent cause conceivable with auxiliaries

It is interesting to enquire into the question of how Śaiva Siddhānta comes to derive the concept of *karaṇa*. The notion of auxiliary cause is the direct outcome of a review of the Buddhist's dialectic against a permanent and universal cause and of a criticism of its *samudāya-vāda*. For Śaiva Siddhānta as for the generality of orthodox Brahminical substance-philosophy causation is not admissible without the admission of a permanent transcendent cause.[3] The Buddhist dialectic against substance by the application of the criterion of causal efficiency wrests from the substance-philosopher the admission that the permanent cause, self-sufficient as it is, is yet conceivable to exercise its causal efficiency in conjunction with auxiliaries.[4] A successive-execution of past and future actions by a permanent agent is conceivable because of conjunction with auxiliaries occurring in succession.[5] The occurrent nature of the auxiliaries accounts for the occurrent character of the effect; the permanent nature of the cause distinct from the auxiliary is unaffected by the production or non-production of the effect.

Admission of auxiliaries to the permanent cause does not, however, mean that the permanent is a collocation of causes. The latter is, indeed, the Buddhist's position according to which several factors combine to produce a self-identical effect. The self-identical on this theory is indeed an illusion, its oneness being like the oneness of a heap of corn.

But the philosophers of being, of the orthodox (*āstika*) tradition, would not accept *samudāya-vāda*. For the latter, cause and effect are strictly equivalent and therefore mutually implicatory. But for a philosophy of being cause and effect are inseparable with one term remaining independent as in the case of *vyāpti* relation. Just as the major term exists without the middle term, and not *vice versa*, even so a cause can exist independently of the effect even though the latter cannot exist independently of the former. The relation of causality is asymmetrical; one term is wider than and hence logically independent of the other. Orthodox systems have held fast to this pattern even though differing among themselves in their interpretation of the logical independence of the cause.[6]

The theory of a permanent cause exerting causal functions successively in association with auxiliaries has not gone unchallenged by the Buddhists. Either the permanent agent mutates or does not mutate in association with an auxiliary. If there is no mutation the contingence will be either constant production or constant non-production. If however there is mutation there is no permanence. The problem concerns the function of the auxiliary and its relation to the permanent. Is the auxiliary an instrument (*sahakārin*) to the causal entity in the sense that it produces some supplementation (*atiśaya*) in it, or is it instrument only in name and means nothing to the cause ? Again, either alternative seems unsatisfactory.[7]

A permanent cause exerting causal function in association with the power of producing all its effects simultaneously, also is not free from difficulties. Does the permanent, endowed with the power to produce the entire effect; continue to exist *after* a simultaneous production of the effect or not ? If it does there will be production of the entire effect again, at one time as at another.

The solution to this problem seems to be either (i) to accept two entities, the permanent cause and the auxiliaries which produce supplementation in the permanent cause and to conceive of the supplementation not as distinct from the permanent but as co-inherent in it, or (ii) instead of having two distinct things which are later on related to recognise two aspects distinguishable but not separable in the nature of the permanent, namely the permanent causal entity (*karaṇa*) and the permanent causal function or power (*karaṇa*) integral (*samaveta*) to it.

The theory of co-inherence of two distinct entities has to face all the objection raised against the doctrine of external relations implicit in the refutation of *asatkārya-vāda*. How can the utterly distinct be related without first being related to the relation? The relation which couples together and 'couples apart' distinct entities, will for ever fall apart and there will be an infinite chain of relation in each and every case. The alternatives to avoiding infinite regression seem to be either to accept momentary units each self-sufficient and self-contained and dismiss relations as fictions of the mind, or to reorient co-inherence (*samavāya*) in terms of identity (*tādātmya*) and accept a polarity of self-existing and self-relating functions within the permanent. The former, namely, the Buddhist's theory of flux, for reasons already stated, is unacceptable and the other one is, therefore, the only plausible interpretation of causality and substance. The concept of *śakti* is the solution implied in the question of the causal means (*karaṇa*). The means by which causal operation takes place cannot be external to the cause in so far as causal operation is of the nature of self-becoming or self-unfoldment. In the last resort it can be nothing other than the intelligent will which is inalienable with spirit the intelligent cause of all becoming.[8]

The *karaṇa* is not of assistance or benefit to the cause, independent as the cause is. It is called the auxiliary (*sahakārin*) from the standpoint of the effect which is dependent upon it for its very being. The effect cannot be conceived to be except as willed by the causal agent; it exists in and through the will. Śaiva Siddhānta in fact distinguishes two kinds of auxiliaries: the natural auxiliary which is the inseparable aspect of the cause and the adventitious auxiliaries which are separable subsidiaries and from which the cause is intrinsically different.[9] In spite of the continued presence of the will the effect is not always produced because of the non-presence or non-functioning of the subsidiary. Nor may it be questioned how, when the cause or causal power is present, the causal subsidiary can be non-present. The presence and the function of the causal subsidiary are themselves adventitious required by the exigency of the 'bound' nature of the creature; with the disappearance of this 'bound' nature the subsidiaries too have no justification to function, just as cause itself has a purely relative function.

The argument that a cause should discharge all its future functions even while it discharges its present function, as future efficiency is also present in it, is also therefore void of force.[10] The will even as it is non-spatial is also non-temporal; time itself is of the nature of a 'subsidiary' conditioned by the will;[11] the function of time is bound up with the effect.

Causal power distinguishable from cause

The Nyāya rejects the view that *śakti* is the determinant of causality. Cause is nothing other than the unconditional invariable antecedent of causal conditions and effect is nothing more than the consequent phenomenon resulting from the conjoint operations of antecedent conditions. The Nyāya admits *karaṇa* over and above its scheme of three causes, but its *karaṇa's* uniqueness consists of its being immediately followed by the occurrence of the effect.[12]

The explanation of fire burning lies not in its potency or power to burn but in the 'nature' of fire. A thing's nature, however, should be non-variant; fire sometimes does not burn when under the spell of the presence of a gem or a magical incantation. Such are, no doubt, counteractions or obstructions to burning, not different from negative conditions like an absence of oxygen; their absence has to be counted as part of the cause. Why posit *śakti* as *karaṇa* ? By cause is meant the totality of conditions necessary for producing the effect; the absence of counteracting agent is but one of these conditions.[13]

This view Śaiva Siddhānta opposes. The postulation of *śakti* is a necessary part of the acceptance of causality. The antecedent conditions of effect are relevant to the effect only when taken as media or vehicles of the causal power which is instrumental in the production of the effect. The existence of *śakti* as a category is logically implied in the concept of cause. There can be no cause which does not include a determinant, namely a specific cause which produces a specific effect.[14] The formulation of the theory of pre-existent effect rests on the admission of the category of causal power. The causal power is not however to be postulated as an independent factor[15] but as inherent in the cause itself.

The suggestion of Nyāya that absence of negative conditions is but part of the condition that produces the effect is unacceptable. Absence or negation cannot be the determinant of effectuation. The argument for the postulation of *śakti* in terms of the action of the counteracting agent is not disproved by the opponent.[16] The operations of the counteracting (*pratibandhaka*) and the reactuating (*uttejaka*) agencies with regard to a sensation of burning by fire cannot be adequately explained without the postulate of *śakti*. The *śakti* of fire is the dynamic cause of its operation of burning. *Śakti* is implicit in and as cause, and effectuation consists of *śakti* 'becoming' *vyakti*,[17] the will positing its content.[18]

Instrumentality (*karaṇatva*) of causal power

The meaning of the notion of *śakti* or agent's will as the world-cause may now be analysed.[19] There must be some means through which the agent brings about the result as, for example, his body, without which the agent cannot will anything into action. In the case of Deity which is spirit, body cannot be the means as spirit is bodiless (*aśarīrin*). Nor can it be *karma*, the merits and demerits of the creatures. Firstly because *karma* presupposes conditions when the creatures are with body and so cannot be the means through which embodiments are brought about. Secondly, assuming that somehow it can, it can only serve as an occasion and not as a direct means of the activity of the agent. The hammer, anvil etc. of the smith are not the immediate means of the smith's actions; it is the smith's operation of raising and lowering of the hammer continuous with his wish to bring about certain results that immediately accounts for the production of the results. Nor can it be *bindu* or *māyā* whose scope is defined by that of material causality. The *karaṇa* and the *upādāna* cannot be identified. Just as 'body' cannot be the 'means' for spirit, so the question of senses external and internal, the psychic functions of desire,[20] discrimination, intellection etc. as 'means' also stands ruled out.

What then remains as the plausible 'means' for spirit to exercise causal function, is its dynamic will itself (*cit-śakti*) which is integral to it. A distinction has to be made between being and will in spirit as otherwise spirit cannot be conceived of as the cause of the world process.

Cit-śakti also, which is of the form of *icchā* (desire) *jñāna* (knowledge) and *kriyā* (action) cannot, it may be objected, be the *karaṇa*.[21] It is only when *cit-śakti* becomes determinate in the form of a *specific* resolve and is again conjoined with suitable instrumentalities[22] that it can bring about a result. Otherwise an agent like the potter will be all the time producing pitchers even because of the continued existence of his *cit-śakti* in the form of *icchā*, and again if the potter's *cit-śakti* were a necessary and sufficient condition—the *karaṇa* for the making of pots, he must be able to create pots at the mere fiat of his will, dispensing with clay, stick and the fly-wheel. Again, *icchā* or desire is an aspect of causal agency constitutive of an agent in his role of agency so that it cannot also simultaneously be the means by which one, already an agent without it, brings about some result.[23]

That *icchā* (desire) cannot be *karaṇa* may be shown in another way also . Is *icchā* identical with the agent or different from him? If identical it cannot be *karaṇa* lest the distinction between *kartṛ* and *karaṇa* gets annulled. If different then it must be non-intelligent being different from the intelligent agent and also diverse as one identical *karaṇa* cannot bring about diverse results. The consequence will be being non-intelligent and many, it will fall to the side of effect. *Karaṇa* and *kārya* will become identical.

To conclude therefore that *karaṇa* be dispensed with is a counsel of despair. An effect without a *karaṇa* is as little possible as without a causal agent (*kartṛ*).[24] The same consideration which makes it necessary to posit a causal agent also makes the positing of *karaṇa* necessary.

There is indeed a gain in simplicity in first arguing to a *karaṇa* from *kārya*. *Kartṛ* is proved only vis-a-vis *karaṇa* . A definite relation of concomitance may be established between *kārya* and *karaṇa*: there can be action if and only if conceivably there is the means by which the action comes to pass. An agent is brought in again by another concomitance between the means of operation and an agent for whom it is means and without whom it cannot be conceived to function as means.

Neither can *karaṇa* and *kartṛ* be simply identified. Just as agent and the material cause may be identified in one sense, namely, in the sense that the agent's being is continuously present in the effect,[25] may we not also identify agent with *karaṇa*? Cannot *nimitta kāraṇa* and *karaṇa* be identical?

The *karaṇa* by definition is an auxiliary dependent on a *kartṛ* (*svādhiṣṭheya-karaṇa*). How can the ground also be that which stands on the ground for its being?[26] The *karaṇa* must be distinguished from *kartṛ*; the distinction may not imply ontological difference as is the case with material cause. A distinction has nevertheless to be made to make causation intelligible.

Such being the difficulties in the way of accepting or not accepting a *karaṇa*, how can *śakti* be intelligibly regarded as *karaṇa*? One objection is that will is instrumental in bringing about a result but only through suitable accessories; a potter's will to make the pot has to depend on clay and flywheel. In answer it may be said, that the will of the potter may be rendered inane due to the non-manifestness of his intelligence which could be obstructed by something alien. His agency is consequently limited and unfree and is contingent upon external accessories. The divine will being always unobscured by *mala* is free and can will anything freely into being.[27] The creative will which alone is the means by which creation etc. takes place is unique in this sense that it is unthwarted by any obstruction and unobscured by dualities of any kind and unhampered by any conditioning by a material cause.[28]

It has been argued that *karaṇa* is nothing but the result of the operation of a causal agent and that therefore *cit-śakti* as different from this is not the *karaṇa*; In reply it may be asked: if *karaṇatva* consists of being strictly a content of some agent's operation, it follows that *karaṇa* is what the agent is in relation with, only indirectly vis-a-vis some operation; one's bodily movement brought about by one's volition will not be an instance of *karaṇa* according to this notion; bodily movement being itself the operation, is not *what is brought about*; it is 'bringing about' itself. That *icchā* etc. constitute agency and that, therefore, are not *karaṇa* is also refuted by this instance.[29] It is true that causal agency involves *karaṇatva* just as material causality also is necessarily implied by it; for an effect there must be causal agent as well as a material cause. In the same way *kartṛtva* also implies *karaṇatva*. But what is available together in the order of being is analysed and discovered separately. It is therefore not a valid objection to say that the concept of agency presupposes as part of its meaning, instrumentality (*karaṇatva*) and that the latter therefore is not intelligible as an independent concept. It is only after knowing the real cause first as distinguished from a mere condition that even the mediated causal role for the condition becomes evident. Being a causal condition (*karaṇatva*) is implied by, but does not imply, causal agenthood (*kartṛtva*).

Causal power as a unity

It has been objected that desire (*icchā*), cognition (*jñana*) and action (*kriyā*) being many, and non-intelligent (as different from the intelligent spirit) could be effect (*kārya*). This is also not tenable. *Śakti* is intelligent and is in relation of identity (*samāvedya*) with spirit.[30] Just as *upādāna kāraṇa* is necessarily non-intelligent, *karaṇa* being nothing other than the *śakti* inherent (*samaveta*) in *nimitta kāraṇa* has necessarily to be intelligent.[31] *Śakti* is a unity which 'becomes' manifold through adjuncts. Desire, knowledge, action are variations determined in answer to or in relation to variations in the objects and the objectives, and do not imply a modification of *śakti*.[32] The latter being *cit-śakti* inherent in spirit can admit of no real diversification and duplication. Desire, knowing and will are not psychical acts discrete and perishing, as they appear in human experience but 'symbols' for *śakti* in its creative role. They are not distinctions within *śakti* but are its symbolic modes viewed in the context of specific functions. The intelligent principle of *śakti* itself of the form of knowledge (*cid-rūpa*) is called *śakti* that desires (*icchā-śakti*) when in free collaboration with such factors as the requisite 'ripening' of the *karma* of the selves it *resolves* 'let me create' (*kariṣyāmi*). Similarly when it wills 'let this be so' (*idamitthaṁ bhavet*), so that things come to pass, it is called willing (*kriyā-śakti*).[33] The forms of the specific resolve and the specific volition define *śakti* but only symbolically. They are only specifically imposed points of view (*vyapadeśa*) from which *śakti* is conceived to function. Otherwise if they were to constitute actual determinations, firstly they could not be variable as resolving *and* willing and secondly there must be either *always* a creation of the world or *always* conservation. Even the Naiyāyika who treats knowledge, desire, will etc. as discrete qualities of self considers them as eternal in the case of God and as specified by the particular object with which they are severally related.[34] Unspecified knowledge and unspecified will can never be creative.[35] The will to create, the will to destroy etc. are all, on the view of a self-identical *cit-śakti* symbolic specifications of Intelligence or Spirit.[36]

IV

GOD AS THE ONLY CAUSE

God as the Material Cause of the World

The concept of Destroyer combines within itself efficient causality (*nimitta-kāraṇatva*) and also material causality (*upādāna-kāraṇatva*). God is the ground of being, the creative ground of all that exists. By this we mean that He is the ground that *transcends* that of which he is the ground. He is the Destroyer.

The concept of Destroyer applied to God suggests that God cannot be a cause along with other causes. Rather He must be the infinite ground of the world, at once the resolving as well as the creating ground of all that exists. There must be however a distance between the totality of the world and God. The distance between every finite object including pre-eminently man, and the infinite ground which is one with it and yet *different* from it, is a decisive element in religious experience which, surely, is alive to the immanent presence of the infinite will in the world process. God is alongside things and is also simultaneously 'above' them.[1]

The metaphysical approach to the reality of God conceived as cause expresses this tension within the God-concept between extreme immanence and extreme transcendence in the following form : Is God *only* the efficient cause (*nimitta kāraṇa*) or is He the efficient *and* material cause (*nimittopādāna kāraṇa*)? The issue is not whether God is *nimitta kāraṇa or* the *upādāna kāraṇa*. God as spirit is the *nimitta kāraṇa*, the intelligent principle of effectuation. The question is whether He is also to be conceived of as the *upādāna kāraṇa*, in so far as He is the *sole* cause of creation and nothing exists *without* Him. The God, the metaphysical argument is in quest of, is not the 'demi-urge' but the Destroyer in whom all things resolve – things, worlds, aeons and even deities.[2]

Śaiva Siddhānta's answer to this question is to admit *māyā* as the *upādāna kāraṇa* and God as the *nimitta kāraṇa*, implying thereby that *upādāna kāraṇa* is at all cause, only in relation to *nimitta kāraṇa*. However, to the question whether God is as such *upādāna kāraṇa* in an unequivocal sense, the answer will be in the negative. *Māyā* is the *upādāna kāraṇa* and God is the possessor, lord of *māyā*.[3]

The attribution of material causality to God is one of the accepted doctrines of Vedānta. Śaiva Siddhānta in claiming to be Vedānta therefore cannot ignore the evidence of the scriptures cited in its support. The issue here is one of literal admission of material causality. Do scriptural evidences clinch the issue in favour of God being the material cause quite in the sense upheld in the cosmo-pantheistic and acosmic pantheistic theories of Vedānta.[4] Let us examine closely the alleged scriptural evidences in support of God's material causality.

The use of the ablative

The Bhṛgu-Vallī[5] begins defining *brahman* as 'that from which beings are born, that by which when born they live, that into which when departing they enter'. The investigator concludes proceeding from the outer to the inner, in causally accounting for the universe, considering respectively the alternatives of '*from* matter', '*from* life,' '*from* mind,' '*from* intelligence' and ultimately '*from* Bliss'. The suggestion everywhere is that the 'cause' *from* which arises the universe is *material* cause. The Śaiva scriptures – Purāṇas[6] and Śaivāgamas[7] too following the lead, say that *from Śiva* arises all this universe, sentient and non-sentient. That, where everything is extended, in which all are secure, *from whence* all began, that is the supreme state.[8] The use of the ablative case in these texts is of great moment.[9] The ablative case-ending[10] is indicative of the relation between material cause and its effect.[11] The term '*prakṛti*', which is used as the characteristic of the ablative case is, it is held, pre-eminently indicative of material causality. The examples adduced by the commentator, namely, of a blade of grass sprouting from a horn, of scorpions emerging out of cow-dung leave one in little doubt of this.[12]

Does the use of the ablative termination in '*yataḥ*' indicate material causality? Surely Pāṇini's aphorism (I.4.30) gives the name *apādāna* to that from which a thing is born. But it may be observed that the fifth, case-ending denotes cause in general; the significant term used by Pāṇini namely *prakṛti* is but a synonym for cause — intelligent cause (*nimitta kāraṇa*).[13] In the Vedic text which is repeated by the *sūtra* along with *yataḥ* occurs *yena* (whereby) and *yad* (whom); *yataḥ* should not be taken in isolation, as relating only to material evolution. Bādarāyaṇa significantly repeats *yataḥ* only, and implies by *brahman's* causality that it is the cause of evolution as well as of sustenance and dissolution of the world. The ablative accordingly refers to the ground of all the operations, the terminus *a quo* as well as the terminus *ad quem* — in a word, the Destroyer. In so far as *nimitta kāraṇa* is inclusive of, and is the *implicans* of *upādāna kāraṇa*, it is perfectly intelligble to say that all this universe *arises* from Śiva.

Scriptural analogies

The different metaphors used in the scriptures descriptive of how the universe arises from the substance of *brahman* are further adduced in support of God's material causality. From a blazing fire sparks similar in nature issue forth in thousands, similarly many kinds of being issue forth from the immutable and they return thither.[14] As a spider sends forth and draws in its entrails, as herbs grow out of the earth, as the hair grows on the head and body of a living person, so from the imperishable arises here the universe.[15] Even as the sea contains foam, waves and bubbles which rise from and subside into it, the absolute spirit is the substratum whence arises the world animate and inanimate and thither it tends.[16]

These metaphors used in scriptures illustrative of God's causality, it is said, are suggestive of material causality. The question is if these illustrations are to be taken literally[17] and as supporting identity between material cause and its effect ? The fire-spark analogy certainly cannot be taken on all fours : the *brahman* and the world are different as spirit and matter. The examples of the scorpion and spider are certainly misconceived, if meant literally, in so far as life does not come out of the non-living and vice versa.[18] The sea-wave illustration also must be understood to imply the relation between ground and its consequences rather than material cause and its effect. The foams, waves and so on, which arise from and subside into the sea-water are by an appropriate transference said to arise from, and subside into, the sea itself which is its base (*ādhāra*).[19]

It may be argued that compatibility between cause and effect need not mean identity and that it is intelligible to conceive of the non-intelligent world as evolution on the part of an intelligent spirit. What is true of cause may not be as such true of effect in spite of their continuity. The properties of milk are not the properties of curd; the properties of the scorpion, a form of life, are not the properties of the lifeless cow-dung. So again with the cases of spider and its web.[20] Yet do we not say that one is the material cause of the other in each case?

The admission of discontinuity of characteristics in spite of continuity of substance is rejection of *satkārya-vāda* on which is made to rest the edifice of *brahman's* causality. What is true of the cause may not be true as such of the effect; continuity is not sameness. But the properties of the effect should not be at variance with the properties of the material cause.[21] If *satkārya-vāda* does not mean this the implication will be that substance (*dharmin*) is different from attribute (*dharma*) as difference of attributes is held not to militate against the identity of substance — an implication that may be seen to be subversive of *satkāryavāda*[22].

The will to become many

The ascription of will (*abhidhyā*) to God, the nature and content of the willing as revealed in passages like 'He wished may I become many' [23], 'He reflected may I become many,' [24] taken together are said to be eloquent evidences of the truth of God's material as well as efficient causality. He is efficient cause as the agent of activity preceded by wish (*kāma*) or insight (*aikṣata*) and at the same time material cause as *becoming* many (*bahu syāṁ prajāyeya*). The latter feature *constituting* multiplicity indicates that God is not merely efficient cause, like the potter who does not resolve 'let me become the pot'[25].

The question here is: does 'may I become many' imply material causality? If it does, is it not contradicted by the *resolve* to become many? It is true the potter who makes the pot does not say 'let me become the pot'. But can also a material cause like clay *resolve* to become pot? It is on the issue of the ability to resolve attributed to *brahman* that Bādarāyaṇa rejects *prakṛti's* candidacy for being the cause of the world.

The real meaning of a resolve to become the manifold world is that God causes and controls the manifold world not as an external agent but as the immanent will;[26] in creating the world God is 'one' with the world; though different, as cause is different from effect, God is non-different from the world because He pervades it as the ground of its being.[27]

Attribution of self-becoming to God

Bādarāyaṇa devotes an entire section[28] towards vindication of the doctrine of *brahman* as the material and efficient cause of the world; here he draws our attention to the scriptural use of the active, non-causative verb in apposition to self (*ātmakṛteḥ*).[29] The Taittirīya says that *ātman* transformed *itself* into its own self[30] (*tadātmānaṁ svayam akuruta*). Action denoted by active (non-causative) verb excludes the possibility of *brahman* being *not* the material cause of the world.[31] The occurrence of expression like *abhavat* (literally became) in the text when it says that *brahman* became the visible and the non-visible (*sacca tyaccābhavat*)[32] is one of the main considerations for Bādarāyaṇa to entertain *brahma-pariṇāma vāda* as a plausible doctrine of Vedānta and thus bequeathed a serious problem to his commentators to account for transformation of *brahman* compatibly with *brahman's* eternity and immutability.

The Śaiva hymnists themselves, whose utterances are authoritative for Śaiva Siddhānta, similarly identify the causal agent of the world with His creation and seem to imply that He is also the material cause of the world: 'Thou art the body, the self, its consciousness and everything'.[33] 'Śiva stands verily as the expansive earth, fire, water, air and the ether, the *yajamāna*, the sun and the moon—the eight forms.'[34] 'He is the fruit, its juice and even the taster thereof; the 'thou' and the 'I'.[35] 'Earth, water, fire, air, ether, vast, the wandering moon, the sun and the man — to sense revealed: eight ways He joined Himself to me throughout seven worlds and as regions ten He moves, alone *Himself*'.[36] 'He is the knower; He is the revealer; He is the knowledge; He is even the known; He is also this vast world, sky and so on'.[37]

It seems to be suggested in these citations that God is of the form of the sentient and non-sentient world alike. The world is a veritable unfoldment of Śiva; subject and objects alike are his parts. There is a real transformation, and tranformation in the reverse of the world into Śiva.

In further support of this it may be observed that the Śaivāgamas trace the creation and dissolution of the world to the different parts of Śiva's own form. An oft-quoted *Vātula Āgama* text derives the realms animate and inanimate, item by item, from each part of Śiva's form.[38] Dissolution is explained similarly as resolving into His respective parts. Again the *āgamas* treat the six *adhvan* comprising the realm of '*śabda*' and *artha* as the 'corporeal' form of Śiva.[39]

Brahman is likewise spoken of literally as the locus of the origin and dissolution of the world.[40] The Chāndogya,[41] after considering sound, breath, food, water, the other world and this world itself as the ultimate ground of the world, clinches the case in favour of 'space' because all these aforementioned effects are produced from space and return back into space. Space[42] is the 'archetype' of *brahman* precisely on the ground of being the direct locus of the whence and the whither of the world. Effect cannot be absorbed by anything less than its material cause.

Brahman is, therefore, aptly celebrated as the *yoni*—the birth-place of all beings.[43] The Muṇḍaka describes *brahman* as the *bhūta-yoni*, the birth place of the elements,[44] *brahma-yoni*, the birth place of the creator of the world-soul.[45] In like manner, Bādarāyaṇa affirms that *brahman* is *Śāstra-yoni*, the source of the world of speech,[46] as a complement to the earlier assertion that *brahman* is the 'whence' of the origin of the *spoken* world by the suggestive use of the ablative.[47] In the Śaiva-Purāṇa too the suggestive expression *yoni* is used appositionally with Śiva.[48]

The use of the active verb and the expression of God *becoming* the world surely lend some plausibility to *brahma-pariṇāma-vāda*. Not only the Upaniṣads, the hymns of the Śaiva saints are replete with such expressions. Śiva becoming eightfold forms that encompass the world of sentience and insentience is one of the recurrent themes of the Śaiva hymnal literature in Tamil. Again this must be understood in a manner that is compatible with the distinction between cause as spirit and effect as non-spirit. The underlying idea in all these passages which identify cause with the effect is that nothing falls outside the unity of cause and that effect arises, subsists and resolves in the cause. Besides, God as cause is non-dual (*advitīya*).[49] It is this feature of non-duality understood to imply not 'one' in a numerical sense but only denial of duality that is emphasized. Śiva is verily 'one' with His creation. This is, in particular, true of the passage which identifies Him with the knower and his knowledge, with the enjoyer and his enjoyment. The relation of cause and effect in the ultimate analysis is one of subject and object, or more correctly, of agent and his doing, of will and its willed-content. There is, therefore, no contradiction in cause being synchronous with and identified as the effect. In being 'the seven worlds and the ten regions' as He is extolled, He no more 'becomes' them than the potter 'becomes' his pot. It is not a case of God himself becoming but becoming in a truly causative sense.[50] It is what lets becoming take place by its being and will. The expressions like 'Thou *art* the ether', 'Thou *hath become* all this' are of the implication that Śiva as agent precisely *is not* all this,[51] as otherwise it will be a non significant assertion. Identifying Him with the fruit, its taste and even the taster again only suggests that He is the creative ground responsible alike for the creation of the fruit, of its taste and also of the taster.[52]

The world is an unfoldment of Divine will and subject and object, enjoyer and enjoyment alike may be looked upon as God's parts but in a figurative sense. There is no literal dispersal into parts of a literal transformation or re-transformation, as these are inconceivable in the case of Śiva who is indiscernible and immutable. In distinguishing material cause which transforms, from a non-transforming efficient cause, it may be recalled that Śaiva Siddhānta implies no dualism such as we have in the Sāṅkhya because the two — material and efficient causes stand in the relation of the depending and the dependent (*vyāpaka* and *vyāpya*), the grounded and the ground (*sthānin* and *sthāna*).[52a] Matter in its gross or subtle form exists but as appropriated and grounded in spirit.[53] Śaiva Siddhānta derives the world from the very form of Śiva in the sense that Śiva is the ground of the material which evolves into and constitutes the gross world. It also means that His agency with regard to its derivation is intelligible only in terms of a personality which He, himself a super-personal principle, freely assumes. The same consideration underlies the conception of Śiva as of the form of the *adhvan* (*adhvamūrti*). It is symbolic (*upacāra*), not literal.[54]

Identification of *brahman* with *ākāśa*[55] brings out the fact that *cit-śakti* is the cause of the origination, duration and dissolution of all beings. Just as elemental ether is the abiding locus of the origination of the elements and the elementals, *cit-śakti* is the abiding locus of *māya*, the material causal *śakti* which unfolds and enfolds on the background of *cit-śakti*.[56] The image of ether is itself suggestive of the disparity between the intelligent cause, namely the will that contains (*ādhāra*) and the material cause contained by it (*ādheya*).

The expression *yoni* also when rightly understood supports only the Siddhānta view. *Cit-śakti* in relation of identity with *śaktimat* in its role as underlying *bindu* (Root matter) assumes the name of *yogamāyā* and is known in this characteristic role as the genital or the birthplace (*yoni*) of the entire created order, of speech and the spoken.[57]

Equivalence between God and the world

Another important *āgama* text expresses the equation of the sentient and insentient world with its cause, God in a significant manner. He is all this world of moving and the non-moving; whatever there is, is He alone.[58] The co-ordinate equivalence (*sāmānādhikaraṇya*) it is argued is conclusive evidence of the identity (*tādātmya*) of the cause and the effect; different things like the pot and the potter's stick are not equated in like manner.[59]

The Śaivāgama text which speaks of the world as effect and Śiva as cause in a language of co-ordinate equivalence (*sāmānādhikaraṇya-nirdeśa*) is indeed significant. The material cause and effect alone can be hyphenated as, for example, clay-pot or copper-wire. The testimony of the *āgama* text seems likewise to imply that the 'Supreme I' and the phenomenal world moving and unmoving alike are hyphenable and the presumption is that the two are intrinsically identical as clay and clay-pot are identical. Were God and the world *different* the hyphenated usage becomes unwarranted.[60]

In reply it may be observed that attributing material causality to God in a literal sense would offend against texts wihich speak of Him as unchanging (*nirvikāra*). The relation suggested by co-ordinate equivalence can only be that of efficient cause and its effect (*nimitta-nimittitva*).[61] Material cause and effect relation (*upādāna-upādeya-bhāva*) is comprehended, and not excluded by efficient cause and effect relation. One is a determinate causal relation and the other determinant relation. Spirit-causality is always of the latter kind and is inclusive of the instrumental and material causalities.

Knowledge of one entailing knowledge of all

The scriptural assurance of knowledge of everything following from knowledge of one thing (*eka-vijñānena sarvavijñāna-pratijñā*)[62] is meaningful only with regard to the material cause. The distinction between efficient and material cause is about being different or non-different from the effect. If God were only the efficient cause, then being different from the world, knowledge of God cannot entail knowledge of everything of which God is cause. If one knows the pot it will not entail knowing cloth also. Knowledge of one particular does not lead to knowledge of another with which it is unrelated. The assumption of a relation between cause and effect which is presupposed in the claim that knowledge of the one leads to knowledge of all is incompatible with God being the efficient cause *only* of the world.

Against the weight of these scriptural evidences which include the Upaniṣads, Purāṇas, Śaivāgamas and even the hymns of the canonised Śaiva saints, it is idle to argue that God being spirit cannot be material cause, or being agent like the potter He cannot also be the material 'clay' of the world. Such speculations of reason stand contradicted by the declarations of *Śruti.*

Nor may it be objected that it is only what is *not* 'inhering cause' (*samavāyi-kāraṇa*) that can be efficient cause (*nimitta kāraṇa*) and *vice versa.* Such disjunction is unacceptable. The real basis of the distinction between the two types of cause is about their function; being substance which transforms itself into the effect is the characteristic of the material or inhering cause, while being endowed with requisitive knowledge and will is the function of efficient cause. As both these are attributed to *brahman* it is legitimate to say that *brahman* is *upādāna kāraṇa* as well as the *nimitta kāraṇa.*[63]

The metaphysical doctrine of all being known when the one is known, of the Upaniṣads as well as of the Śaiva Purāṇas taken along with the significant illustrations given, is interpreted above to imply material causality for Śiva. The argument, briefly, is that knowledge of the supreme being entails knowledge of all its effect (*Śiva-jñānena sarva-kārya-vijñānam*). The presumption here is that the supreme being and the all are neither absolutely identical nor absolutely different but are in identical *relation* (*tādātmya*) as material cause and its effect.[64] The clay being known all clay-products are known.

The difficulty in accepting this interpretation is that as spirit (Śiva) is not as such the material cause of the world and only *māyā* is the material cause, knowledge of the material cause cannot literally entail knowledge of its effect; knowledge of Śiva cannot include knowledge of the material products of *māyā*, the latter being not products evolved out of Śiva. The statement taken without qualification will involve some contradiction. The only plausible interpretation would be: If the pre-eminent (*pradhāna*) is known, all the world being secondary to it, as effect is to its efficient cause, is *ipso facto* known. When a chief of the state is known his subordinates are also in effect known. That is if one knows the king, then by implication one may also claim to know about his subjects.[65] So it is to be taken more as suggestion of pre-eminence (*prādhānya-jñāpanārtha.*) than a literal admission of identity.

To take it as suggestive of material causality lands us in difficulties: does knowledge of Śiva lead to knowledge of what are expressly not the material evolutes of Śiva? Even assuming that knowledge of Śiva involves knowledge about the selves and about *māyā* and its evolutes with all of which Śiva is in relation, what about knowledge of *avidyā* or *mala* with which Śiva is apparently unrelated ? It may be replied that the 'all' in knowledge of all refers only to the manifest and the non-manifest world which stands in the relation of effect to the Supreme Being which is its cause.[66] But even *mala* in so far as it is admitted as real must admit being known, and ultimately, it is by the knowledge by which God is known, even *mala* paradoxically, is also known. On our interpretation of the text that by knowing One all else is known on grounds of metaphysical pre-eminence, the 'all' may be understood even to include *mala* which metaphysically depends (*vyāpya*) on Śiva though not related to it.[67]

What about the illustrative texts? By knowing a clod of clay all that is made of clay become known; by knowing one nugget of gold all things made of gold are known; by the one instance of a nail clipper all that is made of iron become known. The latter in each of these illustrations is a modification and its difference from the former is only nominal, due to speech.[68] Does this not clinch the issue in favour of Śiva's material causality?

The text should be interpreted in a manner which does not conflict with other texts which declare that Śiva is immutable.[69] Texts affirming immutability of spirit (*nirvikāra-śruti*) are unequivocal, while those affirming identity between spirit and the material world have at least an apparent equivocation. The latter must accordingly be interpreted consistently with the former.[70] Keeping this in mind if we approach the *eka-vijñānena sarva-vijñāna-pratijñā* text and illustrations, it may be seen that the illustration and what is illustrated are not quite of the same order.[71] By knowing the very ground of the material cause we know all the effects of the material cause as well as by knowing the material cause itself. Though different as spirit from the material world, by knowing spirit the latter is indeed known as well as by knowing a clod of clay all products of clay are known.[72] Just as from knowledge of the one there ensues knowledge of the rest non-different in nature as in the case of clay and clay-products, even so, where there is difference as between spirit (efficient cause) and the material world

(effect), knowledge of the latter follows from knowledge of the former.

God as the Subject of Existential Judgements

One very striking proof of the immanence of God as the stuff of all that exists is the linguistic evidence provided by existential judgments. In such judgments as 'the pot exists', 'the cloth exists' etc., it is undisputed that existentiality is commonly given (*sattvākārānugata-pratīti*).[1] To what does this recurrent phenomenon refer? Does existence refer to a *sui generis* existence (*svarūpa-sattva*) in each case? That will mean there are as many *sui generis* existences as there are existents. 'Pot exists', interpreted thus, will be a tautology implying that pot is a unique existence as pot.[2] Moreover each existence will be so unique that it being incommensurable, we could not know whether or in what way 'A exists' differs from 'B exists'. Neither can it be co-inherence in universal existence (*sattāgata-tādātmya*). Just as we predicate existence of particulars we predicate existence of the universal also as when we say that 'potness is or exists' (*ghaṭatvaṁ sat*). To admit coinherence in universal existence for universal existence itself will lead to infinite regress. To say that while pot is characterised by existence, potness is only indirectly qualified by existence (*ekārtha-samaveta*) being coinherent with it in a common substratum, is arbitrary.[3]

Therefore, the only plausible way of explaining existentiality common to perceptions of existents is: existentiality with which the pot is perceived to be qualified is *identical* with Being that is God. Just as pot which is perceived as qualified by clay material is identical with clay material the world qualified by existence is identical with its first cause,[4] namely, Śiva. Śiva is identical with existence which all existential judgments imply as material cause is identical with its effect. That Śiva is Being (*sat*) needs no proof: the Śaiva scriptures themselves speak' of it as the one essential definition of Śiva.

The existentiality of existents common to our judgments of perceptions, it is said, evidences the material causality of Śiva: the argument used is that what is perceived to be qualified by existence is identical with its first cause (*upādāna kāraṇa*). What is perceived as commonly present in a number of things is ultimately identifiable with the material cause of those things.[6] Exceptions can easily be cited to the rule suggested by this general proposition. When different cows are perceived as cow A, cow B and so on shall we say that the commonly present factor of the cow is the material cause of A, B etc.?[7] Even less can a universal be the material cause of the particulars.[8] Likewise, in 'the hare's horn does not exist', 'the square-circle does not exist', the common factor present in these negative judgments, namely, non-existence is not the material cause of the hare's horn and the square circle.[9] Existence or existentiality is only a generic quality and is not identical with being. It is of course one thing to say that all existential judgments *derive* their existential support from Śiva who is Being itself; all that exists, the world as well as its material cause, exists *because* of Him. But it is quite another matter to say that existence characteristic of 'pot exists' is identical with Śiva. The latter involves, what is unacceptable, that Śiva is the material cause of all that exists. Moreover, Śiva as Being (*sat*) is unmanifest,[10] supersensuous, so that existentiality which is perceived in such perceptual judgments as 'pot exists' cannot be equated with Him. Being is not grasped by senses; the latter can only be in contact with particulars. The Upaniṣad says[11] : 'His form does not fall within the ken of vision. None can see Him with one's eye but only by (his) heart (*hṛdaya*)'.[12]

The underlying view that existence as a universal is constitutive of reality is not really acceptable. Reality does not consist in relation of existence, direct or indirect such that it might be held that existentiality is commonly present *prior* to all existents. A thing is real without existence as the thing's 'determinant'. The real is that which exists.

It is argued that if the character of existentiality does not 'determine' a continuant like the self, it follows that the latter is non-existent like a 'mare's nest' which also is unpervaded by existence.[13] Besides, if a predicate like existence were not admitted to be continuously present in all existents, how do we account for the use of the common name 'existent' to denote different objects ? In reply[14] it may be observed that things exist because of an inherence of existence in them. Existents have *sui generis* existence and are not determined by the inherence of a common existence. Otherwise it is legitimate to extend the question to being itself and demand the inherence of another being for it; this would make being effect. The use of common appellation does not imply the continued presence of a common factor. Particulars are required only to resemble each other in being called by the same name.[15] If the name 'pot' were to apply to pots because of the continued existence of a pot-character it would follow that pots have evolved from pot-character and not from clay-material, which is absurd.

Although in one sense all existents may be said to be the 'same' in another sense they are different: each existent is private and peculiar and the sense in which one is said to be the same as the other can be explained by saying that existence in 'pot exists' is exactly *like* existence in 'cloth exists'.[16]

Qualified Interpretations of God's Material Causality

Another variant of this mode of arguing, ascribing material causality to the Agent is : the intelligent agent of the world is not as such the material cause of the world but only as related to the non-intelligent *māyā*. This view differs from the earlier one in not ascribing material causality exclusively to God but to God associated with *māyā*, which together transform into the world of sentience and insentience. The merit of this view over the other is obvious. Instead of deriving the non-intelligent from the intelligent and explaining away the apparent discontinuity it derives the non-intelligent from a cause which has the component of materiality in it. It is also in keeping with those texts which speak of material cause and efficient cause in distinct terms[1] besides those texts which speak of the two indistinctly.

The passages cited from the Śaiva hymns in support of this view[2] deserve to be quoted :

Fivefold Thou dost in earth extend—praise !
Fourfold Thou dost exist in the water—praise !
Threefold in fire Thou shinest—praise !
Twofold in the air Thou art all glorious—praise !
One in the ether Thou hast sprung forth—praise !
Day by day He to the Sun its lustre gave
In the sacred moon He placed its coolness;
Kindled in the mighty fire its heat;
In the pure ether placed pervasive power;
Ended the ambiant wind with energy;
To the streams that gleam in the shade their savour sweet,
And to the expanded earth its strength He gave;
For ever and aye, me and millions other than one
All in their several cells hath He enclosed.[3]

Here in these passages the suggestion is that Śiva in his role as the cause combines both material causality and agency simultaneously without antagonism. He is not the earth, water and so on, but *extends in them* as earth, water etc.

The modified version of *brahma-pariṇāma-vāda,* as the present view under discussion is, however, fares no better for the same reasons, namely, that the difference between *nimitta* and *upādāna* is not adequately appreciated. What is meant by saying that *māyā* and Śiva are both material cause of the world ? Are the two each in its own capacity a material cause like the two strands of a rope ? That will be to treat material cause not as unitary but to be understood more as of the form of a tress into which two different strands of cause have been plaited. Or is one of them only, *inseparably qualified by the other* the material cause ? Or is *māyā* the real transforming cause and Śiva the *ground of māyā,* the material cause ?[4]

The first alternative is not a significant modification of *pariṇāma-vāda* because it merely assumes two causes in the place of one. It cannot be said that *māyā* and Śiva are conjunctively the cause of the world, because the two do not have a parity of functions. *Māyā* is coeval with the phenomenon of change, while Śiva is its ground.[5] If the two — Śiva and *māyā,* are alike the material cause even in their functions, then how can they be distinguished ? For Śaiva Siddhānta a difference in substance with identity of nature, as much as difference in nature with identity of substance is hardly intelligible. This is in addition to the other difficulty of conceiving the unchanging intelligent spirit as material cause in itself or in association with *māyā.*

As for the second alternative[6] that the material and efficient causes stand in relation of attribute (*viśeṣaṇa*) and substance (*viśeṣya*) it requires a more detailed consideration. The causative agent of the world is, it is said, a whole or unity (*viśiṣṭa*). It is efficient cause which is also material cause by virtue of its being inseparably qualified by *māyā.* An example of this synthesised unity is afforded by the body-soul relation. The soul, in itself immutable, in association with body is born with its birth and deceased with its decease.

The *prima facie* value of this new concept over the transformation theory (*pariṇāma-vāda*) cannot be gainsaid. *Brahman* the whole never in any sense *becomes* the world. The whole never *precedes* the part nor do the parts *succeed* the whole. *Brahman* always exists as a whole possessed of parts and never becomes parts and therefore does not become subject to the finitude and limitations of the latter. Spirit as the unity qualified by latent matter becomes spirit the unity qualified by manifest matter. During Creation the latent becomes manifest as the effect. The change implied by causation is not immediate or direct but mediated. The *nimitta kāraṇa* in itself does not suffer change but only through the material cause (*māyā*) by which it is qualified.[7]

This is the interpretation of *viśiṣṭādvaita* the identity of one substance existing in two real forms as cause and effect *sub specie aeternitatis* is affirmed. This view is an attempt to harmonise the scriptural references to Śiva (Spirit) as transcendent (*viśvādhika*) and immanent (*viśvākāra*).[8] The efficient cause assumes the form of the world as material cause by *transforming* itself into the sentient and non-sentient forms of existence. And the transformation is of a unique kind[9] such that the efficient cause, eternally pure, immutable, is not affected by the change in spite of the fact that it becomes material cause (*prakṛti*) of the empirical world. How is this accomplished?

The answer is given in an analysis of the concept of *viśiṣṭa* as applied to the cause of the universe:[10]

> In Dissolution, as the text goes,[11] there was Śiva alone left by Himself without a second with the potentialities of the sentient and insentient existence inseparable from His being. From such being went forth the *jñāna-śakti* — the Great light dispelling all darkness (when arose the desire 'may I become many').[12] The cause embodied in the unmanifest, causal form of the sentient and insentient being undifferentiated yet in name and form *willed* that it should become embodied in the manifest form of sentient and insentient existence differentiated in name and form. ('All this did He create, and whatever else there is').[13] He entered of Himself as their soul into the sentient and insentient which had differentiated from Him ('Having created it, He entered it').[14] He becomes thereby transformed into the universe sentient and non-sentient, respectively, the *paśu* and the *pāśa* ('He became the manifest and unmanifest being').[15]
>
> Even as a man has first childhood and then youth, *brahman* of the form of the universe exists in two forms, as cause and as effect.[16] The text[17] aptly distinguishes between '*prakṛti*' (*upādāna kāraṇa*) and Maheśvara (*nimitta kāraṇa*) as respectively *māyā* and *māyin*[18] and also affirms that 'by that which forms His limb is all the universe

pervaded'. What forms an aspect, a free particularisation (*tasyāvayava*) of *brahman* is the *cit-śakti* which as the world-soul (*puruṣa*), of the form of 'I' the supreme Enjoyer pervades the entire universe.[19]

Just as the hair and the nails etc. are not born of the body alone (insentient) or of the soul alone (sentient) so the universe is born not of *māyā* alone or Maheśvara alone, but of the Embodied unity which is accordingly described as the 'womb of all elements' and also as the 'supreme lord, the Mighty etc'.[20]

Śaiva Siddhānta finds itself in agreement with the spirit of this interpretation which is to conserve the sole causality of God. Yet there are differences. Śaiva Siddhānta labels this position as *nimitta kāraṇa-pariṇāma-vāda*. *Brahman* is accepted as *nimitta kāraṇa*, which admits *pariṇāma* of a unique kind, and in this sense alone *brahman* is held to be *upādāna kāraṇa*. On the intelligibility of this distinction — the distinction suggested between *nimitta kāraṇa* in itself and *nimitta* come to be *upādāna kāraṇa*, rests the plausibility of the concept of *apūrva-pariṇāma*. One is the qualified as such (*viśeṣya*) and the other the qualified whole, inclusive of the quality (*viśiṣṭa*). The intelligent immutable Being (*akṣara*) considered in itself is the *viśeṣya* and the same considered in its 'embodied' nature, which indeed is its inseparable feature, is *viśiṣṭa*.

What is this *viśiṣṭa*? Is it anything apart from the *viśeṣaṇa* and *viśeṣya* and their 'inseparable' relation? Is it only their unity or is it held to be something over and above these three? If former, the *viśiṣṭa* being nothing new cannot be absolved from the difficulties which beset the notion of spirit being the material cause of the world. If it is something new, the question of spirit being the material cause does not arise, the *viśiṣṭa* being not identical as such with *māyā*[21] which is only *viśeṣaṇa*.

The concept of *pariṇāma*[22]

The notion of *pariṇāma* implicit in the view that Śiva, qualified by *māyā* is the material cause of the world also deserves to be analysed. The concept may be analysed from the perspective of the 'effect' evolved or from that of the cause which undergoes evolution. To take the first: What is meant by saying that effect is an evolute of cause?

Pariṇāma may be defined as consisting of change of form in the cause — cessation of the previous form and acquiring emergence of a form different from its previous one but conforming to it.[23] This definition will entail the admission that when the effect comes into being the cause has ceased to be. But in the case of the 'transformation' of clay into pot there is no cessation of the clay material. Nor again may it be said that the new form acquired in transformation is a continuation of the discarded form. The world, a 'transformation' of Śiva its alleged material cause should then be a kindred of Śiva, that is, of the nature of spirit. The concept is thus inadmissible in whichever sense taken.

Let us look at the question from the angle of cause. Is *pariṇāma* meaningfully predicable of spirit as cause? Is the evolution of the world from spirit partial or total? It cannot be a part of it as that will mean admission of parts for spirit. If it be total evolution then such problems as follows will arise: as spirit evolves into the first of the thirty-six tattvas[24], namely, *śiva-tattva,* whence can the evolution of other tattvas from *śakti-tattva* onwards proceed, nothing being left unevolved of spirit in a scheme of total evolution? Nor can it be that spirit first evolves *śiva-tattva* and again evolves *śakti-tattva* and so on. The clay material which evolves into a pot is not again perceived to evolve into another pot. Nor again may it be held that only initially the first, namely *śiva-tattva* is the evolute of spirit and that each other *tattva* thereafter evolves from the preceding one: *śakti* from śiva, sadāśiva from *śakti* and so on. This will contradict the scriptural declaration that śiva is the *upādāna*, in whichever way conceived, of *all phenomena*. The *āgama* speaks of the evolution of *tattvas* one from the other and also says that *śiva* is the proximate *upādāna* of all *tattvas*.[25] Material causality is attributed to spirit, sole cause as it is, in an ultimate and also in a proximate sense.[26]

It follows therefore, that Śiva's material causality is inconceivable if interpreted in the ordinary sense of a material cause that undergoes transformation (*pariṇāma*).

The concept of *apūrva pariṇāma*

But the view which attributes material causality to Śiva qualified by *māyā*, does not admit *parināma* for the material cause in the ordinary sense. Transformation of Śiva qualified by *māyā* is of a unique kind. *Apūrva-pariṇāma* is intended to be a reorientation of the concept of *pariṇāma*[27] so that it does not conflict with the unchanging nature of spirit to which the notion is applied.

But this 'unique' transformation is still transformation. If it were not and spirit could be still viewed the material cause somehow commensurate with its immutability, then even the potter could be viewed the material cause of pot.[28] It would be a verbal question only whether we choose to call it the material cause or the efficient cause. If, however, 'unique' transformation *is* a case of transformation although of a unique kind then the difficulty of conceiving it has to be faced.[29] In no conceivable sense could the world be a transformation of the *nimitta kāraṇa* without the implication of materiality (*jaḍatva*) for the latter. Body-soul relation is only an instance and no proof; it presupposes and does not prove the case. The issue before us being ultimately the relation of spirit and matter, the body-soul relation itself cannot be suggested as the solution to the problem implied by it. Childhood and youth in relation to the individual, the growth of hair and nail in relation to the embodied — are only different versions of the body-soul relation.

Nor may it be supposed that if we cannot conceive it with the help of an example, so much the worse for our conceptions. After all there are scriptural evidences, and *āgama* is weightier than *anumāna*.[30] But this is entirely to misjudge the role of reason in relation to revelation. *Anumāna* cannot contradict *āgama*. If *āgama* were to conflict with reason there would be an illicit regress to infinity; there will be no means of decisively settling an issue at any time by reason as it can always theoretically prove to be wrong. When the *āgama* seems to contradict itself, *anumāna* helps resolve it in terms of the weightier of the 'contradictory' declarations and as such *āgama* cannot itself come into conflict with reason.[31]

The concept of *vṛtti*

Material causality seems inadmissible in the case of spirit because spirit is by definition impervious to change (*vikāra*). But the concept of change itself needs to be analysed. Is material causality incompatible with change as such or only with change of a particular kind?[32]

There are at least four distinguishable metaphysical uses of the term 'change'. One is in the sense of origination or creation (*ārambha*) as when we say that the threads have 'changed' into cloth. Another is transformation (*pariṇāma*) as in the case of milk turning into curd. A third meaning of the term is: several particulars combine to produce the impression of a self-same effect (*samudāya*) as for example grains collected in the form of a heap. In none of these senses of the term, for reasons already explained at length,[33] is Śiva conceivable as the 'changing' material cause. But there is a fourth meaning also of the term 'change' which may give us a foot-hold in the way of understanding material causality in the context of spirit. And that is *vṛtti*, a kind of 'change' which does not really involve change in any of the accepted senses of the term. A rolled cloth is unfolded, say, into a tent; this involves only a 'change' of state (*avasthā*). A coiled serpent uncoiling itself into a totally different form neither 'evolves' into an evolute nor 'emerges' as a new effect.[34] Nor may it be said that a tent is nothing but the rolled cloth itself. A rolled cloth is not a tent.[35] A real process is implied involving 'change of form' (*avasthā-viśeṣa*). Likewise in the case of spirit we may talk of 'expansion' or exteriorisation (*vikāsa*) and 'retraction' or inwardisation (*saṅkoca*).

The question that naturally will arise here is, how can spirit which is ubiquitous admit change of states like expansion and contraction?[36] In answer to this question it may be said that these 'changes of states' are only symbolic and the causal function of spirit is described as differentiated because of adjuncts. Or it may also be said that the 'change of states' pertains only to *māyā* by which Śiva is qualified, and that in so far as the qualifying *māyā* (*viśeṣaṇa*) exteriorises and retracts, the qualified whole also may be said to undergo these changes of states. According to the first, it will follow that spirit is not the material cause as change of states are only symbolic 'differences' in spirit, ideal differentiation in the function of will. The second answer is plausible but only by reverting to the doctrine of '*viśiṣṭa*' which has been shown to be not quite intelligible. The notion of *vṛtti* therefore is not really an advance on that of *pariṇāma*.[37]

The objection that change pertaining to the qualification (*viśeṣaṇa*), namely, *māyā* will also affect the qualified (*viśiṣṭa*) may be met by the argument that change belonging to the sphere of *māyā* is not of the order of known cases of 'transformation' such as is involved in the transformation of milk into curd; change exemplified by this illustration is certainly not of the sense in which *māyā* undergoes 'change'. In the transformation of milk into curd there is irreversibility about the transformation, but in the case of *māyā* there is involution as well as evolution.[38] But this argument overlooks the idea that the reversible nature of the cause-effect relation of the self-becoming characteristic of *māyā*[39] is to be traced to the intelligent will underlying the function of *māyā*. Taken physically involution is a causal process in reverse, a self-resolution of the effect into the cause, an enfolding of the actual back into the potential, implying a process in time, whereas, taken metaphysically, involution is the freedom of the will to suspend causality.[40] The manifestation and retraction of the ground of being are really functions of spirit, and not a mechanical process as, for example, it is for Spinoza. They are ultimately linked with the cosmic functions of self-concealment and self-revelation. Far from supporting material causality of spirit[41] the concept of *vṛtti* as distinguished from known instances of transformation really goes to support will-causality.

However the motive underlying the suggestion of *vṛtti* as plausible interpretation of effectuation cannot be doubted. The two extremes which it seeks to avoid are 'creation' as transformation, direct and indirect, which make effectuation real but at the cost of the unity and integrity of spirit, and creation as illusory appearance (*vivarta*) which preserves the integrity of spirit but makes effectuation unreal.[42] Even quality (*guṇa*) and action (*kriyā*) in relation to substance (*dravya*) are brought under the category of effect in relation to material cause. This means that what is minimally required in material causation is the admission of real 'change' of form; association with a '*new*' form[43] is a necessary implication of material causality in so far as quality (*guṇa*) and action (*kriyā*) are not as such identical with substance (*dravya*). The 'new' form or quality by which the material cause comes to be 'qualified' may be either of similar or dissimilar nature. While *guṇa* and *dravya* its material cause, are homogeneous, *kriyā* and *dravya*, though related as material cause and effect, are heterogeneous. It may likewise be held that the world of change and plurality though of dissimilar nature from spirit can originate from it.[44]

This argument is plausible superficially only. It is true that a change of form is all that is demanded about a material cause, but from this admission of a *change* of forms does it not necessarily follow that it is non-intelligent (*jaḍa*)? How can it be an attribute of spirit? Just because spirit has to be admitted as material cause in a literal sense, to reinterpret the very notion of material cause as applicable to spirit is not legitimate. A literal attribution of material causality to spirit invites all the objections raised against the transformation theory. The relation of *kriyā* and *dravya* is not an instance of material causation alone. If the world of dissimilar nature from spirit arises from spirit, the presumption is not that spirit is the material cause which undergoes change of form or function without a transformation of substance. The presumption rather is that spirit is the agent, the world-ground, which brings about change of form. In conceiving the cause as agent whet is implied is the rejection of a dualism of doings and happenings — the 'I do' and the 'it happens'.[45]

The concept of *vivarta*[46]

According to Advaita Vedānta dual causality pertains to *brahman* in a univocal sense since it is conceivable that material cause can also be efficient cause. The parity and even identity of the two become intelligible on a revision of the notion of cause itself. Material causality of spirit is conceivable if by cause we mean not the originating or transforming cause but the unmodified ground of world-appearance.

The material causality of spirit is implicitly contained in the notion of spirit as world-cause; the attribution to spirit of the three-fold processes of effectuation-creation, conservation and dissolution implies that Spirit is efficient as well as material cause.[47] And the material causality of spirit can only mean that the effect is an unreal appearance, not a real transformation. Transformation of the same grade of reality is *pariṇāma*; not of the same grade of reality is *vivarta*. Transformation of the same nature as the cause is *pariṇāma*; not of the same but of a different nature is *vivarta*. Effect non-different from the cause is *pariṇāma*; not non-different and yet what cannot be told apart from the cause is *vivarta*.[47a] It is only change conceived as *vivarta* that is compatible with the eternal existence of cause and the eternal existence of effect-form in the cause.[48]

Vivartopādānatva of *brahman* is conceivable because of the primal hiding principle *māyā* which is co-eternal with *brahman* and through which *brahman* phenomenalises into the form of ether, water and other elements. The latter are in themselves unreal appearances and real only as *brahman*.[49]

Śaiva Siddhānta also believes in the *sole* causality of God. Primarily the ground of the resolution of the world, God is also the cause of its creation. By conceiving such cause as essentially, not accidentally, Will, Śaiva Siddhānta implies that the world, the willed-content, shares with the Will which is its cause the same order of being (*sat*). Although wholly conditioned and determined by Will, the world does not lack in being though it lacks in value — the value of permanence, and therefore is described as non-being (*asat*).[50] Its reality is in fact bound up with and derived from the reality of its cause. The cause is not bound up with or derived from the world. The dependence of the world on

God and the independence and integrity of God in relation to the world — this relation of one-sided dependence is central to religious consciousness.

The theory of *vivarta* is also a rigorous formulation of one-sided non-difference. But from this follows according to the theory the falsity of all relations. To admit that relation is between the false and the real is to say that all relation is false.[51] *Brahman* as the transcendent ground of the world and the world as nothing without *brahman* logically implies the falsity of the latter whence also follows the falsity of the relation in which *brahman* stands to the world. The concept of material causality applied to spirit may be seen to imply that the effect is only appearance. The doctrine of self-becoming (*satkārya-vāda*) is admitted but only as a first step to a negation of becoming as such and the establishment of Pure Being through negation.

Śaiva Siddhānta understands Being as implying will. The cause to which the given world as effect points is both a *kartṛ* and *karaṇa*, spirit and power, form and function.[52] Śiva as spirit is essentially transcendent but through the instrumentality of his will (vis-a-vis *māyā*), He is also the immanent cause of the world-process.

The conception of non-dual *brahman* as the reality of which the world is but appearance is not tenable.[53] Acosmism in a literal sense runs counter to the verdicts of all evidence, of revelation and reason not to speak of the verdict of sense.[54] The implication of the falsity of the world is that its cause, *brahman*, is non-being.[55] The negations of the *Śruti* must be construed along with other texts which speak of *brahman* in personalistic terms. The same *Śruti* which admittedly is the ultimate source of our knowledge of *brahman* as real and *māyā* as unreal also speaks of the world as real. If *Śruti* is to be relied upon, the *Śruti* alone is to be relied upon for one's knowledge of *brahman* and *māyā*, and *māyā* must be interpreted compatibly with other declarations of *Śruti*.

The legitimacy of the notion of illusory appearance is also open to question. There is no compelling instance which is both a content of valid perceptual experience and of negation as well. The snake-appearance, the stock example, may be variously explained as either a case of projection of memory, and not a perception, or, if perceived, not also subsequently negated, or if perceived and also negated, still not undisputedly evidencing the category of appearance.[56] Even granting that what appears is not real, that it appears at least should be of moment. Water in the desert may be appearance but the water-appearance, the mirage, has to be accounted for.

The material cause of world-appearance is allegedly *brahman* and not *māyā*.[57] *Advaita* is foresworn against cosmology; there is no real becoming. *Māyā* which is co-eternal with *brahman* is a *śakti* of *brahman*; itself nothing, like the 'blue tint around objects seen through blue glasses', *māyā* is the seed or potentiality of germination and individuality. God allows himself to be the ground of the power of *māyā* to play.[58]

World-appearance in its manifest or unmanifest form is present in *brahman* but really not of it. But the question that arises here is: *brahman* is absolutely simple and *māyā* is present in Him. How is it conceivable if *brahman* were simple ? How can absolute Being co-exist with absolute 'seeming' ? How can absolute knowledge co-exist with absolute non-knowledge ? *Vivarta-vāda* brings incurable contradictions in the being of God, and a wilful monism that underlies its use is paradoxically also a radical dualism.[59]

If the notion of ground and appearance were only to mean denial of the immanence of the ground in the appearance in any but an axiological sense, it is acceptable and Śaiva Siddhānta has no reasons to reject it.[60] Acceptance of *māyā* as a *śakti* of God and the conception of God itself as both Being and Will also imply axiological immanence of the ground in the phenomena and a rejection of immanence of existence as conceived in pantheisms. If *vivarta-vāda* is a re-interpretation of *pariṇāma-vāda* of all shades, and is implied by them,[61] *vivarta-vāda* itself may likewise be 'religiously' re-interpreted and reoriented to mean freedom of Act, not merely freedom of Being.

The last alternative to be considered is that the non-intelligent *māyā* is really the cause that transforms into the world, and spirit, the ground of *māyā* is also the material cause.[62] This is the most plausible way of vindicating the claim of the material causality of spirit. The efficient cause is both itself, and also the ground of the reality of matter in its gross as well as its subtle form. As ground of matter, spirit is also the *upādāna kāraṇa* (*pariṇamyamāna-māyādhiṣṭhānamātreṇa śivopādānatvam*), while it is also spirit, the *nimitta kāraṇa*.

The grounds for assigning two causalities to spirit are different with differing accounts.[63] They all however agree in according recognition to the truth that spirit is the ultimate ground of being. Śiva and *māyā* of which Śiva is ground, are both material causes of the phenomenal world. The world as existence (*sat*), intelligible (*sphūrti*) and endearing (*priya*), and also as mutable and inert has Śiva and *māyā* respectively as its material causes. Śiva coordinate with *māyā* shares with the latter its role as material cause, and as the ground of *māyā*, He is not mere material cause but efficient cause.

An example[64] will make this position clear. The phenomenon of smoke or soot is the effect of two material causes, fire and wet-fuel. Though both are material causes, only the characteristic of the wet-fuel is visible in the smoke and not the light and brightness of the fire. The phenomenal world is mutable and objective. These characteristics derive from *māyā*. The spiritual characteristics of intelligence and bliss of Śiva are not manifest in the world. But this is as it should be because Śiva is not merely material cause but also the efficient cause; the characteristics of spirit, efficient cause that it is, are not communicated directly in the effect.[65]

It cannot be said that fire is only the efficient cause of smoke and it is the wet fuel alone that is the material cause. As wet fuel *per se* cannot be the material cause of smoke, but it is so only in association with fire, the presumption is that fire is also the material cause.[66] Similarly, immutability, self-luminosity and bliss do not characterise phenomena but spirit. Nevertheless spirit together with *māyā* is conceivable as material cause of the phenomenal world. *Māyā* alone unassociated with spirit is inconceivable as material cause.

It may be objected that if spirit were also the material cause of phenomena it must be perceptible in its effect; the clay material is perceived in pot, being its constitutive stuff. Why is spirit not perceived in its effect? In answer it may be observed that though spirit as such is not apprehended in its effect, its characteristics (*dharmas*) like existentiality and intelligibility are indeed so apprehended; its bliss-nature is of course hidden. The luminous nature of fire is hidden in the smoke, but other qualities, such as heat etc. are communicated.[67]

Another example[68] is cited to bring out the sense of dual 'material' causality: parents in relation to the physique of their offspring. Both parents may be considered the material cause in the sense that their cells conjointly contribute to the formation of the limbs and the bones of the offspring. The male parent at the same time is also considered the 'agent' as regards the 'gift' of the child. In a like manner Śiva is considered pre-eminently agent, the 'giver' of the world, though He is also its material cause.[69]

The example of the spider-web also is illustrative of the dual causality of spirit. The material cause of the web cannot be said to be the body alone of the spider. The *Śruti* says that the spider sends forth as well as draws in its web (*gṛhṇate ca*). To be the ground of resolution or retraction is compatible with material causality only. At the same time the spider is also the *nimitta kāraṇa*.[70] The spider and its material body are both material causes in relation to the threads sent forth and the spider is also the efficient cause.

The difference between the above mentioned positions, and the standpoint of Śaiva Siddhānta is only terminological. One affirms that God is the material cause and the other terms it the efficient cause. No conceptual difference seems to be involved. Even according to the view that God is the material cause, material cause is understood in effect figuratively only. In distinguishing material causality ascribed to God from other known instances of material causality, it is affirmed and also in a sense *denied* of God. All interpretations of God's material causality agree in a striking manner in holding that God is material cause but in a unique sense. Even the pan-organismic view which conceives of the 'growth' of the world of sentience and insentience from spirit, implies by the analogy of the organism, that spirit is the underlying, indwelling *ground* of the manifestation of the effect.[71]

Śaiva Siddhānta is in disagreement only with that view of attributing material causality to God which would conflict with God's immutable nature. If God can be material cause without prejudice to his nature as spirit, with such a view it need not dissent.[72] It does not disagree, because it is with the same end in view that it holds that Śiva is the *nimitta kāraṇa* and *māyā* the *upādāna kāraṇa*. As it was observed elsewhere, *nimitta kāraṇa* is not merely a cause[73] along with other causes; it is also the ground of the cause-effect series. It is the *adhiṣṭhāna* of the retraction and re-emanation of the effect.

God is the cause of the world (i) in being the ground of its existence and also (ii) in pervading and constituting the world.[74] This is the purport of ascribing material *cum* efficient causality to God. God as spirit is the ground of *māyā* and its evolution into the world, and God 'constitutes' the world through his characteristics like existentiality, luminosity and blissfulness. Śaiva Siddhānta, also by its recognition of a three-fold cause, material, instrumental and efficient, subscribes to the same truth. Admission of *māyā* as the material cause, *śakti* (will) as the instrumental cause and Śiva as the efficient cause implies that (i) God is the ground of the world *qua* the ground of *māyā*, the material cause of the world, and that (ii) God is immanent in the world as Will.[75] God's pervasion of the world is not to be understood on the analogy of material cause and its effect pantheistically or on the analogy of a passive, inoperative substratum and the superimposed, as it is understood in the acosmistic Vedānta. It is immanence of will rather than immanence of being.

Śaiva Siddhānta seeks to reconcile the sole causality of God as spirit with the recognition of the observed difference between the sphere of material cause as that of matter and the sphere of efficient cause as that of spirit. *Māyā* is the material cause of the world and Śiva too, being the ground of *Māyā*, is, while being the efficient cause, also the material cause in a transferred sense. Let us take again an example: *paṅkaja* (lotus) literally born of mire (*paṅka*), in growing out of its roots indeed may be said to grow out of the mire which is both the ground (*nimitta kāraṇa*) of the root, as well as the operative condition (*karaṇa*), on account of its moisture inducing the growth of the root into a lotus-creeper.[76] The Agent of the world is conceivable as its 'first cause' only in this sense without involving a compromise of His immutable nature as spirit. It may not be thought that this is virtually to deny material causality and admit mere efficient causality (*kevala-nimitta*) for the creator. The latter being also the material cause is very real, although in a transferred sense. God being the sole cause of His creation is not less true on account of His being material cause in a transferred sense. In fact it is the only sense in which God can be conceived the sole cause of His creation.

The examples cited earlier may be seen to support the present view if properly interpreted. Fire is the efficient cause of the phenomenon of smoke and may also be considered the ground of the wet-fuel in as much as the wet fuel would not cause smoke unsupported by fire. In this sense it may also be called material cause of smoke. The parent is the efficient cause of the offspring *qua* the 'ground' of the germ-cell and also as latter the material cause.[77] The spider, itself the efficient cause, in being the 'ground' of its body from which issues forth its threads, is also the material cause transforming into threads. In all these instances it may be seen that the term 'ground' ('*adhiṣṭhāna*) is used in the sense of intelligent self which both supports and controls what has only a consequent existence in relation to it.[78] The self which permeates every atom of living matter may be said to be more legitimately the constitutive stuff of a living body than matter itself.

V

GOD AS THE LORD OF COSMIC FUNCTIONS

Five-fold Cosmic Operations

Our 'general' account of the reality of God must include definitions; in addition to merely showing that God exists as the causal ground of the world, we should also be able to define the nature of God. God is certainly not the 'given', to be known discursively as this-what. But He may be defined, that is, distinguished by characteristics which are unerringly indicative of His being. It was shown that God as Destroyer of the world was its primary cause. This thesis contains implicitly the definition also; as primary cause God may be distinguished from what is not God in terms of a differentia — the differentia suggested by the concept of Destroyer, namely, one that performs *all* cosmic functions *qua* performer of the pre-eminent function of universal dissolution.[1] This, then, is the 'general definition' (*taṭastha-lakṣaṇa*) of God.[2]

The validation (*pramāṇa*) of the central reality of Śaiva Siddhānta, namely, Śiva, is contained in the notion of cause applied to it. The defining characteristic (*lakṣaṇa*) of Śiva as the lord of all cosmic operations is a logical extension of the same idea. The two together comprehensively indicate the 'general' nature of God. In our knowledge of the real we proceed from the phenomenon of relatedness to the reality of what is in relation; in this quest arises the demand to know the real in itself, unrelatedly. The ultimate essence or nature (*svarūpa-lakṣaṇa*) of Reality, what Śiva is, represents the culmination of knowledge.

The self-existent, self-luminous Reality in its absolute unconditioned essence is Reality, Being or Spirit (Śiva). Considered with reference to the creature, (*paśu*) with whom it stands in a relation of non-difference, it is also will (*Śakti*). Being and Will are related as identity (*tādātmya*) of two distinguishable aspects of the self-same reality. The same, considered in further relation to the exigence of 'cosmic' functions of creation, maintenance and dissolution together with the two 'micro-cosmic' operations of self-concealment and self-revelation, is the Lord or the Sovereign (*pati*).[3] Spirit or Being, in other words, is conceived from the phenomenal perspective as the supreme Person — the Lord (*pati*). That by virtue of which He is the Lord is identical with His essence. Lordship presupposes possession of *Śakti* as the integral nature of spirit. The freedom exercised through Lordship comprises an unlimited freedom of will (*icchā*) and an absolute freedom for carrying them out in actuality, namely, the freedom of act (*kriyā*). Spirit stands as the inalienable basis or background of this freedom.[4]

Lordship exercised in a five-fold cosmic operation through the instrumentality of *karma*, constitutes the general definition (*taṭastha-lakṣaṇa*) of God. And this itself is intelligible only on its being shown (i) that the 'instrument' of *karma* by reference to which Divine will may be conceived to perform the cosmic functions, is only an impersonalised self-concealed form of the Divine Will itself; (ii) that the Divine Will which is an integral part of Divine reality stands immanently in the will of the individual for whom the cosmic functions are meant. God as it were stands unfractionably 'oned' with the individual self such that it could be said that God is as much he (the individual self) as Himself. This is the *advaita* doctrine implicit in the notion of God as the sovereign-Lord of cosmic functions.[5]

The two definitions of god

The *taṭastha-lakṣaṇa* comes first in the order of our understanding and as a step towards *svarūpa-lakṣaṇa* because, implicated as we are in bondage, it is only by reference to the condition obtaining in the bound state, that we can begin our quest for God. We know Śiva in His unconditioned self-existent nature as we know Him in relation to our present condition of existential estrangement, as the source and support of our existence, as law and as love, as, in short, our ultimate fulfilment. It is only from such a perspective that we proceed to a knowledge of God considered in Himself. Before perceiving the moon as what it is in itself, namely a luminous body, we first view it from our point of vision.[6] From our point of location, inevitably the moon is just what sits skirting the bough of the yonder tree. All knowledge, one may generalize, is structured in these two ways bearing necessarily on the existential situation of man in his present 'bound' condition and a future state of freedom from bondage which is his destiny. What we know from the perspective of the bound state of man, bound by the metaphysical, moral and physical bonds of life and existence, is 'general' knowedge (*taṭastha-lakṣaṇa*). What we know in this way leads to a culminating insight which as such is unrelated to our immediate condition of bondage. This is how God is perceived by 'liberated' consciousness, which is knowledge of essence (*svarūpa-lakṣaṇa*).[7] This knowledge unlike all empirical knowing, is knowledge *by being*; as such it has to be realised in the context of spiritual life. In the ultimate analysis vision of God is inseparable from becoming like unto Him, which is not a possession but has to be won by 'purification', by purifying ourselves spiritually even as He is Pure. Purificatory process, that is what spiritual life is, is also negatively removal of the obstacles to our union with God. In one sentence there is no knowledge or 'vision' which does not also involve 'mystical participation.' Knowledge from the ideal perspective of Freedom by definition precludes realisation as long as one is not freed or liberated. A 'secular', 'general', exoteric knowledge of the ultimate essence of spirit is a contradiction in terms.[8]

In Advaita Vedānta, cause and effect as applied respectively to *brahman* and the world are understood in a manner that makes effect an unreal something that is mistaken for the cause. The world, as it were, substitutes itself as reality in the place of *brahmān*. Our discovery of *brahman* accordingly involves a calling off of this substitution. We know *brahman* only as we negate the world of which *brahman* is the unmodified ground. *Svarūpa-lakṣaṇa* involves a rejection of the *taṭastha-lakṣaṇa*.[9]

But as already explained, *brahman* as the world-cause is Will according to Śaiva Siddhānta, that freely wills the world into manifest existence bringing to pass its dissolution and re-evolution. The effect is not an appearance but an exteriorisation effected by Will without undergoing modification; the effect lives, moves and resolves into the reality of the cause. Discovery of Śiva's or *brahman's* essential nature does not therefore involve negating the world as a necessary step in the process. It is true that Śiva and the world are not two co-ordinate realities existing in their side-by-sideness. Knowledge of Śiva surely involves rejection of the world if not as existence as a value in its own right. Were it not so, were Śaiva Sidhānta a philosophical pluralism according to which all are real in the same sense, there would not be any necessity for the two *lakṣaṇas*.

Nevertheless, *svarūpa-lakṣaṇa* does not imply the falsity of *taṭastha-lakṣaṇa*. The two are continuous[10] and mean growing from the merely 'exoteric' to a more inward, 'esoteric' knowledge of God. The transition is from a state of dependence, bondage and finitude to one of independence, spontaneity and infinitude, involving a growth from empirical knowledge to a life of spirit. The two *lakṣaṇas* are not merely two stages within knowledge, two 'definitions' to be contemplated by mind in a detached manner. They are distinguishable respectively as knowledge, and the destined end of knowledge which involves coincidence of essence and existence. Knowledge *by being* is a species of life in which life comes to be immediately aware of an underlying, deeper dimension of reality. It is this ecstatic awareness that is described as the experience of bliss characteristic of the life of spirit. It is to this end the way is paved by knowledge of *taṭastha-lakṣaṇa*. When darkness is dispelled the eye which was shrouded in it comes to know the light, by becoming 'one' with light. But before that it has first to locate the source of light with its focalised vision; the location is a necessary moment in the process of the eye comporting itself in the presence of the luminous effulgence.

Even locating it, it may be noted, is possible because of the commonplace condition of light. It is as if light unobtrusively or 'generally' reveals to the focalised visual sense its own source and leads it onward to union therewith. Union with light by which the eye as it were becomes light is a necessary precondition in order to comport itself properly in the face of light.

The *taṭastha-lakṣaṇa* may only define the 'that' and not the 'what' of Śiva. Still *qua* definition it must unmistakably differentiate Him from the rest. God must be distinguished from what is not God. *Pati* must be distinguished from *paśu* and *pāśa*. *Patitva* (lordship) being relative may not be adequate for expressing the absolute essence of Śiva, and yet however 'generally' considered it cannot serve to characterise any one else. It must exclusively though not exhaustively characterise Śiva. The adequacy of our definition of Śiva as the lord that performs cosmic functions, judged from this test would therefore require as its evidence (*pramāṇa*) a compound assertion to the effect that the Destroyer is the cause of world-creation *and* that Śiva the Destroyer is *alone* such cause.[11] Śiva may be the cause of the world, but unless it is also shown that Śiva alone is, absolutely, the cause, to describe Him as the lord that performs all cosmic operations will not be to 'define' Him; sovereignty of Śiva will not be a proprium exclusively characteristic of His being.

Śiva, in other words, is identical with the *brahman* of Vedānta; He is God as well as the Absolute; no other deity, not the creator Brahmā nor again the world-soul Nārāyaṇa can claim the same supremacy. As the recurrent being underlying all that exists, as the destroyer of all as possessing illimitable lordship, as the most adequate ruler who is immanently present in the creature and guides it towards its fulfilment, as one that drives away the miseries of a never-ending cycle of rebirths, as the light that knows no eclipse, as one that instils fear in the minds of the evil-doers, as the Supreme Being of infinite splendour Siva is *brahman* itself.[12]

Śiva is the 'divine ground' and 'abyss' in which even the gods disappear and re-emerge. The gods of the trinity in charge of the offices of creation, preservation and resolution are swallowed up in the ultimate Being which transcends them. The creator creates the universe and the conserver conserves, but the supreme Destroyer destroys everything, the worlds created and maintained by them as well as the gods themselves. Destroying them He creates them again and brings to pass through them the operations of creation.

Even as there is no being higher than *brahman*, no god is higher than or equal to Śiva who is identical with *brahman*. Though parallel attributes are ascribed to Śiva and Viṣṇu in scriptures, Śiva alone is the Supreme Lord, and qualities indicative of lordship ascribed to Nārāyaṇa must be differently interpreted.[13]

The gods are indeed the operative aspects of the Supreme Lord and their functions are partial manifestations of Śiva's power. Śiva is more the divine ground rather than the god-monarch that rules over a hierarchy of gods. The spirit of the Śaiva affirmation of the supremacy of God considered as the Lord of cosmic operations is a mystical monotheism and not a monarchical monotheism.[14] The one Supreme God who is Ruler (*pati*) rules from within man's being. He does not function as creator from without, but as 'one' with self for whom He creates.

The Concept of *pañca-kṛtya*[15]

The five-fold cosmic functions of the Lord (*pati*) is the answer implied in man's finitude (*paśutva*). The semblance of difference between divine wrath implied by Destruction and divine compassion implied by Creation and Preservation exist not in the reality of God's being or will but exists in and through the medium of the 'existing' finite self. Admission of this must not however be taken to mean that Divine Forms and Functions are therefore not ontological. They are part of the dynamics of 'concealment' and 'unconcealment' characteristic of Divine Reality. It is with reference to the finitude of man that we have to understand the concept of cosmic operations and of the five cosmic operations that Śaiva Siddhānta attributes to God. Man is 'fettered' from the beginning of time by the impurity of *mala* and consequently, though intelligent in essence is unaided and unredeemed, ignorant and inactive. As long as the connate Impurity of the soul remains 'green' (*āmam*) there is no scope for the emergence of the soul's action and knowledge and consequently no way to be rid of the Impurity. The Impurity is inert and the soul already a victim of it can exercise no freedom or knowledge to dispel it. It thus follows that the initiative must come from the transcendent God by whose benevolent Will alone the soul may be made to engage in action with the help of a body and in a world in which to live and move about. Embodiment in its turn implies cycles of birth and death in so far as the Impurity underlying one's birth remains as yet not fit for removal. And the entire cosmic scheme through which the soul is made to pass must have the ring of reality and an intrinsic meaning so that the self may be renewedly motived to engage in action. This involves concealing God's identity in the soul and objectifying the soul's action and knowledge.[16] By all these inter-connected processes the 'green' unripe condition of the primordial Impurity slowly gives place to a condition of ripeness (*pāka*). The potential evil becomes as it were actualised[17] and thus fit for removal. When some thing potential becomes actual God's will is implied as the ground of such possibility. The will, itself neither potential nor actual, is the actualiser of all that is potential. Such is Grace. Neither bondage nor liberation can be understood except as phases of Grace thus interpreted.[18] A successive performance of action and enjoyment of its fruitage contributes to the 'ripening' of the unripe *mala*. Then ensues the bestowal of Grace when the condition of Impurity together with action and the cycle of birth and death which in its turn is occasioned by the beginningless circumstance of Impurity, is set to nought and the soul comes to its undefiled inheritance of freedom.

The five-fold cosmic functions of the Lord refer to a pre-cosmic

Impurity of the soul, namely *mala* and also to two 'adventitious' impurities through a conjunction with which the 'green' *mala* is made 'ripe.'[19] These are *māyā* and *karma*. They are also conjoined from the beginning of time with *mala* in the soul, but they are adventitious in the sense that their functions are to be understood in relation to the function of *mala*. *Mala* functions as the constricting and veiling principle, while *māyā* and *karma*, as willed to 'evolve' and act, serve partially to unconstrict and unveil.

These agencies that bind, being themselves non-intelligent function as media of Divine Will. Cosmic action on the part of Divine Will has broadly speaking, two phases one in which these bonds—the primordial one (*sahaja mala*) as well as the consequential (*āgantuka mala*) are quickened to action and sustained in their functions. The consequential *mala* are willed to effectuate from their original dormant state into their effect forms, and by this means the original *mala* in the soul is matured and ripened. The other phase consists in bestowing Grace through a revelatory manifestation. The initial phase involves a self-veiling of true being of God and simultaneous energising of the Bond as it were as a conniving witness to its function of obstruction.[20] Thereby is set in operation the entire cosmic process.[21] The subsequent phase implies a self-revelation of God's true being which coincides with a dissolution of the bonds. Creation and other world-processes follow upon the self-veiling of the divine power and cease with its self-revelation.

The initial phase of operation, technically the *tirodhāna*, again in its turn implies a grouping of certain 'co-operative antagonisms', namely creating 'body, sense, world and worldly enjoyments' and conserving them out of the creative ground of life on the one hand, and destroying on the other hand, what has been created and conserved, resolving everything into its abysmal ground. These again fall within the single process of maturing or ripening of *malas*. Dissolution is calculated to mature *karma mala*[22]— the stockpile of cosmic *sañcita*, and creation-conservation is intended for bringing about the ripeness of *āṇava mala* through a fructification of *karma* already matured and rendered fit for bearing fruit.

The central theme of the doctrine of five-fold cosmic functions of God is the continuity and congruence between the creative and destructive processes at work within phenomenal life, and also the great continuity between phenomenal life considered as one long enjoyment (*bhoga*) and a life of spirit involving transcending of phenomena (*mokṣa*).[23] All cosmic functions, manifest 'simultaneously with the pulse of every moment, and in sequence through the change of time' are, essentially, expressions and embodiments of grace. The meaning of each of these functions, not only the fifth one which is grace expressly, can become intelligible if looked at as an expression of Divine Grace.

To consider the operation of Dissolution first. Dissolution (*saṁhāra*) seems to be at the farthest remove from grace. Is performing of *saṁhāra*, implying death and destruction, compatible with grace?

Destruction, technically, is giving respite to the self as for example in the case of sleep.[24] It involves bringing about a disjunction of the senses from self during the interval between eating the fruit of a matured *karma* and the maturing of another *karma*.[25] Resolution is being temporarily restored to the state of 'pre-biographic' isolation (*kevala avasthā*) which antecedes a life of empirical enjoyment and suffering and therefore constitutes in a sense the 'native' unmitigated existence of the bound self. To be restored to this 'nativity' after 'consuming' of the fruit of a particular *karma*, as a kind of rest and preparation for the experience of fresh *karma*, is the 'micro-cosmic' significance of Dissolution. A continuous state of experience, an endless activation uninterrupted by suspension and rest cannot betoken a kindly God. There are the accumulated consequences of deeds due to pre-existence and they will have to be matured and liquidated. Otherwise, if a particular experience against a matured *karma* alone were to endure for an indefinite span, other *karmas* from the store-house cannot mature, and cannot consequently be removed. According to the theory of *karma*, no *karma* is liquidated except through its fruits being experienced. What is true of the individual is true of the world in the collective. Without the cosmic *sañcita* maturing during intervals of cosmic dissolution the cosmic process cannot be conceived to serve a purpose.

If Resolution means respite, and respite for the soul is an act of grace in the above sense, then Re-Creation (*punassṛṣṭi*) also cannot be grace, it may be said. Why is Dissolution followed by Creation again? The answer, again, is that a state of perpetuated Resolution also cannot be an act of grace. An eternal condition of rest and inactivity will leave the original Impurity unripe and the souls consequently will remain bound till eternity. Evil, then, will be an invariable necessity instead of a mere potentiality. *Māyā* — the Root matter is quickened into evolving body, senses etc., and souls are subject to births in order that their connate Impurity may actualise from its dormant condition on its way to become 'ripe' and fit for eventual decease.[26] Hence it is that Creative function has to be conceived to follow Resolution.

Is Conservation, then, grace? The function of Conservation (*sthiti*) is 'continuous creativity'[27] which, in our terminology, would mean preserving the self's subordination to *māyā* through whose evolution it comes to be provided with embodiment. *Māyā* is also *mala* in the sense that it 'binds' the soul to matter even though it binds in order that the soul may eventually be liberated from *mala*. But if this 'bondage' to *māyā* were 'preserved' enduringly by means of a continuous creative function (*sthiti*) how can this be an expression of grace?

In answer, it may be said that it is not only by being enabled to take birth but by being made to enjoy and suffer[28] that the process of actualisation of *mala* is accomplished. The Lord causes *mala* to ripen by making it possible for the soul to engage in an unending succession of experiences in each birth. Preservation is, therefore, continuous with the inner 'telos' of creativity, namely that of actualising of the potentialities of finitude (*paśutva*) with a view to its ultimate removal.[29]

If the aim of cosmic operations be to redeem the self from its state of blindness due to *mala*, how is the function of Concealment (*tirobhāva*) compatible with that aim? How can veiling be considered an expression of grace? The cosmic function of Concealment is paradoxical. It inhibits and conceals with the powers of the self, and facilitates the powers of the bonds (*mala*) by stimulating the bonds into action.

The real significance of cosmic concealment lies in bringing eventually to pass for the *malas* a condition when they shall cease to be potent.[30] Till the advent of that condition the *malas* are not only not removed, being not fit for removal but, on the contrary, their hands are as it were strengthened. Both the aspects of Concealment, of omission and of commission, are acts of grace, compatible with the inner aim of liberation and fulfilment for the soul.

The Lord that performs the cosmic functions is omniscient, and knows the miseries to which one becomes heir as one is born. He is omnipotent and it is conceivable that he can liberate all the souls at one stroke. And He is not wanting in goodness either; He is Śaṅkara,[31] one that wills nothing but good for the souls and is the very apotheosis of love.[32] If that Lord does not at once eliminate suffering by liquidating all *karmas* and dissipating the powers of *mala*, the presumption can only be that it is so again because of His Will—the negative will to sustain and stimulate the Bond in its function of concealing and obstructing till such time as it begins to wear thin, ready for total dissipation. It is this negative will of the Lord that is characterised as the concealing operation.[33]

Finally, remains the question: if all these four operations of creation, conservation, dissolution and concealment are functions of grace why admit the fifth Grace (*anugraha*) as a distinct operation? If that is Grace it follows that others are not equivalents of grace; if others are equivalents of grace there need not be a fifth operation in our list under the title of Grace. In answer we may distinguish two forms of grace, the grace which characterises the first four cosmic activities and the grace characterising the activity of revelatory manifestation which accomplishes pre-eminently the fulfilment of the inner aim of 'telos' of all cosmic activity on the part of Divine Will.

The first form of grace is the paradoxical one which helps or fulfils the soul by 'helping' the bonds; cleansing the soul by adding to its original Dirt more kinds of dirt, even as a washerman washes dirty linen by soaking it in washing materials also a kind of impurity. He cures the soul of its disease by inflicting sufferings and sorrow just as a physician seeks to cure by adding to the misery of the patient by administering bitter medicines.[34] But by this form of grace *mala* is only ripened and not removed. The linen soaked in the washing grains only attains to a condition fit for the wash; it has still to be cleansed alike of its initial dirt and of the dirts added in the form of chemicals.[35]

The Impurity brought to an attenuated condition, 'fit for the surgeon's knife', the surplus *karma* that still remains unliquidated and matter (*māyīya*) which has been serving as the vehicle of embodied existence and experience—all these are yet to be 'removed'. The cosmic operations so far considered are not equal to 'removing' them. They have served only to prepare through the cosmic processes for the final bestowal of Grace. It is only by the direct application of the *jñāna-śakti* and the *kriyā-śakti* of the Lord in the guise of a preceptor, that their 'removal' is effected and final liberation from the evil of finitude—from even a potentiality of evil, is accomplished.[36]

The continuity of the five-fold cosmic functions outlined above is unbroken and direct but only from the absolute point of view, which is the point of view of one who has risen to the divine status, to a conscious communion with God. From the point of view of man fettered by bonds and under the sway of the Impurity of *mala* the continuity is necessarily disrupted. Finite existence is not only different from the Absolute being of God but in a sense even implies its denial. Man grows in his individuated separative consciousness and it is part of the cosmic scheme to nurture and foster this self-affirmation of life and a consequent denial of infinite existence with which it is 'one' ontologically. There is no 'natural' transition from this denial implied in the attitude of self-affirmation, to an affirmation of Infinite reality through a self-noughting; and yet this denial itself cannot be ultimate, for from the Absolute standpoint this denial on the part of the creature is also facilitated by the will of God as a necessary moment in the process of redeeming the soul from its Impurity. The latter is responsible for the connate ego-centricism of the finite consciousness and the consequent rejection of its oneness with Infinity. God may be said to will into actuality this initial act of denial and separation as an act of grace as without this act the self-centredness and the obliviousness of divinity in the self due to *mala*, will continue for ever without any hope of dissolution. But by bringing it into existence the creative Will provides for its dissolution through growth and ripening. The alienation from and the reabsorption into the Divine is a continuous process but from the point of view of the *paśu* there is an abrupt disruption, an unconditional leap into the Divine Abyss at a particular point of its worldly career.[37]

God and Non-duality

God is conceived as the Lord that creates because God is Will. It is therefore pointless to ask whether creation is 'necessary' or only a contingent event. God is a being 'existing' *a se* and His aseity is the source from which flow all His other perfections.[1] "Everything which God is, He is through Himself". The question, therefore, 'what is the purpose of God's performance of the cosmic functions ?' has no meaning. Divine will is essentially creative and does not create for a purpose beyond itself. The question however can be raised and also answered meaningfully when viewed from the perspective of the existing 'me'. Considered in itself it surely makes no sense to ask 'why' about God's action. But God as 'identified' with me can be conceived to act for the sake of my good. The 'purpose' of creation is the self itself with which the creative Will stands non-different. Ultimately from the point of view of the self the aim of Creation is the aim of fulfilment, growth in the spiritual sense involving actualisation of its otherwise unactualisable potentialities and an eventual attainment of a *conscious* union with the Lord which is its destiny. The issue may be clarified by raising the following question from the angle of the *pūrvapakṣa.*

Motive of creation

The assertion that God creates the world surely is intelligible only on an adequate explanation of the 'purpose' of Creation. The anti-theists even of the 'orthodox' group hesitate to admit a creative God because of the difficulty afforded by the problem of motive.[2] If God creates, for whose sake does He create? He either creates for Himself or He creates for the sake of others. Or more plausibly He creates for nobody's sake; there is no 'telos' about God's creativity, inner or outer and he just creates as a sport.[3]

If God creates for His own sake it will mean that He lacks something which He must secure from His creative function or from what He creates. That God is in need of something to be accomplished is incompatible with His plenitude and perfection (*nitya-tṛptatva*).[3a] Creation must be an act of spontaneity, not the result of a 'dialectical necessity'.[4] It cannot even be 'the glory of God' that motivates creation because as God possesses His glory eternally in Himself He does not need to create the world to give him glory. There is nothing that God needs or lacks that He could not have without His cosmic functions.

Nor therefore can it be for others' sake, presumably, the individual selves. Because this will raise the further difficulty of defining the relation in which He stands to them as He creates for their sake. Does God create as an individual in the midst of other individuals standing apart from them, for whom He creates?[4a] Or does He create by being existentially, that is, in existence identical with the self or does He create possibly by being both, standing at once distinct from and also identical with the self? In other words, is the relation of God and the self one of identity, or difference, or both identity and difference?

If it is one of identity as between gold and its ornaments,[5] the alternative really amounts to the previous one we have discarded, namely God creates for His own sake. It is suggested by the analogy that the difference between God and self is not real; His creative function will accordingly have to be understood, if at all, for an end which can only be His end, there being nothing really beside Him. If, however, it were one of difference, difference total and uncompromising, as between light and darkness, then again it is inconceivable that He creates for the sake of what is totally different from Himself. God's action can be for anything but not conceivably for the sake of what is utterly different from Himself. Pure difference like pure identity is a denial of relation. If God were 'wholly other' to the self He can be anything but not its Creator.[5a] Can the relation be both identity and difference as, for example, between speech and what is spoken (*śabda* and *artha*) where both are identical and also different.[6] Though different *śabda* and *artha* are mutually implicatory, in which sense they may be said to be identical as well. But this is not really a plausible alternative, because of the obvious logical inconceivability.

The last alternative that cosmic functions are performed for 'no purpose' whatever also seems not tenable. It is one thing to say that a '*purpose*' of Creation is unintelligible implying, as it does, a purpose beyond itself. But it is quite another to say that Creation is 'purposeless'. The difficulties afforded by the problem of motive are avoided by this alternative which considers God's 'unmotived' action after the models of sport and artistic creation. Sport is not, strictly, an unmotivated activity. It is if for nothing else at least for recreation and the joy of doing. Similiarly, the artist seeks consciously or otherwise to express himself in his creations; there is something compelling about them. The artist cannot be supremely detached from his work.

Bādarāyaṇa raises the difficulty pertaining to the possible motive of Creative activity:[7] an all-sufficient God cannot have motive, but no activity can be conceived as unmotivated. His solution[8] is that it is merely a sport or play and of the motiveless nature of sport we have instances in our empirical life (*lokavat*). People indulge in sport apparently for no gain. But the question here is not about the presence or non-presence of motive; motive is continuous with activity and is already part of it. The illustrations can only serve to differentiate between overt motive and subtle motive of action, between motive in the sense of extraneous purpose or motive in the sense of 'inner telos'. But they do not illustrate 'purposeless' action.

When God's activity is described, the descriptions make a natural use of the concept of play.[8a] One saint sings: "by conserving and creating and by hiding all the Heavens and earth do thou *play*". The cosmic functions are described as divine sport. The same saint also sings: "O Lord ! from the sport of Thy grace by which Thou redeemeth, we have been blessed in all ways the Blessed have been blessed".[9] Here by 'sport' seems to be meant, not action devoid of an end — the saint confesses to the experience of blessedness and fulfilment flowing from Lord's cosmic activity — but action that means no effort or exertion for the Lord. The saint seems to heave a sigh of relief when he says in effect, "we are at long last saved, and saved in every possible way as men can be saved" implying the toil and effort and the 'dark nights' it costs one who pursues the arduous spiritual path to rise equal to and become aware of and benefit by Divine Grace ever at work in the soul of man. For the redeeming Grace in contrast, it is just 'play' involving no effort.[10]

In whichever sense taken it is undeniable that we appeal to the creative nature of Divine Will which is identical with Grace. By grace we refer to an activity that is unconstrained by any necessity outer or inner; it is an activity which by definition can have no purpose beyond itself. It is a free phenomenalisation, taking place when it need not take place. It is not in fact legitimate to raise the question of final cause in the context of will-causality. The Will is essentially self-conscious (*ahaṁpadārtha-rūpa*) of its function but consciousness of this function is without any motive. It is a consciousness of one's freedom and means nothing more than an overflow of the joy within.

But this is only the negative side. The Will is also describable as gracious love. The actuality of Will is, humanly considered, life phenomenal and transcendental, and the process of life as such has the uniform character of 'gratuitous' love; it therefore follows that Divine Will is grace in the positive sense of love. Phenomenal life emerging from the night of oblivion to the day of vigil and action, and from the night of empirical wakefulness to the day of Divine Presence, are processes alike conditioned by the actuality of Divine Will. In both it has the character of love. Ontologically God as Will may be conceived to 'act' toward, the other-and-yet-not-the-other creature which *is* therefore if anything the purpose of God's activity.

Interpretation of *advaita*

There is a demand in the conception of God as creative will to conceive of the relation between God and self — the Creator and the creature, neither as identity advocated by acosmisms nor as difference as dualisms interpret nor even as a juxtaposition of the two as advanced by immanental pantheisms but as one of 'non-duality' (*advaita*), inseparable existence. The Divine Will is ontically what it is, namely itself and yet it permeates the will of the individual selves so intimately that it may be said to be, verily, their wills themselves. God is Himself. He is also the selves. He is both.[11] It is not Himself that God creates, nor Himself that He redeems. It is for the purpose of the self's fulfilment that He performs cosmic functions and yet in so far as the selves are not 'different' from Him, He does not perform for a purpose beyond himself. Activity for the sake of the 'self' coincides with activity for self's sake.[12]

This brings us to the most central of the doctrines of Śaiva Siddhānta — the *Advaita* relation. The entire issue about the interpretation of the term *advaita* hinges on the relevance which the question of man's identity with God bears to the human situation. If man were what his core is said to be, if he is Spirit (*ātman*) *per se*, and his 'potentiality' is identical with his 'actuality' the question of a God (*pati*) infinite and absolute, different from the finite creature (*paśu*) will not arise at all. The term '*advaitam*' occurring in Creation texts, if it were interpreted merely to mean that man is in essential though untested *unity* with God it will not bear significantly on anything that exists. Concepts or notions not grounded in a direct sense of existence as it is lived in its everydayness have no real significance. Man is also ineluctably part of existence, estranged and alienated from God. God is the creative ground of the spatial temporal and causal structure of existence, and is not identical with the structure positively or negatively, though He may be freely identified with it as an actor identifies with his role or a mother bears with her suffering child. Identity there surely is but in the sense of a free identification on the part of God with what exists.

The Creation text of the Upaniṣad makes use of the expression *advaitam* in apposition to *sat*, along with *ekam*: *ekam evādvitīyam*.[13] That *advaitam* is not a mere negative everyone admits; what its complement is, is the question. Identity, difference, or identity-in-difference ? An unequi-vocal affirmation of any one of these or a combination of these does no justice to the mystery of God-self relationship that underlies the conception of God as the Lord of cosmic functions. What it then negates is a quality of existence, namely its dividedness, alienation from the divine ground, and what it affirms is God's inalienable indwelling (*ānusyūtatva*) with man.[14]

Before analysing the different senses of *advaita* the following may be said by way of a general anticipation of the standpoint of Siddhānta. Unlike expressions to which is affixed 'not', *advaita* is a word with a negation prefix built into it (like 'intolerable', 'impolite' 'non-aggressive'). It does not have the same function of explicitly rejecting a suggested description. The function of exclusion is implicit in all descriptive uses of language. The device that language often however adopts for making the function explicit is to use prefixes. Of this the word 'not' and its equivalents is the common place. The words beginning with negative prefix instead of emphasising differences serve to underline complementariness. In calling a thing 'unblue' we emphasise its similarity to other 'unblue' things as its difference from blue things. The motive of the texts using the expression *advaita* is less to correct a false impression than to have a constant and persistent interest in 'what is not two', to describe something that is most positive. *Advaita* is in this sense one of those irreplaceable 'primary' words which no other, especially no philosophical term, can ever supersede.[14a] Its occurrence in the text quoted above along with the expression *ekam* which means one, is significant and demands to be interpreted in the light of its uniqueness of reference. Briefly, it refers to the fact that existence is not completely isolated and disjointed from each other, that it is not strange or alien but that it stands within a relationship.[15]

Śaiva Siddhānta arrives at this conclusion through a careful analysis of the semantic issues that arise from the classical interpretations of the notion. The negative particle *nañ* has several meanings[16] of which three seem to be relevant in the context of the expression *advaita*: *abhāva* (privation), *virodha* (opposite) and *anya* (otherness).[17] The metaphysical-theological differences among the various classical Vedānta schools may be shown to be foreshadowed in the meanings that they assign to the negative prefix in *advaita*. The monistic schools (*ekātma-vāda*) understand it in the privative sense (*abhāvārtha*), so that not-two in the sense of non-existence of two implies really oneness.[18] The term *advaita* used to describe *brahman* implies the secondless unity of *brahman* whether the unity be understood as rigorous unity (*kevala*) or a rich unity (*viśiṣṭa*).[19] By a strange paradox the dualist (*dvaitin*) too understands the term *advaita* to imply numerical oneness although this in turn necessarily implies according to him by contrast the existence of a second to it. The sense of the *nañ* that is adopted here is that of the opposite (*virodha*).[20]

The monist interprets the negative particle in the privative sense: in the instance of *a-prakāśa* (non-luminous, that is, opaque) the negation relates to simple absence of *prakāśatva* (luminosity); likewise not-two means one, as a simple denial of two or two-ness. The dualist understands by the denial of two in not-two its opposite one, as for example, in the term *a-dharma* (dis-value), where the negative signifies the *opposite* of *dharma* (value). Though according to this interpretation *advaita* means 'one' it is in turn suggestive of the necessary existence of two and more. Opposition implies the independent reality of the terms between which there is opposition.

Śaiva Siddhānta in adopting a third meaning of negation, namely *anya* (other than), understands *advaita* to mean, not oneness but literally, non-duality (*ananyatva*) neither more nor less. It is not negation of two but a case of negation of duality entailed by 'two'. Not-being-two, in the sense of a positive oneness is not affirmed of *brahman*, but only duality is denied of it. *Advaita*, according to Śaiva Siddhānta, affirms neither the absence of a second (monism) nor implies the being of a second (dualism), but affirms only the secondlessness of the second. What appears to be second to *brahman* in the order of existence is, nevertheless not essentially second to it, because *brahman* is Presence involving union, pervasion and relation. What is therefore denied of the two is their *otherness* which alone furnishes the basis for duality and what is affirmed, by implication, is their inseparability, inalienability, a positive condition of invariable 'co-presence'.[21] The co-present God is not first some one who is, and then co-present with the self. He is always a 'co-present some-one'.[22] They are two but there are never two, or rather, there are two but they are never two.[23]

As examples of this sense of the negative particle are cited *a-brāhmaṇaḥ*

(non-brahmin), *an-aśvaḥ* (non-horse), *an-ekam* (non-single). The nonbrahmin is, strictly, one who is indeed a brahmin by birth but not a brahmin by profession and brahminical ways of life.[24] The 'non-horse' refers to mule which is not, and yet is, something of a horse. The term an-ekam likewise means 'other than' one, signifying two etc. which do not exclude one as such but only the *exclusiveness* of one as one.[25] Similarly, *advaita* does not exclude the ontic being of the two but excludes only their exclusion, duality.

The expression '*advaitam*' seems to be in answer to the problem of how the supreme self and the individual self, two entities real and even different presumably, could yet be *related* at all. Are they to be related by a *tertium quid* which somehow could relate them ? Such a device is notoriously unsuited in philosophy. The mediator has to be mediated. The term *advaita* seems to suggest the answer. The two—the individual and the universal are to be so conceived as containing as part of their essence the ground of unity which would relate them together non-dually. *Advaita* as referring to their relation implies that the relation is unique as being neither just external nor just internal. The two terms of the relation are not devoid of mutual implication such that each would be an 'other' to the other (*bheda, saṁyoga*) as in that case they cannot be brought together in a relation. Nor are the two terms implicatory on a mutual or reciprocal basis strictly speaking, such that each term of the relation is at once implicans and also implicate in relation to the other (*bhedābheda*). If in the former case the two fall so apart that they cannot be *coupled together* as two, in this case the two are so mutually dependent that they cannot be *coupled apart* as two.[26]

Nor is the relation to be conceived as identity (*abheda, aikya*) so that *advaita* may be taken to mean one in a numerical sense. If 'non-dual' were to imply absolute oneness, the one eternally and absolutely one cannot know itself as one.[27] There must be another thing thus thinking. Scripture declares not only that it is one but that it is consciousness.Unitive consciousness is also at once consciousness of its unity; the Will to become many cannot be unreflective will. How would the 'merely' one always and invariably so know itself as such ? Some self-alienation will have to be presupposed in the assertion of one. Pure identity cannot even be uttered. Its very assertion will be proof positive of its mediated character. The very declaration '*ekam evādvitīyaṁ brahma*'[28] in scripture is proof that the term means only and barely denial of otherness.

The advocates of the meaning of one, understand the term not as it is in the text as a unique category of valuation of Being as sacred or holy, but metaphysically as determinative of the number and nature of the real.[29] The expressions *kevalādvaita* (pure monism, non-duality of pure Being) *viśiṣṭādvaita* (monism with qualification, non-duality of Being but with qualification) and *virodhādvaita* (the opposite of monism) indicate pre-occupation with the ontic problem of the number of being. The Śaiva Siddhānta interpretation has the merit of not importing anything to qualify the simple notion as it occurs without adjectives in the text. In its estimate, 'the advocates of the meaning of one have missed the significance of the *negative* expression *advaita*;[30] a more direct *ekam* in all the places in the *Śruti* in its stead would have served the purpose. Even in the texts where the terms '*ekam*' and '*advaitam*' occur appositionally together the distinction drawn between their meanings amounts to a distinction without difference : both the terms mean one, one explicitly and the other implicitly. The former is reinforced in significance by the latter.

For the *advaitin* the nature of secondless Being (*ekam*) is further defined as Pure Being (*advaitam*) devoid even of qualities.[31] For the *viśiṣṭādvaitin* there being no other controller (*advaitam*),[32] the Being which is the ultimate material cause of the universe (*ekam*) is further characterised *qua* sole cause as also its efficient cause. The implication is, according to the *viśiṣṭādvaiṭin* that both terms denote secondless Being —there being nothing outside its unity (*viśiṣṭāntarbhāva eva aikyam*), but not to the absolute exclusion of other things than *brahman*. Other things—the worlds of *cit* and *acit* are latent in Him as in a material cause. The two words *ekam* and *advaitam* both denote qualified Being (*saviśeṣa brahman*).[33]

The *dvaitin* too, although opposed to monism, understands both *ekam* and *advaitam* alike to mean one, of course in the sense that neither is suggestive of a secondless Being. *Ekam* means the one in the sense of the supreme or the chief (*mukhya*) or being different from the rest (*anya*) or being unaided or unsupported by others (*asahāya*). It does not mean one precluding the being of a second. Similarly '*advaitam*' which reinforces the same idea signifies that there is no second to Him of His class (*sajātīya-dvitīya-vastu-rahitam*). The meaning of the negative prefix of *advaita* that he adopts is, simultaneously suggestive of the reality of species belonging to *different* classes (*vijātīya-bheda*).[34]

Śaiva Siddhānta finds these interpretations unsatisfactory. The term *advaita* is understood to be essentially of the same significance as *ekam*. While certainly it cannot be taken to mean something which will conflict with *ekaṁ*[35]— the two notions being alike predicated of *brahman*, it does not follow that they are to be interpreted as synonyms. *Advaita* is not a periphrasis for *ekam*. The term moreover occurs without qualification in *Śruti*, and the direct sense of the term is reflected in the meaning of *anya* (other than) indicated by the privative prefix. The term meaning other than two or non-dual, defines the nature of relation and not the number of Being, that is, whether it is dual or non-dual, not whether it is one or many.

The purport of the use of the expression *advaita* seems to be to expound the meaning of God's relatedness to self which is the theme of the celebrated *mahāvākyas* of Vedānta : 'I am *brahman*' (*ahaṁ brahmāsmi*),[36] 'That thou Art' (*tat tvam asi*),[37] 'This self is *brahman*' (*ayam ātmā brahma*),[38] and 'Intelligence is *brahman*' (*prajñānaṁ brahma*).[39] These propositions dramatically express the non-dual *relationship* of God and self, the relationship affirmed significantly in all the three persons (*aham*, *tvam* and *ayam*), with the suggestion that God is not an impersonal non-relating 'That',[40] but is trans-personal as well as inter-personal. The verbs (*asi*, *asmi*) express some determinate relation, not relationless identity. The problem that arises here is: the self and *brahman* being two in sense as well as reference how can one be or become the other ? How can there be co-ordinate equivalence between the two ? The term *advaita* suggests the answer;[41] it defines the characteristic relationship between the two which permits their identification, union in spite of their being two. It is a species of relation which must be different from simple identity of two identical things (*aikya*) lest the two really become one and render the description non-dual (*advaita*) in the negative, void of significance. It must be different again from identity as between substance and attribute (*tādātmya*) as there are not two things in that case but only two aspects of one and the same thing and their identity could well be described as one and not non-dual. It must be a relation between two things which are yet not two in the sense of being characterised by mutual otherness.

The classical interpreters of *advaita*, however, offer different explanations for the *mahāvākyas.* The *advaitin* as we saw, takes the word *advaita* to imply absolute unity or oneness, as two-less-ness (*dvitvābhāva*) cannot be predicated of things numbering more than one, and here again lest this secondless unity be only in name, it is defined as devoid even of qualities (*nirdharmaka*). *Advaita* denotes Pure Being (*nirviśeṣa brahman*) and the *mahāvākyas* are understood accordingly as identity-judgments (*akhaṇḍārthaka-vākya*) and not as relational (*saṁsargārthaka*) judgments.[42] 'That Thou Art' and other major texts inculcate negation of difference between *brahman* and *jīva* and impliedly assert their identity: the infinite, but not the immediate (*tat*), is identical with the immediate, but not the infinite (*tvam*).[43] The identity between the individual self and the supreme self is indicated by means of a deduction of the two conflicting determinants 'individual' and 'supreme' from both sides and retaining only the common factor, namely Self.[44] The purport of the proposition then is with regard to one element only and not about two elements in some way related.[45]

Rāmānuja too, who interprets the text as expressive of relation, says that it establishes equivalence between the subject and the predicate. The 'that' refers to *brahman* which is to be taken not as Pure Being but as a person with perfections and also modes. The 'thou' though referring directly to the individual self (*Śvetaketu*) refers in fact, extendedly to the supreme self (*paramātman*) of whom the individual self is body (*śarīra*). *Brahman* having qualities is non-different from the Self of all the selves. To take the sentence literally, as expressive of the identity of *brahman* who has such qualities as infinitude, omniscience etc. and self (*jīva*) who is finite, is contradictory. Therefore 'thou' should be taken to extend to the *paramātman* who has self as his mode (*śarīra*).[46] Both the referents of *tat tvam asi* pertain to the self-same *saviśeṣa brahman,* despite their difference of 'sense'.

From the perspective of Siddhānta, the differences between *advaita* and *viśiṣṭādvaita* are much smaller than their similarities. Both seem to adopt the negative sense of the privative prefix in *advaita*: *advaita* means unity, oneness. The only difference, significant no doubt, is that while for one it is Pure Being devoid of qualities and relations, for the other it is Being qualified *sub specie aeternitatis* by attributes and relations; for both the terms *tat* and *tvam* alike refer to *brahman,* to *nirviśeṣa brahman* for one, and to *saviśeṣa brahman* for the other.

Madhva splits the terms of the text *śvetaketo tat tvam asi* by putting the negative prefix before '*tat*' and reads it as *atat-tvam asi*—That, Thou *art not*;[47] the purport of the text is to emphasise the fundamental difference between the finite and the infinite. Madhva's commentator supports the thesis of absolute difference by appealing to nine illustrative instances[48] in the same context. He also suggests a motive for this teaching of difference. However exalted one may be, one is not the supreme being whose majesty as the Lord of Creation is unsurpassed. To know the unbridgeable difference between God and creature is to feel a sense of dependence.[49] To surrender autonomy or independence yielding to 'theonomy' is not only no evidence against difference between finite and the infinite but difference is actually demanded as its metaphysical complement. The term '*advaita*' accordingly is interpreted to mean 'one'[50] so that it implies necessarily the reality of things besides the one; the purport of the teaching of *advaita* is identical with the teaching of the *mahāvākya*, namely to inculcate ontological difference.

Śaiva Siddhānta finds elements of truth in these interpretations but sees no basis in them for an adequate distinction between '*advaita*' and '*eka*'. The *advaitin's* 'denial' and the *dvaitin's* 'assertion' seem to be metaphysically on par; they are euphemisms respectively for assertions of pure identity and pure difference. Śaiva Siddhānta finds *advaita* rather to be adumbrative of the truth of union of the individual with the supreme. God and self do not exist as two realities independent of one another but exist in most intimate union without any possibility of disjunction.[51] What is therefore negated by the term *advaita* is the quality of existence, namely its separateness and independence from the ground of existence. The world of separation is the illusion[52] and inseparable union of existence with its ground, namely Being, is reality.

The dialectic of divine-human relation

Śaiva Siddhānta in answer to the three-fold interpretation to which concept of *advaita* has been subjected, finds three dimensions of relationship which co-exist as dimensions of the self-same truth—those of unity, difference and unity-and-difference.[53] Where others see scope only for a dialectic of difference, or a counter-dialectic of identity and respective vindications of unity or difference each to the exclusion of the other, Śaiva Siddhānta sees only at work a dialectic of divine-human relationship in which unity and difference, difference and non-differenec demand, but do not exclude each other. The 'inner movement of divine life' is disclosed in the dialectic of God-man relation.[54]

The use of dialectical terms in describing the Divine-human relation is necessitated by the infinite tension which characterizes it. The same concept is used in the same sense without any equivocation. If the meaning of the concept changes, the intrinsic necessity for it is described in a logically coherent way. The meaning of unity drives us by an intrinsic necessity beyond itself to difference and similarly, difference in turn points beyond itself to non-difference.[55]

The only way of explaining this self-transcendence implicit in the right meaning of a concept is through a kind of *analogia entis*. It is only by the use of analogies, and different analogies, that changes in the meaning of the concepts of identity, difference, and identity-and-difference, can be explained.[56] Śaiva Siddhānta explains the three dimensions of the relation of *advaita* accordingly with the help of suggestive analogies.

The 'unity' aspect of *advaita* may be understood with the help of the analogy of body and soul.[57] The 'unity' or oneness of body and soul is not a metaphysical fiction; it can be demonstrated in a rather naïve but significant way.[58] When A and B stand in tightest embrace, it is a commonplace that despite their physical proximity they do not lose their self-identity; A does not respond when it is B who is called to attention. No physical proximity, no psychological or social feeling of tele between persons can be so close so that the related persons would be literally *identified* each with the other. A's personal identity never by mistake knits itself on to that of B no matter how close the two are. Now take the case of body-soul relation. The soul does not keep aloof as distinct from the body when the latter is addressed; it is 'one' with the body in the sense that it is wholly identified with the body without any reservation. It is in this sense the Supreme is 'one' with the individual. It is a case of free identification or union and not identity or unity as between gold and ornaments made of gold. The latter case is one of relationless identity and not a relation. In the case of body-soul relation the 'oneness' does not amount to identity; while the soul identifies itself with the body the self is still the self and body the body. While the identification is no doubt unreserved and complete, it will be technically incorrect to say that one *is* the other in the sense in which we can say the ornament is itself the gold.[59]

In the same manner though the Supreme is 'one' with the individual, He is still the Supreme self; the individual does not cease to be an individual. And yet there is 'identity'. The identity or identification is, as may be seen, one-sided. It is the freedom of the Supreme to be the self and also other than the self, while the self's destiny is fulfilled in its oneness with the Supreme.[60] This is the element of self-transcendence suggested by the analogy of body-soul relationship. The very notion of identity implied here points beyond itself. God who ensouls the entire world *is* the world and also different from it. He is different from it in the sense in which the world cannot be different from Him. The latter is exhausted in the relation while the former while being freely in the relation, also simultaneously outlives it.

The moment of 'difference' to which identity points is the difference between what exists and the ground of the actualisation of its existence. It is to this element of unbridged difference that the Vedic assertion of *ekam* refers. If *advaita* were to mean 'inseparability', *ekam* cannot be understood to mean pure unity; inseparability implies that there are two entities between which obtains a relation of inseparability. The two, to the extent they are thus related, may not be quite two, but in ceasing to be quite two they do not become one. If so, the scriptural declaration that Being (*sat*) is one only (*ekam eva*) should be interpreted to mean monism not with regard to existence but about the reality of God-head.[61] The One of the Veda signifies the unequivocal oneness of the Lord;[62] the Lord (*pati*) it is that is one. 'Thou, who sayest 'one' understand that thou art *paśu* in the company of *pāśa*'.[63]

The illustrative analogies bring out the sense of distance or difference so vital in the experience of the holy. The vowel 'a' in relation to other letters—other vowels and consonants, brings out the sense of difference. The difference is not as between two things (or two letters of the alphabet) but as between all and any thing and no-thing or that which cannot be understood as one more thing. It is like the 'ontological difference' between the implicitly uttered 'a' and other letter-utterances.[64] Such difference, religiously speaking, forms the ground of our preference for one over the other : one is fundamental and foundational while the other exists and articulates but in dependence on that one. The visual sense in relation to illumination of light is another impressive analogy. Light is the condition or the ground of the very possibility of vision and is as such necessarily different from the visual sense. Here again the 'difference' is indicative of the intrinsic transcendence of one of the two in relation to the other, and existentially providing the basis for our evaluative preference.

While 'God' is surely the Other, He is not to be equated with the absoluteness of the other. He is 'wholly other' while at the same time He is the not-other, the here, the now and the mine. The 'difference' between God and man suggested by the analogies, it may be noted, does not amount to opposition; it is not like the 'difference' between light and darkness. Just as identity does not mean abstract oneness difference does not mean 'abstract' opposition and duality. The analogies themselves bring out this idea; the difference points beyond itself. The initial vowel 'a' while being different from other letters is not also wholly different from them. As the primary sound that human voice can utter it is present in every other sound vowel or consonant. Itself free from all vocal modulations, it is what makes for the evolution of all vocalisations. The illumination of light is different from the visual sense but not absolutely different; they are species of light[65] and one permeates and interpenetrates the other. Goethe wrote : "If the eye did not partake of the sun's essence it could never perceive it; if God's own power did not lie in us how could the divine delight us ?" God is 'different' from the soul as the Lord (*pati*) is different from the creature in bondage (*paśu*) and yet He is not 'wholly other' ; His very 'difference' understood in the way suggested by the analogies demands as a necessary moment its change into its opposite, namely, non-difference.

The 'third' dimension which gives real depth and meaning to the relation of *advaita* is, then, the element of Divine co-presence or co-working which is the religious counterpart of the metaphysical notion of 'identity-in-difference'.[66] It involves a denial of difference in respect of function. God is non-different from the soul in respect of being and also in respect of will. The felt presence of God in the soul as the will behind its will cannot be expressed in terms of mere co-existence or togetherness. God is not *some one* who is co-present in the spirit of man.[67] This will mean only the dimension of difference, but by the category of 'co-presence' is meant a new dimension of relation involving a *denial of difference*. God as 'some one who is strictly a denial of a co-present God. The concept of co-presence is higher than and inclusive of the concepts of identity and difference; co-presence or co-working negates difference which itself is a negation of identity. The 'co' relation involves negation of negation.[68]

Co-presence can be described in the language of metaphysics as the relation of substance and mode.[69] Of the two terms one depends on the other for its *function* — the other with which it is inseparably related as its mode. Like fruit and its sweetness, melody and sound God is related to self.[70] But self is, at the same time, not a mode. The mode can only be a part of and cannot be in 'union' with the substance. To be in union is to be or become 'one' with the substance from inside and not merely qualify its actuality. The relation of mode (*prakāra*) and substance (*prakārin*) does not represent the heart of the relation but only an element of it. This then is the aspect of self-transcendence about the 'third' moment of Divine-human relation.[71]

This concept of a 'three-dimensional relation'[72] between man and God brings out also God's nature as Being (*sat*), Intelligence (*cit*) and Bliss (*ānanda*). Being 'identical' is in answer to God's nature as Being. Being 'different' is entailed by God's nature as Spirit (*cit*) in so far as Spirit's function is to *reveal*, and knowledge and revelation cannot be reduced to one structure. Active co-presence likewise is the basis of the Experience of God as Bliss. We say God is Bliss through our *having* Bliss in union with God, and this involves our being not different[73] from Him even as difference implied being not identical.[74]

VI

GOD AS THE MORAL SOVEREIGN

Divine Providence and *Karma*

The conception of divine providence implied by the moral argument based on the operation of the law of *karma* is acknolwedgement of the view, that from the sphere of existence, God is the *supreme* and not the sole ordering power in the world.[1] The world is comparable in this respect to a living organism. Disorder is not a valid reason against the *supreme* power of God. To reject this is to accept an existence whose fundamental principle is chaos. This is not so much to pay the logical price of disbelief as violating meaning itself. God is, it may be noted, the supreme ordering factor. It is he who as it were enacts the laws of nature. It is he who makes possible reaping of the infinite long-range consequences of human actions, the principle underlying an 'ordered' world. Thus understood no empirical fact can count against the reality of divine providence.[2]

The conflict between appearances and a belief in Providence is really speaking a mystery to our finite consciousness. The theory of *karma* amounts in the end to an acceptance of this conflict and its character of mystery[3] but it seeks to 'resolve' it by placing it in the setting of Divine justice and Divine compassion between which there is an existential and not an essential difference. The 'order' that we perceive both 'within' and 'without' us is expressive of the unconditional character of a law or command (*ājñā*) in the face of natural processes which seem to contradict it. It is intelligible in the final analysis as grounded in the being and will of God.

The deeper significance of the 'moral argument' making use of the notions of the law of *karma* and of the agent-god in whom the law is grounded and founded consists of the demand for the recognition of an inner revealer of human knowledge and guide of human action, a transcendent condition of man's freedom. This corresponds to a 'free' cause for the cosmic operations supported by the metaphysical argument from the world to the world-ground.[4] In both , the appeal is to the freedom of Will which is the source and sustainer alike of 'becoming' in the case of the world without and of freedom characteristic of the moral world within.

The moral argument for God

In the form in which the moral argument is actually propounded it takes a negative form. It is a counter-argument against the one that argues God cannot be the cause of the world, so full of inequalities.[5] Some of the metaphysical grounds on which anti-theistic arguments were put forward have been examined; on moral grounds too, God's existence has been doubted and denied. There is so much pain and suffering in the world, and such unequal distribution of happiness and unhappiness, that a God that creates and maintains the world in utter indifference to this anomaly seems inconceivable.[6]

The charge of cruelty becomes specially applicable to a God who destroys the world after creating it. Does not universal Dissolution bring out the utter meaninglessness of world-creation? If creation entailing such anomalous distinctions and disparities is suggestive of iniquity, universal Dissolution implying *inter alia* destruction of mankind by cataclysms of cosmic proportions, is suggestive of cruelty of unimaginable proportions.[7] How is a God conceivable who dispenses fruits in unequal measure and eventually destroys everything?

The counter-argument proposed in reply to this antitheistic argument is that these diversities of experience which are factual indeed are not intelligible on any other theory save the one which admits God as the cause of the world. The creator of the world-process is also the 'wise, benevolent and just' moral governor who governs by dispensing in the form of 'happiness' and 'sorrow', fruits of man's own past action. The metaphysical argument, considered earlier, was indicative of God as Destroyer. The moral argument points to His role as Creator-Conserver included under the concept of moral governance or more simply Lordship, Sovereignty (*patitva*).[8]

The cosmic operations of a God-agent involve the paradoxical functions of creating and destroying what has been created; destroying and creating what has been destroyed. Likewise His governance too is paradoxical : causing happiness and unhappiness through such disparities as prosperity and adversity, long life and early mortality, health and disease, and so on. What sense do we make of this?

The metaphysical argument implied that these 'differences' of operations are not intrinsic but occasioned; though all cosmic functions are homogeneous expressions of Grace their paradoxical nature is occasioned by the exigency of *mala* which is the real *raison d'etre* of cosmic operation attributed to God. It is the presence of this metaphysical factor that explains why at all God should be conceived to engage in cosmic operations, and operations of apparently diverse nature. In the same manner the moral argument also is suggestive of the truth, that while God 'governs' his governance implies enjoyment for some and suffering for others because of a two-fold nature of the adjunct which mediates as the freely employed condition for God's dispensation of experience (*bhoga*) to the souls.[9]

The *inequalities* of creation originate not from the Lord Himself but from the merit and demerit of the creatures. Man's suffering or enjoyment is the fruit of his own deed, a 'harvest' sprung from his own actions done in transgression or otherwise of the moral law. The cloud is the neutral cause of the production of rice, wheat and barley; differences of the latter are due however, to the potentialities of the respective seeds themselves, not due to the caprice of the rain-cloud.[10] God too is the common cause of creation, while inequalities of creation are due to the seeds of merit and demerit of the doing, willing and choosing individuals.

The charge of cruelty too in relation to performance of the operation of *saṁhāra* is ill-founded. 'Death and destruction' open the way at once to a re-creation of the world and to a regeneration of humanity.[11] It was explained earlier that *saṁhāra* though ostensibly associated with death and destruction involves giving rest (*viśrānti*) to selves from the strenuousness of *saṁsāra*. Nor may it be asked how in Creation following Dissolution, there can arise inequalities: *saṁhāra*, like death, is the great leveller so that it is not conceivable that 'differences' arise from thence. For by rest is meant not a mere suspension of activity; the suspension itself is negatively a preparation for the soul's experience of fresh *karma*. By *pralaya* is meant only cessation of the operations of creation and conservation in a gross, manifest form. In *saṁhāra* the Lord is said to 'rehearse' in a subtle form ensuing operations of creation in order to prepare and make fit *māyā* and *karma* for their roles.[12]

Differences and inequalities therefore originate from the two-fold *karma*, which is the accumulation of one's merits and demerits earned in previous existences and as it were stored up in the primal material source of the macro-and the micro-cosmic reality, namely *māyā*. The guiding principle of this *karma* renders possible the operation of the 'law' underlying the relation between the accumulated merit and demerit of all past and present experiences with their inequalities and diversities. The latter cannot be explained without postulating an omniscient God-agent as cause and without also positing *karma* as a freely employed auxiliary (*sahakārin*).

Let us now attend to the terms proper of the argument. The moral argument like the metaphysical argument makes use of the principle of causality in tracing the effect (happiness and misery in man's life which typifies all heterogenities of phenomenal life and existence) to a cause, *vis-a-vis* conditions, or auxiliaries. There is also the existential premise asserting that there is a law of moral causation to the effect that there is the factor of *karma* bearing on the life and destiny, here and in the hereafter, of the individual selves.[13] From the general law of continuity adopted in our metaphysical argument, namely that from being alone 'comes' being, and something does not come from nothing,[14] it may be supposed that enjoyments and sufferings of the present life as well as one's embodied existence itself to which they are incident, are but extension and continuation of the 'two-fold *karma*' of a past; the latter it is that has conditioned present birth and it is the individual self that is born and is subject to such experiences. Incarnated in a particular form of birth it 'experiences' the fruits of its previous deeds—deeds and actions performed in previous incarnations. In the same order in which present experience follows in the wake of 'previous' deeds of *karma*, 'future' *karma* is likewise generated by present deeds; there are rounds of rebirths and deaths as a 'consequence' of moral action. The individuals will not cease to be with the decease of their present embodied existence but shall be reborn and reborn again apparently in a non-terminating succession like the unending circle of a fire-brand.[15] The form of life and experience which they will assume in future births is being determined by their present 'moral' life consisting of right and wrong doings in the context of sufferings and enjoyments. The latter, namely the experiences in the context of which alone arises moral action are themselves conditioned[16] by the 'two-fold' consequence of moral acts of previous lives.[17]

The datum from which the operation of the law of *karma* is derived is man's sentient experience involving (i) sensible experience of pleasure and pain, and (ii) reactions and responses of a moral nature arising in their context. Even the naturalist who may not accept the moral distinction of right and wrong action will admit that human experience is marked by a polarity and not a mere relativity of happiness and its opposite.[18] The recognition of the presence of a two-fold goal-direction in all animal behaviour expressible in forms of satisfactoriness or otherwise (or their behaviour-correlates) is acknowledgement of this polarity characterising sentient life.

Now these experiences and births in the human and other forms in their appropriate milieu, point forward as cause points to its effect, to future births and future systems of enjoyments and suffering incident to such births; likewise, by the same logic by which they point to future life they point backwards too, as effect points to its cause, to previous lives and life-experiences.[19] Our present experience of happiness and suffering is, in other words, 'fruit' of actions extending backward to previous lives and are also continuous with fruits of actions in the future which in turn they condition.

Man's life is indeed a 'chain of infinite embodiments' linked in the form of actions and fruits. It is indeed a chain of actions and fruits that is grouped into large number of systems called births or embodiments. The pleasure-pain experiences and their anteceding circumstances constitutive of the ebb and flow of the tide of life, and their antecedents in turn, viz., the general conditions of prosperity and adversity[20] — these in their potentiality constitute the 'nucleus' of embodied existence. Man's birth in a particular socio-biological milieu together with all that it implies is not just an accident but a definite link in a chain of deeds and consequences deserved, and meted out as deserved by man. *Karma* is pre-eminently a principle of continuity. Man is born with these predispositions or potentialities and his present life of moral endeavour is only in the service of 'fructifying' these innately endowed predispositions. The efforts which man freely makes arise but in response to 'experiencing' the 'fruits' of his previous actions. In this process the efforts which consist of actions condition future endowments of happiness-unhappiness, and so on.

These fruits of actions which are coincidental with embodiments, and vary with them cannot by themselves attach spontaneously to the selves. Acts pass away as soon as they are performed and they have no power to bring about their fruits at some future time. Even assuming that acts do not perish but persist in a mysterious manner, how can they bear fruit in another birth ? The sequence of acts and their fruits involve difference of time and difference of place also. Acts performed in one birth bear fruits in another birth. The giver of fruits as there must be one must conserve and synchronise consequences with the deeds.[21]

It may not be said that our experiences are not fruits of actions but only natural, uncaused phenomena. The natural must be of one homogeneous nature.[22] Experience (*bhoga*) must be of a piece and not consist of heterogeneous elements like enjoyment *and* its opposite, namely suffering. The heterogeneity is evidence that such experience is not 'natural'. Water is warm or cool, fragrant or otherwise, not by caprice but rather in conjunction with certain adjuncts.[23] Our multiform experience too is due to the adjunct of a multiform *karma* which operates so as to give rise to diverse experiences.

Granted that such experiences are 'caused' what need is there for assuming *karma* as cause ? Unmanifest Nature (*prakṛti*) which is the source and stuff of our body, sense and objects can itself by its inherently heterogeneous but mutually compatible *guṇas* cause diversities of experience. But this is not admissible. *Prakṛti* and its evolutes are the *content* of experience (*bhogya*). How can they also be *determinant* of experience (*bhojaka*) ?[24]

Nor can it be argued that *prakṛti* in its modification as intellect (*buddhi*) and its dispositions (*bhāvas*) is the determinant of experience and in its other modifications the content of experience. For, the dispositions of *buddhi* are always known to function diversely due to the relative preponderance of the three *guṇas*, and never in a homogeneous manner; the argument merely explains one set of varied phenomena in terms of another set also varied and equally in need of explanation.[25]

The diversities of experience may well be of our own making it may be argued.[26] It is but a case of effort or lack of effort. In this competitive world it is commonplace that the hard-working and the industrious survive and prosper while the indolent and lazy perish. The man of efforts is never really aggrieved and the inactive is never really prosperous. But this is not, however, always the case. The incommensurability between effort and reward is indeed so glaring that it strikes one rather as a rule than as an exception. The most hard-working with the best of will sometimes lapses quite unaccountably into lassitude, and even if active misses his reward, or what is still more puzzling, comes to unmerited grief. Conversely, the most indolent becomes the most blessed.[27] So we have to look for an invariable cause operating prior to the immediately preceding human efforts.

There is no doubt that what causes the present fruits of actions causes them to fructify only through the mediacy of one's efforts. It is not that because of past *karma* experiences of happiness or sorrow befall man like a bolt; man strives in natural response towards such experiences which however are transcendentally conditioned. Effort or exertion is symptom of constructive good *karma*; and indolence or sloth its opposite. One experiences the fruits of one's past deeds but through exercise of one's efforts in so far as one cannot have experience of satisfaction and unhappiness without exertion and effort. Even an immobile form of life like a plant, sentient as it is, exhibits purposive striving when its roots spread in the direction of water and its stalk rises above the earth's surface to absorb sunshine.[28] The latent impressions inherited morally from previous deeds become manifest through one's efforts. Efforts are, in short, a necessary condition (*sahakārin*) of moral action and enjoyment. But a condition must be distinguished from 'cause'.

Just as fruits, which we consume, serve the purpose of our present enjoyment and also serve incidentally another purpose, that is they provide seeds for future fructification, one's efforts serve a two-fold purpose.[29] Efforts as actions made with a sense of '*I* do' contribute towards one's experience of happiness and misery which follow upon one's previous deeds. In the wake of such self-assertion comes as consequence, a fresh influx of actions. It is not that one can be without any effort so that there can be no future births. Striving is inescapable so long as there is experience due to that share of *karma* which has already begun to bear fruit (the *prārabdha-karma*) and striving entails conditioning of the future. In a life of action, therefore, there is no escape from a commitment towards one's future. Man's action commits him and indeed the rest of mankind; it also commits his future.

Therefore the question remains : what is the efficient cause that 'metes out' as it were the fruits of actions and the appropriate births in which the latently present fruits become manifest with the efflux of time, mediated by moral efforts? Some enduring, intelligent, compassionate agent is required[30] to 'own' and acknowlegde the moral deeds of man, an unfailing witness to man's action,[31] and bestow appropriate fruits in every case. Some agent who, unlike the deeds themselves persists as a common factor and spans distances of time and place involved in rebirths; who is also intelligent to know what is good for the souls and also compassionate to liquidate *karma* by meting out experiences by which it may be lived out, so that the souls may eventually be liberated from bondage.

Though it is man who is responsible for his acts and enjoys or suffers in consequence, some one without him owns his acts and dispenses rewards and punishments. The acts or deeds require a recipient who shall bear eternal witness to all that a man does and accordingly dispense the fruitage of the deed. It is the ground that bears unfailingly the fruit of the toil of the cultivator, though it is the cultivator who puts forth the toil and is entitled to the fruits of his toil.[32]

What about the doer himself? Is he not also the common factor between the time and place of a deed and the time and place of its consequence? Acts leave their impressions it may be said in the doer's mind and from these impressions alone the fruits accrue later on. But this is not a tenable view. What do we mean by 'fruitage' ? It is not the subjective feeling of joy or unhappiness as such but a life of enjoyment and suffering incident to the environment in which one takes birth. Are these things projected into existence by the impression-ridden mind?[33] The ground of the law relating action with fruits must be sought in a cosmic-spiritual and not an anthropological-psychological principle.

Shall we not say, as the 'ground and the tiller' analogy seems to suggest, that actions bear fruits through the enduring medium of some 'accusative' of the actions? Like the ground in relation to tilling there is for example the world to 'receive' all actions; the world remains while particular actions perish. But this is not true. Everything connected with a man's act perishes like the act itself. The benefit, the beneficient, the benefactor and the benefactor's claim all perish along with the world. A transcendent ground transcending the finitude of the doer and the circumstances connected with his deed is required.[34]

The action of an agent depends, according to grammarians, on many factors which can be estimated only by an intuitive analysis of syntactical usage such as the time, the place, the circumstance, the productive agent himself. A 'metaphysic' of self as person and agent of action accordingly conceives of agency as exercisable with certain necessary concomitants: the person from whom action issues (ablative of locality), his accessories by means of which he performs actions (instrumental), the time when the action takes place (ablative of time), the object of transitive action (accusative), the purpose and the goal (dative) and the action itself.[35] Man acts and enjoys but in dependence on these concomitants, taking his place with them as one more concomitant of action (nominative, *kartṛ-kāraka*). It is true that these concomitants exist *for* the agent; but it is also true that the agent exercises his agency and enjoyership but in no other conceivable way. Man, metaphysically, has no privileged position as agent. As enjoying and acting self he has to be aided by the objective *tattvas* for a manifestation and articulation of his knowledge and action, and his own position in relation to them is one *tattva* (*puruṣa-tattva*) besides other *tattvas*.[36] These *tattvas* are material, objective and have no spontaneity of action; they function but in relation with self which is spirit; the 'spiritual' self, however, knows and acts but in no other way without dependence on the *tattvas*. Therefore, it follows that God the free active agent that performs the cosmic operations alone is equal to the task of moral governance, conserving moral causation. It is God that takes account[37] of the deeds of the self and awards their due fruits by bringing about a conjunction of the dis-incarnate self lacking in initiative without accessory on the one side, and the location, means, objects of enjoyment as well as the vehicle of body on the other: in short by the cosmic functions of Creation and Conservation.[38]

The two-fold *karma* together with the circumstances connected with it and inclusive of the person who is responsible agent is perishable. One's efforts elicited in the context of one's enjoyment and suffering, result in the deeds which should they bear fruit in another place and time, in another embodiment must, lest they go unacknowledged, be 'owned' by Some one who, unlike the finite agent of *karma*, is enduring, all-knowing and is intrinsically free from the thraldom of birth due to *karma*, and is, above all 'with' the active self in an inalienable relation.[39] Such is the moral governor (*pati*) who alone is competent to vouchsafe enjoyment and suffering in accordance with the two-fold *karma*.

Rival points of view and their inclusion

Having stated the terms and meaning of the moral argument for *pati*, let us review the historic *pūrvapakṣas* with regard to this question and see how Śaiva Siddhānta true to its grain uses them as illustrations rather than refutations of its own position.[40] Objections to moral argument for God may be anticipated from the quarters of naturalism and materialism which may deny the principle of causality involved and affirm a 'spontaneous origination' of the so-called imperfections and inequalities of the 'moral' world, and from what may be described as 'religious' naturalisms which accept a metempirical, superphysical principle as the explanation of the inherent diversity in nature but deny any relation between that and 'God'.[41] Anti-theism in the second case will rest, not on a rejection of the causal principle but on identifying the 'cause' with an autonomous, self-explanatory moral law which governs and conditions the cycle of births and deaths and the infinite variations to which life is subject.

Indian Materialism and its variants categorically deny the bearing of *karma* upon the destiny and life of the individual and of the world and deny, therefore, 'moral' governance. The concept of moral as distinguished from the natural, it is implied, is not legitimate. In contrast to this stand those 'heterodox' systems which take their stand on moral consciousness and find in man's moral action an inexhorable law of moral justice operating impersonally and autonomously. The Pūrva-Mīmāṁsakas too among the 'orthodox' group believe in the doctrine of *apūrva* and its autonomous operation. These systems uphold the validity of moral law but reject the necessity of a moral governor conceived as the law-giver and the custodian of the law. There is appreciation of the moral category as distinct from the natural but the moral as such is here transformed into the spiritual.[42] The 'moral' in this group does not involve obedience to the command of God but consists merely of an awareness of the inner propriety of things—*dharma* to be intuitively realised or as it is held by Mīmāṁsaka revealed in eternal scripture. There is therefore no demand from a moral sense for recognising the existence of God.

Śaiva Siddhānta like other theistic advaitic systems rejects this interpretation of the moral law. The moral law is not an impersonal law. There is no law without an intelligent law-giver. Moral law cannot be conceived without a will behind the law which lays down duty for man in the form of ought. Like the created world and its laws, the law of *karma* too is an expression of divine decree. *Karma* is God's will, His Grace.[43] The will of the Lord implies His knowledge of what is truly right and wrong for man which he declares in a code of injunctions and prohibitions.[44] Man ignorant and swayed by passions is not equal to a knowledge of what is intrinsically right.

The law relating to deed and consequence like the physical law expressive of causal determination is comprehended in the concealing dynamism of *Śiva-śakti* (*tirodhāna-śakti*) which freely employs the accessory condition of *karma* in its performance of cosmic operations; the condition (*sahakārin*) is not external to the divine will but an externalised form which the will takes to regulate the lives of selves through rounds of diverse experiences with a view to 'ripen' their *mala*; the same metaphysical consideration which explains the relevance of cosmic functions underlies the concept of moral governance. The analogy of temporal law which regulates man's social life and its identity with the legislative and executive authority without which the law cannot function brings out the sense in which *karma* may be identified with Divine will or command (*ājñā*).

The idea of a moral 'ruler' of the world which Śaiva Siddhānta espouses through the concept of *pati* must not at the same time be understood to mean an external authority. It is not the circumstance of imposition from without by a fiat of will that goes to constitute the moral in moral action.[45] In fact admission of an external ruler may even take away the very foundation of morality and ethics. How can there be moral life or any ethical principle if there is compulsion or determination from an agent outside ourselves ? The ruler must 'reign' from within as 'one' with man's spirit and affirm man's freedom as moral agent. The freedom underlying law of *karma* is governed by a norm; it implies the possibility of choice and guarantees man's accountability; hence his 'rewards' and 'punishments', sufferings and joy. But at the same time the freedom is determination from within. In principle it does not depend on any external norm; its exercise is not a mere choice between good and evil standing over against oneself; it is indeed one's own norm though revealed externally in the form of 'thou shalt' and 'thou shalt not'. It is more a case of an omniscient and gracious God revealing what is good for man as unaided man cannot discover it.[46]

The real authority of the moral law is explicable only if it can be thought to be not merely 'moral' but spiritual. This means that the moral law, in so far as it is not natural — analysable in terms of natural science as an instance of physical causation, and is also not subjective, bespeaking merely the state of one's mind, is of ontological validity and is an integral part of the cosmic scheme, in terms of which God as spirit is conceived. Moral law is autonomous only as immanent in the autonomy of the spirit. We require a knowing or willing mind — an all-knowing omnipotent Spiritual being in which it is eternally realized and without which the *categorical* nature of the moral imperative would be inexplicable.

From the standard of Śaiva Siddhānta, those who deny the moral law and its bearing on man's life and destiny, are advocates of uncompromising determinism; they deny freedom even in the empirical sphere itself; in denying the moral law they make man a fortuitous creation of natural forces; his sentient life too is but a sequence of physical events governed by the same natural law. Human suffering becomes on this view a brute fact unexplained and therefore incapable of removal in any conceivable manner. Inequalities and diversities are mere natural occurrences as the unequal length of the fingers of our palm.[47]

In contrast stand the systems which accept the moral law (*karma*) and its profound implications for man's life. Man is a moral agent; he acts freely and is as such ethically responsible. The moral act of man is evidence of the immanent freedom in his empirical life. *Karma* though speciously like scientific law stands really for the freedom of man's will. The law of *karma* is more like the law of a state; when a law of the state is broken it still remains a law. *Karma* implies freedom.

The point of view which admits the principle of *karma* as the explanatory factor of life and existence with all their diversities makes for greater optimism. Human suffering is a fact but is not a brute fact; that man can suffer is itself evidence of his inherent freedom.[48] This freedom in empirical life can itself be made absolute by insight into the norm of the moral law. Such was the insight of Buddha.[49]

There is a moral law, a cosmic order of deed that decides the content of each life. What we sow that we shall reap here and in the hereafter. That man must accept. Man has only to perceive the Norm, to accept the cosmic law; it would work with him instead of against him. Let man surrender the desire, the craving to live, to possess and enjoy and submit to the inexorability and universality of the Norm. This immanent freedom felt and experienced in man's striving and moral struggle itself gets transformed into the transcendent freedom (*nirvāṇa*). "I realized that destroyed is rebirth, the religious life has been led, done is that which was to be done, there is nought for me beyond this world".[50]

Nevertheless to accept *karma* without accepting the 'transcendent freedom' eternally exemplified in God does not make for real optimism in life. It does not mean real optimism because it does not imply real freedom. *Karma* taken as an autonomous blind force infringes upon empirical freedom. Man is a play thing in the hands of blind destiny,[51] so long as he is not able to work out for himself through renunciation and discipline, his liberation. Moral consciousness has no direct intuition of the reality of freedom. Factually law of *karma* taken by itself implies nothing more than pure succession and a dependent or relative origination. A consciousness of the inalienability of the means and the end is, only negatively, a search for freedom and implicitly a demand for transcendent freedom.

Real freedom is discovered and revealed in the experience of the Divine reality.[52] If moral law is to be an eternal ruling principle it must be found to exist in its ideal perfection eternally in someone who exemplifies transcendent freedom. The moral law is absolute because God is absolute and the law is but the manifestation of His being. Man's moral endeavour and achievement is made possible by the eternal perfection that is already an accomplished fact and is operative incessantly in human affairs. God's freedom is not acquired or achieved through effort or exertion. The hypothesis of an acquired perfection is a denial of the eternity of divine justice and grace which are the moral foundation of the world-order.[53] Transcendent freedom involves the notion of *freeing* others through grace which is the prius and presupposition of man's moral life. Both for a life of immanent freedom in subservience to the law of *karma* and for a 'life' that transcends *karma*, it is man's relationship or kinship—his identity with the transcendent Spirit or Freedom accessible to him within his inmost core,that serves as the metaphysical foundation.

The comprehensiveness and adequacy of this view according to which freedom is meaningful here and now in the phenomenal world in which we live, relatively to the views which look upon freedom as only transcendental or noumenal cannot be denied.[54] The real is real as immanent in the actual. The eternal is in eternal touch with time.

Infinity indwells and underlies the finite. Such is the concept of grace and is the solution implied in the problem of transcendent freedom and empirical determinism. Transcendent freedom is meaningful to us because we ourselves are 'identical' with it in our core even while we are empirically determined. The transcendent is not a closed system.[55] In the empirical sphere itself where necessity seems to reign freedom is meaningful to us. Even where determinism is the law it is not unqualified determinism, so that a complete break off from the actual is not necessary. The insight into the freedom which one has even in the empirical realm subject to the law of deed and consequence, the freedom to rise above it by a consciousness of one's oneness with that interior source of freedom, helps one to realise that transcendentally spirit is Freedom or Will. The empirical is not closed, but *continuous* with the transcendent. The continuity of *saṁsāra* and *mokṣa* which is the inner significance of the 'five-fold cosmic operations' attributed to God is a corrective of the tragic interpretation of finitude which equates necessity with temporality as such and conceives freedom as an escape from time and a destruction of the individual who is a mere product of finite existence.[56]

Karma and Grace

The working of God's justice then takes the form of the Law of *karma* according to which man is 'rewarded' in strict accord with his doings. If he does evil, unhappiness — suffering befalls his lot. Divine justice is only a facade of divine love. It is the exoteric version of divine compassion. It is divine love adapted to man who is still only part of nature and oblivious of his status as spirit. The same unmotivated 'motive of love' which explains cosmic operations, underlies the functions of 'owning' of man's right and wrong doing and dispensing of happiness and misery. The law of *karma* is Grace in disguise. Its operation is for the ultimate good of the souls— freedom from the connate evil or impurity of *mala*. Evil has to be lived out by man himself in freedom by means of his free decisions and he must bear the full responsibility for his decisions. God who is conceived as the very apotheosis of self-less compassion ensures the system of justice according to which due fruits are bestowed in accord with man's free choice and decisions.[57]

What is the metaphysical basis for God meting out the fruits of one's moral endeavours? Śaiva Siddhānta answers this question in a distinctive manner. Endeavour or effort which man puts forth is indeed free in the sense of being unconstrained by an external factor, but is not free in the sense of being freely initiated into existence by man who is metaphysically speaking unfree and had to be invested with body, senses and the world before he can know and exert: invested not by blind Nature, nor by blind destiny but by the omniscient, merciful God. Therefore, man's moral endeavour is, metaphysically, of the nature of duty or service at the gracious behest of the Lord's will, elicited in a free manner in response to the Lord's command. In no other theory is the spring of man's action intelligible. But the active man is unaware of the source of his freedom; he is assertive and ego-centric in his attitudes. Self-affirmation in a separative consciousness seems to be the law of his being in his incarnated existence. Disincarnate, he is inert like matter without the initiative of effort and incarnated, he is self-assertive; he is conscious only of his right of action and is oblivious of a sense of duty in relation to a transcendent command which metaphysically attaches to all his action.[58] God's grace, therefore, does not rest content with investing the ignorant and inactive self with body and senses so that it is able to know and act. Rescuing it from its state of isolation and impurity Grace proceeds also to cure it of its moral egoism by meting out the fruits of merit and demerit that accrue as a necessary consequence of the self's action.

There are two things attributed here to God in His role as moral governor. Omniscient as God is, it is God alone who knows about the inherent goodness of ends and moral rightness of actions. The moral ends are declared for man in the Vedas and doing what is enjoined as duty in the Vedas is therefore right action and doing to the contrary is wrong. The moral code for man is necessarily the code of scriptural commands; man with his congenital ignorance and impotence cannot be conceived as capable of knowing and striving by himself for the realisation of his good. Morality consisting in doing right is absolute and is determinable only by what the omniscient lord has revealed in the scripture. Therefore, it is only the Lord who knows from inside what is good for the self that can also judge the moral act of man and apportion due fruits. He 'owns' all actions of man in transgression, as well as in conformity to the law and metes out the due fruits of happiness and sorrow in order eventually to cure him of the disease of his self-will.[59] As the determiner of moral ends for man only God knows what merits and demerits accrue upon a particular right or wrong action, and accordingly it is He who can cause their liquidation through appropriate fruits. Consequences of an unseen nature (*sañcita*) accrue to man's action because of the sense of 'I' which the doer brings to bear on his action with the inevitable accompaniment of the sense of personal appropriation and attachment. God, therefore, is not merely witness to the deeds of omission and commission of man, 'owning'[60] them silently, but apportions out of super-abundant grace experiences in the form of happiness and sorrow. He apportions so that the accrued consequences of man's egotistically motived actions may be liquidated.

God as the Inner Illuminer of Experience[1]

The requirement of the moral argument for a moral governor or apportioner of the fruits is in the final analysis for an inner enlightener of knowledge. Human knowledge is both genetically and structurally[2] finite; it is not self-contained but receives its initiative and guidance from without itself from a source which is not likewise finite. The finite self being united with the impurity of *mala* from eternity though spirit cannot self-initiate the knowing process.[3] A demonstration of this can only be negative;[4] a positive instance of concomitance is not citable from the nature of the case. That the intelligent self cannot initiate of its own accord its function of intelligence can only be illustrated by the negative example of not-self. The non-intelligent sense organs do not sensate their respective objects except as 'informed' by the indwelling self. The senses are only channels *through which* takes place knowledge. Not possessing the quality of knowledge inert (*jaḍa*) as they are, they do not *initiate* the knowing process.[5] Behind them stands a principle which not only possesses the quality of knowledge in its own right but also initiates knowledge for the senses.

Perceiving their respective objects by the help of this intelligent principle, the senses[6] nevertheless cannot apperceive themselves perceiving in this manner.[7] Even less can they perceive the spirit (*ātmacit-śakti*) dwelling in them stimulating their function. In the same manner the self in its turn though spirit in essence, stands in need of inculcation from a yet deeper source of initiative with respect to its knowing process. Self has to be enlightened and guided by Spirit (*cit-śakti*) for the articulation of its functions of knowledge and action. The self's enjoyment of the fruit of its works is accomplished through a life of *avasthās* oscillating between the vigilance of wakefulness and the oblivion of sleep, by the abiding assistance of an unvarying, ever-vigilant Spirit[8] which is, therefore, the Light that illumines one's consciousness. And just as the senses function as duly informed by the intelligent self but are nevertheless unaware that they function in this manner, the self, too, is conscious because of the unfailing assistance of Spirit within, but is at the same time, due to Ignorance, neither self-aware of its consciousness nor aware of Spirit that indwells and pervades its conscious function. To be illumined from an interior presence of Light is its essential nature but to be self-oblivious thereof, and be in consequence an 'I' unto itself[9] (epistemologically and morally) is its existential predicament. Though consciousness is illumined by *cit-śakti* unfailingly, under the beginningless circumstance of Impurity, Consciousness becomes outwardised in orientation. The indwelling Spirit however cannot be known in an outwardised or objectivised mode of knowledge.[10]

The analogy of senses in relation to the self that operates as the principle of knowledge in union with them brings out the unique sense in which God is understood as the inner ruler or governor, as the enlightener in the spirit of man revealing knowledge and making possible experience in its wake, even at the finite level.[11] The self that 'informs' the senses making them agents as it were of knowledge is not a mere transcendental presence on account of which condition the non-intelligent evolutes of *prakṛti* 'know'. The senses 'know' but as being actively operated on by the principle of agent-self (*puruṣa*) being in identification with them. It is self's identification with them — *in* and *as* the senses,[12] that enables the latter to 'know'. According to the other explanation, namely that the senses know but in the proximal presence of spirit, what is unexplained is that the senses while thus knowing are not also self-aware that they know in the presence of spirit.[13] That the senses do not thus apperceive spirit lends support to the presumption that self activises the senses not by its detached, inoperative presence but by standing united with them and identified as the senses themselves and orienting them towards their respective objects. Their manifestation and their objectivised articulation — neither is conceivable without self, active and intelligent *being in union with them*.[14]

In the same way, it is suggested that without the active 'help' or 'assistance' (epistemological and moral)[15] of an indwelling God, the self in turn cannot be conceived in its role of subject of knowledge or agent of action. An active and enduring assistance in actualizing knowledge that remains otherwise unmanifest and also of outwardising the orientation of knowledge by pervading it.[16]

That the senses and intellect being material do not sensate without a knowing self functioning in unison with them, is plausible. But self is acknowledged to be conscious spirit. Why does it require the help of another spirit (*cidantarāpekṣa*)? A self that is not self-sufficient in its knowledge for which quality indeed it is claimed to be spirit, can hardly be called self. What it may need is the assistance of senses for a manifestation of its knowledge. Like the eye in association with external light the self too should be able to assume the role of agent and enjoyer merely through the assistance of senses. What facilitates the experiencing self (*bhoktṛ*) to enjoy forms part of that which is experienced (*bhogya*). Why need an initiator (*preraka*) for the intelligent self? If intelligence is in need of inculcation from another resource of intelligence we may raise the same question with regard also to the second intelligence.[17] Is divine initiative in relation to self's knowledge a self-contained process, without being in need of an initiative and guidance from yet another source? If so, why can it not be the same in the case of the self too?

In answer it may be said that though certainly on the basis of the distinction of intelligence and non-intelligence, the self and the not-self (the senses *etc.*) are distinguishable, they also resemble each other in a striking manner. Both are devoid of self-intuition. One is constitutionally incapable of it, namely the 'knowledge' that is due to the mediation by the not-self (*pāśa-jñāna*) and the other too namely the knowledge that is intrinsic to self (*paśu-jñāna*) is incapable of self-intuition because of the accident of *mala*-obscuration. Like the sense organs which are themselves blind, but perceive by the help of spirit identified with them and therefore perceive only outward and not themselves, the self too though spirit cannot in the natural course invert its orientation of consciousness which is toward the object, and turn its gaze inward.[18]

Nor does this lead to infinite regress. The Spirit that from within initiates knowledge for the self is self-luminous. Being self-initiated it initiates others' knowledge. Spirit is all-knowing and is, therefore, also the enlightener of self's knowledge by being in free association therewith. The self, on the contrary, does not know unguided nor does it enlighten or initiate knowledge in other selves. The difference between spirit that is dependent for knowledge and the spirit that knows independently is the difference between the two ontologically distinguishable orders or categories of being. They are not merely distinguishable as two but are related complementarily as the principal[19] and the subsidiary in their co-working. The self that knows is by definition[20] subordinate to Spirit which presence makes possible self's knowledge. The eye that gazes and the sunlight that shines are alike luminous but the eye can neither see of itself unaided by the sunlight nor can it illumine another eye and aid it to gaze. The sunlight on the other hand as it were both comprehends and also reveals.

If divine revelation were the general condition of all knowledge how is it that, with that invariable condition present there is variation (*tāratamya*) in the revealed knowledge? If variations in knowledge are accountable in terms of variations due to the factor of *karma*[21] then an additional divine source of revelation for knowledge is superfluous. To this objection the reply is, as it has already been explained at length, that *karma* being non-intelligent cannot enlighten knowledge but can only serve as a factor or auxiliary of enlightenment. The blossoming of lotus requires something from without besides the blossoming flower itself, namely sunshine which is the condition of its possibility. Similarly, the fruits of one's toil like cultivating of land requires in addition to the necessary factor of toil itself the factor, namely the cultivable land also as it were to guarantee the yield of the toil. In fact the 'land' is not a factor in addition to toil but is the condition under which there could at all be toil. Likewise, *karma* points to God who is 'from without' it, non-intelligent that *karma* is, both for maturing (*paripāka*),[22] and for issuing in fruits.

The distinction between God and creature is expressed by the key concept of knowledge. The distinction is between Spirit that knows as well as reveals on the one side, and the self which knows that which is revealed and is consequently incapable in its turn of revealing knowledge to another self. Just as in the case of cosmic creation God is looked upon as activating and energising the world into existence through self-activity,[23] in the same manner in the context of knowledge God the Revealer may be looked upon to initiate knowledge also by self-knowing. God as spirit both knows and reveals, and reveals by knowing.[24] Human knowledge, therefore, involves as a necessary condition of its possibility, divine initiative to manifest it into being (*niyamana*) and also a prescient divine knowledge to articulate or sustain its function (*pravartana*) of knowing.

God's function of initiating knowledge through itself knowing, in free conformity with the *karma* of the self and duly vouchsafing experience (*bhoga*) to it is on par with His cosmic functions and may likewise be understood as involving a five-fold operation, each serving an identical purpose as betokening gracious love, covertly or overtly. Thus the rhythm of a cycle of the inception of sensory function followed by its conservation through remembrance and continuous revival and ending in obliviscence will correspond to the three cosmic functions of Creation, Conservation and Dissolution. Investing of knowledge with the feeling-tones of pleasure and pain converting knowledge into an absorbing, self-forgetful experience (*bhoga*) will correspond to Concealment while Knowledge commensurate with the nature of inculcation undistorted by egoism will be Revelation.[25]

Such is the 'anthropo-genetic' operation of Grace as it may be described happening as part of the aforementioned cosmic operations.[26] With the worlds themselves as His body, the multifarious forms of life as His limbs, with His Knowledge, Will and Action as His psyche, the Lord performs the operation of initiating knowledge and making possible experience to all living existence. What is the outcome of this? In the case of cosmogonic operations it was seen that the immanent intention was to actualise a potential condition of pre-cosmic Evil (*mala*) and when the latter thus becomes fit for removal its removal was effected by the direct bestowal of Grace which is the culminating operation in the scheme. The 'anthropo-genetic' operations of God, on the other hand, including its culminating phase, forge only empirical life without enabling the self to go beyond the vicious circle of *saṁsāra*.[27] In reply it may be observed that in so far as the operation of knowledge-initiation is integral to the scheme of the cosmic operations its aim too is eventually to redeem the self from bondage. God initially initiates knowledge discursively (*ekadeśa-jñāna*) through such instruments of discursiveness as senses and vouchsafes in its wake discursive, empirical experience (*bhoga*) for the embodied selves, and subjects them as a consequence of their experience to rounds of births.[28] This is but part of the cosmic scheme which ultimately is to bring about a condition of 'ripeness' of the Bond of Impurity of the Self.[29] When that condition shall be reached, when the knowing self shall be pure receptivity itself,

God then initiates 'absolute' knowledge which is as it were the threshold of absolute unitive experience.[30] Discursive knowledge and experience is a necessary preparation for the eventual advent of non-discursive knowledge and experience.[31]

The above account of divine sovereignty emphasises the absoluteness of the nature of God. Though God is supremely related, He is 'unadulterable'.[32] He participates unreservedly in finite experience and yet is untouched by finitude. Different examples are adduced to explain how God's integrity as the Absolute remains unaffected by His cosmic operations and his exercise of his sovereignty epistemological and moral. An actor impersonates many roles on the stage yet remains at the same time essentially himself. God too does not suffer change though he assumes different forms in order to perform different cosmic functions. The forms of personality that He freely assumes are those of His *śakti* from which He is non-different 'like a tree and its pyth': what appears in His *śakti* appears in Him as well. God appears in different forms figured in His *śakti* just as a crystal which reflects golden, blue and other hues appears golden, blue, and so on identical with those hues. The compatibility of texts which glorify His immutable nature as spirit with those which describe all activity as *due to* His presence is similarly brought out by other examples. In the neutral presence of the sun a lotus is seen to bud, another to blossom, yet another to droop and another again to wither.[33] These variations characterise only the flower and not the sun which shines unvaryingly, impersonally. In the same way, variations in knowledge which God initiates in self pertain only to self's knowledge conditioned as it is by its *karma* and not to the initiating God who is transcendent. 'Do you suffer all the agonies that the micro-organisms may be said to experience in your stomach? Yet surely you 'participate' in their experience as they are part and parcel of your organic existence'. The sufferings of the self are also likewise shared but not 'suffered' by god.[34]

An interesting question that these illustrations raise may be considered.[35] These illustrations of God's unsullied nature are surely in the interest of His absoluteness but do they also betoken a 'compassionate' God ? The question is not if God is not affected or touched by things outside Him, but if he is at all touched in some sense or not. Is not God, His unconditionedness notwithstanding, love? The similies employed to bring out the unsullied nature of God do not seem to make God's compassionate nature intelligible.[36] The analogy of the worms in one's stomach surely is nearer the point. Indeed we do not suffer the agonies of the worms that squirm in our belly or intestine but our body is, nevertheless, brought into relation with the suffering of the worms. Some 'sympathetic' suffering is suggested. But still God remains untouched by the actual suffering. If man's suffering as such is foreign to the nature of God and God is a mere witness in relation to it, then it is contradictory to define divine providence as will that is freely involved with finite experience (*kāryonmukha*).

The one answer to these objections is that true love or compassionateness which consists in effecting a removal of the finitude of the self and recovering its authentic selfhood of unhindered conformity to God is the very substance of divine actuality. We cannot conceive God without reference to the function of Grace. Grace pertains to God under the veritable form of eternity. It is not anything different from Will (*śakti*), which is inalienable with Being.[37] There is no Grace without God and no God without Grace. Though the two appear different and pose a problem in respect of their relatedness, to the discerning eyes of the wise it is a distinction without difference.[38] We do not, in fact, first conceive of a God and then attribute the quality of grace to Him understood in the sense of kindness or favour to one who is in distress. The very conception of God is in terms of a creative 'movement' or Will[39] which freely vouchsafes a field of experience to self in which it may enjoy and suffer in accord with its *karma*, again an impersonalised form of Divine Will. The ascription to God of the cosmogonic processes of Creation etc. and the anthropo-genetic processes that underlie man's awakening to knowledge, presupposes divine compassionateness as the basis of 'theogonic' processes in God Himself, His *śakti*. Without it the above-mentioned functions cannot be conceived to take place.[40]

It is also to be noted that the notion of grace of God indwelling in the spirit of man does not involve a destruction of self-hood. The congruence between self-hood and spirit indwelling self is of the closest imaginable kind. The 'desire, knowledge and will' of the two are in unalienable union and unity. The self is metaphysically 'subordinate' to spirit and its will has its being in the Will which is an integral part of divine reality. Human will is neither identical with Divine will nor 'other than' it, but is in union with it as the light of the evening star is in union with the light of the sun.[41] The analogy brings out the sense of fulfilment by resources which are not self's own but by grace eternally accomplished in the self.

A question that will arise in this context has to be faced. The individual self is analogous to the senses as regards knowing; it has knowledge and experience as revealed by and also simultaneously 'enjoyed' by the indwelling spirit. It would follow from this that just as the effects of the functioning of the senses affect the self, the pleasure and pain experiences of the self must likewise affect God. The indwelling self is the real subject of knowledge which knows in unison with the senses. The subject of knowledge is also the subject of the ensuing experiences of pleasure-pain; the senses are only the channels of such experience. In the same manner, the self's experience in turn must communicate to the Spirit that underlies self and is the ultimate 'subject' of all knowledge and experience. Does God as the participant in the experiences of the self have pleasure and pain experiences?

The answer to this objection is briefly as follows. Senses, indeed, function for the sake of the self, and the character of their experience is not controlled by anything in themselves, non-intelligent as they are.[42] The body is not an end for itself; its organs experience things not for the sake of the body as such but for the sake of the embodied intelligent self.[43] The self that experiences is precisely unlike the body in this regard. Metaphysically its 'experience' is made possible through an illuminer of experience from within but what it experiences is *for* itself. It does not merely transmit its experience as do the senses for another putting itself in service to that thing. It knows and experiences as duly illumined by the indwelling Grace but in accord with its *karma*. Its experiences even thus limited are however made possible through the factor of divine enlightenment and even divine participation. Its experiences though 'founded' by the participative experience of God are still only the fruit of its ego-orientation. Karmic experiences constitute the sphere of pleasure and pain[44] and God's participation in them is like the participation of sun in the function of sight.

The Upaniṣad says : The One inner Self within all is unaffected by the miseries of the world just as sun is undefiled by the faults seen by one's eye, and the 'inner' self is really outer to the sorrows of the world.[45] God is untouched by the pain of the world not because the latter is unreal but because 'pain' is peculiar to the 'unfree' condition (*paśutva*) of the self, its egotistic self-assertion and its identification with the not-self (*tattva*) consequent to its ignorance of its true nature.[46] *Pati*, on the contrary, is *freely* identified with the self, and His participation is an act of grace. This is what invests the notion of 'grace' with associations of attractiveness[47] as well as those of majesty and power which are implied by world-causality.

In God's benign presence (*sannidhi*) the world of self lives, moves and has its being.[48] When He shines everything shines, by His light all this is illumined.[49] Not only the material processes but all 'processes' of life and mind are rooted in the ever-abiding 'living', 'thinking' and 'willing' God. Divine providence implies the idea of good as the ultimate power of being and knowing and is suggestive of the metaphysical attribute of Bliss. It is the nature of God as the source of Bliss that makes it significant to say that He activates all selves by His presence.[50] Providence is not, however, mere presence but a benign will that directs everything towards its fulfilment.[51] It is the 'inner directedness' present distributively in every action as the incipient Will, and also simultaneously as the transcendent Eye that *sees* everything[52] to make possible all sight. The metaphysical attribute of knowledge or omniscience of God is implied by the admission that He is the revelatory source of all intelligence, the 'sight' and light of all knowledge. At the same time, while participating in human experience as the sight behind seeing God is transcendent. The effect or affects of experience befall only to the self that experiences and not to God, who as the transcendent participant does not *appropriate* the experience for Himself. What is phenomenal (*asat*) cannot be the 'experience' of God.[53] It is this feature of God who participates in phenomenal life without being affected by its phenomenality that accords with the metaphysical attribute of God as Being (*sat*).[54]

VII

GOD AS WILL AND BEING

The Concept of Divine Will : *Śakti.*

In our account of God's moral governorship, a distinction was implied between Divine will (*ājñā*) which is instrumental in the performance of the cosmic functions, and Divine being or Spirit (*Śiva*) the transeunt causal ground of the function. Lordship (*patitva*) is conceivable with reference to Spirit only because of a more initial distinction between two main aspects in its essence, that of Will and Being. The ground of all becoming and the will to 'become' are correlatives, not contraries; they are typical of other metaphysical 'contraries': simplicity and complexity, absoluteness and concreteness, being and becoming, actuality and actualisation, consciousness and self-consciousness. God conceived as world-ground and Lord cannot be 'pure' being to which becoming as such is foreign; 'pure' unity devoid of differentiation ; pure actuality with nothing 'possible' in Him; in short He cannot be the Absolute in the sense of being *devoid* of relationship.[1]

Śaiva Siddhānta develops its argument for *śakti* from a premise of God's relatedness to the world of self[2] which is accepted as basic to a doctrine of *advaita.* God pervades the latter in a manner which defies conceptualising in terms exclusively as unity or multiplicity. From this factual relationship of God with self which a theory of Divine creation and Divine governance necessarily presuppose, we may derive the concept of Divine Bi-unity, of *Śiva-śakti.* The Divine will which operates in and indeed even as the self of man—'one' with it, 'different' from it and 'along' with it all in one breath, and the Divine Being are the distinguishable but inseparable aspects of the self-same Supreme Reality.

Let us look at the argument more closely. The premise of the inference is that God is 'one and yet not one' with the individual selves, and the conclusion that this premise entails is that God has *śakti* 'non-different and yet different'—inseparable and yet distinguishable from Him.[3] The argument thus stated is a form of implication (*arthāpatti*). That a cause has an inner invisible nature, supersensible and yet inferable is an accepted doctrine among the speculative systems of orthodox thinking.[4] Applying the same argument we may validly postulate causal power as a necessary implication of the law of causality and conceive of God the supreme cause of the world-process, accordingly, as being endowed with the power to become.

God in relation to his power (*śakti*) is such that He is, strictly, neither one nor not-one, but neutral, numerically speaking between one and not-one.[5] And this is so because He is all-pervasive, omnipresent. What is all-pervasive is entailed by that character which is neither one nor not-one in an exclusive sense but neutral to one and not-one. That is, it partakes of being one *and* not-one, just as the sun that pervades all distant objects is, likewise, self-related to its own rays in such a manner that it may be said to be both one and not-one.[6] To state it negatively: what does not stand thus 'neutral' between one and not-one is not also all-pervasive as may be seen in the case of a particular, say a jar or a stone. Without ceasing to be a unity it 'overflows' or steps out of unitive existence and pervades as the ground of being. The one without ceasing to be one ceases to be one *in particular*, being also 'everything' through self-relation.

The universality of God is compatible neither with His nature as 'pure' identity nor as 'pure' difference. Pure identity will exclude universality understood in the sense of all-pervasiveness, pervading of things 'non-differently'. A thing self-identical in point of space or time cannot also pervade another point without at the same time sacrificing its self-identity.[7] Pure difference again will exclude universality. What is different *inter se* cannot pervade all things 'non-differently'. If there is duality within the structure of Being how can Being be non-dualistic in its relation with all that exists?[8]

Nor can it be said that God is not universal. Nothing, nowhere can exist without Him. He is the ground of all being.[9] It has been said that he is like the vowel 'A' symbolising the fore-most articulation of human voice which underlies the pronunciation of all other letters and words. He is the ground of the existence of *paśu* and *pāśa*.[10] How is this conceivable if God were not universal?

The conclusion then is, there is dynamics in the ontological structure of Being itself. It is because of this dynamic element, God could be conceived of as the agent performing cosmic functions and as the Participant in the spirit of man in his life of enjoyment and suffering (*bhoga*) no less than in his life of spirit (*apavarga*). God who is the Lord of the creature (*paśu-pati*) is 'bi-unal' as *Śiva* and *śakti* like the sun which is a 'bi-unity' of sun, the luminous body and its luminous rays.[11] The God who pervades the entire creation as creative will pervades the content of creation and pervades the individual selves by its immanent presence in their wills, is itself a transcendent unity of spirit and freedom, Being and Will.

One self-identical real admits of a two-foldness within its being, a two-foldness which does not disrupt its self-identity; it is two-fold between which the relation is one of identity (*tādātmya*). The sun, for example, has a two-foldness, when it is self-manifest and when it manifests other objects.[12] In being self-manifest and also other-manifest it does not cease to be identical with itself. When illumining objects it is named the ray or radiance of the sun; when self-illuminig it is named the sun. Notwithstanding difference of names, the denoted object is identical. In the same way spirit (*caitanya*) may be conceived of either as consciousness *per se* (*cit*) when considered in itself, or as conscious power (*cit-śakti*) considered with reference to something in relation to which its reality is appreciated, as *that of which* it is conscious. Spirit, the supreme reality likewise stands self-related by relation of identity as substance and attribute between two distinguishable aspects within itself.[13]

In fact in everything, a two-foldness of form and function is discernible, determined by the respective circumstances of not being related and being related to something without. To know a thing is to know it either in its relations or to know it as itself, unrelated. This is true in a sense of all knowledge empirical and non-empirical alike. Knowledge of material objects and knowledge of spirit too *qua* knowledge admits of this distinction. A non-conscious object like fire *has* the function of burning, which is latent when unrelated to combustible objects and manifest when related; at the same time it *is* fire in form, considered in itself when its function of burning is latent in it. Similarly in the case of consciousness, usage pemits us to distinguish between what it is and what it has or does. Consciousness *has* the conscious function when it is *conscious of* something; it is objectified, exteriorised consciousness. Consciousness *is* conscious spirit when it is consciousness *per se* (*svaniṣṭha*).[14]

The *advaitin* understands by universality of being not its relationship to another but infinite being. Being is infinite in space, in time as well as in intrinsic nature; it is the counter-correlate of absolute negation, anterior negation and reciprocal negation;[15] it is infinite spatially, eternal with respect to time and universal in nature in the sense that it is the ground which makes all differences (*bheda*) possible. Particulars themselves arise but as particularisations of the universal being which is the prius and in relation to which the particular is an accident. The individual self is accidental in so far as its individuality is to be understood as a limitation of the universal.

Śaiva Siddhānta interprets universality of being indeed, to mean what spans all difference; being is continuous with all particulars as their common medium and does not itself partake of their differences even though 'identical' with them, with each, in its uniqueness. From this does not follow the unreality of the particulars or the accidental nature of individual self. The particulars are not also unique monads utterly unrelated. It is in refutation of monadism that Śaiva Siddhānta argues that being is infinite, universal. Being is the universal non-different medium sharing in which the particular ceases to be a mere particular. Just as the enduring presence of God is not implicated in space or in time, it is also not implicated in the intrinsic distinction of things, neither in the distinction between one self and another. Without being 'distracted and diversified' God participates as the all-pervasive Presence.

God's relation to space-time as well as to individual natures must be interpreted qualitatively. God's universality, all-pervasiveness[16] does not mean being extended through all space or endlessly reiterated or repeated on the scale of time or again being spread out to constitute as such every individual nature. Even though we conceive God as a personality as it were without a ego-centre we cannot put Him 'alongside Himself' sacrificing the personal centre of divine life. By all-pervasiveness is meant God's non-dual presence in all things. He is that which is central as well as that which is peripheral.[17] This imagery that God is the centre as well as the circumference in so far as a circle is nothing but a centre writ large, is of special significance. It is with the help of a radius that a circle is described, a centre is spread out. Divine participation in the life and existence of the individual self can be conceived to be accomplished by means of Divine will (*śakti*).[18] From God's omnipresence we draw the conclusion that God must be, not a mere centre but a centre as well as a radius, the fixed as well as the mobile point, both necessary for making up a circle.[19] He is of the nature of term as well as relation. He is not only *what* is related but also the relation itself.[20]

Śakti and the dialectic of difference[21]

The *advaitin* espouses between *brahman* and *śakti* bare unity which is not conscious. The *śakti* and its phenomenalisation are unconscious processes of *brahman* but not in *brahman*. There is no *real* dynamics in Reality. The process in relation to Reality is of the nature of illusory superimposition and subsequent rejection. *Śakti* is indeed the principle of illusion (*māyā*). The function of fire is not the fire nor is it of course nothing (*śūnya*); it exists and functions but only as an adjunct (*upādhi*) of fire. *Śakti* exists as the attribute of the substance and constitutes metphysically substance's unreality; substance is the reality of *śakti*. Creation and other cosmic processes are beginningless processes due to *māyā-śakti* and the latter is superimposed on *brahman* which merely reveals it. *Cit-śakti* is really *māyā-śakti* blazed by the presence of Spirit. Just as the rope does not actually create into existence a snake but merely causes its appearance *cit-śakti* too while being itself self-same brings to pass the appearance of the manifold. *Cit-śakti* identical with spirit (*brahman*) is the reality of all appearance. The creation of the manifold on the part of Will has to be understood as illusory creation and consequently, bondage and liberation are 'caused' by *śakti* but only in a figurative sense. Neither bondage nor the bound nor the Will that redeems from bondage is real. The real is indeed to be understood in terms of their unreality.

The observed differences of the empirical world are therefore false constructions of the mind. Difference as such indeed is never perceived. It is only indeterminate perception that may be said to be determined by the object. All determinate perception, involving, as it does, the relation of speech (*śabda*) is conditioned by senses and the two forms of sensory intuition, namely space and time. Perception can only apprehend a thing positively; it cannot apprehend it *as different from other things*. Difference is being different from other things; it is reciprocal negation (*bheda*). How can perception evidence negation? If, therefore, difference is not validly perceived it follows that it cannot be validly known by other avenues of knowledge; reason and revelation alike as evidences of knowledge depend on apprehension of relation which involves reciprocal negation but as the latter is not validly perceived it follows that it cannot be validly known by reasoning or revelation.

Bondage and liberation are, therefore, epistemic and the power which causes both is also consequently epistemic.[22] Ontologically there is no dynamics in *brahman*. *brahman* is pure being devoid of function.

The absolutistic interpretation of *śakti*, outlined above is unacceptable. From the very argument by which the pure identity of spirit is sought to be proved, it follows that it is not 'pure' or sheer identity.[23] It is not so pure as not to admit of knowing it and even demonstrating it as pure. Or if knowing it as pure were not real knowing then it follows in the absence of the possibility of *real* knowledge, that spirit is not pure identity. Every attempt to prove non-difference involves the use of difference. The use of inference presupposes that the major term is different from the middle and minor terms. One is unascertained and the other necessarily ascertained. The *pakṣa*, for example, there is fire on the hill (a statement of the *probandum* which is open to doubt) and the *sapakṣa*, for example, there is fire in the kitchen present along with smoke(a statement expressive of the positive concomitance between the *probans* and the *probandum*) must be necessarily different and their being different is a necessary condition of valid inference. Were they non-different there would be no illustrative instance where the two, the *probans* and the *probandum* coud be together available; and in their absence there could be no knowledge of invariable concomitance. Therefore, the very use of inference to prove pure non-difference is disproof of its 'purity'.[24]

What is then suggested by the oneness of *cit-śakti* declared in *Śruti*, is that there are not many *cit-śakti* but one only. Its difference from what is not *cit*, namely *jaḍa* is, on the other hand, a necessary implication of the oneness of *cit-śakti*.

The scriptural evidence also it may *a priori* be said, cannot prove non-difference. If scripture were accepted as affording real evidence for oneness, such acceptance in turn will tacitly involve the admission of the reality of the different words which go to compose the scriptural text and also the different meanings of the words – the subject as different from predicate and *vice versa*. In the very acknowledgement of scripture as a means of valid knowledge difference is assumed[25] so that an attempt to prove non-difference on the basis of identity-texts (*abheda-śrutis*) would involve contradiction. The texts which seem to say that *cit-śakti* is pure identity must accordingly be interpreted in a manner which does not conflict with the initial acceptance of empirical difference. Scriptural declarations about *cit-śakti* being pure being and pure identity should be interpreted to be a eulogy for its eternity and ubiquity; taken literally they will conflict with reasoning which supports difference.[26]

It has been argued that the evidence in support of difference of determinate perception (*savikalpaka pratyakṣa*) may not be accepted; determinate knowledge is only a construction involving the use of *a priori* forms and categories. But in reply it may be said that although determinate perception, admittedly is caused by a preceding indeterminate perception it is no less valid than the other; as it is valid evidence of difference the indeterminate perception also must be taken implicitly to assert difference of one thing from another thing. Since there can be negation only of what is implicitly affirmed it even follows that knowledge of non-difference involving negation of difference, is secondary and conditional upon a prior knowledge of difference;[27] the knowledge 'pot is not different from cloth' is contradicted by future empirical experience while 'pot is different from cloth' is never so contradicted. Does it not follow since non-contradiction is the criterion of truth, that indeed perception of difference, not non-difference is valid ?

Not only does reasoning involve difference but unless difference is accepted reasoning ceases to be 'efficient'. Generalization, concomitance (*vyāpti*) which is the nerve of reasoning rests upon perception of *specific* difference. One term is invariably connected with *another* term so that we could say on perceiving one, the other is inferred to exist while it remains unperceived.

Moreover, the advocate of absolute non-difference cannot assert non-difference significantly, so that its contradictory may be denied.[28] Is non-difference different from difference ? If different, what is sought to be denied is implicitly asserted. If non-different, that is also the view of *śakti-vāda*. *Sakti* is non-difference so as not to exclude difference, difference permeated by non-difference.[29]

The illustration of rope-snake is cited in support of the theory that *cit* is non-dual reality, and difference, plurality and particularity are its appearances. An illustrative example alone cannot make for a valid inference.[30] The illusion of snake in a rope is cancelled by true knowledge of the rope and therefore it is plausible that the snake-appearance was not real. But the appearance of pot and cloth with their reciprocal difference is not likewise cancelled by another knowledge; it persists in other space-time too. Empirical difference which underlies all our beliefs and constitutes the very texture of discourse, is not unreal. The *cit-śakti* of the self as qualified by the mode of the intellect (*buddhi vṛtti*) which assumes the respective forms of the different objects which it confronts, becomes differentiated as it were through the adjuncts. While the adjuncts of determinate knowledge become different with different objects which it pervades, the agent of determination is a self-identical unity always of the form of the knowing subject and never of the object. It is eternal, being spirit and immutable.[31] Its self-identity is compatible with its assumption of different determinations only because it is not an abstract identity or unity but an identity wih the *freedom* of differentiation, a unity with the *freedom* of 'othering' into and as the manifold.[32] It is Spirit distinguishable as knowledge and will, consicousness and freedom, form and function, being and dynamics.

The *advaintin's* dialectic of difference betrays an inadequate conception of the unity of God. God's unity is not *opposed* to multiplicity in so far as God has no opposite by which he is conditioned and limited. His unity has to be understood compatibly with his being the transcendent 'I' (*ahaṁpadārtha-rūpa*). The I that is transcendent is also the 'transcendent ' I so that it cannot say 'I' as *against* you and me. The dialectic of difference proceeds on the application of unity in an exclusive sense which has an opposite, and it is claimed that that is the only legitimate sense of unity.[33] Unity cannot be conceived without the contrast of diversity. But the non-duality of God is a demand for a different notion of unity. God's unequivocal 'oneness-and-all-inclusiveness' is the presupposition of his non-duality.

God's 'oneness' must be comprehensive of multiplicity. Exclusive 'one-ness' of the God of pantheisms tends to rejection of multiplicity as illusion. Pantheism tends inevitably toward acosmism. The alternative that all things are not God is as dualistic as the alternative 'all things are God'. Multiplicity is not privation of being. Diversity is not difference or duality.

Śakti as the theogonic process[34]

Śakti is the solution implied in the paradox that what is one cannot be God and what is God cannot be one. *Śakti* is admission of 'diversification' in the absolute unity of God without subjecting the unity to division. It is the notion which envisages a 'process', in, eternity, which initiates transcendentally all processes within and without empirical time.[35]

The idea underlying the concept of theogonic process—eternal processes taking place through Will, is that there can be no *bhoga* or *mokṣa* without Will. Just as the authority of the ruler vests with the members of his government in the discharge of their respective duties, the power automatically differentiated according to the different activities for which it is required, so is Divine *śakti* the one central authority differentiated three-fold, five-fold, eight-fold and so on,[36] according to functional differences underlying processes in phenomena, both those leading to enjoyment here (*bhoga*) and those leading beyond it (*mokṣa*). This means that 'processes' in *śakti* are to be conceived necessarily with reference to self, its bondage and liberation.

The concept of a plurality of function as manifestations and articulations of one Divine Function (*śakti*) suggests the possibility of distinguishing a 'general' and 'ultimate' nature with regard to *śakti*. To take the example cited in the Ṛg-Veda, *Agni* has these functions or energies; heat-energy operating in the sacrificial fire, gastric energy operating in the growth of plants and so on; electric energy operating in lightning, and solar energy operating in the sun. These functions form the 'general' (*taṭastha*) feature of fire called forth in response to specific requisitions, while its 'ultimate' nature (*svarūpa-lakṣaṇa*) is just energy. There is no discontinuity between the two natures, the ultimate nature as energy being pervasive of all its other functional differentiations. In the same way, in *śakti* we may distinguish between its specific modes of functions answering to differences of cosmic operations and an ultimate, essential, invariable form present unconditionally through all 'differentiations'.

The essential nature of Will in its generality as underlying all specifications is not definable in terms of a purpose beyond itself. It is nevertheless Grace, in the positive sense because its actuality is not conceivable except in terms of life. We can describe it negatively, as Knowledge which does not amount to inhibition of Grace.[37] It is deobstructed knowledge. It is Knowledge as the foremost process of 'othering' of Being and, as Knowledge it is conceivable again as at once knowing and revealing. This is *parā-śakti*, Knowledge *per se*, Revelation *per se* — in short, Grace itself.

Admission of this pure form of Grace as Knowledge that knows and reveals unconditionally implies that further specifications of this 'pure' process are Knowledge that *do not* reveal unobstructedly, but involve withholding of revelatory manifestation of Grace.[38] Pure Knowledge becomes Pure Action; a general Will becomes a specific Function in the direction of performing cosmic operations in order to cause maturing of the Impurity enveloping the self. This is the First *śakti* (*ādi or ādyā-śakti*), or the Concealing *śakti* (*tirodhāna-śakti*). The remaining three specifications of *icchā-śakti*, *jñāna-śakti* and *kriyā-śakti* are the aspects of this Initial *śakti* intent on the specific function of maturing or ripening *mala* through rounds of operations.[39] *Icchā* and *kriyā* are determinations of *jñāna* so that these specifications are in congruence with the nature of the foremost manifestation of Will as Knowledge *per se*. Affection and conation are distinctions within Knowledge, the synonym of revelatory Grace. Affection (*icchā*) is Grace involved in the removal of *mala* and vouchsafing *śivatva*. Knowledge co-ordinate with affection implies knowing of the means thereof, and conation is the specific will or resolve to do, in that direction.[40]

Classification of *śakti* into five or more, presupposes a theogonic process of divine self-manifestation, initiating of the five-fold cosmic functions in a serial order and causing their operation at levels below the Pure, through other agencies. The process is described as a kind of Divine Genesis [41] a nine-fold variation through which takes place the genesis of Will, each arising continuously from the preceding, and the most initial arising in turn from *Parama-Śiva* which is beyond every concrete predicate. The entire thing is also looked upon as a Divine Drama[42] in which the Lord is the mono-actor impersonating different roles by assuming the forms of his *śakti* and yet remaining Himself. Cosmic operations, the manifest one as well as the subtle (*sūkṣma*), which precede the manifest is the revelation of this Divine Drama, involving assumption of different forms of *śakti* serially emerging, one from the other.

Broadly, we may distinguish three phases in this theogonic process: (i) the phase of a preparatory rehearsal of the five-cosmic functions, sustaining, in consequence the selves in their 'life' in *kevala avasthā* — a pre-biographical, pre-transmigratory state of Isolation from which state they emerge with the advent of the *sthūla pañca-kṛtya*; (ii) the phase of association with the 'gross' self-posited distinctions of form, namely *icchā*, *jñāna* and *kriyā* implying a *specific pre-disposition* for the 'overt' Creation of the world from the respective *māyās* to be followed by the four other 'overt' operations of *pañca-kṛtya*; and (iii) the phase involving the cosmic activity of Creation setting into actual motion the operations by sheer will. These correspond, respectively, with the three States (*avasthā*) which God freely submits to, out of super-abundant Grace, namely *laya* (literally, absorption), *bhoga* (enjoyment), and *adhikāra* (assuming of Office). The three distinguishable phases of any creative action are exemplified here, the phase of initial absorption with a theme, being suffused with its contents, mentally creating it into existence as it were; the next phase of a preparatory set prior to action and following suspension of absorption, constituting the joy of creative function about to be exercised; and the third stage of consummatory action.[43]

Each of these three phases including the initial one *laya* constitutes a 'process' with its implication of redeeming self from *mala*-obscuration. The one theme of the drama pervades and dominates all its phases from its very inception to its distant end. The theme translated in terms of our life is the emergence of life from a state of lifeless inconscience (*kevala avasthā*), of consciousness from its oblivion, of will from its condition of inanity — in short, of the emergence of self from its primordial condition of ignorance and inaction due to *mala*, to a life of action. The life of action includes a life of affirmation and enjoyment leading to more enjoyment, and also a life of withdrawal leading to a cessation of enjoyment as preparation for the life Eternal. Both these moments presuppose emerging from the night of oblivion and inaction. Divine processes taking place in eternity are the pre-condition of this emergence and enjoyment.[44]

To return to the three phases of the theogonic process. The first phase of self-absorption again admits of a distinction of two stages: the stage when śiva is self-absorbed as all *jñāna*, and the stage when he is self-absorbed as all *kriyā*. The first is 'subtle' self-absorption (*sūkṣma-laya*) describable as pure 'awareness' or concern for Re-Creation (*punassṛṣṭi*) from a state of Pre-mergence. The second stage typifies 'gross' self-absorption (*sthūla-laya*) describable as implicit activity immediately following pure awareness. The activity is of the form of incipient performance of the five-cosmic functions[45] with the help of an incipient differentiation of *śakti* in so far as doing *different* functions even incipiently, entails the serial exercise of the moments of affection, cognition and conation.[46]

The second phase of Enjoyment (*bhoga*) of God forms the intermediary between implicit five-fold functions and overt five-fold functions,[47] and in terms of the life of self, the point of inter-section between *kevala* and *sakala* states of existence. What is distinctive of this phase is the presence of proneness to overt function through association with overt differentiations of *śakti*, namely, *icchā*, *jñāna* and *kriyā*.

The third phase of Office (*adhikāra*) again consists of two levels, respectively termed *sūkṣma adhikāra* and *sthūla adhikāra*, distinguishable in terms of the two orders of existence recognised in Śaiva Siddhānta cosmology — the Pure and the Impure.[48] The difference is that in the one case, God sets into operation the cosmic functions by sheer will with regard to the Pure Realm of existence of which God is himself agent, while in the second He initiates the cosmic operations *through* sub-divine agencies and brings about the evolution of the Impure Realm.[49]

Cosmic operations — both cosmological and micro-cosmological leading to the genesis of the world and the genesis of man as a conscious, willing being, thus imply also a process of Divine genesis, an eternal process involving distinguishable moments but subserving the same purpose of redemption, or conquest of non-being. It is of interest to note that Divine functions are conceived in this scheme as transcendent and yet continuous with the phenomenal process. This is suggested by Will functioning in continuity with finite will operating at lower levels through the agency of the latter.[50]

The distinction between *laya-śiva* or simply, *śiva* and *parama-śiva*, on which this doctrine of Divine genesis proceeds is of special significance. It is the distinction between Being in its level of utter indetermination, as Spirit *per se prior* to the inception of the Divine process and Being as distinguished by Will. The cause of all manifest functions or processes is Will, a process, in eternity and the 'cause' of the Will in the same sense of the term cause, is the Nothingness of *parama-śiva* in which the Will is as yet unborn. As all the modal distinctions of

Will are resolved into non-distinction, the distinction of Will and Being also ceases to be articulate.[51] This raises the problem of the relation of Deity and Absoluteness.

God and The Absolute[1]

The 'definition' of God in terms of functions or operations which belong uniquely to Him as belonging to no one else serves to differentiate the noumenal reality of God from the phenomenal reality of the world. But it is more of a descriptive knowledge in which the characteristics of our phenomenal existence are used as the basis from which to reach god. It is 'knowledge' from the inevitable perspective of Bondage. What is demanded in this kind of knowledge is a direct immediate experiential awareness of deity, as deity is self-aware, free from all hindrances of bonds. Such would be knowledge of God as Absolute, that is, detached or disengaged from any limiting relation, pre-eminently from the basis of all particular relations namely that of the subject and object. Positively stated, knowledge of Absolute is given in a non-discursive supra-relational experience in which knowing and being, knower and the known become fused.[2]

Such knowledge of the Absolute, being a case of knowing by being, is to be accomplished through a progressively unfolding life of freedom from constraints and impurities (*śuddha avasthā*) and rising to the level of being the Absolute through union. When formulated and defined it takes a negative form: Śiva, as the Absolute is termed,[3] is described in these terms: unobjectified, indeterminate, the incomparable, the untainted, the uncognised, the non-finite, the uncaused, the immovable and the non-relative.[4] It is neither perceived nor inferred nor indeed revealed.[5] Śiva is neither possessed of form nor formless, neither indeed *cit* nor *acit*.[6] He creates not, nor does He do other functions. He neither performs austerity nor does He enjoy. He freely assumes these and other forms and yet He is indeed without them.[7]

The essential incomprehensibility (*acintyatva*) of God in the midst of all attempts at comprehending Him as transcendent self, Will and so on is a necessary element of a fully developed religious consciousness. God remains a mystery — the unfathomable — even when He is 'revealed'. Śaiva Siddhānta asserts the paradox of Divine hiddenness even to Revelation.[8] God is essentially mysterious. He is beyond the reach of the Veda and the Vedānta.[9]

A genuine mystery is experienced not in an attitude of ordinary cognitive experience but when experience turns inward to apprehend itself and fathom its ultimate implication.[10] Mystery characterises a dimension which transcends and precedes the surface phenomenon of sense-conditioned knowledge; it precedes even one's *immediate* inwardness — the *yogin's* dream and the philosopher's ideal. The 'abysmal' element constitutes the mystery of the ground. The mystery appears only when 'self' is driven beyond itself to its 'abyss', beyond its matter-conditioned reason, beyond even self-intuition of its matter-free essence as spirit.[11]

The central burden of all the different accounts in praise of the greatness and glory of the Deity seems to consist in the affirmation of the mystery and the inscrutability of its essential nature. The *Śatarudrīya*[12] hallows in the same breath, the world-transcendence (*viśvādhikatva*), world-causality (*viśva-kāraṇatva*), world-controllership (*viśvāntaryāmitva*), and the world-form (*viśva-rūpatva*) of the Divine Reality denoted significantly as the *Rudra*. The Purāṇas, likewise, make use of conflicting and paradoxical images of description: The 'timeless' *event* of *Śiva* growing in the form of a column out-measuring the movements of both Brahmā the Creator, flying upwards in the form of a gander in a vain effort to reach the top, and of Viṣṇu the Conserver, plunging down as the boar to fathom the beginnings of the column; the Supreme event of the gods of Trinity emanating from the 'parts' of Siva; the creation of the world represented again as emanations from His different limbs; and the half-male half-female form of the Lord typifying the 'he-she-it' nature of the world. These apparently conflicting notions and images point to the truth that they are symbols, not concepts of human understanding. The Deity to whom they point is beyond simple assertions or their negations.[13]

Even saintly consciousness which is sensitive to the personalistic presence of God is aware of the central 'hiddenness' in God's nature which defies all categorisations.[14] The Śaiva saints to whose utterances we owe the most vivid and personalistic images of Godhead also glorify by use of paradox the abysmal element in it: He is the nearest and the farthest,[15] the end and the beginning;[16] the most easy to approach and the unapproachable;[17] the night and the day;[18] the yea and the nay;[19] the low and the lofty;[20] the cause and the cure of suffering;[21] the good as well as the 'evil;'[22] the subtle and the gross;[23] the tallest as well as the tiniest;[24] the separate and also the united;[25] inside and outside;[26] the earth and the heaven;[27] the old and the young;[28] different and identical.[29] The hymnal literature abounds in such paradoxes which point to the ineffable and inexhaustible essence of the Deity which no knowledge seems capable of whittling away. It is ineffable as inherently transcending the context of bondage and the structure of knowledge and communication defined by such context.

We speak of God as the Destroyer, the abysmal ground of all that exists but by this is meant that the supreme Reality underlies all that exists in a manner which can only be symbolically asserted as the Destroyer. He is the inner illuminer of life in the sense that He underlies life as its ground, and in this sense we say God is 'living'.[30] He is the moral Governor in the sense that we understand Him in relation to our 'moral' life, in response to the demand that every man be treated exactly as he individually deserves and so as the Dispenser of justice. Similarly, He is Self in the sense that He is not a thing but one that has self-hood persisting in the midst of and comprehending all that changes; relatively to that, even the individual 'I' is not self.[31]

Although no predicate from our repertoire of empirical knowledge can apply to God in a literal sense, religious consciousness, nevertheless, attributes 'predicates' to Him which purport to state the positive nature of God considered as Absolute.[32] Such are the descriptions of God as Being (*sat*), Spirit (*cit*) and Bliss (*ānanda*). These are uniquely connotive of God's absoluteness. If the finite also has being, Being as connoting the supreme Reality transcends in significance the mere negative of the concept finite being; the latter relatively is non-being (*asat*). In the same way if self also is spirit, Spirit as defining God transcends the negative meaning of the term as applied to the self; the latter relatively is, non-spirit (*acit*). Similarly with Bliss. When applied to God it is understood as a fullness transcending the negative of empirical pleasure.[33] All the 'absolute' predicates used as connotive of the essence of God such as omniscience, omnipresence, infinitude, eternity, unconditionedness, beginninglessness, wisdom and unceasing power[34] may be treated as synonyms for this metaphysical triad of *sat*, *cit* and *ānanda* used to describe the positive Divine.[35] These paraphrases, negatively, refer to its essential uncomprehensibility either through a sense-conditioned knowledge or through its cessation. Positively they mean the spontaneity and freedom which are the essence of divine infinitude and its realizability in non-dual intuition (*ananyasākṣātkāra*).[36]

Two considerations stand out prominently in the Śaiva Siddhānta conception of the Absolute: its utter inaccessibility to a knowledge that is finite and 'unfree' (*asvatantra*), to *vāc* and *manas* in short,[37] and its apprehensibility through non-dual intuition, a knowledge that is free, indeterminate, eternal, all-comprehending, non-symbolic, non-objective apprehension.[38] As it has already been shown, no knowledge, indeed, can arise for the self without the aid of Grace which is the general precondition for the manifestation of knowledge. But the natural orientation of self's knowledge is towards the object, like that of sense because of the beginningless predicament of obstruction. By making 'objective' knowledge and experience possible for the finite self, Divine grace ripens the 'source' of finitude so that it becomes fit for removal. Now by the help of what is known by objectification surely it is not conceivable that one can hopefully come by a knowledge of the transcendent condition of such knowledge. The outwardised senses cannot be aware of the self in the way it is aware of its sensory objects. Spirit which is the ground that makes self's knowledge possible is at the same time outside the ken of self's knowledge. The objective orientation of self's knowledge precludes it from knowing the indwelling Spirit (*śivam*).

But this is not the same as saying that Spirit is unknowable to self. The absolutely unknown cannot be asserted to be something.[39] Its knowledge in some sense must be within the realm of possibility. To be Spirit and yet not knowable are contradictory. To assert that the unknowable exists is not significant because no appeal can be made to the unknowable.[40] The Absolute cannot be *śūnya*, a non-entity like the square-circle, no more than it can be an objectively knowable entity.

The Absolute in other words is neither *śūnya* (non-existent) nor *asat* (objective existent).[41] It is not *asat* in the sense that it is not objective, phenomenal. It is the noumenal Spirit (*cit*) which is unknowable as object, and is free from origination, decay and death which define the nature of the object. The Absolute again is not *śūnya* in that it is not the absolutely unknowable. It is Being (*sat*) which is knowable as super-existence (*jñeya*) to intuition, to a spontaneous, self-revealed Divine knowledge (*pati-jñāna*).

The self can have no knowledge without the aid of Divine grace. And what aids it can itself be 'known' again surely by Grace's self-disclosure in the spirit of man. It cannot be known as an object to a knowing subject that stands sundered from the object.[42] It is true that in every type of knowledge a knowing subject and a known object are logically distinguishable, but in the case of our knowledge of that which makes knowing possible by itself initiating knowledge through self-knowing,[43] what is demanded is the surrender even of our subjectivity while we 'know' it. It must be 'known' as it 'knows' itself, an 'object' if at all to its own subject.[44]

God as Being

The Upaniṣad says: Not by speech, not by mind, not by sight can He be apprehended. How can He be comprehended save by one saying that He is?[45] Śaiva Siddhānta points the Absolute negatively by the word *Śiva* which is a synonym for *cit* (Spirit), technically, that which is inaccessible to knowledge which is *mala*-ridden, namely *pāśa-jñāna* and *paśu-jñāna*;[46] and positively by the word *sat*, that which is immediately self-revealed (*gocara*) to a knowledge that is inherently free from the taint of *mala*, namely, *pati-jñāna*.[47] Being (*sat*),[48] therefore, sums up all uniqueness of God considered the Absolute.

The question of Being is the central ontological question. It is the question which man can ask, being himself, separated from it while belonging to it. Man as the representative of phenomena belongs to being. He would not otherwise *be*. But he is also alienated from it. That is why he is also given to wonder at being: Why is there something, why not nothing? He is a mixture of being and non-being (*sad-asat*). That is what explains at once that he is bound and that he can be liberated. Being itself is neither bound nor liberated. It is Absolute in the sense that unlike man it has the complete power of being and is indeed the answer to the question of man. Śaiva Siddhānta understands Being, not abstractly as what is implied by the sphere of non-being as negation thereof (*asad-vyāvṛtti*) but as the power which 'resists' or conquers non-being. *Sat* implies *śakti*.[49] It is the sun which stays the potential darkness.[50] It is only an abstract absolute that is incompatible with an active God, the Lord (*pati*). But *sat* implying *śakti* is at once Absolute and God. It precedes all concreteness and dynamism and freely implies them.[51]

The description of God as Being is offered as definition—'essential' definition. Being should be the essence of God in an unequivocal sense.[52] That means, the self and world in its manifest, gross form in the sense of phenomena (*māyīya*) as well as in its causal undifferentiated form, namely *māyā*, cannot have 'being' in the same sense in which we say God is Being. What is here asserted is that neither the known object (*pāśa*), nor the knowing subject (*paśu*) can be said to 'be' in the same sense in which the transcendent condition of knowledge which knows with the subject and reveals the object to it, may be said to have being. It is true that the self and the world are real existents. Śaiva Siddhānta advocates the realistic theory of pre-existent effect (*satkārya-vāda*). There is nothing like non-existence other than, or as opposed to, existence. Nevertheless, the world is described as *asat*, not in the sense that it does not exist but in the sense that it exists with a difference. The difference is that its existence presently in a manifest form will soon be followed by existence that shall no longer be manifest. It is existence which under conditions appears and disappears. It is, indeed, not in principle different from avowed appearances like conjurors' trick, mirage, dream etc.[53] They all come and go with no assignable 'stay'. The appearances of mirage etc. are no more illusory than the world of facts is real. They are all of the same species, real and yet not being. Just as in relation to what appears through error and is later on cancelled, the world-appearance has a more solid, distinguished 'being', noumenal realities like *māyā*, *karma and mala* may, in relation to the world, be said to have 'being' in a still deeper sense. Their 'being' is less precarious than the being of the world; the world perceptibly passes from manifest existence to non-manifestness, while *māyā* etc. can only be conceived to undergo change from their unmanifest, causal form to their manifest, effect form. *Mala*, the principle of 'non-being' too is being, though what kind of being may be attributed to it is not obvious.[54] In whichever sense understood, its being too oscillates between an actualised condition when its 'powers' are manifest—what constitutes Bondage, and a dormant condition when its concealing powers are reduced to nought — what constitutes Liberation.[55]

Therefore, phenomenal and noumenal realities alike, those empirically perceived as well as those cognised by transcendental reflection are being but only conditionally. They are part of 'objective' experience (*anubhava*). Even the unobjectified subject of experience, namely, self, to the extent that its existence is implied by experience as the transcendental unity apperceiving it, is 'objectively' known, and is therefore not Being.[56] Though self as spirit is surely being its history also involves a change from a condition when its 'being' has been swallowed up in non-being (Bondage) to freedom from such condition when it regains its ground in Being unmixed with non-being (Liberation). The self too, therefore, to the extent it shares a mode of existence which is there for a time but ceases to be thereafter is not Being.

Being, therefore, defines God univocally. God Eternally Free is not subject to change. Conditions of bondage and liberation introduce no difference in His nature as Being. He is, therefore, not *a* being being exclusively above the vortex of change involved in the transition from Bondage to Liberation[57]. He is beyond the categories of finitude and is beyond all process being without beginning or end.[58] He is indeterminate Being, being not affirmable as this and *a fortiori* as not-this.[59]

Sat is identical with unconditioned self-existence. What has no self-existence and exists under varying conditions varying with them is *asat*. The epistemological basis of this distinction is that everything knowable in the (sense) experientially certified manner is *asat*, while what is *sat* is never knowable in that manner. By applying this norm, *sat* may be distinguished from *asat*. Being differs from what is not Being because of a difference in the mode of their being known. The difference is, briefly stated, in respect of falling or not falling within the ambit of human experience. Human experience with its relational mode of knowledge involves contrast and alternation of the known and the unknown — the known foreground as against the unknown background . This is the predicament of human knowledge and is a reflection on (i) the nature of the object experienced and also (ii) on the nature of the experiencing self. Both imply finitude which again means their partaking of the nature of *asat*.

Two questions may be raised here, one about the 'mystical' experience of God the possibility of which is admitted in the system. Is it also 'human' experience, and will that not make God given to such experience, *asat* ? Secondly, is not to know God as what is not knowable, itself to know God ? What about the knowledge of God as cause ? Was it not argued in the case of self, that even to know self as the transcendental condition of knowledge is to know it, however, generally ? Just as the word 'I' experientially certifies to self's existence, does not the word God' that we use as when we say 'God is', denote God ?

To take the second objection first. God can certainly be spoken of even as an immature maiden can *discourse about* sex-experience. To be able to speak is not certainly to have knowledge. The speakable is not necessarily the presentable.[60] When it is said that God cannot be 'given' to experientially certified knowledge, what is ruled out is His presentability as object. God may be the referent of the word 'God' in a discourse, but nothing is 'given' corresponding to the referent. To speak or think of God as cause etc., or as what cannot be known, is not to 'know' Him. Or, we may say that it is to know God verbally (*vācaka-jñāna*) and not experientially (*anubhava-jñāna*).[61]

But is not again to know God experientially the possibility of which is admitted, to unsay that God is Being ? This brings us to the second question. Experience of God is intuitive, immediate knowledge (*ananyasākṣātkāra-jñāna*). It is not 'objective' experience to which God is 'given'. It is an experience where knowing and being commune together. It is only discursive experience where the 'object' confronts a knowing subject that spells 'non-beingness' for what is thus experienced.

Being and knowing

The norm, that what is *sat* can never be discursively experienced while what is thus experienced is necessarily *asat*, needs supplementation.[62] Otherwise, while *sat* may be distinguished from *asat* it cannot also be distinguished from the unreal (*śūnya*).[63] The latter, namely the unreal like the hare's horn, is not 'discursively experienced'; and like Being it also admits of neither beginning nor end. Being is, therefore, further definable as what is its inapprehensibility notwithstanding accessibility to non-discursive, non-dual intuition.[64]Both unknowability to discursive reason and accessibility to non-dual experience, define the concept of Being as applied to God.[65]

Being is thus brought within the sphere of some 'accessibility' (*gocaratva*) notwithstanding its inapprehension by objective knowing. Just as Being has to be distinguished from the world evident to sense and reason it has to be distinguished also from the never-evident. The one essential presupposition of a philosophy of spiritual life seems to be that Being which is the goal of spiritual endeavour is in some sense truly accessible. And in being accessible it is at once distinguished from both the evidenceable and the never-evidenceable. What is evident to knowledge does not have to be also the object of the quest of spiritual life, while the never-evident is never the object of knowing or striving.[66]

Being is, therefore, non-apprehensible and yet accessible. What is further implied in this admission may be stated as follows. Being *qua* the accessible, is not quite indeterminate. It is not indeterminate in a strict sense because, though it is devoid of predicates literally speaking we are, indeed, not precluded from saying that it is Being (*sat*). Being certainly cannot be object of thought as *a* being. But Being is Being, and not nothing. The alternative to *sat* is not the indeterminate but *asat* — *asat* in the sense of *śūnya*.

The dilemma seems to be : If we assert that the Absolute is *sat*, then it becomes the known (*jñeya*) to a knowledge — the object (*asat*). If we are precluded from asserting that it is *sat* then it becomes *asat* again — in the sense of *śūnya*. But admission of the possibility of a spiritual realisation of the Absolute, on which account all absolutisms show a curious agreement, implies that the Absolute can be *asat* in neither of the two senses of the term. If it is a knowable object it can be known in the ordinary way. Why should there be a spiritual effort (*sādhana*) to realise again what is already known ? If it is the unknowable, of what avail is spiritual effort in quest thereof ?[67]

One solution to this problem seems to be to say that the Absolute from the ultimate standpoint is pure immediacy. It is Intuition itself (*jñāna-mātra*) not *that* which is intuited as *sat* or *asat* though from the empirical standpoint it is approached *through* spiritual knowledge.[68] This distinction of levels or standpoints is forced on us because of *avidyā*. It is *avidyā* that invests the indeterminate with the distinction of knower and known, and this distinction, though not real in itself, can be used as a means to reach the ultimately real. When *avidyā* is removed, there being no distinction of *jñāna* and *jñeya* in the Absolute, there is strictly, neither Being nor Non-being.

Śaiva Siddhānta does not accept this approach to spirituality, the approach involving a distinction of standpoints. A strict application of this distinction will abolish the immanence of the absolute in the phenomena, its role of activation and illumination of phenomenal things — in short its inseparability with Grace. The absolute from the ultimate standpoint, it is said is indeterminable either as *sat* or as *asat*. But the Indeterminate, neither Being nor Non-being, *is*. The most ticklish question about the unknowability of the Indeterminate is the question of its evidence. On what evidence is it said that the Indeterminate is present? Negation of determination is not negative determination. The Indeterminate is admittedly not the denial of reality. If so, on what evidence is it asserted or implied *to be* real?[69]

If it is evident to some knowledge,it is not Indeterminate, but Being *accessible* in some sense. If it is not evident at all, how can it be distinguished from the never-evident *śūnya*? To reply that while the never-evident is dispensable the Indeterminate is indispensable as the ground, is no answer because it presupposes that the Indeterminate is Being. To argue that the evidence in question here is self-evidence and not a case of being evidenced by another knowledge again presupposes the reality or the Being of what is self-evident.

Śaiva Siddhānta finds this concept of the Indeterminate with its inevitable implication of *śūnya* in conflict with the *sat* of the Upaniṣads. *Sat* is the Being 'unknowable to knowing,[70] and accessible unequivocally to the experience of intuition through non-dual union with Grace. To the extent, the *sat* of the Upaniṣads may be distinguished from the Indeterminate, it may be identified with the personalistic God of the Śaiva Upaniṣads.[71] The personalism of the Śaiva religion is implicit in the philosophical ontology of the Vedānta with its notion of *sat*.

Does not the view that the Absolute is 'neither the evident nor the never-evident' which Śaiva Siddhānta espouses, also amount to saying that the Absolute is indeterminate? In answer it may be said that this exclusion for him is proof, not of the indeterminateness of the Absolute even with regard to Being and Non-being but, on the contrary, its nature as Grace amenable to man's knowledge in union therewith.[72] The Absolute is accessible to intuition through non-dual union with Grace which is inalienable with the Absolute. Though transcending the subject-object structure of knowledge it is intuition it is also self-distinguishable in terms of seer, seen and the *revealer* so that it is meet to speak of the Absolute as Being, as *jñeya* to a *jñāna*.[73] The subject-object relation of finite knowledge is now replaced by another *ecstatic* relation where the infinite 'object' serves also as the relation.

Absolute is at once the term and relation of its 'knowledge'.[74] Being is *jñeya* (known) to a *jñāna* (knowledge) that is non-dual with the *jñāpana* (revelation of knowledge). This view of intution of the Absolute is in consonance with, and is indeed implied by, the two notions of Divine bi-unity (*tādātmya*) and Divine relatedness (*advaita*).[75]

Divine bi-unity explains how it is conceivable that Absolute Being is knowable through itself. That through which it is known and that which is known are not the same and are not different. God and *śakti*, Being and Will are neither one nor not-one, but 'neutral to one and not-one'. This answers all objections from a spirituality that does not feel the need for Divine assistance. If Being has to be known through Being, has it not to be known first? And through that it is known again? This objection is met by the conception of Will as immanent in Being. The Divine will underlies all our knowing function even in phenomenal life. It does not have to be known, as objects previously unknown are brought within the knowledge relation. As it is ever at work as the Will underlying man's will all that he has to do is to surrender his 'egoistic' subjectivity. Grace then, hitherto incipient in him reveals Being.[76]

Divine will being ever at work in man is the doctrine of *advaita*. Man is in indivisible unity with God. This view is the presupposition underlying the conception of cosmic functions, of God as the Governor and the Redeemer. The problem of the knowledge of Absolute also receives its answer from this key notion.

In advocating this view of a 'non-dual' knowledge of the Absolute being possible through surrender of subjectivity and union, Śaiva Siddhānta defines its position in sharp contrast from (i) the view that God can be approached like an objective, existing thing, and known through a 'dual' knowledge in which the knower stands over against the known, and (ii) the view that the knowing self, with the surrender of its subjectivity, 'becomes' one with God, so that it is not correct to say that Absolute is accessible to a non-dual knowledge of the self.

Against the first view it may be said that our bond or Kinship with God which as one of 'inseparable union' is ulterior to everything that we can stand over against it. What ever is thus known from outside is *asat*. But God is *sat*. A 'dual' knowledge of *sat* is a contradiction in terms.[77] The concept of 'non-dual knowledge of God through union with God's knowledge of Himself' is the solution implied in the distinction between *sat* and *asat*.

Nor is God as Absolute known through the self's own contemplation. This alternative admits that God cannot be known by standing over against Him but rejects the solution of a non-dualistic union with God's knowledge. The questions that become pertinent in this connection are:[78] is the soul-contemplation of God accomplished by means of the mind or is it accomplished without it? Or possibly in neither way? Or is it again, a contemplation in none of these senses, but meditating on what is avowedly beyond one's knowledge with an inward assurance of its being through such repeated efforts of meditation? None of these solutions are open for knowing the Absolute. It is knowable neither through senses, nor through a withdrawal from the senses. It is knowable neither in the wakeful condition of life nor in the suspension of the wakeful, neither in half-sleep which is our empirical life nor in the full sleep of pre-empirical isolation. A new awakening or vigilance is needed, a transition from empirical consciousness mediated by senses and directed towards the world struggling for synthesis and integration, to an integrated super-consciousness which is alive to the reality of Grace immanent in it. The true contemplation of the Absolute consists of non-dual intuition of God through inward union with Grace.[79]

One other 'dualistic' point of view which Śaiva Siddhānta is at pains to refute is the view which puts forward what may be called a perfectionist theory of grace.[80] The formula, of God's accessibility not withstanding His inapprehensibility, is admitted in this point of view, but different implications are drawn from it, implications that amount to repudiation of the notion of Absolute itself. While it is admitted that neither *pāśa-jñāna* nor *paśu-jñāna* can be adequate to a knowledge of God it is at the same time suggested that self may outgrow its association with *pāśa*, and attain to a standard of perfection after a due cleansing of its innate Dirt. *Śivatva* is the name of a non-conditioned mode of being, a state of absolute freedom into which the self shall be reborn. Thus the freed man who has appropriated another mode of being transcending finite condition, is no longer in need of Grace. Man has the potentialities of fulfilling the meaning of life within himself, aided no doubt in the initial stages by God from without. But in the end, the freed man is God unto himself equal in every respect with God, and 'knows' the latter without the implication of Grace.[81]

This view exhibits the contradiction between admitting *advaita* relation between Deity and man and rejecting the absoluteness of Deity. Man is in unalienable relation with the Deity at the very root of his being. In order to be able to know it as object to a subject, he should stand over against it, which conflicts with his being 'one' with it in being. *Cit-śakti* (Grace) stands immanently in man's spirit as the Subtle within the gross, as soul-light indwells in the light of the eye so that it is not conceivable that he can know it through *his* own knowledge (*ātma-cit-śakti*). The eye-light is incapable of gazing at the soul. How can man even when he is perfected, be conceived to know God with his unaided knowledge? How can the light of his soul (*ātma-cit-śakti*) perceive the Light within and reveal it to itself ? Even when the eye is freed from all obstructions to its sight, how is it conceivable that it can gaze into the transcendent condition of its very sight?[82]

If man is 'one' with God ontologically, and the Śaivāgamas are unanimous in asserting it, it follows that God cannot be anything less than Being, having primacy over knowing. Being can admit of a knowing that is only interior to it. The *Śivatva* is not a perfection to which man aspires and achieves but represents the spirit of God indwelling in man. It represents Being in the sense of a supernal Perfection having resources of love through which it is accessible to man's knowledge.[83]

Lastly may be considered the view that self merges in Being with the surrender of its 'I'-ness and that therefore it is not correct to define Being as what is accessible through Grace.[84] The answer to this question was already given in anticipation. The really vital question is: Is Being the Indeterminate? If, as was shown, it cannot be in the strict sense of the term indeterminate, that is indeterminate even with regard to being and non-being, then it follows that the 'I' that has become 'one with Grace through conscious union, does not cease to exist though it ceases to persist as 'I' in relation to 'that'. For, the self that intuits Being is as much itself as it is also Being.[85]

BOOK THREE

ON BOND : PĀŚA

VIII

INTERPRETATION OF *MĀYĀ*

The Concept of *Māyā* : Approach and Analysis

For a proper understanding of the doctrine of *māyā* in Śaiva Siddhānta and particularly of the reasons that lead to its postulation, one may start from the basic ontological structure of the system.

The phenomena of movement, change and multiplicity are the result of an inner creative process of a spiritual principle, the noumenal reality whose being is non-different from free creativity. This is the true significance of the doctrine of *satkārya-vāda* enunciated in the context of the evolution of the material world.[1] The doctrine consists in the recognition of an inner factor of change and development, a free activity, a spontaneous self-becoming which accounts for the creativeness in and of the world.

The Sāṅkhya-yoga philosophy indeed recognises self-becoming from within as the principle underlying all evolution. It advocates a 'first cause' for the world and its existential continuity with the effect. That which becomes and that into which something becomes are identified. Only this involves a 'bifurcation' of reality itself into two ultimates[2] ultimately disparate. We have *prakṛti* as the changing real which is independent, and co-eval with the unchanging *puruṣa*. It is non-intelligent but non-intelligence carries no implication of dependence on, and pervasion by, the intelligent spirit. It is real in its own right, self-contained and can well be termed Being itself. In the Yoga philosophy we have a slight modification of the theory. *Prakṛti* is in a sense dependent on an external agent at least for its evolution; the dependence is however negative. God only removes the barriers to the modification of *prakṛti* into its effect, but does not move it to action (*aprayojaka*)[3]. *Prakṛti* is the first cause of the world being dynamic in its own right, although its dynamism in the creation of the world is controlled negatively from without, by God.

Though the Sāṅkhya-yoga is an attempt to reach the inward in explaining change, the core possessing creative energy according to it, is a self-contained matter foreign to spirit. The Yoga corrective in the form of God's causal role remains an external occasioning factor. Does this not defeat the very purpose for which the notion of 'self-becoming' is employed to explain evolution? To attribute change and development to the intrinsic dynamism of matter sounds naturalistic. Matter is endowed with qualities which belong to spirit. These inadequate attempts emphasize the fact that, while the phenomenon of development has indeed to be explained with reference to an ultimate material cause, namely *that* which changes, the latter cannot have a separate, independent existence. The dynamism of development must be rooted in that of spirit.

The postulate of *māyā* and its significance for Śaiva Siddhānta may be best understood when viewed in the light of these requirements. In Śaiva Siddhānta *māyā* represents the first cause but only as an expression of God's will. *Māyā* is neither independent nor dynamic in its own capacity and is therefore *asat* in character. It is the assumptive power (*parigraha-śakti*) of God. Its evolution into the world as well as its very being is inconceivable without *śakti* which is its ground. *Māyā* itself is a kind of *śakti* of the Lord. The use of the notion of *śakti* with reference to *māyā* is quite significant. The term *śakti* does not necessarily imply co-inherence (*samavedya*) with spirit. Irrespective of whether it is inherent in spirit or not it certainly implies ontological dependence on spirit (*śaktimattantratva*).[3a] The being of *śakti* consists of its being under the autonomy of *śaktimat*.

Admission of *māyā* as *śakti* of God amounts to a rejection of metaphysical dualism. Though *māyā* and *Śiva* are distinguished, and distinguished sharply as non-intelligent and intelligent respectively they are not dual as subject and object where the existence of each is said to be independent of the other. Recognition of *māyā* as *śakti* implies that the nature of the object is understood with necessary reference to spirit (*cit*) while spirit is understood to be intelligible by itself and therefore in free relation with the object. The Sāṅkhya-yoga also, admits that the nature of the object consists of its being *for* spirit, its manifestness is to the self[4] but Śaiva Siddhānta appropriates its very existence and function to the existence and function of spirit. Agency (*kartṛtva*) with which knowership (*jñātṛtva*)[5] is identical may be attributed to *māyā*[6] but only in a secondary, derivative sense.[7] The manifestness of matter as well as its very existence is comprehended 'non-dualistically' in that of spirit. The relation between God and *māyā* is that of will and the content freely intended by the will. There is continuity between the two[8] unlike the case of knowledge and the known. The relation between God and *māyā* is more like that of an agent's will and what it wills unalienably into being, rather than that of a subject in relation to an object confronting it from without.

Willing as a mode of attending to the object, must be distinguished from knowing.[9] In knowing, the object is independent of knowing and even may be said to exist without being known actually or even possibly, while in willing the reverse seems to be the case. Willing is a mode of consciousness which is prior to its content, determining the latter regarding its very existence and function. The content exists under the form of eternity but only as the content of will, is not a fact already determined for the will but a contingency which is being determined by the willing and therefore as it were nothing apart from the willing. The world is not an existent fact which God confronts, but is one about which there is on the one hand, consciousness of freedom in bringing it to pass and on the other, in abstaining from doing so. *Māyā* is not an accomplished fact which God *knows* and fashions; it is his freely assumed *śakti*.

In the hierarchy of agencies beginning for example with the potter's at one end, an advance is implied here regarding the possession of freedom and knowledge characteristic of the function of agency at the other end of the scale. Ananta[10], the representative agent of cosmic functions, may be said to approximate and typify infinite knowledge and freedom (as the name suggests).[11] Ananta however remains a representative *paśu* and shares the inherent limitations of finite agency. *Śiva* who is the ultimate *causative* agent effects a disturbance in the equilibrium (*kṣobha*) of *māyā through* the agency of Ananta; the latter under the stress of Divine will, disturbs the condition of *māyā* and evolves *kalā-tattva* and so on. Such an agency, finite as it is, can be exercised only by an embodied agent. The account that the Saivāgamas give of Ananta's instrumentality (will) affecting *māya* naturally sounds dualistic; the agent embodied and determinate, contingent in knowledge and action, work on a pre-existing *māyā*. Causal action here means a determinately conscious relation of the agent with the object to which his action relates. So far it is not different from the instance of the potter producing pot from the pre-existing clay-material.[12]

But in the case of Śiva's direct agency (*sākṣāt kartṛtva*) in relation to the pure realm (*śuddhādhvan*)[13] which encompasses and exceeds the realm presided over by Ananta, *bindu* (the pure counterpart of *māyā*) undergoes modification under the immediate stress of *cit-śakti*. *Cit-śakti* pervades *bindu* as its ground. The action of *cit-śakti* upon *bindu* is not a contingent event, but in a sense, constant. Though the language of 'disturbing of equilibrium' (*kṣobha*) is still employed[14] in analogy with Ananta's agency, *Śiva* as the agent and *śakti* as the instrument eternally pervade *bindu* the material cause. Being eternally pervaded by *śakti* which stirs it into action, *bindu* and its first evolute, *nāda*, are only logically successive but factually simultaneous. The distinction between *bindu* in its essence and *bindu* in its stirred (*kṣobhya*), awakened condition is an ideal distinction. To anticipate in brief an exposition given in greater detail below: The *kalās* which include *tattvas* and *bhuvanas* as well the three stadia of *śabda*, namely *mantra*, *pada*, and *varṇa* evolve from the stirred material cause but only as reflexes, as indeed the obverse and the reverse sides of the 'changes of states' *laya*, *bhoga* and *adhikāra* symbolically attributed to *śakti*. The evolutes and extensions of *bindu* are named after the underlying functionaries which are only aspects of *cit-śakti*. While these states (*avasthās*) are symbolic, not literal when applied to spirit which is immutable, the ensuing 'modifications' in *bindu* are however literal. The names of the 'evolutes' of *bindu* are identical with the respective names of the functional differentiation of spirit which underlies *bindu*. *Śiva*, *śakti*, *sadāśiva*, *maheśvara* and *śuddha vidyā* are primarily the names of the functional aspects of the Agent, and by transference also the names of the five *śiva-tattvas* which are 'evolutes' of *bindu*.[15]

Śiva's instrumentality (will) affects *bindu* as the self affects the existence and movement of body. Causal action is not the relation of subject and object but an act of free creation unhampered by the existence of an intractable 'other'. *Bindu* and *māyā* are the powers which create the world but essentially as 'one' with the Divine will that is the 'home' of the conditions of the possibility of the world. The will underlies existence in its possible and actual forms. Though *bindu* or *māyā* is admitted technically as the transforming cause of the world, Divine will, directly or otherwise is the 'fulcrum'[16] of that cause even in its unevolved condition, and the dynamism characteristic of its evolution is but the 'exteriorisation' or concretisation of the dynamic will. God unmoved is the Supreme mover, in Himself giving the impulse to all movement. Matter is not a principle of externality, that which spirit has not been able to quicken and transform. Matter does not stand in front of Him, 'outside' Him as His 'other', but constitutes a unity with Him in a special way. The state of being in 'union' with matter is an eternally accomplished state of the Divine will. It does not occur in evolution at a stage but is the very presupposition of evolution. There was never a moment when Lord had to *become* the Lord of *māyā*. The two exist together, in one another, one comprehended in the being of the other.[17]

Matter is not a 'given' to spirit. The latter does not have to 'know' it by becoming acquainted with it. God's 'knowledge' of the material cause (*upādāna kāraṇa*) is the eternal link which sustains the latter's very life and existence. What may be called 'knowledge *of*' in relation to an object existing prior to knowledge and conditioning it is not the knowledge which God may be said to have of material existence. In His case it is not a knowledge of what is 'other' and what is 'prior' to the act of knowledge.[18] It is indeed part of knowledge of God about Himself as the 'whole filling the whole'[19] limited by nothing, mediated by nothing.

In the words of a text, the paradox of creation is: God who is the prius (*munnavan*)[20] creates everything out of the non-intelligent (*māyā*) but the latter assumes no priority over or even parity with Him. There is strictly no parity of existence or function between the material cause and the agent. The agent is the Prior one whose initiative and freedom to create and unfold the world out of the world's material cause antecedes the material cause itself. The agent is indeed prior to it, eternally conditioning its existence freely unfolding everything out of it as freely as out of Himself. And yet *māyā* as the eternal content of willing is distinct from the act of willing itself. The supremacy that is implied by being the cause of the world does not derive from the material cause which is permitted to transform into its effect by its Agent-ground. Instead the value and role of material cause derives from the Agent-ground.[21]

It may be said that Śaiva Siddhānta adopts a dynamist theory of matter in recognising that *māyā* is an assumptive power (*parigraha-śakti*) of God.

Material reality is not a substance confronting spirit but a process and a potentiality which is being actualised into creation of sense qualities, and psychic functions on the one side and acts of attraction and repulsion on the other.[22] One and the same agent is the activating source of the 'mental' process (desire to produce a pot) and also of a 'material' process (fashioning of the pot). An agent is an ideal super-spatial super-temporal entity and as such transcends the distinction between mental and material process. Will is itself neither a continuant in space (physical) nor an occurrent in time (mental), but neither the continuant nor the occurrent is possible, much less actual, apart from it.[23]

Rejection of *māyā-vāda*[24]

According to *māyā-vāda*, the absolute alone is real and free from all objectivity and duality and therefore the world with its multiplicity and division cannot be merged with or included in the Absolute. The world utterly different from *Brahman* cannot therefore be real but only appearance. Our perception of the world is an illusion.

Ignorance is lack of knowledge of the real object, and also a positive attribution or projection of something else in the place of the real object. The illusory object is not made up of real constituents; it is an effect of ignorance itself. Consequently the world is literally of the stuff or substance of ignorance and as long as ignorance is operative the illusion of the world also persists. The world is indeed 'something' but that which 'disappears' at the mere touch of knowledge.

The ultimate principle of cosmology according to *māyā-vāda* is the principle of cosmic illusion — *māyā*. Every fact or event in the world, physical and mental is a mode of *māyā*. The character and constitution of the world subjective and objective have to be defined by reference to this principle of illusion.

Two main arguments are advanced[25] for the view that underlies advaitic 'cosmology', namely the view that *māyā* in the sense of cosmic illusion is the source and stuff of the world and because it is not reality, the world too, its effect, shares with it the character of unreality. Therefore there is really no *valid* means of knowing a world of difference despite one's faith in its existence. Neither perception nor reason nor, revelation is evidence, in a strict sense, of the reality of such world. Perception, strictly, can vouch as evidence only what is co-terminously present not a world of which one can say that it has been real or that it will continue to be real in the future. Real in the sense of being uncontradicted in past and futute alike as well as in the present, the world's 'reality' is only a fiction. Inductive reason — the question of deductively proving the empirical world not arising, also fails being dependent upon perception for standing on its feet. So there is *no valid means* of knowing the world of difference and consequently presumably no world of difference for there to be known.[26]

One may however argue: It may be that from the very complex nature of the case of a 'world' as such that it defies our understanding of it as 'object' of knowledge (*prameya*). Not that there is no world. In answer to this objection it is further argued that by no conceivable relation can such 'world' be rendered intelligible to one's understanding. That is to say, even were the perceived world of difference 'validly' perceived and perception thereof is valid perception, not misperception, there is no way of intelligibly relating such valid knowledge (*pramiti*) with the object alleged to be validly perceived namely the world (*prameya*).

Absence of a validating means of knowledge (*pramāṇa*) and absence of any recognised relation (*saṁbandha*) between a knowledge of the world and the 'world' itself are the dialectical grounds for viewing the world of difference which we happen to perceive an appearance only (*mithyā*). The originating source of the appearance namely *māyā* is also, therefore, only appearance, not reality.[27]

On neither of these grounds,[28] however, Śaiva Siddhānta is prepared to concede that the world is only appearance. Perception is valid evidence of the world of difference and arguments and scriptural evidence against it is not univocal.[29] Regarding the relation of valid knowledge of the world (*pramiti*) and the world validly known (*prameya*) it has been argued that the relation can be neither of identity (*tādātmya*) nor of cause-effect relation or conjunction or inherence or any other conceivable relation. It cannot be identity because pot and knowledge of pot belong respectively to the spheres of the object and of the subject. Neither can it be a species of causal relation. When cause is present the effect cannot be unavailable and *vice versa*, but in the case of knowledge we have knowledge without the corresponding object as for example in dreams, and also object without its being necessarily known. Conjunction and inherence too imply invariable co-presence of the two terms of the relation. The relation cannot also be the relation of knowledge and the known considered as ultimate and indefinable for the 'known content' (*viṣaya*) remains for ever indeterminable all our knowledge of it being only *qua* the known. In reply to this dialectic of relation, Śaiva Siddhānta holds that the relation of knowledge and the known[30] is indeed *sui generis* and should be acceptable even to the opponent. For example, the knowledge that the world is illusory and its content are not certainly unrelated. As for the objection that the content remains undefined being unknown except as the content of knowledge, it may be replied that content may be defined precisely as that which becomes manifest in corresponding to a particular event of conscious state occurring in the mental history of an individual.

Does *māyā* delude ?

The world of manifoldness is not illusory, in its manifest or non-manifest forms. It is 'public' reality not a private idea in the mind.[31] It is 'object' of valid experiential knowledge as such free from being contradicted. Not being spirit it is not itself a value, but it exemplifies all values of spirit and serves as a lamp unto the way of one blinded by darkness and a vehicle for ascending to a life of spirit. It is the supreme antidote provided by the gracious Lord to counteract the effects of the congenital Ignorance and Impurity of *mala*. It is an expression of Divine grace itself, though a disguised expression.[32]

But Divine grace as we have seen functions with a polarity of expression. It bewitches and lures by projecting the temporal process, letting it swell gigantically and usurp the mastery and the rule and letting it as it were to shut off from us the light of Heaven. Not the temporal process itself is delusive; it is 'gracious' in intention; without it no earthly persistence of human existence is conceivable. Time's hybris outstriding all measure is what is meant as the feature that bewitches. The demonic power here is what we in our blindness have ourselves rared, thanks to the connivance of God, overstriding the gracious aspect which lets things be.

Śaiva Siddhānta calls the material cause of the world, corporeal and incorporeal, of speech and of the spoken by the expressive word *māyā*. It has been asked whether denoting a real cosmic principle by the name of *māyā* is not historically an anomaly.[33] That it is not so can be seen if we keep in mind the polyvalence that the word enjoys without detriment to its sense of unity.[34] Principally the word *māyā* has two different senses: it implies art, an artifice, extra-ordinary power, power of making wonders. It is a noun from the root *mā* which means 'to measure' or to lay out, and the word *māyā* thus derived suggests a measuring, formative consciousness. The word also implies cunning, artfulness, deceit, fraud or enchantment. Śaiva Siddhānta takes it in the first sense.[35] By *māyā* is meant power or energy which has possibility of developing as a free determination of will in which its being is rooted. The second sense of the term *māyā* signifying, 'cunning' also is implicit in the concept of development of *māyā* as material cause in so far as it is a development or unfoldment of something consequent on *veiling* the true nature of spirit. Spirit wilfully loses itself in the appearance of multiplicity and in the operation of a law governing the discordant rhythm of pleasure, pain and delusion. *Māyā* is also a *mala*,[36] a form of impurity by association with which the self is ultimately freed of its connate Impurity. *Māyā* is the principle which 'deludes' the individual subject to the law of *karma*; the delusion which confounds self with not-self is the contributory cause of enjoyment (*bhoga*) and *māyā* by means of its material evolutes occasions the illusion (*moha*) of eternity, purity and blissfulness which are qualities of self in the non-eternal, impure and painful not-self.[37] In one sense, *māyā*-evolutes serve to partially unveil the *mala*-veiled self by facilitating a manifestation of the three-fold aspects of consciousness, namely 'knowledge, will and action'. In another sense it 'deludes' consciousness by its very formative structure, constricting and limiting consciousness' sweep by its very provision of the senses of the body, the world and objects of enjoyment. Thus it contributes to the experience of sorrow and misery by helping to articulate the law of *karma*.[38]

Māyā is pre-eminently non-intelligent (*jaḍa*). Itself non-intelligent, 'blind', it serves not only as the cause of the being of things but also as the cause of one's knowledge of phenomenal existence. It is the cause of the word and its meaning. It is the source of all worlds and their constituents, of all corporeal forms and their sensori-motor equipments which facilitate knowledge and action, and of all revelations of knowledge articulate and inarticulate, and yet it is 'blind'.[39] To this blind, material cause of Creation Śaiva Siddhānta adds another blind principle, that is *karma* which is the 'auxiliary' cause. The admission of these 'blind' causal principles which nevertheless are comprehended under intelligent *śakti* suggests the idea that the creative principle operates as it were with its face hidden. Creative operation involves self-concealment while its 'opposite', namely, the operation of recovery is self-revelation. Creation is part of 'natural' willing; God, who wills does not say 'I am creating' but wills to the effect 'let this be done' (*idam ittham bhavet*). *Māyā* the creative principle like the cognate one of *karma* is consequently 'blind'. When God wills to abstain from this natural willing, when in other words the cosmic process is reversed, the 'blind' principle is no longer blind. *Māyā* is *jaḍa* in the context of 'natural' freedom and *cit*[40] in the context of spiritual freedom.[41] The reflecting medium of spirit at work as the cause of the cosmic operations is opaque, not transparent and the 'blindness' or darkness of the cosmic principles of *māyā* and *karma* is but part of the 'opacity' of spirit. When the latter is perceived as Grace as such, in its transparent self-effulgence, *māyā* and *karma* too cease to be dark but become translucent.[42]

The element of wonder and inscrutability in the notion of *māyā* also deserves attention. *Māyā* is an 'identity of opposites'.[43] It is eternal (*nitya*) as the conserving material cause of the world and yet its various forms 'rise' and 'perish'. It is one numerically and yet it *constitutes*, each uniquely, multifarious bodies subtle and gross, worlds and objects. It is always invisible and formless and yet the 'home' of all visible forms; indeterminate and yet housing all determinations. It is the 'support' of the existence of *karma* and of its articulation, by providing the means and materia where-with the individual self ekes out the fruits of its past deeds, and at the same time it undergirds *karma* in the process. It is *acit* (non-intelligent) and yet it functions as a manifesting medium of knowledge like a lamp that pierces the encircling gloom of night. It is infinite and yet is finitised as respective body and so on.[44] The 'discordant' elements of *māyā* constitutive of its nature are, however, harmonised in the dynamics of Divine will which in its self-consistent nature as Grace adjusts all that is conflicting.[45] Even the polar functions of concealment and revelation, picturesquely described as the opacity and transparency of spirit, are at bottom one, like expressions of grace.[46] All opposites are exemplified by this polarity of functions in spirit and are therefore fundamentally of one essence.

Is *māyā* as a category of explanation dispensable ?

It can be readily granted that there is no causal efficiency conceivable in a material cause unpervaded by the will of an intelligent agent. What should be equally obvious is that the latter cannot be conceived to evolve the world out of nothing. The world can originate as little without a causal continuant which evolves as without spirit which makes evolution possible.[47] A tree can spring up as little without its seed as without the soil or the ground which is its support. A house can be erected as little without the bricks as without the earth's gravitation to support it.

It has been argued that this demand for a stable material cause of the world is not legitimate. The only evidence phenomenologically sound for the existence of objective reality is after all one's stream of cognitions out of which one cannot jump.[48] And as a flux, the constitutive stuff of which it is made cannot be anything but the void, or nothingness (*śūnya*). An enduring substantial entity is unthinkable as it cannot conceivably exert causal efficiency in succession or simultaneously. A mere stream of events in an objective (*kṣaṇika-vāda*) or in a subjective sense (*vijñāna-vāda*) also it cannot be, because of the felt discontinuity and disruption for the stream during sleep. The cosmic night (*mahā-suṣupti*) with which *māyā* is compared as the womb of all wakeful existence is therefore made of the stuff of *śūnya* (void). From nothing emerges the world and into nothing it resolves.[49]

The Śaiva absolutist who does not belive in the intrinsic objectivity of existence,[50] also opposes the argument for a material cause for phenomenal reality. Spirit manifests objective world in the manner of a yogin who, it is said, creates objects — city, army and so on,[51] without material causes. True, the yogin's creative activity is proverbially uncommon in that he creates by a fiat of his will without requiring material cause. But, if this is conceivable even exceptionally, from such uncommon instances, it will be plausible to conceive of the creation of the world without a material cause.

It cannot be argued that the yogin's creation is also due to a cause not different from what we consider to be responsible for ordinary everyday creations. It may be said that a pot made of gold differs but little from a clay pot *qua* effect produced from a material cause. But this need not be accepted. It is pointed out,[52] that after all the pot is not the outcome of its so-called material cause alone, as for example, atoms. On the contrary, without the intervening stages of the pot-halves, the accessories of movement of hands and feet, time *etc.*, the pot does not come into existence. There being so many things necessary for making a pot, does a yogin too create a pot by acquiring all that is necessary for the creation of the desired object? If he does, he would be no better than the potter himself. If he does not, that is, if he creates without these well-known intervening steps, then why at all think of atoms *etc.* to be the material cause? The world too like the creation of a yogin may well be a sheer manifestation of the will of God, the yogin *par excellence*. *Śruti* also says that God who is spirit manifests objects out of sheer will like a yogin, without a material cause.[53]

In reply to these objections it may be said, firstly, that it is not really conceivable how the world could resolve into nothing or evolve from nothing. Existence without *that* which exists which the theory of void signifies is contradictory. Causal efficiency which is the mark of the real is inconceivable without a permanent, substantial something. The discontinuity for the cognitive stream and for the object-series in deep sleep is not evidence of voidity of existence. Instead, variations in the objective—the palpable physical thing given to wakeful consciousness and the impalpable, sub-sensible world given to dream and sleep-consciousness, point to the reality of a material order as distinguished from the reality of the sphere of non-material, non-variant subject. A theory of pre-non-existent effect, of which *śūnya-vāda* is a variant, is untenable.[54]

The Śaiva absolutist's objection too is answerable. The substance of the objection is that while a 'becoming' without *that* which becomes, namely the material cause is not unplausible as may be seen in the instance of the yogin's creation, postulates of material cause like atoms are, on the contrary, notoriously destitute of any certainty. But in reply it may be said that the postulate of *māyā* unlike those of *paramāṇu*, and *prakṛti* as the material cause is 'accepted in faith' and acknowledged by thought.[55] Free causality of will does not mean exclusion of material causality as such but only of a material cause that stands over against it limiting its freedom as is the case in the instance of clay-material in relation to the potter. Where nothing has being of its own independent of intelligent will, where everything that is, is but a content (*vyāpya*) to one omnipresent will (*vyāpaka*) how can admission of *māyā* as the material cause make any difference to the freedom of the supreme Will? Instead of its obstructing its freedom, we may say that it serves to manifest it.[56] What is 'given' to will is not a given something; it is consumed by the will as a free means to itself as end. If it is not so consumed it has to be taken as an opposed will.[57] That is why Śaiva Siddhānta admits *māyā* as freedom and yet as intrinsically inert or inane (*jaḍa*) in rejection of pan-psychism.[58]

Analogies of creative imagination, dreaming ideation and the magical creation of the yogin are cited[59] to illustrate the spontaneity of will-causality not conforming to the known pattern of creation out of a pre-existent material. It is doubtful how far these illustrations can go to support a repudiation of the sequence of cause-effect relation. In creative imagination though things are produced spontaneously there is no production *ex nihilo*.[60] The creative ideas are perhaps, 'the stirring of a breath that comes from without'. In dreaming, obviously it is the latent impressions that manifest themselves. Even if it were a 'conscious dreaming' its freedom only means that it does not follow a preordained plan. In ideation too what is germinal in the depth of consciousness[61] rises to the conscious level.[62]

In the case of the creation of the yogin again for which the Śaiva absolutist holds special brief, it is not that the yogin has to create things 'out of nothing' in order to stand distinguished from say, a potter. The creations of the yogin in so far that they may be analysed intelligibly at all, are no exception to the rule of a cause-and-effect relation. They do not exemplify a counter principle that effect arises from what is not its assigned cause;[63] the pot which the yogin creates by his sheer will is presumably not identical with, but certainly is similar to the potter's jar. It is a product one may say although it may not have been produced from clay. Similarly it may not be argued that God's creation is like the yogin's , similar and yet different from all known instances of creation from some assignable material cause. There is no positive evidence to assert that cosmic creation is necessarily different from all instances of creative activity.[64] The notion of God's causality is put forward as an aid and not as a limit to our understanding of God's transcendent nature.[65] When it is denied that God creates the world from no material cause, by implication is also questioned the validity of such illustrations. A denial of God creating out of nothing implies a questioning of the validity of such illustrations as the yogins, alleged to be instances of creation without a material cause.[66]

It may be argued that the yogin's creations are *prima facie* non-different from other natural creations; they last till their purposes are served; they possess forms as are compatible with their essential nature.[67]

In what way do they differ from 'natural' effects of causes? It may be replied that to the extent they are not different, they are also like the 'natural' jar produced from their respective material causes. The text which says that God manifests the world without a material cause like a yogin[68] must not be understood as an assertion of creation *ex nihilo*;[69] it on the other hand refers by means of the significant analogy of the yogin, to the freedom of the creative will which consists in its unhindered spontaneity to unfold the phenomenal world out of its material cause as spontaneously as out of itself, thus differing in this respect from other known cases of an agent exercising causal efficiency through and in dependence on appropriate material causes.[70] God's raising of the world-crop without a seedling must also be likewise interpreted.[71]

Admission of *māyā* as the cosmic material cause rests also on a previous acceptance of *karma* and individual selves that are subject to its law.[72] The 'bearer' or support of *karma* as there must be one could be *māyā* alone. *Māyā* alone can be the material support for the existence and articulation of *karma* so that admission of *karma* will not be compatible with non-admission of *māyā*. That *māyā* alone can be the material support of *karma* may be shown in the following manner. The deed itself cannot be the bearer of *karma* because it is seen to perish as the deed is done. Nor can it be the doer,[73] intelligent as he is, plausible though it seems that the doer here and in the hereafter being identicale, his present deeds may leave their impressions in him so that in the hereafter they may unfold themselves therefrom. Nor may it be objected that deed and consequence of deed being of the nature of cause and effect must obtain in the same locus; *māyā* and self the doer are heterogeneous. According to the law of deed and its consequence, consequences of one's deeds residing with the doer but benefitting another person, and similarly such consequences residing in some other locus but benefitting the doer of deeds of which they are consequence, are both plausible. We have an instance of the first kind in the *śrāddha* ceremony where the merits of the deeds of one generation are said to be yicariously acquired by another generation. The merits accruing from the *śrāddha* rites performed by the son while residing with the son are said to benefit his parent and similarly the rites done by the father reside with him and benefit the deceased son. As an instance of the second kind we have the commonplace case of soil-cultivation The fruits of cultivation inhering in the locus of the field cultivated benefit the cultivator. Even as the fruits of the labours of tilling the soil lie and arise not from the tiller but the soil tilled, the fruits of *karma* have as their support not the doer but *māyā*. Again, the one which stands in the relation of a support to *karma* must be like *karma* itself inert, non-intelligent. Moreover, how does the law of *karma* operate in the case of an individual self ? The corporeal form, sensory-motor equipment, natural environment—these are the channels through which operates the law of deed and consequence, and these are evolutes of *māyā*. If *māyā* does not evolve into appropriate 'means' and 'objects' of enjoyment for the self, *karma* cannot be conceived to operate. From this too it follows that *māyā* is the supporting medium of *karma*[71].

IX

DOCTRINE OF THIRTY-SIX TATTVAS

The concept of *Bindu* : Evolution of Siva Tattvas

The need to postulate 'pure' *māyā* (*bindu*) arises because of the following considerations. God as Agent who performs cosmic functions is pure spirit, immutable and His direct instrumentality cannot be in relation to the 'impure' realm of *māyā* where impurity derives from the presence of *mala* and *karma* and consequently entails pleasure as well as pain, knowledge as well as ignorance, for selves under its sway. The 'material' principle which, śiva as the Agent and *śakti* as the Instrument, pervade and quicken must approximate to spirit in its transparency, unlike the material principle involved in the case of non-divine agents like Ananta. The 'material' cause which Śiva's instrumentality (Will) affects non-dualistically, as one's will affects one's body, must necessarily be different in quality from material causes operated upon by finite will-causalities.

Divine will initiates the cosmic process by freely undergoing certain processes spoken of as theogonic states (*avasthās*), such as *adhikāra*, *bhoga* and *laya* and this is intelligible only with reference to the presence of an adjunct in the immutable Will (*śakti*). The three 'archetypal' cosmic processes are distinguishable in terms only of differences in the adjunct. The latter, however, must be real difference in contrast to which the Divine 'processes' may be understood as symbolic. The adjunct of Spirit must, in other words, be material though of an attenuated kind. Such is *bindu*. In *bindu* we distinguish threefold processes that the creative Will undergoes as it creates. When *bindu* is in a state of readiness to evolve awaiting the 'quickening' of the will which underlies its existence as its ground, the state is of *bhoga* for the Divine will. When *bindu* is 'quickened' and brings to pass its effect, it is *adhikāra* for the will. Will is conceived as executing its authority. When *bindu* is in its causal unmanifest form with all its effect retracted it is *laya* for the will, that is, will devoid of any operation.

The Pure Realm (*śuddhādhvan*) of which *bindu* is the causal form must be conceived as a universe of experience consisting of planes of life and consciousness analogous to our own. By *bhuvanas*, as they are called, are meant the abodes of beings endowed with corporeal bodies and senses made of the substance the materiality of which corresponds to the degree of their perfection.[2] The most perfect beings mature with regard to their impurity in all but one sense for which they have to await their saving illumination till the beginning of the next aeon. They serve by virtue of the *adhikāra-mala* still left in them as agent-instruments in the performance of the five-fold cosmic functions of the Lord[3] in the Impure realm (*aśuddhādhvan*). A 'Pure' material cause is required to serve as the stuff of the materiality of the body, senses, world and objects of the world for enjoyment commensurate with the spiritual perfection of these souls. *Māyā* cannot serve this purpose because it is awaiting to be stirred or quickened to evolve the 'impure' realm from *kalā* to *pṛthvī* by one of the above mentioned agentinstruments, Ananta.

The universe of *māyā* is impure as well as inert; it is also a source of delusion (*moha*) and pain (*duḥkha*); in association with the triple *malas* which provide worlds bodies and so on for souls bound by them it serves as the vehicle for (i) the bond which creates the delusion of self in what is not self (*māyīya*), (ii) the bond which is of the form of desire and creates the cycle of pleasure-pain-torpid experiences (*karma*) and (iii) the bond that is of the form of finitude (*paśutva*) veiling souls from eternity. It is, again, as a consequence of its association with the three *malas*, indifferently the 'object' of experience (*bhogya*) of all souls alike; it is lastly, what undergoes evolution (*pariṇāma*) and is subject to the vicissitudes of change.[4]

Māyā cannot come under the immediate stress of the Pure will of Śiva. The Impure realm of *māyā* is encompassed by a super-principle of matter and is again subject to mutations. It therefore, points to an agent who is under the command of an agent above him. A corporeal agent who has determinate knowledge and exerts causal agency externally to the matter that he wields.[5] Just as gold in becoming a crown points to a goldsmith that makes the crown to order, *māyā* points to an agent who exercises his agency necessarily at another's behest.[6] *Māyā*, in other words, is 'object' of determination, and fashioned by a corporeal agent as clay is fashioned by a potter with hands and feet. What follows from this is the need for the admission of a material source for energises *māyā* into evolution. It must be *prior* to *māyā*, as it is inconceivable that the agent energising it is already provided with body and also with the ingredients of determinate knowledge by which he initiates action. Such is *bindu*. *Bindu* provides the corporeality for the will that creates the Impure realm and evolves the word-form (*śabda*) of the will to constitute its determinancy.[7]

Another argument for *bindu* is: the 'knowledge' of individual self admits of variations.[8] Some are of very limited understanding; others are exceptionally discerning. Self is admitted to be spirit, eternal, immutable, and self's consciousness (*cit-śakti*) too, must be free from mutability. Substance and its attributes are non-different. But how are we to reconcile this with the phenomena of growth and decay, expansion and contraction in the empirical knowledge of the individual self? Surely such modifications cannot *inhere* in the self.[9] Self is spirit. They must be due to an adjunct which serves as the seed of knowledge signified by words at the empirical level.[10] The variety of forms of knowledge are the forms of this adjunct so that though in one sense it may be looked upon as a limiting condition it may be viewed more correctly as what negatively serves to preserve the eternality and the immutability of self.[11] The adjunct cannot be *karma* for *karma* introduces difference in empirical experiences *vis-a-vis* the material accessories of tattvas and *bhuvanas*. *Karma* accounts for *bhoga* but variety in the latter is occasioned by the variety of accessories, just as it does not also *allocate* the experience of its fruits to the respective agents. The adjunct which accounts for the phenomenal variety of knolwledge, therefore is not *karma* but that through which *karma* brings about inequalities in experience. Such is then *bindu* or more correctly an evolute of *bindu* (*nāda*) diverse like the diverse selves conditioning in each the occurrence of empirical knowledge.[12]

Indeed not only as a requirement for the determinate knowledge of Ananta, and in general, as the constituting condition of individuality and variety in human knowledge but even more generally, for everybody's knowledge, *bindu* or *nāda* is required as the 'cause'—the *cause cognoscendi* (*jñāpaka-hetu*).[13] It is accepted by the generality of thinkers that all determinate knowledge through universals is interpenetrated with words. Determinancy in knowledge free from word-association is impossible. Knowledge and the word are co-extensive. The latter is the light and life of all 'living' knowledge. Now by word we mean the word-form and not the overt sound. Equating word (*varṇa*) with *overt* sound (*dhvani*) will rob the word of its distinction, namely possession of meaning. Sound is the physical vesture of word, its manifestor (*vyañjaka*), while the word is what is manifested (*vyaṅgya*).[14] The word is the cause of inner speech, a kind of inner voice as it were which arouses the consciousness of meaning. External articulate sounds are only a vesture for it. It is also physical like the overt sound[15] but is pregnant with meaning which may be said to be immanent in the form of intention. It is what underlies communication. Setting up in the hearer an identical arousal of meaning like the vibration of a violin by another similarly strung. The causal source of this *nāda*, structured as many and material, is *bindu*.

Bindu is conceivable as the causal source of two parallel but interdependent lines of evolution, that of word (*śabda*) and of meaning (*artha*) intended by the word. The realm of *śabda* subsists in dependence on the realm of meaning in so far as *śabda* has no significance other than the symbolic.[16] Like the universe of Pure Realm (*śuddhādhvan*) emanating from *bindu*, the world of *śabda* too is 'pure' due to dissociation from *mala* and *karma*[17]. Both are sources of happiness unmixed with sorrow. The two orders of evolution, therefore, proceed from one identical substrate which, therefore is looked upon as a complex of causal potencies productive (*kāraka-śaktis*) as well as informative (*jñāpaka-śaktis*). The productive causal potencies evolve into the sphere of meaning and the information into the sphere of words.

It may be objected here that while Pure Creation is essentially supersensuous, its different tattvas and their *bhuvanas* being very subtle and the residents thereof being supernatural beings, the sphere of *śabda* which also is said to be part of Pure Creation, is not super-sensuous in nature. The letter-sounds are audible to the hearer, otherwise according to the theory the sense of the meaning cannot be produced in him. In reply it may be said that the letter-sound or *vāc* as it is called is in essence super-sensuous but because of adjuncts becomes audible as the articulated sound. In the sphere of *śuddhādhvan* (Pure Realm) it remains through all its ramifications 'subtle' like the *śuddha-tattvas*. In the sphere of *miśrādhvan* (Mixed Realm) because of association with the adjunct of physical sound it becomes gross and in the sphere of *aśuddhādhvan* (Impure Realm) grosser still as the differentiated articulate sound is manifested with the help of the vocal argans.[18]

Evolution of the speech-world

The evolution of the speech-world (*śabda-prapañca*) can become intelligible if we understand it in its reverse order. The order of progression is from the external, overt gross speech-sound to the Transcendental Silence of Pure speech. We have accordingly three stages, the first where it is gross sound (*sthūla-nāda*) produced by the help of physical elements like ether and air and audible to the ear; the second where speech becomes incipient and indistinct as the contents of a peahen's egg contains within itself the colours of the peacock in their sequence but indistinctly and at the same time potent with thought or discursiveness and lastly the stage where it is devoid even of discursiveness and is the ultimate cause of all objective knowledge and is present in every form of life as the determinant of consciousness and means of communication.[19] This is Pure Speech in relation to its externalised forms and is called *nāda* or *sūkṣma-nāda*,[20] the intermediary form is *bindu* or *akṣara-bindu*,[21] and the gross form is *varṇa*.

The problem of the evolution of the speech-world is at bottom the problem of distinguishing different levels of language.[22] And always the frame of reference from which such distinctions and gradations are made is the finite self *for whom* language is. It is with reference to the condition of finitude that we understand all evolution. The different stadia in the evolution of the universe of speech account for 'differences' of knowledge, in depth and in amplitude, and individual beings are broadly classed in the light of these differences under three categories.[23] But for a progressive association of speech in its different levels no knowledge is possible for all the categories of beings.[24] Speech of the overt, articulate sound-form, of a form which is inarticulate but differentiated, of a form which is undifferentiated as well as inarticulate and yet relatively gross and finally of a form which is subtle as well as undifferentiated and inarticulate — these form the hierarchy of levels of speech, spelling 'bondage' in varying degrees to the individual beings[25] through differences in the arousal of meaning. For spiritual attainment there is the urge to advance and ascend from the phenomenal diversity and division to transcendent unity, although the goal of such an urge clearly falls outside the sphere of speech.[26]

Vaikharī is the speech-form in which the letter-sounds already differentiated become manifestly pronounced as letters of the alphabet in their various combinations through suitable aids become audible to the hearer. This is the word used as the articulate symbol. It is a commonplace that symbols require as a basic condition of their functioning that they be understood by the listener. The *vaikharī* in being the word capable of denoting meaning evokes in the listener the same sense. That which is the denoting capacity in the *vaikharī* evokes in the hearer the same capacity and through that the sense of the meaning intended.[27] It is thus of greatest assistance, in that it makes communicability the soul of a language, possible.

Another interesting thing to note about *vaikharī vāc* is the role played by the ideo-motor force of vital-air (*prāṇa-vāyu*) in the process of its outwardization.[28] It was observed that pure sound becomes differentiated and also articulated through suitable physical agencies. The inner sound (*dhvani*) becomes assembled into internally differentiated letter sounds by the functioning of *udāna-vāyu*. However, in order to become articulate it requires an additional impulsion which should be equal to outwardizing it and rendering it audible to others. The teeth, lips, tongue and palate are there to give its shape and form but the main impulse to outwardization must come from some inner force similar to and yet different from *udāna-vāyu* which is adequate for manifesting the unmanifest letter-sounds but not for dispersing them overtly and making them articulate. This is done by *prāṇa-vāyu*. It may be noted that the real motive force behind ideation as well as articulation is the ego-sense (*ahaṁkāra*) under whose resolve the different bio-motor forces control the life of the body. What is specially significant here is that the unerring, determinate character of the knowledge due to *vaikharī* derives from the fact that the vital air responsible for its articulation is activised, not by the doubting aspect of mind, *manas*, but by its determining aspect, *ahaṁkāra*. Determination, indeed the function of *buddhi* arises solely through a subjective resolve provided by the ego-sense.

In relation to *vaikharī* all other levels of speech may be described as transcendental. While *vaikharī* is empirically perceivable, *madhyamā* and those beyond it are implicit and are to be understood by transcendental reflection. There must be a level of speech preceding articulation but succeeding the stage of homogeneous non-diversified sound-content. To put it in terms of the resulting knowledge it is what stands intermediary to indeterminate knowledge on one side and the fully determinate articulate thinking on the other. More positively, it is the implicit speech-form causing determinate knowledge to the speaker in whom it is manifest sub-vocally. The connection between the word and meaning is midway between a level where it is indistinct and the level where it is differentiated. As it is prior to the operation of vital air it remains inarticulate but it represents to intellect the object intended assuming as it does, the form of a subjectively contemplated combination of letters. What helps in the process of 'inward' combination is the *udāna-vāyu*. While *prāṇa-vāyu* facilitates articulation by pushing the sound complex from the larynx to the mouth where the tongue and palate mould it, *udāna-vāyu* facilitates differentiation by raising it from the lungs to the larynx.[29]

Paśyantī is the speech-form with the impulsion to concretise into the overt and the empirical. The stage of differentiated letter-sounds points as its cause to *paśyantī* (literally, 'looking for') where letter-sounds are present in their order but without distinctions. The yolk of the egg which conceals within it the different colours of the peacock is the usual example cited. Another example is sunlight containing unmanifestly within itself the entire colour spectrum. In all these examples it may be noted that differentiation is implicit in the sense that all the different elements along with the *pattern* of their differentiation are implicitly contained in this level of speech. *Paśyantī vāc* contains in itself in an undifferentiated subtle condition all the letter-sounds in the order in which they are analysed and synthesised under the impact of *udāna* at the larynx. Though undifferentiated, *paśyantī* is self-luminous;[30] its denoting capacity takes the form of an indeterminate thought-form. All determinate knowledge presupposes an indeterminate awareness which is due to the functioning of *paśyantī*. From this it follows that indeterminate knowledge, the awareness of the bare 'that' does not represent a level of knowledge where determination of the 'what' is absent. The name, class, quality of a known content constituting the 'what' of the knowledge are revealed implicitly in the revelation of its bare 'that'.

The *parā* or the *sūkṣmā vāc* is the ultimate source of the denoting capacity of speech. This is *nāda*. It is the prius of all discursiveness. If *paśyantī* is the cause of determinate knowledge (*nirvikalpaka-jñāna*), *parā* is the source of knowledge as such (*bodha*) without regard to determinancy or its absence. The difference between the two corresponds to the difference between the possible and the actual. Nor may it be thought that as prior to *madhyamā* which stands for determinate knowledge, either of *parā* or *paśyantī* would do to represent the stage of indeterminate knowledge and that to have both, one in turn the cause of the other is prolixity. The principle underlying the concept of 'pre-existent effect' which is throughout adopted in the account of evolution is: the manifestly differentiated elements of the effect could be conceived to be latent in the cause as a possibility but only through an intermediary stage where these differentiated elements are first actualised at an ideal level, that is unmanifestly.[31] This naturally follows from viewing the theory of pre-existent effect (*satkārya-vāda*) as but the reverse side of will-causality. The will holds within itself its content always as a possibility and its exteriorisation into the overt and the empirical is mediated by a stage marked by the impulsion to concretise.

Parā vāc or *nāda* is the highest aspect of speech-form; it is what possesses unconditionally and ultimately capacity of denotation. It is highest in the sense that it is higher than and therefore different from *paśyantī*.[32] It may be said to be eternal in the sense that it is ever manifest in the individual as a general condition of intelligibility even when all its more concrete modifications remain unmanifest.[33] It is what is present even during deep sleep. It is also said to be the light within.[34] It is said to be the 'self' itself because of its proximity by virtue of its inwardness to self.[35] It is peculiar to each individual being constitutive of his individuality in knowledge, and therefore not eternal; being non-intelligent in itself, it remains only a product. To be more precise we can say that *parā vāc* forms the nexus between *bindu*, the eternal substratum of speech, and its perishable manifestations. Viewed as a product of *bindu* or *bindu* in its quickened state, *parā* is non-eternal being many present in each, having its locus in each inmost body (*para-śarīra*), and it is material *qua* a product. *Parā* is *bindu* itself come to be endowed with a competence (*adhikāra*) to unfold into *paśyantī* and occasion knowledge in different degrees of determinancy. It is this *adhikāra* that is perishable.[36] In itself *qua bindu* when it is not as such related to the individual, and therefore unitary, it is eternal. It resembles *śiva*, the first of the thirty-six tattvas in this respect.

Theory of *nāda*

Nāda is what accounts for intelligibility independent of the conditions of person, time, space etc.[37] It is the cause of the expressiveness of all knowing, propositional or otherwise and as such, is not to be identified with propositions. It is what makes propositions possible. It is the transcendental condition of the categorising function of the mind.[38] It is the living 'voice' in forms of life as an incipient motivation for response which in the case of the human beings translates itself into the categorised expression of the mind. This is intelligible if one considers the truth that expression or communication is part of life process itself. Life indeed reduces to the medium through which we communicate.

If *nāda* cannot be identified with the categories of human understanding, still less can it be identified with its vocal expressions, namely sentence, word or letter or the unity of letters. It is what makes use of these in the service of knowledge.[39] If these are spoken of sometimes as generators of meaning, it is only in the sense that they serve to manifest *nāda*, which alone possesses absolutely the capacity to denote meaning. The *Parākhya-Āgama*, for example, says that it is the last letter of a word with the revived residual impressions of the preceding letters that is expressive of meaning.[40] If by this were meant as Nyāya would say, that literally, the accumulated impressions of the past letters roused in memory convey meaning,[41] this is untenable because the revived residual impressions can arouse only the memory of something that was previously known, and not the knowledge of a new thing.[42] Nor can it be in the sense that it manifests what is a unity of all letters and is itself unperceived, eternal and partless. The first letter, it is held, rouses this latent symbol in the mind vaguely and the succeeding letters as they are gradually heard, manifest it more clearly till the last letter fully reveals it. This view too is not tenable because here again the old objection arises, namely that residual impressions can arouse only a memory of what was experienced, and cannot present to consciousness what is yet to be experienced. Again, this perceived unity of letters which is said to possess the denotive capacity is intelligible neither as identical with the letters, whose unity it is said to be nor different from them.[43] If identical with the letters, it cannot perform a task which the letters as such are incapable of performing. If different, when perception is *ex hypothesi* evidence that the unity of the letters is not different from the letters themselves, an inference to the contrary can really be of no avail.

The statement of the *Āgama* cited above should, therefore, be understood to mean, that *by manifesting nāda*, is meaning generated. The last letter of a word in being the manifestor of *nāda* is eulogised as the manifestor of meaning. The *varṇa* of the *varṇa* theorists, and the *sphota* of the *sphoṭavādins* are admissible as generators of meaning, only as manifestors of *nāda*.

Rejection of *śabdabrahma-vāda*[44]

The Śaiva Siddhānta view of the relation of word (*śabda*) and meaning (*artha*) is that word is a means for the understanding of the meaning, just as a lamp lights and locates the things shrouded in darkness. *Śabda* is not eternal and its function is strictly contingent on *artha*. Without the latter it has no *raison de etre*. Speech does not figure separately as a factor of illumination of self's knowledge but is always implied by the mention of the factor of *artha*.[45]

On a different view, namely according to the absolutistic philosophy of language, the position will be reversed. *Artha* is the appearance of *śabda* and *śabda* is the reality of *artha*. One is generated by the other without the other degenerating in the process. It is *śabda* itself that is projected out as *artha*. There is no object except that which is conceived through word. Therefore the object is only a refinement or perfection of the word;[46] meaning overflows the word, the same word having different meanings. This only shows that words are themselves pregnant with meanings and have a freedom to denote any meaning.[47] With the emergence of the word emerges the meaning and not *vice versa*. It is the word which has to be used even when the meaning has to be explained.[48]

The *śabdabrahmavādin*, therefore, looks upon *parā* as the fundamentum of speech as well as the spoken, the Absolute itself. It is *śabda-brahman*, self-luminous, impartite, immutable and eternal. When realised in its pristineness through right discernment the self is lifted from the thraldom of individuality. *Parā vāc* is related to the phenomena of sound and sense alike as Reality is related to its appearance.[49]

Śaiva Siddhānta rejects this view of *parā* and rejects also the underlying assumption about the relation of word and meaning. It will look upon *parā* or *nāda* not as *brahman* but as *śakti* —*parigraha-śakti* of *brahman* and its unfoldment into concrete and overt speech forms as a case of real change of states, modal change (*vṛtti*) not unreal appearances. If phenomena were only appearances of *śabda* then *śabda* will be the source not only of its appearances but also of the delusion which causes the appearance. And this leads to infinite regress.[50] If it is a case of real transformation — the word giving birth to meaning, then there can be no reversibility, a re-transformation of the meaning into word again, which is ruinous to the eternity of the word.[51] If the word is creative of meaning it ceases to be eternal. The meaning is said to be only a 'refinement' of the word, not its 'other'. Now is this meaning also a refinement of the word? Or is it the other way about?[52] The same word has different meanings. If from this it is concluded that meanings are immanent in words themselves, then a word meaning two very different things should entail that the latter are identical. If *artha* be approached from the side of *śabda*, and not *vice versa* this predicament cannot be avoided.[53] Word is pregnant with meaning it is said, as rice contains within itself its fry. But does the fry come out of the rice unfried on fire?[54] The word is in fact learnt to span meanings so that the latter are prior to the word. Again between the two, it is the meaning that persists through a word so that we are able to 're-collect' it through the word. Does this not show that it is the meaning and not the word that endures and outlives the other?[55]

Evolution of Siva *tattvas*

The emergence of the first principles is one of the most fascinating problems of philosophy. Śaivism looks upon the universe of experience as made of ultimate principles hierarchically arrangeable in the order of increasing subtlety and pervasiveness, with a series of 'planes' of living affiliated to them, differing mutually but possessing the common characteristics of the principles as their predominant features. These principles are called tattvas, and are definable and distinguishable by reference to the souls for whom they are constitutive of their experience (*bhoga*). Whatever contributes to the experiences of the selves, all of them bound in different degree, contributes directly or indirectly, and endures till they are 'dissolved' (*pralaya*), are called tattvas.[56] They may be grouped and arranged accordingly in respect of their central function of contributing to the 'experience' of the individual selves, and this will also be, in the reverse, the order of their dissolution.[57] By experience (*bhoga*) is meant sentient experience, knowledge.[58] And knowledge for the Śaiva siddhantin is always conative and effective as well as cognitive. *Icchā*, *jñāna* and *kriyā* — this is the pattern of knowledge. *Jñāna* and *kriyā*, understanding and will, discernment and function are concretisations of an initial aspect of knowledge, namely *icchā*, intentionality which is the 'motive' to know. It is with reference to this 'motive' that knowledge is understood as experience (*bhoga*).[59] For a manifestation of this sentient experience[60] three things are needed: objects to serve as the 'food' for the experience, structured in terms of their being potential occasions for the feelings of *sukha*, *duḥkha* and *moha*; excitation of the *icchā*, *jñāna* and *kriyā* of the self by suitable agencies, as without them awareness will remain inhibited, being arrested by *mala* from eternity; and lastly, and certainly most importantly, activation of the knowing function of the self by *tirodhāna-śakti* which reveals or initiates knowledge to self, as sun's light is revealing for the eye. The light reveals by uniting with the eye, suffusing it and 'seeing with' it. In the same manner *Śiva-śakti* also conceivable in terms of triple aspects — *icchā-śakti, jñāna-śakti* and *kriyā-śakti* should activate self's knowledge by uniting with it, its *icchā* with self's *icchā*, its *jñāna* with self's *jñāna* and its *kriyā* with self's *kriyā*. Then only is experience possible for the self.[61]

Keeping this in mind, let us return to the tattvas. Those of the tattvas which though mutually differing[62] yet agree in providing for the objective side of experience constitutive of the pleasure-pain-delusive contents of knowledge may be grouped together, as the 'objective' tattvas (*bhogya-khaṇḍa*). Those serving to manifest or actualise the cognitive potential of the self by effecting partial unveiling of the self and predisposing it to experience are of one group, the experience-generating group (*bhojayitṛ-khaṇḍa*). Lastly comes the group of tattvas which transcendentally activate the experience-generating tattvas by union therewith. Such is the activating-group (*preraka-khaṇḍa*).

The last mentioned group of tattvas is, however, the first in the order of their function. They encompass and exceed the other tattvas, and are logically prior to them though in the order of one's discovery they come in last. They are the transcendental conditions of experience and are discoverable through reflective analysis. From the data of knowledge to the knowing function and its excitatory conditions and from them again to the transcendental conditions of such conditions, this is the order of analysis.

The order of enumeration of *śiva-tattvas* which constitute this group becomes intelligible when *bindu, śakti* and *śiva* — the three 'jewels'[63] are taken together into account. These are the three ultimates distinguished in terms of causation, respectively as the material, instrumental and efficient causes.[64] The three converge at the level of this group and their convergence is less apparent at the two other levels. *Śiva* is the transcendent unity and so is *śakti* but with this difference that *śakti* has distinguishable aspects in terms of which it appears either as *jñāna-śakti* or *kriyā-śakti* or both. Such distinctions arise, however, because of the adjunct of *bindu* the eternal material principle outside *śakti* and yet one with it, and they do not imply modification. *Bindu*, however, is modificatory and its modification is set into operation by the Divine will (*śakti*) at the end of cosmic Dissolution. The modification initially takes the form of the rise of *kalās* in the order of increasing expansion like concentric circles each subsumed under the next. These *kalās*, five in number, constitute as it were the framework of the entire evolution and precede further progressive structuralisations called tattvas and *bhuvanas* on the one side and *mantra, pada* and *varṇa* on the other.[65] The tattvas are constituted by *kalās* and *kalās* are immediately under the *śakti*, directly stirred into existence by it.[66]

When at the end of cosmic Dissolution *bindu* retracts to its original condition as the matrix of Pure creation, *Śiva* the transcendent unity underlying *bindu* also stands without 'differentiation' from His *śakti* in terms of *jñāna* and *kriyā* and therefore also without the differentiation of *Śiva* and *Śakti*.[67] With the advent of the will to resume cosmic operation again, tension sets in *bindu*. This advent takes the form of the rise of *jñāna-śakti* from *Parama-Śiva*. The Will barely 'knows' *bindu* with the intent to make *bindu* fit for evolution. *Bindu* is disturbed out of its equilibrium under the immediate stress of *jñāna-śakti*. Activated (*adhiṣṭhita*) now in a special way by Śiva *qua jñāna-śakti*, *bindu* in its quickened formation is called *śiva-tattva*. This is the first change of state (*vṛtti*) that *bindu* undergoes. *Bindu* is *kuṇḍalinī*[68] in its essence and Śiva is the same *kuṇḍalinī* in its awakened state.[69]

Following the indeterminate knowing of *jñāna-śakti* arises an indeterminate willing of *kriyā-śakti*. If the intention behind knowing was to make *bindu* fit for evolution the present intention is to make it evolve. The resulting 'modification' in *bindu* is the emergence of the second *tattva*. *Śakti-tattva* is the second change of state that *bindu* undergoes.[70]

Then ensues a combination of *jñāna-śakti* and *kriyā-śakti*, knowing in a determinate manner and willing in a definitive sense which is accompanied by the emergence of the third *tattva—sadā-śiva*. This *tattva* typifies the state of readiness and impulsion towards Creation (*unmukhīkaraṇa*) preceding actual creation.[71]

The emergence of the fourth and the fifth tattvas may be likewise understood in the following manner. When the state of a combination of *jñāna-śakti* and *kriyā-śakti* gives place to a new combination with *kriyā* prevailing over *jnāna* in order to arouse cosmic activity in its subtle form from the *sadā-śiva tattva* already predisposed to create, the ensuing modified state of *bindu* is termed *maheśvara-tattva*.[72] When this gives place again to the will to arouse cosmic activity in its overt form on the part of *śakti* with its *jñāna* aspect prevailing over *kriyā*, there follows the rise of the fifth *tattva*—*śuddha-vidyā*.[73]

The five śiva-tattvas share with other tattvas the character of experience[74] having *bhuvanas* affiliated to it for the two classes of (*i*) *adhikāra-muktas* already referred to, and (*ii*) *apara-muktas*. The latter are the liberated selves who are freed also from the burden of office (*adhikāra*) through worship of the divinities that preside over these tattvas. While free from *adhikāra* they are not, however, free from the *vāsanās* of *bhoga* and *laya* and have, therefore, fallen short of the supreme ideal of Freedom which is achieved only through *Śiva-jñāna*. From the account given of the emergence of the five tattvas it is also obvious that they serve as the freely improvised loci for the three theogonic processes of *laya*, *bhoga* and *adhikāra* already explained.

These tattvas provide also for the unfoldment of the Śaiva-āgama[75]—the transcendent source of knowledge accepted co-ordinately with the sources of reason and perception. This, of course, follows from their inclusion of the parallel evolutes of the speech-world. Thus *Śiva-tattva* is the 'home' of the Śaivāgamas in the form of *sūkṣmā vāc* undifferentiated into *Kāmika* etc. while *śakti-tattva* houses them in the form of *paśyantī*. In the *sadāśiva-tattva* they exist as *madhyamā* along with *praṇava* and other agencies that are responsible for their organization under twenty-eight names. In the two other tattvas the Śaivāgamas obtain in the form of *Sūkṣma-vaikharī* and *sthūla-vaikharī*, with their further differentiations and recensions into upāgamas and with all attending *śāstra* literature.[76]

The evolution of the five tattvas must be understood as evolution not in the sense of transformation (*pariṇāma*) but in the sense only of changes of states (*vṛtti*) of one self-identical material cause. The reason should be obvious. *Bindu* is *śuddha-māyā*, unmixed with *mala* and *karma*. A simple entity cannot be conceived to undergo transformation. That is why *aśuddha-māyā* has to be understood as undergoing transformation. Evolution or simple extension (*vṛtti*) is always understood as partial (*ekadeśa*).[77] Effectuation consists in the transition from the stage of 'potency' (*śakti*) to that of actuality (*vyakti*). And the stage of potency or power is ever-conserving. That is why in the evolution of tattvas *māyā*, for example, is conceived to function as *māyā* and also differently through its evolutes simultaneously, continues to exercise this function even as it extends or evolves into *vaikharī*.[78]

Mayiya[1] Evolution of *Vidyā* and *Ātma* Tattvas

1. Are there two *māyās* ?

Enumeration of the two orders of evolution, the pure and the impure, rests on the recognition that finite selves are not all of like finitude. As *bhoga* is linked up with finitude, differences in the quality of *bhoga* call for the recognition of different orders of existence.[2] This in turn necessitates the recognition of two causal material principles as the matrices of the two orders. *Bindu* is Pure *māyā*, while the impure order of evolution proceeds from a *śuddha-māyā* or *adho-māyā*. The special title of the latter to delude[3]— to bring empirical experience home to the self and bind it — is reflected in its appellation — *mohinī*.

From this it seems as if two material causes are recognised in the system. *Śuddha* and *aśuddha* are not only different but even opposed. One enlightens without deluding and the other deludes without enlightening. Moreover, admission of two dissimilar agents, one infinite and the other finite, is evidence of a radical discontinuity between the two *māyās*.[4]

There are two ways of opposing this point of view. One is to hold a view just to the contrary. Not only are the two not opposed but they are continuous. The two are alike material (*jaḍa*) their difference in being pure and impure notwithstanding. Texts also speak of the evolution of one *from* the other.[5] In spiritual *sādhanā* also *kalā-śuddhi* entails *śuddhi* for the *bhuvauas* and the tattvas of the impure world. Again *aśuddha-māyā* is counted as one of the tattvas like *prakṛti*, the presumption being that it is only an evolute like every other *tattva* of *bindu*. There are, therefore, no two orders of existence. The one slides into the other without disruption.

There is another way of opposing the view of the two *māyās* and this may by implication oppose also the second view of one *māyā*.[6] If there are two *māyās* they cannot be causes. What are many and material, being effect, cannot also be cause. Moreover, admission of a dual realm of phenomena is not compatible with the recognition of one cause in

God. If the material cause is different *inter se* how can God be conceived to combine in Himself efficient and material causality? The dissimilar agencies of the two *māyās* are not two wills. Agency is of one only, that of God though it may involve delegation of it in consideration of the nature of the bound souls. Though *bindu* enlightens and *māyā* deludes, both indeed enlighten. One enlightens without deluding and the other enlightens by deluding, just as non-knowledge, like knowledge is also a *buddhi-guṇa*.[7] *Bindu* causes happiness (*sukha*) and *māyā* causes sorrow and delusion (*duḥkha* and *moha*). But both agree in causing experience (*bhoga*). There is no discontinuity.

Nor does this mean that there is only *bindu*, and *māyā* is only an evolute thereof. For this abolishes all differences between the pure and the impure spheres, and, therefore, also abolishes degrees of finitude. Existence of *different* planes of life and mind has no meaning if they are meant to subserve the *bhoga* of selves of the same degree of finitude.[8]

The conclusive view then can only be that there is one material cause — *māyā*[9] which in its phase 'unmixed' with *mala-karma* is *śuddha-māyā* and in the other phase with this admixture, is *aśuddha-māyā*. Nor does this introduce heterogeneity in the nature of *māyā*. For *śuddha* and *aśuddha* are not mutually opposed. The relation between the two is of one-sided dependence[10] pointing to the nature of the distinction between the two as one of levels. This interpretation keeps in the foreground the basis of the distinction between the class of tattvas evolved from *bindu*, namely the directive tattvas (*preraka-khaṇḍa*) and the two other groups in relation thereto, namely, the directed (*prerya*) which brings out their compatibility and the self-transcending nature of the distinction.

The *vidyā* tattvas

In order to understand the evolution of the tattvas generative of experience for the self (*bhojayitṛ*) the presence of the two *malas*—*karma* and *āṇava* with *māyā* has to be taken into account. The one inner function which all tattvas subserve, namely *bhoga* for the self, needs to be understood here against a basis or background where the tattvas are required to manifest knowledge for the self not unrestrictedly but in accord with the self's *karma* and accordingly by effecting a partial unveiling of its knowledge against obscuration by *mala*. The 'partial' removal of the obscuring power of *mala* is dictated by *karma*.

The tattvas which engender *bhoga*, broadly speaking, help the individual self bereft of knowledge and action, come by the initial competence to experience, or have 'experiencership' (*bhoktṛtva*). The self is assisted to become the agent of experience (*puruṣa*) fit to experience the object (*prakṛti*) and its modes. How does the self become the experiencer?

Two conditions seem necessary. The self must first attain to a general condition of being able to experience. This requires a 'general' manifestation of its cognitive,emotive and active aspects dormant under the obscuration of *mala*. These aspects from their non-manifestness shall not be concluded to be non-existent. What is non-existent is that which remains unmanifest to knowledge, despite the presence of the manifesting agency or means. We say for example that the table is non-existent in this room when no table is manifest inspite of the availability of the manifesting means of broad daylight. We do not say of the chair or table which remains hidden or concealed because of the condition of darkness that it is non-existent.

Secondly, it is also required that the self which can now have experience is also actually oriented towards the object. It must be set for the experience. It is the presence of this set, constituting as it does the 'specific' condition of experience that leads to a consummation of experience. How can the self be 'set' about its cognitive and conative experience? A manifestation of its 'faculties' (*śakti*) is, of course, necessary but not sufficient. Experiencing function which consists of a conative appropriation in the wake of cognition involves a certain non-distinction (*avidyā*) and a consequent self-assertion and similar other 'hindrances' (*kleśas*). Only thus equipped the self becomes fit in a specific sense for its life of experience.

The function of general manifestation of self's knowledge involves (i) a *serial* arousal of the conative, cognitive and emotive *śaktis* into action and impulsion of them towards the *buddhi-tattva*; (ii) a determination of the intransmissible *specificity* of the self's *bhoga* by way of a qualification of the principle of *karma*, and (iii) a determination about the duration of self's *bhoga* again in the service of the operation of *karma*. These are achieved by the functions of *kalā*, *vidyā* and *rāga* tattvas in the first case, by the *niyati-tattva* in the second and by *kāla* in the third. These constitute a permanent vesture (*kañcuka*) for the self in its empiric career, not varying during the variations of its states (*avasthā*)[11] unlike *buddhi* and other tattvas which unite and separate. The self conditioned by the five *kañcukas* acquires specific orientation to *bhoga* through a further acquisition of the 'human impurity' (*puṁstva-mala*) of five *kleśas* from *prakṛti-tattva*. The 'empiric man' equipped with the five *kañcukas* and five *kleśas* is the *puruṣa-tattva*.[12]

Kāla and *niyati-tattva* deserve our attention first. *Kalā*, *vidyā* and *rāga* configuration is of direct consequence to the self, serving as it does, immediately to manifest self's *bhoga*.[13] They are constituents of the 'body' of self—the subtle body serving as the intrinsic means of *bhoga* of the individual. *Kāla* and *niyati* relatively speaking are of indirect consequence;[14] they assist in *bhoga*[15] through delimiting and determining *karma*. The self becomes related to *karma* only after its *jñāna* and such are manifest. Though thus kalā *etc.* are logically prior to *kāla* and *niyati* from the point of view of the self, still *kāla* and *niyati* come after it, and are the cause of the tattvas and their derivatives. While *kāla* is the pre-condition of the rise of other tattvas, *niyati* acts as the determinant, as well of kalā etc. manifesting self's knowledge.[16]

If *kāla* is the pre-condition of the rise of other tattvas, what about its own advent? Can there be a beginning of time? The answer that is suggested is: empirical time has a beginning *in* transcendental time (*śuddha-kāla*).[17] Transcendental time precedes empirical time, not temporally, but through 'eternal' existence; its 'eternal' essence is not, of course, eternity. That from which the world events derive their chronological order, exists by participating in the essence of 'archetypal' time.[18] The postulate of *śuddha-kāla* is necessary to explain Ananta's agency in relation to *aśuddha-māyā*. His agency unlike the agency of God is in time and yet not in empirical time for the latter is yet to come into existence. All theogonic processes are 'out-side' time—empirical and transcendental.[19]

Kāla should be admitted as real and independent of things that are temporal. Even when all the necessary causal factors are available, the potter, wheel, clay and so on the pot now produced, was not produced before now.[20] Time is the condition without which the presence of all the necessary factors do not amount to the production of the effect. Even *karma* is the causal condition but through the instrumentality of time. The mango does not blossom except in its time. Flowers do not wither except when their time comes. If time does not exist these must arise irrespective of consideration of time or perish as soon as they arise.[21]

The reality of time following from its meaning is an indispensable presupposition of a philosophy of spiritual life.[22] It is what makes the philosophy realistic. Time is the presupposition of *karma* theory, of fruits accruing to the deed long after the deed. It is the presupposition not only of growth or modification characteristic of the physical but also of growth in a spiritual sense, the 'ripening' of the soul and so on.[23]

At the same time, while time is real it cannot be the Reality (*sat*) itself. Spiritual life involves also a conquest of time. Its philosophy asserts the paradox of the temporality of time. Time is not eternity. It is the effect of cause.[24] Śaiva Siddhānta denies the eternity of time by denying its unity. Time is manifold. If it were taken as one, and beginning and end in time are only accidents of time, what is this empty husk of time which can never be conceived without its accidents? Distinctions of past, present and future are not always relative distinctions. A pot broke, it breaks or is breaking, it will break—this distinction which is a commonplace of our life is intelligible in itself without reference to other scales of time. While such units of time as day, hour, and year are apparently measured in relation to the unit of the sun's movement, the past-present-future distinctions are not of that category.[25] Distinctions in the phases of motion are really the distinctions in time and not *vice versa*.[26] Because time is not spirit and is also manifold it follows that it is effect (*kārya*).

Niyati-tattva is the allocating principle which functions as the determinant of the experience of the fruits of deeds for the respective agents.[27] Like the law of the land which provides against improper filching of another's fruit or neglect of one's own, *niyati* enforces the right to one's *bhoga* negatively and positively.[28] But for this specificity with reference to one's *bhoga* determined by the law, the principle of deed and consequences cannot become articulate and the self consequently cannot be tied to *bhoga*. Hence the need for *niyati-tattva* as one of the five invariable 'vestures' (*kañcuka*) for the experiencing self. The underlying assumption here is that *karma* can yield its consequence as toil yields its fruit but it cannot also cause it to attach to the agent of the deed,[29] any more than one's toil necessary for the fruit is also sufficient to guarantee its accruing to the person that has put forth the toil. In the latter case such guarantee is provided by the law of the land and similarly, *niyati* the cosmic law provides the guarantee for experience of *karma*[30] specifying non-transferably the fruit to the one that is entitled to it.

There is an unbreakable continuity between deeds and their fruits in the *doer's* experience. To admit promiscuity in this relationship cuts at the very root of the theory of *karma*. Nor does this, strictly speaking, exclude a like continuity between one's deed and their fruits in *other people's* experience, as it has been urged by critics of the *karma* theory.[31] One's deed does not constitute the fruit of another person, because that will be to deny any relation between deed and consequence between one's past and one's present, but this does not exclude one's suffering for another's sake or foregoing one's joy for the sake of another. For the other person whose suffering I may take upon myself is related to me by love. I freely suffer for his sake. The rites performed by the son can benefit the father because the son and the father are related. For example, I can freely give away all my wealth to some one I choose and this does not offend against the principle of *niyati*.

The admission of *kalā*, *vidyā* and *rāga* tattvas rests on the following considerations; *bhoga* for the individual consists of its cognitive 'assimilation' of the 'objective' through mediation of *buddhi*. This becomes possible only on overcoming the obscuration of *mala* under the effects of which the individual has been a victim from without beginning bereft of the sense of I and mine—*kartṛtva* and *bhoktṛtva*. The de-obscuration process consists of counteracting the veiling effects of *mala* in the self's *cit-śakti* as the effects of burning of fire are counteracted by the presence of a gem.[32] There is a consequent sub-activation of *ātmacit-śakti* to effect its functioning as the agent and enjoyer. Counteracting of the veiling powers of *mala* implies manifestation of the *kriyā-śakti* of the self so that it attains competence with regard to the foremost requisite of agency. Just as the human eye recovering from the effects of blindedness is under a daze and has to recover again from the effects of the daze before it can perceive objects, the individual even with his *kriyā-śakti* restored to function is still unable to grasp the *buddhi-tattva* and apprehend objects. His *jñāna-śakti* also has to be manifested so that he may be able to 'perceive'. Perception again has to be followed by intention or desire as without the latter there can be no 'enjoyment' (*bhoga*). And this involves sub-activation of the *icchā-śakti*. Now only the individual self may be considered to have become competent, in a general sense at least, to have *bhoga*. He is now equipped witn general *bhoktṛtva*.

The proof of the existence of a *tattva*, we saw, is also the proof of its exclusive capacity to exercise a *specific function*. If a *tattva* exists it is there to serve a definite purpose in the scheme of reality.[33] We may accordingly posit the three tattvas of *kalā*, *vidyā* and *rāga* against the three specific functions of (i) removal of the obscuration of *mala*, (ii) removal of the daze of the removal of obscuration, and (iii) removal of the obscuration also of the desire or will.

Kalā-tattva as the name signifies[34] effects the 'removal' in a partial manner of *mala*-obscuration and manifests the *kriyā-śakti* (*kartṛ-śakti*) of the self.[35] The *kriyā-śakti* obscured by *mala* is de-obscured partially by *kalā*.[36] Removal (*nivṛtti*) in the context of the all-pervasive *mala* must be understood in the negative sense of de-obscuring. The example of a gem de-obscuring the burning effect of fire on the person of a man was already given.[37] It is, literally, nullifying the arresting powers of *mala* in the *kriyā-śakti* of the self. The function of 'partial' removal is to be understood by reference to *karma*.[38] De-obscuring of the obscuring *śakti* of *mala* is about those contents which become object to the function of *buddhi-tattva* but strictly in commensuration with one's *karma*.[39]

The 'exclusiveness' of the capacity of *kalā-tattva* to function in this manner may be demonstrated in the following way. Its function of de-obscuring *mala* and sub-activising *kriyā-śakti* cannot be accomplished (i) by *buddhi-tattva* below it, (ii) by śiva-tattvas above it, and (iii) even by *Śiva-śakti* which is beyond all tattvas, though all the three are indispensable for the function of *kalā*. *Buddhi-tattva* is required to function as the medium for *bhoga*, and yet because it is non-intelligent (*jaḍa*) it has itself to be activated by the intelligent self.[40] The latter, therefore, must first become agent of this function of activation of *buddhi* and for that *kalā* is required. *Kalā-tattva* is, therefore, logically prior to *buddhi-tattva*.[41] How about *Śiva-śakti* which is spirit itself? Can it not serve to activate *buddhi-tattva*? The answer is that just as one's body is activated by one's own self, one's psyche too is activated by one's self alone. Because *śakti* is the cause of all effect it does not mean that it is *śakti* and not the potter that fashions the pot. It may be asked : is not *kalā* itself *jaḍa*? Has it not to be activated by a self again? The answer to this objection is that *kalā* and other tattvas, *jaḍa* as they are, are activated in their turn by śiva-tattvas presided over by the intelligent *Śiva-śakti*. The śiva-tattvas themselves cannot take the place of *kalā-tattva* because as it has been explained, the 'pure' śiva-tattvas cannot function as revealers for impurity-ridden selves.[42]

Vidyā and *rāga* tattvas are more complex than *kalā* in their function. Both will have to be understood in relation to *buddhi* and its dispositions. In the wake of *kriyā-śakti*, *jñāna* and *icchā-śakti* are aroused. While in the former the self acquires agency of action, in the latter through the exercise of *jñāna* and *icchā* the agent acquires competence for enjoyer-ship.[43] *Jñāna-śakti* aroused by *vidyā* accomplishes a kind of internal knowing—the immediate knowledge of every kind. The principle underlying its function seems to be that neither the senses nor the mind (the internal senses) are capable of self-function. They have to be activated by the intelligent self and the mode of self's activising is through uniting with them. And for activating them in this manner it requires, in order to apperceive, to be aided by a *tattva*. For example, we admit the possibility of indeterminate perception as the stage preceding determination by *buddhi* and this involves activising the sense directly unmediated by *buddhi*. *Vidyā* assists the self in this by manifesting its *Jñāna-śakti*. *Vidyā* also functions as the instrument for self to apperceive *buddhi* itself when the latter modifies into pleasure-pain experiences. *Vidyā-tattva* occasions apperception of feelings to the effect 'I am happy', 'I suffer'.[44] It is interesting to note that for the siddhāntin, feelings are not self-perceived by the *cit-śakti* of the self unmediatedly, as it is held in Advaita Vedānta.[45] The argument is that self's *cit-śakti* as such can experience only the unlimited Bliss of *Śiva* and therefore empirical feeling of pleasure and its opposite has to be mediated by the *upādhi* of *vidyā-tattva*.

Rāga-tattva evolving from *vidyā* manifests *icchā*[46] and causes the incidence of attachment which is one of the dispositions of *buddhi*.[47] While *rāga* manifests 'object-less' attachment—a general predisposition or set, *avairāgya* of *buddhi* is specific attachment. The latter presupposes the former.

One interesting question that is discussed in connection with this concept is:[48] can we not say that the object itself is sufficient to excite the *icchā-śakti* of the self? The object is surely the occasion for the experience (*bhogya*) of pleasure and pain. Is it not also adequate to excite a general 'attachment' on the part of the self? The answer that is suggested evidences rare discernment into psychology. Unless there be something in the self answering to its attachment to pleasure all like objects must excite attachment in a uniform manner. Moreover, there can be no renunciation of attachment if objects and not man were to determine attachment. Conversely, with the non-availability of object there should be automatically renunciation, which is not however, the case.[49] The pleasure-occasioning nature of object is not quite the exciting cause of man's attachment.[50]

Puruṣa is the nodal *tattva* in this group. It involves as explained earlier an aggregation of all the aforementioned tattvas which the self takes on as its cloak—an inseparable cloak, and emerges as the *kartṛ-kāraka* to take his place by the side of other *kārakas*.[51] The self now acquires a complexion[52] and a name. What distinguishes *puruṣa-tattva* is the presence of the impulsion to *bhoga*[53] precipitated by the five hindrances of (i) ignorance (*avidyā*), (ii) egoity (*asmitā*), (iii) desire (*rāga*), (iv) identification (*abhiniveśa*) and (v) aversion (*dveṣa*) arranged in the order of their sequence, the egoity arising from the error of taking non-eternal as the eternal, non-pure as the pure, pain as pleasure, desire arising from egoity, identification from desire and anger or aversion from identification. These 'hindrances' constitute the 'special' ingredients of *bhoktṛtva*, the more general being provided by the *kañcukas*.[54]

The stage is now set, with the full accomplishment of *bhoktṛtva* for the self, for the emergence of phenomena (*bhogya*). The *bhogya* stratified from *guṇa-tattva* down to *pṛthvi-tattva* has to be evolved into existence. *Prakṛti* an evolute of *kalā-tattva* is intelligible against this function. Its function is to evolve the objective tattvas on the one hand, and also be the substratum for the five *kleśas* accruing to *puruṣa-tattva*. That it is required for evolving the world of objective tattvas which constitute the *bhogya-khaṇḍa* implies that it is not itself the primal objective *tattva*. The view that *prakṛti* is *guṇa* in equipoise and is the 'rootless root' of phenomena is rejected.

The logic of the mediation of *prakṛti-tattva* between *kalā* and *guṇa-tattva* was already anticipated. Differentiations in the *kārya* cannot derive without obtaining implicitly in the *kāraṇa*. *Guṇa-tattva* with its manifest differentiated structure cannot evolve from *kalā-tattva* to which *guṇas* are wholly foreign. Hence the need for the intermediary *prakṛti* where the *guṇas* are in unmanifest balance.

Nor is *prakṛti* conceivable as derived from *māyā* instead of from *kalā* an evolute of *māyā*. If it does not derive from *kalā* it cannot constitute the immediate *bhogya* for the *kriyā-śakti* aroused by *kalā* but can only function like *kāla* and *niyati* as external forms of experience. The principle of deriving one *tattva* from another is that it should be manifest (*sthūla*) precisely in relation to the other which is its latent condition (*sūkṣma*). *Prakṛti* is undifferentiated and unmanifest relatively to *kalā* which is barely devoid of these features and is 'alone' (*kevala*). *Prakṛti* is *sthūla* in precise relation to *māyīya* (*kalā*) and not to *māyā*.[55]

Atma-aattvas

Prakṛti and its evolute *guṇa-tattva* and the evolutes of the latter, respectively, imply *guṇas* in unmanifest balance, manifest balance and manifest imbalance. The relation between *prakṛti* and *guṇa* is similar to the relation between *māyā* and *kāla*, the first evolute of *māyā*. *Guṇa* implies immediately the agency of will under whose stress it precipitates into manifest *guṇas* as it emerges from its cause.[56] The agency is of *śrīkaṇṭha rudra* subsumable under the authority of the agency of Ananta.

Guṇa is the generality of the three *guṇas* of *sattva*, *rajas* and *tamas*. It is a commonplace that the three *guṇas* function in unison as mutually implicatory and hence the justification for a *tattva* of *guṇa* as such.

The three *guṇas* and their permutations is one of the interesting topics for study. From the qualities and actions associated with each *guṇa* it is obvious that the three *guṇas* typify respectively the three categories of *pati*, *paśu* and *pāśa*.[57] This becomes apparent when the three *guṇas* are said to manifest three modes of *bhoga*—*sukha*, *duḥkha* and *moha* (*prīti*, *aprīti* and *viṣāda*), that is *sattva sukha*, *tamas duḥkha* and *rajas moha*. Feeling of happiness is typical of *pati*; feeling of suffering of *pāśa* and the feeling of 'affective insensibility' (*moha*) is typical of the indeterminate nature of *paśu*.

The three *guṇas* are substantial and not 'attributive' as the term *guṇa* may suggest.[58] They are of the character of object in being the constituent of the object and being for the *bhoga* of the *puruṣa*. The evolution of the objects (*guṇin*) from *guṇa-tattva* implies a novel metaphysical theory of the relation of *guṇa* and *guṇin*, which may be considered a little later..

The three *guṇas* manifest their respective nature in the *jñāna-śakti* and *kriyā-śakti* of the *puruṣa* already predisposed towards *bhoga*. *Sattva* implies the quality of illumination, uninhibited revelation of knowledge which it manifests in the *jñāna* of the self. Similarly, in the *kriyā* of the self is manifested an inward quality of buoyancy and sense of fulfilment characteristic of unobstructed will. *Rajas* manifests in the *jñāna-śakti* the quality of drive which accounts for quickness and immediacy of comprehension, and in the *kriyā-śakti* the sense of appropriation, the feeling of 'I' and 'mine' and the consequent quality of dynamism in personality. *Tamas* contributes to *jñāna*, inertia coupled with pride which subjects knowledge to distortions. In *kriyā-śakti* its impact results in indolence, antipathy, deceptiveness and so on. These six qualities—light and lightness, affection and appropriation and inertia and indetermination,[59] together with the three primary modes of feeling—happiness, suffering and delusive insensibility constitute the nine *guṇas*. These *guṇas* colour the orientation of the self by dominating its *icchā*, *jñāna* and *kriyā*. The self's knowledge at a time is determined by the predominant *guṇa* in its conation and affection.

When *sattva* predominates and *rajas* and *tamas* are subordinate, the result is the evolution of *buddhi-tattva*. The *jñāna-śakti* already manifest by *vidyā* is manifested determinately in relation to objects and endowed through the categories of class with assertive certitude by *buddhi*. *Buddhi* is itself also the 'object' (*bhogya*) for the self, in its modal transformation into the forms of the objects. The latter are not as such experienced but the feeling-modes into which their apprehension is converted are experienced. *Buddhi* is at once a mode and a datum of knowledge . From this it also follows that accumulations of the twofold consequence of the deeds of *puruṣa*—merits and demerits, which determine the function of *buddhi* as a mode, are grounded in *Buddhi*. *Buddhi* consequently also is the seat of all modes of referring to the content, dispositions (*bhāvas*) determined by *karma*. Such modes of reference are contingent and variable and therefore cannot be *ātma-guṇas*, as it is for the Naiyāyikas.[60]

It also follows from the last mentioned point that *buddhi* is the seat of impressions for the revival of past experience in the present. The contingent impressions cannot inhere in the eternal self. The Buddhists deny the existence of a permanent self and refuse to distinguish between consciousness and cognitions on the ground that they are absolutely indivisible in experience. But memory defies explanation on this denial. Memory requires more than mere dating of a fact in the past. It must be dated in *one's* past. One must think that he directly experienced its occurrence. At the same time, of course there is also the other side to the issue. A permanent, unvarying self will resist all change. There can be no recalls and revivals in its knowledge. *Buddhi-tattva* as the seat of memory impressions is the solution implied in the problem.

The admission that *buddhi-tattva* is the seat of merit (*puṇya*) and demerit (*pāpa*) contains implicitly all its division of dispositions and determinations (*bhāvas* and *pratyayas*). The latent impressions of man's deeds (constituting the contents of his Unconscious) are grounded in *buddhi* characterised by non-discrimination and lead to activities which are 'deserved' at the respective times. Intellect's modes of reference to a content or dispositions are determined by this factor. Accumulated merit (*puṇya*) takes the form of the disposition of *dharma* and accumulated demerit (*pāpa*) takes the form of *a-dharma*. *Dharma*, *jñāna*, *vairāgya* and *aiśvarya* belong to 'pure' *buddhi* while *a-dharma*, *ajñāna* and *anaiśvarya* belong to *buddhi* with the *uparāga* of *tamas*. *Avairāgya* (*rāga*) pertains to *buddhi* under the influence of *rajas*.[61]

Determination, judgment involves the element of subjective resolve which appears in the gross form as 'who can compare with me'. Subjective resolve is different from the certitude of judgment which is content-determined. It is the implicit 'I' in all assertorial certitude, the self-assertiveness in assertion, the ego-motive in perception.[62] *Ahaṁkāra* is, accordingly, evolved from the *rajas* element of *buddhi*. Another difference between *buddhi* and *ahaṁkāra* is that while *buddhi* is 'instrumental', *ahaṁkāra*, like *kalā-tattva* is 'nominative' in relation to self's action.[63]

Ahaṁkāra differentiates because of the distributive emphasis of the *guṇas* again, into *bhūtādi*, *vaikharī* and *taijasa*,[64] the first giving rise to the luminous evolutes of *manas* (mind) and *jñānendriya* (sense), the second to *karmendriya* (motor organs)[65] and the third to *tanmātra* (subtle elements). The function of distinguishing the determinant (*viśeṣaṇa*), from the determinate object (*viśeṣya*) indeterminately given through the senses, is the work of mind (*manas*).[66] *Manas* mediates between the outer senses and *buddhi* and the swiftness of action that this mediating role entails, explains its *sattva* nature. The three internal organs — *manas*, *buddhi* and *ahaṁkāra*—are specific modes of exercise of *icchā, jñāna* and *kriyā* of the experient self (*puruṣa*).

The outer senses of knowledge and action—the sensorium and the motorium both are derived from a variety of *ahaṁkāra*, not from the *bhūtas*. The five *jñānendriyas* stand for the function or faculty of vision, audition, olfaction, ductatory and tactile sensory functions rather than their physiological counterparts. Śaiva Siddhānta advocates *prāpyakāri-vāda*[67] according to which the sense pervades or relates to the object and knows. Immediate contactual relation is a precondition of experience at the sensual as well as intellectual levels. The eye alone because of its translucence due to relative preponderance of *sattva*, of the *sattva*-predominant group of five senses 'goes over' to its data while the other senses 'stay' and pervade their respective data.

One peculiarity of the visual sense significant in Śaiva Siddhānta account is the recognition of its nature as a sepcies of light and yet as dependent for its illumination on the external physical light. The relative preponderance of the *sattva* component of the sense explains its 'luminous' character. But *tamas* as the counterpart of *sattva* is also present, the evolute of which , namely physical darkness is congenital to the visual sense; while luminous it cannot illumine unaided by physical light. The latter is the evolute of the *sattva* preponderant aspect of *tamas ahaṁkāra* and therefore proves a complement for the visual sense.[68]

The sensory organs manifest the *jñāna-śakti* of self while the motor organs manifest *kriyā-śakti*.[69] Just as one self-identical knowing function is modalised into different functions as visual and so on, becausa of differences in the data of knowledge, one self-identical conative function is distinguishable as various motor functions in terms of differences of activity. The Sāṅkhya-Vedānta tradition conceives spirit in terms only of the function of knowledge and relegates *kriyā* to what is outside spirit. Śaiva Siddhānta rejects the view on the ground that spirit being ubiquitous, action that takes place in its presence must also be unexcepted in the case of inert objects. This is not however the case. All action is, therefore, willed action directly or otherwise.

From that variety of *ahaṁkāra* where the quality of darkness and inertia are preponderant are evolved the five *tanmātras* (subtle elements which are attributive[70] and the five *mahābhūtas* (gross element) which are substantial. Introduction of this distinction of attribute (*guṇa*) and substance (*guṇin*) is distinctive of Śaiva Siddhānta metaphysics. All physical and psycho-physical 'substances' are indeed evolutes of three *guṇas* where *guṇa* stands for quality. This is admissible as substance is not a sub-quality. This is admissible as substance is not a substrate of qualities but only the latter in the collective.[71]

The *māyīya* in brief comprises the sphere of the tattvas which constitute (i) the accessory to knowledge in the broadest sense, the ten elements gross and subtle at the outer periphery being the outermost accessory, the ten senses, sensory and motor being the outer accessory, the four inner senses being inner-outer and the *vidyā*-tattvas the innermost, and (ii) the correlates of experience, tattvas of the form of universes being 'common' correlates for experience for all selves, those of the form of 'incorporeal bodies' (*puryaṣṭaka*) being the 'uncommon', that is, specific correlates of experience unique for each self, and of the form of corporeal bodies (*sthūla-deha*) being the 'common-uncommon' correlate of experience. *Māyīya* is the macro-cosmic and micro-cosmic reality which serves as the medium for the operation of the three-fold bonds of *māyā*, *karma* and *mala*.

X

THE DOCTRINE OF MALA

The problem of the real core of bondage has been shelved while considering the nature of the 'bondage' of body, sense, worlds and its objects (*māyīya*) on the one hand, and of deeds arising from a sense of agency (*karma*) on the other. What is that which when present, the aforementioned agencies of bondage are also present as bonds binding man, but when overcome cease to bind him ? *Māyā* and *karma* do not bind the free, neither the eternally free God, nor the 'freed' man. These are indeed bonds binding man already 'bound'. This primordial bondage is *mala*.[1]

Mala is characteristically described as utter darkness, 'darkness beyond all darkness'[2] which is not to be perceived or plumbed by any human device. *Mala* is pre-cosmic — pre-macro, pre-micro — cosmic, 'occasioning' the sequence of cosmic functions and also the sequence of states (*avasthā*) of consciousness obtaining between the two poles of oblivion and memory. In either of them *mala* functions 'from without' conscious man, its presence unfelt and unperceived by the 'I'.

Like the concept of *māyā*, *mala* also can be studied as regards its existence through a critique of the concept of *ajñāna* of Vedānta,[3] to which it bears some resemblance. What is chiefly disputed about the Vedāntic concept of *ajñāna* is the underlying notion of self as Pure consciousness. That the self exists as an entity dissociated from its somatic and even psychic condition of existence is granted. It is by reference to such experience indeed that we are able to tell discriminatingly *paśu* apart from *pāśa*. What Śaiva Siddhānta will dispute is that the self resting in itself is immediately conscious. The Śaiva Siddhānta view of *paśu* must be kept in view. The self is in theory consciousness, and yet factually unconscious. Its knowledge and action will have to be permitted to manifest themselves from within reactivated from a condition of inhibition. The material accessories constituting the physical and the psychical organism serve to manifest consciousness, and manifest in accordance with the instinct for action and disposition for knowledge provided by the seeds of *karma* which are present beginninglessly. The span of its manifest consciousness, its emergence and subsidence are determined by the auxiliary of *karma*. Even though in theory self is infinite and is identical with consciousness its existence and knowledge unmediated by the operation of material accessories are as good as non-existent (*asat-samāna*, *śūnya-kalpa*).

A contrast of this view with the concept of *sākṣi-caitanya* of Vedānta will provide the right perspective for a critical understanding of the meaning of the concept of *mala*.[4]

Ignorance and the problem of evidence[5]

For the *Advaitin*, *ajñāna*, (unlike the *mala* of Śaiva Siddhānta) is the cause of world-illusion. Transcendental ignorance indeed is the cause of the empirical world. Phenomena, subjective and objective alike, are derived from Ignorance. 'Cosmology is only a cosmological history of belief.'[6] A positive Ignorance is the cause of the empirical world. In support of this theory it becomes necessary to demonstrate the existence and knowledge of Ignorance apart from the empirical world. The cause must be shown to exist logically prior to its effect. Such a claim — the claim to demonstrate not only its existence but also its knowledge, necessitates also the postulation of a consciousness to apprehend the causal Ignorance.[7] Accordingly all the available evidence are pressed into service simultaneously of such a cause and of a consciousness in witness thereof.

Of perceptual evidence two kinds of avowals of ignorance are noted — one of general 'objectless' ignorance as in 'I *do not know*', and the other of ignorance of something specific, as in 'I *do not know myself and others*'. Both, it is claimed, evidence a direct acquaintance with Ignorance as something positive, and not privative on the part of a transcendental consciousness (*sākṣin*).

Evidence of Ignorance is sought in a more impressive manner from an analysis of the sequence of states (*avasthā*).[8] Here again the enquiry into positive Ignorance resolves into enquiry about the transcendental knower *through* the *avasthās*.[9] A consciousness confined to one state cannot know the state *as* a state.[10] Attempts which equate one or more of the physical accessory of consciousness functioning on the different states will have to face this problem, namely how in that case can it know that state *as* a state. The *advaitin's* solution of this problem is to recognize Ignorance the object *par excellence* as that which modifies into diverse objects. Differences in the states are traceable to differences in the object.[11] The gross physical thing of the wakeful consciousness, the sub-sensible world of dream, and the attenuated 'object' in deep sleep are all of the objective realm—the realm of Ignorance. From such differences in the object the distinction of the knowing subject (from the different objects) emerges—a non-variant, transcendental consciousness. Memory judgments like 'I slept well; I did not know anything' evidence direct acquaintance with Ignorance on the part of such a consciousness.

So *ajñāna* and *sākṣin*—Ignorance and Witness-self are two interrelated concepts, and evidence of one is also evidence of the other. By implication, the legitimacy of the concept of *mala* is denied as the latter implies that Ignorance could be evidenced without simultaneously bearing evidence to a Witness-self. A detailed consideration and criticism of the Advaita analysis of the twin-concepts is therefore in order. It will also bring out the difference in the quality of evidence that Śaiva Siddhānta adduces for *mala*.

Perceptual evidence and *ajñāna*

The question is whether these perceptual and memory judgments about Ignorance may not be more plausibly interpreted in ways which do not imply an existent *ajñāna* and consciousness thereof.[12] 'I do not know' is evidence of a mere factual privation or absence of knowledge, as may be seen from the use of the negative prefix in the aforesaid and similar perceptual judgments.[13] It is a commonplace assumption that prior to the rise of any specific knowledge a factual absence of that knowledge exists. All such expressions assertive of one's knowledge of ignorance, general or specific, merely imply a simple negation and a 'perception' of that negation.[14]

But then an assertion about the negation of knowledge, is somewhat paradoxical. The problem is: does the assertion imply or not a prior knowledge of the negated (*pratiyogin*) before there arises a knowledge of negation. On neither count, negation of knowledge seems assertible.[15] If there is a prior knowledge of the absent (*pratiyogin*) before an assertion of absence, this very knowledge will militate against the claim to know absence as such of all that there is. If, on the other hand, there is no prior knowledge of the absent, an assertion implying knowledge of the absence of knowledge itself cannot arise. Without a prior knowledge of the counter-correlate (*pratiyogin*) there can arise no knowledge of absence.

The dilemma stated in simpler language amounts to this: To know absence presupposes a prior knowledge, a knowledge presumably of that very object whose absence is claimed to be known. The presupposition is necessary in so far as absence is always absence of something and knowledge, knowledge of some object. All affirmation is affirmation of *something* (in the logical sense of some) while negation is absolute negation. But then, to grant this will mean a contradiction. To know something and also claim to know its absence are contradictory.

It cannot be held that 'I do not know' merely pre-supposes some knowledge, say knowledge of a pitcher as against which I say I do not know. As the disavowal of knowledge in 'I am ignorant' is general, not of anything in particular, a previous knowledge of, say a pitcher, it is thought, may be safely pre-supposed as the counter-correlate without offending against the claim not to know a thing. But this is not tenable. On the analysis that 'I do not know' implies absence of knowledge a prior knowledge of even a pitcher will be proof against the claim of absence of knowledge.[16] This will be so whether 'absence of knowledge' is understood as generic absence (*sāmānyābhāva*), or as a conjunction of specific absences (*abhāva-kūṭa*). A generic absence of knowledge cannot be unpervaded by one of its specific absences implied by the prior knowledge of a pitcher. A 'composite or heap' of absences, again, is equivalent in truth value to a generic absence only when it is a product of *all* specific absences. Denial of even one specific absence will not be compatible with the assertion of a composite of absences considered as a logical product.[17] There will, otherwise, arise the contingence of accepting the plausibility of one's disavowal to know something at the same time while he has knowledge of that something.[18]

The same difficulty will make it impossible to apprehend the absence of a particular knowledge (*jñāna-viśeṣābhāva*). To perceive the absence of a thing, *it* has first to be brought within consciousness. The negative judgment 'I do not know myself and others' need not presuppose an affirmative judgment, it may be thought. It only presupposes the presentation perhaps in imagination or memory, about myself and others. But is this plausible? If there is even a presentation of an object to one's consciousness, how can one assert in the same breath its absence?

It may be thought that the counter-correlate or the 'describer' (*nirūpaka*) of a perceptual knowledge of absence of an object is, apprehension of the perceptual knowledge and not an apprehension of that object whose absence is to be perceived. In apprehending the perception of, say a pitcher, one has only an apprehension of *some* perception and not of a specific pitcher-perception. This also is not acceptable. An apprehension which 'describes' the perception of the pitcher's absence will necessarily involve apprehension of the *determinant* of that perception, namely the pitcher. Absence of a knowledge of the pitcher will presuppose not merely a general knowledge of the counter-correlate but a determinate knowledge of the pitcher.[19]

Yet another defence of the position that 'I do not know' evidences only 'absence' of knowledge can be as follows: The proposition 'I do not know' does not of course involve negation of a particular object previously known as such, but negation of some object that may be given some determinate predicate, say that it is man. Remembering a thing which is both given and of the form of a person, I say, 'I do not know' meaning by it that I do not know if the given were a person or not. As negation here only presupposes only a recollection of what is given as possibly a person, the latter is compatible with a negation of the same implied by the assertion that I do not know if the given were a person. It is only if there is a previous knowledge of the given as the person, that 'I do not know that the given is person' will be a contradiction.

In reply, it may be observed that as negation cannot be given apart from the twin factors of knowledge of the thing negated (*pratiyogin*) and locus of the negation (*anuyogin*), in the above analysis a knowledge of the absence of a person as characterising the given, will entail also a previous knowledge of (*i*) the person, as that of whom there is absence and of (*ii*) the 'given' as that whereof something is absent. Therefore even if the counter-correlate of negation be only a memory-judgment there is no escape from self-contradiction. In the very negation itself is involved a knowledge of something and simultaneously a disavowal of its knowledge.

Nor may it be argued that a knowledge of the negated which negation entails is only a prior knowledge, that is knowledge pertaining to some other time, so that the latter may not be contradicted by its being disclaimed in the present negation. A negative judgment of perception pertaining to the present must imply an affirmation pertaining to the same present. A perceptual judgment by definition apprehends what pertains neither to the past nor to the future, but only to the present occasion of the experience which that judgment directly reports. The *pratiyogin* of a perceptual negation accordingly cannot relate to some other time.[20]

The question of how both knowledge and ignorance with regard to an identical content are compatible on the hypothesis of *bhāvarūpa ajñāna* remains, however, to be discussed. *Ajñāna* is understood on a parity with *jñāna* as a positive something rather than as the privation or absence of *Jñāna*. The problem then will be about the relation of this positive Ignorance to knowledge. It is one of opposition or no opposition? If latter, that is, if Ignorance were compatible with knowledge, when one comes to know a pitcher one may also at the same time well claim to be ignorant of it. Knowledge of the pitcher must be simultaneously compatible with ignorance of the pitcher, as not opposed to it. If, however, Ignorance were the *opposiet*[21] of knowledge the old difficulty raised against the 'privation' theory will have to be faced. To be ignorant is to be aware of its opposition to knowledge[22] and therefore ignorance of the pitcher will presuppose simultaneously a knowledge of the pitcher[23] no less on this theory than on the theory that ignorance is a factual privation of knowledge.

In reply, it is pointed out how knowledge and ignorance can be compatible with regard to the same content, and that indeed, because it is possible that there is consciousness of ignorance. The same content may be known, negatively as well as positively, as unknown and as known. The object of ignorance is not indeed known through the senses and the connected factors of the mind (*vṛtti-jñāna*) and yet it cannot be said to be not known at all.

The *Advaitin* postulates a transcendental consciousness (*sākṣi-jñāna*) besides the empirical, which knows *all* things always. It is independent of the instruments of knowledge and disappears no more with the latter's disappearance than it is produced with them. It is by the acceptance of this eternal knowledge that even one's ignorance becomes manifest to oneself. Ignorance is really not incompatible with this *sākṣi-jñāna*; the latter, actually reveals ignorance along with its locus and object.

There are then two kinds of knowledge, one compatible with ignorance, the other not. The non-empirical witness-consciousness is compatible with ignorance; it reveals it *qua* opposite of knowledge. Ignorance of pitcher, for example, is illumined by *sākṣin qua* opposite of a knowledge of pitcher. Ignorance of pitcher, the knowledge regarding which it is ignorance, and the 'determinant' of the knowledge namely a pitcher — all are indifferently illumined by *sākṣin.* An indeterminate knowledge is not, therefore incompatible with a determinate ignorance.

It may be asked whether an indeterminate knowledge of ignorance of a pitcher must not again be preceded by a determinate knowledge of pitcher. Without a previous determinate knowledge of the pitcher how can one be conscious of being ignorant of the pitcher? That an 'indeterminate' knowledge of pitcher can co-exist with a determinate ignorance of the same, therefore stands unproven. An indeterminate knowledge of pitcher will point in its turn to a determinate pitcher as its cause. Even though *sākṣi-jñāna* may be compatible with ignorance, the *vṛtti-jñāna* which it in turn presupposes will, therefore, conflict with the ignorance.

The answer to this objection is simple. This order, that before the manifestation of the 'pitcher-qualified ignorance' there must *first* be determinately manifest the pitcher, will hold good only in the case of occurrent or originated instances of knowledge. But transcendental consciousness is eternal and it eternally manifests all things.[24] Therefore, even though a 'determinate' (*avacchinna*) manifestation may point to a 'determinant' (*avacchedaka*), in the case pertaining to *sākṣi-jñāna* there is no time-relation of first and later between the two. The two are simultaneously manifest to *sākṣin.*

This answer will also adequately meet the objection that even as ignorance is known as a positive something it is also known as the opposite of knowledge and that therefore on this theory too one is not free from the presupposition of a militating counter-correlate. The problem of ignorance arising neither with nor without the knowledge of what one is ignorant of, namely, the *pratiyogin* does not simply arise on the assumption of a transcendental consciousness which *simultaneously* manifests ignorance and its so-called counter-correlate. The difficulties arising from either accepting or rejecting a counter-correlate for negation become irrelevant on the hypothesis of a positive ignorance

Nor may the claims of the theory of 'absence of knowledge' be buttressed with a similar defence. Accepting a transcendental consciousness one may profitably defend the theory of 'absence of knowledge' instead of surrendering it to that of 'positive ignorance'. But this is not tenable for transcendental consciousness is indeterminate by definition while all cognition of absence is determinate as implying cognition of the absence of *something*.[25] The postulate of transcendental knowledge cannot be pressed into service to solve the problem of the apperceiving of the absence of knowledge. Transcendental knowledge apperceives negation in its generality while the particular knowledge of the thing negated, which is rightly opposed to negation, is acquired extraneously, by the operation of *vṛtti*. That this explanation cannot hold for 'absence' may be seen from the fact that there is no such thing as a generalised absence as all absence is essentially determinate.

The upshot of the discussion is, briefly, that the judgment 'I am ignorant' evidences a positive Ignorance which is being attributed to me, and that therefore it has parity with 'I know'. The solution to the paradox of my knowledge of *what* I am ignorant of, is that 'knowledge' of Ignorance is transcendental knowledge which simultaneously illumines contents as well as ignorance of the contents. The main point of dispute in this account is the contention that *ajñāna* is never opposed to the *sākṣin* or what is same, the *sākṣi-jñāna* never opposes but on the other hand, always is revelatory of *ajñāna*. But is *sākṣi-jñāna* always revelatory?

Take the instance of the experience of pleasure. This is, admittedly, a case of transcendental intuition (*sākṣi-jñāna*). How is it that a 'delusion' of pleasure is never as a rule experienced? It is idle to say that pleasure is *intrinsically* free from obscuration and that therefore it is meant, that it is revealed by transcendental knowledge ever as unobscured. For, in that case, it is pertinent to ask how when pleasure is not, as a fact, experienced one says 'I am unaware of pleasure'. If pleasure *qua* an internal state is ever unobscured it should always be manifest to one's consciousness and not only when it is in fact experienced. Pleasure is not experienced when it is not manifest, and when it is manifest it is never 'unexperienced' such that one may feel one is ignorant of it. The legitimate presumption, then, is that the unobscured nature of pleasure-experience, is due to the circumstance that it is revealed by the transcendental consciousness. The latter no less than all empirical knowledge is inimical to obscuration by ignorance. It is not 'conducive' to it.[26]

The opponent holds that while transcendental knowledge is unopposed to ignorance, empirical, relational knowledge is the opposite and constitutes indeed the termination of ignorance. Is this always so? When one fails to recollect, say a pitcher seen on a previous occasion, one's ever present transcendental knowledge alone does not suffice to reveal one's non-recollection of pitcher. Even as one is, transcendentally, conscious of one's forgetfulness, one is not specifically conscious of one's *forgetfulness of pitcher*. For the latter, what is required is a relational knowledge of the form of memory.

Again take an instance of a valid inference to the effect that a yonder hill is fiery. This inferential knowledge which is a case of *vṛtti-jñāna* is not, however, a *vṛtti* which can terminate ignorance and unveil the inferred fire to the eye of the percipient. Accordingly, it is not a counter-positive of *ajñāna* and should take the form of the judgment 'I do not know' instead of 'I know it is fiery'.

The contention that *vṛtti-jñāna* is terminative of ignorance while *sākṣi-jñāna* is tolerant, and even conducive to ignorance, therefore, stands unproven. On the one hand, in the presence of *sākṣi-jñāna* there is no obscuration, no ignorance. On the other, even when *vṛtti-jñāna* functions ignorance persists, unaffected by the former's presence. What does this show?[27]

Instead of therefore accepting a questionable *bhāva-rūpa ajñāna* which *sākṣi-jñāna* reveals, it can be more plausibly held that it is only a negation of knowledge (*jñānābhāva*) that is being borne witness to by *sākṣin*. The argument that *sākṣi-jñana* is indeterminate cognition while all cognition of absence is determinate presents no special difficulty on this theory, no more than on the theory of *bhāva-rūpa ajñāna*. For even in the case of the positive Ignorance its counterpositiveness to a prior knowledge makes it no less determinate. That Ignorance is, as such, apperceived by *sākṣin* while its counterpositiveness to knowledge can be perceived by an extraneous *vṛrtti-jñāna* is a plea which can be urged as well in defence of 'negation of knowledge'. The generality of all negation is determinate and so it may be argued that there can be noapperceiving of negation as such as in the case of Positive Ignorance. But an indeterminate *sākṣin*, unlike an occurrent *vṛrtti*, can apperceive negation as such, because *ex hypothesi sākṣin* is not generated, say, by a previous knowledge of the object of negation.[28]

Remembrance and *ajñāna*

Remembrance of *ajñāna* directly experienced during sleep-state (*suṣupti*) is embodied in the memory-judgments 'I slept soundly', 'I did not know anything', which one has on waking. This is adduced as yet another perceptual evidence of *ajñāna*. Remembrance or recollection to that effect on waking after deep sleep is evidence of direct acquaintance with *ajñāna* during the sleep state which is being remembered in the form 'I was absolutely ignorant then'. The commonplace memory-judgment bears evidence to (*i*) the existence of the positive *ajñāna* during sleep and also (*ii*) experience of it in an unself-conscious way during that state. Were there no *ajñāna* and were it not also apprehended one cannot *recall* having had no knowledge.

The Vedāntic analysis of deep sleep is with a view to demonstrate the continuity of witness-consciousness and also the presence of *ajñāna* as a positive something homogeneous and indeterminate, as pure objectivity shorn of all empirical variety. Śaiva Siddhānta, as it shall be made clear, does not accept this analysis. There is no positive 'objective' experience in sleep[29] and *ātmacit-śakti* already individualised as agent-subject of experience is characterised by absence of knowledge of the empirical world in the absence of a functioning of the means of knowledge. During deep sleep the *ātman* in its individuated form as 'I' exists but without knowledge of any object and feeling of pleasure and the factual absence of knowledge and feeling in that state is known only by inference on waking from sleep.

Had there been knowledge during sleep, there would be memory-impressions of the same on awakening; but the judgment 'I did not know anything' is proof of the paucity of any memory. The content of the judgment in fact is itself evidence of the utter *absence* of memory about the sleep-state preceding it. From the absence of memory can we not infer in retrospect the factual absence of any knowledge during the condition of deep sleep?

But this inference surely is open to question.[30] Firstly, while all remembrance necessarily points to a previous experience, all experience need not have to be accompanied by remembrance, so that from an absence of remembrance one may infer the absence of a previous experience. From the absence of any remembrance it is legitimate to infer a presumed absence of previous experience as but a possible explanation of the present absence of remembrance. There is no necessity or invariability about absence of remembrance being preceded by absence of previous experience.

At the most, from the non-remembrance of anything it is plausible to infer the absence only of that kind of intense experience which is generally accompanied by residual impressions in the mind. An impressionless experience might well have been characteristic of sleep. It cannot be argued that memory impressions of a previous experience are in the mind but are unrevived for want of the cues (*udbodhaka*). For the memory judgment 'I knew ***absolutely nothing***' certifies to the non-availability of the impressions. With intense thinking and meditation which is also one of the cues for reviving memory impressions one is yet never as a rule able to remember any previous experience during sleep.

Absence of knowledge during sleep may be inferred from the circumstance of the non-availability of the necessary conditions of knowledge at hand, so it may be argued. But this is not tenable. For how is one to know about the non-availability of the conditions of knowledge during sleep? The conditions of knowledge are never known directly but inferred from the resulting knowledge. Absence of knowledge is inferred from the absence of the conditions of knowledge and from the latter is inferred the absence of knowledge — a veritable vicious circle.

In sleep there could have been no knowledge because of the express non-functioning of the sense organs, it may be said. But is it 'non-functioning of the sense organs' at the time of sleep but as known now, that proves that absence of knowledge or is it non-functioning of the sense organs but as known immediately at the time of sleep itself? Not certainly the second. If knowledge of the non-functioning of senses was present during sleep then it is not true that the self is then characterised by absence of knowledge. Nor can my knowledge now about the non-functioning of the senses at the time of sleep be proof of the absence of knowledge at that time.[31] My present knowledge cannot be used as a middle term to prove the absence of something in the past.

The paucity of the operation of the senses during sleep might be inferred from the refreshed sense of well-being which characterises the body and mind on awakening, it may be urged. From the datum of the felt refreshedness of the senses and the fitness of the body on awakening, the paucity of all sense operation and a consequent absence of disturbance in deep sleep may be inferred; and from this again may be inferred absence of any knowledge during the condition of sleep. But this argument too is faulty. For what evidence is there regarding the connection between the refreshed condition of the senses and their previous non-functioning? Not certainly direct experience. The two must be both given at the same time to one's direct experience before a connection between them can be established. Nor can it be from others' experience. It is not after perceiving a non-functioning of senses being followed by their refreshed condition in others' cases that one feels on awakening not to have known anything while asleep.

Other physiological explanations for the non-functioning of *manas* and the consequent unconsciousness may be sought to be used as the middle term for inferring absence of knowledge during sleep.[32] The problem with such explanations is, how does the middle term come to be known. Every suggested middle term has in turn to be inferred with the help of some other middle term. And this launches us on an argument which is viciously circular.

Let then, 'I did not know anything in sleep' be a case of memory (*parāmarśa*) but why should it be memory referring to an objective experience? The aforesaid objections are only against taking it as inference but this itself is no proof of the experience of *bhāva-rūpa ajñāna* during sleep. The memory, as the negative form of the memory judgment indicates, may well relate to the *absence* of any cognitive experience. To demand a knowledge of the presence (*pratiyogi-jñāna*) for the knowledge of absence (*abhāva-jñāna*) will not avail in this case; any knowledge in the sleep-state is *ex hypothesi* ruled out. This is the substance of the objections raised against all attempts to infer with the help of some middle term the factual absence of knowledge during sleep. Absence of knowledge may be characteristic of the self in sleep without a knowledge of the counter-correlate.

In reply it may be shown that the main point of objection against inferring absence of knowledge during sleep was the non-availability of a middle term which mediates between the two states and is itself immediately known. On the theory of a positive Ignorance (*bhāva-rūpa ajñāna*) no such difficulty can arise because Ignorance itself which is immediately perceived by *sākṣin* takes the place of the middle term. The ever available Ignorance which is immediate is the 'middle term' for evidencing absence of knowledge during sleep.

It is, therefore, plausible to hold that there is remembrance with regard to the presence of *ajñāna* during sleep and from its presence, absence of any specific knowledge is to be inferred; *ajñāna* is adequate as the middle term because of its invariability and immediacy. As Ignorance and *specific* knowledge are incompatible, from the presence of the first the absence of the second may be inferred.[33]

Examination and criticism

Absence of specific knowledge during sleep is a fact. What is disputed is the positing of an *ajñāna* to account for the absence of specific knowledge. The main consideration for interposing *ajñāna* between the self and absence of specific knowledge is that the latter, namely 'absence' cannot as such be known except as a consequence of *ajñāna*. A knowledge of the absence of knowledge in any other sense seems inconceivable.

Plausible as this position seems to be, it is not, however, free from dialectical difficulties. The alleged relation between the presence of Ignorance and absence of knowledge in sleep remains unproven. Ignorance is the middle term and absence of knowledge is the major. Now, is the 'absence of knowledge' 'described' by Ignorance in the sleep-state absence of all knowledge or is it of some specific knowledge?

Not the first. A general proposition to the effect that *all* absence of knowledge is related to Ignorance cannot be asserted; no illustrative instance can be found in our waking life where the relation may be perceived. What waking life can illustrate is a relation between Ignorance of a particular thing and a specific absence of knowledge about that thing; with the latter can co-exist other knowledges. But to assert a relation with the absence of all knowledge — absence of knowledge with which no knowledge co-exists, is not possible on the basis of any evidence from wakefulness.

Nor can the absence of knowledge in sleep which ignorance 'describes' be specific absence. A specific absence of knowledge is compatible with the presence of other knowledges; so that it is not established that during sleep the self is characterised by absence of *all* knowledge.

To say that Ignorance in sleep is related to a generic absence of knowledge in the sense of constant absence, will also not do. As the absence of knowledge characteristic of sleep is either prior absence of knowledge which is to follow after waking or a posterior absence of knowledge preceding sleep, in either case there cannot be constant absence of knowledge.

It may be argued that a generic absence of knowledge in sleep caused by Ignorance, may be inferred in the following manner. In every individual case of ignorance in waking life we may perceive its relation to a respective absence of knowledge; ignorance in respect of a pot is correlated with absence of a knowledge of pot. From this it may be generalised that in the state of sleep which is marked by Ignorance there is a corresponding absence of knowledge in its generality.

Every case of ignorance is necessarily related to a respective absence of knowledge. And the condition of primal, objectless Ignorance in sleep may likewise be known to be related to a general absence of knowledge. Ignorance is immediately apprehended by *sākṣin* and from Ignorance may be *inferred* absence of knowledge. Thus while absence of knowledge during sleep remains unexplained on other hypotheses, on the hypothesis of Ignorance and a transcendental consciousness (*sākṣin*) which apprehends Ignorance, it is adequately explained.

This claim too cannot pass muster. Let us examine this position with care. There is alleged a necessary, universal relation between positive Ignorance and a negation or absence of knowledge, as there is between smoke and fire. The relation may be apprehended in any instance of waking life; ignorance of pot and an absence of pot-knowledge are apprehended as mutually implicatory. Apprehension of the absence of say, pot-knowledge is open to all the difficulties alleged against a knowledge of ignorance in so far as it is a discursive apprehension of absence; knowledge of absence of knowledge can arise neither with nor without its counter-correlate. In the case of apprehension of positive Ignorance this difficulty does not arise because of the availability of transcendental consciousness but in the case of apprehension of absence of knowledge with which positive Ignorance is apprehended to be correlated, the difficulties urged by the opponent himself on the earlier occasion will arise. And without a knowledge of absence the alleged universal relation between the two will be uninstanced and therefore unevidenced.

If a knowledge of the major term, namely absence of knowledge, is unintelligible, still less is a knowledge of the middle term, namely ignorance, intelligible. In the example cited above, the middle term is ignorance of pot; to be precise, it is apprehension of 'pot-ignorance' as characterised by the universal of ignorance, just like the knowledge of smoke in the universal relation (*vyāpti*) between smoke and fire; the terms of the *vyāpti*, the pervaded and the pervader are not mere particulars but determinate particulars 'determined' by their respective universals. But *sākṣin* can give an indeterminate perception of ignorance and cannot reveal determinately 'ignorance with regard to pot'. The *sākṣin* can know Ignorance, not as a term in a relation, but as essence in its intrinsic character.

And lastly about the necessity of the relation between ignorance and absence of any knowledge: is the one necessarily related to the other, and if so, on what ground? As ignorance and specific knowledge are contradictories, Ignorance can co-exist but only with 'absence' of all specific knowledge. From this follows, that in sleep with Ignorance coexists, not a general absence of knowledge but only absence of that kind of knowledge which is incompatible with Ignorance. Memory-knowledge, for example, is not incompatible with Ignorance; memory impressions of pot may well be co-present with 'ignorance with regard to pot' and likewise, memory-impressions of all objects can well be present with Ignorance during sleep.

Such are, in brief, the difficulties in inferring 'absence' of any knowledge on the assumption of the existence of a positive Ignorance. The difficulties are as insuperable on the assumption of it as without it.[34] To them are in fact added the difficulties inherent in the concept of positive Ignorance.

But this is only a *tu quoque* argument. How does Śaiva Siddhānta explain the inference of the absence of knowledge during sleep? Can it be said that because of the non-functioning of the causal apparatus necessary for knowledge during sleep, there was absence of knowledge? If so what about the difficulties already raised?

In answer[35] it may be suggested that (*i*) from the invariable absence of memory for any knowledge during sleep-state — which is so tellingly expressed in the form 'I did not know anything' it is plausible to infer the absence of any 'impression-leaving' knowledge, (*ii*) from the absence of such knowledge it is plausible to infer the absence of the causal apparatus necessary for engendering knowledge and (*iii*) lastly, from the inferred absence of the causal apparatus it is plausible to infer the absence of knowledge. It may be noted that circularity is avoided by arguing from the absence of a particular type of knowledge to the absence of the causal factors of knowledge and from thence again to the absence of all knowledge. This seems legitimate in as much as, the objective causal factors of knowledge are identical be it for knowledge that leaves behind impressions or for knowledge that does not do so.

Inference and *ajñāna* : [36]

The same spirit that Ignorance cannot be the unknowable — that it is "itself an object beside many others though it cannot have any other as its object, it being Ignorance" — inspires the *Advaitin* to undertake to adduce 'inferential' proof for *ajñāna*. *Bhāva-rūpa ajñāna* is inferred from the datum of knowledge of knowing something that was not previously known. All knowledge is of the nature of manifestation and manifestation implies removal of some positive veil that covered what is being manifested.

But surely the inference evidencing *ajñāna* cannot be of the ordinary syllogistic type. What is sought to be established through inference is something which is not evident except, if at all, through this inference. It is not like fire which we already know by perception and now infer to be present, say in the yonder hill. The very existence of *ajñāna* has to be evidenced through inference so that no observed instance of it can be cited and on the basis of it a general rule framed.[37]

But the *Advaitin* is not deterred by these considerations. He offers demonstrative proof of a sort quite different from the syllogistic type. It does not take the form of demonstrating that *ajñāna* exists but that there must be something which is capable of being destroyed by right knowledge. The reason (*hetu*) must be intrinsic to knowledge, something in virtue of which right knowledge is knowledge. There must be something which is beginningless other than the previous absence of right knowledge which is capable of being destroyed.

This is what right knowledge of, say A, invariably accompanies, the reason being that it is right knowledge — the cause of the manifestation of the previously unmanifest object. In similarity with the case of the right knowledge of say, B where the incidence of *his* right knowledge may be seen to involve a destruction of the previous absence of his right knowledge, the case of A's right knowledge also may be seen to involve or imply destruction of some positive Ignorance, akin to and yet different from the previous absence of A's right knowledge. Something which is beginningless in nature unlike a different knowledge which also exists before the incidence of right knowledge and is destroyed or terminated by it.[38]

The inference is, indeed, very odd; it is made with so many stipulations and supported by an illustration which itself is expressly not an instance of what is sought to be proved by the inference. The stipulations are apparently necessary to exclude the candidacy of the following from claiming the place of *bhāva-rūpa ajñāna* (i) the previous absence of right knowledge which also invariably precedes and is terminated by right knowledge, (ii) the supersensible dispositions (*adṛṣṭa*) in the locus of the self which too generally precede and are terminated by the effect and (iii) the preceding item of knowledge which a succeeding right knowledge invariably supersedes (all knowledge being *svottara-guṇa-nāśya*). What every right knowledge *qua* knowledge implies, on the other hand, necessarily and invariably is the existence of a positive, beginningless Nescience which it (the right knowledge) duly destroys.

The above inference though very ingenious, and technically free from formal errors may be criticised on grounds of wanting in pursuasiveness. A demonstrative inference must not merely demonstrate the necessary presence of the minor term (*sādhya*) in the major (*pakṣa*) but, to be pursuasive, also demonstrate that it is present unconditionally except for the condition of the middle term (*hetu*). If what is sought to be proved is available in the *pakṣa* not in virtue of the presence of *hetu* but because of some condition (*upādhi*) other than the *hetu*, the proof will consequently fail of its purposes as an effective clincher. In the inference about A's right knowledge being invariably preceded by something which it (right knowledge) destroys because of its being a right knowledge, the alleged precedence of 'something destroyed by A's knowledge' may be due to the circumstance of that something being non-related to A and not necessarily to its preceding a right knowledge.[39]

Again take the illustrative instance (*dṛṣṭānta*) of the inference. A's right knowledge is said to be a terminator of some positive beginningless ignorance which is different from a mere factual absence of A's right knowledge which in turn is also terminated. And the example illustrative of knowledge in the role of a terminator, is B's right knowledge which is known if only to terminate the factual absence of B's right knowledge. The argument is more ingenious than pursuasive. And the illustrative instance is surely the least convincing part of the argument.[40] The entire argument rests on the assumption that manifestation of an object consists merely in dispelling what is opposed to its relation. On the contrary, can it not be said that it consists as much in defining the object ?

Mala and the problem of evidence

The upshot of the entire discussion is to deny that Ignorance can be established by perceptual or even by inferential evidences. Any attempt to prove *mala* will presuppose a consciousness of the difference between bondage and liberation. It is only in the felt contrast between the two states that the real causal factor underlying the distinction can be known. *Mala* is significantly described as 'darkness' — 'darkness beyond all darkness' which is not to be perceived or plumbed by sense or reason. The one point of difference drawn between physical darkness and the Darkness of *mala* is that while physical darkness veils all things but unveils itself, the second one unveils neither.[41] Picturesqueness apart the suggested difference excludes an exoteric understanding of the function of that which constitutes our bondage. That it is 'darkness' implies that it cannot be known from the point of view of the eye 'in darkness' but only from the viewpoint of the eye 'in association with light'. Darkness has to be searched out by the help of light.[42] Though 'perception' is ruled out of court — the *paśu* cannot *perceive* the transcendental condition of his *paśutva* while conditioned by it. Inference and implication may be used to elucidate what is entailed by the contrast of bondage and liberation.[43]

Arguments for Mala[1]

By what evidences does Śaiva Siddhānta establish *āṇava mala*? Though no perceptual evidence is admissible from the very nature of the case, reason can certainly help us to conceive of this principle of obscuration. The self must be obscured by *mala* in so far as the self while being unlimited is *de facto* only of limited knowledge. One who is never of limited knowledge is never also obscured by *mala* presumably as it is, for example, in the case of God.[2] If self were not obscured by *mala*, whence comes his desire for experience?[3] The will to live and enjoy which underlies a life of affirmation (*pravṛtti*) characterising all living beings proceeds from a state of primordial privation and obscuration.[4] It is the latter state of deprivation that drives or impels one into activity. From this experience of felt impulsion we infer an antecedent state of obscuration and arrest. The rise of this impulsion to act will be unaccountable. If this desire (*āsakti*) for *bhoga* can arise in one who is unobscured by *mala* it can arise too in the case of the liberated (*mukta*). By liberation (*mokṣa*) we mean termination of *bhoga*.[5] Attachment (*rāga*) is ofcourse the immediate cause of the desire for 'enjoyment'. But why does attachment fail to lead the liberated into *bhoga*?[6] Neither the ever free Lord, nor the freed or liberated soul suffers from longing for 'enjoyment'.

The chief argument for the admission of *mala* is, that its presence is the implication of the distinction between bondage and liberation. On no other valid presumption can liberation be told apart from bondage.[7]

The liberated man (*mukta*) is one who is liberated from something which was throughout with him during bondage and, presumably, constituting his bondage from which he is now said to be liberated. Freedom from *mala* alone it may be shown constitutes freedom from bondage as such.[8] It is not mere freedom from embodiment because in death and again in the states of world-dissolution such freedom is achieved. For the same reason it cannot be also freedom from cognition *etc.*[9] because the latter are contingent on the embodied condition. It cannot also be freedom from good (*dharma*) and evil (*adharma*). As self is always intrinsically free from them — *dharma* and *adharma* being only dispositions of *buddhi*,[10] even in the bound condition itself, such freedom is secure. It cannot be freedom from the *karma* which is causatively constitutive of respective experiences. Freedom from *karma* which is actively causative (*phalopadāyaka*) of *bhoga* is achieved in the state of Dissolution also. Freedom from *karma* which is *potentially* causative (*savarūpayogya*) of *bhoga* on the other hand is not achieved even in *mokṣa*, because a potential cause being identical with essence is never terminable. Moreover, freedom from a potential, undifferentiated *karma* may be said to be achieved in a measure by every one here itself; for example, one is free from the potentiality of another's *karma*. Nor may it be said that by *karma* should be meant the respective *karma* of persons causing the respective *bhoga*. It is simpler to assume a causal relationship between *karma qua karma* (*karmatvena*) not necessarily one's *karma* (*svakṛta-karma*) and *bhoga*.[11] Śaiva Siddhānta assumes *niyati* as the allocating principle conditioning the experience of the fruits of *karma* to the *respective* agents.

Nor does freedom from impression of delusion (*bhrānti-vāsanā*) constitute *mokṣa*,[12] such freedom being in a sense always achieved so far as the self is concerned. *Buddhi* is the seat of impressions and self *per se* is always free from it. Freedom from *māyā* also is not the cause of *mokṣa* because one particular self may be freed from the sphere of *māyā*.[13] *Māyā's* existence is necessary for evolving the tattvas in the form of the common world as well as for evolving the uncommon tattvas which constitute the *puryaṣṭaka*, the vehicle for each individual self's enjoyment. To be freed from the enjoyer-enjoyed relationship (*bhogya-bhoktṛ-bhāva*) between *māyā* and *puruṣa* is also not *mokṣa*. For here again if it is freedom from actual relationship such freedom is available in *pralaya* itself. If it is freedom from a potentiality (*svarūpa-yogyatā*) of it even the freed one is not free from it as potentiality persists without end.[14]

By the method of elimination it thus follows that what one is freed from when one attains *mokṣa* is an unconditioned condition obstructing unconditionedly again the unbroken continuity of bliss-experience; termination of this condition alone implies Freedom.[15] The argument for *mala* thus narrows down to one point: a primordial non-manifestness of the experience of Bliss constitutive of one's very Being (*Śivam*).[16]

But this argument is quite vulnerable. As *mala* is one, as one is liberated from *mala* the latter must cease to exist. If it be argued that *mala* though one has many concealing *śaktis*[17] and that it is only one *śakti* that is called off as a result of one attaining liberation, the same may be said about the already accepted principle of *māyā*; *māyā* is one but it has innumerable 'individual' *śaktis* which go to constitute the *puryaṣṭaka* of individual selves; one such *śakti* disappears on one ataining liberation, but *māyā* itself continues. Why posit *mala*?

Again, one may not at all admit the intelligibility of bliss-experience. To say that it is characteristic of attainment of Freedom makes no sense. What after all is the evidence of the presence of such experience in *mokṣa* when we have, admittedly, no inkling of it now? Assuming that it is present in *mokṣa*, it may well be that it originated with the advent of *mokṣa*. Why have we to assume its existence even now and also posit some obstruction for it to account for our non-experience of it? Nor may it be argued that an originated experience might have also to end, and that, therefore, there may be a relapse to bondage. On independent grounds, for example, from scripture, we know that *mokṣa* is interminable and that one never swerves from that condition. Neither may one argue from the eternity of *mokṣa* to the eternal unoriginated nature of bliss-experience. By the same logic one may have to say that *mokṣa* itself is unoriginated.[18]

If bliss experience is unintelligible its non-manisfestness (*aprakāśatva*) is even less proved. A privation or absence, in a literal sense, of self's luminosity,[19] cannot certainly be what is meant by non-manifestness. As self's luminosity is eternal its absence is non-available even in Bondage in spite of the presence of what allegedly conditions its non-manifestness. Non-manifestness cannot also mean a modified state of self's luminosity.[20] The latter, identical with self is immutable (*apariṇāmin*) and if it can be modified it can be as well originated. Nor can non-manifestness imply absence of relation with the object.[21] Neither self-relation (*svarūpa-saṁbandha*) nor identity relation (*tādātmya*) can admit of its own absence. An external conjunction which admits also disjunction is unthinkable as the relation between self's luminosity and the object illumined by it. Non-manifestness cannot also be interpreted to mean being related to darkness (*tamas*)[22] because to do so is to beg the very question at issue.

As self's nature is of the essence of manifestness (*prakāśātmaka*) to admit non-manifestness for it is indeed contradictory. Therefore, by non-manifestness what is meant one may say, is absence, not of self's luminosity, but the luminosity due to *vṛtti*[23] — a *judgment* of the feeling of bliss considered a mode of *buddhi*. To this the objection is: such non-manifestness is available in the state of *mokṣa* also, as for example, in the case of the Freed self who also does not have a *judgment* of bliss, and conversely, even in the state of bondage non-manifestness in the above sense of the term is not available: one has an inferential *judgment* or a *judgment* through the evidence of testimony, to the effect that one has the feeling of bliss.[24] A judgment about one's feeling of bliss one has even when one is not liberated from bondage, and paradoxically even the Liberated has no *judgment* of bliss-feeling.

By non-manifestness is meant, it may be said, what is conveyed by the significant expression:[25] *it is not, and it is not manifest* (*nāsti na prakāśate*). What is implied by this expression is, that which should be patent as existent is covered and made to seem non-existent, which presumably is the work of an obstructing principle, namely *mala*.

Just as one expresses on returning to wakeful condition after deep sleep, that he did not know anything in the previous state, it is a commonplace experience that the blissful nature of self is non-existent and non-evident. To explain the unmanifest character of bliss compatibly with one's acceptance of its existence we have to appeal to a positive obstruction, which covers or veils what should otherwise be manifest and makes it seem non-existent. Such is *mala*, so it may be argued.

But even this does not seem convincing. The very experience to which bliss seems non-existent, it can be said, *a priori*, cannot arise and the expression "*it is not*; *it is not manifest*" is, consequently, inept. Admission of the nature of essential manifestness (*svarūpa-prakāśa*) to bliss is incompatible with even a seeming experience of its non-existence.[26] In so far as consciousness *is* self-luminous bliss and not merely *has* bliss, its existence cannot be abstracted from its self-luminosity such that one might suspect that only the latter was obscured and later de-obscured.

If this expression (*abhilāpa*) of a feeling of non-existence and non-manifestness were to clinch the argument what about persons in the bound state itself whose 'bondage' precisely precludes a confession to such feeling? Shall we say that in their cases there is absence of non-manifestness? Again, an expression like 'it is not; it is non-existent' is a judgment of thought, expressed in a sentence. How can the cause of it be a thing like *mala* ? From the evidence of a judgment we can only argue to a state of knowledge; we cannot jump to a conclusion about the existence of a substance. A positive substance may have to be posited as the cause of the condition of a loss of manifestness of bliss, it may be said. A real and not a seeming loss of self-manifestness of bliss is inconceivable without detriment to the integrity of spirit whose essence is bliss.

There seems, in short, no way of explaining non-manifestness of bliss in the face of the following dilemma : it cannot be opposed to self-manifestness; it cannot also be unopposed to self-manifestness. If it is opposed to it, manifestness (*prakāśa*) ceases to be invariable and consequently the self too, identical with self-menifestness will cease to be 'self'. If it is *not* opposed to it non-manifestness has no meaning, the difference betwden the two being merely terminological (*pāribhāṣika*).[27] It thus follows that the argument for *mala* on the ground of 'unintelligibility otherwise' of non-manifestness of bliss, is without force. This dilemma, that the obstructing principle of consciousness cannot be *opposed* to consciousness, and is at the same time nothing if it is not opposed to it, will have to be faced by all those who argue that consciousness in principle omniscient, is *de facto* limited because of an obstructing adjunct.

The critic may not stop here. He may even have positive reasons against entertaining the concept of *mala*: (i) Self is spirit and its self-manifestation *cannot conceivably be* under a veil. How can a lamp be veiled by darkness? (ii) Is the veil of consciousness natural (*svābhāvika*) to consciousness or is it adventitious (*āgantuka*)? If it is natural and intrinsic to consciousness, it cannot be terminated. If it is adventitious it will mean that initially there was absence of non-manifestness; consciousness originally self-manifest subsequently became unmanifest. Can this be acceptable? Moreover, if veiling or obstruction can be adventitious why not accept the passions of *moha*, etc., whose distorting role in perception is recognised, in the place of a transcendental condition of obstruction? If *mala* is transcendentally deduced as the cause of these passions etc., one can more plausibly explain them (passions etc.) as contingent upon empirical factors like errors of judgment. (iii) If consciousness were under a veil the veiling principle must be coeval with consciousness, infinite (*vibhu*); if so how is it conceivable that it does not also veil God's consciousness? As infinite, *mala* cannot but be related to *śiva*, also infinite. Nor may it be argued that conjunction of *mala* and *śiva* is eternal or uncaused (*aja*). It can be so in the case of *mala-jīva* conjunction also.[28]

These objections may now be considered. It may be pointed out that the experience underlying the expression "bliss is not; it is not manifest" is unexceptionable and one cannot gainsay the factual meaning of the expression on theoretical considerations. The expression suggests there is bliss and yet it is not felt to be present or manifest. Were not bliss present as implied by this expression it would follow that it is not present in *mokṣa*, which is contradictory.[29] Neither can it be said that bliss originates anew in *mokṣa*. What is originated must have an end. It cannot be argued that for the same reason *mokṣa* itself must be unoriginated. For *mokṣa* is another name for the manifestation of bliss-experience and the issue under discussion is identical.[30] The 'origination' of bliss-experience is but the termination of the constituent condition of bondage, namely *mala*.

Difficulties have been raised about the intelligibility of the concept of non-manifestness of bliss (*ānandāprakāśatva*). By non-manifestness is meant what is present and yet not felt to be present or manifest as conveyed by the expression "it is not; it is not manifest". Literally, it implies privation of the self-luminous *cit-śakti* (*cicchaktyabhāva*). Nor may it be questioned how this is conceivable. For it is not privation of *cit-śakti* as such — that is certainly unacceptable but privation of *cit-śakti qua* qualified by the absence of a veil.[31] *Cit-śakti* qualified by the absence of a veil is manifestness (*prakāśatva*) while a privation of *cit-Śakti* qualified by the absence of a veil will be non-manifestness (*aprakāśatva*).

Being the condition which causes this privation or non-manifestness is the characteristic of *mala*. The existence of *mala* is derived from the unintelligibility otherwise of the circumstance of a privation (*abhāva*) of *cit-śakti qua* characterised by the absence of a veil. Though *cit-śakti* as such is eternal and can admit of no privation, in its circumstance of being characterised by something, it can point to a state when it has been deprived of that circumstance.

The 'generating' condition of this privation must accordingly be understood not as the cause which brings about a new result but as the occasioning factor which (i) secures the privation of the determinate whole (*viśiṣṭa*) by (ii) inhibiting or arresting the determinant part (*viśeṣaṇa*).[32] A determinate (*viśiṣṭa*) implies the determinant (*viśeṣaṇa*) without whose existence, the existence of the determinate is not intelligible. Accordingly the privation of the one implies the privation of the other; the relation between the two, it may be said, is the relation of 'intention-intended' (*prayojaka-prayukta*).[33] The *viśeṣaṇa* here is 'being characterised by the absence of a veil' and the *viśiṣṭa* is '*cit-śakti* characterised by the absence of a veil'. The *viśeṣaṇābhāva* will be 'absence or privation of being characterised by the absence of a veil'; when stripped of the double negative, it stands for the presence of the veil (*āvaraṇa*).[34] The *viśiṣṭābhāva* will be *privation* or non-presence of *cit-śakti* as characterised by the absence of the veil. *Mala* is derived as the causal factor which secures the presence of the veil and a consequent non-presence of *cit-śakti qua* characterised by the absence of the veil.

But the critic may object to the very notion of a veil in the context of *cit* or *cit-śakti*. How can even the possibility of the incidence oo *āvaraṇa* be conceived? In answer it may be said that from the *de fact*f experience of a felt absence of bliss and an absence of its manifestness it is legitimate to posit a general condition which thus obstructs the bliss experience, and from this valid presumption of a general notion of veil it is legitimate again to define what is implied in this general admission. As *cit-śakti* per se (*viśeṣya*) cannot be veiled so as to bring about its own privation (*abhāva*) *cit-śakti* as defined by some adjunct (*viśiṣṭa*) may be considered to be veiled and from this can be inferred the veiled state of the adjunct (*viśeṣaṇa*) itself.[35]

Non-manifestness of bliss (*ānandāprakāśatva*) it was argued, cannot be intelligible in the face of the dilemma: it cannot be either opposed or unopposed to self-manifestness.[36] If it is really opposed to it, self-manifestness is not invariable to self. If not really opposed no 'veil' is, then, implied. This objection also can be met in the light of the distinction that we have made between *viśeṣya* and *viśiṣṭa*. The self as what is defined (*viśeṣya*) is unopposed to non-manifestness but *qua defined* (*viśiṣṭa*) it is opposed to it.[37] *Mala* the condition of non-manifestness is not opposed to the intrinsically self-manifest *cit* or *cit-śakti* but is only opposed to it in its 'embodied', qualified nature.[38]

It was argued by the critic that a distinction between bondage and liberation can be made with the help of *māyā* itself and that it is not therefore necessary to posit *mala* in addition. *Māyā* too like *mala* may be conceived to have individual *śakti* corresponding to the individual 'physical' vehicle of experience (*puryaṣṭaka-deha*) which it evolves for endowing each form of life, and that in *mokṣa* there is termination (*vigamana*) for the individual *śakti* and not for *māyā* itself. This argument too it may be shown to rest on a mis-conception. *Māyā* is not *śaktimat* but *śakti* itself,[39] the causal unmanifest form of the manifest world and so its 'termination' is not conceivable without also involving a termination of the entire world process.[40] The only factor which when present conditions and constitutes bondage and whose absence ensues liberation, is *mala*.

The critic suggested certain positive reasons against *mala*: one was a counter-argument to the inference given for *mala*[41]— self-manifestness cannot be veiled by *tamas* just as light cannot be concealed by darkness (*tamas*) and that self-manifestness is a kind of illumination. The fallacy of this argument is quite apparent: there are four terms; *tamas* is used in two very different senses[42] between which there is no community of meaning.[43] If the middle term were understood in either of the two senses alone, the argument though formally valid will yield a conclusion that is either a truism or positively untrue.[44]

Another reason given for the non-acceptance of *mala* was: it cannot be natural to self and it cannot also be non-natural, that is adventitious. If natural it will be eternal and if otherwise it is a self-contradiction: *mala* in the sense of an unconditioned condition of bondage is only adventitious, it points to a state beyond itseslf. In examination of this argument, it may be conceded that *mala* is *svābhāvika* (natural) not certainly adventitious; the argument that the natural must be non-terminable (*avināśin*) however, may not be accepted.

The argument implied by the critic is either an inference of the following form: *mala* is non-terminable (*avināśin*) because it is 'natural' (*svābhāvika*) or, it may not be inference, but only a kind of *reductio ad absurdum* (*tarka*) of the form: if *mala* is natural it is non-terminable but as it is not non-terminable it follows that it is not also natural. Either way, it may be shown that the argument is not free from formal defects.

To explain. The *inference* to the effect that *mala* is *avināśin* because it is *svābhāvika* is, strictly, inadmissible. Either the subject (*pakṣa*) of the inference exists or it does not. If it exists *mala* is thereby accepted so that it becomes pointless to argue to show that there is no *mala*. If it does not exist there will be the fallacy of uncertainty about subject (*āśrayāsiddhi*). If the subject of the inference "were *mala* assumed to exist by the siddhāntin" there will be contradiction (*bādha*), absence of the thing to be inferred in the subject. For by the same evidence by which *mala* is assumed to exist its terminability is also assumed.[45] To say there is *mala* but it is non-terminable is contradictory.[46]

The *tarka* of the form that *mala* if natural will be eternal, and that in the absence of its eternity its 'naturalness' also is rightly in question, is also formally invalid. What is *tarka*? It is a supposition of the presence of a *hetu* (which must be actually absent) necessitating the supposition of the presence of the *sādhya* (whose presence is an absurdity).[47] But here the supposition of naturalness of *mala* is not supposing what is actually absent. By the same reason by which *mala* is inferred to exist its naturalness, (*svābhāvikatva*) also is inferred. *Mala's* unconditioned nature is part of the meaning of the concept.

The last objection to *mala* was that admission of *mala*, also infinite (*vibhu*) like the self that is veiled by it, must veil *Śiva* too who is infinite.

Just as we could validly presume and hypothesise about *mala* veiling the self from the datum of self's transition from a previous state of ignorance to the present state of knowledge, and from the factuality of the distinction of bondage and liberation, we have no similar datum phenomenologically available from which to presume that God could also be veiled by *mala*. On the contrary we are led by the arguments for *mala* to view God as eternally unveiled by *mala* in precisely the same sense the self is eternally veiled by it. The presumption of *mala*-obscuration for God runs counter to the arguments by which we are led to envisage the concept of *mala*. Moreover, there can be no obstruction or veil of the non-material (*ajaḍa*) by the material (*jaḍa*). *Śiva* is *pure* spirit and is the counterpositive of *mala* that veils.[48]

Nor may it be held that by the same logic the self too as non-material be not veiled by *mala*.[49] We presume, by implication and elimination of the other alternatives, a state of beginningless obstruction for the *ātmacit-śakti* notwithstanding its non-materiality. The obstruction, surely, cannot come from another non-material source. The non-material being a kindred of self cannot be its opposite causing obstruction. God, for example, cannot be conceived to veil the self being of homogeneous nature (*svajātīya*) 'as neem is of homogeneous nature with sandalwood with its arrested fragrance'. If self cannot be veiled by the non-material *mala*, by what else then can it be veiled? Not by another self, because that will mean terminability for the other self. The liberation of the self that is veiled implies a complementary *cessation* of the veil. We, therefore, conclude that only by *jaḍa* can *ajaḍa* be veiled. And from this we are led to make a distinction between the nature of God as non-material and self also as non-material but one constitutionally impervious to *mala* and the other open to its obstruction.[50]

The sense in which the concept of veil must be understood was already explained. It is not strictly 'veil' in the sense of screen which obstructs (*āvaraṇa*) and it cannot also be what actually effects a condition of non-illumination (*aprakāśśīkaraṇa*). Neither is compatible with the nature of *ātmacit-śakti* which is all-pervasive and eternal like self of which it is *guṇa*. What is its nature then?

The nature of *mala*-obstruction, precisely stated, is a de-functioning of the twin functions of knowledge and action of self towards the content (*kāryāpravartana*). Like fire which continues to exist unobstructed and manifest and yet its 'scorching' effect is 'arrested' or inhibited by *mantra-śakti*, the self too, without obstruction or destruction to its being, is nevertheless 'veiled' regarding the content-orientation of its knowledge-function (*śakti*). The concept of *śakti* as a distinguishable and yet inseparable aspect of a thing has already been explained.[51]

We may again distinguish[52] in *śakti*, between the aspect of content-determination which constitutes its functional differentiation and an aspect that is prior to it, constitutive of its undifferentiated function. It is the distinction between *kartavya-śakti* that is in relation with the content (*jñeya*) and *dṛkkriyā-śakti* that is different from and prior (*itara*) to the content (*parārthamātra-saṁśaktirūpa*).[53] It is the former that is arrested or obscured by *mala*. The self's content-directedness which is part of its being is unobscured but its *orientation* to the content is arrested. Just as the luminous visual sense enshrouded in darkness is not in consequence bereft of its luminosity or even its directedness of vision to external objects but is 'in itself' (*svaniṣṭha*) without the actual orientation; self too under the veil of *mala*, is neither bereft of its nature as illumination nor is at the same time illuminative of the content. It is in this sense obstruction (*bādhaka*) for knowledge is admitted as constitutive of its primary Bond (*pāśa*). It is Primordial obstruction (*pratibandha*) and *karma* and *māyā* too, are bonds (*pāśa*) only as consequential obstructions, *karma* as immediately accompanying it (*anubandha*) and *māyā* as the ensuing relation (*saṁbandha*).

BOOK FOUR

ON SELF : PAŚU

XI

THE SELF AND ITS KNOWLEDGE

The Self, its Existence and States

In the order of discovery, the notion of selfhood presupposes knowledge of the existence of the transcendent God and the phenomenal world. The contrast of the two orders gives rise to the concept of a *third* reality which, in participatively mediating between the two at the same time ceases to be a *third* something. Selfhood is a distinction without difference. In the very process of distinguishing the 'real' given in sense-experience from the reality implied by but transcending experience yet another distinction is suggested, namely, that of the self, to be distinguished alike from either of them. A 'self' whose being is to be understood phenomenologically speaking neither as different from that of phenomena nor as identical with that of the trans-phenomenal God. The *ātman* is characteristically named *paśu.*[1]

However in the order of understanding, of defining characteristics definition of self-hood with its implication of 'existence' individuated, isolated and estranged from the presence of Being by which it is, takes precedence over the definition of the two contrasted realities namely *pāśa* and *pati*. The two conditions or states of existence in and through which the realities of *pāśa* and *pati* respectively become evident to oneself, are meaningful against the perspective of a primordial transcendental state (*atīta avasthā*) of Ignorance and Inaction typified by the notion of *paśu*. To aniticipate what is to follow the *sa-kala* and *śuddha avasthās* in which one has the respective cognizance of *pāśa* and *pati* presuppose a *kevala avasthā* in relation to which *paśu* is known and defined.

The argument given as evidence (*pramāṇa*) for the reality of *paśu* resembles the argument used to elucidate the reality of *pati*. The same argument served to suggest or show both that there must needs be a Causal Agent for the world of becoming and also that it must be one having absolute Lordship over all cosmic functions and as such identifiable neither with any species of *pāśa* —*parmāṇu, prakṛti, kāla karma* or *svalakṣaṇa,* nor with that of *paśu*— the intelligent *puruṣa, puruṣa viśeṣa* or even *puruṣottama* in the heirarchy of selves. In the same manner the arguments supporting evidence of the reality of self or self-hood are also suggestive of the fact of experience that the self, thus arrived at, is of the nature of *paśu*, *not* identifiable with *pati* even as it is not identifiable with the realm of *pāśa*—body, senses, super-senses, vital air and so on.

The method of transcendental reflection used for discovering selfhood is employed by the generality of Indian philosophical thinking, orthodox and non-orthodox alike. The transcendental proof is the indication as it were, of a subjective experiment with the knowing function. Knowledge of self does not come *after* reasoning, as a conclusion following the premiss but shines in the very process of reasoning itself. It is not a case of proving or demonstrating that self is an entity that exists but one of distinguishing. The distinguishing may be *expressed* in the form of reasoning: *because* the self is said to be nought, the self is;[2] because it says 'my body' the self as different from body is. That this is so may be seen from the circumstance that the self is defined in terms of those very characteristic 'states' as subject thereto (*avasthā-pañcakastha*) which are employed in reasoning about the existence of an embodied, sense-endowed self as distinct from body, sense etc. The *pramāṇa* and *lakṣaṇa* are co-incident here as in the case of God.

The method of realising the conclusion in the very act of arguing, of 'seeing in the doing' may be seen to be a commonplace of reflective thinking. In the imaginative presentation of a motion, the path of the motion emerges into being. The line is there before oneself as one draws it . To 'prove' that the line is present as imaginatively apprehended or traced, is in fact to prescribe to others, to subject the apprehension to a recalling or imagining of one's own act of having drawn a line. Adducing of transcendental proof is likewise a phenomenological experiment involving a deepening and extending of the 'knowing' of knowing activity.[3] In the reasoning employed in demonstrating the *a priority* of self-hood or rather self-relatednesss the call is for inwardising or reflective introspection of knowledge by which one comes by an understanding of oneself.

The reality of self like that of God is in the final analysis accepted in faith and interpreted, distinguished by self-reflection. Although in one sense intelligible to thought as the subject of 'I consciousness', the reality of a distinctive self-hood eludes the grasp of all natural evidence. What is closest in existence is in a sense farthest in thought. The known categories of the object cannot be applied to what forms the very precondition of objectivity itself. The self being a transcendental condition of experience cannot be evidenced in the same manner in which any content of experience becomes evident to our understanding. It is like the sense organ eye being expected to turn its gaze at the seer by whom and at whose service it is able to see.

The most radical form of the denial of self-hood we have is the assertion that self is *śūnya*. Nought is its essence. The position of scepticism or nihilism about the reality of self as meriting consideration can, however, only mean not that self as such is not real but that self in any of its alleged meanings may not be conceived to exist. The *śūnyavādin's* denial may be thus analysed: the body, senses, objects, none of these can be 'self'; nor can the self be the immutable consciousness that underlies them. The 'self' so-called is, therefore, *śūnya*. The difference between the naturalist's and the materialist's denial of self, to be considered presently, and the *śūnyavādin's* denial of self is obvious. The 'body is self' theory (*dehātma-vāda*) denies self understood as something different from body. The 'psyche is self' theory (*antaḥ-karaṇātma-vāda*) denies self understood as different from one's psychical being. The vitalist advocating the theory that vital air is self denies self understood as different from the principle of vital life. The 'self is nought' theory however denies self understood as *anything*, as body, senses, objects as immutable entity or alternately that it is a complex and a continuum of *skandhas*. When it asserts that self is 'nought' in the final analysis it means indeed to deny that it is something or nothing or that it is both or neither.[4] No view of self or combination of view is tenable.

The advocates of the reality of a permanent *ātman* as well as those denying its permanence, equate it with a 'stream' of cognitive states employ the well known device of 'transcendental' epistemology and a similarly oriented psychology in support of their views. But an unbiased use of these methods would only evidence, the *śūnyavādin* suggests, that *śūnya* or nullity is the essence of self-hood. The self-theorist (*ātmavāḍin*) anchors his proof for *ātman* on the demand for an unsublatable basis (*adhiṣṭhāna*) in all cases of sublations or negations. In the classical case of 'this is not siliver'[5] the negation applies to silver-relation only so that the terms of the relation are intact with their reality unaffected by the negation of their relatedness. Or, the negation may be taken to apply to 'silver' as well as to silver-relation in so far as the relation itself cannot be negated if at least one of the terms of the relation too were not negated. The real then is that other term which is not negated and indeed stands as the basis of negation. Such is self.[6]

The Non-self theorist (*anātmavadin*) too interprets the negation in a typical negative judgment like the one considered above as applying to a feature ascribed to the ground, not to the ground itself. In 'this is not silver', the 'not' is a denial of 'this'. Negation removes objectification or externalisation as 'this' and also at the same time shows the identity and the reality of the other term as thought-content (*vijñānarūpa*).

The *śūnyavādin* finds these interpretations dogmatic. The pure epistemology of error-apprehension is vitiated by a hidden ontology: the ontology of self or the no less reprehensible ontology of states in the place of self. The mode of cancellation which supervenes on a univocal perception of the specific quality implies not merely that the silver apprehended no longer appears but it indeed was not there even when it did seem to appear. It is the correlate of total negation of the past and the future no less than of the present. The negation even as it is total in respect of 'where' and 'when' must apply totally in respect of 'what' also. The negation for all times applies not only to the 'silver' seen in the example but to all the factors without exception that seem to be intrinsic to the error-situation. What are negated in 'this is not silver' are : (i) the seer (ii) seeing or sight (iii) the sense-datum of silverness (iv) its relation to silver and (v) the silver itself.

The concept *śūnya* indeed derives its meaning from this typical situation of 'cancellation' of error: what admits of being negated totally for all times is *śūnya*; the 'self' approached through the idea of a subject that knows in a knowledge-situation comes under the sweep of total negation, and is therefore *śūnya*. That negation applies only to the perceived 'silver' and not to the perceiving subject admits of no proof. It is futile to try to salvage either the 'this' or the 'silver' in the context of which the real may hopefully be encountered. The one is as much 'false' (*śūnya*) as the other, as much negated in so far as the one is not come across without the other. It is idle to say that one-half of the 'illusion' only is negated and that the remaining half outlasts its sweep. Either the entire error-situation, inclusive preeminently of the 'perceiver' is negated or nothing indeed is negated. There cannot be a middle course no more than there can be between having a hen for laying eggs and cooking it for eating.[7]

The appeal to psychological introspection in evidence of the reality of self is equally unavailing. The self is said to be the unvarying residuum persisting through the variable states of wakefulness, dream and sleep (*avasthātrayāvyabhicārin*). What is this never-defunct residuous reality? It cannot be body or senses or mind or ego-sense as these admittedly become defunct in one or the other of these states. Nor can it be the momentary cognition (*kṣaṇika vijñāna*) as there is, presumably, discontinuity for it in deep sleep. The *anātmavādin* substitutes the temporary discrete mental states in place of the 'self' of the *ātmavādin*, and alleges their continuance in deep sleep as well as in the two other states of quasi-wakeful and wakeful experience. But this is not tenable. Is this 'stream of cognition' in sleep determinate or indeterminate? Determinateness in cognition can arise only through objects and in the absence of sensory-function in deep sleep, there is no question of the alleged persisting cognition being determinate. Neither can it be indeterminate cognition. Cognition being by definition of the mode of a *relation* of a 'that' and a 'what'. Even assuming that there can be modeless consciousness it does not stand to reason to say that in sleep, consciousness of the undifferentiated form of I, persists. For on waking there is no memory of a conscious experience of 'I'. Moreover consciousness being a series of self-aware cognitions (*vijñāna*) must be introspected in sleep also which however is not the case. These considerations show that there is definite discontinuity for the stream of cognitions during sleep. The attempt to find a continuant conserving through all the three states is a wild goose chase.

Even assuming that there persists in some mysterious way an I-consciousness during sleep, such consciousness can have for its content only nullity or nothingness (*śūnya*). It is generally contended that all determinate cognition differentiated by name, form, class etc. emerge from the background of an indeterminate cognition which is opposite in nature, that is, a base cognition devoid of differentiation. May it not like-wise be held, with equal phenomenological justification, that the indeterminate stage of knowledge preceding determinateness is in turn likewise preceded by an abysmal consciousness of nothingness. If a knowledge of what logically and psychologically presupposes its counter-correlate, namely knowledge of 'that' as its source, the knowledge of 'that' as well as 'what' characteristic of wakeful awareness may well be taken by the same logic to presuppose as its source or matrix an awareness having nothing for its content. This is what is indeed exemplified in sleep-awareness. From a primordial nothingness emerges cognitive life itself and nothingness, therefore, is the reality that really persists through the states of wakefulness and dream as well as through sleep. The alleged ego-consciousness present invariably in all states of one's existence is mere consciousness of nothingness. Therefore *śūnya* indeed is the real stuff or substance of self (*śūnyam ātma-tattvam*).

Against this extreme position of the denial of the reality of selfhood it is no answer to advance a view of self and argue for its plausibility. The *śūnyavādin's* equation of self with *śūnya* involves a refutation of all conceivable views. The *śūnyavādin's* own method of refutation does not consist in advancing one view against another but self-convicting every conceivable view of contradiction. The only way open for the advocates of the reality of selfhood then to confront *śūnyātma-vāda* is to show the self-contradiction if any in the position of *śūnyātma-vāda*. Is there any self-contradiction entailed in the assertion that the self is *śūnya*?

Surely a denial of self involves contradiction no matter if the denial is asserted as one more position or point of view or asserted transcendentally as the conclusion of a dialectical rejection of all positions or points of view concerning self. A simple way of demonstrating it is the stock in trade argument of the Idealist. Non-existence of self like the non-existence of a jar must be known to someone who witnesses to it lest the assertion of non-existence goes unevidenced. If it must be known the one that knows it at least exists. To say that that too is non-existent makes no sense for *that* non-existence must be known to someone and so on. A more viable way of showing the contradiction involved in the *śūnya* theorist's position is: is there a consciousness of *śūnya* or not? If there is not, on what basis of experience is self alleged to be *śūnya*? If there is *śūnya*-consciousness then that at least is not *śūnya* and will unassailably constitute selfhood.

The point is that selfhood is involved in the very act of the denial of self. Self is of the very nature of consciousness underlying the denial of body *etc.* as self and the consequent assertion that self is *śūnya*. This becomes specially apparent when the denial of self, methodologically speaking, proceeds on the basis of a *successive* elimination of different things like body, senses etc. as self. When each one of them with some credentials for being considered 'self' is subsequently discarded on the basis of whatever is normative for selfhood, that thing which is common to the different acts of discarding is there. That cannot be discarded. The generic element in our acts of denials that the self is body, senses etc. is that which denies or rather the denial itself, an act of consciousness. The denier or denial too may not be denied for in the very act of denying *that*, it is again presupposed and so on without end.

Therefore as proof if any for the reality of selfhood against those denying it we do not have to seek anything beyond the very act of denial itself. The denial of self paradoxically affirms the reality of self. It is an instance where the consciousness of a wholesale denial is itself the reinstatement of the content of the denial. The denial of a square-circle or hare's horn does not involve contradiction and therefore does not evidence the reality of what is denied. On the contrary their denial is itself the evidence of their unreality. But the denial of self or what is same the affirming of its mullity is self-contradictory. Even the most extravagant denial of consciousness presupposes consciousness of denial.[8]

The conclusion that follows from this may be set forth briefly as follows: There is something who knows, who having first become un-selfconsciously one with the body, senses etc. rejects each of them by conscious reflection as 'this is not I'. The knower in the form of *sūkṣma pañcākṣara* is the self. Such is *paśu.*

It may here be thought that what ensues from this confrontation with the self-nihilist is that self cannot be denied. It does not follow that it is *paśu* different on the one side from *pāśa* and from *pati* on the other. The existence of these have already been shown or demonstrated to be real as the implication of one's experience. Can either of them not assume the role of selfhood? In answer it is pointed out that *māyā* which is the constituent stuff of body, senses etc. and is possibly considered competent for the role of selfhood is material, non-spirit. It is not itself self but which in association with self in bond helps or aids in manifesting its knowledge from out of its unmanifest condition. Just like spectalces aiding the eye that is short-sighted but are themselves devoid of sight, *māyā* and material evolutes play their role in the manifestation of knowledge but the knowing self is different from them. By the same consideration it also follows that the self that stands in need of the aid of *māyā*, like the eye in dependence on the spectacle, is not God who is spirit the ever-knowing and the independent epistemologically speaking. God is like the light which makes vision possible but the agent of the visual function is not light though it necessarily and inalienably partakes of its nature, both in its function and in structure too.

The body is the most plausible condidate for mind or self-hood. The mind or self, whatever it be, is perceptibly dependent on the brain for its ability to think at all and not merely for its outward expression of the thought in words and deeds. The possessive sense is so unmistakable and yet while one is ready to see the distinction between the possessor and what is possessed in the case of 'external' things like house, estate, wealth etc. one is not able to perceive a similar distinction in relation to body despite the use of the possessive 'my body'. The most effective refutation of this prejudice lies in showing that while one certainly implies some identification of oneself with one's corporeal existence as when one says 'I am fat', 'I am lean', 'I am a brahmin', 'I am a woman' one is never known to identify oneself with the body like 'I am my body', 'I am my hand'; with regard to the body it is always 'mine' and not me.[9]

There is something which says 'my hand', 'my body' and 'my knowledge' as well as 'my house', 'my state' and my wife'. That something is the self which tends to contemplate thus as 'my hand', 'my leg', 'my body' despite the fact that these are not itself, just as previously it contemplated in a more pronounced state of self-obliviousness as 'mine' other external things without the suspicion that what is thus felt to be one's own is not indeed oneself.

The 'sense is self' theorist relatively has a more plausible case. The senses by definition are associated with the intelligent function. Between the different senses modalised no doubt in terms of different functions, the cognitive function is spanned adequately without the further need for a 'self'. In rejection of this over-simplification it may be pointed out that the sensorium leaves out of account the other spirit-functions of desire and will. Selfhood involves the conincidence of desire and will as well as cognition. Each of the senses can perform only *its* function and cannot overlap in respect of others' functions. Self is precisely that which experiences all the sensations without the limitation of modality. There is also in addition the limitation of sensory function, namely, that though unlike body it is by definition associated with manifestation of intelligence it is nevertheless devoid of reflective self-awareness or apperception. They have 'objective' consciousness (*para-prakāśa*) but do not have consciousness or awareness in the sense of being aware of itself. The eye is not conscious to say 'I see' or the ear 'I hear'. That is self which is not only conscious, manifesting objects like light but is also conscious of itself like light illumining itself (*sva-prakāśa*) at the same time as it illumines things.

More interesting than all these considerations phenomenologically is the issue that if the senses were self how dream-awareness which *prima facie* is also experience is to be explained. In sleep the wakeful sensorium surely does not function. That there are varying 'states' of self beneath the threshold of the wakeful is the phenomenological evidence for distinguishing self from body, senses, vital air etc. on the one side and also as it shall be shown presently from spirit which precisely is what is *not* subject to varying states of consciousness.

The psychic or the subtle body-complex which is operative in dream state as well as the wakeful, it might be thought, could lay claim on phenomenological grounds to selfhood. In answer it is pointed out that on those very grounds it follows that the bodily complex operative in dream experience is *not* the self.[10] The issue relates to one's consciousness of one's dream state. There is no introspective awareness of dream as dream. It is recollected in the wakeful. Dream, it may be observed is vaguely recollected, that is, as one's *dream*. It is not just a species of recollection but recollection as of a dream implying a qualitative distinction between dream and wakefulness.

The implied argument for self here is that there is a retrospective knowledge in the waking state of what was experienced during a state when the senses were not at work. This is evidence that even the subtle body composed of the psychic complex is not self but like the gross physical body what the self is identified with. If that which knows in the waking state the occurrences in the dream state were the subtle body, it would be conscious of the dreams quite in the same manner as it recollects within the wakeful state itself past wakeful events. Waking consciousness of dream state which is precisely not the same as the dream consciousness of dreams is the experiential basis for not equating 'self' even with the more subtle, less variant and mutable complex of corporeality.

The internal senses themselves though they are relatively to the outer senses, more inward and more expressly in some sense 'means' of knowledge and even interchangeable with 'self' still fall short of the ideal of selfhood for a variety of reasons. Themselves made of the luminous constituents of Nature which in turn is an evolute of *māyā*, they are no less non-intelligent despite the fact that they are more integral to the function of intelligence. The inner faculties are secondary epistemologically to the outer senses and are themselves differentiated like the outer senses in respect of different functions. Just as a king governs in conjunction with his ministers who assist him by their counsel because he is finite in knowledge as well as action, the self, with knowledge obscured by innate impurity is associated even with the inner faculities not differently in principle from association with outer senses and body. The inner senses are not self but what assist self with their counsel so that self may have 'discursive' knowledge. They are like the window in my study which 'assist' me to see the sky by my seeing through it. Because under the present condition of 'defilement' the self cannot know and act without the aid of the internal senses it does not of course follow that it shall be unable to think and act without these aids. In union with one or more of these aids the self is what is systematically subject to varied states of consciousness. But being thus subject to states or 'mutations' of consciousness is a predicament that is due to self's connate, not innate, impurity from which it can in principle be, though not in actuality, free.

The idea can be brought out differently also by applying the epistemological criterion of self-and-other consciousness (*sva-para-prakāśatva*). The internal functions of reflection, intellection, recollection are indeed 'conscious' processes but they are not self-luminously conscious. Their 'consciousness' is of external data presented to them by sense. The consciousness of self is of that which appears in the medium of the internal functions. These two forms of consciousness, the object-oriented, sensory kind and the one relating to discursive reason, alike are occurrences taking place one after the other so far as the 'self' is concerned. Like waves arising in the sea and reaching the shore in systematic succession they appear one after the other in the self so that the latter is not any one or all of them. The self is what time may be said to be in relation to the solar and the lunar bodies. The latter also pre-eminently have their special role in measuring day and month. But it is time as it were in association with these bodies that make for these divisions so that it is not identical with any or all of these bodies. The upshot of this is that what is called mind is intelligent only in a relative sense. It is intelligent when compared with the sub-mental stratum of evolution of tattvas. Viewed in relation to 'self', however, it is no more intelligent than the senses and body. It has 'objective' consciousness, exemplified in its functions of doubting, determining and remembering. But these functions do not also include as part of them the consciousness 'I am doubting' or 'I am determining or remembering'. To account for this new horizon of self-awareness is required 'self' in addition to mind.

The vitalist points to the invariability of the vital function which is rightly synonymous with life itself and is therefore *prima facie* qualified for the role of selfhood. Why need a super-experiential 'self' to explain experience? The reply to this objection is simple enough. Experience of pleasure and pain should be always available for the alleged self namely the vital function which is at work invariably, in wakeful as well as in sub-wakeful states. But these experiences are not present introspectively at least in sleep — that is what we mean by deep, sound sleep, though vital function does not de-cease in that state. The latter correlatively co-exists with such experiences but these experiences are not 'for' the vital function. They are manifest when self is awake and are in unmanifest abeyance when the self is at rest, thus functioning 'for' the self which, therefore, is not identical with vital function.[11]

The most interesting sidelight that the above analysis throws on the question of the reality of self is that it provides also at once the ground for the distinction of self from God. The obvious conclusion that would follow from the considerations which preclude one from identifying one's 'self' with one's bodily, vital and even mental existence, is that one's 'self' is in the final analysis, spirit itself eternal immutable and all-knowing. That, however, is not tenable can be shown on grounds again of phenomenological introspection. The I of my experience is one that knows if and only if it is shown or revealed. When self is devoid of assistance of the operation of accessories like body, sense, mind and even vital air, when, in other words, the self is driven beyond even the nether limit of subliminal sleep-awareness when even the vital function ceases as it were, the self is supremely without knowledge. But when these accessories emerge on the horizon of experience, slowly and gradually they manifest knowledge for self. This is not compatible with the picture of an unvariant, unflagging consciousness or spirit that is alleged to be self. The self of one's experience which knows but as strictly commensurate with being shown or aided does not approximate to the ideal of an omniscient, omnipresent and eternal God whose knowledge is perfect and unchanging.

That spirit is subject to the limitation of *avidyā*, and that therefore it is conceivable that under the spell of such limitation it is, out of association with material aids, devoid of intelligence, will not suffice. Even when thus associated contingently with material manifestors it suffers from a kind of self-obliviousness that gives no inkling whatsoever to its nature as spirit. Self is not *brahman* but precisely the one that is open to instruction by scripture and preceptor about *brahman*, namely, that it is immutable spirit and unflagging light, that *brahman* in contradistinction to the self that is instructed, knows no obstructive Ignorance (*kevala*), needs no manifestors to neutralize the obstructive function (*sakala*), and equally significantly, needs no instruction or inculcation (*upadeśa*) from a transcendent source about knowledge of itself (*śuddha*). Even when self is aided by material accessories its 'knowledge' remains radically finite in structure thus not deserving the title of knowledge: it is categorised and limited by considerations of space and time and also by the circumstance intrinsic to its knowledge-situation, namely, that it identifies with each of the thing that it knows so that knowledge becomes by nature determining, finitely discursive in character, knowing each thing 'by being that'. Its knowledge structure, cross-sectionally analysed at any instant of its occurence, reveals a spectrum of states ranging from total oblivion to 'peak' alertness. Just as even in the state below that of dreamless sleep there is rudimentary 'experience', in the midst of the most wakeful moment also there is unconsciousness. Wakeful unconsciousness and unconscious wakefulness both alike are built into the nature of human knowledge. How can this be assimilated to the notion of pure consciousness which is constitutive of the nature of God?

There are two kinds or orders of states to which 'self' is by its very structural predispositions subject: the causal states (*kāraṇa avasthās*) of the pre-biographical pre-empirical isolation (*kevala*), of the empirical and the transmigratory existence *sakala* and of the supra-empirical (*śuddha*) characterised respectively by total veilment, partial unveilment and total unveilment of the cognitive, conative and affective life of the individual. And the effect-states (*kārya avasthās*) like wakefulness, dream etc. through which the individual self passes in its empirical existence and indeed in every moment of its empirical existence.

Though it is only in the context of spiritual life where the focus shall be on the actual dissolution of bondage in and through a life of pure states (*śuddha avasthās*), the key for the understanding of this essential ingredient of self-hood, namely, self's subjection to fluctuation of states is provided, possibly from an inspection of one's day to day experience itself to see how a life of *avasthā* is in the service of a *progressive* dissolution of bondage for the self, its conquest of knowledge which is only a moment of its Ignorance and its winning of a condition of readiness for the advent of true knowledge.

Nature of knowledge

Before we proceed to the main problem of the nature of the evidence of knowledge it is necessary to consider briefly the nature and forms of knowledge recognised in Śaiva Siddhānta. Knowledge implies the commonplace distinction of the knower, knowing and the known; its logical aspect consists in the reference to the known object, and its psychological aspect involves reference to the knowing subject. Indian epistemology discusses the psychological aspect as a preliminary to the objective or the logical side of knowledge to which belongs the problem of truth.[1]

Psychologically, knowledge may be seen to be an 'attribute' of an enduring self. The selves are many, each infinite and uniquely individual, the individuality in the epistemological sense being constituted by *nāda*[2]. The self is conceived as what knows and feels (*jñātṛ*, *bhoktṛ*) and also is agent of actions (*kartṛ*). What makes for the epistemological *subjectivity*, is inherent in the nature of the self which is the knower.[3] It is not correct to say that the experience of knowing (*jñapti*) rather than knowership (*jñātṛtva*) belongs to self.[4] The Sāṅkhyaite separates the two and attributes knowership to *buddhi*. Knowership cannot be an attribute of the non-intelligent *buddhi*; the latter is an aid for the manifestation of knowership. All individual selves are as such knowing subjects.

In the terminology of Śaiva Siddhānta, knowledge is *cit-śakti* and is the essence of self; it is, therefore, called 'self's knowledge-function' (*ātmacit-śakti*). It is not merely what belongs to self as its inseparable accidens; it is its *guṇa*; the relation of *guṇa* and *guṇin* is of identity. As knowledge is essentially, and not contingently, related to self, self is sometimes referred to as knowledge for consciousness (*caitanya*) just as *paśu* is so called because of its relation with the quality of *paśutva*.[5] As *guṇa* and *guṇin* are identical they can be denoted interchangeably.

Knowledge or knowership consequently cannot be an occurrence in time and space. Finiteness with regard to space, time etc. (*kvācitka*) cannot be the intrinsic characteristic of what constitutes the essence of self which is infinite. The eternal and infinite self cannot be the substrate of a non-eternal finite knowledge-event. The presumption that we make accordingly about the phenomenon of knowledge-occurrence is that its occurrent nature is adventitious, conditioned.[6] This implies admission of (i) an initial condition of obscuration or arresting of knowledge with no assignable beginning for such a condition, (the obscuration being an unconscious process) and (ii) a subsequent partial reactivation of the arrested knowledge by means of material accessories which are particular and variable in nature. All empirical knowledge are species of this partially manifested knowledge reactivated from an original state of arrest; their extent and duration are strictly commensurate with the extent and duration of the manifesting media. This provides for the infinite variation and gradation in empirical knowledge.

Ātmacit-śakti, in other words, is beginninglessly veiled by *mala*. *Mala*-obscuration does not, however, remain static and constant, thanks to the initiative taken transcendentally as part of the cosmic operation of God. The obscuration is partially removed by the help of *māyīya* which both partially unveils, on the subjective side knowledge and also on a parallel evolves on the objective side objects of experience (*bhogya*). The mannet in which knowledge results varies with the variations in the modes of activity of *buddhi*; the latter in turn vary according to the degree of the 'unripeness' of *mala*. This accounts for the phenomenon of knowledge coming to us in different empirical modes like perception etc., even though all modes are identical with *cit-śakti.*

The logical side, knowledge in its reference to the objcet may now be considered. A subjective fact is nothing in itself but the relation of knowledge to the object.[7] Knowledge consists of its relatedness to the object. Knowledge is consequently characterisable as self-and-other illumining. Its *relation* to object as intentionality is an essential quality of self and is its eternal and inalienable function.[8] Self's apprehension (*grāhakatva*) which is of the nature of self-and-other-illumination is not its separable accidens. It is neither separable nor is it accidens. It is its very essence. This means that in the sphere of knowledge no distinction can be made between the subjective and the objective; there is no bifurcation into the world of ideas and the world of extension.[9] There is no cognitive state but which is without a reference to the object; there may be grades of objectivity corresponding to the states of knowledge, but at no state of knowledge is reference to object absent.

This means that objects precede knowledge and exist before they are known. They are there for the self and their order of evolution, their manifestness and unmanifestness condition a sequence of states in self's knowledge. The reference to object which characterises all knowledge receives a special interpretation in Śaiva Siddhānta in the light of its metaphysics of self.

Ātmacit-śakti is all pervasive, but its pervasion is of a unique kind. In cognitively pervading an object it identifies with the object and assumes its character; of course, assumes it intentionally and not substantially: it becomes 'one' with it and in relation to the object whose 'colour' it wears as its own, it remains the 'determinate' (*vyāpya*). Though ontologically everything has its being in self as spirit and is, therefore, 'determinate' in relation to self, epistemologically the determinant self comes to have its being in every object with which it is in cognitive relation and becomes determinate.[10] The knower or knowledge becomes dependent on the known, and surrenders its being to that of the known object. Knowledge cannot 'know' anything by keeping aloof; to know is to become identified with the being of the object for the time being and to a limited extent.

The analogies of a crystal assuming the red colour of a ruby in its proximity and of the visual sense which 'assumes' the form and colour of the object it pervades, brings out the two features of self's cognitive reference; to become identified with the object immediately presented, and then 'know'[11] it, even as the eye after pervading the visual shape and form of the object 'perceives' it. Knowledge, in other words, is not merely like a lantern which shines or a light which shows; it also *knows*. This fact of knowledge by identification is consciously known when a particular identification has already ceased to exist. When distinctions arise in the object given in the same state, and in the levels or grades of objects given in different states, by constrast the self also becomes consciously aware of its mode of knowing.

The knowing self is both knowledge and will; it is cognitive as well as conative (*jñāna-kriyātmaka*). It is not a mere subject but also agent. Understanding and will are not two different functions. The two point to an initial aspect of knowledge prior to the distinction into discerning and functioning — the 'intention' (*icchā*) which may become concrete as an intellectual determination or as a decision. Intentionality or the will to knowledge precedes other conditions of knowledge. Without this will to accommodate the object, the 'motive' to cognise, there is no 'experience' of knowledge. The word knowledge stands for the intention and its concrete embodiments in the form of a specific knowledge and specific volition.

Both the concrete function of *cit-śakti*, namely the cognitive and the conative fulfil a function in the acquisition of knowledge.[12] The conative removes the hindrance or the veil to the object becoming known; its cognitive *śakti* invests the object with a competence which is conducive to its manifestation in knowledge. Whenever one is referred to the other also is to be understood as implicity present. The 'intention' (*icchā*) behind knowledge brings about the identification of the subject and the object and accomplishes the 'experience' (*anubhava*). The intelligence becomes pure ardour. To enjoy or experience is interchangeable with ' to know', the latter being only a *nomen abstractum* of the former.[13]

The most significant detail and yet the least obvious one from the standpoint of empirical epistemology is the factor of illumination in knowledge. Illumination by *Śiva-śakti* is the eternal presupposition of knowledge. This is consistent with the metaphysical view that self is grounded in the being of *Śiva-śakti*, the relation being one of inseparability (*ananya-tādātmya*). The eye-analogy which recurs very often bears a distinct significance. Eye is used in the sense of an apparatus that 'receives' what is given it; notwithstanding its active role as the *seer* it is only a sensory receptor in the sense that it is not also the source of light which illuminates the object. Illumination by light is the condition of the possibility of vision. The crystal-analogy also bears the same significance. The source of the light of the crystal as well as of the colour of the red object which is reflected, that is, the physical light is the unobstrusive precondition which makes reflection possible.

The physical illumination 'aids' visual sensation in two characteristic ways. It dispels darkness and unveils the 'object'. and also at the same time it enables the translucent eye to 'reach out' to the object. Likewise *Śiva-śakti* illumines knowledge as it were from within and from without in its reference to the object. *Ātmacit-śakti* and its eternal condition of illumination namely *Śiva-śakti* are used interchangeably in the epistemological literature of Śaiva Siddhānta.[14]

When *Śiva-śakti* is introduced as the invariable condition of illumination of knowledge one is not very far from raising the question of the nature of God's knowledge, and its place in our epistemological study. By *Śiva-śakti's* illumination what we mean is not merely the divine light which unveils objects and aids the eye but also divine knowledge; the function of *showing* cannot be separated from *knowing*, as is also the case of *ātmacit-śakti*. God's omniscient knowledge underlies all knowledge. If so the question that naturally arises is: does God know self and self's knowledge which He 'illumines'? If he does not he is not omniscient; if he does, what is said to be an unobjectified subject becomes 'object' of knowledge; the distinction between knowledge and the known becomes relative.[15]

The question may be raised in the more evident context of self's knowledge of itself. Does *ātmacit-śakti* know its own *ātman*? And when it is said to become omniscient, freed from *mala*, does it know otherselves? If any one of the three categories of real accepted in the system, namely *pati, paśu* and *pāśa* were to be unknowable the concept of omniscience would be void of meaning. The admission of a threefold ontological reality carries the implication that they are knowable in some sense of the term 'to know'. Distinctions in the modes of knowability are obviously in demand.

Śaiva Siddhānta accordingly makes a distinction between what is experientially known (*prameya*) and what is barely known (*jñeya*) without being experienced.[16] It is difficult to illustrate this distinction from human knowledge which by definition identifies with and imbibes the character of the given. Nothing seems to be known without also being experienced and therefore there seems *prima tacie* no justification for making this distinction. However, consider the following example: in the case of a valid memory-cognition there may be said to be a bare acquaintance with the memory object such as there must be one,[17] in so far as it is *valid* memory-cognition. There may be images in memory but the images are not numerically distinct from the thing or event remembered in valid memory;[18] the manner of acquaintance is not different in remembering and perceiving and yet the 'acquaintance' with the object which correct remembering seems to involve is not 'experience'. It is quite different from perception in this case. When something is determinately perceived there is acquaintance accompanied with participation; the perceiver and the perceived are identified. In memory or retrocognition one is not acquainted with the represented object. In the one there is direct acquaintance and a consequent identification. In the other, the acquaintance is oblique which accounts for its non-experiential character. This follows from the truism that in the one case the objectification is ontological while in the other it is merely logical.

A better example of this mode of cognitive reference will be indeterminate knowledge[19] which is admitted as the prius of all empirical modes of knowledge. Determinate knowledge is judgmental and carries the reference of a what to a that identified with the real, and presupposes logically a prior acquaintance with the bare predicate (*viśeṣaṇa*).[20] This reference to an indeterminate predicate will be another illustration of a knowledge that barely refers without grasping and identifying.

The bare content of these cognitive references is not like the content of perceptual cognition. It is surely object — as without it cognition will be phantasy, and yet it is not, strictly, an object of knowledge (*prameya*). It is object in the sense that it is known by immediate acquaintance and yet it is no object of experiential knowledge. It is a species of what is known (*jñeya-viśeṣa*) wtihout being objectively *experienced.* The content given is not a 'given' content. It is *jñeya* and not *meya.*

The corresponding cognitions also may likewise be distinguished as *jñāna* and *māna.* In *pramāṇa-vāda* it is only the second kind of knowledge and its content that is generally taken cognizance of. It is with reference to the circumstance of a possible objective experience that knowledge, namely *cit-śakti* is called *pramāṇa*; the subject which knows is called *pramātṛ*; the object known is *prameya*. In the context of a real that cannot possibly become an 'object' of knowledge even though knowable, the 'knowledge' is no *pramāṇa* or *pramiti*; the 'knower' is no *pramātṛ*; what is known is no *prameya*. The entire subject-object scheme of cognitive reference becomes inapplicable in this case.

Can *ātmacit-śakti* be object to itslef ? Can it become object to a self (*ātman*) to which it belongs as attribute ? Can it become object to other *ātmacit-śaktis* ? Do not self and its *cit-śakti* become object at least to *Śiva-śakti* which illumines and informs it as light illumines the eye ? The answer to these questions without prejudice to the rule that *pramāṇa* technically is never *premeya* and *vice versa*, and also to the claim of omniscience which belongs inherently to *Śiva-śakti* and also 'soteriologically' to *ātmacit-śakti* through union with *Śiva-śakti*, is to be derived from the distinction made between *jñāna* and *pramāṇa*. The *ātman* or *ātmacit-śakti* is never *prameya* to a *pramāṇa*, but for that reason it does not mean that it is unknown to *Śiva-śakti*. When self too knows itself and knows other selves and their knowledge, its knowledge is not of the epistemologically cognisable category of *pramāṇa*.

With regard to self's cognitive encounter cf God also, the scheme of *pramāṇa* is strictly, not applicable. Firstly, it is no knowledge of a particular; God is universal being. Secondly, there is no *pramāṇa* by which to know God except as He is revealed to self by *Śiva-śakti*; the 'means' and the 'end' of knowledge coincide there. That is why God is spoken of as the supreme *jñeya* (*paramaṁ jñeyam*). He is *jñeya* to a *jñāna* to which self's knowledge is elevated by *yoga* (*parāśakti-yoga*)

Though thus God is not known as object to a subject but rather as identical with the subject of knowledge itself, one important characteristic of the epistemological situation endures, the 'experiencing' of what is known.[21] Self's knowledge of God is no exception to the rule, that is 'experiences'—in terms of a will to enjoy (*icchā*) which is part of its knowledge-structure, what it is in cognitive relation with. That it is supra-relational knowledge involving a coalescence of esence (*jñāna*) and existence (*jñeya*) only makes for a supra-relational non-objectified 'experience' involving co-incidence of the *knower* and the known—what is technically called the *bhoga*. *Bhoga* is 'ecstatic' experience involving the agent standing out of itself. But in standing out of itself it does not also cease to be itself. The supernal Experience is still the experience of self, the erstwhile *pramātṛ* stays no more individuated,[22] the primary condition of individuation as knowing *subject* namely *nāda* being transcended.

General Conception of Means of Knowledge (*pramāṇa*)

The word *pramāṇa* derives from the root *mā* which implies measurement or assessment. Measuring knowledge with respect to its correctness or truth is called the 'measure' of knowledge.[1] Qualitative measurements expressed in terms of volume, density or length tell us about the nature of the object[2] but the very truth about the object, its reality itself would also have to be measured.[3] Investigation or scrutiny is necessary in order to establish the truth about objects. The 'logical' means of investigation in respect of truth value has parity with the ethical or the evaluative judgment without which one does not know right action and also with the aesthetical without which there is no appreciation of beauty.[4] *Pramāṇa* is the scale of measurement which philosophy uses for gauging what all empirical measurements tacitly assume, namely the truth or the reality of a thing and the untruth or irreality of the nothing or nonentity.[5]

The recognised definition of *pramāṇa* as the means or the avenue of valid knowledge (*pramiti-sādhanam*) derives from the suffix *ana* in *pramāṇa* which is indicative of its function as the instrument of correct knowledge.[6] The instrument view of *pramāṇa* adopted by the generality of Indian logicians, errs on the side of being too wide, rendering the term *pramāṇa* an equivalent of any and every accessory to knowledge.[7] Factors, physical and physiological like say, light and the visual sense organ involved in the occurrence of sensation will become the rightful claimants for the title of *pramāṇa*.[8] Indian epistemologists do not, of course, use *pramāṇa* in this loose, non-technical sense.

Objection to *cit-śakti* as *pramāṇa*

The empirically minded Instrumentalist (the Nyāya) can turn the table against the theory that *cit-śakti* is the *pramāṇa*. While an empirical understanding of *pramāṇa* in terms of the observed means of true knowledge may err on the side of being too wide (*ativyāpti*) the view that the intuitive power of the intelligent self is as such *pramāṇa* may be shown to involve the error of impossibility (*asambhava*) of there being at all a *pramāṇa* as thus understood. As *cit-śakti* is identical with knowledge and is *ex hypothesi* eternal, being the attribute of eternal self, the question of its being also something which *gives rise* to true knowledge does not arise. *Cit-śakti* is also right knowledge (*pramiti*) itself and so must be eternal like the knower of whom it is the very essence. Therefore the question of a *pramāṇa*, of a means of knowledge whereby a previously unknown thing comes to be now known itself cannot arise.[9]

The above objection may be shown to rest on an uncritical equivocation of terms: *cit-śakti* is used in the sense of *pramiti* and the same term is used in the sense of *pramāṇa*. *Cit-śakti per se* is not the *pramiti* but *pramāṇa*, and this must be distinguished from *cit-śakti* come to be limited or defined by an object, when it is *pramiti* and not *pramāṇa*.[10] *Cit-śakti*, by itself, without relation to any object which it reveals, is eternal and universal, but *qua* defined by the 'limitor' of some object it is particularised and admits of being said to be produced by some means. The revelatory function *per se* of consciousness and the same as revelatory of one object or other by which it may be said to be 'defined' as light may be said to be defined by the thing that is lighted, are clearly and unequivocally distinguished. It is therefore meet to speak of *cit-śakti* as *pramāṇa*.

The above objection has of course one merit, that it elicits the admission of reference to objects for defining a *pramāṇa*. This means that the advocate of *cit-śakti* is not very far from including senses also under *pramāṇa*. Even so, accepting this distinction made between *cit-śakti* as *pramāṇa* and the same as defined by an object, as *pramiti*, the critic may hold that it still fails to meet adequately the requirement of a *pramāṇa* for knowledge.[11] If *cit-śakti* were itself, independently of sense organs etc. a necessary and sufficient condition of knowledge, it being universal and eternal, with the coming into existence of every new object, knowledge of the same must ensue even prior to and therefore presumably, without a need for, sense-object contact. The emergence of an object must coincide with its emergence in the field of one's knowledge and of right knowledge at that, without regard to the contingence of its coming into contact with the senses. What is still worse, the all-pervasive *cit-śakti* will have to be defined indiscriminately by the limitors of all objects, of the future as well as of the past and present, and even of doubt and of error. *Cit-śakti* as *pramāṇa* thus seems to be a worse offender in respect of being too wide. What is claimed to be the unique condition of true knowledge will be the condition of all knowledge actual and possible and of even doubt and error.

On the other hand, the theory of *pramāṇa* as *pramiti-sādhana* may be seen to be really not wide. By 'means' (*sādhana*) of knowledge is meant not any and every means, but the special cause (*karaṇa*) without which valid knowledge can never arise. A distinction between different kinds of knowledge like perception, inference etc. can be made by reference to the difference in the specific methods of acquiring knowledge, and within the perceptual the different kinds of sensory knowledge can likewise be accounted for by reference to the differences in the sense modalities which are the specific means (*karaṇa*) of the respective kinds of knowledge. So ultimately senses alone, can adequately evidence knowledge, it may be argued.[12]

Some definition of *karaṇa*

In reply, before vindicating the claims of *cit-śakti* as *pramāṇa*, it may be useful to enter into a brief discussion of the meaning and plausibility of the concept of *karaṇa* as distinguished from a *kāraṇa* used in defining a *pramāṇa*. The instrumentalists' use of the notion of *karaṇa* may be in one or the other of the following senses of which none, it may be shown, is tenable.[13]

One such meaning of *karaṇa* by which a specific means of acquiring knowledge may be distinguished from other means is to define it as 'different from what is not immediately connected with the result.'[14] Positively stated *kāraṇa* is the causal operation which is instrumental in *immediately* producing the result.[15] The operation of conjoining the two halves of a pitcher cannot but result in the immediate creation of the whole pitcher.[16] In criticism of this, it may be pointed out that while every *karaṇa* may be a case of 'being other than not immediately connected with the result', the converse is not true: every case of the *definiens is not coeval with the definiendum.* Take the case of pleasure or happiness as an experience. Happiness is not identical with, but strictly the 'accusative' (*karman*) of the *experience* of happiness as may be seen in the judgment 'I am happy' (*ahaṁ sukhī*). At the same time happiness and experience of happiness are inalienably connected;[17] either of them is 'different from what is not immediately connected with the other which is its result', thus deserving, according to the definition, the title of *karaṇa*. But happiness as the *object* of the knowledge 'I am happy' cannot also be the *means* of such knowledge. The *karman* and the *karaṇa* — the accusative and the instrumental are mutually exclusive.

On the other hand, some of the acknowledged 'means' of sensory knowledge, as for example, the sense-organs, are not covered by the definition; these are expressly not the *invariable* and immediate antecedents of sense knowledge; they may function without immediately resulting in knowledge. The eyes may stare and yet nothing may be perceived.

Another view of *karaṇa* which may be considered is to define it in terms of *possession* of some active function through which the effect is produced (*vyāpāravatvam*).[18] While the first view seeks to define *karaṇa* as what is most indispensable for the effect, for want of which the effect is not produced even when other causes are present, the present one seeks *karaṇatva* in a cause come to be associated with its intermediate function (*vyāpāra*) through which it causes its effect.[19] The intermediate factor which a cause causes which in its turn contributes towards producing the effect (*tajjanyaḥ tajjanyajanakaśca vyāpāraḥ*), is called *vyāpāra* and possession of this by a cause constitutes *karaṇa*.[20] This definition too errs on the sides of omission and commission. It is inclusive of such things as light whose illuminative operation arises from light and in its turn contributes to seeing, which are expressly not means of knowledge; it on the other hand excludes an express means of knowledge like reflection on the middle term (*parāmarśa jñāna*) from the title of a *karaṇa*;[21] itself a function, *parāmarśa-jñāna* does not possess a further function. Nor may it be argued that it is only the sign (*liṅga*) available at the time of the inference, and causes the *vyāpāra*, and not the *parāmarśa* that serves *karaṇa*. For from a sign that is yet to come into existence or has ceased to be, no inference should be possible, the alleged *karaṇa* being then non-available.[22]

The definition which combines the two aforementioned views, namely, *karaṇa* in association with a *vyāpāra* is necessarily and invariably productive of the result, may be thought to fare better. Mere possession of *vyāpāra* may not constitute a *karaṇa*; even physical light possesses illumination which originating from light 'originates' vision and so can pass muster as *karaṇa*. Therefore, it may be qualified: possession of a *vyāpāra* which will invariably lead to the result; light's illumination is not a function leading invariably to a result (*phala-niyata-vyāpāra*) and therefore is no *karaṇa*, unlike sight or seeing of the eye which is invariably productive of the result of vision.

That this modified account is not adequate enough may be seen from the following case. In the dark, notwithstanding the activity and the conjunction of the eyesight with the object there is no vision. In this instance there is the active function of the sense of eye and the function is also presumably accompanied by its end (*phala-niyata*), namely, conjunction with the object in the dark. And yet there is no resulting vision. The definition therefore becomes inapplicable in this typical case which meets the requirements of the definition and yet admittedly is not a means of knowledge.

To say that the function of sight aided by some extraneous factor like light which dispels darkness, is *karaṇa*, will not suffice. Any function (*vyāpāra*) in that case could become a *karaṇa* subject to being assisted by some extraneous factor. The stipulation about the causal function that it should be necessarily geared to its effect becomes void of significance.[23]

So much for the omission. Its error of commission will be its inclusion of cases which cannot be *karaṇa*. The object of knowledge expressed by the accusative case (*karman*) in answer to 'what' or 'which', also in a sense is a case of 'function issuing necessarily in a result' (*phala-niyata-vyāpāra*). In the example 'the rice is cooked' the function which results in rice being cooked actually consists of a softening of the rice;[24] but rice is what is cooked and is not also the chief means (*karaṇa*) of cooking. Indeed all the *kārakas* — the accusative, ablative, dative, genitive as well as the instrumental, are related to the functions directly resulting in action (*phala-niyata-vyāpāravattva*), and can lay claim to being *karaṇa*.

Instead then of defining *karaṇa* either as the immediate operation or as the operative cause or as both we may push the analysis a little further and say that *karaṇa* consists in being willed by some agency (*kartṛ-preryatvam*).[25] Here again the questions to be asked are: is all *karaṇa* a concomitant of the function of an agent, and secondly, are all cases of 'being willed by an agent' a *karaṇa*? Neither seems to be the case. The psycho-physical organism is *kartṛ-prerya*, that is, it exists and functions but as willed by its agent-self. But it is not *karaṇa*. *Parāmarśa jñāna*[26] is a *karaṇa* in respect of *anumiti* but being knowledge is not conditioned by the will of an agent (*puruṣa-tantra*) but by the object (*vastu-tantra*) or by another knowledge which serves as its means (*pramāṇa-tantra*).[27]

The entire collocation of the conditions of valid knowledge put together, it may be thought, is *karaṇa*.[28] Though individually the sense organs etc. may not under any view of *karaṇa* be adequate means of knowledge, their *conjunction* may be what is denoted by *karaṇa*. From the knowing agent at one end onwards to the fruit of knowing at the other, a conjunction of all these factors can be *pramāṇa*. The argument is that only where all causal collocations are available, there is effect and even if less by one there is no effect. It can therefore be presumed that the collocation in its entirelty is *pramāṇa*.[29]

That this view too is unconvincing, may be shown. If the conjunctive whole, and not the individual conjunctives, were *karaṇa*, it follows that senses etc. are not *karaṇas*. It may be replied that conjunction is not something over and above the conjunct elements (*samudāyin*) and that therefore the two may be equated;[30] the senses etc. too, *qua* non-different from the conjunctive assemblage or aggregate include the entire spectrum of factors ranging from the subject at one end to the object on the other; the two extremities, the knowing subject (*mātṛ*) and the known object (*meya*) can also lay similar claim to the title of *karaṇa*, the conjuncts taken individually being non-different from the conjunctive whole. This will annul all distinction between the subject and the object of knowledge, a distinction on which however rests all empirical usage.[31]

Again, the causal assemblage (*sādhana-sāmagrī*) must be so to a percipient. It must be object to some subject. What is 'object' of knowledge cannot also be the means of knowledge.[32] What is known cannot also at once be the means through which it is known.[33]

Such then is the impasse to which an 'instrumental' approach to the general problem of *pramāṇa* leads.[34] The 'instrument' of knowledge is sought to be defined variedly as obtaining between the *kartṛ* (subject) and the *phala* (object), namely, *vyāpāra*, or as *kartṛ* in association with *vyāpāra*, or as *kartṛ* associated with *vyāpāra* that is invariably related to *phala*, or what the *kartṛ* wields by way of exercising agency, or finally, as a name standing for all these factors in the collective. What is really demanded in these attempts to distinguish the 'means' from the 'end' is that while a 'dualism' of subject and object is surely untenable a radical distinction, however, between the invariable knowledge or the knowing process and the variable known objects, be admitted. A process is involved in knowing, and its condition is that *the knowing act, itself originated but only figuratively, stands transcendent to the known object.* The 'instrument' which evidences the objects' reality, must accordingly be sought from the non-objectified side of knowledge. What *evidences* knowledge of objects (*māna*) cannot be object of knowledge (*meya*) but knowledge.

The claim of being a *pramāṇa* cannot be made even for intellect or mind (*buddhi vṛtti*) which, unlike sense, seems invariably involved in, and even identical with the processes of manifesting objects. *Buddhi* is matter, a material evolute of *prakṛti* and its mode (*vṛtti*) cannot illumine objects.[35] Itself non-intelligent (*asaṃvidātmaka*) it only aids as an accessory in the manifestation of intelligence. The multifarious modifications of *buddhi* are called consciousness (*bodha*) but in a figurative sense. What 'helps' manifest consciousness is eulogised as consciousness itself.[36] *Buddhi* is a manifest objective *tattva*, objective in the sense of what is objectively known as any known object and manifest in the sense of being self-identical involving the process of becoming itself. *Vṛtti* is self-identical with *buddhi*; the pleasure-pain modalities of *buddhi* are objectively apperceived and therefore *buddhi* too with which they are self-identical is an object of knowledge.[37]

Cit-śakti as *pramāṇa*

The valid means of knowledge of object will have to be in the last resort identical with valid knowledge itself. The solution to the vexed problem of *karaṇa* of knowledge accordingly is that it is not anything other than *cit-śakti* which is identical with consciousness.[38] As *cit-śakti* is unconditional unlike lamp, senses etc., it coincides with knowledge without over- or under-pervasion. The objections raised against other definitions of *karaṇa* consequently become inapplicable. The direct, innate intuitional function of consciousness as defined by objects is what constitutes valid knowledge (*pramā*) in respect of those objects and *a fortiori*, also the 'means' of valid knowledge (*pramāṇa*) in their cases.[39]

A question that naturally will arise here and anticipated in an earlier objection is: only were the *karaṇa* a limited and finite entity it could enter into relations with objects which are limited and finite, and also vary those relations. But *cit-śakti* which is the inseparable essence of consciousness, is, like consciousness, unlimited and infinite;[40] as *pramāṇa* it must evidence *all knowledge all the time*. The occurrent quality *kadācitkatva*) of knowledge which permits us to speak of knowledge-events cannot be accounted for. It is only as occurring events, knowledge is categorised under different modes, as perceptual, inferential etc., in terms of differences in their mode of genesis; but the theory that the all pervasive *cit-śakti* is *pramāṇa* will not explain the existence of the diverse empirical modes of knowledge.

The answer to this objection is as follows: Only when *cit-śakti* is defined by its relation to an unveiled object—unveiling being effected through the operation of *buddhi vṛtti* (*anāvṛta-viṣaya-sambandha-cit-śakti*) that it is said to be *pramāṇa*. Consciousness is beginninglessly obscured by the impurity of *mala* and so even though omnipresent, all-pervasive, its relation to objects is *de facto* non-existent. Everything in the world is a *possible* object to the self as everything has its being in the all-pervasive being of the self. The predicament of the self is that under the condition of *mala*-obscuration the possible object is never also the catual object of its knowledge except as and when mediated by *vṛtti*.[41] *Cit-śakti* despite its universality fails to illumine the object even though in factual relation with it till some *vṛtti* arises *via* the senses and rends the intervening veil between the object and apprehension. When, the *vṛtti* occurs and functions through the channel of senses, to that extent, strictly, there is removal of the condition of obscuration of consciousness. There is consequently illumination through relation with object, now unveiled by means of the *vṛtti*. This accounts for the contingent and variable nature of knowledge.

The relation between *cit-śakti* and the object may be defined in yet another way.[42] *Cit-śakti* as defined by *buddhi vṛtti* which is of the nature of valid experience, is the means in respect of that valid knowledge (*yathārthānubhūtirūpa-buddhivṛttyupārūḍhatva*). A true knowledge of a pitcher for example is knowledge identified with the *buddhi vṛtti* which is of the form of a valid experience of the pitcher. And the same is also the 'means' in respect of that knowledge. The limited and contingent nature of illumination is explained in the context of knowledge through its identification with *buddhi vṛtti* which is limited and contingent[43] and is also capable of being *either* true *or* false.

A second question that arises here is: *cit-śakti* thus defined will be a neutral condition of manifestation of all knowledge, of doubt and error as well as of truth.[44] Truth or falsity marks the nature of *buddhi vṛtti* but the illuminating factor underlying it can only be a neutral condition; it cannot be partial towards true knowledge. How then, can we say that *cit-śakti* is the evidence of *true* or *valid* knowledge ?

20

The point of the objection is that as doubt and error too like true knowledge are knowledge and imply illumination, although indefinite and even positively distorting, the conscious function of *cit-śakti* cannot be said to be the means of only valid knowledge and be 'free from doubt etc.' That this objection has only a seeming plausibility may be shown. Consciousness is identical with truth and even though it is only a judgment of *buddhi* that is said to be true, the *source* of its truth is consciousness which underlies the act of judgment. The implied concept of truth is ontological; it is identical with revelation or unhiddenness of Being, consciousness being another name for the 'where' of the eternal occurrence of such revelation. The 'validity' of all valid knowledge is to be traced to *cit-śakti* the manifesting source or ground of knowledge, while in case of non-valid knowledge, non-validity is present in spite of the presence of *cit-śakti* and is to be attributed to the element of *vṛtti* with which *cit-śakti* is identified.[45] The truth character of a judgment is due to the circumstance that it is an unmediated function of consciousness while its erroneous or doubtful character is due to being mediatedly *vṛtti*. Erroneous and doubtful knowledge too are functions of consciousness, but the 'error' and 'doubt' about them are to be attributed to the cooperating factor of *vṛtti*. In the case of true or valid knowledge on the other hand the 'truth' of the knowledge flows from what constitutes being knowledge, namely consciousness which is invariable, and not from the co-present variable factor of *vṛtti*.[46]

The Pauṣkara Āgama defines *pramāṇa* accordingly as the *cit-śakti* which is free from doubt etc., free from the doubtful, the erroneous and the merely recollective.[47] That is to say, *cit-śakti* 'defined' by *buddhi vṛtti*, determined indubitably, unerringly and also immediately, that is unmediated by a previous knowledge, constitutes *pramāṇa*. In so far as *cit-śakti* is not as such identical with the defining *vṛtti* which is material, it is intrinsically free from the elements of doubt, error and mediacy. The stipulation that only a doubt-free, unerring *cit-śakti* can be *pramāṇa* must be accordingly understood to refer to *buddhi vṛtti* which in its reference to the object can be uncertain or erroneous or be mediated. A *cit-śakti* that is free from the co-operation of a *vṛtti* in the forms of doubt, error etc. or to state it positively, a *cit-śakti* that is defined by a *vṛtti* of the form of valid experience is, then, the *pramāṇa* in the sphere of what is revealed in that experience.

XII

VALID AND NON-VALID KNOWLEDGE

The Nature of True or Valid Knowledge

The notion of truth or error is ascribed to *cit-śakti via* the intellectual mode of activity (*buddhi-vṛtti*) in which it may be said to be 'embodied' as self is embodied in the physical organism. Just as the life principle incarnates in flesh and articulates as living organism, subject to the laws of life, consciousness is incarnated and not merely expressed, in *buddhi-vṛtti* for articulation as judgment; the same metaphysical view underlying the relation between body and self underlies also the relation between consciousness (*cit-śakti*) and the knowing act (*buddhi-vṛtti*) in knowledge. Valid or non-valid to be defined by its relation to object given it through sense. The mode of the intellect, of the nature of *valid experience* (*yathārthānubhūtyuparūḍhavṛtti*) *qua illumined by cit-śakti* constitutes valid knowledge and the same of the nature of non-valid experience (*a-yathārthānubhūtyuparūḍhavṛtti*) *illumined by cit-śakti* is constitutive of non-valid knowledge.[1]

Therefore 'validity' of knowledge will have to be defined by the relation of *buddhi-vṛtti* to the object given it through sense. The etymology of the term for valid is quite suggestive. It implies concordance or absence of discordance with a given object or event (*artham anatikrāntaṁ yathārtham*). The 'validity' of the intellectual act consists in some kind of accordance obtaining between it and the objective fact. The success with which the concept of validity may be analysed will therefore depend upon the intelligibility of the meaning of 'accordance'. Without the help of this notion of accordance with what is given, there is from the very nature of the case no way of defining validity of knowledge. Truth or validity with which we are concerned in our present analysis, is what is characteristic of knowledge expressible in the form of judgment.

It is useful to recall here the realistic postulate about knowledge, namely, that all knowledge (as different from fantasy) points to an object which is necessarily 'real' and independent of it. Knowledge merely discovers its object. This reference to the given may be known as valid or otherwise not at the level of bare knowledge undifferentiated as 'that' and 'what' such as we have in pure sensation but at the level where we refer an idea content to reality—ascribe a 'what' to the 'that'. The senses do not err just as spirit (*cit-śakti*) as such does not err. The senses do not err because they do not judge and relate. *Cit-śakti per se* being universal also does not err, because nothing can be given it *from without.* It is only with reference to the given and also with reference to a predicate which is ascribed to it by the interpretative activity of mind that the question of truth or error can arise.[2] Only the judging act, which is particular and non-eternal and to which something is given, can err or not err. Truth, then, is a significant characteristic of judgment determined by a determinate relation of its predicate to its subject rendered so by its referential translucence. It is significant as implying as false what is contradictory to it. When applied to the prejudgmental level of awareness, truth becomes a non-significant description.[3]

The precise nature of the relation between *vṛtti-jñāna* and objective reality is, by the very nature of the case, unanalysable. Though we say that a proposition's truth consists of being in accord with fact, it is a commonplace that we cannot get away from propositions to the realm of pure facts in order to make the comparison. We do not have *vṛtti-jñāna* on the one hand and facts unencumbered with *vṛtti* on the other. *Vṛtti-jñāna* is not an experience of 'what' without 'that' though such an experience may be said to be logically presupposed as in indeterminate knowledge.[1] A *vṛtti-jñāna* refers to 'that' by ascribing a character; what is thus referred to by it cannot itself be a character, a 'what' as judgment will then cease to be knowledge. All that we can say then about the nature of *vṛtti-jñāna* is that it consists of predication of a character or qualification (what) to a qualificand (that).[5] A knowledge of either without the other is *ex hypothesi* not available for *vṛtti*-defined knowledge.

Some Definitions of Validity

Though 'accordance' between knowledge and fact constitutive of truth defies analysis in terms logically simpler, the terms between which a truth-relation obtains in *true knowledge*, may be defined. A critical examination of the various possible modes of conceiving the relation may help us to formulate the relation between 'that' and 'what' of a true judgment adequately.[1]

The most simple way of conceiving the nature of accordance between the given and the activity of the understanding (*vṛtti*) is to view it as a case of resemblance.[2] Such a view rests apparently on the common-sense belief about the 'similarity' between knowledge and a given situation which makes it valid knowledge. Although with the simple view of common-sense one may not disagree, its simplicity and naïveté as a common-sense *theory* does not need a detailed demonstration. The alleged similarity cannot obviously be total, so that there can be a one-one resemblance between the activity of the mind and what lies outside it. Neither can it be bare similarity of structure. It may not be thought that the two may bear resemblance to each other at least as mere existents. For this resemblance will not be adequate for constituting validity as some degree of it will be present in error too.

Nor can validity be defined as consisting in being of practical value.[3] A *valid* cognitive activity, it is said, is, what eventuates in useful action. Validity is what favours or fulfils attainment of purpose. But if one were to question on what ground the usefulness of knowledge is ascertained, the reply will have to be that it is presumably on the ground of its being valid. The very notion of fruitful activity cannot be made intelligible without implicitly at least referring to validity and therefore cannot be used for defining it.[4]

It may be useful to anticipate here the distinction between the problem of the nature of truth or validity and the problem of its criterion. Knowledge is useful or works may be a useful criterion for testing its validity, but this is not what is meant by saying that it is valid. The usefulness of a belief may be symptomatic or confirmatory but not also constitutive of truth. If it were constitutive then a non-valid belief which proves useful should be, according to this view, a contradiction in terms. Such is however not the case. It is not only not contradictory but it is quite plausible to think of non-true beliefs as useful and useless beliefs as true.[5]

Another possible way of defining validity is, as what is non-available except with fact.[6] Non-presence of the one without the other (*avyabhicāritva*), literally, absence of promiscuity, may mean non-presence of the intellect's function other than at the locus of the fact, even as in an inference the middle term is an invariable concomitant with the major term in the sense of being present but only 'in' it. This is not quite true, because the *buddhi's* function, that is, *buddhi-vṛtti* is known to be present at least at one locus other than that of the fact to which it relates, namely, *buddhi* itself from which it is never sundered even when it pervades the objects through its mode. Non-presence of *vṛtti* without the corresponding object may not also mean that the intellect's function is non-present except where it is *related* to fact. For its presence at a locus *related* to fact is available in the case of valid knowledge;[7] the 'given' in doubt and error is in some way certainly related to fact.

Yet another way of defining validity will be: that attribute which is not the correlate of the absence of the qualificand — where such attribute is characteristic, there is validity.[8] This definition will not cover instances of valid knowledge where the attribute happens to be a correlate of the absence of the qualificand as, say, in the instance of cognising that 'the floor has or possesses the vase' (*ghaṭavat bhūtalam*). Here though 'the floor having the vase' is not the correlate of its relational absence (*saṁsargābhāva*) it is the correlate of its mutual absence (*anyonyābhāva*). With all existents, difference (*bheda*) from others exists, just as their own difference from others exists in other existents.

Nor may it improve the case by stipulating about the 'absence' in the above definition as absence which is constant (*atyantābhāva*). The attribute which is not the counterpositive of its constant absence in the qualificand is, it may be said, the characteristic of validity.[9] When red apples are perceived rightly as red, the predication of redness will be an instance of an attribute which is not the counterpositive of its constant absence in the qualificand, even as fire is the counterpositive of its constant absence on the surface of say, a sheet of water. Likewise, wrong predication of 'silverness' in nacre will not be an instance of such predication as 'silverness' is the counterpositive of its constant absence in nacre.

However, the inadequacy of this definition to define the sphere of validity will be evident in the following example which, being a clear case of non-valid cognition still involves predication of what is not the counterpositive of its constant absence in the qualificand.[10] Take the case of a false predication of redness of apples which, in fact, being unripe, are only green and not yet red. Here too, no less than in the valid case of predicating redness of red apples, redness is not the counterpositive of the constant absence of the qualificand (which, in this case of non-valid knowledge are green apples). Redness falsely perceived of apples yet to turn red is only the counterpositive of its prior absence in them and to that extent, shares the character of 'not being the counterpositive of its constant absence in the apples'. A character which is alleged to be the characteristic, exclusively of validity.[11]

Nor may the 'absence' be therefore 'prior absence'. Truth or validity, one may say, is that attribute which is not the counterpositive of its prior absence in the qualificand.[12] The case that this definition will rule out will be the very instance where redness is predicated of red apples, which can be said to be counterpositive of its own prior absence. In so far as the question is not expressly about predication of redness of apples at a given point of time, the predicate is equivocal and can conceivably be the counterpositive of its own prior absence. At a given moment of course the predicate red in 'apples are red' cannot be the counterpositive of its prior absence. But without this stipulation about time, redness predicated of red apples in a temporally unspecified sense, will certainly be counterpositive of its prior absence.

Shall we, then, attribute truth or validity to the predicate which is not the counterpositive of its prior absence in the qualificand *qua* limited by the time of its content?[13] This amounts to an unwarranted restriction of predication to cases where the time of the content is taken into consideration. All propositions surely are not propositions of time. All predications may be in time, without reference to which surely it may not be possible to distinguish between true and false predication. But this is not the same as admitting that all predications are *about* time.

Assuming that predication is made with reference to time and that in this instance of predicating redness in 'apples or cherries are red' the present tense is indicative of their (the cherries) contemporaneity with the time of predication, the aforesaid instance of knowledge may be shown to be uncovered by the definition despite the fact that it is a case of valid knowledge. In the proposition 'cherries are red' a time-element may be said to be involved in either of two senses; according to one sense of the term, time is unperceived but according to the other, perceived. Time may mean either the moment[14] which is the infinitesimal nether limit of time as ordinarily understood, and a content as qualified by time in this sense, namely, the moment is, *ex hypothesi*, unperceived. The absolutely momentary is imperceptible. The precise moment when a not quite red cherry turns red is thus never perceived. Time in the sense of gross, perceptible time, however, refers to a combination of some moments[15] which may be said to qualify perceptibly a content of knowledge, as when we say 'the cherries are *now* red'.

In this latter sense, predication of redness in 'cherries are red' may be said to involve perception of the time-factor and may be expected as valid knowledge to fulfil the condition of the definition. But alas, no. Even when made with an express reference to time, the predicate red is not the counterpositive of its prior absence in the qualificand.[16] The qualificand, here in the example, the cherries *qua* limited by the time of reference (in above sense of the term, time) will imply a minimum of four moments which are inclusive of the moment of the previous absence of redness. Hence, the predicate red being not the counterpositive of its previous absence in the cherries, will not be true predication even when made with an express reference to time (as in 'the cherries, now, are red').[17]

Moreover in the case of valid conjunct cognition of 'flower and vase',[18] neither being not the counterpositive of the *relational absence* of the other, neither conjunctive of the conjunct cognition will be valid according to the proposed definition[19] and so will be yet another case of valid knowledge under-pervaded by the definition.

Leaving aside these sophistications due to the notion of 'absence', why not define validity more simply, as just being of the nature of the characteristics of the qualificand ?[20] The characterisation of a qualificand by the attributes pertaining to it constitutes vaild knowledge. A definition of this kind without further stipulations will err by over-pervasion in the following case which involves assertion of an attribute that pertains to the object, and yet is no valid cognition. A heap of transparent scarlet beads is perceived by the side of a glowing red live coal and the two alike are perceived as fire—a clear case of erroneous cognition. In this instance, though there is available the circumstance of the characterising of the qualificand by the attributes pertaining to it—the predication of fire in the subject which includes fire, the cognition as a whole is not valid. In the same manner, mis-perceiving fire as beads and beads as fire, another variant of erroneous cognition, may claim validity in the name of the predication of attributes present in the qualificand taken as a whole.[21]

Valid knowledge if defined as that where the object constitutively, not merely epistemically, happens to be the substrate of the characteristics predicated,[22] also begs the issue. A formal way of showing the fallacy is to indicate that the definition is wide, wide enough paradoxically to include error. In the perception of silverness in nacre, the substrate of the characteristic perceived constitutively is nacre, no less than in the perception of silverness in silver.

Nor may the definition be improved by substituting in the place of 'is' in a constitutive sense by a non-constitutive 'is qualified *as*'.[23] According to this, it is qualification by the substrate of predication (*viśeṣyatva*) and not being the object thereof (*viṣayatva*) that constitutes validity. In the instance of predicating silverness in nacre, being substrate of the predication of silverness does not constitutively belong to nacre though it is believed to be such. The instance in which this definition may be shown to over-extend, will be again an erroneous, simultaneous cognition of a heap of scarlet beads as fire and *vice versa*. Here though each of the two items mis-perceived as the other taken severally, may be said to be unqualified by 'the substrate of the two respective predicates', as a single complex cognition, the qualificand, namely scarlet beads *cum* fire, is qualified constitutively indeed by the substrate of either predicate, and, therefore, will have to be construed as valid knowledge according to the definition.

If we in despair turn to a negative formulation of the same definition in order to avoid its over-pervading the instance of a non-valid conjunct cognition and say that validity consists of not being qualified by what is not the substrate of the characteristic predicated,[24] we are still no better off than before. The instance of a genuine valid cognition that this definition will under-pervade will be a conjunct cognition of, say, a table and a cloth wherein the characteristics of either of conjunctives is affirmed of the other, and therefore fails to qualify as true according to the definition of 'being qualified by what is not the substrate of the characteristics predicated.'

Truth as Correspondence between Judgment and Fact

What, then, about the classical definition of truth stated in its simplest form as that which is characterised by what is characteristic of it?[1] Truth lies in the affirmation of that predicate, where there is correspondingly an object qualified by the same characteristic. There are two elements in cognition, the 'that' (*viśeṣya*) and the 'what' (*prakāra*) and an accord or consonance between the two constitutes truth.

We seem to have certainly made some advance towards a plausible view of true or valid knowledge. To know validly is to know the qualificand as qualified by what *is* its quality. In so far as it is possible at all to talk in the abstract of 'valid knowledge' as such apart from instances of knowledge which we recognise severally to be 'valid', we cannot define the common factor better than as correspondence obtaining between the manner of predication in judgment, no matter what is predicated and the manner in which the relation actually obtains.

But to state it thus—as correspondence between such-and-suchness in our judgment and the same in fact, surely leaves much to be desired as a logical definition. It would not be difficult to cite in the same strain as before cases of over-pervasion and under-pervasion even of this definition, stated without being properly formulated in terms of a determining relation (*avacchedaka saṁbandha*).

An erroneous cognition—simultaneous misperception of beads and live coal each as the other—will satisfy the formula of 'asserting a predicate of a subject which has that predicate'; the 'that' and the 'what' of the erroneous judgment accord with the 'that' and the 'what' of reality. Conversely in the following example '*here is the* universal of pot' (*atra ghaṭatvam*) the order of the 'that' and the 'what' is changed[2] and will fall short of the formula of truth as correspondence between what is expressed as the subject of a judgment and its predicate.

How then shall we qualify the statement to make it logically precise as a definition of correspondence? The definition, to begin with, must be such as to avoid all equivocation. The subject of the assertion must be unequivocal; it must not be 'determined' or 'limited' by an attribute which is in conflict with its nature.[3] In the statement 'the trunk of an electric post is in conjunction with some human hand', 'the trunk of an electric post' of which something is predicated must not be determined by a character that is contrary to its own; the post-trunk should be exclusive of, say, the post-top. Otherwise, if the trunk of the post were also to include the 'top of the post' what is asserted of the former will over-extend to the case of the latter. A stipulation of this nature secures for the definition of correspondence a great measure of freedom from over-pervasion.[4]

Another stipulation will be: the condition that the thing asserted should not be determined by a nature incompatible with its own, should be positively known. A mere absence of knowledge to the effect that it is 'determined' by what is incompatible with its own nature, will not do. The need for a qualification like this may easily be shown. Take the example of judgment in which it is known that there is no correspondence with fact: the crystal is red-coloured; here the crystal only looks red; redness, in fact, is inherent in *what is associated with the crystal*, and not inherent in the crystal itself.[5] The condition of a knowledge that the qualificand should not be determined by contradictory nature will rightly exclude this case from the purview of valid knowledge. Knowledge to that effect presupposes that the relation between the subject and the predicate is direct (*sākṣāt saṁbandha*) and not mediated as in the example.[6]

So much for the first part of the formula of correspondence about the givenness of the qualificand (*viśeṣyasya tadvattvam*), in knowledge as well as in fact. Now about the element of predication (*tatprakārakatva*). Instead of stating it merely as possession of the predicate it may more plausibly be restated as *possession* of relatedness to the predicate. The advantage of stating it as a relation rather than as possession of quality is that such instances where a predicate itself is referred to as the qualificand (for example, 'here is the universal of pot') may be covered by the definition. On a different view we have seen that such judgments involving a transposition of the 'that' and the 'what' as ordinarily understood, will fall outside the scope of valid knowledge. This will not be so on the present view where 'whatness' is defined as 'what is *related* to the subject term'.[7]

The introduction of the notion of relation as a necessary feature of correspondence serves to differentiate valid knowledge from erroneous knowledge.[8] The subject must be in determinate relation to the predicate attributed, *constitutively* not merely epistemically. In an erroneous perception like 'this is silver' though silverness and its relation to 'this' is perceived the constitutive counterpart of 'this', namely, the nacre is not perceived; the correlateness (*anuyogitva*) is there but it does not figure in the judgment. The very concepts of 'that' (*viśeṣya*) and 'what' of a judgment may be seen to be derived from the phenomenon of relation; the two necessary terms — the termini of a relation are, that which is related (*pratiyogin*) and that whereof something is related (*anuyogin*). The constituents of a cognised judgment of relation are the adjunct (predicate) and the subjunct (subject) *both of which are also cognised*.[9]

Lastly, the predication of 'what' to the 'that' must not be left indeterminate. The particular subject which stands in a *determinate* relation to the predicate, and not a subject just in some relation to the predicate—such must be the nature of a valid judgment. This stipulation helps to interpret the erroneous nature of the conjunct cognitions both of the true and the erroneous kinds, already referred to, consistently. In the conjunct, wrong cognition of red beads and fire, each as the other, there are two conjunctive pairs of 'that' and 'what' which get mixed up and hence the error. If the particular 'what' is predicated of the 'that' to which it bears a *determinate relation* and not to the other, there would be no error.[10]

It has been asked whether a correspondence theory of truth can be free from the main difficulty of having to offer a test of its truth. 'A predication is made of a subject which is in relation to the attributes in question in the manner in which predication is made. But how are we to know whether the relation between subject and predicate is actual or whether the manner of the predication is also the manner in which the relation obtains'?[11] Throughout the discussion of the subject what has been suggested is that the manner of predication in thought must, in every detail be such as to be congruent with the manner in which the relation obtains in fact. A question like the one raised above, namely, how the alleged correspondence is to be tested is never contemplated. This is, however, as it should be. We cannot get outside of our knowledge to test correspondence. If the element of correspondence were not intuitively grasped with the grasp of knowledge, by no extraneous test can it be ascertained; such tests, which we do actually make are with a view to demonstrating and conforming the claim of truth which knowledge with its 'that-what' structure makes as it occurs. That such tests sometimes fail to confirm will only prove that the want of accord between the manner of predication in thought and the relation in reality has arisen presumably because of incorrect apprehension.

Affinities and Differences with Realism

The Śaiva Siddhānta definition of true knowledge is identical with the standard classical realistic doctrine of the Nyāya. However, it is useful to digress here to show the conceptual differences between the two systems.[1] The elements in a judgment for the Nyāya, namely, the *viśeṣya* and the *prakāra* are two distincts though connected by a relation; and relation itself is another distinct entity. The knowledge-content and knowledge are comparable because knowledge itself is knowable as an object. Hence a positive implication of its advocacy of the correspondence theory of truth consists of its doctrine that no knowledge is self-valid. Śaiva Siddhānta differs from the Nyāya on almost every one of these counts. The *viśeṣaṇa* and *viśeṣya* in a judgment are, for it, identically related (*tādātmya*); and the relation of identity itself is not to be distinguished as separate from the terms; the sense of knowledge (*viśeṣaṇa*), that is, the terms in their totality constitute the substance (*viśeṣya*).[2]

The identity of the character and the characterised, and the consequent identity of knowledge and the knower are among the absolute presuppositions of a transcendental epistemology. Without them no 'true' knowledge is conceivable even though these principles themselves may not be demonstrated by true knowledge. Knowledge in its empirically defined form as *buddhi* is in its turn knowable as any known object, and empirical truth may be defined as correspondence between the immediate content of knowledge and the object referred to by knowledge. But this does not prevent Śaiva Siddhānta from admitting self-evidence to knowledge at the same time. The 'truth' of true knowledge is the determinate of which the determinant is the self-luminous *cit-śakti*. It is only in the case of erroneous knowledge the 'error' is caused externally though as knowledge it too is of course evidenced by *cit-śakti*. Consistently, Śaiva Siddhānta joins issue against the Nyāya for its advocacy of non-self-evidential theory of knowledge (*parataḥ prāmāṇya-vāda*).

It may be recalled that one of the accounts of the nature of truth which Śaiva Siddhānta rejects is that truth is what 'works'; workability as a possible account of truth presupposes correspondence in so far as knowledge has first to be knowledge before it can lead to action; that it leads to action, and the action may confirm the 'truth' of the knowledge, are not organic to knowledge as knowledge. Workability can be neither the definition nor a criterion of truth. There is no scope for indirect testing of the truth of knowledge; truth is self-evident, evident with the evidence of knowledge. This also sharply distinguishes the position of Śaiva Siddhānta from the Nyāya which in admitting fruitfulness as the criterion of truth rather inclines towards a view of coherence.

What howevér lends utmost plausibility to a suspicion that Śaiva Siddhānta theory of truth too borders on systematic coherence is its doctrine of the identity of *guṇa* and *guṇin*.[3] A thing is nothing more than a character-complex. The sense-data of perception, the 'what', and the 'object' perceived — the 'that' are really non-distinct. The object is not an unknown substrate of qualities but is merely constituted by the qualities so that they are no more different from each other than, say, a forest and its trees are *inter se* different.[4] This is implicit in the view that truth is correspondence between knowledge-content and the object; how can we assert this correspondence if we have two closed though parallel spheres having nothing to do with each other?

The Nyāya realist finds in the qualificand (*dharmin*) a nexus between knowledge and the object;[5] the predicate-element alone has scope in respect of doubt or mistake. Consistency, however, requires that to be able to assert correspondence or lack of correspondence, the predicate too must be in a sense 'given ' as the subject; doubt and mistake will necessarily have to be explained like truth from the side of the predicate but this itself rests on the positing of non-distinction between the unseen subject and the seen predicate. Deny their identity, knowledge becomes a pure act of faith; being always open to question a predication can never be validated by more predications because *ex hypothesi* at no stage can the element of predication claim validity on intrinsic grounds.

It may be argued that if the two were non-different the question of factual relevance in knowledge should not arise at all, all knowledge involving predication should be *eo ipso* relevant.[6] In answer it may be observed that while no knowledge is indeed without some factual relevance not all the predicative elements of knowledge can be equally relevant to the 'subject'. One element alone can belong to or to be more correct, 'be' the subject intrinsically at one time, constitutive of the uniqueness of the thing (*svarūpa lakṣaṇa*).[7] In relation to this, other elements are extrinsic and are, therefore, its accidens (*taṭastha lakṣaṇa*); they are factually relevant and yet not relevant to the requisite degree to be 'true'. The 'intrinsically' relevant predicate 'qualifies' the subject as its differentia and therefore constitutes it; it is the norm of truth in comparison with which all predication in knowledge about that subject will have to be judged.

In relation to the standard predicate which is constitutive of the thing intrinsically, all other predicates about it may be grouped under two headings: the 'class' of predicates which are homogeneous with the standard predicate which they 'resemble' and the class of predicates not homogeneous with it; the common feature about them is that they do not bear any resemblance to the standard predicate. While the standard predicate will be indeed the thing itself, predicates falling under the first class are relevant to a degree to warrant for themselves a 'general' truth; those falling under the second, though relevant theoretically in the sense that 'all things are everywhere' (*sarvaṁ sarvātmakam*) do not serve to 'define' the object even with a 'general' measure of truth. Such predicates when not discriminated from the other class and when also positively 'attributed' to the subject, constitute error.

It may still be asked how one is to know whether a given knowledge is true or not, whether its predicate belongs to one class rather than to the other. The answer to this is: every knowledge comes with the claim that its predicate is the constitutive element of the subject, that, in other words, it is true predicate; there is otherwise no way of 'knowing' the truth of knowledge. From the known compatibility or otherwise of the predicate with other predicates known about it we may infer the presence of an epistemological excellence (*guṇa*) or its opposite (*doṣa*) to account for the origination of true or erroneous knowledge. But in respect of knowing, if knowledge is true, self-evidence seems to be the only plausible solution.[8]

Śaiva Siddhānta is realistic and its theory of the non-difference of substance and attribute is not idealistic neither is its theory of truth coherence theory in the accepted sense of the term. A coherent system of proposition can only confirm the truth of what was self-evidently known and even this confirmation presupposes evidence for the truth of its proposition independently of coherence with other propositions. In rejecting a causal theory of perception according to which the sense-datum is held to be the effect of a material thing different from it, Śaiva Siddhānta does not necessarily give up realism or become idealistic. The existence of a particular sense-datum is *prima facie* evidence for that of the material thing to which the sense-datum belongs; unless this is so, no confirmation of our original acceptance would ever be possible. We cannot go beyond perception for our assurance of the existence of material things.[9] Śaiva Siddhānta admits a discursive activity of the mind which distinguishes and relates the variegations of a sense field; sensory knowledge is apperceived by mind, along with its structure but it is not this fact which constitutes the truth of knowledge; the given in knowledge determines its truth. All knowledge is knowledge of the given remains an indispensable presupposition of the realistic epistemology of Śaiva Siddhānta.[10]

Non-valid Knowledge : Forms and Theories

The indispensable evidential source of valid knowledge is *cit-śakti*; *cit-śakti*, in association with valid determinate knowledge, with knowledge which is 'free from doubt, error and remembrance' is *pramāṇa*; this statement gives us an idea of the kinds of non-valid knowledge in relation to which *cit-śakti* is not *pramāṇa*. The question of a *pramāṇa* arises only in the context of *pramā*. When *cit-śakti* is said to be the source only of such knowledge as excludes doubt, error and remembrance, it is suggested that doubt etc., though, as forms of knowledge, are illumined by *cit-śakti*, are not validated or *evidenced* by *cit-śakti*; being non-valid knowledge they derive *qua* non-valid knowledge from the presence of certain external factors. Doubt arises from a cognition of a common character in two objects; error from the presence of some defect in the knowing self or in the knowledge-apparatus; remembrance from a previous experience. In all these cases though it is self as *cit-śakti* that doubts, errs and remembers, its intrinsic nature of *evidencing* knowledge as valid is obscured by association with certain extraneous factors.

Forms of non-valid knowledge

(i) *Remembrance*—We 'may start with remembrance or memory in our account of non-valid knolwedge, because it seems to be the least 'non-valid' of the three forms.[1] Memory indeed admits of classification into valid memory (*yathārtha smṛti*) and erroneous memory (*ayathārtha smṛti*) on parity with valid and erroneous knowledge, and its exclusion from 'valid knowledge, as such, seems on purely technical grounds. It is knowledge generated by past impressions (*saṁskārajanya-jñāna*) and is not presentative (*na tu yathā śruteḥ*).[2]

On a different view of memory,[3] memory is also a species of presentative knowledge in which one directly apprehends the object of memory. Instead of perceiving a sense-datum in memory one perceives the images, but the 'image' is in some mysterious sense constitutive of the past object even as sense-data constitute the thinghood of the object perceived. On this view the distinction between valid memory and erroneous memory is a distinction within erroneous knowledge.

Memory is only retro-cognition, not cognition. Even the most valid form of retro-cognition will fall short of the self-evidential character of direct cognition.[4]

On the view that memory is only representative knowledge produced by impressions of old experience, the distinction between valid memory and erroneous memory will rest upon whether it is a revival of a past valid knowledge undistorted by imagination or of a knowledge that is represented faithfully.[5]

In whichever sense taken memory by definition does not give 'new' knowledge. A *pramāṇa* should give knowledge which is immediate and therefore previously unacquired. Immediacy and novelty go together. It may be said: in a 'persistent cognition' (*dhārāvāhika-jñāna*) of an identical object cognition in the second and succeeding moments are impression-generated. Shall we, therefore, exclude it from valid knowledge on the same ground as that of memory? The answer is that in a persistent cognition there is only a possession of impression (*saṁskāratva*) and not generation by impression (*saṁskāra-janya*).[6] The knowledge of the second moment is not caused by impression but by those very conditions which cause the first knowledge. Therefore, there is no question of the exclusion of 'persistent cognition' from the sphere of valid knowledge on similar grounds.[7]

(ii) *Doubt*—Doubt is conflicting apprehension in respect of one and the same subject —the predication of conflicting 'whats' to the same 'that'. The conflict implies mutual incompatibility, contradiction. Doubt is not negation or absence of knowledge, but a positive mental *vṛtti* in respect of something given though the *vṛtti* alternates between mutually incompatible features of the given. It is, therefore, a cognition lacking in decision (*avadhāraṇavarjita*) and oscillating between two mutually exclusive alternants.

Doubt is a 'mental' cognition (*mānasa-jñāna*).[8] The self cognises first the undifferentiated without mediaticu by name, class, etc. Such is indeterminate knowledge. This is followed by observation of characteristics or (whats), and conjectures, of the form 'this may be a man', 'this may be a stump' arise in the mind. The conjectures of course presuppose a previous experience that only a man and a stump possess those characters. The conjecture-alternatives which mind contemplates themselves lead to an enquiry into the nature of the object for a determinate character by the help of which a decision may be reached in favour of the man or the stump. A failure to discover such a character, and the resulting indecision is doubtful cognition.

Doubt thus mediates between *nirvikalpaka-jñāna* which is pre-judgmental and *savikalpaka-jñāna* which is alone either valid or non-valid. Doubtful cognition, non-valid cognition as well as valid cognition are all modes of *buddhi-vṛtti*. Doubt is a *judgment* which apperceives two alternatives as a consequence of perceiving their common character, just as error is *judgment* which apperceives what is not there, as being there.[9] As judgment again it is ultimately *cit-śakti* as defined by the *vṛtti* that really doubts.[10] As it was observed elsewhere, the element of indecision and also that of wrong decision, as in the case of error, are to be attributed to the cooperating factor of *vṛtti*, material (*māyika*) as *vṛtti* is, rather than to the all knowing *cit-śakti* even though it is *cit-śakti* that may be said to doubt and err.

In the example where the cognition with regard to a presented something alternates between say, a man and a stump, the cause of the alternation is the perception of height etc., which is common to both the alternatives. We can even say that perception of the specific characters (*asādhāraṇa dharma*) of the alternatives too is the cause of mental oscillation characteristic of *saṁśaya*, for it is the apprehension *at once* of the specific characters of a man and a stump in the given that accounts for one not being able to decide in favour of either of the alternatives.

According to the first interpretation, *saṁśaya* will be a species of valid Knowledge; doubt perceives the common character and is to that extent valid. According to the other interpretation *saṁśaya* will be non-knowledge; in respect of one specific character it is sure to be erroneous as both specific characters cannot be true; a conjunct proposition in which even one of the conjuncts is false, is false.[11]

(iii) *Error*—Error (*viparyaya*) is the cognition of an object as *other than* what it really is. If valid knowledge consists in perceiving a thing as *what* it really is (*tadrūpa*) error lies in perceiving it as *what* it is *not* (*atadrūpa-pratiṣṭhita*).[12] It is attributing to a thing such predicates as are not found in it , as for example, attributing silverness in nacre.

Error, in other words, is incidental to the relating of two or more objects given in knowledge. If the complex content of a judgment corresponds to what is in the objective world, it is valid; otherwise it is erroneous. The elements involved in an erroneous judgment are all facts of the objective world, but while they are not *related facts* in the world, they are however perceived to be related. In the case of perceiving the conch to be yellow because of a jaundiced eye, the yellow colour and the conch are presented to the mind, but their perceived relation is not factual. In the case of nacre-silver illusion also, silverness is presented, but presented more as a representation through the impression of a former experience; the shop-silver is 'implicitly' perceived (*alaukika pratyakṣa*). The nacre-silver illusion is, therefore, a case of a wrong relation of terms one of which is presented in the visual field itself and the other presented elsewhere and elsewhen; or, more plausibily it is some defect in the sense-organ relation which accounts for erroneous perception.

The chief features of the *anyathākhyāti-vāda* which Śaiva Siddhānta advocates in the company of Nyāya-Vaiśeṣika, Yoga and also the Bhāṭṭa Mīmāṁsakas, may be brought out by a cirtical review of some classical theories of error with which the system comes to grips.[13]

Rival Theories of Error and the Perspective of Siddhanta

Error has been a subject of endless debate and analysis in Indian-thought. Broadly speaking, the different theories of error may be grouped under two headings, those views which agree in admitting that what appears in error is in some sense or other real and those which deny that it is real. The second group will include the view which characterises the content of error outright as *asat* (*asat-khyāti*) and also the view which if it does not characterise it as *asat* does not also characterise it as *sat* (*anirvacanīya-khyāti*).[1] To this group also belongs the view of the idealist (*ātma-khyāti*) according to whom error consists in the external projection of a subjective fact. Knowledge of objects has a form, but objects do not have specific forms of their own.[2] Form is attributed to what has no form. These views including the last one are critical in their attitude of the view of the reality of the given and tend to pronounce cognitive experience as such erroneous by its very nature.[3]

The other group of theories of error which assume a realist's attitude to the question, inclines to look upon knowledge as capable of becoming erroneous under characteristic circumstances; by this is implied that knowledge is capable of being valid also and that indeed it is so intrinsically. This attitade of optimism towards knowledge and the trust in its value as the means, and the only means at man's disposal for achieving liberation from bondage at least to the extent it is achieved by means of knowledge, is the true spirit of religious philosophies like Śaiva Siddhānta.[4]

The element of realism notwithstanding, Śaiva Siddhānta is critical in its consideration of rival theories, specially in its treatment of rival realistic views. This is because it admits a distinction between truth and error from the cognitive standpoint itself unlike the realistic theories which it criticises. There is an objective basis for error which cannot be gainsaid, just as there is an objective basis of evil which lends poignance to moral struggle. An erroneous judgment is a judgment; it is not non-thinking (*akhyāti*), nor is it a judgment which *from the cognitive point of view* is never negated (*sat-khyāti*). Error is real error and cancellation of error is real cancellation in knowledge. Disillusionment in knowledge is a pointer to the fallibility to which the cogniser is prone congenitally, and to the defective and misleading nature of the physical medium of knowledge.[5]

(*i*) *Theory of akhyāti* : The 'no-erroneous-knowledge' theorist (*akhyātivādin*) holds that error is not a unit of knowledge at all, but indeed a composite judgment whose components are two judgments—a judgment of perception and a memory judgment having their respective contents. The want of discrimination between the two, or to use the theorist's own jargon, non-apprehension of their difference (*bhedāgraha*) results in error. The so called erroneous judgment is thus dissolved into two judgments, neither in its own sphere invalid. A non-distinction of the two and their objects constitutes the 'invalidity' of the knowledge. It is a case of memory not aware of itself as memory (*pramuṣṭa-tattāka smaraṇa*) and therefore as different from perception.[6] The implication of this super-realistic point of view is obvious; knowledge is as such veridical. Consequently activity that knowledge issues in, is never as such suspect.

It may be objected that if error were no unit of knowledge—a single determinate cognition, but only non-apprehension of distinction, it could not be the cause of activity or inclination as, for example, in the case of the erroneous perception of nacre as silver. Non-apprehension does not urge one to activity. Apprehension, inclination and activity must function in unison.[7] If activity consists in securing of the silver, there must be the preceding desire to have the silver which in turn presupposes apprehension of it as silver. Activity, in other words, involves a positive apprehension as its prompting base.

In reply, the *akhyātivādin* says that this need for a prior determinate cognition (*viśiṣṭa-jñāna*) as a condition for activity arises only in the case of fruitful activity to which all 'true' cognition leads, but precisely, not in respect of an activity which is baulked of its fruit (*visaṁvādi-pravṛttisthala*) as the one relating to 'silver'. For the latter, a mere non-discrimination of the difference between memory and percept (*bhedā-graha*)[8] would suffice. On the other hand it can even be shown that even those who speak of *viśiṣṭa-jñāna* in error will have to accept *bhedā-graha*, as in turn the condition thereof. For, to perceive nacre positively as silver (*abheda-graha*) presupposes negatively, a prior non-perception of their difference (*bhedāgraha*) had to be admitted. The advocates of *viśiṣṭa-jñāna* will have, in other words, to accept (1) *bhedāgraha*, (2) *abheda-graha* or *viśiṣṭa-jñāna* as leading to (3) *pravṛtti*. The *akhyātivādin* can explain error without this prolixity, in terms only of *bhedagraha*.[9]

About *viśiṣṭa-jñāna*: Whence comes this *viśiṣṭa-jñāna* like 'this is silver' ? In every cognition where the content is a 'this-what' as for example, when we perceive a *daṇḍin* (one having a stick) there should be (i) sense-relation to the 'what' (*viṣeśaṇa-sannikarṣa*), namely, the *daṇḍa*, (ii) sense relation to the '*this-what*' (*viśeṣaṇa-viśeṣyayoḥ sannikarṣaḥ*), that is, *daṇḍa* characterising the *daṇḍin*, and (iii) non-apprehension of an absence of sense-relation between 'this' and 'what' (*tadubhayorasaṁsargāgrahaḥ*) as eventually leading to a determinate perception (*viśiṣṭa-jñāna*), namely, 'this-what'. It is obvious that, of these conditions the first is more fundamental as without it the second and the third do not follow. Now in the nacre-silver knowledge where is the *viśeṣaṇa-sannikarṣa*. Do not admit actual contact with the sense-datum of 'silver', and there is no determinate cognition to the effect 'this is silver'.

If it be replied that this condition — no *viśiṣṭa-jñāna* without *viśeṣaṇa-jñāna*, holds good only of *pramā*, not of *apramā*, the question of prolixity arises; one set of conditions for *pramā* and another for *apramā*. Besides, if there is no sense-relation in *apramā*, how will one distinguish between inferential cognition (*anumiti*) and this case of perceptual knowledge (*pratyakṣa*), there being no *viśeṣaṇa-sannikarṣa* in either of the two?

Śaiva Siddhānta vindicates its own stand by showing that these charges are not unanswerable.[10] To take the last objection first. It can be maintained that there is no 'contact' in the case of erroneous perception in the sense in which it is demanded by the opponent, and it is in this respect different from valid perception. To convict it of prolixity (*gaurava*) is no real charge because prolixity can be sometimes a contingence of the acceptable.

There is an actual sense-relation involved in the illusion of silver; only it does not involve the ordinary sense-contact. It is implicit perception without a perceptual relation but where there is a sort of cognitive relation (*jñāna-lakṣaṇa-sannikarṣa*) between sense and the silver. Relation not only with the subject (qualificand) but with the predicate silverness. Impression of a previous experience serves as the means of contact between sense and the silver — silver not in the immediate visual field but of elsewhere previously perceived.[11]

That it is still perception may not be questioned. Though dependent on a previous experience of 'shop-silver', the idea of silver is sense-bound in 'this is silver'. Nor may it be said that a perception of this nature involving 'complication' and no literal *viśeṣaṇa-sannikarṣa* is non-different from inference. In the inference of fire from perceiving smoke too there is absence of *viśeṣaṇa-sannikarṣa*. An inference rests on its own causal conditions like knowledge of *vyāpti* etc. and when these conditions are fulfilled, we have inference. In the instance of illusion of silver there is no inference involved.

It is true that in cases which seem to be amenable both to perception and inference the decision should always be in favour of the first. But perception in whose favour the ruling is here given, is, it may be remembered, of the normal kind and not of the 'implicit' variety.[12]

There is also the alternate explanation[13] which does not involve the use of this questionable sense-object contact brought about by the revival of a past impression of an object. There can be *sannikarṣa* with a *viśeṣaṇa* which is of the form of a defect (*doṣa*). The determinate cognition of 'this' as qualified by 'silverness' is generated by the sense of being for the moment in contact with some *doṣa* that accounts for the error of the judgment.[14] Perceptual errors may all be traced to a relation to some defect in the perceptual mechanism or in the physical medium. Even the body-soul error (*dehātma-bhrama*) may likewise be traced to a relation with a congenital 'defect'. What is needed to meet the objection of the opponent is to admit relation (*sannikarṣa*) in some form or other as a plausible explanation of error as a case of knowledge.

To come to the first objection. The *akhyātivādin* contends that non-apprehension of the difference between 'perceived' nacre and 'remembered' silver (*bhedāgraha*) itself will suffice to prompt activity and that it is not necessary to feel the contents of the two cognitions, namely, the nacre and the silver, to be a synthetic whole as a condition for activity. Let us accept this and see what it implies. Non-knowledge of the difference of a 'desired' silver from the presented (*iṣṭa-bhedāgraha*) acounts for an exertion (*pravṛtti*) in the direction of the 'silver'; shall we not expect then that a similar non-knowledge of the difference of silver that is not desired from the presented (*aniṣṭa-bhedāgraha*) should lead to the opposite of *pravṛtti*, namely a recoil from exertion (*nirvṛtti*). Such seems indeed the case in rope-snake illusion. Non-apprehension of the difference of the 'snake' which is not certainly desired, from the given rope, leads to a negative exertion (*nirvṛtti*) in relation to it, that is to say it leads to running away from it. There is no cancellation (*bādha*) from the perspective of *jñāna* according to *akhyāti-vāda*; the *jñāna* remains intact. *Bādha* refers to *pravṛtti*. Cancellation is 'practical', that is obstruction or frustration of empirical activity.

The *reductio ad absurdum* of this explanation can be seen in the following example.[15] Take the case of an erroneous conjunct cognition involving a simultaneous perception of two or more things — erroneously. Lead and silver by the side of each other are simultaneously misperceived. Here the explanation that a non-apprehension of the desired A's difference from B leads to an 'adient' activity in respect of the desired (*pravṛtti*) and conversely, a non-desired A's difference from B leads to an 'arient' activity[16] towards the non-desired (*nirvṛtti*) will lead to the contingence of the occurrence *at once* of *pravṛtti* and *nirvṛtti* in respect of lead and silver simultaneously given in knowledge.[17] The upshot of this criticism implied by this case of erroneous conjunct cognition is to the effect that *pravṛtti-nirodha or nivṛtti* is only a 'practical' analogue of the cognitive error consisting in a positive apprehension of the given as otherwise than it really is. Therefore, the claim that non-apprehension of distinction is on a par with apprehension and that it is indeed even more basic than the other being its presupposition, is not acceptable.

As for the objection that the *akhyātivādin* could explain *pravṛtti* with one factor only, namely *bhedāgraha* whereas the advocate of *anyathā-khyāti-vāda* has to reckon with two factors, namely, *bhedāgraha* and *viśiṣṭa-jñāna*, it may be replied that though in one sense the latter view seems prolix, in another sense it may be shown to have the advantage of parsimony (*lāghava*) on its side. The issue translated in plain language amounts to this. One says that it is the perception of silver in nacre that promotes one's activity. The other view is that it is not perception of silver—there being no silver percept there, but really non-perception of it as different from silver that prompts one's activity. Now which of the two is less presuming? Certainly the first, because it uses the comparatively simple notion of perception of nacre as silver instead of the awkward notion of non-perception of it as non-silver. A positive factor (*bhāva*) has the advantage over the negative (*abhāva*); negation unlike affirmation is incomplete; it necessarily points to its correlate, as negation *of something*. So it is more in keeping with the requirements of parsimony to account for *pravṛtti* in terms of a positive determinate cognition (*viśiṣṭa-jñāna*) rather than in terms of a negative non-perception (*agraha*).

When we thus establish a relation between *jñāna* and *pravṛtti*, we may not necessarily have to anticipate erroneous instances where activity does prove 'false' (*asatya pravṛtti*). Knowledge always comes with a truth-claim and inspires activity as a rule. That this relation between *jñāna* and *pravṛtti* does not cover the case of *apramā* (error) as conceived by the opponent is no objection. The *akhyāti-vāda* account of error is not certainly the only explanation nor even, for the reason stated above a plausible explanation. Knowledge (*jñāna*) and activity (*pravṛtti*) are of one piece.

(ii) *Asat-khyāti*: To pass on to other theories of error: The Madhvites advocate *asat-khyāti* as the explanation of error. Although subscribing to the form of *anyathā-khyāti* in defining error as cognition which apprehends one thing as of the nature of another,[18] the *asatkhyāti-vādin* further contends that it is the apprehension of *asat* as *sat*[19] that constitutes error. The arguments are as follows: when the perceived silver is sublated as 'this is not silver' (*nedaṁ rajatam*) it is implied that the content of error is non-existent (*asat*). It is also seen after cancellation that what is cancelled, namely silver, is not only what is not, but what never has been; the content of error is really the counter-correlate of non-existence in all times[20] and in all places. The Madhvites define absolute non-existence rather paradoxically as what is *present* in all the three times and contend that it is this *asat* that appears in error. How can a non-existent content be an object of knowledge? The reply is that we refer to men who are dead and to events that are past. In such instances the non-existent is the 'describer' of knowledge, even though being non-existents they do not produce the knowledge.[21]

In criticism of the above view, it may be asked how, firstly, *asat* can at all appear and secondly, what is still less conceivable, how *asat* can be perceived.[22] For, the Madhvites contend that on the strength of *nedaṁ rajatam* that in the erstwhile cognition of silver, the silver that never was at any time was presented and also perceived as such. There is it is claimed 'givenness' (*pratīti*) for *asat*. This we question. The argument for *asat* being perceptually cognised verges on the absurd. When you say that a thing is not *asat*, does not such exclusion (*vilakṣaṇa-jñāna*) imply *pratīti* of *asat*, asks the *dvaitin*. To know that something is not *asat*, is to know *asat*. But our question is not if *asat* can be inferred or known by implication, but if it can be *perceived*. In the nacre-silver illusion, the silver is perceived. The *dvaitin* has only taken his stand on *nedaṁ rajatam*. What about the affirmative cognition *idaṁ rajatam*, which constitute error proper? How will he account for the perceptual character of error if the content thereof were *asat*? How can there be *sannikarṣa* with *asat* without which its being perception cannot be explained?

The *dvaitin*, however, replies that the sense-organ affected presumably in some way, being in contact with what is in fact presented, causes the rise of cognition representing it as something which did not exist at all. But this is not convincing. To admit knowledge without an object is, strictly, not compatible with the assertion of self-validity of knowledge. If a self-certifying *sākṣin* were admitted as the *pramāṇa* in knowledge (error in knowledge being attributed to the presence of *doṣa*), the explanation tallies with the one given by the *siddhāntin* himself. However, the criticism stands that the *asatkhyāti-vāda* of the Madhvite rests only on *nedaṁ rajatam*.[23]

(iii) *Sat-Khyāti* : In sharp reaction to the theory that the non-existent appears in error, is put forward the theory of *sat-khyāti* as it were as its *reductio ad absurdum*. The content of error is not *asat*; no knowledge indeed refers to an unreal object. Rāmānuja himself seems to have favoured *anyathā-khyāti* as may be seen when he defines error as consisting of a thing appearing to be other than that it is (*anyasya anyathābhāvaḥ*).[24] However this is only the epistemic condition; the constitutive condition of error, meant as a counterblast to the *asat-khyāti*, is embodied in the theory of *sat-khyāti* or *yathārtha-khyāti*.[25]

The knowledge of silver in nacre is not false or unreal but is real and points to a real object, the silver element being present in the nacre as its constituent. The presence of silver content in nacre should be understood on the principle of determining similarity by real representation, known as *pratinidhi nyāya*.[26] The suggested substitute for *Soma* in its absence, for purpose of performing a sacrifice is a more readily available plant (*pūttika*) which can take the place of *Soma*. The implication of suggesting this alternative seems to be the fact of the actual representation of the *Soma* element in its substitute. Two things similar to each other, capable of serving mutually as a substitute each for the other, and also of being mistaken, are so by virtue of the actual representation of each in the other in varying degrees.

In fact not only are things similar, being actually represented in each other, but indeed all things are in all things (*sarvaṁ sarvātmakam*). This is the ontological basis of the view that all apprehension erroneous or otherwise, refers to a real object, and that what is real is alone apprehended. That, this is the ascertained view or the Vedic tradition, may be seen by reference to the Vedic texts relating to the process of *pañcīkaraṇa*—the quintuplication of the different elements, the implication being, that in each element there are present all the other elements in some measure.

In criticism of *sat-khyāti*, we may say that on this explanation of error, there can be nothing like cancellation of error. If the '*idam*' actually possesses the silver content in it for which reason it is perceived as *rajatam*,[27] how is it subsequently cancelled as *idaṁ na rajatam* ? It may be replied, that not silver (*na rajatam*) does not involve total negation. The negative particle (*nañ*) has many meanings of which the one applicable here is partial negation (*alpa*), *na rajatam* therefore means *alpa-rajatam*, so that what is thus denoted in its negative aspect is 'nacre' even as 'nacre' itself denotes the positive aspect.

But this defence is unconvincing. The issue here does not hinge upon a verbal interpretation, such as the one involved in the meaning of the term *advaita*, but concerns actual perception. Moreover, if all things are everywhere available negatively or positively, how does 'this is not' contradict 'this is' ? Even after cancellation as 'this is not silver' how is it that one is not in quest of the silver-element that is present undeniably in the nacre?[28]

The statement that similarity is due to, and in fact another term for, partial identity of material content fails to apply to the commonplace error of mistaking body for the soul. Nothing of the body is represented in the self or *vice versa* constituting the basis of similarity. The advantage of *anyathā-khyāti* over *sat-khyāti* as adequate explanation of error is obvious in such instances.[29] Even in errors arising through perception of similarity, therefore, there is no need to postulate identity of material content, as a significant factor accounting for the rise of error. The principle of *trivṛtkaraṇa* and *pañcīkaraṇa* applies to the intermixing of the *tanmātrās* and not of the *bhautikas*. The *pratinidhi-nyāya* explanation is also untenable; *pūttika* is recommended as a substitute for *Soma* not necessarily because of structural identity.[30] If it were on grounds of identity there are better claimants, for example plants of the same species as of *Soma*, to serve as substitute of *pūttika*, which are not however mentioned in the Veda.

With the underlying postulate of *sat-khyāti*, Śaiva Siddhānta realism cannot certainly be in disagreement. The correspondence between knowledge and its contents should be in respect, both, of the *that* and the *what* of the presented. This is true in the case of non-valid as well as of valid knowledge. The *satkhyāti-vāda* explains it by positing structural affinity between things of the world which make for their unity. Error arises because of similarity, and similarity is identity in structure. The principle underlying *pañcīkaraṇa*, Śaiva Siddhānta would argue is the principle of '*guṇin*' conserving with its unity unbroken, through all its *guṇas*. It is the invariable presence of the *guṇin* in the variable *guṇas* that is explained by the Vedic theory of 'all things in all things'. Śaiva Siddhānta accordingly differentiates error from truth in terms of its theory that *guṇin* is wholly composed of *guṇa*;[31] in the erroneous perception of nacre as silver, the *guṇas* like the peculiar lustre which are sensed, are real; the *guṇin* too, namely, the given nacre and the '*perceived*' silver are real. It is only the relation that constitutes the error of commission.

For the *satkhyātivādin* strictly speaking there can be no error of commission. Knowledge is for him of the given and of *nothing but the given*. *Satkhyāti-vāda* admits at the same time that knowledge is not of the whole of what is given; like *akhyāti-vāda*[32] it also admits that incomplete knowing may give rise to errors; in the erroneous perception of the yellow conch it is non-apprehension of its whiteness that constitutes error. Śaiva Siddhānta will also admit that konwledge, perceptual, inferential and even scriptural is never of the *whole* of the given; every *guṇin* is composed of an indefinite number of *guṇas*, classifiable under the two categories of what belongs to it unrelatedly (*svarūpa-lakṣaṇa*) and what belongs to it in relation to a perspective (*taṭastha-lakṣaṇa*). One consequence to be drawn from this view is that no empirical knowledge can span the entire conspectus of the *guṇas* constitutive of a *guṇin*. Knowledge always sub-apprehends. But there is also the other conclusion to be drawn : knowledge can also over-apprehend; failing to discriminate between the relevant and the non-relevant *guṇas* it may mis-relate, as in the case of nacre-silver illusion.

(*iv*) *Ātma-Khyāti*: The *ātma-khyāti* of the Yogācāra idealist conceives 'silver' in the erroneous cognition 'this is silver' as but an idea that is externalised and projected out; 'this is not silver' cancels only the idea's externality and indeed even reinstates, by implication, the subjective character of the idea.[33] This theory of error is part of the idealistic doctrine that awareness and its content are one inseparable whole and that there is indeed no external reality. What is needed then to accomplish a refutation of *ātma-khyāti* is, with Kumārila,[34] to show that knowledge is grounded in the objective, and is indeed inconceivable without this objective basis. What knowledge refers to, may not invariably be present *there* and *then*, but that it has to refer to something 'given' in order to be knowledge, cannot be gainsaid. All knowledge is knowledge of the object; the latter is *revealed* or discovered by knowledge.[35]

The main argument for idealism is that a cognition and its object are always known together. The object cannot be conceived without reference to consciousness of object. From their invariable simultaneity it is legitimate, argues the *vijñānavādin*, to posit non-difference between them; an extra-mental object is a figment of imagination.[36] Consciousness is something which is by itself; the 'objects' vary but consciousness is invariable. The *viṣaya* can be denied but *vijñāna* cannot be denied; consciousness cannot be denied without denying in order to do so, and that is again consciousness.

Illusion merely consists of externalisation. Why are dream-contents 'illusory' ? Not because they are ideas, forms or modifications of consciousness, but because of the claim which the dream-content makes to be 'out there' existing in its own right. It is the same with perceptual illusion also. It is the 'thisness' — the objectivity that is 'erroneous' in 'this is silver' and is cancelled as in '*this* is not silver'; 'this is not silver' really means, silver is not *this*, but only 'silver' (idea); cancellation shows its identity with the thought-content.

In criticism, it may be asked how there can be consciousness or cognition without the object to be cognised. That consciousness is real and cannot be denied Śaiva Siddhānta surely accepts, but that consciousness is also constitutive of reality is not acceptable. The 'this' and the 'silver'— the that and the what of erroneous judgment must belong to the same order on parity with any valid judgment. Error is also judgment. Neither of the two elements of the judgment can be absolutized to the rejection of the other.

In so far as knowledge is defined by the content, knowledge cannot be absolutized to the exclusion of the content. That, content defines knowledge, does not require any special proof. In our knowledge of blue as different from knowledge of yellow, it is a commonplace that element of 'knowledge' is experienced as the common factor. The specific elements of blue etc. are *inter se* different is also a commonplace of experience. From this, does it not follow that the differents are also distinguishable as different from what is common to them?[37] Two conflicting predicates cannot belong to one identical subject; to what the predicates of identity (of knowledge) and the difference (of determinations in knowledge as blue, yellow etc.) belong, accordingly, cannot be one but two, namely, knowledge and its content.[38]

(*v*) *Anirvacanīya-Khyāti*: The slant of the *siddhāntin's* denunciation of *anirvacanīya-khyāti* is in respect of the implied conclusion that the world is a superimposition (*adhyāsa*). There can be no rational deliverance of the falsity of the world deductively or inductively supported. If therefore *Śruti* is to be cited in support of the reality of *brahman* and the 'falsity' of the world these questions can be raised : (1) whether *anirvacanīya-khyāti* is adequate as an analysis of empirical illusion and (2) whether admitting its adequacy it still follows that the world as such is illusion or 'false'. Facts are, the theory seems in effect to say, no more evidence in the resolution of philosophical problems than fancies.

The *anirvacanīya-khyātivādin* agrees that error, like truth, points certainly to an object which is other than consciousness, but as it cannot be memory image, or an elsewhere, elsewhen-existent, or the chimerical, or a real existent in the locus of illusion, by the method of elimination it has to be admitted to be the utterly indeterminable (*anirvacanīya*).[39] It cannot be memory image because what is presented in error is perceived and not remembered. There is no *smaraṇa* but only *saṁskāra*. It cannot be an elsewhere-existent object which is implicitly perceived in error, because the content of error may be like an empirical object previously experienced, but in so far as its location coincides with the location of the ground spatially and temporally, it is a unique object which is false in the very instant of its appearance. It is not *asat* because of the undeniable presentation of 'silver'.

The status of the 'false', then, is that it is neither real in so far, that, it is cancelled as *nedaṁ rajatam*, nor unreal, in so far that it appreared as *idaṁ rajatam*, but only *anirvacanīya*. Śaiva Siddhānta's criticism of this theory seems to be in substance this: the notion of 'neither real nor unreal' involving a simultaneous negation of being and non-being is contradictory.[40] If you deny, you *ipso facto* affirm, and *vice versa*. That there is really no contradiction however between what appears and what is real is sought to be demonstrated by the *advaitin* in various ways.[41] If the two are not contradictories, it, of course, follows that the law of excluded middle does not apply.

But the question is: is there any intrinsic difference between the *anirvacanīya* and the *asat* ? The 'false' is the correlate of negation in all the three times not with standing the fact that it appeared at the time when it was 'perceived' as *idaṁ rajatam*.[42] Not only does it have no before or after, but its appearance as being at the time and place of its appearance is also only appearance. Therefore, the difference between the *asat* and the *anirvacanīya* is only epistemic, not ontological. The status of the negated silver is not different from that of mere nothing. This is of course accepted only after cancellation. Ontologically, what appeared is not real; what is real does not appear.

If so, does not the law of contradiction demand that the illusory 'silver' must be either real or not real, either unreal or not unreal ? The *advaitin* while seeming to differ from the *asatkhyātivādin* inclines metaphysically to the view of the *asat*; the false and the unreal are metaphysically on par, both the 'correlate of negation in all the three times'. Śaiva Siddhānta and other orthodox systems incline to the realistic view that the content of error is a species of the real. The error-content is also a 'what' related—misrelated to a 'that'. Śaiva Siddhānta admits non-empirical *cit-śakti* as the central factor in knowledge but that some thing can be given to it in its pure form, unmediated by *vṛtti*, it does not accept. *Cit-śakti* is, *ex hypothesi*, under the veil or obscuration of a connate impurity and it is only the unobscured focal centre of *cit-śakti*, deobscured by the interposed *vṛtti* and its precedent accessories, as defined by the said *vṛtti* (*vṛttyuparūḍha anāvṛta cit-śakti*) that knows,[43] everything is given but to the *vṛtti* defined *cit-śakti*. Error therefore like valid knowledge is only a *vṛtti-jñāna*; it is 'false' knowledge. In valid knowledge the 'what' is at one with the 'that'; there is accord between quality (*guṇa*) and being (*guṇin*); a content is related to some fact which accepts its qualification. Error on the other hand is a content loosened as it were from its own reality and 'related to a reality with which it is discrepant'.[44]

XIII

SELF-VALIDITY OF KNOWLEDGE AND REVELATION

The realistic theory of knowledge rests its case on knowledge's claim to be veridical; to deny this claim will be to deny self-revelation to knowledge. There can be no real unknownness in knowledge. Revelatory in essence, knowledge necessarily carries its own certitude. If, then, knowledge is necessarily valid, and yet knowledge does also happen or turn out sometimes to be 'invalid', the presumption can only be that there are variable factors helping or hindering the free functioning of knowledge.

To hold a correspondence theory of truth and accept coherence or pragmatic test as the means of verifying truth is not compatible. At least it is not realistic epistemology. The Nyāya-Vaiśeṣika realist holds somewhat inconsistently that validity, no less than invalidity is 'extrinsic' to knowledge: every knowledge in itself is neutral in an epistemological sense, and has to be known again as valid or otherwise. Defining truth as consisting in something being characterised by what is characteristic of it, the Nyāya-Vaiśeṣika proceeds, in an unrealistic manner, to hold that what guarantees truth of a knowledge, however, is coherence of one knowledge with another knowledge. The criterion employed here amounts to finding out, not whether knowledge is really knowledge, for example, in its apprehension of an object as the object in reality is, but in ascertaining whether there is 'coherence' between two experiences. The advocates of epistemological realism — the Mīmāṁsakas, the Vedāntin, therefore maintain the doctrine of self-validity of knowledge by directing their arguments against the Nyāya-Vaiśeṣika.

It is useful to recall at the very outset the distinction to which Śaiva Siddhānta adheres in its 'transcendental' epistemology, namely, the distinction between consciousness which is meta-judgmental, and is the inalienable essence of self, and knowledge in the sense of judgment or content-cognition, which belongs to self through self's identification with the modal operation of intellect. Consciousness (*cit-śakti*) is, in principle epistemologically independent of any external illuminer and is, therefore, termed self-illumining or self-evident (*svayaṁprakāśa*) though factually it depends on 'external' accessories for a manifestaion of its knowledge. This as we have seen is due to a primordial Impurity (*mala*) with which consciousness has been tainted and clouded.

Now it is a commonplace assumption that in whichever way consciousness is 'evident' its 'truth' consisting of its determinancy (*viṣayāvacchinnatva*) is also thereby evident. While admitting self-evidence for consciousness we do not say that its truth consisting of its manifesting of a given content is extraneously evidenced. To be conscious, and conscious 'validly' are not different. What is true of consciousness should also be true of conent-cognition of which consciousness is the implicate. By the very act by which a judgment is cognised, the judgment's validity too is cognised, it (cognition of judgment) being the necessary and sufficient (epistemic) condition of validity no less than of valid *knowledge*.

Theory of Self-Apprehension of Validity

When truth or validity of knowledge is said to be self-evident (*prāmāṇyaṁ svataḥ*) what is suggested is that the characteristic of validity is 'self apprehended' (*svataḥ grāhya*).[1] But what does self-apprehension, again, mean ? Stated simply, self-apprehension of validity of knowledge means that the truth of a true judgment is apprehended in the very apperception of the judgment.[2] The theory does not assert unmeaningly that validity apprehends itself as valid. It does not even assert that as something is known it is *ipso facto* known infallibly. It does not say for instance, that it is never the case that we know something but can be mistaken. Such caricatures of self-evidence as one may see, rest on specious 'verbal' arguments.[3]

The doctrine of self-apprehension of truth or validity states something much simpler in meaning and without equivocation, though it is possible to disagree with it. What it precisely asserts may be shown by reference to three possible ways the concept may be analysed.[4] Self-apprehension of truth may mean either (*i*) truth coming to apprehend itself as true (*prāmāṇyatvena grāhakam*),[5] or (*ii*) apprehension by a true judgment itself of its truth also; as a true judgment 'truly' reveals the given, it reveals also its 'truth' (*prāmāṇya-gocara-jñānena grāhakam*),[6] or (*iii*) apprehension by that, which apprehends or apperceives a true judgment, also of the truth of the judgment (*svāśraya-grāhaka-grāhyam*).[7] The first meaning will reduce the theory to the questionable view that, to know something truly is necessarily to apperceive such knowledge; as if to know otherwise cannot imply self-apperception. The second view too involves the assumption that a self-same initial mode (*vṛtti*) both reveals a content and has itself too for content; this is attributing self-luminosity to the non-intelligent *vṛtti*.[8] It is, therefore only in the third sense that a theory of self-apprehension of validity can be meaningfully stated. A judgment has to be apperceived, in so far as a judgment cannot at once also be a judgment about itself. There can be judgment about judgment just as judgments are about facts. What the theory states is that one cannot apperceive a *true judgment* without also apprehending in the same act, its truth. What it denies is that there can be apprehension of knowledge but without an apprehension of its truth characteristic.

The statement of the theory, of course, rests on certain assumptions regarding the truth or validity of knowledge and secondly of how such knowledge is known. To cognise a content as itself, that is, as possessing the characteristic that it does indeed possess, is true cognition. In a content-cognition the manifold, given to the senses and grasped by the different sense-modalities is drawn into introspective awareness by the mind (*manas*); mind is the principle of unity which apperceives and synthesises the unsynthesised cognitive data given through the avenue of sense. It follows, therefore, that what apperceives the cognition of the given content apperceives it also at once as valid cognition; the 'that-what' structure of the initial cognition in which lies its 'truth' is also apperceived as the cognition is apperceived.

The Concept of Cognition of Cognition (*Anuvyavasāya-jñāna*)

A question that may arise here is about the legitimacy of admitting a cognition for cognition (*anuvyavasāya-jñāna*). When I perceive the pot I may also apprehend that I perceive. If the first is through a *vṛtti*, is the second experience also likewise due to *another vṛtti*?[1] This has been an interesting subject of debate in Indian Philosophy. The Nyāya solution which Śaiva Siddhānta seems to approve of and adopt at least so far as *vṛtti-jñāna* is concerned, is: there are two cognitions —primary and reflective, *mūla* and *anuvyavasāya*. While the former is brought about by sense the latter implies conjunction of the mind.[2] There is firstly, a cognition of things, as 'this'; this is accompanied by cognition of that cognition, as 'I know'. Themselves devoid of self-revelation but only of service in illumining objects, cognitions — sense-conditioned cognitions are cognised by reflective or second-order cognitions (*anuvyavasāya*); cognitions are objectively 'intentional' (*paraprakāśa*) unlike consciousness.[3]

When 'cognitions' are said to be objectively 'intentional' (*paraprakāśa*) it is not however meant that they are essentially non-perceptible (*parokṣa*) as it is held by Kumārila. For Kumārila, cognition is to be known like the senses by an inference from the phenomenon of cognisedness (*jñātatā*).[4] This is an extreme position which makes cognition uncognisable except as an inference from effect to cause; the existence of *jñāna* as cause is to be inferred from the effect of the form of a manifestedness (*prākaṭya*).[5] We have also the other extreme view, that all cognition is *ipso facto* self-cognised; all cognitive and emotive states are 'phosphorescent', self-revealing; there is no *state* of consciousness which is not self-revealed. The Buddhists who hold this extreme view oppose that cognition reveals objects by keeping itself in the background like the sense-organ. It is indeed in this respect that cognition is to be distinguished from matter.[6] The material entities like the 'senses' or *manas* are only the efficient cause and not the *causa cognoscendi*, revelatory of objects; the latter function is that of cognition itself.

The solution suggested by the concept of second-order cognition (*anuvyavasāya*) steers clear of these extremes. There is a constitutional limitation about the sense-conditioned knowledge that it cannot turn upon itself. Cognitive states as such are not self-cognisable. At the same time as there is the self-luminous *cit-śakti* they do not become like objects an 'other' (*parokṣa*), such that their existence will have to be mediately inferred; it is a mediated perception.

But this solution surely has its own difficulties. If we admit a fresh cognition for the cognition of the original cognition, for the cognition of that, another one will be needed thus involving us in infinite regress.[7] Does the second cognition arise when the initial one continues to exist or has ceased ? Cognitions being instrument-conditioned are only successive events; they cannot be continuous; again, neither can the second cognition arise when the first one has ceased to be, because with the first one non-existent, on what will the second cognition bear ?

These criticisms have been faced by the Naiyāyikas. The sequence of two cognitions is not like the pure succession of unique particulars (*svalakṣaṇas*) of the Buddhists; there is the continuant soul which is qualified by *jñānatva* that survives a particular *jñāna* which ceases to exist.[8] The charge of infinite regress also presents no insuperable difficulty. Phenomenologically to perceive something is not the same as apprehension of that perception. All our activities imply this distinction between cognition of things and cognition of that cognition. The charge of infinite regress is therefore an academic sophistication. Moreover, the charge can be legitimate only if it were held that a cognition has necessarily and invariably to be cognised by another cognition;[9] even without regard to the second, with the first one itself apprehending objects, our activities can proceed. What the admission of *anuvyavasāya-jñāna* amounts to is that a cognition can also become a content in its turn to another cognition.

Such answers, it must be admitted, are not very convincing. The great question of epistemology remains unanswered by the Nyāya: Can knowledge reveal something without revealing itself ? The Naiyāyika admits of nothing which is intrinsically intelligent, self-revealing; the object, sense, internal sense and even the self is as such devoid of intelligence. How can their relation result in revelation of intelligence or knowledge ? It is, therefore, quite pertinent to raise the question: does not the admission of a cognition of a cognition to do the role of what the original cognition is incapable of doing, invalidate all cognition ? If knowledge were not self-revealing in essence how can *anuyvavasāya* reveal the original cognition ?[10]

What makes for the truth of introspective cognition, like that of any cognition, is the identity of the cognition and the content; identity in respect both of 'that' and 'what'. But in the case of introspective cognition the identity between it and what it cognises, namely, the original cognition, can never be proved, for the idea underlying admission of *anuvyavasāya-jñāna* in the Nyāya system is that no cognition cognises itself at any time, and consequently, no cognition cognises also its own truth.

It should be clear that for Śaiva Siddhānta which advocates 'self-apprehension of validity', admission of *anuvyavasāya-jñāna* cannot be on the basis that knowledge is intrinsically devoid of self-luminosity. The self, and the other-luminous *cit-śakti*, identical with the eternal and all-pervasive self, is the central factor of knowledge, its measure as well as method. The order of manifestation of its knowledge due to the instrumentality of less or more of material accessories makes it possible to distinguish different levels of knowledge. Objective orientation following in the wake of obliviscence regarding itself is the predicament of knowledge due, as we have seen to a primordial clouding of the self. The object-oriented *cit-śakti* in its monadic form when sub-activated by the partial unveiling effected through the principles of '*kalādi*', pervades the sensory function unmediated by the psychic complex. The result is sensory knowledge, which takes the form of 'this'. When it next pervades the three-fold psychic complex the resulting knowledge, even as it becomes determinate, becomes also self-conscious, as 'I know'; the subjective resolve is a necessary moment of determination in knowledge. The psychic senses are themselves devoid of intentionality being evolutes of matter, but *cit-śakti* using them is intelligent spirit and is alone therefore truly 'intentional'. To admit a cognitive apperception for cognition does not, therefore, lead to infinite regress in Śaiva Siddhānta which admits against the background of every knowledge event, the self and the other-luminous *cit-śakti*.

Statement of the Theory

To return to the problem of validity: self-validity of knowledge means that, as a true judgment is apperceived the truth of the judgment also in the same act is apperceived. For a discussion of this issue indeed it is not necessary to be dogmatic about what truth of knowledge means or how knowledge is known. One can define truth as ultimately a case of accord between the sequence of 'that' and 'what' in thought and in fact the same, as it has been argued at length by the *siddhāntin* himself; or as a mere case of non-contradicted knowledge, or consilience between propositions, or as what is efficient and useful. Similarly, regarding introspection of knowledge it may be argued that to know a thing is the same as being introspectively aware of that knowledge (*sva-grāhya*), or that it is inference from the datum of knownness (*parānumeya*), or that it is apprehended by witness-consciousness (*sākṣi-grāhya*), or, more simply, by the mind which reflectively cognises cognition (*mānasa-grāhya*). The theory of self-apprehension of truth or validity merely asserts that truth be defined as it may and the knowledge which is true be known in any manner, apprehension of the truth of knowledge is part and parcel of the apprehension of that knowledge.[1]

Śaiva Siddhānta itself demonstrates the thesis of self-apprehension of validity against that of the Nyāya on the bases that (i) knowledge is known introspectively by the mind, and (ii) validity of knowledge consists of correspondence between knowledge and fact; with these assumptions the Nyāya is in agreement. Accordingly, demonstration of *svataḥ prāmāṇyatva* may take the form of showing that there is incompatibility between acceptance of the two aforementioned propositions on the one hand, and non-acceptance of *svataḥprāmāṇya-vāda* on the other.

But before we go to the argument proper in support of the theory, it is useful to attempt, briefly, a statement of the theory of 'self-evidence' (*svatastva*) with such qualifications as will bring out the chief features of the theory. Subject to the condition that there is as yet no contradiction of the knowledge whose validity is in question, validity in all cases is apperceived along with the perception—a normal explicit perception, of that of which a valid predication is made.[2] The thesis of self-evidence of knowledge has to be hedged in with these stipulations in order that the theory may be freed from over- and under-statement; these stipulations also help us to see what the theory *denies* meaningfully. The advocate of *paratastva* argues that just as in the case of error (misperceiving nacre as silver), the erroneousness (*apramātva*) is apprehended by the mind with the help of a contradictory knowledge (*bādhajñāna*) which cancels the original knowledge, in the case of valid knowledge also validity is apperceived, extraneously by the congruence of the knowledge with an inference based on successful activity. This, however, the theory of *svatastva* denies. While denying it in the case of valid knowledge, it of course, accepts it in the case of error; by the help of an extraneous cancellation only, it is open for knowledge to know invalidity. It follows, therefore, that the self-evidence of validity in a valid knowledge is acceptable *provided it is not contradicted by further experience*.[3] Till such time as a judgment is contradicted by another judgment it is necessarily known as valid judgment.[4]

That validity must be self-perceived in *all* instances of a knowledge of another knowledge is also a significant stipulation. Even the rival theorist (*paratastvavādin*) admits that the validity of the original knowledge is perceived in a subsequent knowledge, where of course the second knowledge is duly supported by an inference based on successful activity. But what distinguishes *svatastva* from this position is its demand that self-evidence must be an invariable feature of *all* subsequent knowledge; not only knowledge which receives confirmation from an extraneous source, grasps the validity of the original knowledge; *all* subsequent knowledge *qua* knowledge apperceives the validity of the original valid knowledge.

The *paratastvavādin* while holding that validity of knowledge has to be known mediately by an inference, validity as such, considered as a class-character is 'implicitly' perceived. The class *pramātva* like all classes is perceived, not in the normal way, but 'implicitly'; when the smoke in the hearth is perceived, the smoke-class also is implicitly perceived; invariable concomitance which forms the basis of inference, is between two such perceived class-characters. It is not such 'implicit' knowledge of validity that forms the issue between *svatastva* and *paratastva*. The 'implicit' apprehension of the class of validity may be accepted, but self-revelation of knowledge's validity may be denied. Therefore, the theory of self-perception of validity has to be stated expressly with reference to 'normal' perception.[5]

Two conditions are necessary for the mind to be introspectively aware of its knowledge. One is that it must be naturally the content of its own operation, not possibly of other minds. Secondly, it must be contemporaneous with, not removed in time from, its operation;[6] otherwise introspection will become a species of memory which, as was shown above, is not valid knowledge.

The Chief Argument for Self-Apprehension of Validity

When the two conditions are present, and under circumstances stipulated in the aforementioned way, the mind should be able to apperceive knowledge as validity as the original knowledge perceived its own datum. The central argument in support of *svatastva* may now be stated. All the factors necessary for the apprehension of validity are available *in full*[1] in the introspective reflection of knowledge. If and when the causal factors, necessary and sufficient for the generation of knowledge, are available, the resulting knowledge cannot be unavailable. Likewise, when all the causal factors which go to define validity, are present, it is inconceivable how validity could be non-present.

The initial cognition of the form 'there is pot on the ground' arises through sense-object contact. Introspection of the form 'I know there is pot on the ground' arises through a relation of inherence of what is in contact with the mind. There is thus a parity between the structure of the initial cognition and the subsequent introspection. As the sense is in contact with its datum, so (original) knowledge stands in relation to introspection. The original cognition with its structure as such becomes the content of the second cognition. If so, does it not follow that validity in whichever sense is characteristic of the initial cognition, is also, along with the latter, content of the second cognition ?

Introspection manifests the initial cognition which is of the form of the attribution of a predicate to a subject. To manifest initial cognition but not manifest attribution of a predicate to a subject is inconceivable. And truth or validity as already shown consists of the apprehension of the predicate in relation to a subject which has that predicate. Therefore, apprehension of validity follows from those very factors which yield the apprehension of cognition.

Introspection, it is significant to remember, encompasses not merely the subject and the predicate of the original cognition but also of the relation of the two; the cognition grasped by introspection is indeed cognition of a predicate *in* some subject. While cognition is immediately given to the mind, the determinate content of the original cognition is also at once given to it through a sort of contact; *anuvyavasāya-jñāna* is a species of *pratyakṣa*.[2]

The advocate of *paratastva* is not however to be overawed by this argument. After all, what does introspection manifest? Does it manifest a cognition in which a predicate is *cognised* to belong to its subject, or does it manifest a cognition in which a predicate really belongs to its subject? What the mind seems to be in contact with, is not the being (*asti*) of a 'that' as qualified by its 'what' but a 'belief' (*jñāta*) to that effect. The question whether the predicate does belong to its subject, as it is believed, has still to be decided on pragmatic or other grounds. The *svatastvavādin* confuses the epistemic with the constitutive grounds of validity of knowledge,[3] belief with knowledge. A belief is belief *as*, whereas knowledge is 'independent' apprehension (*svātantryeṇa grahaṇam*). When the intial cognition (*vyavasāya-jñāna*) perceives its content directly, that is, when the *dharmin* is immediately given to *vyavasāya-jñāna*, *anuvyavasāya-jñāna* only apperceives it, *as* this, in dependence on *vyavasāya-jñāna*.[4] Apprehension of validity is, therefore, not implied or involved in the apprehension of cognition.

Let us, in reply, examine the view that while original cognition at all does, *anuvyavasāya* does not immediately, independently apprehend the content of the original cognition. The *paratastvavādin* seems to be satisfied with his view that the subject of a knowledge is immediately and by itself given in original cognition and that it is only in the case of introspective knowledge that such direct, independent apprehension is not available. But is not this distinction arbitrary? Is 'truth' apprehended immediately and independently in the original cognition?[5] And if it is, in any conceivable sense, is it not apprehended likewise in introspection?

'Independent' apprehension of truth may be understood in any one of the following senses: as something is apprehended, the apprehension precisely does not consist in apprehending it *qua* a content of cognition. Or, in apprehending something the apprehension is indeed of something but not of a determinate something as 'this'. Or, independent apprehension may mean not apprehending something implicitly, as for example, universals.

If the first meaning were true, namely to apprehend truth 'independently' is not to apprehend a thing as the content of cognition,[6] then even where something is *validly* inferred, such inference will not amount to an 'independent' apprehension of truth in the above sense of the term. The inference on grounds of workability in proof of the 'truth' of a cognition is to the effect; the cognition, say, there is water in front of me, is true. Here the inferred cognition — inferred, let us say, validly, has, like any cognition, two sides: the epistemic side consisting of knowing or believing that there is water, and a constitutive side consisting of the fact of there being water; the compatibility between the two sides indeed constitutes the 'truth' of a cognition. Of these distinguishable sides, the constitutive one, namely the fact itself is known of course, as 'what is not apprehended as the content of cognition' (*jñāna-viṣayatvenāgrahaṇe grahaṇam*). But what about the epistemic side? The *belief* to the effect there is water certainly constitutes 'apprehension as content of cognition'. Therefore, if this interpretation of independent apprehension of fact in knowledge were adopted, an inference like the one which the advocate of *paratastva* makes to prove the truth of a cognition will itself fall outside the scope of factual knowledge; inference can have formal coherence but will be, *a priori*, without factual relevance which constitutes truth, in so far as it involves as part of it, believing something as a content of cognition.[7]

If, however, the second sense were to be adopted, namely to apprehend truth independently is to apprehend it, but necessarily *as not* the content of cognition, the above difficulty, of course, would not arise. An inferred cognition, in respect of its constitutive side will come under the purview of factual knowledge, if by an independent knowledge of fact were meant, knowing expressly *as not the content of a cognition* (*jñānāviṣayatvena grahaṇam*). But for the same reason for which a valid inferential cognition can claim truth as implying a direct acquaintance with fact, why can not the same claim be made on behalf of introspection? In introspection also there are two sides relating to belief and to fact; in respect of the presence of the second element why not admit there is independent apprehension of fact? Why make this arbitrary distinction that, while in the initial cognition there is independent apprehension of the *dharmin*, in introspective cognition there is no independent apprehension?[8]

The third meaning of 'independent' apprehension is that it consists of a non-implicit apprehension or what is same, a non-apprehension in an 'implicit' way with the help of some extraneous knowledge. On seeing a rose we become aware of its fragrance by virtue of the impressions from a previous experience. This is not normal but implicit perception. Independent, direct apprehension as different from a belief may mean, negatively not knowing a thing in the above mentioned manner by some implicit 'complication' but apprehending 'independently'. Is this intelligible? Take the following example which is expressly a case of '*belief as*' and not direct knowledge. 'I know that a flower vase is on my desk at my house': here the knowledge is not immediate perception but is only verbal knowledge. It is not also 'implicit' perception but knowledge arising through words. Shall we then say that because it is not apprehended 'implicitly', that is by complication with some previous knowledge, it is a case of independent apprehension of fact?[9]

The upshot is that a distinction between belief, as only *belief as* and knowledge as implying a direct acquaintance with the *dharmin* is wholly unwarranted. Consequently, the distinction between an initial cognition as constitutive knowledge and introspective cognition as only epistemic knowledge also falls. The distinction between 'belief' and certainty is untenable in the ultimate analysis. There is no warrant for saying that while the latter is a quality of knowledge, the former is only subjective. Once you admit this distinction it then becomes difficult to say how or when ascertainment of truth which is epistemic can be said to become logically complete so as to become knowledge in the constitutive sense. All valid mediate knowledge claims not mere formal consistency but truth where, of course, it is factually true as well as formally valid. It is agreement with fact that makes a formally valid mediate knowledge factually true. In the same manner it is the presence of the fact that makes introspective knowledge true knowledge.[10]

A sounder view that seems acceptable is that with the act of knowledge itself knowledge of its truth, not a mere belief as to its truth, takes place simultaneously. It is so in perception and in introspection and it is so in all mediate knowledge as well. Every belief in the logical sense of the term, is not a mere *belief as*, but knowledge claiming logical certainty till it is doubted or falsified. When grounds for doubting or disbelieving the truth of knowledge are suspected to exist, the non-truth of such beliefs is inferred; non-validity is extrinsically apprehended.

Does self-apprehension of validity rule out doubt?

A plausible objection that is raised against self-apprehension of validity is that if the theory were true, validity of knowledge can never at all be doubted.[11] Doubt pertaining to a knowledge as to whether it is valid or not, should not arise under any circumstances if in the very act of cognising knowledge its validity too is cognised.

Look at the structure of a doubt-cognition: 'Is this knowledge valid or not'? The interrogative form typifies doubt. There are in this form two conflicting 'whats' attributed to a 'that' — the qualificand. Take away the qualificand , and there is no doubt. For, of what shall the conflicting attributes be predicated? In 'Is *this knowledge* valid or not?' *this knowledge* whose validity is 'doubted', must first be cognised. But if it were cognised, its validity too on the theory of self-apprehension of validity, is cognised, so that it becomes pointless to doubt again whether it is valid or not. The dilemma before the *svatastvavādin* is: doubt can arise neither without, nor with, the cognition of 'that' (*dharmi-jñāna*). Without it of course no doubt can arise, and with it too, no doubt can arise unless it be on grounds subversive of the theory of self-apprehension of validity.[12]

The objection raised here, however, is not peculiar to this theory. The difficulty of having to account for the possibility of doubt supervening on a cognition has to be faced by the opponent too. Let us again consider the structure of the interrogative form of doubt; is my cognition, say, of a typewriter on the table true or not? Here the initial cognition consists of a provisional assertion of knowledge of the existence of the type-writer (*tadvattva-viṣayaka*), but introspection takes the form of a doubt pertaining to the possible non-existence of the typewriter (*tadvattvābhāva saṁśaya*). Is there not a contradiction between the two making it equally difficult even for those denying self-apprehension of validity, to explain the supervention of doubt?

To say that the initial cognition of the typewriter's existence on the table passes away before doubt as to its possible non-existence arises, and that therefore there is no preclusion of the second by the first,[13] is no escape. For even with the live impression left by the passing away of the initial cognition (of the existence of the typewriter) still not rendered obliviscent due to a time-lapse (*apramuṣṭita-saṁskāra*), there is preclusion of doubt (about the possible non-existence of the type-writer).[14] Otherwise, if supervention of doubt is still possible one has to admit as a rule, the possibility of doubt arising in the third instant after the occurrence of every certain knowledge.

The real difficulty with the opponent is his want of appreciation of the mechanics of doubt. Does doubt arise automatically in the mind after the rise of every knowledge, like a reflex action? Why does not doubt arise about what is at hand in the same way as about what is seen at a distance? Normal doubt arises only when there is a suspicion of defect in the origination of our knowledge. 'Is this knowledge valid or not?' does not supervene after every knowledge. It is only on the suspicion of the existence of some counteracting factor (*pratibandhaka*) that one begins to entertain the doubt whether one's knowledge is valid or not.

The dilemma posed by the opponent about doubt being able to arise *neither with nor without*[15] a knowledge of the 'that' (*dharmi-jñāna*) is not real. *Dharmi-jñāna* is not the originating ground of doubt. When you doubt whether something is A or not -A, it is not that you first know that something, and then pause to consider whether it is A or not-A. The 'that' is already part of the doubt, and does not precede it.[16] Doubt, like all determinate knowledge (*viśiṣṭa-jñāna*) can originate from only a knowledge of the predicate (*viśeṣaṇa-jñāna*). The cognition of the subject (*dharmin*) does not have to be there first as a necessary precondition for the rise of a cognition of the subject-predicate.

It may be argued, that when so many trees are perceived on one's way it is only with reference to one particular tree a doubt possibly arises as to whether the 'given' one is a cedar or a juniper. Does this not show that doubt originates only with a prior 'that' given in knowledge?[17] Otherwise when all the trees have been in the field of one's vision, it is inconceivable that doubt could arise only pertaining to *one* tree in particular. The legitimate presumption is that atree is first cognised and then it is doubted whether the given tree is, say a juniper or a cedar.

But it may be asked in reply how when all the trees have been in the visual field only one tree was cognised. Was it because of some of its arresting features? But if so why not admit that doubt could arise about the tree merely on perceiving those features? It is simpler to trace the inception of doubt to the observed features of the object rather than to the object itself, an unknown something, which has to be postulated. The thing (*dharmin*) itself is never as such a datum; what give rise to knowledge are the sense-data. Doubt, also a species of knowledge, is generated by the perceived sense-datum. How can a sense datum occasion both knowledge and also doubt, it may be asked. The reply is that sense-data of object can occasion (i) valid knowledge, (ii) doubtful knowledge, and even (iii) erroneous knowledge in so far as knowledge may be free from or infected with elements which occasion a suspicion of the presence of conflicting predicates or a definite misrelation of subject and predicate as a positive source of error. The distinctive sense-data of the object are themselves the ground of the origination of knowledge as well as of doubt or error.

Be the cause of the inception of doubt as it may, how can introspection infected with doubt reveal the validity of the initial cognition? In reply to this it may be recalled that one of the stipulations made about the universality of *svatastva* was that introspection in apprehending the initial cognition cognises also its truth so long the latter is not contradicted. When it is contradicted, that is, when one case of absence of relation between the object and the attribute comes to be perceived, truth ceases to be apprehended. Absence of relation between the object and what the object has (*tadvattva*) is the content of doubt, just as a mis-relation between the two is the content of error. Apprehension of the absence of relation (*tadvattvābhāvopasthiti*) is the cause of the rise of doubt.[18]

Examination of Extrinsic Apprehension of Validity

So much for the thesis of *svataḥprāmāṇya-vāda* in defence. Let us now examine the counter-thesis of *parataḥ prāmāṇya* (extrinsic apprehension of truth). Truth has to be made known by other means; it is not self-evident in knowledge. The truth of a judgment is inferred from successful activity. That there is water in the tank before me, I know to be valid or true from my 'successful activity'; my activity based on the 'knowledge' proves fruitful and this validates in retrospect the knowledge. The question that naturally arises here is: what is the example on the evidence of which can rest a universal relationship between successful activity and truth? Can it be from this instance itself? There is water in the tank, is true, I know from my being able to reach the fact successfully whatever this may mean. But how are we to know the truth of this example itself? By reference to another example?

The advocate of *paratastva* will have either to repeat this process *ad infinitum*, consistently, without at any stage seeking to validate inference on grounds of self-evidence, or to avoid infinite regress, give up the thesis of extrinsic apprehension at least in one instance of the validating inference.[1] If validity of one knowledge is to be evidenced by another knowledge and this, by yet another , and so on infinitely, we cannot even assert at any stage that one knowledge is evidenced by another knowledge. The other alternative, namely, of giving up *paratastva* and accepting self-evidence at least in the case of initial validity, also, is equally unavailing. If initial validity could be self-evident, what prevents validity itself being self-evident? If validity is intrinsically determinable anywhere, the truth of *paratastva* is given up. If validity is not determinable intrinsically there can be no positive demonstration of the truth of *paratastva*.

Now what about a negative inference ? Where there is no validity, it may be argued, there is no successful activity, as may be seen in the case of the 'nacre' which is mistaken for silver. There is no difficulty about the example here,[2] its validity is ascertainable from perceived instances of non-validity. Therefore, if a positive concomitance could not be asserted between validity and successful activity on the hypothesis of extrinsic determination of validity, at least a negative concomitance could be established as between the absence of validity and the absence of successful activity.

In answer it may be asked : how can there be a knowledge of the absence of validity without a knowledge of its correlate, namely validity?[3] Negation presupposes a knowledge of what is negated; so, if we know validity first before knowing its absence, the old difficulty persists : how do I know that my knowledge of validity is valid knowledge?

To this the Naiyāyikas reply that ordinarily expected objects do not require any test about their being true or valid, in the absence of any legitimate misgiving about their existence.[4] On seeing a sheet of water in a desert one has a natural doubt about the validity of this perception but on reaching the actual water surely one does not doubt if his knowledge is valid; one's expectations are fulfilled and no test of validity is, therefore, called for. It is not that without a previous knowledge of validity, knowledge of absence of validity cannot arise or that there cannot be successful activity. To act successfully we must only *believe* in the validity of knowledge. If it works the belief on which it is based, becomes 'true' knowledge.

But these answers are not satisfactory. If it is said that no test of validity is called for till one suspects some scope for error, the presumption can only be that knowledge's validity is self-evident. Again, the distinction between belief and knowledge rests on treacherous grounds. What is it that converts a mere belief into logical certainty, the *paratastva-vādin* cannot say. By a curious paradox, the *paratastvavādin* comes to believe in the 'self-evidence' of inferred knowledge while rejecting it in the case of perception and apperception. What is exactly the ingredient of 'certainty' present only in valid inference and absent in perception, he cannot say.

If absense of validity cannot be used as the major term concomitant with absence of successful activity, the critic may suggest another inference[5] in which the concomitance may be between absence of invalidity (major term) and successful activity (middle term). There is in this *vyāpti*, no *sādhyāprasiddhi*; the counter-correlate of 'absence of invalidity' is invalid knowledge which is available in error. And negatively too a concomitance could be shown to obtain between an absence of the 'absence of invalidity' and an absence of successful activity.

The critic may, by this new generalisation of concomitance (*vyāpti*), escape from *sādhyāprasiddhi*, but this victory will cost him his *paratastva* doctrine itself.[6] For, it may be again asked how the inference about an absence of invalidity is itself validated? The contingence of having to sacrifice *paratastva* at least in an initial case will have to be faced. Moreover, the critic began with a demonstration that validity of knowledge is determinable extrinsically but ends by demonstrating that absence of invalidity is extrinsic to knowledge. The issue before us is about validity (*prāmāṇya*). Of what use is an inference in which 'absence of invalidity' (*aprāmāṇyābhāva*) is the major term (*sādhya*)? The inference will be significant only if absence of invalidity is equivalent to validity but such equivalence is presuming without warrant. The only legitimate postition, therefore, is to accept self-evidence of validity.

Extrinsic Apprehension of Invalidity of Knowledge

We have so far discussed the positive implications of *prāmāṇyaṁ svataḥ*—validity is self-apprehended. A valid judgment is not perceived without its validity. A negative implication of this theory will be that non-validity of non-valid knowledge is apprehended 'extrinsically' (*aprāmāṇyasya parato grāhyam*). All orthodox systems with the possible exception of the Sāṅkhya[1] uphold *paratastva* as regards invalidity of knowledge. Error is not self-evident. It is so, not because knowledge of which errror is a species, is, apart from external conditions, logically neutral. Knowledge determines itself always as valid. Self-evidence is an inseparable quality of knowledge. Invalidity is not self-evident because its self-evidence will be incompatible with the self-evidence of validity.

Invalidity of knowledge is apprehended mediately from the experience of contradiction and from an awareness of some defect at work in knowledge. What helps apprehension of the error of a judgment is 'extrinsic' to the factors needed to apprehend the judgment itself. Just as there is no apprehension of knowledge without an apprehension of its truth, no knowledge is apprehended as well as its falsity; the latter when present, is inferred from an experience of contradiction between the *prima facie* validity of knowledge with which claim it comes as it occurs and a subsequent activity (*bādha-pratyaya*).

While truth has no external criteria, the criterion of falsity is a contradiction. Non-contradiction as such is not the criterion of truth because to know the absence of contradiction is not alone to know the validity of knowledge. Knowledge is self-valid. But in respect of non-valid knowledge, to experience contradiction is to know the non-validity of knowledge as against the earlier presumption of its validity.

The chief argument for *paratastva* in respect of apprehending invalidity is : invalidity cannot creep into introspection when the original cognition happens to be innocuous.[2] Even in the case of erroneous perception immediate introspection perceives it only *qua* valid. Error is not a given datum but a construct. Pre-introspective cognition communicates 'being that' (*tadvattva*); 'being not that' (*tadabhāvavattva*) is brought home by perception of contradiction (*bādha-pratyakṣa*). Mind (*manas*) whose function consists of relating and apperceiving, apperceives invalidity as being constituted of 'being not that'. Immediate introspection which is only a reflex of the pre-introspective cognition is innocent of invalidity.[3]

The positive and the negative implications of self-apprehension of validity (*prāmāṇyaṁ svato grāhyam*) have been set forth. The upshot of the discussion is that self-evidence is the only criterion of truth. Knowledge must vouch for its own truth, on pain of ceasing to be knowledge *if it ceases to vouch for its truth*. Doubt and denial, which are commonplace, assail, not self-evidence of knowledge but knowledge itself. Validating inferences are in order because knowledge itself can be undermined by contradiction and other vitiating factors. Verification merely reinstates knowledge by dispelling the suspicion of contradiction.

Theory of Extrinsic Generation of Validity of Knowledge

But this is not the whole story. There are certain secondary implications of this doctrine which, from the point of view of Śaiva Siddhānta epistemology,[1] are of primary importance. If invalid knowledge were conditioned by considerations *extrinsic* to the conditions of knowledge, it is meet to consider valid knowledge too as *constituted*, though not apprehended, by extrinsic factors. The truth of perception, inference etc. is *apprehended* intutively, but *arises* from considerations which are in addition to the objective grounds of perception, inference etc.

To admit that all knowledge is veridical and self-revealing is not the same as to admit that its verity proceeds from the very conditions which go to *constitute* it as knoweldge. To say there is no unknownness in knowledge's validity is different from the denial, that knowledge and valid knowledge do not *originate* from identical conditions. A theory of self-apprehension of validity does not commit one to say that validity is likewise self-*originated*. A distinction has to be made between the order of knowing and the order of being. The order in which truth as characteristic of knowledge is known, is not, and, for reasons to be stated presently, indeed cannot also be of the order of being *true* knowledge. A justification for this departure from the classical interpretation of Vedānta shall be attempted in the sequel.[2]

What, then, is the main thesis of 'extrinsicality' (*paratastva*) in the sphere of origination of validity? The theory avers that validity as such arises from without (*anyasmājjāyate*) resembling in this respect non-validity which also originates, not from the conditions originative of knowledge themselves but from outside those conditions.

Accordingly, validity or truth like error may be described as something which has for its defining characteristic the nature of being a specific effect, determined by a specific cause, the latter, of course being determiner of validity only and not also of non-validity[3] (as it will be the reverse in the case of error). This sums up the theory of the 'extrinsic' origination of truth in the neological tradition of stating such issues with reference to the quality of 'defining characteristics' (*avacchedakatā*).[4] When it is said that the nature or character of effect (*kāryatā*) uniquely defines validity, it is implied that, corresponding to such nature there is also the character of a cause (*kāraṇatā*) and that the two stand in the relation of determinant (*nirūpaka*) and the determinate (*nirūpita*). That is to say the causal conditions adequate for engendering knowledge like sense-object contact, knowledge of the *hetu* etc. are not, as such adequate to engender *valid* knowledge. The general conditions of knowledge are generative of knowledge, valid as well as non-valid, so that validity itself uniquely defined as it is by the 'character' of being effect can only be generated by some *specific* causes which shall not be in common with the causes of non-valid knowledge.

Argument for Extrinsic Generation of Validity

The argument for the 'extrinsic' genesis of validity is implicit in the very statement of the theory. Knowledge's validity, it is said, is of the nature of the limitor or determinant of being effect (*kāryatāvacchedaka*).[1] The 'determinant of effecthood' implies that it is 'described' by a cause, a unique cause that shall be expressly exclusive of non-valid knowledge.

The points to be noted in this definition of 'extrinsicality' are : (i) validity or valid knowledge is a unique determinant of 'effecthood' (*kāryatā*) (as for example, the potter's stick is the unique determinant of the instrumental cause, and the pot-halves the unique determinant of the inherent cause of the pot). (ii) The 'effecthood' of validity is 'described' by its cause, even as the locus resident in mountain (*parvata-niṣṭhādhikaraṇatā*) may be said to be 'described' by fire (*vahni-nirūpita*). (iii) The cause which is the 'describer' (*nirūpaka*) of 'effecthood' is a unique cause as expressly exclusive of being the cause of non-valid knowledge.

The use of the concept 'determinant' (*avacchedaka*) is no mere logical sophistication. It is suggestive of an argument. The demand behind its use is the demand for coincidence or concurrence (*saṁnidhatva*) of what is said to be the determinant with the entity determined by it. The two must be mutually co-implicant; neither should out- stretch or under-stretch the locus of the other.[2] The property of jar (*ghaṭatva*) is, for example, determinant of 'effecthood' which means, being a jar and being the effect of a unique cause, are concurrent; there are no eternal jars. Substantiality (*dravyatva*), on the other hand, cannot be determinant of being effect, because being a substance and being the effect of a specific cause are not concurrent; there are unoriginated substances, for example, atoms which have the property of substance (*dravyatva*) and yet are never the effect of a cause. Being determinant of effectness, therefore, cannot be attributed in apposition to things of which some of them only, or which is some aspects only, are effect of a cause. It cannot in other words, be, in apposition to things which can be both eternal and non-eternal.

Now, all valid knowledge (*pramā*) are, like the generality of jars, originated.[3] And validity (*parmātva*) is characterised by the coincidence of originated-ness (*kārya-vṛttitva*). The property (*dharma*) characteristic of it, 'occurring in' (*vṛtti-dharma*) it, is the property of being, and *only* being, an effect (*kāryamātravṛtti-dharma*). Now every effect must needs be determined or 'described' (*nirūpita*) by its corresponding cause, lest there be nothing like adventitiousness (*āgantukatva*). It is what makes intelligible that something, having not been, comes into being (*abhūtvābhāvataḥ*). To say there can be effect which is not 'described' by its cause will imply the contingence of an unoriginated thing remaining for ever so without origination. A 'describer' (*nirūpaka*) is, therefore, necessary which shall 'describe' unequivocally, its effect. Accordingly, valid knowledge, in so far that it partakes of the character of being *only effect* is necessarily determined by a cause which shall be uniquely sufficient to generate the validity of valid knowledge.

Being an effect and not being due to a *specific* cause are not compatible. In so far as *valid* knowledge, like knowledge itself is an effect, and never also in any sense unoriginated, and is at the same time different from knowledge as, say, a pot is different from a piece of cloth, it must have been occasioned by a specific cause besides the generic causes sufficient for engendering knowledge as such. Differences in the effect must be accounted in terms of differences in the cause. We distinguish a paddy crop from corn by reference to their different seedlings. Even so the observed differences between knowledge that is valid (*pramā*) and bare knowledge neither valid nor non-valid, must arise from different sets of causal conditions.[4]

Such, in fine, is the argument for an 'extrinsic' genesis of validity. There must be a specific cause of the form of some excellence (*guṇa*) and a consequent nature of effectness (*kāryatā*) 'described' by it, and validity (*pramātva*) is the 'determinant' (*avacchedaka*) of such 'effectness'. The cogency of the argument rests on (i) validity being 'only' effect and also on (ii) the presumed universal relation between 'being only effect' (*kārya-vṛttitva*) and 'being *determinant* of effectness' (*kāryatāvacchedakatva*), that is, being the effect of a specific cause.[5] Objection to the argument can accordingly take the form of doubting the truth of one or both of these assumptions.

Some Objections Considered

To take the first assertion, is validity of valid knowledge 'always and only' an effect? Cannot validity be unoriginated? The non-eternity of valid cognition derives from the circumstance that all cognition is originated by a set of causal factors. But have we not scouted an instrumental theory of cognition and upheld the view of *cit-śakti*, eternal, *inerrant* and immediate, as the constitutive stuff of cognition? Are we then justified in assuming categorically that all valid knowledge is, *qua* knowledge, non-eternal, and produced by a set of causal factors? Moreover what about the valid nature of God's valid knowledge? Is it also originated and contingent on causal factors?

In reply, it may be said that as the issue of 'origination' is germane only to judgmental cognition (*vṛtti-jñāna*), the case of *cit-śakti* or of God's cognition may not be cited in disproof of the non-eternity of validity.[1] While discussing the problem of self-apprehension of truth also it was shown that the issue was about apprehension of the truth of judgment over which alone there was scope for difference. Those admitting consciousness as the evidential basis of knowledge ill doubt its nature as self-illumining or as eternal. The problem of validity of knowledge is essentially a problem about the valid or non-valid judgmental mode of cognition. This suggests that *paratastva* of validity in respect of origin (*utpatti*) is, strictly, due to the *vṛtti*-defined nature of knowledge and that knowledge in its ideal condition of freedom from *vṛtti*, when it for example, apprehends God, is only self-evident; in such condition the question of origination of knowledge does not of course arise.

Validity (*prāmāṇya*) taken as the attribute of a judgment, then, is necessarily and invariably a product (*kārya*) originated by a cause. Now every effect which is 'only' effect and never also non-effect may also be said to be the determinant of the genre of effect as such. Validity too being 'only' effect is determinant of effectness. Being effect of its corresponding cause must, in other words, be coincident with every instance of valid cognition, and must not coincide with any instance of non-valid cognition.

The presumed universal relation between what is 'only' effect and being the effect of a correspondingly unique cause may however be questioned. Take the following example: a vase that is blue-tinted or a fleeting cognition,[2] say, of a tree as when one has while driving by — these are avowedly characterised by the property of being 'only effect' (*kāryamātra-vṛtti-dharma*). Can we, therefore, demand for them a 'unique' causal determinant? The vase or the cognition as such can be determinant of effect and points in turn to a determinate cause. But a blue vase or a fleeting cognition of a tree cannot likewise point to a correspondingly determinate cause which shall be different from the cause of 'bare' vase or 'bare' cognition.[3]

Besides, there can be no common element of validity underlying all valid cognitions such that one may say that validity as such has a unique cause of some excellence. The 'class' of valid cognition does not seem to admit of a property to determine its nature as class.[4] Why then posit a causal excellence for validity as such?

A specific unique cause to 'describe' valid cognition, accordingly, is not also necessary; what do we mean by valid cognition? A cognition must ascribe some predicate to a subject and the subject must indeed be characterised by the predicate. This makes for validity. If so, does it not follow that, as in the case of a blue tinted vase, here also, that is, in the case of a valid cognition, by a conjunction of the two causes — one that of a 'what', appearing to belong to a 'that', and the other, of the same 'what', *really* belonging to the 'that', validity is generated exactly as in the case of 'the blue-tinted vase'.[5]

The argument that differences in effect must be explained as having been generated by different causal conditions each unique to the different elements of the effect, also is not tenable.[6] Take the two cognitions: cognition of a blue vase and flower, and the cognition of a vase and flower of some other colour. Though both are cognitions and, as cognitions, are generated under identical conditions as effects, they are different, as different as belonging to two species. Specific differences in the effect can follow from generic affinity in the cause. That valid cognitions, like non-valid cognitions must have unique causal determinants, is therefore not tenable.[7]

Now these objections may be met in the following manner. The argument for *paratastva* may be stated in the form the of an inference, an inference that will make due allowance for cases which have been cited by the critic as exceptions to the rule under which *pramātva* is sought to be correlated with unique causal determinants. Validity is determinant of effectness because of its having the character of being 'only' effect, as may be seen in the instance of, say, the universal jar. The general proposition on which it rests, namely, 'given something having the character of being 'only' effect, it is determinant of effectness' may, however, be expressly restricted to apply only to cases which do not involve contradictions.[8] Two are the sources of such contradictions, as may be seen from the critic's objections and they may both be excluded.[9]

Instances like 'blue vase' are already known to be determined to be effect of cause or causes which are not over and above the relation of conjunction (vase) and the relation of inherence in the conjoined (blue). Such instances where the cause is already ascertained in the above manner, no doubt, contradict the premise on which *paratastva* rests, namely, what is 'only' effect, is determinant of causality. Such cases involving contradiction may accordingly be excluded from our generalization.[10]

But how are we to make this distinction between exception and the rule? If blue-vase is generated not by a unique cause but only by a conjunction of its two respective causes, so may it be the case with all valid cognitions; in valid cognitions also there are two components: thatness (*tadvattva viśeṣyakatva*) and whatness (*tatprakārakatva*). When the two are 'compresent', by virtue of their compresence itself, is perhaps, generated validity. No extraneous 'excellence' may be needed to constitute the validity of valid cognition.

It may be observed, in reply, that while, it cannot be gainsaid that there are the two components in every valid cognition, from a mere circumstance of their availability validity is not generated. In an erroneous cognition of the type examined elsewhere involving multiple contents which are all simultaneously misperceived, the elements of 'that' and even the relation of 'in'-ness obtaining between the two are all available and yet the cognition is not true. The *determinate* relation between the elements is not constituted by the elements themselves or even by their conjunction.[11] It must be traced to some specific excellence over and above the conditions necessary for the generation of valid *cognition.*

Instances where, by the very nature of the case it is idle to seek for a common source must also be, likewise, excepted from the rule that what is *only* effect is determinant of effectness. Now, will not the exception made in such cases of absence of a common cause of diverse effects undermine the claims of validity itself, validity being only a name for instances of valid cognitions? In answer it may be conceded that there is no common recurrent phenomenon like validity and that therefore it is not meet to look for a causal determinant for validity as such. But from this what follows is, not that validity is not constituted by some causal excellence but only, that we cannot point to one 'excellence' as the determinant of validity amongst all the different instances of valid cognition.

Extrinsic Conditions of Validity

Although it may not be possible to ascribe the validity as such of knowledge to some common excellence inhering in all conditions of valid knowledge, such impossibility should not itself be deemed a sufficient ground for the rejection of the theory of extrinsic genesis of validity.[1] Those admitting extrinsic genesis in the case of non-validity do not ascribe non-validity as such to a generalised 'defect' (*doṣa*) present with all conditions of non-valid knowledge but, complacently, point to specific defects relevant to specific kinds of non-valid knowledge.[2] The difficulty indeed arises from the impossibility of determining the conditions of knowledge as such, as valid knowledge is but another name for the generality of valid perception, valid inference and valid testimony. The general conditions of knowledge can only be a generalization of the different conditions of perception, inference and testimony, the three comprehensive modalities of knowledge. In the same manner the specific excellences (*kāraṇaguṇa*) of the conditions of valid knowledge which make it valid, too are unique to each modality of knowledge.[3]

Perceptual validity

Thus, take the case of perception. While it is commonly accepted that perception is a case of sense-object contact, it is a commonplace that theoretically at least the contact can never be complete, a good part of the spatial configuration of the object not forming part of the perceptual field.[4] Therefore, while some senseobject contact is necessary for the generation of perception, maximal contact of the same as will preclude the possibility of illusion,[5] alone can generate *valid* perception. If sense-object conjunction is a *necessary* condition of perceptual knowledge, the additional excellence with which alone it can become also a *sufficient* condition for valid perceptual knowledge will be maximal conjunction of the object with the sense.

It should not be objected that this excellence does not condition validity in cases of perception of qualities and actions.[6] Or as it has been pointed out, that it fails where a person with jaundiced eyes perceives white objects as yellow in spite of an adequate contact of the eye with the surface of the white object.[7] What is given here as the constitutive excellence of visual perception must be understood only as but an instance of its kind (*upalakṣaṇa*) and is extendable in other cases with necessary modifications. Regarding the erroneous perception of the white shell as yellow, it is a case of mis-relation due to *doṣa* notwithstanding the circumstance of maximal contact of the eye with the surface of the shell and is no more a problem for the *siddhāntin* than for the critic.

Validity of inferential knowledge

Coming to inference and testimony, we have likewise to point to those features that are additionally present in their causal conditions. Unlike perception which is cognition not derived through the instrumentality of another cognition,[8] inference and testimony are mediated cognitions having for their conditions another cognition like knowledge of the middle term etc. It is accordingly easier to point to the causal excellence of valid inference or valid testimony. One or the other of the causal conditions generative of inference or testimony, when 'excellent' generate *valid* inference or *valid* testimony even as when 'defective' they are generative of nonvalidity.

To take inference first. The causal condition of inference is the knowledge that the middle term (*hetu*) in its character as concomitant is present in the minor (*pakṣa*).[9] A knowledge, in other words, in which the *hetu* as determinant of the concomitanthood (*vyāpyatāvacchedaka*) is a chief qualifier (*hetu-prakāraka-jñāna*). Now if that of which it is the chief qualifer, were *actually* endowed with possession of the major term (*sādhyavad viśeṣyaka*) and not merely judged to be such, then this causal condition of inference will also make for valid inference. If the knowledge that *hetu* is the attribute of *pakṣa* were, in other words, true in the sense in which truth has been defined, as corresponding to fact, then the resulting inferential knowledge will be unequivocally valid.

Even valid inferential knowledge thus arises from a knowledge in which there is accord between the 'that' (*viśeṣya*) and the 'what' (*prakāra*), the 'what' here being the what of the middle term (*hetu-prakāraka*) and the 'that' that which is possessive of the major (*sādhyavad viśeṣyaka*).[10] Even thus stated, it is observed that the ideal of an unambiguous statement of fact is still not reached. For what is stated amounts to a simple ascript which associates a predicate with a subject whereas we need assertion of predication as a fact. A mere knowledge of the attribute of *hetu* as inhering in what does actually have the *sādhya* may be seen to obtain even in the case of a non-valid inference. In a case of a joint-cognition as when one infers on perceiving live red cinders and a heap of red beads by their side, when the qualificand is fire because it is red, the inference is 'constitutively' invalid in respect certainly of the beads. We have nevertheless in this instance the validating condition of an association of the attribute of redness and the subject in real possession of fire.

In order, therefore, to exclude such errors we may reformulate the aforesaid condition of validity as hereunder: the knowledge in which *hetu* is the chief qualifier and is 'limited' by the qualificand qualified by the actual possession of the major term — only such assertion of predication can make exclusively for valid inference.[11] Introduction of the notion of 'limitor' (*avacchedaka*) serves to emphasise the determinateness of the relation between the qualificand and the chief qualifier; that alone as chiefly qualified by the middle term, also is qualified by possession of its corresponding major term.

It has, however, been argued that reflection on the *valid* middle term can itself be sufficient to guarantee validity of inference.[12] This view is indeed in harmony with the demand for a knowledge of the middle term universally related to the major and characterising the minor, as the immediate cause or the operative cause (*karaṇa*) of inferential knowledge. On this view, inference rests on (i) a knowledge of an occurrence in the minor term (*pakṣadharmatā-jñāna*), and (ii) the knowledge is qualified by pervasion of the middle and the major (*vyāpti-viśiṣṭa-jñāna*). If a consideration of the occurrence in the minor term of that which is qualified by the pervasion, were a *true* or *valid* consideration, the resulting inference would also be valid.

The difficulty in accepting this view is that it is possible to arrive at a non-valid conclusion even with the help of a valid 'consideration', and conversely to reach a valid conclusion despite such consideration being not valid.[13] In the first instant after the production of a pot, to infer that the pot is odorous on the valid consideration that it is earthy and earthiness is universally pervaded by odour, is to infer falsely, because in the first instant of its production it is bereft of qualities and action though not bereft of the universal of earthiness.[14] An example where the inference happens to be valid when the instrument originating it is avowedly non-valid, would be where a fiery hill is rightly inferred to be fiery but on a wrong consideration which mistakes dust for smoke. In this instance reflection on the middle term is illusory reflection and yet the conclusion reached, is valid.

It is ingeniously argued that as God's knowledge which is eternal, universal and inerrant is a compresent, *conditio sine qua non* of all events, mental as well as physical, even when one's 'reflection on the middle term' happens to be deluded as in the above case, God's knowledge which is compresent with that even cannot be deluded.[15] *His* reflection on the middle term, may be of the valid form: because of, say, brightness which is invariably pervaded by fire, there is fire on the hill, so that it is with the help of reflection on the true middle term[16] as concomitant with the major, alone the true conclusion is reached even in this instance. In reply it may be observed that when a well accepted basis of inference is already available, namely, one's consideration of the middle term, it is idle to posit an extraneous basis in God's knowledge merely for the sake of supporting a theory. To argue that because 'true reflection on the middle term' has to be admitted as the cause of true inference, therefore God's reflection on the middle term which is ever true, be postulated as the basis in such cases, seems a case of *non-sequitar*.[17] Moreover, God's knowledge which is acknowledged as the general cause of all occurrences is only of the form of a direct eternal knowledge of the material cause of things and events, and not as of a determinate reflection on the middle term etc. The charge of stating an unestablished theory in order to bolster up a preconceived notion about the cause of valid inference, therefore, stands undefended.

Another alleged 'causal excellence' of valid inference is *uncontradicted* knowledge of the presence of the major (*sādhya*) in the minor (*pakṣa*).[18] An inference arises not merely under the circumstance of knowing the middle term as characterising the minor but on a negative knowing of the absence of any contradiction or incompatibility to the presence of the major in the minor. To know that fire is not present on the mountain is contradiction (*bādha*); to know that it is not the case that fire is not present on the mountain is non-contradicted knowledge (*abādhita-jñāna*). Now if this non-contradicted knowledge were true, in the sense that it occurs when under the real circumstance of the actual absence (not mere belief of absence) of contradiction, then the resulting inference will be valid.

A difficulty arises in accepting this view. The question is: does the uncontradicted knowledge of the major as present in the minor amount to a certain knowledge (*niścaya*) or not? If a certain knowledge of the major were available before arriving at the conclusion, the latter would surely be redundant. If, on the other hand, it were not certain knowledge, then there can be no uncontradicted *true knowledge* (*abādhitatva-pramā*).[19] It may be replied that uncontradicted knowledge of the presence of the major in the minor is in fact a doubtful alternation of the form: either a non-contradicted major (*abādhita-vahni*) or its absence (*abādhita-vahnyabhāva*) is present in the minor. In all cases we infer a conclusion not when we already know of the presence of the major in the minor but only when we doubt whether the major does so exist. As the positive alternant of this doubtful alternation is of the form of *certain* knowledge, we have what is necessary for the rise of uncontradicted true knowledge; while in respect of the negative alternant of the alternative judgment, the conclusion about the presence of the major in the minor cannot be said to be redundant.

This ingenious reply too is singularly unconvincing. It assumes, what is not obviously true, that every inferential knowledge is preceded by a doubt about the presence of the major term in the minor. A man merely on hearing the rolling of thunder concludes about the existence of rain clouds. A doubt about the presence of the major term in the minor does not obviously enter his knowledge before making the inference.

The opponent has the burden of proving an unproven theory that every inference is necessarily preceded by a doubt pertaining to the presence of the major in the minor. And secondly, he has to show that the validity of inference derives but only from this previous consideration. The advantage in our favour, on the other hand, is that, as it is already well proven that a previous knowledge of the middle term as characterising the major is the generating condition of inference, we have only to prove that its validity will be unestablished without some additional feature of 'excellence'.

In such inferences where the presence of the major does not apparently enter into our knowledge as for example, in the inference of the existence of rain clouds from the rolling of thunder, the omniscient God at least knows of its presence and that, therefore, *His* knowledge of the uncontradicted major in the minor, it may be argued, provides the basis of valid inference. But this is again to leave a well-accepted basis of inference in one's knowledge and seek it in an extraneous factor which is a neutral condition of all knowledge and does not participate in the purely discursive mode of human thinking.

Moreover, this is precisely the difference between unaided reason and scriptural revelation as evidences of knowledge. While in the case of sense and reason, God's knowledge which no doubt is a commonly present factor does not go to constitute or contribute to their validity, in the case of the transcendent source of knowledge, namely Revelation, it constitutes the validating source. Without the latter source of knowledge available, human knowledge subject to its constitutional limitations cannot aspire for absolute truth. This of course takes us to the problem of the validity of scriptural knowledge.

Validity of scriptural knowledge

In the case of *śabdapramāṇa* (testimony) it may be seen that what guarantees its truth is the circumstance that it originates from the *speaker's knowledge ofthe truth* of what is spoken.[20] The truth of the speaker's knowledge is the causal condition (*karaṇa guṇa*) which uniquely determines the validity of verbal testimony.

Does not this interpretation about the 'excellence' of valid verbal testimony make its scope limited by applying only to the testimony of the spoken word? What about the *unspoken* word, namely, the eternal Veda? The answer is that it is precisely because of validity's demand for an additional causal excellence besides the general conditions necessary for the origination of valid *knowledge* that we have to say that there must be a 'speaker' for the Veda also.[21] Veda is valid verbal knowledge and its validity has to be traced to a causal element over and above such conditions as are necessary for the rise of verbal knowledge (*śabda-bodha*).

It may be argued that the demand for an 'extrinsic' *guṇa* for valid verbal knowledge (*śabda-pramā*) can be met without having to postulate God as the revealer of the Veda. Compatibility or mutual fitness of words (*yogyatā*), for example, can itself be its *guṇa*. And one may say that it can be *guṇa* even more plausibly. Firstly, the feature of 'mutual compatibility' of words characterises the perception or perceptual judgment of the knower and can rightly go to constitute the validity of *his* perception. The *guṇa* and the *pramā* must have the same locus. How can the speaker's knowledge be a constituent element of the hearer's cognition? Secondly, it also wins on the side of parsimony (*lāghava*). The knowledge of a speaker of the word does not figure among the acknowledged causal conditions of verbal knowledge, while mutual fitness of words is a commonplace condition. 'Moisten with fire' (*agninā siñcet*) is no verbal knowledge not because the man who uttered it did not know well or knowing it, did not speak well, but because of a simple absence of syntactical fitness between its constituent words. The latter being clearly a more empirical condition of verbal knowledge it is meet to define the constituting *guṇa* of *valid* verbal knowledge also, in terms of it.

Therefore, either the mutual compatibility (*yogyatā*) between constituent terms of the proposition itself or one's valid knowledge of such compatibility (*yogyatā-pramā*) may be the *guṇa* of *śabda-pramā*.[22] Why posit God as the source of the validity of verbal knowledge?

In answer let us analyse the meaning of compatibility, the alleged *guṇa* of *śabda-pramā*. One meaning of the term is not to be aware of the absence of a contradictory relation of the objects denoted by a sentence. Compatibility consists of the absence of an ascertained lack of relation.[23] When the meaning of a sentence is uncontradicted, there is *yogyatā*. But this meaning though intelligible, is not adequate as an exclusive *guṇa* of *pramātva*; in erroneous knowledge too there is 'absence of ascertained lack of relation'. In error there is certainly a belief in the absence of a decisive lack of relation; had there been a knowledge to the contrary, that is to say, if one were to previously know the absence of relation, error could not conceivably have arisen.

Nor can 'compatibility' mean a positive presence of relation.[24] In error while there is 'absence of a lack of relation' there is certainly no relation present of the objects denoted by a sentence. Still take the case of a valid verbal knowledge to the effect 'the ground possesses the pot'; according to the definition, validity of this knowledge must arise from the presence of a relation immediately precedent to the rise of the knowledge, neither before nor after. There can, in other words, be no 'valid', verbal knowledge about past or future relations of objects.[25]

Compatibility of words may be defined in a more trenchant manner to avoid the defects of the two meanings. Compatibility consists of a lack of valid knowledge of the constant absence of the relation of one object to another[26] denoted by a sentence. The restatement rests on equating 'there are no pots on the ground ' with 'the absence of pot is there on the ground'; instead of a thing being absent it is more a 'presence of its absence'.[27] The meaning of compatibility suggested in a roundabout way here is absence of contradiction (*bādhakābhāva*) in the relation of objects. But as we had already observed even erroneous verbal cognition does rest on a *prima facie* knowledge of absence of contradiction. Unless an omniscient knower whose knowledge is always valid were accepted as a constant factor present in all knowledge, it is not plausible to assert absence of contradiction (constitutively and not epistemically) as the validating factor of verbal knowledge.[28]

The other alternative suggested as the *guṇa* in lieu of the revealer's knowledge may now be considered. When the condition of compatibility of words is *validly known* (not merely believed to be such), from such *valid knowledge*, may be derived the validity of verbal knowledge. This seems certainly more legitimate as the validity of one's verbal cognition is traced to one's own *valid* knowledge of *yogyatā* between the referents in a sentence, instead of being traced to valid knowledge of some one else. But on a closer examination this may be seen to be not really so.

Which of the above two explanations is to be accepted as the *guṇa* will have to be decided by applying the two criteria of invariable precedence (*niyatapūrva-vṛttitva*) and 'non-establishment otherwise' (*ananyathā-siddhatva*)? That all knowledge arising from the spoken word is preceded by the speaker's intention or knowledge is unquestionable; the precedence is necessary and invariable. A parrot may repeat words which may cause knowledge to the hearer and yet the parrot does not 'know'. But some one who knows must have said the words to the parrot. What, therefore, remains to be accepted complementarily is that the invariably preceding factor is the 'cause' which 'serves' the effect; the intention of the intelligent speaker is the causal determinant of the validity of the spoken word. In the case of the constitutively valid compatibility (*yogyatā-pramā*) it has first to be established that it precedes necessarily all verbal knowledge; before knowledge through a sentence arises it is preceded by 'valid' comprehension of the compatibility of its words. But this is by no means established.[29]

That a speaker's intention precedes all spoken words considered as sources of knowledge, does not obtain in the case of the unspoken Veda, is no objection. Because that is precisely the issue before us. A decision about the nature of the *karaṇa-guṇa* which serves *valid* verbal knowledge, alone can settle the issue about the Veda, namely, whether as verbal knowledge it also must be understood as 'revealed' by a knower. That in the case of the Veda its knowledge does not depend on its being 'spoken' by a speaker is no more a legitimate objection than one's doubting the universal relation 'all smoke is pervaded by fire' on the suspicion that in the yonder hill the observed smoke is perhaps not pervaded by fire.[30]

It thus follows that the entire discussion as to whether validity is intrinsic or extrinsic, originates from the issue of the validity of verbal testimony, of Vedic testimony in particular. Śaiva Siddhānta throws its weight on the side of the *svataḥprāmāṇyavādins* who uphold self-evidence of knowledge in general as against (i) the heterodox systems for which Vedic testimony has no validity,[31] and (ii) the Nyāya-Vaiśeṣika who accepting Vedic testimony as a valid source of knowledge and also accepting divine origin for the Veda, concludes that all validity is wholly extrinsic and knowledge is intrinsically neither valid nor invalid. With the latter the disagreement is in respect of the conclusion but not in respect of the premise. Śaiva Siddhānta considers the validity of testimony to arise from the circumstance that it is the evidence of the reliable authority of one who knows, and alone knows, things rightly. The most reliable authority epistemologically is the one whose word serves as the source of the absolute validity of knowledge. The *āgama* which is a generic name for the highest revelation of knowledge is typical of all knowledge in the respect that it is self-valid. It is self-valid in the negative sense that the circumstance which renders knowledge invalid, or leads to a discovery of invalidity arising from incompatibility with subsequent experience (*bādhaka-pratyaya*) does not exist in the case of the *āgama*. There is no *karaṇa-doṣa*, for the source or genesis of invalidity is usually the invalidity of the speaker's knowledge and in the case of the *āgama* the speaker or the revealer is the omniscient Lord whose knowledge cannot be defective.[32] Nor is it possible for the *āgama* to conflict with *anumāna* and *pratyakṣa*; the latter relate to empirical experience and *āgama* relates to the trans-empirical. Nor can one part of scriptural revelation conflict with another part. Revelation being homogeneous, coming as it does from one identical source cannot be divided against itself. Conflicts within revelation, and between revelation and reason are therefore only apparent; such 'conflicts' come with a demand for resolution and removal, consistent with the identity and the authenticity of the validating source.

BOOK FIVE

ON LIFE OF SPIRIT : MOKṢA

XIV

SPIRITUAL LIFE AS MEANS : SĀDHANA

Śaiva Siddhānta is a religion of gnosis or knowledge (*jñāna*).[1] If all religions may be said to be oriented towards realization of the Holy, Śaiva Siddhānta is a religion where this is explicitly understood as knowledge (*jñāna*). It is in full accord with the Vedāntic dictum—'through Knowledge alone is Release.'[2] Knowledge of Spirit (*pati-jñāna*) is integral intuition of the truth of existence at its source, which entails freedom of the self from the thraldom of bondage. To grasp the oneness of things in eternal spirit, 'all in each and each in all' is freedom from Privation the source of all evil, and is a portal to the Experience of unitive life.

Spiritual knowledge is experience where the states or stages of 'knowing' may be distinguished from the resulting knowledge. The stages of knowing correspond psychologically to the stages of perception in empirical life. This is intelligible since knowledge or gnosis which issues in liberation is understood on the model of perception rather than demonstration through reasoning. The latter results only in 'probable' knowledge while perception, is both immediate knowledge and under correct conditions of apprehension, gives certainty. In perception there is an advance from a state of undefined awareness of objects to an intelligible discrimination of them in terms of their specific and generic characteristics facilitated *inter alia* by the process of naming (*nāma*). The senses present the object undiscriminatingly and in an inarticulable manner; understanding determines its nature, form etc. with precision. The unmanifest becomes manifest, the unknown known. Language in its latent and manifest form plays its role in effecting this transition. In spiritual knowledge too there is a similar passage from an 'indeterminate' to a 'determinate' awareness. Only here the transition is from the 'gross' to the 'subtle', from the merely known to the dimension of 'realisation' or 'experience'. The role of language is also reversed in this transition from general insight typified by the hearing of the word (*śravaṇa*) to the ultimate intuitive realisation (*niṣṭhā*) which involves pre-eminently transcending language, even its latent essence (*bindu*).[3] The example illustrative of this procedure was already considered in another context.[4] The crescent moon in its most initial phase is spotted with effort and ingenuity on the horizon and the well-known way in which it is 'shown' is as follows: first attention is drawn towards the branch of a tree lying in the line of vision of the moon. Then the gaze is lifted up towards say, a floating mass of clouds. Finally the eye-sight can focus on the all but invisible moon.

The stages involved here are (*i*) perception of the gross, which is 'general', exoteric, uncritically dogmatic, (*ii*) perception alternating between the 'gross' and the 'subtle', between the uncritically general and a critical and specific awareness and (*iii*) the true perception of the thing in terms of its specific being, 'esoterically' determinate, that is without the indistinction of a general view. The passage is epistemologically speaking, from false knowledge through incomplete, speculative knowledge to right knowledge.[5] The distinctions of error (*viparyaya*), doubt (*saṁśaya*), and truth (*yathārtha*) applicable to knowledge may be said to correspond to the three stages involved in this transition. The journey is from darkness through twilight to light.

Accordingly there are three discernible stages of spiritual knowledge (*jñāna*) : The initial one of 'indeterminate' awareness, a perceiving of oneself, the world and God as one continuum: God as indwelling the self as self within the self, and the self as microcosm in turn comprehending within itself the entire cosmos. This will be the stage of 'difference' perceived undiscriminatingly without even a conscious co-ordination of the knowing subject, known object and knowledge relating the two.[6] The next stage is one where the subject surrenders to the object and experiences 'identity'. The focus shifts from the continuum of God—self—world to the transcendent factor of God exclusively. The stage is described as the middle-ground between indeterminate knowledge of 'what' involving difference and the determinate experience of 'that' involving non-difference. The culminating stage of knowledge is the determinate vision of Being 'identical with all and yet as the groundless, different from everything.'[7] The non-separate *śivam* disengages itself from the general setting, 'identical' with the world of plurality and difference while at the same time 'not' being anything of such a world. Being is intuited as the non-other which is in the same breath also the 'wholly other'.[8]

In the terminology of Śaiva Siddhānta these stages of knowledge may be called (i) *rūpa*, (ii) *darśana*, and (iii) *śuddhi*.[9] *Rūpa* implies *prima facie* definition (*lakṣaṇa*) of things with its twin edges of differentiation and designation[10] in which there is a general comprehension but no self-critical understanding. The knowledge is useful practically and is the function of reason or intellecct which enumerates and categorises in the interest of comprehension and control.[11] *Darśana* is metaphysical reason which is knowledge quickened by the incipient revelation. All knowledge is as stated above, concomitant with 'revelation' as eyesight is with light. Metaphysical reason is that stage where knowledge becomes conscious of this concomitance, and is aware of its subordination to something higher or deeper which is the condition for the very possibility of its functioning as knowledge. In effect, it is knowledge by contrast. All contrast involves an element of revelation or illumination which inspires the contrast. *Darśana* is indeed insight, self-critical and contemplative yet it does amount to integral knowledge. It is prone to 'misplaced concreteness', as the knowing self detaches itself and views things abstractly.[12] In *śuddhi* we have consummatory knowledge where knowledge is undistorted by hindrances of impurity. Impurity in the context of perception is a figure of speech for obstructions to the vision and also intervention of the material media of perception that have their roots in the obstructing agency and, consequently, are infested by it.[13] *Śuddhi*, therefore, implies vision 'cleansed' of all impurities. It is direct perception where the perceived content is perceived immediately, an Awareness which is above knowledge.

Now, as there are three modes of reality distinguished in the system —*pati*, *paśu* and *pāśa*, each of the three is perceived in a three-fold way—erroneously, doubtfully and truly so that we have nine distinct but inter-dependent stadia of knowledge which together with the culminating Experience (*bhoga*) constitute the *daśa kāryāṇi* of Śaiva siddhānta.[14] This doctrine sums up in a single formula the philosophy of spiritual life —Means (*sādhana*) as well as the Fruit (*phala*). These ten 'actions' constitute the sphere of spiritual activity, ten functions of spiritual life. It is marked by the self's unquestioned 'oneness' with the tattvas (*tattvarūpa*)—where everything from God to a blade of grass including the knower himself is viewed under the category *tattva*,' at one end of the scale and its all-embracing Experience of the Plenum (*śiva-bhoga*) at the other.

Now a question arises as regards the sequence of these *kāryas*. Śaiva Siddhānta is not a pluralistic system. In pluralism we know one fact after another in succession as it were; each item of knowledge is logically independent of the rest and is possible without a knowledge of any of them. But in Śaiva Siddhānta as it has been made clear there can be no knowledge of *pati*, or of any of the three modes of reality without knowledge of the others. Knowledge of the one entails knowledge of the other though the nature of entailment varies with the quality of the mode. The ten *kāryas* or knowledge-occurrences do not take place in the sequential order in which they are enumerated. They synchronise in characteristic combinations in terms of their mutual entailments. Thus it may be said, in broad outlines, that *tattva-rūpa* and *tattva-darśana* go *pari passu* with *ātma-rūpa*; so do *tattva-śuddhi, ātma-darśana* and *śiva-rūpa*. *Ātma-śuddhi* and *Śiva-darśana* go together. The ninth and the tenth, following *ātma-śuddhi,* namely *śiva-yoga* and *śiva-bhoga*[15] are distinguishable as the penultimate and the ultimate spiritual 'gains' (*ātma-lābha*), the two standing respectively for union and unitive life. The last two consequences (*phala*) constitute Freedom (*mokṣa*) for which the preceding stages are means (*sādhana*).

One notable feature of this concept of spiritual life as graded ascent is the continuity between the spiritual Means and the spiritual End. The concept of the spiritual involves the identity of the means and the end. This is the paradox of spiritual realisation. Realisation is *eternal* realisation.[16] The goal of spiritual life also is a kind of life and involves no change in the modes of existence or even behaviour. What one has been doing hitherto with a sense of spiritual 'ought', one now does spontaneously. The example that is given is significant : milk is taken by the convalescent as indicated for nourishment and also by the healthy against no prescription for conserving health.[17] *Mokṣa* is also an effortless, eternal conservation of spiritual value and is continuous with its means. Conversely, *sādhana* has something of the accomplished character of *Mokṣa.*[18] The dawn of the saving knowledge (*pati-jñāna*) which is the means for *mokṣa* is itself in principle co-incident with the advent of *mokṣa,*[19] though in practice this has to grow into a steady intuition to constitute Freedom.

The orienting concept for a comprehension of the *daśa kāryāṇi* is self. The dialectic of spiritual life that is called knowledge circles round the attainment of self-consciousness by the ego by which it becomes aware of itself as existent and so wins reality.[20] Paradoxically the recovery of its ultimate reality consists in a surrender of its egoity which becomes possible through encounter with God. It is knowledge of *ātman* that holds the key for comprehending the sphere of tattvas on the one side and the sphere of spirit on the other. Without the emergence of the distinction of self and not-self there is no insight into the tattvas. Likewise, spirit emerges from its hiddenness in self in strict proportion to the self's openness to it. It follows from this that there is a growth or deepening of self's knowledge of itself. In the process of comprehending *pāśa* and *pati* the self's understanding of itself undergoes a change of levels. In *ātma-rūpa*, *ātma-darśana* and *ātma-śuddhi* we get the clarification of the other *kāryas*. The scope of spiritual discipline is defined by the comprehensive scopes of *rūpa*, *darśana* and *śuddhi* with regard to self.

Self-understanding of Self (*ātma-rūpa*)[1]

The transcendental gulf between spirit and phenomena is overcome in the principle of self which participates in both realms. The element of 'participative experience' (*anubhava*) is unique to the cognitive life of self; it is this which qualifies it for its role of mediator between what otherwise would fall apart as mutually incompatible. The antithesis between the empirically cognised world of plurality and the one which is amenable only to a non-empirical realisation is intelligible only through recognition of a principle in whose cognitive structure are discernible the two modes of experiencing the real, empirically and non-empirically. Even for maintaining the distinction between the two orders a *third* category has to be admitted which is capable of partaking of the two natures.

As *sat* is distinguished from *asat*,[2] the self is distinguished in the same act from either of them, distinguished as neither *sat* nor *asat*, and still in a sense, necessarily, as both, as *sadasat*. The argument is : the *sat* and the *asat ex hypothesi* cannot experience each other, and lest this distinction remains unknown, in which case it cannot be asserted, there should be a self which can experience the one sensuously and the other in a trans-sensuous manner and whose reality is therefore coeval with the reality of the distinction between *sat* and *asat*.

The meaning of this statement becomes clear when we look into some of the significant ways in which its truth can be denied. The problem here is : is accepting a distinction between *sat* and *asat* incompatible with denying *sadasat*, a third mode of reality ? One alternative is to hold that *sat* be so conceived that it can apprehend *asat*.

Another alternative is to conceive *asat* to be able to know *sat*. Either way *sadasat* distinction becomes intelligible without the concept of a *sadasat* mediating between the two.

The Śaiva monists[3] and absolutists do not concede independent status to the self as knower. The monists' contentions are that the self and the world are really the *sat* itself just as branches, stem etc., are indeed the tree itself. Knowledge of the self and knowledge of God reduce ultimately to one knowledge. *Pāśa-jñāna* and *paśu-jñāna* are species of *pati-jñāna*. It is a case of the whole itself comprehending its parts. Nor may it be said that everything is *non-est* before *sat*. The scripture declares without equivocation that God is of the form of this world. How can one say that there is no world as such for God? The contention that *sat* alone is, and that there is nothing beside it means, not that *sat* does not know *asat* but that there is nothing outside the complex unity of *sat* to know.

The Śaiva Absolutist[4] too does not accept *paśu* as an independent centre of knowledge. *Paśu* is no doubt admitted. The particularised spirit dwelling within the gross body is *paśu* (*dehi-paśu, pramātṛ*). It is the enjoyer (*bhoktṛ*) of pleasure and pain but this is Śiva himself.[5] Śiva enters into the diverse modes of existence and freely assumes the condition of *paśu* (*paśu-bhāvanā*), while assuming it his transcendence remains unsullied by the distinctions of finitude. Therefore, as the individual knower envisages an object, it is the universal consciousness (*saṁvid*) itself, and not any *sadasat*, that manifests its presence. The omnipresent consciousness reveals its presence as subject in a knowing context just as *Rāhu* is seen only in times of eclipse when he is seen negatively upon the moon's orb.[6]

The Śaiva Dualist[7] for reasons opposite in nature would deny a knowing self as implied by the distinction of *sat* and *asat*. True, *sat* cannot know *asat*, but *asat* can conceivably know *sat*. *Pati* is immutable spirit; it does not have to know anything. *Paśu*, being immutable spirit like *pati* also knows relationally. The illumination of a lamp does not itself 'see' objects but makes visibility possible by its presence. And yet relational knowledge is a fact to be accounted for. Therefore, it has to be accepted that it is the material sensorium (*asat*) inner as well as the outer that really 'knows' things. Just as iron is magnetised in the proximal presence of magnet matter (*asat*) too becomes 'intelligent' in the presence of spirit. Nor may it be thought that this is perhaps a plausible account of empirical knowledge only, and that it is not adequate for a knowledge of Being itself (*sat*). The same mechanism of knowledge operative in Bondage operates in Freedom too, with this difference that corresponding to a 'transmutation' (*saṁkrānta*) of the self into *sat* in *mokṣa*, the sensory media (*asat*) also become transmuted into spiritual media in order to perceive Being. The point is, either way, it is the *asat* that knows — when freed as well as when bound. The self is only a presence falling under the category of *asat* during bondage and under *sat* during liberation; in its presence it is the *ι sat* that knows, like reflection of light in a mirror illumining the objects in front of the mirror.

The Śaiva Siddhānta concept of self as *sadasat* will have to be understood in the context of these two alternative points of view. The main objection to these positions is, that neither view brings out the nature of the self as qualified to know and realise the supreme ideal. If *pāśa-jñāna* and *paśu-jñāna* are really moments of *pati-jñāna*, many scriptural statements to the effect that the self achieves its freedom from *pāśa* through knowledge of *pati*, become pointless.[8] There would be no point in the concept of awakening from the slumber of empirical half-wakefulness to spiritual vigilance, implied in the transition from *sakala avasthā* to *śuddha avasthā*. These considerations apart, there are inherent difficulties in the aforementioned positions. Can *sat* really 'know' *asat* ? It is as inconceivable as light illumining darkness.[9] Everything is void (*śūnya*) from the point of view of *sat*. Indeed, the *sat* can have no private point of view. Everything is nought from the context of *sat* since nothing stands out determinately or manifestly before the *sat*. The *sat* cannot know the *asat* as 'this is the pot', 'this is cloth'. If it does, it will have to be itself a species of *asat* identifying itself with one of them and viewing others from that prejudiced position.[10] *Sat* as pure consciousness cannot 'judge'. It is always impartite (*akhaṇḍa*).[11] Nor does this feature of *sat*, namely, its not 'knowing' *asat* detract from its omniscience. Demonstrative knowledge or knowing perspectively as subject of knowledge confronting the object is denial of pure consciousness. Its absence constitutes, instead of detracting from the nature of *sat* its nature as *cit* also.[12]

Precisely for the same reason the *asat* cannot know *sat*. Firstly *asat* cannot *be* in order to know *sat* if everything from the context of the latter is nought (*śūnya*).[13] Besides, the *asat* is *acit* and therefore *ex hypothesi* cannot know. It is what is of service in the hands of an intelligent subject and is not itself intelligent.[14]

It may be argued that when *asat* may be said to know *sat*, by *asat* may not be meant the fleeting world which obviously is *jaḍa*, but its underlying metaphysical principles, namely tattvas; as the name itself indicates, they are real and sentient if at least because of the proximity of spirit. The tattvas are indeed the noumena, fontic ultimates. They are present invariably in all experience.[15] The *āgamas* also speak of *paśu-jñāna along side* of *pati-jñāna* and *paśu-jñāna*. Again, of the thirty-six tattvas the śiva-tattvas are explicitly termed *caitanya*, and the *puruṣa-tattva* is described as *cidacit*.[16]

The reply to this clarification is that it is only a *prima facie* understanding of the tattvas (*tattva-rūpa*). On further analysis it may be seen that they are *asat* (*mutable*) and therefore *acit* (non-intelligent). The appearance of intelligence in the tattvas is only due to an illusion that the tattvas are immutable as against their mutable effects (*tāttvika*). Philosophic wisdom (*darśana*)[17] must discriminate the real from its appearance. The tattvas are 'real' only for the untutored eye. For the enlightened they are objective (*jaḍa*) and therefore non-intelligent (*acit*). The terms *caitanya* and *cidacit* which are used to denote some tattvas should not be understood literally. The śiva-tattvas constitute the 'Free Forms' (*svatantrādhiṣṭhāna*) of Śiva and are, therefore, termed *caitanya* by courtesy.[18] So with *puruṣa-tattva*, which on account of its inseparable relation with self comes to be denoted as *cidacit*. As extensions and transformations of *māyā* they are all non-intelligent.[19] They are objectively known and are, therefore, other than the subject, the self.[20] Similarly the term *pāśa-jñāna* should not be taken literally. *Pāśa-jñana* is knowledge of *pāśa* where the 'of' is objective-genitive and not subjective-genitive. It is really *paśu's* knowledge of *pāśa* through the accessory of *pāśa*, even as *pati-jñāna* too is *paśu's* knowledge of *pati* at the self-disclosure of *pati*.[21]

So by inference through elimination we arrive at a conception of *sadasat*.[22] The self knows *sat* and *asat* which are incompatibles; the self's own compatibility with both, arises from the circumstance that it is of such a nature that while being different from them is at the same time capable of having its being in them, as fragrance resides in a flower neither unmanifest nor distinctly manifest. When the self cognises *pāśa* its identification with it is so complete that its cognition may be termed *pāśa-jñāna*; similarly when it 'knows' *pati* it is indeed *pati-jñāna*. Therefore, unlike *sat* and *asat* the self which is a *sadasat* is known, not independently by itself, but only in the context of its knowledge of *asat* and *sat*.[23]

The concept of *sadasat*[24] may be analysed thus: It means: (i) the self is a knower who can have true knowledge (*pramātṛ*), (ii) it is what ruly knows *through* an inculcating medium (*upadeśin*) and (iii) it is what knows by identification, by 'being' or 'becoming,' the thing known (*tadbhāva-bhāvita*).[25] The self apprehends by relation (*pramātṛ*), since neither *pati* which is consciousness (*jñāta* or *jñāna*), nor *pāśa* which is only object (*prameya*) can be the *pramātṛ*. The reason why Śiva and self though alike spirit are distinguished as consciousness that is revelatory and as subject that receives revelation is because the latter can know if and only if 'shown' (*upadeśin*), and again can know a thing only by identifying itself with it and therefore is only 'gross' spirit (*sthlūa-cit*) in relation to Spirit (*sūkṣma-cit*); while Spirit knows by itself, and again 'knows' without experiencing, that is, without identification, and therefore is revelatory (*upadeṣṭṛ*) to a recipient (*upadeśin*), like what light is — the external light or the light of the soul, in relation to sight.[26]

The notion of *sadasat* brings out the paradoxical nature of self. The self must be neither *sat* nor *asat* and still it must 'be' in a sense both. In virtue of its paradoxical nature it justifies its own proper being and also rescues the appearances and saves the phenomena on the one hand, and also makes spiritual realisation possible as an experience.[27] This characteristic nature of the self gives us the clue to the meaning of spiritual realisation in Śaiva Siddhānta. While the notion that the self is *pramātṛ* qualifies it for a life of *jñāna* as one for whom true, saving knowledge is a possibility, the self being an *upadeśin* explains why such *jñāna* should be *pati-jñāna*. The forms of inculcation (*upadeśa*) may vary depending upon the degree of spiritual maturity attained, but the self has to be 'shown' in order that it may know what is true. The last feature of the self, namely its 'becoming' of the nature of what it experiences, explains why even after dissociation from *pāśa* there is the lingering of *paśutva*, against which the only available means of *sādhana*, again consists of a conscious mediation of identity with *pati*. It also explains why the stage of *nididhyāsana* should culminate in *niṣṭha śiva-yoga* in *śiva-bhoga*.

Self-Insight (*ātma-darśana*)[1]

Self is the *sādhaka*. Now, what is the *sādhana*? Is it *jñāna* or *bhakti* or *dīkṣā*,[2] or a co-ordination of all of them, or any one of them with the others as accessories? The answer is already anticipated in the observation that Śaiva Siddhānta is a religion of *jñāna*. When we determine the precise nature of *sādhana* we must distinguish between the end or objective of which it is constituted, from the means whereby such an end is sought to be achieved, without forgetting the means-end affinity characteristic of all spiritual endeavours. The end is *jñāna* so that the *sādhana par excellence* admitted in the system is the path of knowledge (*jñāna-mārga*). *Jñāna* is the true path (*sanmārga*).[3] All other means are means as only leading to *jñāna*.[4] All spiritual disciplines only by leading to *jñāna* lead to *mokṣa* so that they are *sādhanas* only in a secondary sense. *Karma, dīkṣā, bhakti* etc. are, indeed, accredited spiritual disciplines recognised in Śaivism, but Śaiva Siddhānta conforming in spirit to Vedānta holds that all of these are of service in occasioning knowledge which alone is the means of attaining release.[5] What is not knowledge is non-knowledge (*ajñāna*) and as such can only bind and not liberate.[6] It is self's knowledge of Śiva as revealed through Śiva himself—*pati-jñāna*, so that all other species of knowledge — *pāśa-jñāna* and *paśu-jñāna* by the same logic fall under the category of *ajñāna* and therefore can only bind and not liberate.

The classical, picturesque illustration given in the traditions of Vedānta,[7] to convey that *jñāna* is the means of release is also given here with significant modifications.[8] A prince brought up since birth amongst poor hunters grows up as one of these without even the suspicion of his royal blood and of his being the heir to a kingdom. Neither can he so much as discriminate between the stations of a hunter and a king. The king always full of love for his son nevertheless awaits the moment when the latter would be equal to recognising him, and at the ripe moment reclaims the prince explicitly from his surroundings by revealing his identity by saying 'you are my son' and restores him in all honour to his royal inheritance.

The points of the analogy are very obvious. The self is from ever in the company of *pāśa*, and being completely in the dark about its redeemer without even a suspicion about him and knowing much less of its own identity as *cit* suffers from the evils of finitude, vice and suffering. The Lord who hastens its spiritual development standing at its back as it were, appears in front at the 'ripe' moment of maturation. God alone being the eternal intuitive witness from inside can know of the moment and as the preceptor reveal self's true identity by lifting it from its sensory surroundings, transforming it into Himself under the shade of His flower-like feet.[9]

This is the *darśana* of the self — a contrast between its erstwhile existence in the company of sense (*asat*) with its present life of spirit (*sat*).[10] It may also be noted here, that even as *tattva-darśana* — discrimination of the 'objective' and 'non-intelligent' character of the tattvas, followed in the wake of *ātma-rūpa* — the perception that the self is neither *sat* nor *asat* but what knows them as such, *ātma-darśana* follows in the wake of *śiva-rūpa* — perception of Śiva in the guise of the Preceptor — *sadguru* who vouchsafes this true vision. Also, as a corollary to this *śiva-rūpa*—*ātma-darśana*, there follows *tattva-śuddhi* — freedom from the sense of 'I' and 'mine' in relation to tattvas consequent on a felt disillusionment of their 'reality' through inculcation of the Preceptor.[11]

The other significant points implied are: (*i*) The direct means for effecting the dissolution of all evil and the ensuing realisation of the Good, is *jñāna*. *Mokṣa* is, pre-eminently, an experience of discovery and 'disillusionment'. It is discovery in the sense of revelation. Revelation or unveilment and not a blind effortfulness or even devotion is the *sādhana* in the true sense.

(ii) The revelatory source of such knowledge must be Śiva himself. That is to say, the *jñāna* that effects dissipation of *pāśa* (*pāśakṣaya*) and grows into *Śivānubhava*—(*a*) cannot be itself a species of empirical knowledge (*pāśa-jñāna*) with its subject-object abrogation but must be non-empirical, intuitive;[12] (*b*) cannot also be self-knowledge (*paśu-jñāna*) which, though encompassing the divide of subject and object (*vyāpaka*), by the very nature of the case cannot be the means of the knowledge of spirit because self-knowledge implies self's knowledge of itself — self-intuition, but self-intuition[13] follows and does not precede, Śiva's revelation of Himself. Self's transparent nature as it has been explained, cannot be directly intuited. It shows itself only as the light of the Divine rends the intervening veil of obscurity.

Are There Alternative *Sādhanas* ?

Two alternative paths of spiritual realisation suggested in lieu of *jñāna* may be considered. They are the paths of action and devotion, neither of which will endorse this unequivocal exhaltation of *jñāna* as the ultimate means to release. The view that action etc. is contributory to knowledge, it is urged, detracts from the independent value of the scriptural texts relating to *kriyā*.[1] To say that *jñāna* and *kriyā* stand in the relation of a whole (*aṅgīn*) and a part (*aṅga*) which is organic to the whole is, it is urged, even to invert the order of precedence in this case. *Āṇava* is obscuration of a positive kind and its removal has to be worked at through action only.[2] Ignorance or obscuration is not itself the *mala* and but only the effect thereof as darkness is the consequence of an obstruction to vision.[3] If ignorance as such were the *mala* it is either a nought (*tuccha*) or a real attribute (*dharma*) of the self and in either case its removal is inconceivable. If it were a nought then there *is* after all nothing to be removed and *jñāna* will have no function. If it were a quality of the self, again *jñāna* will be of little avail for removing it, as little as for removing the other qualities of the self like its eternity etc. This will mean there is no release. Therefore, we have to conceive *mala* as a positive something (*vastu*) which *causes* ignorance, even as an opaque film on the pupil of an eye obstructs the vision of the eye and *causes* darkness. A thing (*vastu*) and knolwledge (*jñāna*) are not contradictories. In the nacre-silver illusion it is true that the illusory silver is dispelled by the knowledge of nacre. But here the nature of ignorance accounting for the illusion is susceptible to removal by knowledge. There are indeed two kinds of ignorance:[4] one where, due to the impression of a former kind, the predicative element (*dharma*) of a thing is perceived as presented in a like thing owing to lack of discrimination. The other kind is one where it is precipitated by the presence of a positive factor: a jaundiced eye perceives the conch as yellow; one suffering from an optical disorder perceives two moons. Of these kinds, the first one is removable or sublatable by knowledge. It is by the dawn of discrimination that it is nacre and not silver that ignorance of nacre is conquered. The other kind of ignorance which is due to some positive factor is removable only on the removal of its cause and not by *jñāna* alone. The defects due to jaundice are not to be traced to the intellect, wherefore it cannot be cancelled by discriminative knowledge. At any rate there is only an 'ideal' freedom from such illusions through knowledge.[5] The man who perceives a double moon can be made to know through discrimination that what he perceives is illusory. But actual freedom from such an illusion results only when its constitutive cause, namely, the disease itself is removed. Similarly the illusion that the body is self is not overcome by mere subjective disillusionment born of the knowledge that the self is different from the body. For that the root cause of such illusion, the *mala* should be removed.

The removal of *mala* is therefore to be effected by *kriyā*—by *dīkṣā* or the divine act of initiation, even as the killing power of a snake's poison is neutralized by the snake charmer through suitable antidotes.[5a] The obstruction of vision due to the presence of an organic factor like the formation of a film (*paṭala*) on the pupil can be averted only by surgical intervention and not by a mere process of 're-education' as in the case of some functional disorders. Blindness due to a formation of cataract is somatic, not a 'hysterical' blindness. An opaque condition of the lens of the eye occasions blindness by obstructing the passage of the light. Similarly, *mala* a positive condition of Ignorance is removable only through the application of *dīkṣā* which is as it were the knife of the Divine surgeon.[6] Knowledge regarding the nature of *mala* and its removal is only ancillary to the application of *dīkṣā* even as theoretical knowledge concerning the growth of *paṭala* and its removal is to the actual surgical operation.[7] Therefore knowledge is subordinate to action[8] and wherever knowledge is extolled as the supreme *sādhana* we should understand it in the sense of *kriyā* in which it finds its fulfilment.[9] *Dīkṣā* itself may be regarded as *jñāna* because it is 'intelligent' action (*citkarma*). It is the will of *Śakti* in the form of *dīkṣā* (*Śivadīkṣā-śakti-saṁkalpa-cit-karma*),[10] that effects *mokṣa*. *Mokṣa* or Freedom of the self is really the prerogative of God. Neither the freed nor what it is freed from can be the one who effects *mokṣa*.

The *āgama* says in clear terms that it is *dīkṣā* that secures the destruction of *pāśa* and the attainment of *mukti* which is union with Śiva.[11] The word *dīkṣā* itself is indicative of its role. It is a significant singular name implying action with a dual effect: a gift (*dāna*) and a loss (*kṣaya*)—gift of the fruits of *mukti*, and loss of the bonds of *mala*.[12] Does not Umāpati also say that of the three kinds of *dīkṣā* the incomparable *nirvāṇa-dīkṣā* steers the self clear of the six *adhvans* and leads it straight to its supreme ideal.[13]

Such are, in brief, the arguments of the activist (*kriyā-Śaiva*). Śaiva Siddhānta opposes this interpretation: The arguments overstate the case, either saying what is untrue or merely proving the obvious. What exactly is the significance of *dīkṣā* ? If by that is meant a species of rite performed with the accessories of *homa* etc., then it excludes one recognised mode of initiation, that is, *niradhikaraṇa-dīkṣā* — Initiation rite performed expressly with no accessory whatever, which is employed in the case of souls belonging to the categories of *vijñānākala* and *pralayākala*. Again it is enjoined in the scriptures that the initiated should not give up his daily and other rites as long as he continues to live; if he discontinues it the effects of Initiation would be set at naught and what is worse, he is condemned to the underworld after the decease of the body.[14] But how are the *jīvanmuktas* described in the system? "They have no distinctions of 'good' and 'evil'; they seek not anything; they have no duties to perform; they have no fasts and rites incumbent on specific stations in life".[15] The *jīvanmuktas* are described to be above all obligations. The *jñānin*, says an *agama*,[16] has no duties to perform, no rites to do and no obligations to discharge. The advocates of *dīkṣā* would have to count these traits of the *jīvanmukta* herein described as slips or sins of omission and therefore regard them not only as not liberated but as defaulters who deserve to be consigned to the netherworld.[17]

If it be replied that this condition attaching to *dīkṣā* prevails till the onset of the intuitive experience only, which once achieved renders one immune from all obligations secular as well as religious then it amounts to giving up the case on behalf of an independence of *dīkṣā* as *sādhana* for release; for it is admitted that intuition is the direct means of that experience with the implication that *dīkṣā* is auxiliary (*aṅga*) to that intuitive knowledge.[18]

What is really implied by the term *dīkṣā* is not a species of 'action' but refers to Will and its function (*kriyā-śakti-vyāpāra*). The modes through which it manifests or externalises itself are only *upakāra-dīkṣā*. They are no more *dīkṣā* in their own right than *pratyakṣa* etc. are *pramāṇas*. The latter are *pramāṇas* only in the extended sense of being auxiliary to the real *pramāṇa*,[19] that is, the *ātma-cit-śakti*. Once this is conceded, namely that *dīkṣā* denotes primiarly *kriyā-śakti* it cannot be maintained any further that *dīkṣā* and not *jñāna* is the means for *mokṣa*. For *kriyā-śakti* is but at its core *jñāna-śakti* only. *Jñāna* is more fundamental than *kriyā* as its necessary presupposition.[20] It should, therefore, be evident that *dīkṣā* which is subsidiary to *jñāna* is a *mokṣa-sādhana* only *through jñāna*.

The argument that *mala* is a substance and as such its removal has to be worked at through *kriyā* is, again incorrect. Is not snake-poison, which is a substance, counteracted by knowledge, of the nature of meditation on Garuḍa, rather than by some action, (*kriyā-vyāpāra*).[21] The more suggestive illustration of the substantive nature of *mala*, commensurate with its characteristic destructibility of *śaktis*, and the one used in the *āgamas*, is darkness which is positive[22] and is dispelled just by the illumination of a lamp and not by a thousand 'acts'. All action in this context is of service in the removal of darkness facilitating the incidence of light which alone can dispel it. All acts of initiation contribute toward effecting release from *mala* only through occasioning the dawn of knowledge. The analogy of cataract in the eye (*netra-paṭala*) also proves to be a broken reed. The blind whose vision is obstructed by an opaque film in the eye, is helpless even when it is operated upon unless he is able to see with the aid of external light, and therefore, even when it regains its vision the objects have to be shown or revealed to it by a light from without.[23]

Umāpati defines *dīkṣā* as an exteriorisation or manifestation of the power of Śiva (*Śivasya vyāpārātmaka-śaktiḥ*) which enables one to discharge his duty with regard to the performance of daily and other rites duly as enjoined in the *āgamas*, and also with regard to a hearing of the revealed Word.[24] The word *dīkṣā* itself is used as a synonym of *kriyā-śakti*. It does imply a gift (*dāna*) and a loss (*kṣaya*), only the gift is of knowledge, and not directly of *mokṣa*.[25] It is what undermines the bond of *mala* by making possible conferment of *jñāna*, and through that of *mokṣa*. Of the three well-known varieties of *dīkṣās samaya-dīkṣā* confers fitness to enter a life of ritual (*śaivācāra* or *caryā*); the *viśeṣa-dīkṣa* to do *kriyā* and *yoga*, while the *nirvāṇa-dīkṣā* which some consider immediate means of *mokṣa*, really speaking qualifies one for directly receiving *jñāna*.[26]

What is achieved in *dīkṣā* is a spiritual purification issuing in the dawn of knowledge. This is what takes place in *adhva-śuddhi*[27] which constitutes the main feature of *nirvāṇa-dīkṣā*. The *adhvan* represents the entire universe of speech (*śabda*) and sense (*artha*) which serves as the locus for the performance of *karmas* (*hita* and *ahita*) in the three modes of thought, word and deed; the 'cosmic-material' pathways for their transmutation into the cycle of merit (*puṇya*) and demerit (*pāpa*) which constitutes the karmic life of self.[28] In the 'purification' of *adhvan* which is accomplished by the operation of *kriyā-śakti* the sum-total of stored-up *karmas* (*sañcita*) together with its material locus (*māyīya*) is set at naught so that the self freed from the weight of *karma* and *māyīya malas* becomes qualified for the dawn of *jñāna* for the *jñāna-śakti* to operate upon. Therefore, it is *jñāna* that dispels the darkness of *mala*. If, therefore, *jñāna* is operation of *jñāna-śakti* and *jñāna-śakti* is but a function of Will (*śakti-saṁkalpa*) of which *dīkṣā* is only a synonym, then the overdrawn distinction between *jñāna* and *dīkṣā* really turns into a distinction without difference.[29] But with this extended significance of the term *dīkṣā* Śaiva Siddhānta has no reason to be in disagreement.

Therefore, textual citations to the effect that it is *dīkṣā* that secures the attainment of release, should be understood to imply that it is a means of release *through jñāna*. *Ratna-Traya* says : *mala* is removed only by the act of *dīkṣā* associated with meditation of Śiva *and not by a thousand jñāna*, even as disorders like *timira* are cured only by action laid down in books on medicine.[30] The *jñāna* impugned here is the intellectual knowledge which is only penultimate (*apara-jñāna*), not the intuitive experience (*anubhava*) which is ultimate (*para-jñāna*). The phrase 'in association with meditation' (*śiva-praṇidhānena karmaṇā*) which qualifies *dīkṣā* in the cited text is itself suggestive of the idea that *dīkṣā* devoid of association with *anubhava-jñāna* is as futile as the intervention of the surgeon who is without the requisite experimental knowledge.

The upshot of the discussion is that 'action' as such has no privileged position in the scheme of liberation envisaged in Śaiva Siddhāuta. *Kriyā* has only a purificatory value. To regard it as central and make *jñāna* a means to it is to misjudge the spirit of Śaiva Siddhānta, offered expressly as the synthesis of Vedānta. While it is true that there is no metaphysical discontinuity between *kriyā* and *vidyā*, at the same time *kriyā* is only an occasioning fulcrum (*nimitta*) for the dawn of *vidyā*.[31] The *āgama* which consists of sections on *vidyā* as well as on *kriyā*, *yoga* and *caryā* go by the name of *jñāna* (*apara jñāna*) by reason of the primacy of *vidyā*.

The other suggested alternative path of spiritual realisation is devotion (*bhakti*).[32] Devotion itself includes knowledge within it. The Śaivāgamas too speak of *jñāna-pūjā*, *jñāna-yajña* etc.[33] Aruṇandi Śiva says while admitting, that *jñāna* is the means of attaining *Śivatva*, a small act of devotion shown unto a Śiva-*jñānin* is, however, sufficient for performing the same miracle.[34] The merits of such act will increase to the magnitude of a mountain and will surely lift man from the throes of birth. He attains knowledge without having to submit to the tortuous pursuits of *caryā* etc. The pursuits of *caryā*, *kriyā*, *yoga* as well as *jñāna* as such make no difference if the pursuant is gifted with that love which comes from utter selflessness.[35] The whole of Periya-Purāṇam blazes forth the glory of the devout (*nāyanmār*) who exemplify the truth that loving surrender to the abiding will of God can accomplish what no amount of learning and reflection can achieve.

Śaiva Siddhānta, indeed, is a philosophy of devotion, but *bhakti* for it differs from what it is for the pursuants of the 'path of love' (*bhakti-mārga*). *Bhakti* is not the path but the prize, standing at the end rather than at the beginning of spiritual life. Devotion is no mere 'discipline'. It is the very substance of *parā mukti*.[36] Love is nothing but attenuated will, and the positive experience of bliss in *mukti* implies exercise of will which constitutes the essence and not merely the attribute of self. The lives of the Śaiva saints portrayed in Periya-Purāṇam illustrate not devotion as a disciplinary value (*sādhana-bhakti*) but devotion *descriptive* of the nature of released (*sādhya-bhakti*).[37]

It should at the same time be remarked that *bhakti* is no substitute for *jñāna* as a *mokṣa-sādhana*. Devotion to God and the Godly, as a path is extolled only as leading to knowledge through a process of 'unselfing' so essential to knowledge. Aruṇandi's reference to the merits of men pursuing the path of devotion actually brings out indirectly the supremacy of *jñāna*; the alleged merits of the *bhakta* arise out of devotion to a Śiva-*jñānin*.[38] Again, his statement to the effect that the *bhakta* becomes a man of knowledge without having to go through the labyrinthine pursuits of *caryā* etc., should be understood to mean, not that *bhakti* itself would take the place of *jñāna* in their cases, but that for the devout the pursuits of *caryā* etc. are no longer arduous.[39] What is demanded in the states of 'hearing' of the word (*śravaṇa*) etc., namely the surrender or emptying of the self as a condition for the dawn of knowledge, is equally secured through means other than the intellectual in the case of a fortunate few, for whom inculcation of *jñāna* takes place as immediately as for the souls of the categories of *vijñānākala* and *pralayākala* mentioned in the *āgamas*.

With the exception of Mānickka Vācagar whose inculcation by the Guru looks quite 'human' and conforms to the standard laid down in the texts, and is perhaps omitted for that reason in Periya-Purāṇam, all the Śaiva saints about whom the latter talks are indeed 'exceptions' to the standard; they are initiated immediately into *śiva-jñāna* either from within as in the case of *vijñānākala* or from without, as in the case of *pralayākala* classes of selves. Aruṇandi reckons with this possibility when he prefaces his *Siddhi* with the words[40] that, 'for those blessed devotees who out of great merits earned in the past instinctively yearn for spiritual freedom, God is Himself the immediate guide to truth and that there is no need of the Book for them; therefore, he addresses himself only to those earnest beings (*vainayika*) who are eager to learn and reflect upon spiritual values'. Therefore, while it is true that it is only *jñāna* that rends asunder the snare of *pāśa* and reveals the *pati*, the means to its attainment need not be through speculative knowledge. Though with some, intellectual method is a principal way of 'experiencing the deity' it by no means follows that speculation upon truths is superior to other methods.[41]

The *Pauṣkara-Āgama* makes a distinction between *para-jñāna* and *apara-jñāna* ,between ultimate gnosis and the non-ultimate knowledge of *Śruti* leading to it[42] — *Śruti* whose contents need to be correlated by speculation (*yukti*) and confirmed by individual insight (*anubhava*). The *Śivadharmottara-Āgama*[43] speaks of *jñāna-yajña* as the highest mode of worship[44] (*yaj*—'to worship') and describes it as consisting of (*i*) studying of scriptures, (*ii*) promoting study of scriptures, (*iii*) teaching others (on the strength of one's own individual insight), (*iv*)studying them from the proper Guru (*śravaṇa*), and (*v*) reflecting upon their truths (*manana*). Here, only the last two, namely, *śravaṇa* and *manana* together with their necessary accompaniments of *nididhyāsana* and *niṣṭhā* (*samādhi*) which are significantly, not mentioned under *jñāna-yajña*[45] constitute the scope of *jñāna* extolled as *sādhana par excellence.* The first three stages, re present only the intellectual preparation for it. For a privileged few there may dawn *jñāna* without this intellectual preparation although even for them it is *jñāna* which dawns effortlessly that vouchsafes *mokṣa.*[46] Only in their case, as in the case of selves less steeped under obscuration of *mala* (*vijñānākalas, pralayākalas*) the stages of *śravaṇa* etc. need not have to be gone thorugh successively. Illumination in such cases is at once complete,[47] without involving a process of transition from false knowledge through incomplete knowledge to right knowledge.

Preliminaries and Accessories to Knowledge

The significance of advocating *jñāna* as the ultimate discipline, is that its goal is not to be conceived as something to be comprehended in terms of ethical perfection or even religious endeavour[1] but as pointing beyond them. Such a state has nevertheless to be worked at through an intense course of ethical and religious discipline. The self becomes purified, diaphanous as it were, so that it may fully reflect the Light that reveals itself from within. The disciplines which prepare the self for the onset of *jñāna* are, it may be noted of the nature of responses to an apparently new Impact of divine power which is technically termed *śaktinipāta* in the system.[2]

There are, in other words, two distinguishable stages in the spiritual life of the individual self preceding the dawn of *jñāna*. First there is the active mundane life which is one of voluntary efforts and enjoyment. But a dutiful life (*dharma*) of action and enjoyment with its implication of attachment and passions and of ego-centricism implicit in them, cannot be conducive of *jñāna* for which 'equanimity of mind' is a necessary pre-requisite.[3] There should, therefore, be a transformation of the life of *dharma* such that the self is not tied to bondage, forever hindered in its approach to *jñāna*. This transformed ideal of ethical life is the second stage which 'naturally' leads to a condition 'beyond good and evil'. The transition from the first to the second stage is not natural but spiritual. How is this brought about ? *Śaktinipāta* is the answer implied in the problem.

The underlying meaning is evident. Bondage is too heavy to be removed by self-effort alone. This is the pre-supposition of the admission of *jñāna* as *mokṣa-sādhana*. There must be a 'descent' of Divine Grace. But before this can take place and the saving knowledge revealed by the preceptor, the following must be achieved : (*i*) 'equanimity' with regard to the twin *karmas*, (*ii*) the implied maturing of the veil of *mala*. Descent of Grace becomes a possibility after this. Yet by the same logic by which the Descent is invoked as the condition for the onset of *jñāna*, these two 'pre-conditions' of Descent themselves in turn also presuppose divine assistance. The new conditions or preliminaries of knowledge have themselves to be brought about by Grace.[4] A condition, as it were 'prior' to God's action but which God alohe can fulfil. This paradox epitomizes the Śaiva Siddhānta view of spiritual need and its fulfilment.

To admit a condition or basis for the Descent of divine Grace is not of course to make the latter 'necessary'. We have to understand the 'dualism' of self-effort and grace as somewhat similar to that of *bhoga* and *apavarga* in the Yoga system, or natural will and spiritual will in Vedānta.[5] Although the first is phenomenally continuous with the second, the second implies a rejection of the first. This is what accounts for the 'uncaused' or abrupt nature of the advent of spiritual life which is a mystery. Śaiva Siddhānta only reverts this order and says that while self-effort is noumenally continuous with grace (a polar function of Grace) phenomenally it is discontinuous with it. There is phenomenally a distinction between the active self-assertive life of ethical endeavour, and the advent of a 'religious' orientation to life involving a total transvaluation of the ethical values. It is this transformed or transvalued ideal that brings in its wake (*i*) *karma-sāmya*, and (*ii*) *mala-paripāka*, and the resulting *jñāna*, all alike moments of its own dynamism. Such is, in brief, the underlying significance of the concept of Descent of Grace.

This Descent itself will be unintelligible if Grace cannot be conceived to function prior to the advent of the Descent. It is in the light of the latter, grace as exemplified in natural revelation, that we can understand its advent as spiritual revelation in the form of a 'new' Impact as *śaktinipāta*. It is, in other words, in the light of the distinction between *sakala avasthā* – wakeful vigilance and *kevala avasthā* —the quiescent invigilant state of sleep, that we also conceive of the possibility of a similar distinction between *sakala* (natural wakefulness) and *śuddha avasthā* (spiritual awakening). Spiritual illumination typified by the Descent of Grace must be understood in the light of the process of progressive illumination in natural life.

Progressive illumination is picturesquely compared to the rising digits of the lunar circle.[6] It is not like the sun but the moon which gently reveals in and through the gloom of darkness and reveals in graded ascent, digit by digit. As the moon increases in its luminous shape slowly and imperceptibly, there is a corresponding decrease of the encircling darkness. The moon in its earlier phases or digits shines by being relatively speaking unmanifest, and in its full phase shines fully manifest. Similarly *tirodhāna-śakti* reveals in a 'natural' way during the state of bondage, by remaining hidden in different degrees, and contributing inversely to a progressive dissolution of the screening power constitutive of bondage, and reveals in the spiritual sense only when the bond has become tenuous. The *tirodhāna-śakti* in one sense sustains the grip of *mala* over the self but by sustaining it, it also contributes towards a slackening of the grip necessarily and progressively. The screening powers (*śaktis*) of *mala* operate inversely to the operations of *tirodhāna-śakti*. When this process apparently reaches its ideal limit the obscuring functions are wholly neutralised and they come to 'nought' without a content. The hold of *mala* is loosened, and the grace that was operating by veiling as it were, with the veil of *mala* till now (namely, *tirodhāna-śakti*), becomes, transfigured' into Grace that Reveals (*anugraha-śakti*). The transfiguration from the obstructive to the instinctive phase of Grace is of course only apparent.[7] This apparent change in the role of *śakti* synchronises with the achievement of ripeness of *mala* (*mala-paripāka*) and the latter in turn synchronises with the achievement of an equanimous attitude with regard to the two-fold *karma* (*karma-sāmya*). These co-incident spiritual 'events' again will have to be understood as one of degrees. The Descent, and therefore the two other 'events' which it presupposes, are not abrupt and final, but are gradual and progressive till it becomes overwhelming (*atitīvra*, *mahōgra*). The Descent in slow and imperceptible degrees marks respectively the different stages of the *jīvanmukta* and the *sādhaka*.[8]

A mere life of *dharma*, of action and enjoyment does not, however, bring about by its own momentum the attitude of self-surrender entailed by what has been called earlier, an equanimous frame of mind. The lot of a merely ethical life is compared to that of one who hungers and eats and hungers again after a while, and so on interminably.[9] This shows there is a demand in such a life for something abiding and constant, some enduring source of satisfaction. Virtue is surely to be preferred to vice but there is nothing intrinsically good about virtue itself until it is recognised as Grace. In so far that virtue keeps the self in bondage to moral egoism, hindering its approach to *jñāna* there is little to choose between virtue and vice.[10] They are like gold and iron fetters. The only chance of escaping from this vicious circle seems to be to act 'with skill'; regarding both good and evil alike without attachment; without performing virtue with a view to obeying the law or eschewing evil for fear of transgression; in other words to submit to Grace and act in dedication to *pati*.[11]

Such are the 'austerities' or asceses—*tapas* which are enjoined in lieu of ordinary duties, conducive to the goal of knowledge. They are not like austerities performed for securing unspiritual ends. They are fruitful of the imperishable result of *jñāna*.[12] Unlike ordinary acts of virtue done towards the *paśus*, these practices of *tapas* are necessarily directed towards Śiva. They are action consecrated unequivocally to the service of Śiva — *śiva-puṇya*.[13] Even the Vedic sacrifices wherein gods are invoked for offerings will fall under the category of *paśu-puṇya* the gods too being *paśus* only. Even though Śiva indeed is the ultimate recipient of all offerings it is the attitude of the one making the offerings that counts. The *jñānin's* love for humanity and his 'humanistic' activities, will for example, come under *śiva-puṇya* because the *jñānin* sees Śiva in all. Conversely, the Vedic sacrifices, even if Śiva were among the gods invoked for receiving their offerings or ablations will be considered *paśu-puṇya*,[14] the reason being that Śiva is invoked as one among *paśus* and not as *pati*, that is, *paśupati*. Therefore, such *karmas* although indeed are directed to God, in intention are performed for the creature. This means that even worldly deeds may be transmuted into *śiva-puṇya* if in intention they are dedicated to *Śiva*. Thus even in the very midst of the flux of karmic life, of action and reward, is to be found the clue for eventually transcending the rule of the natural law of deed and consequence. *Tirodhāna-śakti*, in a general sense, provides for a life of action but it also provides a solution for its bondage by making room for *śiva-puṇya* within the scope of such life.[15]

Śaiva Siddhānta, therefore, does not advocate renunciation of work as a means for reaching *jñāna*. Active life (*sakala avasthā*) in itself is an advance in the spiritual history of man over a night of sleep (*kevala avasthā*). And here again there is a hierarchy. Optional duty (*kāmya-karma*) is superior to any impulsive action, and daily duty (*nitya-karma*) marks a still higher stage in the life of action. Nevertheless both species of action come under the category of *paśu-puṇya* which can only lead one into, and not out of the clutches of *pāśa*. No deed, however altruistic, is without its bearing upon the ego of the doer.[16] Above the vocation of duty comes the vocation of service. The scheme of *Śiva-dharma* serves as a means for progressive undoing of the sense of egoism by conscious surrender of one's action to *pati*.

The meaning of the ascetic ideal in Śaiva ethics is not negative. Asceticism is here functional and not formal, its object is not escape from the world but serving self-surrender, self-effacement. And this ideal of self-surrender cannot be achieved effortfully or assertively. It is achieved only through and in proportion to service to Śiva. The

Śaiva ascetic is also at the same time the dedicated devotee of the Lord. The austere sage is also the saint compassionate.[17]

In these acts of service consciously dedicated to God, again there is a hierarchy. There are external acts of worship consisting of an outward adornment of divine images and other rituals where the action resembles those of a devoted servant towards his master.[18] There are again modes of worship which are inward as well as outward, as in reciting of prayer, meditation and performance of fire-rites. Action at this stage in its spirit of spontaneous allegiance is compared to the devotion of a son towards his father.[19] The son serves the father overtly and also spontaneously with inwardness. There are again acts of devotion of a more subjective turn consisting in the performance of yoga. In this stage the *sādhaka* is a 'friend' of God.[20] True friendship is an inward quality not apparent from external behaviour. These stages of *sādhana* — respectively called *caryā*, *kriyā* and *yoga*, imply *progressive* revelation of God (*tirodhāna-śakti*)[21] and negatively a progressive undoing of the screening powers which hide in different degrees self's vision of the Real. *Tirodhāna-śakti* accordingly assumes various forms— the grossly visible form (*sakala*) to meet the requirements of the first stage, the visible *cum* non-visible form (*sakala-niṣkala*) for the second and the non-visible (*niṣkala*) form for the third.[22] In keeping with the natural order of deed resulting in a consequence, these spiritual acts also lead to respective consequences in the form of spiritual enjoyments: becoming an inhabitant of God's world (*sālokya*), becoming or drawing near to God (*sāmīpya*) and becoming his equal in form (*sārūpya*). Only these are the immediate goals of such acts the ultimate goal for which, at the same time, they prepare, is *jñāna*.

By virtue of the cumulative maturation through these stages the self is led to the final stage of *jñāna*.[23] The Formless (*akala*) is intuited (*jñeya*) in this stage. The gross, the subtle and the still subtler forms of the previous stages are now seen to be 'general' in relation to the present intuition of the impartite ultimate nature of God. *Jñāna* is thus a stage of 'action' continuous with the three previous deeds of worship and is also their culmination. This is the Right Path (*sanmārga*) and the devotion implied in this form of *sādhana* is typified in the self-surrendering love between a lover and his beloved. All the different forms of sentiment or attitude through which religious consciousness expresses itself can be reduced to these four forms — that of master and servant, parent and child, friend and friend, and paramour and the beloved.[24]

What is of significance here is, the transition from *caryā* to *jñāna* in all these different *sādhana*, embodies the principle which marks the passage from *śravaṇa* to *niṣṭhā* within *jñāna* itself. For, in *jñāna* itself are again distinguished stages in terms of the gross form of hearkening or hearing (*śravaṇa*), the less gross one of reflection (*manana*) and the subtle form of contemplation (*nididhyāsana*) on the one side and the resulting Experience (*niṣṭhā* or *samādhi*) on the other. These are termed respectively *caryā* in *jñāna*, *kriyā* in *jñāna*, *yoga* in *jñāna* and *jñāna* in *jñāna*.[25] The transition throughout involves the same principle, namely, of proceeding from the sense of the presence *revealed* to a full realisation of its ultimate nature through union and unity. The transition when viewed from the side of resulting Experience is a transition from 'error' through 'incomplete' or 'uncertain' knowledge to Truth.

Karma-sāmya, *Mala-Paripāka* and *Śaktinipāta*

By performing these religious acts the *sādhaka* accomplishes a spiritual ripeness which is typified by his attitude of detachment towards his two-fold karmic experiences. The meaning of the term *karma-sāmya* has been a matter of great controversy in the writings of Śaiva Siddhānta.[1] A literal understanding of the term would give the sense of equality (*samatva*) of one's good and bad deeds. When two equipotential *karmas* — the most meritorious of good deeds like the performance of *Aśvamedha* sacrifice and the most hideous of bad deeds like the murder of a Brahmin — mature simultaneously, the tension ends in the reciprocal cancellation of the two *karmas* and with them of the satellite *karmas* also.[2] Another explanation is its equality with reference to its stored up merits (*puṇya*) and demerits (*pāpa*).[3] Equalisation of the most meritorious and the most hideous deeds as a result of mutual cancellation, even if possible, leaves the other less meritorious and less hideous deeds free to bear their consequences, so that it is not conceivable that good and bad deeds as such stand cancelled. Granting that they are so cancelled, what results is only a 'dissolution' of *karmas* leading to the state of *vijñānākala* (*vijñānakaivalya*) which is without *karma* but not without *mala*.[4] According to this explanation, *karma-sāmya* cannot lead one out of *saṁsāra*. Further, what is meant by good and evil cancelling each other ? The theory is based on the mathematical notion that the sum of two equal and opposite quantities is zero. But are *puṇya* and *pāpa* determinate quantities to be so measured ?

Karma-sāmya, mala-paripāka, śaktinipāta and *śiva-puṇya*, these are events in the spiritual life of man in which setting alone they derive their significance.[5] They are landmarks in the spiritual voyage of the self. *Karma* from the point of view of the self relates always to its desire and aversions.[6] This is what serves to sustain the unending chain of deed and consequence. *Karma-sāmya* as a preliminary to the slackening of the grip of *mala* should be understood to imply a condition when accumulated merits and demerits and their fruits come to entail no difference to the affective reactions of man. For a mind which is unmoved by the pangs of sorrow as well as by the lures of pleasure, *puṇya* and *pāpa* with regard to their results necessarily become identical. They remain infructuous as well because the soil is now unsuited for germination of new *karmas*. When the fruits of *puṇya* and *pāpa* are experienced with discrimination and reacted to differently, that is, with attachment and aversion then and only then they fructify into good and evil consequences and so on endlessly. Pleasure and pain are of the same species so that the 'right' attitude to them must be a uniform 'nay', not discriminately 'yea' and 'nay'. An infinite resignation with respect to finite goods is a negative symptom of living in the finite but solely in virtue of a God-relationship.[7]

It is this state beyond good and evil that eventuates in the accomplishment of the 'ripening' of *mala* (*mala-paripāka*). The same dynamism at work in bringing about neutralization of the twin deeds, accounts for self's sense of disillusionment about its worldly experience.[8] The hold of *mala* is reflected in the self's inveterate impulse to outwardisation and its consequent entanglement in the phenomena.[9] A tranquil frame of mind disinclined alike towards the so-called merit and demerit is, therefore, inimical to the active operation of the screening powers of *mala*. *Mala-paripāka* really means 'conjoining' of *mala* with all those factors instrumental in counteracting its screening powers.[10] The attitudes of attachment and aversion are, for example, factors which tend to rehabilitate and not reduce their potency while the attitude of enlightened indifference which *karma-sāmya* presupposes, will undermine it.[11]

As the screening powers of *mala* are effectively neutralized as a consequence of the *karma-sāmya, tirodhāna-śakti* becomes *anugraha-śakti*. This is *śaktinipāta*.[12] The marks of *śaktinipāta* in a *sādhaka* are his spiritual qualifications which make him competent for *jñāna*.[13] These are, an yearning for Freedom, a passion for discriminating between the true from the false etc. In addition there are certain other characteristics peculiar to a recipient of *śaktinipāta*. They are his attitudes of spiritual reverence which he spontaneously develops towards *Śiva-bhaktas* and *Śiva-śāstras*.[14]

Knowledge and *Śuddha Avasthā*

The *sādhaka* who experiences *karma-sāmya* etc. enters into the *śuddha avasthā* which marks the culmination of the *caryā, kriyā* and *yoga* disciplines. It is the state of illumination as against the preceding stages of twilight (*sakala*) and 'darkness' (*kevala*) in the spiritual life of the self. As the *sādhaka* enters *śuddha avasthā*, Siva reveals Himself.[1] Such is *jñāna*. The source of such knowledge is Śiva, who discloses himself in forms appropriate to the varied spiritual developments of the self. Differences in the spiritual development are ultimately traceable to individual differences of the selves which account for their radical plurality.[2] *Mala* is one but its screening powers hide in varied degress the vision of the selves commensurate with their individual differences. The differences of screening may be classified under three levels or strata *sūkṣma, sthūla* and *sthūlatara*. Śiva reveals Himself accordingly in different degrees of mediateness, when of course, *mala* has become 'ripe', that is, when its screening powers have become because of conjunction with factors inimical to their operation, tenuous, ready for dissolution. Thus for the *sakala* whose vision has been under a heavy screen (*sthūlatara*), Śiva appears in the guise of a Preceptor and imparts knowledge through Instruction (*upadeśa*), Book (*śāstra*) and the resulting Experience (*anubhava*). For the *pralayākala* whose vision is less obscured and who is consequently not bound by *māyā*, Śiva appears directly as the 'Thou' in a Divine form and imparts *jñāna*. For the *vijñānākala* who is under the effect of least screening, and is consequently not bound by *māyā* and *karma*, Śiva imparts knowledge from within as the 'I', making it appear knowledge has dawned of itself.[3]

For the worldly soul,—*sakala*, Śiva reveals Himself *through* a third person, namely, the *guru*. Śiva acts through the form of a freed individual; it is a case of *appearing* in a form and not an incarnation.[4] The shortcomings due to human form do not affect Śiva because when the human preceptor becomes of the nature of Śiva by conscious union, his form has no longer the sting of *pāśa* about it. Śiva is manifest in and appears as a human preceptor; He is not hid in the medium as 'cream is hid in milk', but manifest like the 'creamy crust in curd'.[5] Admission of the advent of *śuddha avasthā* as the basis for revelation of knowledge implies the incompatibility of the latter with the like of sense (*sakala avasthā*). The senses obscure the self's true nature and reveal to it only what they 'objectify', namely, the objects, and here again each sense only its object, just as many colour reflections in a crystal overshadowing the colour of the crystal itself, display only themselves.[6] How can what obscures the self's nature and presents only their own object be the means of revealing the real nature of self ?

True, the senses are at work when the Preceptor reveals knowledge. The senses do not cease to function and yet there is perception of Truth. The *jñānin* is asleep to the world of senses even when the senses are at work but is awake to the Reality beyond the senses.[7] This is *śuddha avasthā*. When the senses, body, etc., with which self is endowed in its 'empirically' wakeful existence, dissociate themselves, as for instance, in sleep, then what results is the *kevala avasthā*. When on the other hand, the self dissociates itself from them, what ensues is *śuddha avasthā*.[8]

Another difference between the *kevala* and he *śuddha avasthā* is that when self rises above its sensory life and attains union with Śiva, there is no return any more to its previous condition. There is no drive from the *śuddha* back to the *sakala* state. When, however, the self lapses into *kevala* it has again to resume its career with the senses (*sakala avasthā*). The reason is not far to seek. The screening *śaktis* of *mala* are susceptible to removal while *Śiva-śakti* is inalienably 'one' with self.[9] This is the presupposition of spiritual realisation.

There can be reverses *within* the *śuddha avasthā* due apparently to the residual impressions of *pāśa*, but there is no return from *śuddha avasthā* to *sakala avasthā*. There is no more return to the senses 'just as the gushing water of a stream with its barriers broken rushes head-long into the sea and never turns back'.[10]

It may be argued that Śiva being the absolute reality the senses etc. go back eventually to the same source, namely, Śiva, the sole reality acknowledged. *Pāśa-jñāna* is not ultimately something in itself different from *pati-jñāna*. Once *pati-jñāna* is attained, *pāśa* (the senses) too become divinised so that even when *mukti* is attained, there is no return to the condition of sensory knowing. The Śaiva *siddhāntin* asks :

is *pati-jñāna*, the 'reality' of *paśu-jñāna* and *pāśa-jñāna*, the latter being only aspects or mutations of *pati-jñāna* not real in themselves (Śivādvaita), or is it the converse, that is *pati-jñāna* into which the other two species of *jñāna* become 'transmuted' (*Śivasaṁkrānta-vāda*) ? Either alternative is fraught with consequences disastrous to spiritual realisation. If *pati* is the sole reality and *pati-jñāna* is everything, if all *avasthās* are *śuddha avasthās*, what need is there for this spiritual endeavour to cross over the *saṁsāra* ? Why is *mukti* said to lie in the *paśu* discarding *pāśa* and realising *pati* ?[11] If, on the other hand, they are different, then *pati-jñāna* is not absolute knowledge. Spiritual realisation demands both that Śiva be absolute reality and *Śiva-jñāna* absolute knowledge.

The solution implied in the acceptance of *śuddha avasthā* is : *pati-jñāna* (absolute knowledge) is identical, and yet in another sense non-identical with *pāśa-jñāna* (empirical knowledge) and *paśu-jñāna* (self-knowledge). *Pāśa-jñāna* is identical neither with *pati-jñāna* nor again with *paśu-jñāna*, the latter two being non-empirical in nature. And still through pervasion *pati* is 'identical' with *paśu* and *pāśa* alike, in which sense the three *jñānas* are one. This position is clarified by the body-soul analogy. Though self indwells in, and activates all the senses, the senses are not therefore on the same footing as regards the function. The eye is qualitatively different with respect to sensing, from other senses. It sees things by reaching them pervasively (*prāpyakārin*). Others do not. The difference between the self and the senses, and within the senses between the eye and the other senses, becomes apparent when the eyesight, having been temporarily lost, is regained. Similarly, the relative supremacy of *paśu-jñāna* over *pāśa-jñāna*, and of *pati-jñāna* over either of them becomes apparent when the Preceptor imparts real knowledge.[12]

Thus there is a coincidence between three of the *dasa-kāryāṇi* namely, *śiva-rūpa, ātma-darśana,* and *tattva-śuddhi*. Real *freedom* from the tattvas—what is termed their '*śuddhi*', and self's insight (*darśana*) into its own nature which flashes to it in the wake of its freedom from an unquestioned identification with tattvas are entailed by the mere presence, in the form of Preceptor, of Śiva (*śiva-rūpa*).

Pāśa-jñāna refers to the entire sphere of word (*śabda*) and meaning (*artha*).[13] All the products of the four *vāc*, the *veda*, *śāstra*, *smṛti* and *purāṇa*, all arts and sciences as well as the *tattva* from *nāda* to *pṛthvī* and the *tāttvika*, comprise the sphere of *pāśa-jñāna*. *Pati* is beyond the sphere of word and meaning (*vāṅmanotīta*). But what about *paśu-jñāna*, self-awareness which is aware of *pāśa* as *pāśa* and is non-empirical and is the prius of the empirical ? The self which is conscious of *pāśa* and knows itself as not-this, is already betraying in this attitude of covert self-assertion vestiges of *paśutva* which it impugnes when dissociating itself from it.[14] Therefore, even this is *paśu jñāna* and is of as little avail in knowing *pati* as *pāśa-jñāna*. Neither consciousness underlying self's dissociation from *pāśa* (*Śivasama-vāda*), nor the dissociation itself (*pāṣaṇa-vāda*) can be the means of freedom from *pāśa*. Self's knowledge of itself as ever in inseparable union with Śiva, *follows* Śiva's revelation of Himself and therefore cannot be the means of knowing Śiva.[15] Self-consciousness may be the ultimate principle of human knowledge and experience but it has only a negative value as negatively pointing to an absolute eternal consciousness which is the implicate of all knowledge and experience. This is positively shown to self by the Preceptor, when finding its affinity with the Presence, the self also knows itself. The so-called *paśu-jñāna* is ultimately only an illusion, a momentary phase in the spiritual history of the individual due to thetransition from bondage to release—from *sakala avasthā* to *śuddha avasthā*.[16]

Self-Purification (*ātma-śuddhi*)

All spiritual *sādhanā* are designed as disciplines for advancing steadily in the life of spirit. Both to progress spiritually and also to maintain what is achieved in the face of reverses possible and actual, *sādhana* is essential. Accordingly, for the *sādhaka* in the *śuddha avasthā* spiritual disciplines are enjoined for remaining steadfast, firmly established in the Knowledge revealed to him as well as to advance farther and farther in the life which is Knowledge. As he advances in this life the disciplines cease to be 'duty'. The 'ought' and the 'is' become indistinguishable. Prescriptions become descriptions.

Advent of Knowledge, though in a sense accomplished and final has to be enlivened by life. Knowledge does not dispel Ignorance at one stroke and for good. It involves a process. When you hurl a stone into a pond overlaid with moss it pierces the mossy surface for the moment but the next instant it is covered again. Similarly, when *jñāna* dawns, the obstruction of *mala* gives way but when it slackens, obstruction sets in again.[1] The slackening, of course, is due to the *vāsanā-mala*. The *sādhaka* does not, by reason of this, return to the *sakala avasthā* but fortifies his position by meditation etc.

How does the *sādhaka* persevere in the vision vouchsafed to him? One of the disciplines suggested for this is to contemplate the non-real world (*asat*) as mere 'nought'.[2] All the 'choir of heaven, and the furniture of earth'—even the supernatural *siddhi* etc. are unfoldments out of a causal condition in which as effect they are *non est*.[3] In such contemplation the real as the 'ground' will emerge.[4] The various colours in a crystal are seen to be not *in* the crystal, and therefore are nothing in themselves: through reflecting on this phenomenon the crystal itself emerges in its native luminosity. When the paintings on a screen are seen to be merely the ephemeral impositions on the screen overshadowing its native surface then what is disengaged with the help of such meditation is the screen alone.[5] This is, then the way of remaining steadfast in the knowledge of *pati* : 'when you negate *pāśa* as a deception like a fleeting mirage, *pati-jñāna* which has dawned comes as a cool shade'. When one is thus established in Knowledge confirmed by the contemplation of the falsity of the world that obtrudes, one in the life of grows Knowledge.

The relinquishing of *asat* (phenomenal) as *asat* (false) is the negative side of the discipline; positively it implies contemplating oneness with the *sat*, appreciated earlier negatively in the process of the devaluation of *asat*. Contemplation or meditation is to be of Śiva as identical with self, not as *another* being.[6] The meditation takes the form of 'He is I' (*so'ham*). An impressive analogy is given to bring out the sense of the contemplation of identity. In the *Garuḍa*-meditation one overcomes the effect of a snake's poison by the power of the divine *Garuḍa* which he invokes through meditation of oneness with it. The consciousness of identity with *Garuḍa* which the reciter (*māntrika*) achieves is real and not imagined (*āropita*).[7] This is evident from the consecquence of the meditation, namely, the nullifying of the effect of poison. In Śaiva discipline, meditation (*bhāvanā*) is never a mere exercise in imagination. A contrived meditation cannot serve its purpose. A hungry man 'meditating', however intensely, on food is little likely to have his hunger appeased.

Now, does the reciter (*māntrika*) actualy become *Garuḍa*?[8] The answer is, the object of meditation here is not the bird but the inspiring divinity thereof, in the form of the *mantra*.[9] When the reciter meditates on the *mantra-rūpa* constantly and becomes 'one' with it, he acquires the functions of that divinity to counteract the effects of poison. The points suggested by the analogy are obvious. The self which is disposed, by its very constitution, towards identifying with the object of its knowledge, identifies itself with *asat*, or alternately with *sat* in knowledge. From the *asat* it dissociates or disaffiliates its identification by contemplating on its (*asat's*) falsity. But from *sat* dissociation is inconceivable, *sat* and self being ontologically 'one' though existentially dis-united. Therefore, in the context of *sat*, the *sādhana* prescribed is meditation of identity, in the same sense in which the 'falsity' of *asat* was meditated upon. The *sādhaka* should meditate on himself as Śiva and perceive that like the eyelight and sunlight, his dedicated service and the Divine in union with him are complementary in nature.[10] In the meditation 'I am *Garuḍa*' (*Garuḍo'ham asmi*) the factors involved are: the *śakti* of the meditated *mantra*, the *śakti* of the meditating self; the presence of both being necessary so that the meditation be effective. Similarly in the meditation of 'I am Śiva', (*Śivo' ham asmi*) the *jñāna* and the *kriyā* of the one meditating manifest in his 'dedicated service' and the *jñāna* and the *kriyā* of the meditated Śiva manifest in union are both present. Haradatta says:[11] *Advaita* is taught as the final teaching of the *āgama*. Now, it cannot mean unqualified identity (*nirupacaritaikya*) because it is evident that *Garuḍa* and the *māntrika* are different. Nor can meditation of oneness be false or imagined because meditation of *Garuḍa* counteracts the effects of snake poison. 'It is this meditation typified in *Garuḍa-bhāvanā* that is taught in the ancient Vedas when the latter exhort one to contemplate That as oneself'.[11a] If the *mantra* '*Garuḍo' ham asmi*' were understood in the secondary sense of its terms to mean pure identity of self, it would lose the character of meditation (*bhāvanā*) and its use in the context of the removal of poison will become unintelligible.[12]

Another *sādhana to the same effect*, that is, towards manifestation of *jñāna* and the perception of the *jñeya* is the recital of *śrī-pañcākṣara*. Spiritual discipline is not adequate till it harnesses our thought, speech and action alike towards the realisation of its goal. Accordingly it takes the forms of meditation (*bhāvanā*), recitation (*mantra*) and action (*kriyā*).[13] Every real meditation involves three points; our mind, feeling and will are all exercised in it. We think the object of meditation; we feel the emotion of the 'creaturely' sense and finally there is *icchā*—the resolve or the renewal of our surrender to God which is an act of will. The need for *mantra* and *kriyā* to reinforce *bhāvanā* arises out of the circumstance that the *sādhaka* may again turn by virtue of habit due to the lingering taints of *mala* to his erstwhile state of bondage to sense, even as a vermin turns yearningly from a sweet sugarcane to the bitter 'neem' it was feeding on before.[14]

The *pañcākṣara mantra* used in this context is formulated in the following order: *śi-vā-ya-na* and *ma*; the letters respectively stand for *Śiva*, *anugraha-śakti*, *ātman*, *tirodhāna-śakti* and *mala*.[15] The illustrative analogues for them are respectively the Sun, its rays, the eye, the light and darkness.[16] This is also called *mukti-pañcākṣara* in view of the fact that its recital is designed to lead one from the state of *sādhaka* to that of the *mukta*. As it shall be presently explained, it is the direct *sādhana* for *śiva-darśana — ātma-śuddhi* which is the portal to *śiva-yoga — śiva-bhoga* in the scheme of *daśa-kāryāṇi*.[17] The significance of the *mantra* lies, as the letters indicate, in the self acknowledging the supremacy of *śiva* and *śakti* and its own insignificance in comparison on the one hand, and of its freedom from *tirodhāyin* and *mala* on the other. The order of recital gives precedence to *śiva* and *śakti* (*śi* and *va*) and relegates *tirodhāyin* and *mala* (*na* and *ma*) to the end to indicate their being 'conquered' : it is because of this fact of their being conquered or overshadowed[18] *na* could be distinguished from *ma* in the recital. It is only through an awareness of the distinction of *va* and *na*, that the distinction between *na* and *ma* emerges. The letter *na* which signifies *tirodhāyi* is understood to comprehend within it *māyā* and *karma*[19] which are the freely employed instruments in its service. There is thus full harmony in import between the contemplation of the *mantra* as thus understood and the *sādhana* previously mentioned, namely relinquishing *asat* as false and meditating on *sat* as identity. The self is the nexus between *tirodhāna-śakti* (*na*) and *anugraha-śakti* (*va*) — between the whirl of cosmic dance (*ūna naṭana*) and the dance of wisdom (*jñāna naṭana*) in the words of Umāpati.[20] Its spiritual endeavour should be directed towards finding itself not between *na* and *va* but between *śi* and *va* in which lies its destiny. When *na* and *ma* are in the ascendent the self is oblivious of and indifferent to *śi* and *va*, and is therefore caught in the vortex of phenomenal life (*ūna naṭana*).[21] When it is disenchanted and disillusioned, *śi* and *va* gain ascendence; with the ripening of *mala* (*ma*), *tirodhāyi* (*na*) ceases to function and is as it were transifigured into *anugrahaśakti*.[21a] As symbolic of this change, the five letters of *mukti-pañcākṣara* are now really reduced to three, the letters of *tirodhāna* (*na*) and *mala* (*ma*) being absent.[22] *Śakti* (*va*) brings about the union of the self (*ya*) with śiva) (*śi*).[23]

It is in this form that the *mantra* is said to embody the meaning of *tat tvam asi.*[24] The three terms of the *mahāvākya* stand respectively for *paśu*, *pati* and their essential union. Similarly, *śi* and *ya* denote *śiva* and *ātman* and *va* their union which is the work of *anugraha-śakti*. Still, in a sense, we can say with Tirumular[25] that Śiva is the ultimate import of the *mahāvākya* by reason of his primacy and absoluteness. The *pañcākṣara* ultimately denotes the one supreme *jñeya.*[26] This point is more clearly brought out in the two other forms of *pañcākṣara* suggested in the hymnal writings of the Śaiva saints.[27] In one of these the self (*ya*) freed from *tirodhāyi* (*na*) and *mala* (*ma*) loses itself in *śakti* (*va*), so that we have only two letters *śi* and *va* left. Māṇickavācakar refers to it in a celebrated verse which is quoted by Umāpati as embodying this supreme truth.[28] At another place also Māṇickavācakar says: 'In him my body, soul and thought and mind were merged. How all myself was lost, sing we, etc.'[29] Finally, we have *pañcākṣara* in the form of one letter (*ekākṣara*), namely *śi* only[30] where the suggestion is that *śakti* with self 'sinks' in Śiva. A popular verse of a saint is quoted in illustration of this truth which defines *niṣṭhā* as consisting in renouncing the associates, that is, delusious, and the company of women, that is *māyā* and seeking the Father through the assistance of the mother, and in the end reaching the Father even oblivious of the mother that led unto him.[31] These two forms of *pañ.ākṣara* correspond to the forms of *śiva-yoga* and *śiva-bhoga* yet to be considered.

Now it remains to be seen how contemplation of *mukti-pañcākṣara* serves its intended purpose of warding off the lingerings of Impurity (*vāsanā-mala*). The ultimate import of *mukti-pañcākṣara* is to show that self and Śiva stand in the relation of owner and owned.[32] The self perceives the inconsequential nature of its body and other possessions (*na*) and the ultimate impotence of *mala* (*ma*) which occasions them consequent cn perceiving the 'absoluteness' and omniscience of Śiva (*śi*) and *śakti* (*va*). *Śakti* (*va*) now is its only prop[33] with which to realise unity of Being (*śi*). The recital of *pañcākṣara* thus carries with it a total disvaluation or depreciation of self, disvaluation in respect of its very being as an independent thing, and a complementary appreciation of Śiva as the supreme Being and value. Meykandar gives picturesque illustrations to show how *śiva-darśana* and *ātma-śuddhi* are achieved at once by means of the *sādhanā* of *pañcākṣara* recital.[34] Of the three ultimates of the system, *pāśa* and *paśu* are perceived immediately as the contents of the judgments 'I am ignorant' (*aham ajñaḥ*), 'I know' (*ahaṁ jānāmi*) respectively; *Pati*, is to be intuited through meditation of *pañcākṣara*. The planets of *rāhu* and *ketu* are preceived, not like other planets, which hover about in space but only *in and through* the planets of the sun and the moon during solar and lunar eclipses. In the same way is *pati* perceived in oneself in and through the contemplation of *śrī-pañcākṣara* in which one becomes immediately aware of oneself as the creature (*śeṣa*) and, by complementary relation, of Śiva as God to whcm one belongs (*śeṣīn*).[35] The real manifests itself as 'light within the light' in that creature-consciousness even as fire appears in the wood when the friction stick is revolved —'like the appearance of oil on grinding the sesame, of ghee on churning the curd, of water on boring the ground, etc.'.[36] The self too freely surrenders its being unto Śiva, in which indeed lies its freedomm, just as iron loses its being consisting of hardness etc., in the fire. Thus it is that the recital of *śrī-pañcākṣara* becomes a *sādhana* for *śiva-darśana — ātma śuddhi*.

Antaryāga-pūjā comes in as an accessory to the recital of *pañcākṣara*[37] and bears the same significance. Although Śiva is the 'wholly other', He is also one with man at the same time so that he can be worshipped in the sanctum of one's heart. The heart in the form of a lotus stands for the microcosm of the thirty-six tattvas which compose the world and the Transcendent (Śiva) is invoked as being seated *on* this lotus seat, which is symbolic of the relation in which the self stands to it.[38] Thus the thirty-six tattvas from *pṛthvī* onwards to *śakti-tattva* are represented in the different parts of the lotus-heart. *Pṛthvī* has its root in the navel, the twenty-three tattvas beginning with *pṛthvī* are its stalks; the seven *vidyā*-tattvas and the *śuddha-vidyā* of the śiva-tattvas are its eight tender petals. *Īśvara* and sadāśiva tattvas are its stamens, *śakti-tattva* is its pistil and ovary, and *śiva-tattva* the (fifty-one) seeds on it. To complete the picture as a Śaiva saint does,[39] the root of this lotus is *māyā*; the mire whence it springs is *karma* and the tank at its base *mala*. Śiva is worshipped as the 'installed' (*sthānin*) of which the *hṛt-puṇḍarīka*, is the seat (*sthāna*.)[40] In this sanctum of worship (*pūjāsthāna*) Śiva is invoked in the form composed of the *pañcākṣara*.[41] The supreme spirit is contemplated as 'dancing' in the sanctuary of one's being in a form made of the five letters of *pañcākṣara*.[42] Thus it may be seen that *bhāvanā*, *mantra* and *kriyā* involving our mind, feeling and will tend towards the same result, namely, *ātma-śuddhi* and prepare it for *siva-yoga—śiva-bhoga*.

XV

SPIRITUAL LIFE AS END : MOKṢA

Recovery of Self : Integration with Śiva (*Śiva-yoga*)

For Śaiva Siddhānta, Freedom or *mokṣa* is primarily freedom from *pāśa* as such , comprising all evil, the unoriginated as well as the consequential. If the sphere of spiritual endeavour represents a state when *pāśa* is brought under effective check, in *mokṣa* it is overcome or 'destroyed'. The text defines this aspect of *mokṣa* in the words that the freed attain self-realisation (*svānubhūti*) being no longer fettered by *mala*, *māyā* etc. *Pāśakṣaya* — literally the wearing out or destruction of *pāśa* is the chief, if only the negative significance of *ātma-lābha* — the fruit of the self's spiritual endeavour, namely the recovery of self.[1]

The advent of *pati-jñāna* marks the steady, progressive and a wholesale dissolution of *pāśa*. The several stages of *pati-jñāna* through which is effected *pāśakṣaya*, progressively culminating in Enjoyment of Śiva (*śiva-bhoga*, *śivānubhava*), *mokṣa par excellence*, are as follows : In *śiva-rūpa*, there is freedom from not-self (*tattva-śuddhi*). In *śiva-darśana* is achieved freedom from assertion of self-being (*ātma-śuddhi*). In *śiva-yoga* is achieved freedom from the root source of 'me' and 'mine' which outlasts all efforts of relinquishing self-assertion and persists by the very act of discriminating self from not-self. And this leads to the Freedom of *śiva-bhoga*. In *śiva-rūpa*, Śiva by the application of his *kriyāśakti* sets at naught the entire residual stock of *karma* remaining accumulated after only a fraction of it has begun to take effect, namely, the *sañcita*, and also therefore the physical loci of the form of *adhvan* which 'house' the *karma*, namely, the *māyīya*. This is done symbolically in the act of *dīkṣā* (*nirvāṇa-dīkṣā*) by the *guru*. In *śiva-darśana* by the application of his *jñāna-śakti* Śiva dispels the primal evil of *mala* which has been dwarfing the potentialities of self from eternity, and also reduces to nought in advance[2] fresh influx of *karma* due to self's earthly life, that is, *āgāmin*. That portion of the karmic life which has already begun to bear fruit and to which is due one's present embodiment, *prārabdha* is destroyed only by experience.

Speaking from the side of self in its journey from the condition of bondage to Freedom, with the advent of Preceptor-given knowledge the gross manifestations of *pāśa* in the form of tattvas cease to obtrude. Still, it must be remembered that *pāśakṣaya* remains as yet an unattained ideal. As a text puts it,[3] the enemy is only stayed which merely means not that victory is attained but that it is in sight. Even after *tattva-śuddhi* the root *mala* still remains as is evident from the dogging illusion of 'I' or selfhood which now after dissociation from not-self assumes prominence. Through *tattva-śuddhi* one is led beyond the tattvas to self (*ātma-darśana*) which now appears to be foundational. There is no freedom from this *paśutva* till one intuits the truly foundational—the *jñeya*.[4] Self-emptying (*ātma-śuddhi*) should supervene on gaining insight into self's reality. Among the *sādhana* prescribed for the intuition of *jñeya* is the recital of *śrī-pañcākṣara*, the significance of which lies in contemplating the absoluteness of *śiva-śakti* and self's own non-significant, inconsequential reality. This contemplation ripens into *yoga* or mystical intuition.

Intuition of spirit implies conformity and union of the perceiving subject and the perceived object. If the union were not complete it only means that the screening effects of *mala* are still at work. *Paśutva* which endures even after dissociation from *pāśa* operates in two ways, the second even more devious and treacherous than the first. Firstly, it manifests itself under the guise of a newly won insight of the self. Self's insight about its reality *in contrast with not-self* is still a case of *delusive* knowledge, the object perceived being only the *paśu* and not the true self 'before God'. When one conceives the real in terms of one's 'I', the real suffers itself to be 'hid' in and as the 'I' so that what is perceived is only the 'I' and not the indwelling reality. It is, therefore, only a case of erroneous cognition of the species of the rope-snake illusion.[5]

Now when the self seeks to overcome this by contemplation of identity with *pati*, *paśutva* still dogs it even more imperceptibly. The illusion now is '*I* intuit *pati*', 'He is I', the sense of me and mine still implicit in *so'haṁ bhāvanā* and the recital of the *pañcākṣara* is potent with seeds of duality.[6] Even an incipient discrimination of 'I' and 'mine' is evidence of persistence of delusion due to *mala*. The structure of 'me'-'mine' consciousness when analysed may be seen to involve again the distinction of the knower, known and knowledge. The consciousness of 'me' is of 'I' as the knowing subject (*jñātṛ*) while that of 'mine' involves consciousness of knowledge (*jñāna*) and of the known (*jñeya*).[7] If the real were known *qua* the known, that is over against the knower then what is thus known is not the Real. Śiva is as surely unknown to one who seeks Him in terms of 'I' (the seeker) and the 'Thou' (sought), as to the one who seeks Him in one's 'I'.[8]

A significant analogy is cited.[9] The sense of vision, namely, the eye is distinguished from other senses for its translucence on account of preponderance of *sattva*. Its distinction is, that while other senses come into contact with objects at their respective centres, the sense of eye itself composed of light reaches out to the objects in close association with outer light. The two species of light—the visual and the elemental although distinguishable *qua* evolutes of *ahaṁkāra* cannot be differentiated in their respective function of seeing and illumining. Functionally the two are so close that all known modes of defining the closeness in terms of identity, difference etc. prove wide of the mark. The difficulty arises because of the peculiar circumstance under which the two orders of light mix eventuating in the sensation of vision. The optical sense which may be conceived to be a subtle, luminous emanation from the eye becomes so completely attuned to the outer light that it would be untrue to view it as preserving any determinate feature of its own other than the feature of the outer light it is in union with. That is to say it has no distinguishable being of its own as it loses itself in and *as* the light which illumines the objects to it.

In this respect the elemental light which merely illumines, presents a contrast. It remains unaffected by the circumstance of the visual light mixing with it and preserves its being, under every circumstance of its union therewith. Therefore, to conceive of the phenomenon of vision in terms of visual light only, is an obvious delusion because only the seeing aspect is recognised in disregard of its necessary complement, namely, the revealing aspect. Now, to conceive it in terms of visual light *and* outer light too is no less delusive. For even here it is the 'seeing' aspect that is prominent, however unintentionally. The truth is that vision is nothing in itself as it were, but for its illumination by outer light.

This then is the first aspect of *śiva-yoga*. Self should be 'one' with God in such a way that it does not regard itself as other than God. Just as in its bound state God in union with it knows without being seen to be other than the self, similarly now self in union with God should become one with Him in being and abide unfailingly in His service.[10] This is at once the means prescribed and also a description of the self freed from the effects of *paśutva* lingering on in the form of 'me' and 'mine'.

The second aspect of *śiva-yoga* is submitting to the will of God which negatively, is giving up of one's own will. When self stands integrated in union with God as 'one' with His Being, is its will which is its essence active or not? If latter, that is if self's will were not to persist, self ceases to be. If former, how can self be integrated in union with God? The answer to this objection is: to do nothing but the will of God.[11] For the eye which is able to 'intuit' light or illumination non-dually—intuit it by submitting to light, there is no more clinging to the contents illumined but only pure apprehension of their 'condition'. The contents for the eye are ultimately raised to the level of the 'condition'.[12] The act of sight is transformed into pure play. In the same manner when self stands with its will also in unison with the will of God—without which 'condition' its will cannot conceivably function, the world present as the content of its will ceases to obtrude as 'this' but gets trnsformed into the condition under which it could possibly be a content, namely, the Divine will itself.

If through a 'union' of being, freedom from the lingering effects of *mala* potent with the seeds of duality is achieved, through a union of will freedom from the lingering effects of *māyā* and *karma* is accomplished.[13] As the 'world' ceases to confront one's will as it becomes one with Divine will, appetition and aversion which are part of life *in* the world do not arise and the scope for a lapse to bondage is reduced to nothing.

Is not to surrender one's will to the will of God, to surrender one's freedom?[14] To recognise external authority even if divine would be heteronomy, subjection to a law outside oneself. What is ultimately 'bondage' but submission to *another's* will?[15] How can 'being united to the will of God' be compatible with the ultimate freedom of self? This question is a demand for the definition of the meaning of the freedom of will. We are thus far led to a position where freedom (*svātantrya*) cannot be interpreted to suggest two different kinds—freedom in the context of God and freedom in the context of self. One single notion of freedom is in demand as we no longer have two wills on hand. What can be the significance of such freedom?[16]

To say that it consists of being unrelated to what is other than oneself (*parānapekṣatva*) is not valid because God's will (*śakti*) is freely related to phenomena. Non-compliance with another's will (*parecchānanuvartitva*) also is not freedom because God's 'activity' of cosmic functions, and of his vouchsafing of fruits is in free compliance with the beneficiary's own will. Freedom is not a matter of being uncoerced or uncontrolled by another (*parā'preryatva*) for God allows himself to be freely 'coerced' or coaxed by the devotees as when they ritualistically invoke His presence in images. Freedom, therefore, consists in what one freely wills (*yad icchati karoti tat*).[17] It cannot be explained in any other term without reference to will which in principle is freedom itself. Freedom is conformity with one's own unrestrained will (*apratigata-svecchānuvartitva*). This meaning of freedom defines at once the freedom of the supreme Will and also the individual will in union with it. Will cannot have a purpose ulterior to itself. Its unhampered free exercise is itself its own end — a joy. Divine will may be described in a figurative sense as the will to self-enjoyment. Will and the will to enjoy are identical. Freedom is freedom of will to enjoy. If so, the will in eternal union with it cannot be described in any other term: the individual will's nature too is to enjoy Śiva. The will or intention to experience the Bliss that is Śiva (*Śivānandānubhavecchā*) is its authentic will (*apratigata-svecchā*) and compliance therewith (*anuvartitva*) without any sort of constraint to the compliance is Freedom. To be unfree means to be under some sort of constraint. To be free means the chooser or the agent is the essential link in the chain of causal events and that no extraneous compulsion — physical, moral or metaphysical, forces him to act in a direction incompatible with his basic desire or intention.

'Thy will be done' is therefore not a source of unfreedom. On the contrary, it alone is exercise of one's real freedom. To submit to the law of *karma* is a necessity; it is to surrender one's freedom or spontaneity towards *Śivānandānubhava* and submission to the consequence of *mala*-obscuration. To 'submit' to the will of God is to exercise one's will unhampered by impediments.[18] He that 'willeth to do the will of God' is alone not only the one that knows the Truth. He is alone also consequently the Free.

But is not to do 'Thy will' a species of doing? How can there be deed without a consequence of the deed? How, in other words, when there is experience due to the deed that has already begun to bear fruit (*prārabdhānubhava*) — no matter if done in union with divine Will, there is escape from its consequence in the form of influx of fresh deed (*āgāmi-karma*)?[19] The solution to this lies in a correct apprehension of the natures of *paśu* and *pāśa*. 'The senses of ear etc., are not 'me' or 'mine' but *māyīya* — the assumptive *śakti* of the Lord. Their function too is at the Lord's initiation not at my will. The contents of sense-function, the world and the means of one's experience of the world, body, mind, universe and its objects are also *māyīya*, of the Lord and are not at my command. I am myself — I, who in association with them eke out and enjoy *karma*, am at divine 'disposal', knowing when he reveals knowledge and not knowing when his revelation is obstructed. Like *māyīya śakti* I am too, not independent will but a free content in relation to divine Will'.[20] When human will is dedicated to the Divine in such spirit, human action ceases to bind. The *prārabdha-karma* too becomes a mere 'deed of the body' in the presence of the supreme self instead of 'my' deed or experience.

In God, law and love meet. He is both impersonal justice underlying the 'relentless' working of the law of *karma* binding the self, and also the personal love with regard to exempting those who are in union with His will from the law. This only means that law and love are to be understood properly as implying neither a meaningless compulsion of causal law nor the equally meaningless irresponsibility of caprice. *Karma* is impersonal and 'impassible' love[21] — the love which gives itself equally to all, of which another name is justice. *Mokṣa* is 'preferential' love. God loves every man with the same degree of love and is also 'partial' to the liberated. There is no contradiction.[22] Divine justice itself in its core is 'preferential' love, not impassible or indifferent love. And conversely Divine mercy exemplified in the case of those freed from bondage is not in truth 'preference' or partiality. Divine Grace is open to all and impervious to none. The God of Grace has no favourites. All are at once His favourites.

For those who can be united in love with His love — whose will is in free unrestrained unison with His Will, He also reciprocates by 'establishing' them in Unitive Life in lieu of the *āgāmi-karma*. For those who cannot be so united because of restraint or resistance, He is not indifferent or non-reciprocating but merciful by meting out *āgāmi-karma* eventually to cure them of their egoism through commission of deeds, which is resistant to union.[23] In the same manner God makes possible present experience of the fruits of previous *karma* (*prārabdha*) for the liberated as well as for the bound in an impartial manner, but entailing different consequences. In the case of the bound it leads in its wake, through the subtle agency of appetition and aversion ever present in the 'bound' man (*atisūkṣma-karma*) to accumulation of fresh *karma*. In the case of the liberated, the one established in union with Divine will, the polarity of appetition-aversion in the form of *āgāmi-vāsanā*, being no longer potent in him, because of conscious union, the *prārabdha* experience becomes infructuous.

The underlying function of God's Grace is identical. In the one case it vouchsafes experiences of happiness and suffering to the assertive, appropriating man with the gracious intention of curing him of his 'disease' of self-assertion. In the case of the other He Himself 'owns' the *prārabdha* experiences which are disowned by the unassertive self established in union with divine Will. The experience not being appropriated is 'God's experience.'[24]

Even the *jñānin*, it is sometimes said, is prone to be affected by *prārabdha* which, admittedly, does not cease to exist. This only means that while there is no experience of *prārabdha* for the *mukta* in the sense that it leads to the rise of a fresh stream of *karma* (*āgāmi*), there may be *prārabdha-vāsanā*. The vessel that contained spices might retain the faint traces or impressions of the aroma but surely such traces are not serviceable as condiments for the purpose of cooking. In the same manner, in the case of the freed, who is anchored in the will of God, due to his embodied condition and also because *prārabdha* has not ceased, worldly desire may arise through sheer force of habit. But as the freed is established in God the Support, the consequences of *prārabdha* do not amount to anything. The *vāsanā* does not get a hold as a seed for the future and consequently does not germinate bue deceases with the products of *māyā*.[25]

To be 'set in the mould of Śiva'[26] unswervingly, in the face of such desires as may arise in relation to the world, is indeed a feat and an achievement. But the *jñānin* is equal to it. He is a spiritual adept. He is like the expert jockey who sits unperturbed by the swiftness of his spirited mount. The senses of the liberated which are his medit of commerce with the world are under his effortless control because he remains steadfast in the 'Divine mould'.[26a]

The problem of how self which is *sadasat* with its proneness to assimilate the nature of its object, may be conceived to accomplish the feat is not insoluble. For, self the participant, participates in the nature of God as *sat* and so does not perceive *asat* notwithstanding its *de facto* relation with *asat* in its embodied condition. *Asat* cannot persist 'objectively' before *sat*.[27] The eye in the full blaze of light cannot perceive darkness, and also therefore 'objects' whose contours in their reciprocal distinctness are determined by darkness.[28]

Recovery of Self : Transcendent Enjoyment of Siva (*śiva-bhoga*)

After attaining conscious union with God, and after *pāśa* and its impressions are warded off, there should be nothing more left for self to achieve. The goal is reached. Freedom from *paśutva* is continuous with manifestation of *Śivatva*. What then is distinctive about this culminating phase of the *daśa-kārya* ? The answer to this is that while union with God in being as well as in will is indeed constitutive of Release itself, the union has still to grow into the Bliss of unitive life for which another name is *Śivatva*. The state of *yoga* marks the fourth (*turīya*) in the five pure states of spiritual realisation (*śuddha avasthā*), while that of *bhoga* stands for the culminating phase (*turīyātīta*) of Experience.[1] In union there is only a fore-taste of Bliss (*sukha-prabhā*), a negative consequence of dissolution of *paśutva*. But Supreme Bliss (*parama-sukha*) is not a negative experience. Not to do ought but the will of God is not Bliss though it is certainly its immediate precondition. A distinction is thus evident between manifestation of Grace and the ensuing manifestation of Bliss.[2]

The constitutive element of Bliss is the *advaita*-experience. The inner significance of *advaita* consists in its being not merely a relation or union but a resulting experience of the relation. We may accordingly distinguish between the stage of 'advaitic' relation with *śakti*, and an ensuing *advaita* experience of *Śivatva*. The difference is brought out by different analogies. Advaitic relation between *cit-śakti* and self is like the indissoluble union of light with sight which cannot be understood in terms more fundamental than the relatedness implied by the analogy.[3] *Advaita* experience into which this relation grows is like the more inward unity of consciousness with the function of seeing or sight.[4] At the finite level itself we have both these phases of grace as relation and as the relationless experience underlying man's cognitive experience. *Śakti* 'shows' by being in union with consciousness, as the condition which makes its experience possible even as external light reveals to eye by being in union with visual light as the condition of its sight. Śiva also similarly pervades the being of self,[5] not merely as an external condition but as *constituting* self's experience. As *śakti* shows or illumines by being in union with man's knowledge and will, Śiva is 'one' with his being or self and knows. If the condition of sight, namely, light cannot be distinguished apart in terms of function from the seeing eye, the self that *sees* is even less distinguishable from the seeing eye. Both may be described as phases or dimensions of one all-embracing *advaita* experience.[6]

When self is freed from *pāśa* and is established and consciously rooted in the will of *śakti*, surrendering its will in freedom typified by the dissolution of bonds, it becomes immediately aware of this second dimension of the presence of *Śiva* in its very being as the knower behind its knowledge; and not merely as what makes its knowledge possible as the necessary and sufficient condition (*karaṇa*) of knowledge. The knower underlying knowledge — like self underlying its sight, is *constitutive* of and not merely the condition of the experience of knowing or seeing. Now this immediate self-awareness of unity of Being, which is as much self being aware of Śiva as Śiva being self-aware, is a more positive experience than the preceding one of union of will. Immediate self-awareness of this interior 'Grace' as Being involves exercise of the will of self previously surrendered. If the state of union with *śakti* may be described as knowledge or will devoid of content, the content being raised to the level of the condition, the present state implies knowledge acquiring a 'content' but in a new and unsuspected dimension. It is knowledge becoming self-aware of the 'knower' of knowledge like the eye turning its gaze from outer light to the inward glow of its soul. This Awareness (*jñāna*) of Śiva as content more immediate than self's own immediacy, involves also the exercise of the two functions that we distinguished in consciousness, *icchā* and *kriyā*.[7] The self is now not merely pure awareness or receptivity but pure Ardour and pure Activity. This is *śiva-bhoga*.

The scope for the exercise of the triple functions of sentience characteristic of self as spirit, constituting bliss experience is defined in the following manner :[8] an inward self-intuitive self-awareness of Śiva as the subject implies uninterrupted memory (*jñāna*); forgetfulness is a privative feature of our experience which can be transcended only in divine experience.[9] Similarly, a perpetual renewal of the resolve to dedicate and the accompanying attitude of ontological dependence (*śeṣa-śeṣi-bhāva*) towards Śiva who is the Transcendent 'I' in the self will be exercise of *kriyā*; and ecstatic love for the indwelling Person within its own personal being; growing from fulness to fulness, will be the reaction of *icchā*. This last element forms the counterpart of the affective factor in our experience which makes it *bhoga* with its hedonic tone.[10]

The difference between empirical experience (*bhoga*) and Unitive Experience (*śiva-bhoga*) is with regard to the content only.[11] Śiva is indeed, for such experience, as much the 'content' as any object is for empirical experience. And just as in self's empirical experience too, divine initiative of the experience takes the form of *experiencing with* the self, so that the self may have experience, in self's transcendent experience (*śuddha-bhoga*) too, Śiva 'experiences' Himself *with* self so that self may experience Him.[12] It is this feature of God 'experiencing' Himself with self in order to constitute the self's unhindered Experience, that gives this culminating phase of spiritual life its character as *eternal* Experience.

Śiva's primordial 'oneness' with self — self having its being 'under the shade of the Divine Feet'[13] is an eternally accomplished fact and is the precondition of experience. Union of man and God is possible only because of a prior unity of Being. God is a *unitas*, a unity that is already accomplished. But in order that it may be *seen* God also implies a *unio*, a union which must be entered into before realising God as unity that he is and always has been. Not only for a manifestation of self's knowledge but for its knowledge knowing the content, Spirit (Śiva) is the prius and the presupposition. Spirit is the Revelation that gives itself unto man as well as the receiving Revelation.[14] Spirit is at once the 'outer light' which reveals vision to the eye of the self, and also the Inner Light which pervades the visual content *with* the vision of the self.

Certain distinctions are, however, to be kept in mind in this account of *śiva-bhoga*. Experience of self, and Śiva's 'experience' inseparably coincident and even coalescent as they are, must still be distinguished in so far as self is not as such identical with Śiva though always 'one' with it.[15] This ontological distinction is implied in the very concept of God as one who knows *with* the knowing self. For, while the knowing self is 'bound' by its empirical knowledge, Spirit which too knows with it, is not however bound. This difference arises from the distinction between Spirit as *sat* and self as *sadasat*. Knowledge for self implies necessarily experience with its twin modes of affective identification and conation. Spirit, on the other hand, knows but does not 'experience' in the latter sense of the term. Experience involves novelty, to be acquainted with something newly and implies previous non-acquaintance. Therefore, for Spirit which is eternally omniscient (*anādi-bodha*) there can be no 'experience';[16] the distinctions of *jñāna*, *icchā* and *kriyā* in the context of spirit are symbolic. They do not answer to a mode of experiencing as it is in the case of self. In fact it is in relation to the latter that we make such distinctions in Spirit.

Śiva's experience which underlies self's experience of Śiva must therefore be distinguished from the latter. Śiva is Bliss itself while self 'enjoys' the Bliss of Śiva.[17] Śiva's eternal nature as the Transcendent 'I' is Bliss *per se*. Spirit as Consciousness is also equally Self-consciousness. It is both Being and Bliss (*ānanda-rūpa*).[18] Therefore, Śiva's experience of Himself which is the implication of *śiva-bhoga* refers only to the eternally realised nature of Śiva as Bliss. Experience in this context is a figurative expression of the essence of spirit. In the case of self, however, experience relates to experiencing. The continued presence of Śiva as the 'knower' in self's knowledge of Śiva accounts for the accomplished character of self's experience, without involving moments of previous unacquaintance. And yet there is an eternal novelty, a perpetual freshness about the experience.

The above is the significance of the paradox implied in the admission that in *mokṣa* (*śiva-bhoga*) there is not only the 'giver' and the 'enjoyer' of Bliss but also *mala* the 'occasioner' of Bliss experience.[19] The presence of all the three is implied in the Experience of Bliss. Presence is never inoperative presence of a witness, but *active* presence.[20] Therefore, just as Bliss experience involves the active function of giving or vouchsafing of Experience on the part of Śiva and the active function of enjoying on the part of self, similarly it involves an active function of *mala* also as in some mysterious sense contributing to, and even constituting the accomplishement of Bliss as an Experience.

But how are we to accept this ? Is not ignorance destroyed by knowledge ? Truth destroys error. It is true that *mala* is substantial; it is not mere 'anterior non-existence' but that on account of which there happens to be anterior 'non-existence' of the ever-existent *jñāna*. But substantial as it is,[21] it is nevertheless destroyed.[22] This is the presupposition of *mokṣa*. How can *mala's* eternity, and still worse, its eternal 'function' be conceived compatibly with the ideal of *mokṣa* ?

The solution of this problem is foreshadowed in the answer to the question concerning the dissolution or destruction of *pāśa*. In what sense is *mala* destroyed ? That it is surely destroyed in some sense is beyond question. Freedom is a fact. The text says : "Just as a cleansing seed precipitates the dust of the water, just as light 'dispels' darkness, just as an antidote counteracts the effect of poison, Freedom implies not the destruction as such of *mala* but only of its screening powers".[23]

The continuance of *mala* after a 'destruction' of *mala-śaktis* is sought to be explained in various ways consistently with self's achievement of Freedom from bondage. For example, it has been said that selves being many in number, when one self attains Freedom, *mala* would be less by one only of its infinite screening powers so that its indefinite continuance is conceivable. This solution is unsatisfactory. What happens when all the *paśus* attain freedom ? If *paśus* are infinite in number, not merely indefinitely large, how can there be a real subtraction from it from time to time ? The achievement of freedom even by one *paśu* would be figurative only.[24]

This criticism is not perhaps fair. Nothing is subtracted nor anything added. *Mokṣa* and *bhoga* stand only for differences of levels. They are continuous stages and do not involve coming in or going out. As Umāpati puts it, perhaps the only way of answering the question of the *number* of selves is: The number of the free and the number of unfree are equal to the number of the days past since creation and the days yet to come.[25]

The real crux by the difficulty in the problem is the meaning of 'destruction'. In what sense is 'destruction' admissible for *mala-śakti*? Can something that *is*, be destroyed ? If *śakti* is destroyed in some sense, how can *mala* escape destruction ? *Śakti* and *śaktimat* are one. If *guṇa* is destructible, *guṇin* cannot be indestructible.

A clue to the solution of this problem is provided in the manner in which self is conceived to be 'de-obstructed' of its primordial obstruction of *mala* in empirical life itself. *Kalā* and other tattvas effect a partial manifestation of self's knowledge by counteracting the obscuring *śakti* of *mala* to a limited extent.[26] An analogy will prove useful. Heat-sensation caused by the stimulus of fire may be counteracted by the presence of an obstructive agent so that heat-sensation is not felt despite the continued presence of the stimulus. Now, there can be antidotes, such as certain gems which are capable of neutralizing the effect of the obstructive agent of the heat-sensation, without tampering with the presence of that agent; in exactly the same manner the latter itself could do it in its turn in relation to the stimulus. *Mala*-obstruction is like the obstructive agent; it obscures the knowledge of self, making self's 'knowledge' unfelt in spite of the self remaining itself. Self is there, but its knowledge remains unmanifest. Now *kalā* and other tattvas act as counteracting antidotes to neutralize, partially of courses the obstructive function of *mala* so that self may be 'de-obscured' and consequently permitted to know and act. In this process of counteraction the obstructing agent whose function is neutralized does not cease to be intact.[27] It continues to exist as before. Only its obscurative function is 'neutralized', that is, rendered impotent; the sting of its 'power' is removed. No difference is introduced in the being of *mala*.

The continued existence of *mala* when its obscurative function is neutralized, is, in a sense, even demanded. The functions of obscuring and de-obscuring are *enduring* functions. It is not that when *kalā-tattva* reactivates the self by 'de-obscuring' the effects of *mala* that it ceases to function thereafter having done its job. Its function is continuous. This is evident negatively in empiritcal life itself; when it ceases to function there is no reactivation of consciousness; sleep follows; when it functions again there is awakening to consciousness. Does this not imply necessarily the continued presence of *mala* also ? *Kalā* etc. *continuously* prevail against the *continuous* presence of *mala* by counteracting its obscurative function.[28]

This may be illustrated also by the analogy of light.[29] Does light 'destroy' darkness ? Surely darkness is dispelled by light, and indeed is so only by light. But when darkness is thus dispelled or destroyed does it become non-existent ? Nothing that exists, merely ceases to exist. It may cease to exist in the same form and under the same condition. But surely it cannot decease. That darkness is not as such destroyed may be seen from the fact that there is reobscuration by darkness when light is withdrawn. Therefore, darkness is not wiped out of existence by light. Instead, we may say that it continues to 'exist' even in the presence of the light. Light does not dispel darkness at one stroke and then withdraw. It *continuously* prevails against the continuously existent darkness by continuously dispelling it.[30]

The concept of *abhibhava*—subdual or arrest, holds the solution for the problem.[31] Knowledge due to *kalā* etc. *subdues* the obstructive function of *mala* which *subdues* the manifestation of knowledge. Light *subdues* the veiling nature of darkness which *subdues* the manifestation of light. The eternity of *mala* too in *mokṣa* should be similarly understood. Bondage and Freedom are in fact continuous and the continuance of *mala* as the 'limiting' factor from the fringe, is identical in both. What after all is the difference between bondage and Freedom? Bondage is 'privation' of one's will, a thwarting of compliance with one's own unrestrained will. Freedom is a privation of this privation, a thwarting of the thwarting of will, or positively, it is Bliss Experience, a free unhampered exercise of will which is joy itself. Bliss, the distinguishing mark of *mokṣa* is Bliss-experience. Infinity in Infinite Experience is actual fulness of living. Plenitude is experience of plenitude. Bliss is *eternally* enjoyed by the privation of Bliss being under *eternal* subdual.

The 'existential' root of the doctrine of the 'eternity of the three in *mukti*' too is not to be forgotten. It is the mystical experience of Reality in terms of encounter as *eternally* new.[32] One always apprehends the ever-accomplished Absolute Reality, as it were in one's primary intuition. He sees it everytime with a 'new' eye. This ever-recurring quality of novelty or renewal is illustrated by the instance of the ever-fresh never-stale fragrance of flower.[33] In the idealised form of love the lover finds in the beloved always the 'new'. His love experience which is ineffable is describable only as a perpetual progress from climax to climax.[34] The mystic's revelation is the revelation of spiritual life and its moments. The life of spirit is not an object of knowledge but life. Life is open only to Life, and can only be known in the concrete experience of spirittual life. Example and not proof, living and not defining are adequate where existential realities are concerned.[35]

BOOK SIX

NOTES AND REFERENCES

BOOK I

CHAPTER ONE

INTRODUCTION TO THE PHILOSOPHY OF ŚAIVA SIDDHĀNTA

The Point of View :

1. Rene Guenon in his *Introduction to the Study of Hindu Doctrines* (trans. Richard C. Nicholson, Luzac, London, 1945) purporting to interpret the spirit of Hindu culture to the west views the issue of historicism not merely as a question of method separating the western approach to problems of existence and value from the Eastern, but one of principle. The crucial distinction is between the 'universal' and the 'individual' orders. 'The contingent, the accidental and the variable belong essentially to the individual domain'. They are what condition 'The individual aspect of things in its manifold modalities' with regard to the quest after the universal, however, 'all that can alter with time and place' is on the one hand the manner of expression 'admitting of indefinite variation' and on the other hand 'the degree of knowledge or ignorance of it to be found among men'. Metaphysical knowledge implies 'permanent and changeless certitude'. Likewise in his other book *Man and His Becoming, according to the Vedānta*, (Luzac, London, 1945) Guenon says that 'in the metaphysical order there can be no place at all for 'specialisation' (p. 3).

For a totally and typically different orientation, see Richard Niebuhr's *The Meaning of Revelation* (Macmillan, 1960). The historical relativist position is spiritedly advocated. There is no such thing as purely objective thought as the scholastics and men of enlightenment may have believed. There is only historically and socially conditioned thought. 'There is no neutral standpoint and no faithless situation from which approach can be made to that which is inseparable from faith' (pp. 37-38).

The two extreme attitudes, in a sense imposed by their respective material for study are not, however, unreconcilable. Knowledge and certitude need not mean uncommittedness and neutrality. Nor does committed attitude mean adoption of historical relativist position. In the existentialist, and not an idealistic, interpretation that is offered here a strictly historical approach with its overtones of scientific naturalism is avoided.

2. The pre-philosophical matrix from which Śaiva Siddhānta emerged historically speaking comprises of poetry, festivals, laws, art and folklore and above all the genius of Tamil language itself without which Śaiva Siddhānta as we know it could not have developed. For an illuminating treatment of Śaivism understood as an outlook on life rather than as a 'sectarian' religion or a 'scholastic' philosophy, from the angle of Tamil language, literature and folklore see Meenaksisundaram, T. P. *Śaivism and Tamil Literature*. Śaiva Siddhānta, Vol. 1, No. 1, 1966.
3. For a concept of structure of religion set forth in generic terms derived from an analysis of human existence see John E, Smith, *The Structure of Religion*, Religious Studies, Vol. 1, No. 1, (1966).
4. The only issue that has engaged the attention of writers of Indian philosophy from the standpoint of historical inter-connectedness is the relation of Buddhism and Vedānta : Symposium on Buddhism and Vedānta, Proceedings of Indian Philosophical Congress, Amalner, 1954; Buddhism and Vedanta, Seminar Proceedings, Centre of Advanced Study in Philosophy, Banaras Hindu University, 1969.
5. Śaiva Siddhānta as a theo-philosophy approximates to the Christian concept of 'theology' — logos about things divine, understood expressly as participation in and reflection upon religious faith even though 'faith' itself here would mean primarily some kind of intellectual or mystical intuition. See Infra. Note 11.
6. For an account of the antiquity of Śaiva Siddhānta see Narayana Iyer C. V. *Origin and Early History of Śaivism in South India*, University of Madras, 1936; Nilakanta Sastri K. A. *Development of Religion in South India*, Madras, 1963; Maraimalai adikal, *Tamilar matam*, 1939.
7. The value of an anthropological or archaeological approach to religion is not minimised. What is questioned is the implied antiquarianism and the attitude to the alleged facts that go to constitute the history as if they are objective, neutral events to be

recorded and repeated. Cults and beliefs relate to meanings which need to be interpreted rather than recorded.

8. 'yat prasiddham anatiprasiddhañca', Śrīkaṇṭha, SKB, Vol. 1, p. 20.

9. Meykandar, the Founder-preceptor of Śaiva-Siddhānta is described by one of his pupils as 'the one that could point at the false, make possible its removal and point at the true or the real of the nature of Intelligence and Bliss', *Unmai Vilakkam*, 1.

10. 'punthi vaṭṭattil pukundu nindrānaip poyyenbano ?' *Appar* 4 31, 4.

11. Faith is used here in the sense of *fides*. awareness of God, not the mere attitude of trust towards God (*fiducia*). It is also an attitude of will without abandoning its primarily cognitive character.

The Upaniṣadic expression of faith is 'bhāva-grāhyam' (Śvetāś. Up. 5, 14) 'the grasping faith, i.e. faith that grasps being, the faith of the Affirmation.

For a fuller analysis of the Śaiva concept of faith as 'bhāva' or 'mahābhāva', see *Vāyavīya saṁhitā* 3, 38 : It is what is attained after the arising of non-attachment to sense in consequence of the advent of knowledge, and what in its turn predisposes towards an intensification or deepening of knowledge in the form of meditation and the ensuing union or integration; integration with Grace, by which Liberation is achieved. Achieving of liberation is a goal in which bhāva cuts across all order and gradation in terms of birth, age, status and even *merit*. *ibid* 39-45.

The *locus classicus* of Śaiva Siddhānta from the point of view of faith understood in this precise sense is *Periya-Purāṇam* which represents, like Upaniṣads in relation to the Veda, the 'end' of the Śaiva canon. See *infra* sec. on 'Śaiva Siddhānta Literature'.

Mānikkavacagar's descriptive phrase of 'belonging to Thy feet' used appositionally to 'faith' brings out the sense of Integration with Grace : 'un tiruvadikkām pavame *aruḷu* kandāi' *Tiruvācakam* 5, 5. 'Pavam', which G. U. Pope rather inadequately translates as 'life' is really the bhāva, the true Occurrence (Cf. the suffix in '*sambhava*') or Happening of Divine Descent.

12. Otto, R., *The Idea of the Holy*, trans. John. W. Harvey 2nd ed. Oxford Univ. Press, New York, 1950.

13. *Tiruvācakam* 10, 13; 11, 18.

14. Cf. 'No other truth there is than *to be Thine*' *Ibid.* 5, 81. The locative ('unkanandri') brings out the sense of continuity. It is the same in sense as the dative of 'etamitaḥ pretyābhi sambhavitāsmi' of *Śrīkaṇṭha* BS 3, 2. 31 which is suggestive of ultimacy as the Good (prāpyatva).
15. Cf. 'ātmaiva hi ātmano bandhuḥ ātmaiva ripurātmanaḥ' *Bhagavad Gītā* VI, 5.
16. Śaiva Siddhānta is critical of all varieties and shades of monism (ekātma-vāda) including the monism of the word (śabda-brahma-vāda). Sarvātma śambhu considers BS itself 'extrinsic' to Śaivism because of its overtones of ekātma-vāda. (*Siddhānta Prakāśikā*, Śāstra prakaraṇam. See below sec. on 'Meaning of Śaiva Siddhānta'). The principle of identification of the Vedic texts, which Edgerton considers as the underlying motive of Vedic 'monism' (*The Beginnings of Indian Philosophy*, Allen and Unwin, 1965, London, p. 22) is elaborated into a sustained doctrine of homology between macro-and micro-cosm in the Śaivāgama and conclusions of a non-monistic kind but non-dualistic in import are drawn from it. Cf. the doctrine of aṣṭa mūrta of Iśāna appearing in its eightfold form of the *Vāyavīya saṁhitā* 2, 2, 12 ff. The doctrine is an attempt to preserve the transcendence of God without overlooking His non-dual relationship with the world of phenomena. For the metaphysical and theological distinction between this doctrine and the Vedāntic monism and pantheism Cf. Dasgupta, S. N. *History of Indian Philosophy*, Vol. 5 (Cambridge, 1954), p. 120.
17. *The Mystical Element of Religion*, Vol. 1. Preface to the Second Edn. p. xvi, London, 1908.
18. This is the upshot of Umāpati's nirākaraṇa of (1) aikyavāda monism, (2) nimitta-kāraṇa-pariṇāma-vāda monism. SN 6 and 12 sections. Cf. also the cynicism of his remarks in refuting the Śaiva-vāda parodying a line from *Tiruvācakam* (22, 7), *ibid* sec. 13 lines 55-62.
19. Indeed the Given is not given except in the intuition and communion of self with it. Though it does not exist otherwise for the self, this communion itself is not effected at the initiative of self. The Given in the communion has the initiative. The religious paradox is that God is at once the content of faith and also what alone can produce or cause such faith. (Cf. 'By His Grace alone,

bowing before His feet' of *Tiruvācakam* 1, line 18). He is at once the End and the Means. For the significance of the concept of God as bi-unal, absolute-concrete, being-will, male-female and illumination-vibrancy See *infra* Ch. 7, sec. on 'God as Divine Will'.

20. This is fully brought out by Meykandār in one udāharaṇa veṇbā SNP 6.2.5.
21. '*adu* ennum oṉru aṉru'. *ibid.* 6.2.5.
22. 'adu anri vērē aduvenrari aṟivum āngundē' *ibid.*
23. 'adu enṟaria irandallaṉ; angarivuḷ *nirral ariyum arivē Śivamumām*'. *ibid.*
24. In the terminology of Śaiva Siddhānta it is the interpenetration of self's icchā, jñāna and kriyā by the icchā, jñāna, kriyā of Śiva-śakti. See Ch. 14.

25 & 26. The homology between the orders of cosmos and the individual which is a recurrent theme of the Brāhmaṇas is systematised into a doctrine in the Śaivāgama literature especially in the yoga and vidyā pādas. This has led scholars like V. V. Ramaṇa Śāstri to trace the origin of Śaivāgama literature to the Brāhmaṇas. See Ramaṇan, V. V., A Synopsis of the Lectures on the Śaivāgamas; *Siddhānta Dīpikā*, Vol. VIII, No. 1., 1909.

27. An outline of Śaiva Siddhānta as a 'phenomenology' of spiritual life is given in chapters 14 and 15, *infra*. by way of expounding the doctrine in Daśa kāryāṇi.
28. For elucidation of the meaning of the concept of pramāṇa See Ch. 11. Sec. on 'the General conception of Pramāṇa.'
29. The classical style adopted in their bhāṣyas by the ācāryas and taken over from the Pūrva Mīmāṁsā, is that of devoting a whole section to a theme and arranging the sections systematically. The sections called adhikaraṇa are factorised in the following order; (1) theme (viṣaya, pratijñā), (2) questioning of the theme (saṁśaya), (3) the *prima-facie* view (pūrva-pakṣa), (4) answers to the objections of No. 3 (Siddhānta), (5) inter-connection of the sections (saṅgati); some scriptural texts are intended as the subject matter for the theme (viṣaya-vākya).

    Meykandar in the vārttika commentary written by himself on his own SNP, follows this classical style with suitable modifications. There are no viṣaya-vākyas of either the Veda or āgama even though Meykandar makes frequent references to them.

The structure of his vārttika is to give the upshot of the sūtra summarily in the beginning and subdivide it under several adhikaraṇas. The adhikaraṇa has three limbs (1) the proposition (merkol), (2) reason (etu), (3) illustration (udāharaṇa).

30. This answers objections often and rightly made that sometimes the positions of rival schools presented are not historically accurate.
31. As examples, may be cited the 3rd and 7th sūtra of SNP.
32. This acquires a special significance in Śaiva Siddhānta for which anubhava is an epistemological category. *infra* Ch. 11. sec. on the Nature of Knowledge.
33. For the overlap of the different parts, each of which reproduces the entire system, from its own angle, see the analyses and structure of Books 2-5.
34. The coherence of the scheme is not to be understood to mean a logical or rational coherence. The necessity and the universality of the scheme do not consist in that violation of it would mean violation of rationality. It would mean violation of meaning itself. From this point of view a title like 'A Logical Presentation of Śaiva Siddhānta' (which is incidentally the title of John Piet's clearly written book) is highly misleading.
35. For example, in analysing the concept of God, Śaiva Siddhānta is exercised in drawing a sharp line between God and the non-God. The latter comprising not only the non-intelligent world of matter but also the intelligent self, SNP. 1. Likewise in analysing self it fights against equating the self with not self of every kind on the one hand, and with God on the other SNP. 3.
36. The first edition of Paranjoti, V., *Śaiva Siddhānta*, Luzac & Co. 1938, is a modern classic on the subject treated as a half-way house to absolutisms of the variety of Bradley and Advaita Vedānta.
37. The modern classic of Śaiva Siddhānta treated as needing to be complemented by a thorough-going theism of the Christian type is Schomerus, H. W., *Der Śaiva-Siddhānta*, Leipzig, 1912.

Formative Concepts of Śaiva Siddhānta :

1. For a general understanding of the term 'Absolutism' used in the context of Indian philosophy see Murti T. R. V., *The Central Philosophy of Buddhism*, Allen and Unwin, 1955, pp. 320-322.

2. Śrīkumāra gives a plausible account of the 'why' of the three categories of Śaivism TP. p. 24 : If paśu, the one subject to saṁsāra, were not accepted, in the absence of a *raison d'etre* for either saṁsāra characterised by the polarities of good and the not-good, birth and mortality, pleasure and pain or, cessation of saṁsāra and its characteristics, the entire corpus of scripture-śruti, smṛti, itihāsa, purāṇa *etc.* bearing on the one theme of Bondage and Freedom, purporting to reveal what is otherwise unknown will become pointless. Likewise were pāśa the source of saṁsāra and stratified as three-fold were not accepted, there would also be in the absence of body *etc.* no question of movement to Heaven and Hell, births and deaths, the self being intrinsically devoid of motion. Pati too, the Lord of saṁsāra, were he not accepted, there could not arise the question of cosmic functions of Creation, Preservation and Destruction, subjection to the bonds of good and the not-good and liberation therefrom, individual selves being non-omniscient and devoid of freedom of taking on bodies.
3. Cf Umāpati quotes as sāmpradāyika vacanam :
'Pauṣkare ca mataṅge'ṣṭa sapta svāyaṁbhuve tathā
pañco'ktāḥ śrī parākhye ca mṛgendrādau trayassmṛtāh.' (PB. 13).
Sivagra yogin cites a similar verse. 'sapta svāyaṁbhuve proktāḥ ṣaṭ pauṣkaramataṅgayoḥ, śrīmatparākhye pañco'ktāḥ padārthāḥ raurave trayaḥ.' Sp. p. 28.
4. It is not surprising that historically speaking the Sāṅkhya proved a point of departure for pluralistic, realistic and empirical developments on the one side and absolutistic developments on the other. The inherent instability of sāṅkhya dualism stimulated evolution of religio-philosophical thought in different directions. See Murti, T. R. V. *The Central Philosophy of Buddhism*, Allen and Unwin, London, 1955. pp. 62-63. For Sāṅkhya as a logically possible basis for the Śaiva Siddhānta metaphysics of three reals, see Sūryanārāyaṇa Śāstrī S.S. *The Sāṅkhya Kārikā* Introduction, p. xiv.
5. Murti, *op. cit.* p. 65.
6. For the distinction between distinction and difference and for rejection of the identity of non-distinction and identity see *infra* Ch. 5, Sec. 'God as Non-dual'.
7. The Śaiva monist will however interpret the three-foldness of beings modes as not ultimate but as internal differentiations of one

plenary Reality, just as water is the only reality which because of adjuncts appear in manifold forms like waves and foams. Śrīkumāra *op. cit.* p. 24.

8. Pati, paśu and pāśa are sopādhika; Śivam, ātman and mala are nirupādhika. SSUM p. 17. For the co-incidence of the three in their 'essential' unity in mokṣa see *infra* Ch. 16.

9. Cf. Sūryanārayaṇa Śāstrī S. S., The *Śivādvaita of Śrīkaṇṭha*, University of Madras, 1930, p. 258.

10. For understanding of Advaita to mean the paradox of the other which yet is not unrelated *infra* Ch. 5, Sec. on 'God as Non-dual'.

11. Though limitation or finitude is conditional (sopādhika) and freedom from limitation or finitude is unconditional (nirupādhika) Śaiva Siddhānta admits the paradox that the limitation or unfreedom of the limited being is unconditionally conditional (anādi bandham) and likewise being is 'unconditionally' unconditional (anādi mukti) See Kiraṇa Āgama opening lines of Māyā paṭala of (vidyā pāda) 'viśuddhaḥ sphaṭikaḥ kasmāt kasmāt tāmraṁ sakālikam; yathāsmin na nimittaṁ hi tathā naiva śivātmanoḥ.' Also cited PB. p. 14; Also N 6 lines.

    Another way of stating it would be : God the creator does not *have* or *possess* freedom; he is free. Likewise the creaturely soul does not have defilement; he *is* defiled.

12. In the minimal sense on sheer 'existence' of the three ultimates of the system only pāśa is existent (sat); in the sense of existence which carries with it the sense of awareness of itself paśu is conscious existent (sat and cit); in the sense of existence understood as ecstatic existence pati alone is entitled to it (sat, cit and ānanda) MNP, p. 74. See also *infra* Note 18, Ch. 15.

13. In answer to the question 'patiśca kiṁ vidho jñeyassādhikārapade sthitaḥ, śivaśca kīdṛśaḥ prokto yo'dhikāra-vivarjitaḥ'? the reply that is given differentiating the two concepts are : 'patissadāśivo jñeyo mantrātmā mantra-vigrahaḥ, sarva-mantrādhipaścāsau sṛṣṭi-saṁhārakārakaḥ. patireva samākhyātassarva-kāmaphalapradaḥ, sthūlassūkṣmo vimisriśca evaṁ rūpastu saṁsmṛtaḥ. Śivo vastu paras tasmān mantrātīto nirañjanaḥ, nirāmayo nirādhāro varṇa-rūpa-vivarjitaḥ, sarvajñas-sarvagaś-śāntas-sarvātmā sarvato mukhaḥ, atīndriyo nirālambhas-susūkṣmaś-śāśvato dhruvaḥ, sa eva bhagavān vyāpī hyaprameyo hyanaupamaḥ, bahirantar-vibhāgena

tile tailamiva sthitaḥ' *Sarvajñottara Āgama,* padārtha vicāra prakaraṇam, verses 43-47.

14. Cf. Sambandar's mode of reference to the divine presence by the demonstrative pronoun 'ivan', he that is close by, in the very first decad sung by him at sirkali.

15. Meykandar makes frequent use of the name, meaning literally the seer of truth, in SNP implying that the real nature of asat cannot be known without a prior knowledge of sat (mey).
Cf. also Nirambavazakiar's invocation to Meykandar : He that could expound the unexcelled Inculcation of Śiva-jñāna by knowing the true path as 'this is the non-abiding, and this is the ever abiding', *Sethu Purānam,* Navalar ed. p. 3.

16. The profane as the 'impure' and the sacred as the pure and also the purificatory receive special attention in Śaiva Siddhānta. The concepts of mala and Śiva are understood as terms of contrast another name for Śivatva being nirmalatva: 'mummalam viṭṭu ninmalanōdu niṁdridal muttiyē', *Parapakkam* 32. Also, 'niarvadhika-paramānandamaya-niṣkalaṅka śivatva-prāptir hi muktiḥ. . . .nirasta-samasta-doṣa-kalaṅka-śaṅkā-niratiśaya-maṅgalāspadaṁ hi śivatvam.' Śrīkaṇṭha, BS 4, 1, 3. Cf. also the upaniṣadic expressions : Śukram (Kaṭha up 6, 17) viśuddham (Śvetāś Up 3, 1).
Śrīkaṇṭha also quotes as the Muṇḍaka text the following (which is not found in the existing texts of the Upaniṣad) : 'yaś-caṇḍālaś-śiva iti vācaṁ vadet tena saha saṁvada tena saha samvasa tena saha bhuñjīta' BS 4, 1, 16.

17. The 'enslaving' character of the world, the determinations of nature are the outcome of objectification due to mala. The 'world' too though a lamp unto one's way in a night of darkness ('vidivām aḷavam viḷakkanaya māyai' TAP 3, 10) is a species of darkness, the overwhelming gloom of the night renders as it were the feeble light also gloomy. SVP 70. See *infra* Ch. 14 Sec. on 'Preliminaries and Accessories to Knowledge'.

18. The contrast of sat and asat is expounded in the sixth sūtra of SNP and then in the seventh the contrast of 'sadasat' from either of them is set forth : the self that is neither of the two ('irandalā ānmā') SNP. 7.

19. Umāpati begins his SVP, with words which imply that acceptance of the three categories of pati, paśu and pāśa is not the point of

view of any particular metaphysique but the structural presupposition common alike to scriptures and also to arts and sciences, in short to any discipline that is addressed to man. *ibid*, 13, first line.

20. Aruṇaṇdi defines the distinctiveness of Śaiva Siddhānta in these words : 'pati paśu pāśam *terittup* pakar *Śivanaik kāttum* nanmārgam' *Supakkam*. 8, 22.

21. Śaiva Siddhānta implies this criticism in its refutation of the Dvaitin's interpretation of 'Advaita', *infra* Ch. 5, sec. 'God as Non-dual'. According to some modern interpreters of Dvaita-Vedānta Madhva is the most consistent monist in the above sense : 'Madhva in his exposition of Brahma-mīmāṁsā brought the *monism* expounded by the vedas and the upaniṣads to its culmination' Raghavendrachar H. N, *Madhva's Brahma-Mīmāṁsā*, 'The Cultural Heritage of India' Vol. III, p. 331, Calcutta, 1953. See also by the same author '*Dvaita Philosophy and its Place in the Vedānta*, Mysore University 1939, and '*Conception of Svatantra*', Mysore University, 1941.

Cf. also Berdyaev's penetrating analyses of Calvinism and Barthianism and of the belief that God is everything and man nothing, *Spirit and Reality* Geoffrey Bles, 1946, p. 133.

22. *infra* Ch. 5 sec. 'God as Non-dual'.

Meaning of Saiva Siddhanta

1. The groupings are made by the Śaivāgamas themselves : 'sthūlaṁ ca sūkṣmaṁ caiva samayam dvividham bhavet, sthūlaṁ *bāhyam* iti proktaṁ sūkṣmam *abhyantaraṁ* smṛtam' *Yogajam* cited NVM p. 2, Also 'lokāyato'tha bauddhaścārhato mīmāṁsā eva ca, māyāvādaḥ pāñcarātraṁ ṣaḍete samaya-*bahiḥ* śaivaṁ pāśupataṁ vāmaṁ bhairavaṁ tu mahāvṛtam kālāmukhamiti khyātam antaḥ samayāṣṭakaṁ' *Ajita* cited *ibid*, pp. 2, 3.
Meykandar makes a fling at the out-group in the opening colophon venba to SNP : 'keḷām *puran*'. Arunandi refers to the outer-fold and the inner-fold schools *Supakkam*, 8, 11 and Umāpati speaks of those belonging to the inner and those who are of the outer. SVP, 7. Māṇikkavācakar speaks of God who is 'far from those without', *Tiruvācakam* 1, line 8 : (purattār). See also *infra* Ch. 14, sec. 'Ātmaśuddhi and Śiva-darśana' Note 14.

2. 'Puraccamayat tavarkkirulāi akaccamayat toḷiyāy' SvP 7.

3. Popular expositions, catechism and polemical writings of Indian religious systems and specially Śaiva Siddhānta adopt a ladder-theory of refutation of rival systems. Ṣupakkam 8, 11 apparently presents a ladder-theory but in another verse (8, 13) the author reconciles it with the ideal of samanvaya which is the true spirit of the Veda and the Āgama.
4. *Infra* sec. 'Formative Factors of Śaiva Siddhānta'.
5. See *Indian Philosophical Annual* vol. 5, Centre of Advanced Study in Philosophy, University of Madras, 1971 for a seminar discussion on the meaning of Liberation as a philosophical ideal.
6. *Māpāḍiam* pp. 41,42.
7. *Supakkam* 8, 13 reflects in spirit if not in letter the samanvaya thus interpreted.
8. For a similar contemporary attempt vide Paul Weiss, *Modes of Being* (Southern Illinois Uni. Carbondala 1958) and for a criticism of its rationalistic overtones consult John Wild's review article, *Weiss's Four-Fold Universe*, Review of Metaphysics, 1958, xi, pp. 610-36.
9. 'siddhānta eva siddhāntaḥ pūrvapakṣas-tataḥ pare' RT, 11
10. Cf. the distinction between 'saṅkalpa' and 'sannidhi' : nā'cit cit sannidhau' SJB, 7 SB p 349; Also pp *ibid* pp 332-333 ; *infra* Ch. 6 sec. 'God as the inner illuminer of experience'.
11. This is what lends real edge to anti-theistic 'heresy' and provokes the wrath of the theist. Cf. 'Sudar vittuḷan engaḷ Sodi....iraiye vandu sārmingale' of Sambandar addressed, presumably, to the heretical Jainas and the Buddhists.
12. The sub-classification under the 'Inner' and 'Outer' groups of schools is traceable before *Māpāḍiam* which handles it with great analytic clarity and rigor to ÑVM : Velliambala vāṇar of Dharma puram in his commentaries gives a highly diffuse exposition of the overlapping group of 'Inner-outer' claiming to begin where *Parapakkam* left off : ÑVM p 2.
13. *Parapakkam* adds to the list the Ājīvaka-mata and gives an exposition and criticism of the school. The Ājīvakas are heretical even according to the 'heretic's' own standard. See *infra* Ch. 6 sec. 'The Moral argument for God *vis-a-vis* karma' for an analysis of rejection of freedom empirical and transcendental alike of the

Ājīvakas. Cf. also Basham A.L., *History and Doctrine of the Ājīvakas*, London 1951.

14. *Sūta Saṁhitā*
15. *infra* Ch. 11, sec. 'The self, its existence and states'.
16. An unchanging self is not incompatible with the notion of self's subjection to fluctuation of states of consciousness. Self is by definition what is impervious to change though in substance and function it is susceptible, to obstruction and de-obstruction. See reference *ante* note 15.
17. For a historical account of these encounters, see Mayilai Seeni Venkatasamy, 'Pauttamum tamizum' (1949 kazakam, Madras) 'Sainamum tamizum' (1951 kazakam, , Madras)
18. Tu (verse,10) and TKP (verses 16-21) interpret the theological significance of these encounters and the revelatory character of the miracles on the lives of the Śaiva Saints.
19. Cf. the refutation of the samudāyātma-vāda of self as skandhas in SNP 3.7
20. Cf. 'tattva-darśanam' *infra* Ch. 14
21. *Māpāḍiam* pp 52-63
22. For understanding of Brahminical darśana as patterned on substance in contradistinction to Buddhism, see Murti *op cit* pp 11-14
23. For the notion of self-understanding through self-transcendence see *infra* Ch. 14.
24. For the ontological distinction of self and Spirit *infra* Ch. 11 sec. 'The self, its existence and states'.
25. Cf. the distinction between the Sāṅkhya concept of puruṣa as cinmātra viśeṣa and the Śaiva Siddhānta concept of caitanya as dṛk kriyātmaka (MA 2,14,15)
26. See Jaimini's loka-vedādhikaraṇa-nyāya. The Mimāṁsā nyāyas are application of commonsense to understand Vedic passages.
27. *infra* Ch. 13 sec. 'Examination of Extrinsic Apprehension of Validity'
28. See SB pp 23, 24 for statement and refutation of the Mimāmsā position.
29. The *locus classicus* is Śaṅkara's commentary BS 1, 1. 1; also the opening words of his commentary on Gītā.
30. Cf. Śaṅkara's distinction of the Śruti texts into parā and aparā.
31. The vidyā-tattvas are accepted with modifications and under different labels by the generality of the Tantric Schools. For extracts

from relevant tantras of Vāma Bhairava and Dakṣiṇa relating to tattvas see ÑVM pp 20-46; 50-168

32. The limiting power of Reality is māyā and its kañcukas; pūrṇatva is not attained so long as māyā and her kañcukas operate. Such is the concept of bondage and liberation of this group.
33. ÑVM *op cit* p. 160-172.
34. The concept of 'special' revelation of Śaiva Siddhānta (see below) derives from the Tantra even though as originally conceived their validity was acknowledged in lieu of that of the Veda
35. Exclusion of Aikhya-vāda from the Śaiva group is due to its non-recognition of mala. ÑVM pp 295-299.
36. Cf. Bādarāyaṇa's rejection of their' 'exclusive' theism as unintelligible (asāmañjasya) BS 11, 2, 37.
37. Likewise the decisive question for Śaiva Siddhānta *vis-a-vis* Schools of Śaivism will be : what does Freedom as Experience mean ?
38. Maurice Cranston, *Freedom* (Longman's) London, 1954, p. 6.
39. *infra* Ch. 15 last part.
40. Albert Schweitzer, *Indian Thought and its Development*
41. For elucidation of the meaning of mala as entailing the distinction of Bondage and Liberation, see *infra* Ch. 10 sec. 'Arguments for Mala'
42. *Parapakkam* 8, 23.
43. For the role of mediation See *infra* Ch. 9, sec. 'The Concept of Bindu'.
44. TAP 6, 2; *Māpāḍiam* p. 45.
45. 'siddhānto vedasāratvāt' (suprabheda) 'vedasāram idaṁ tantram' (Makuṭa) 'vedāntārtham idaṁ jñānaṁ siddhāntam paramaṁ śubham' (Makuṭa) cited Sendilnadaier *Śivajñānabodha vacanālaṁkāra Dīpam* p. 17.
46. Sometimes a Śuddhaśaiva-vāda is added to the list and the first two, namely, pāṣāṇa-vāda and bheda-vāda, identified bringing the total again to six. *Māpāḍiam* p. 44 (Cf. also the Āgamic citation :
'śaiva-bhedaṁ pravakṣyāmi aikhya-pāṣāṇavādinau
bhedavādi samavādi saṅkrānti ca'vikāravān pariṇāmi ca śaivāśca
siddhānti paraīritaḥ' ÑVM p 19.
47. SN Pāṣāṇavādi saṅkalpam and Bhedavādi saṅkalpam; ÑVM pp 299-309.

48. For the Śivasamavāda concept of samatā as the sense of identity *Supakkam* 6, 9. Jñānaprakāsar's Com. Also *ibid* 8, 30 : 'karudaran *pōl* nirppan' and the same commentary.
49. *infra* Ch. 7, sec. 'God and Absolute'
50. SUP, 99.
51. For a refutation of the Sivādvaitin's implied concept of mergence See SN. nimitta-kāraṇa-pariṇāmavāda-nirākaraṇam, lines 122, 123 and śaiva-vādi-saṅkalpa-nirākaraṇam lines 55 to 65.
52. Velliyambala Tambiran (MNP p 169) distinguishes between the goals of abhivyakti of the generality of Karmāvaraṇa Siddhānta (aṣṭa prakaraṇa) and of ānanda of the Jñanāvaraṇa Siddhānta (Meykanda sāstra)

Formative Factors of Saiva Siddhanta

1. The scriptural sources of Śaiva Siddhānta unlike the case of Vedānta include many heterogenous items of not equal importance though ultimately held to be 'one ' in meaning. Scripture as Revelatory source is acknowledged in three levels general, special and personal, the second illumining the first and the third illumining both. They are therefore treated under the title of formative or operative factors.
2. *Republic* VI 508 b-509 b. *The Collected Dialogues of Plato* ed. Edith Hamilton and Huntington Cairns, Pantheon, 1961.
3. *Supakkam* 8, 9 and 10 Śiva Jñana yogin's com.
4. 'aṣṭādaśānāṁ vidyānāṁ bhinnavartmanām' PA 7, 61 ff.
5. *ibid* 7, 63 to 66
6. *Tirumandiram* states it both negatively and positively : 'Vedattai vitta aṛamillai vedattin, ōdattahum aṛamellam uḷa' verse 61.
7. Even for the Neo-Śaivite who tends to dispute the 'vedic' authority for Śaiva Siddhānta it is some Veda, may be different from the existing recensions, that is acclaimed as the normative. See Subramanya Pillai, K, *Tirunānmarai viḷakkam*' kazakam, 1931.
8. SNP 30.
9. The verdict of the generality of Hindu tradition about the Veda that it is one continuous, homogeneous tradition is striking. For a most sustained demonstration of this in relation to Śaivism, Cf. Haradatta's *Śruti Sūkti Mālā*, Kazakam, Madras 1925 and Appaya's *Śiva Tattva Viveka*, Harihara Sastri, 1895

10. The Veda as a single body of doctrine presents difficulties for the exegete. Śaiva Siddhānta tends not to see in it a succession of adoration of Gods all expressive of the same fundamental intuition of one God in different ways. Rather we should see them as a present attempt to clarify what is seen at first only obscurely and hesitatingly. So much so the Śaivite would insist that what is central or crucial in it adumbrated in various ways is indispensable to a correct understanding of the other 'non-central' 'non--crucial' passages, rather than *vice versa.* Thus the task of exegesis that becomes a necessary part of self-understanding of Upaniṣads is demanded for the understanding of Vedas themselves.
11. *Appar* 5, 100, 1, 5, 7, 8.
12. *Sambandar* 3, 108, 7. Also Cf. the descriptive expression used for the Veda by the Śaiva hymnists in general and before them by *Tirukkural* and the generality of classical Tamil literary tradition, namely, *marai.* See *infra* Ch. 7 sec. on 'God and Absolute' Note no. 8.
13. *Vājasaneyī Saṁhitā* XVI; *Taittrīya Saṁhitā* IV, 4
14, 15, 16. *Māpāḍiam* p. 367.
17. Cf. *Sūta Saṁhitā* 4 22.
18. *Māpāḍiam* 370.
19. Cf. 'sūcanāt sūtram'. Appaya's remark 'na sūtrāṇām arthāntaramapi bhavadvaryam uchitam' *Śiva Tattva Viveka op. cit.*, p. 37.
20. The Śaivāgama contains oblique criticisms of the sūtra literature of Brahminical Hinduism, namely, those of Kaṇāda, Kapila, Patañjali, Jaimini and even Bādarāyaṇa, and places them on grounds of common 'exotericism' on par with the heterodox systems classing them together under the label of 'external' (bāhya)
21. 'sugato yadi sarvajñaḥ kapilo ne' ti kā pramā
athobhāvapi sarvajñau matibhedas-tayoḥ katham'
is an oft-quoted verse in the prakaraṇa texts relating to the Śaivāgama.
22. Śaiva Siddhānta as the name of the Śaivāgama is naturally the earlier and more popular use of it. The Trika tradition refers to the body of twenty-eight Śaivāgamas as Śaiva Siddhānta and the pursuants of the tradition as Saiddhāntikas. *Tantrāloka* Vol 1, 37-48 commentary (Kasmir Granthāvali, 1939)

23. Cf. BS 11, 3, 1.
24. SVP 51 and 99 for the equation of general-specific with bondage-liberation.
25. Cf. the connotation of the name Meykandār, the truth-seer. Meykandar is perhaps thus named because of his frequent use of this expression in his vārttika : 3, 6, 1; 6, 1, 1; 6, 2, 1; 6, 2, 2,; 8, 3, 1; 10, 2, 4. Apparently, the use of the expression 'true' to refer to the Āgama in contra-distinction to the Veda amounts to a qualified acceptance of Vedic authority accepting it only to the extent that it does not conflict with the Āgama : The *Kāmika* says, 'vaidikaṁ sarva-saṅgrāhyaṁ śaiva-vākyāvirodhi' (cited MNP p 11). But underlying this condition is this faith that the Veda intrinsically can never be in conflict with the Āgama, no more than it is in conflict with itself.
26. On the Advaitin's view this amounts to a distinction between Reality and Appearance. Appearance is not nothing but what depends on the Real even for its appearance. But if it depends on the Real even for its appearance its dependence is more primary and its character as bare appearence is only an interpretation of its dependence.
27. *Tirumandiram* 2397
28, 29. 'vayaṃ tu vedaśivāgamayor bhedaṁ na paśyāmaḥ. vede'pi śivāgama iti vyavahāro yuktaḥ, tasya tatkartṛkatvāt. ataḥ śivāgamo dvividhaḥ traivarṇakaviṣayas-*sarvaviṣayaś*ce'ti.' SKB. 2.2.38. Śrīkaṇṭha does not say that the Veda is meant for the three castes and Āgama for the fourth. The distinction made in connection with the question of competence is between the initiate and the non-initiate—the śuddha and the aśuddha from *all the four classes* : brāhmaṇaḥ kṣatriyo vaiśyaḥ śudraś-śūddha-kulodbhavaḥ, ācāryāste hi vijneyā nānyeṣāntu kadācana', *Suprabheda Āgama* cited MNP p. 11. PB cites the citation from SKB and interprets it to mean 'vedastvapakvādihikāri-viṣayaḥ śaivāgamastu pakvādhikāri-viṣaya iti, p. 10.
30. The transcendence of social morality in a theonomous way of life is the theme of *Periyapurāṇam*. See below.
31. 'saṁskṛtaiḥ prākṛtair-vākyair-yaś-ca śiṣyānurūpataḥ, deśa-bhāṣādyupāyaiśca bodhayet sa guruḥ smṛtaḥ.' This is the admission of Āgama itself (*Śiva-dharmottara*, cited in NVM p. 31). Tirumular's

Tirumandiram is itself Śaivāgama : 'sindaicheyd*agamam* seppalu-trēnē'. v. 105.

32. Recent focus of interest in the dimension of 'thou' is a reaction or counterpoise to concentration on the world of 'it'—the *Eswelt* and the fatal technocratic developments which are its consequences. But in the case of the Śaiva canons (Tirumurais) the *zeitgeist* which occasioned the rise of a theology of 'thou' as in Tirumurai and Divyaprabandha is not science or technology and an antecedent pre-occupation with it but a spirituality of 'It'.

33. The intuition is of the Thou in vivid concrete imagery. Though the philosophy of Tirumurai is the same as that of the Śaivāgama, the Āgama account is abstract enunciation in the third person about the divine, on the 'thither' side of the confrontation of 'I' and 'thou'. Compare it with the 'pemmān *ivananre*' of *Sambandar* or with 'attā unakkalāi ini allīn inalāme' of *Sundarar.*

34. It is not a historical accident that all religious-theological developments on the Hindu scene claim support from the Upaniṣads. The philosophical ontology of Brahman-ātman is the basis for the personalistic theism of Śaivism and Vaiṣṇavism alike.

35. Cf. also *Tiruvācakam* kīrti, lines 24-26.

36. Cf. 'Revelation, whether it is original or dependent, has revelatory power only for those who participate in it, who enter into the revelatory correlation', Tillich, *Systematic Theology*, vol 1, p. 127 Harper, 1967.

BOOK II.

CHAPTER TWO

THE EXISTENCE OF GOD

God as the Ground of Cosmic Dissolution

1. The significant expressions selectively used by Meykandār, taking them from Tirumurai's to denote Destroyer , world-ground in the sense of the world's 'whither', are : 1. odungi, literally, the Resolving, 2. andam, lit. the End SNP 1. Aruṇandi, in the same strain uses īrumakē, lit. One that also is the End. *Supakkam* 1-1. These verbal nouns, it may be noted are active in form but causative in meaning and the ambiguity is systematically maintained implying the immanence of the cause (in the sense of *resolvum, retractum*) in that which is 'effected' by it. More truly immanent than in the case of material cause in relation to its effect see *infra* note, 7.
2. The concept of Destroyer imports a novel way of combining the two notions of nimitta-kāraṇatva and upādāna-kāraṇatva. *infra* Ch. IV
3. 'pūrvaṁ saṁhāraḥ paścāt sṛṣṭiḥ' SB p. 21. The paradox expresses the temporal aspect of the asymmetry between the dual and complementary notions of creation and de-creation
4. This is the negative overtone of satkārya-vāda as interpreted in Śaiva Siddhānta : 'na hyasaṁhṛtasyā'nāhita-vāsanasya sṛṣṭis-sambhavati, asat-kārya-niṣedhāt.' *ibid.* p. 21.
5. SB gives this interesting exception to the rule: 'asṛṣṭasyā'pi prāgabhāva - paramāṇusyāmikā - māyā - mala - sambandhādes - saṁhārāt.' p.21. The citation of prāgabhāva as an instance of *asṛṣṭipūrvakasaṁhāra* is intelligible because prāgabhāva is not absence but is something positive, another name for prāgavasthā, as it is according to the Later Nyāya school (e. g. Raghunātha Śiromaṇi). For the same reason dhvaṁsābhāva is not a counter-example as one that has a beginning but no end. Dhvaṁsābhāva being itself negative admits of no further negation. There is no dhvaṁsa for dhvaṁsa. See also SB. p. 310. Dissolution, it may be noted, symbolises

self-revelation which is another name for freeing process, while creation-conservation typifies the obverse function of self-concealment. For interpreting saṁhāra in the sense of Revelatory Grace, *Tirumandiram* verses 425 to 428.

6. *Supakkam* 50.
7. This shows that the God of Dissolution is not the God of Deism, being ever at work, conditioning negatively every moment of created existence. The gods of creation and preservation stand contrasted in this respect from Hara. See below.
8. *'ādiyāy naḍuvumāhi aḷavilā aḷavumāhi'—Periyapurāṇam* I.1.The italicised words, literally 'the end without the end' bring out this sense.
9. The procedure which SÑP adopts is (i) to extol the comparative supremacy of the function of dissolution to creation ('oḍungi... uḷadām'), and (ii) to extol the ultimacy of the Destroyer ('andam ādi) where the epithet of Destroyer is expressly understood, more as explanatory of the intrinsic nature (ayoga-vyavaccheda) than as exclusive (anya-vyavaccheda).

   Even the gods of creation and preservation are particular beings like man, having limited freedom to order their own being and the being of nature. They are constituted guardians of Being, having only a steward-like status. Mythological motifs of gods choosing to be for themselves, forgetting their dependent status and ceasing to be manifestations of Being, which it was for them to express, are recurrent in the Śaiva hymns, and is the solution to the riddle of the gods' quest for the God above gods. See *Tiruvācakam*, tiruvundiār verses.
10. *'azibavai seyal'* Ñ 57, last line. The terminator is the Immortal and the Imperishable amṛtākṣaraṁ haraḥ. *Śvetāś. Up.* I. 10. *tirumandiram* uses the names 'irappīli' (25) 'ulappīli' (3) meaning the non-ending, as significant proper names of God.
11. See *infra* Ch. Five. The *Ṛg—Veda* (X.129.6, 7) asks : who really knows ? Who in this world may declare it ? Whence was this creation, whence was it engendered ? 'arvāg devā asya visarjanenā'thā ko veda yata ābabhūva' ? If nothing was before creation, not even the gods associated with cosmic functions it is implied that even gods were among the dissolved.
12. 'Just as a pot dissolves into clay, a wave into water or a bracelet into gold, even so the universe resolves into me. Adoration to

myself ! for when the world from its highest god to its least stem of grass dissolves, the *destruction is not mine*'. *Aṣṭavāhika-Saṁhitā*, cited in Zimmer's *Philosophies of India* (Bollingen Series), p. 11.

Does not the Destroyer also destroy Himself ? There will be kartṛ-karma-virodha. Fire burns only what is not itself. All transitive action involves elements that necessarily are distinct *inter se*.

13. *Śvetāś. Up.* IV.18. See also *Ṛg-Veda* III.62.10.
14. SKB 1.2.9.
15. 'bhuvana-śabdasya kāryamātra-paratvam upapādya samarthanīyam.' SMD 1, 2, 9 Vol. 1, p. 330.

The Purāṇas describe that Primeval Darkness in vivid terms : 'tadā jagad idaṁ sarvaṁ nirūpan niṣkriyaṁ bhṛśam, nā' horātro na vā bhānuś-candro vahnis-surā na ca, tamobhūtaṁ jaḍākāraṁ bhīṣaṇaṁ kevalaṁ dvijāh.' *Śaṅkara-Saṁhitā*, cited in Sendinatha Iyer's Tamil Trans. SKB p. 239. foot-note.

16. 'samasta-sākṣiṁ *tamasaḥ parastāt*' (*Kaivalya Up.*7), cited SKB I.4.28. The italicised term is interpreted to mean 'viśvottirṇatvam (ṢKB), sarva-prapañca-śeṣitvam and mokṣopāya-sākṣāt-karaṇīyatvam' (SMD Vol. I, p. 571).
17. 'brahmaiva sarvasaṁhartṛtvena śrūyate. kutaḥ ? carācaragrahaṇāt yad uktaṁ nikhila-carācara-prapañca-bhoktṛtvam ayuktam iti *tad eva brahmatve lakṣaṇam.*' SKB I.2.9.

Sūta Saṁhitā IV, 28, 32f endorses the view that liṅga applies uniquely to Maheśvara even on etymological grounds : liṅga is that wherein all gods resolve. 'ālayaḥ sarva-devānāṁ layanād liṅgam uchyate'. Everything that is other than Śiva (a-śiva) resolves in Śiva and therefore the unresolved Residuum alone is appropriately liṅga by its very nature, *ibid* IV, 28, 25. Liṅga consequently being the omega is also the alpha of all that there is of the formed as well as of the formless (*Periyapurāṇam*, sākhyanāyanar 8), a point that is signified iconographically by the amorphous shape of the liṅga bespeaking of its indifference to form and formlessness.

18. BS I.2.9.
19. *Kaṭha Up.* I.2.25. 'brahma-kṣatrayor odana-śabdasya gauṇa-vṛttau bhojyatva-rūpaḥ.' SMD. Vol. I. p. 336.

'odanaṃ saṁhāraḥ......mṛtyor upasecana-rūpaṇa-balāt pratīya-mānasya mṛtyunā saha tatsaṁsṛṣṭa-saṁhārasya pralaya eva bhāvāt pralaye sarvasya carācarasya saṁhāraprasiddheḥ.' SMD Vol. I, p. 336.

20. *Atharvaśiropaniṣad*, cited SKB *op. cit.* Commenting on the meaning of Mahāgrāsa, a Śaiva-Purāṇa says :
'sarvagrāso mahādevas-sarvāṇḍānyakhilaṁ jagat
sarvān jīvān vīkṣaṇena hāsena ca parān krudhā
aṭṭahāsena nṛtyena lalāṭa-nayanāgninā
huṁkāreṇa ca hastena pādāghātena līlayā
nānā-rudragaṇais sākaṁ samhāraṁ yaṁ cakāra saḥ
sa mahāpralayo nāma sarveṣān-nāśakārakaḥ.' *Śaṅkara-Saṁhitā* 21, 2-5; cited Sendenatha Iyer *op. cit.* pp. 238-39.

21. 'yā imā viśvā bhuvanāni *juhvat*.' *Ṛg Veda* 8.3.16. cited SKB *op. cit.*

22. *Atharvaśiropaniṣad*, 55.

The unity and immortality of the Lord are features that distinguish Him from the multiplicity and mortal nature of creator-gods : 'nūrukodi piramarkaḷ nunginār......irilādavan īśan *oruvane*.' Appar

23. 'prabhur haraḥ' SJB. 1, 'prabhuḥ prabhavana-śīlaḥ jagatkartā maheśaḥ' SB p. 20.

24. The typically Śaiva way of discoursing about God is not as 'the Alpha and the Omega' (*Revelation* 21 : 6) but rather as the Omega and the Alpha.
'andam ādi' SJB 1. Meykandār's 'andam ādi' which inverts the sequence of beginning and end repeats the sound and sense of a score of such expressions from *Tevāram* :
'*andamāy* ulahādiyu māyinān' 3.2.1
'*īrum* naḍuvum mudalumāvān' 6.17.1
'*piṇḍrānum* muṇḍranum ānām' 6.11.2
'mūvāde yāvarkkum mūttaṇtaṇṇai *mudiyāde* mudal naḍuvum muḍi vānānai.' 6.74.3.
'*muṇṇavaṇ* kāṇ piṇṇavaṇ kāṇ' 6.48.8.
'*mūtt* iḷaiyai' 254.8. Also
'pinmunnāki nindrān', *Tirumandiram*, 28.

25. Śivāgra yogin gives very suggestive parallels: one that performs agniṣṭoma and several other sacrifices is still celebrated after the performance of one particular yāga, viz. satra-yāga which among the sacrifices that he has performed ranks highest; he is celebrated

as satrayāgī. A hamlet inhabited by learned men is denoted pre-eminently as the hamlet of the learned (dīkṣita-grāma). SB p. 21

26. That this is the considered view of Śruti, Smṛti, Purāṇa, Itihāsa as well as of the Śaivāgamas is ably discussed and demonstrated by Appaya in STV, 13 Com.; also CVTS 1, 30.

27. SJS and SVP give plausible reasons : In so far as these deities may not be conceived to exist apart from their functions, if Creator and Conserver were to outlive universal Dissolution it will follow that nothing is really destroyed when creation and conservation persist. Nor can some be exempt from the sweep of *universal* Dissolution. It thus follows that the only enduring ground of the resolved world is the Destroyer who it is that can create it again and conserve. *Supakkam* 1.35; SVP. 17.

28. 'hara-śabdena yogarūḍhyā saṁhartā Śiva ucyate,' SB p. 20.

29. *Māpāḍiam* p. 67; SMD Vol. I, p. 335.

30. *Supakkam* 1.54. There are in other words, two concepts of 'end of things' : the natural end the one that forms an integral part of a cycle standing at the polar opposite of 'beginning'; and also an 'end' that stands outside the cycle alike transcending beginning and end and marking the 'end' of the cycle itself and therefore standing at the ground of the possibility of the cycle's renewal. [Cf. Umāpati's anthropomorphic image of Destroyer-God standing like a colossus and destroying everything that is, SVP. 16.] The two concepts may be distinguished as the vertical and horizontal notions of *eschaton*. The vertical is often, however, used as a symbol for the horizontal. The natural 'end' which comes as the extreme limit of separation from the beginning like sleep in relation to wakefulness is a cosmogonic notion, while the 'end' which lies beyond the end as well as the beginning of things is soteriological in significance.

31. In the Vedas the distinction is only implicit and again not unequivocal. Śrīkaṇṭha, however, suggests that the purport of the atrādhikaraṇa (BS 1.2, 41-42) is to distinguish Śiva as mahā-saṁhāra-rudra from saṁhāra-kalā-rudra (even as Śiva has been distinguished from Brahmā the creator in I.1.17-20 and from Viṣṇu, the conserver in I.2.9-10). SMD ably supports this thesis by showing that Brāhmaṇa, Kṣatra and Mṛtyu whom the supreme eats or consumes typify the realm of created existence in its entirety, pure,

mixed and the impure and that their Consumer thus stands distinguished from guṇi-rudra, the consumer of only the impure realm. Vol. I, pp. 335-37.

32. *Māpādiam* p. 67 ff. The passage under reference concurs with Appaya's remarks in SMD *op. cit.*

While Creator (Brahmā) and Conserver (Viṣṇu) are sakalās, Destroyer (Śrīkaṇṭha-rudra) belongs to the class of pralayākalā souls, the relative supremacy of limited dissolution over limited creation and limited conservation is expressed in terms of freedom from the bond of Māyā. Śrīkaṇṭha-rudra only typifies Mahārudra; to him are attributed the names, forms and even the functions of Pati eulogistically because of his closeness in the hierarchy of Paśus to Pati. His is also the office of revelation of knowledge; all revelations are traced to his agency. *Māpāḍiam* p. 68; SNP 96, 97.

33. The three-fold avasthās of laya, bhoga and adhikāra which God as the Lord of the cosmic functions freely assumes are explained in Chapter 8. They are the archetypes of Creation, Conservation and Dissolution (in the reverse order).

34. *Māpāḍiam op. cit.* ff.

35. *Tiruvācakam* 3 lines 10, 11.

36. *Tiruvācakam* refers to the 'sin' of confusing Śiva with a deity that rules the heavens and the earth and singles out those who describe themselves 'gods moving on earth' as the worst sinners in this respect. *Tiruccadukam* verse 4. The fling here is at brahminical polytheism which is oblivious to the reality of God above gods *concealed* in the Vedas.

37. This is one of the persistent themes of the Śaiva hymns. The world is the work of powers which are mediately descended from the One but do not know it, and indeed even obstruct the knowledge of it in the world over which they rule. Cf. the *Padmapurāṇa* text in which Viṣṇu says :

'namaste devadeveśa namaste śāsvatāvyaya
na *jāne'haṁ* bhavantaṁ ca *tvaṁ tvāṁ* vedya namo namaḥ
śaraṇaṁ tvāṁ prapanno' smi cakṣurme dīyatāṁ prabho
praṇāmaṁ kevalaṁ kartuṁ śaktosmi *nahi veditum*'
cited in commentary SSM, 14.

Sambandar refers to the episode of the creator and the conserver gods not knowing the 'below' and the 'beyond' of Śiva imaged as an unending stretch of a column of fire in the 9th verse of his decads. Appar devotes an entire decad (captioned liṅga-purāṇa) to this theme. Tirumular had an entire section called significantly 'the quest for the Feet and the Crown' (adi mudi tedal') in which he explains the symbolism of head or crown (=knowledge) and feet (=grace) *Tirumandiram*, 2425.

The philosophical motif of liṅgodbhavamūrti is that gods being mediately descended from the God above them cannot comprehend his height or even his tip.

38. The profoundly significant Tamil word for God 'Kadavuḷ' from the root kada to transcend. The diverse modes of transcendence and their paradoxical implications of intimate immanence in the all which is transcended are summed up in *Tirumandiram* 14 which is also elucidation of the meaning of 'Kadavuḷ'.

39. In this sense Śiva is identified with the trinity of Gods. *Cf.*
'padaittaḷittazippa mummūrtihaḷāyinai'
'mūvar kōnāi niṇḍṟe mudalvan' (*Tiruvācakam*)
'mūvar uruthanda mūla mudaṟkaruvai' cited in *Māpāḍiam op. cit.*

Creation and Dissolution are conceived to succeed each other in apparent endlessness. At the end of each cycle the created world returns to Śiva and re-emerges from Śiva at the beginning of the next cycle. In between Great Creations (mahā-sṛṣṭi) and Great Dissolutions (mahā-saṁhāra) are Intermediary (avāntara) creations and dissolutions.

The Ṛg-Veda refers to the revolving of the five-spoked wheels in which all beings abide :

'pañcāre cakre parivarttamāne tasmin na tasthur-bhuvanāni viśvā' (I.164.13). The five 'spokes' (ara), if we look at them through the eyes of Purāṇa (*Kailāsa-Saṁhitā*, 10.77) refer to the five 'limbs' of sṛṣṭi, sthiti, saṁhāra, tirobhāva and anugraha which succeed each other cyclically and five such 'cycles' also going by the same names revolving concentrically with greater and greater expansion, each encompassing the preceding. The outermost 'cycle' refers to *mahā-sṛṣṭi* and *mahā-pralaya* and the others to intermediary ones.

According to the same Purāṇa, the sṛṣṭi-cakra refers to the five-fold functions of sṛṣṭi etc. of the realms of nivṛtti-kalā, presided over by Brahmā the Creator and his four satellites (vyūha) who do the remaining functions; sthiti-cakra refers to sṛṣṭi etc. of the realms of pratiṣṭhā-kalā presided over by Viṣṇu the Preserver and his four satellites who do the four associated functions within that sphere; saṁhāra-cakra refers to sṛṣṭi etc. of the realms of vidyā-kalā presided over by Rudra the Destroyer and his four satellites who do the functions other than destruction within their orbit; tirodhāna-cakra refers to sṛṣṭi etc. of the realms of śānti-kalā presided over by Maheśvara, the Concealer, and his four satellites who perform the four other functions; and lastly, anugraha-cakra refers to the sṛṣṭi etc. of the realms of śāntyatīta-kalā presided over by Sadāśiva, the Revealer whose satellites are Maheśvara, Rudra, Viṣṇu and Brahmā, the very presiding deities of the other cakras who perform the accessory functions of sṛṣṭi, sthiti, saṁhāra and tirobhāva in that sphere. The upshot of this hierarchical conception is that Sadāśiva or Śiva is alone the Mahārudra who destroys during 'great Dissolution' the entire created realm from those of the nivṛtti kalā to śāntyatīta-kalā and that therefore he alone is its Creator too in a fundamental sense.

Kailāsa-Saṁhitā 10, 26-27 citations given in Sendinatha Iyer's *Vacanālaṅkāra-Dīpam* (pp. 3-6).

That Sadāśiva is the Lord (pati) that performs creation as well as Dissolution may be seen in the following :

'*patiḥ sadāśivo* jñeyo mantrātmā mantravigraaḥ
sarva-mantrādhipaś-cāsau sṛṣṭi-saṁhāra-kārakaḥ.'
—*Sarvajñānottara Āgama*, cited *ibid.* p. 8.

40. 'trimūrtīnāṁ kāraṇātmakaṁ sthūla-sūkṣma-śūnya-rūpa-rahitaṁ cidānandaikarūpam.' SP. p. 28 f.

41. 'na sthūla-sūkṣmo na ca śūnya-rūpo jñānaika-rūpo jagadeka-bandhuḥ'. *Devīkālottara Āgama*, cited *ibid.*

42. 'na ca nāmāni rūpāṇi śivasya paramātmanaḥ.'—*Sūta-Saṁhitā* cited *ibid.*

43. 'tathā pi māyayā tasya nāma-rūpe prakalpite
śivo rudro mahādevaḥ śaṅkaro brahma tatparam
viṣṇu-nārāyaṇādīni nāmāni parameśvare
kathañcid yoga-vṛttyā tu vartante na tu mukhyayā'.
Sūta-Samhitā, Yajña-vaibhava-khaṇḍa 27, 28 to 30 cited *Ibid* p. 29; ÑVM p. 694. Also 'eṇṇāyiramkodi perār pōlum', *Appar* 6, 21, 8.

44. *Vāyavīya-Saṁhitā* (Pūrva 32, 23-24) says that 'Viṣṇu' is among the names essentially denotive of Śiva : Śivo maheśvaraś-caiva rudro viṣṇuḥ pitāmahaḥ, saṁsāra-vaidyas-sarvajñaḥ paramātmeti mukhyataḥ, nāmāṣṭakam idaṁ mukhyaṁ śivasya pratipādakam' 'Viṣṇu' is used as connotive of Śiva also : 'śiva-tattvādi bhūmyantaṁ śarīrādi ghaṭādi ca vyāpnoditi śivas-tato viṣṇurudāhṛtaḥ' *ibid.*

45. eko hi nāmagair-bhedais-sthitaḥ sa parameśvaraḥ
bṛhatvād bṛṁhaṇatvāc ca brahmaiva śivayogataḥ
viṣṇuḥ prabhavaśīlatvāt prabhavo jagatāṁ prabhuḥ
rujaṁ drāvayate yasmāt tena rudro rujaḥ kṣayāt.'
Parākhya-Āgama, cited SP p. 29. The term 'prabhu' of SJB is interpreted in this citation.

46. The notion of Destroyer as suggestive of the incommensurability of finite things and God is distinctive of Śaivism and marks the point of distinction from Vaiṣṇava pantheism. To stress the contrast of God and the world Śaiva Siddhānta would describe God as nimitta-kārana. See *infra* Ch. 3. Cf. the viśiṣṭādvaita doctrine that world qualifies and is a constituent of the very essence of God—the divine actuality.

    Cf. Rāmānuja's interpretation of co-ordination of Vedic enunciations as expressive of the relation of mode in which one thing stands to another. *Srībhāṣyam* 1, 1, 1 p. 138. Śaiva Siddhānta understanding of non-duality includes and over-extends in meaning the relation of prakāra-prakārya.

47. For a discussion of the incomprehensibility (acintyatva) of God as Being see *infra* Ch. 7 sec. on 'God as Being'.

48. SÑP. 7. Meykandār says that God does not 'know' the world as the latter is of the nature of non-being, in the presence of God who is Being. Meykandār brings out more clearly the contrast of Being and non-being than SJB 7 : na acit citsannidhau.

    The term Śūnya, however does not mean non-being. Māpāḍiam p. 403 : The particular is non-est in the sense that it is non-persistent *qua* particular before the universal.

49. For interpretation of Dissolution as a cosmic process in relation to the dictum of SJB 'nācit citsannidhau' see upodghāta in Tamil of PB p. 10.

50. 'Thou art not aught in the world : nought is there save Thee' *Tiruvācakam* 22.7.
51. *infra* Ch. 7 'God and Absolute'.
52. Cf. texts like 'sarvaṁ khalvidaṁ brahma' with 'sarvo hyeṣo rudraḥ' and 'ekam evā' dvitīyaṁ brahma', with 'eka eva rudro na dvitīyāya tasthe' of the Śaivopaniṣads. Brahman (Being) and Rudra (Destroyer) are one.
53. This makes God different in principle from what is ordinarily meant by a cause. From a cause one can derive its consequences but from God conceived as Destroyer nothing can be derived. The notion of Destroyer affirms and denies the applicability of the concept of cause.
54. The notion of 'kāla-kāla', destroyer of time, which is a favourite phrase and symbol with the Śaiva hymnists may be contrasted with kāla-kāra (Śvetāś. *Up*. VI-2, 16) creator of time (kālasyāpi kartā). Kāla-kāla means kālasya nīyantā, upahartā. Kālaḥ sarva-vinaśakārī tasyāpi vināśakaḥ, commentary of Śaṅkara.
55. *Cf.* the words of Appar : 'pahaderi varuvār collum paṇiketkak kadavomo ? pattṛattṛōmē'. Also, 'kālanai vīdu ceyda kaḷal' (4.14.6). In one ten (4.14 Daśapurāṇam) Appar describes in each stanza the state of ultimate Dissolution and the Great Śiva who alone outlives it and is therefore our only refuge (śaraṇa). The anguish (Cf. vāttam, avalam, tuyar etc. occurring in *Tevaram*) in the face of the transcendent which death arouses finds vivid description in *Tevaram*. The anxiety of Brahmā and Viṣṇu is the anxiety of the creature, i.è. not having the 'aseity' of the Destroyer.

The Knowledge of God's Existence

1. A false distinction is drawn between Śivādvaita and Śaiva Siddhānta in terms of the alleged rationalism of Śaiva Siddhānta; HIP, Vol. V, p. 11; Schomerus pp. 33, 34; 423; SAS p. 26.
2. Śivāgama is also used as a synonym of the Veda : 'vede'pi śivāgama iti vyavahāro yuktaḥ.' SKB II.2.38.
3. For an account of the knowledge through the source of the Śaivāgama, vide *ante* pp. 33, 34.
4. 'vedānta-vākya-kusuma-grathanārthatvāt sūtrāṇām' etc. *Śāṅkara Bhāṣya* I.1.2. See for a comparative account of the structure of SJB and BS, *ante* ch. 1.5; the name *Śivajñāna-Bodham* itself

indicates that it purports to determine the truths of the Śaivāgamas (Śiva-jñāna). *Māpāḍīam* p. 13.

Revelation as an acknowledged mode of knowledge, it is useful to remember is not something into which the inferential process of reason does not enter—It is not strictly 'non-rational' or worse, 'irrational' any more than it is the case that reason as an acknowledged mode of knowledge is merely rational, exclusive of revelatory elements vide *infra* sec. on prāmāṇyavāda Ch. 14.

5. śabdāparokṣa-vāda which the vivaraṇa school of Vedānta advocates is unacceptable to Śaiva Siddhānta. SB pp. 455-58.
6. The 'silence' of the Transcendental Speech is the source of all speech and all conceptualisation but like the latter it is also pāśa-jñāna. Not even the pure inwardness of the soul beyond that of 'silence' can give the intuition of God. See below.
7. For elucidation of the distinction of the meaning of apara-jñāna and para-jñāna, vide *infra* Chapter 6.
8. 'Śol teriyāpporuḷ śodikkappāl ṉindra śodiyāṉ' Sambandar 154-3; TU 3, 9, 10, 29. 'śorpadam kaḍanda tollōn kāṇga' *Tiruvācakam*, 3 line 40.

   The view of language implied in the metaphysics of nāda is that it is the instrument of objectifiaction, though having transcendent roots. It is the *apriori* condition of the possibility of knowledge and language as such. Mystical intuition of God involves going beyond the reaches of nāda.
9. 'peru nūl coṉṉa aṟattiṟanal viḷaivadāi'. SVP 8.
10. Just as Sun's illumination is the necessary condition for determinate as well as indeterminate vision, for the earthly souls (sakalās) the Book is indispensable both for a discursive understanding and for a non-discursive, intuitive realisation of God. *Māpāḍiam* p. 5.
11. Discussion is here confined to the use of anumāna as a means of demonstrating the reality of God.
12. Cf. Sāṅkhya-Tattva-kaumudī on kārikā 6, for illustrations of this type of inference.
13. Śaṅkara says that scriptural accounts of Brahman as the world-ground from which arises etc. the world, is not for the purpose of suggesting inference because in the inference from the world as effect to a cause, the effect alone is apprehended and it cannot be

ascertained whether it is related to Brahman or to something else :
'kārya-mātram eva tu grāhyamāṇaṁ kiṁ brahmaṇas-sambaddhaṁ kim anyena kenacid vā sambaddham iti na śakyaṁ niścetum.' *Śaṅkara Bhāṣya* BS I.1.2.

14. *Ñānāmirdam* (v. 58) puts the matter thus : Is the transition from the hearth-fire (dṛṣṭānta) to the hill-fire (sādhya) transition from one particular to another particular or is it one of generalization through universal ? If former you have not accepted anumāna at all as a valid means of knowledge. If latter, why not also accept in the case of analogical inference in respect of the existence of a world-cause ? See also *Māpāḍiām* pp 84. Also 'yatra sadubhayor dośaḥ parihāro' pi vā samaḥ naikaḥ paryanuyoktavyas tādṛgartha-viniścaye,' MA vṛtti 3.6.

15. 'dharmeṇa sādhyate dharmī kvacit kāryeṇa kāraṇam,
kāraṇena kvacit kāryaṁ kvacidāmnāya-darśanāt'.
Mataṅga-Sūtra, SRS, p. 13. MA vṛtti op. cit. Also Dīpikā on the same verse.

16. The picturesque illustration given in the Āgama is :
'kṛṣṇāñjananibhair· uccaiḥ sāṭopair niviḍair ghanaiḥ
nirvighnair vipulaiḥ snigdhais taḍinnirghoṣa-saṅkulaiḥ
prāvṛṭsamaya-samprāptair dṛṣṭair vṛṣṭiḥ pramīyate
evaṁ pūrvavatā sādhyam anumānena vṛt sadā'. cited *ibid.* p. 14.

17. 'sthūlāvṛtta-śakṛtpuñja-bhūpṛṣṭhaṁ madagandhi ca
stambhaśayyādibhiś cihnair atrāsīn mattavāraṇaḥ
atīto hyanumānena sādhyaḥ śeṣavatā budhaiḥ'. cited *ibid.* p. 14.

18. The kāryāt kāraṇa and kāraṇāt kārya anumānas as valid pramāṇas belie the empiricist-pragmatist view of pramāṇa as causally efficient (arthakriyā-sthiti); the latter is applicable only to inference pertaining to the present and underpervades the two varieties of anumāna mentioned above. NVM p. 429.

Parapakkam verse 34 cites these forms of knowledge avowedly inferential as typically other than perception, acceptance of which as valid in practice is incompatible with rejection of them as mere speculation. The materialist *cum* positivist however would reduce them to perception. 'kāndalo anumānamāvaṭum kātchi munnadum kātchiyē' *Ibid* verse 35 : their validity or invalidity is none else than the validity or invalidity of the perception involved. Against the materialist's attempt to reduce all inferential knowledge to a species of perception, the Siddhāntin points to the irreducible inferential elements present in perception itself which are admittedly constructions.

19. 'kārya-kāraṇa-rūpa-vyatirekeṇa dharma-dharmi-svabhāvamātrapratibandha-mūlatvād idam anubhayātmakaṁ sāmānyam iti ucyate' SRS p. 13.
20. 'dṛṣṭaṁ sāmānyato dṛṣṭam iti tatsādhanaṁ dvidhā
tatrā'dyam akṣayogyasya padārthasyā' numāpakam
anyat sato'pyadṛṣṭasya padārthasyā'numāpakam' NVM p. 585.
21. 'prapañca-kṛtyaṁ tatkartāraṁ ca kutrā'pyadṛṣṭa-kāryatva-sāmānya-paśu-jñāna-gocara-jagat-kartranumāpakaṁ sāmānyatodṛṣṭa-sādhanaṁ piśācānumānavat'. *ibid* p. 585.

God as Reality : The Central Argument

1. Rev. J. H. Piet : 'Faith in an Inference and Faith in a Person'. *The Indian Philosophical Conference*, 1945.
2. Hara is not mere cause of World dissolution. With world-dissolution 'merit' and 'demerit' are not destroyed. There is creation again after destruction. Hara, therefore, signifies the dissolution of the karmic bond itself, indeed of the condition of bondage as such. *Supakkam* 133. Sivāgra yogin's comm.
3. 'kāryatvād āvayoḥ siddhaṁ kāryaṁ *kumbhādikaṁ* yathā.' PA 1.92. 'asattuḷa karivinai vinaak kuṛivaral pōdal kūda *turuterādi* pōl,' Ñ 58.
4. 'avai mūviṇaimaiyiṇ tōttṛiya tidiye' SÑP. 1.
5. 'ulahamellām varumuṛai vandu niṇdru pōvadum ādalālē' *Supakkam* 1.1.
6. 'tidiyē' SÑP. *op. cit.*
7. 'tōttṛiya tidiyē' *ibid.* Also, 'vandu niṇṛu pōvadum ādalāle' *Supakkam op. cit.*
8. 'ōdārō oṇḍroṇḍrittrṇḍri uḷadāi iṛakkandum aṇḍreṇdrum uṇdeṇṇa āyndu' SÑP. 1.1. udāharaṇa.

The premise of theological argument, that all are perishable—things, worlds, eons, time itself, looks like the conclusion of an inductive argument of the form 'such and such is true in these instances, so it is probably always true'. That, however, it is not an appropriate characterisation may be seen from its *a priori* quality, as a metaphysical conclusion 'all things are *necessarily* perishable. See *Citrurai* SÑP 1. 1st. adhikaraṇa.

9. Even Kant's *Critique* leaves us an exterior world but one about which we can know nothing *except that it exists.* Kant is rightly critical of the age-old belief in ontology the belief that things have essences but this critical attitude is possible on the accep tance of the thing-in-itself.

10. 'unnum*uḷadu* aiyamiḷadu' TP, 1.9. The Tamil root uḷ in ulladu, undu, uṇmai imports self-existence or Being. Another characteristic expression for self-existence is 'tan' as in 'tarcivam' (*SVP* 13) self-existing Śiva, in tani ('avan tāne taṉi', TP, 1, 8) what is uniquely self-existent.

11. Cf. Hume, 'there is no being whose existence is demonstrable' *Dialogues,* Kempsmith ed. p. 189.

12. 'Irum mudalum tuṇaiyākap pedai tidiyāhum' SÑP, 1,1, udāharaṇa.

13. 'payil vittellām kāritamadanir kāttum anguram kaḷiyum venil sīrudait tulaham' *Supakkam* 1,9.

14. Though spuriously like an inductive argument from parallel cases it is not an inference at all. The 'argument' is advanced with the explicit disavowal that it is inference : SNB 1. udāharaṇa. See Śivajñāna yogin's comment on the word 'pedai'. Also *Supakkam* 1.1. The *Svāyambhuva* text 'nā'numānāgamād atra jagat-kāryasya sambhaved ṛṣṭavat sarva-bhūteṣu nāśotpattiḥ pradṛśyate' (NVM p. 588) also makes such disavowal.

15. This is the view of the 'orthodox' anti-theist—the Mīmāṁsaka. *Māpāḍiam* pp. 71. 72.

16. To argue, says the Mīmāṁsaka, from a supposed contingency of the world to the existence of God, is like arguing that the hare has horn because it is born of cow. *ibid.* p. 72.

    The expression 'beginning of time', though linguistically regular, expresses no meaning. It tries to say what cannot be significantly said, namely, that there was a moment before which there was no possibility of anything being before anything else, which is a patent contradiction.

17. Compare Ryle's statement : "If all cloths are concatenations of stitches, absurdity results from saying that all stitches are themselves cloths" Ryle, G. : *The Concept of Mind,* Barnes and Noble, 1949, p. 214.

18. *Supakkam* 1.9. Comm. of Śivajñāna yogin and Śivāgra yogin.

19. 'strīpuṁ-napuṁsakāditvāt kārya-darśanāt'. SJB (S) 1.1.
'strīpuṁ-napuṁsakākhyātaṁ jagat sarvaṁ krameṇajam
sthiti-saṁhārato viprāḥ sarvadā kartṛpūrvakam.'
Svāyambhuva-Āgama, NVM p. 583.

20. The pūrvapakṣa here, is that while compositeness may signify being effect of a cause, the notion of a composite whole itself is not intelligible. A simple conjunction of parts (avayava-saṁyoga) cannot constitute compositeness, as conjunction of say one's apparel with one's self does not make for a composite. Nor can compositeness be inherence of parts (avayava-samaveta) as threads in a cloth are not related to each other by inherence and yet the cloth is an instance of a composite whole. Nor is by composite meant, generator of parts (avayava-janyatva), because that is precisely not the sense in which the world is said to be composite. A composite cannot also stand for mere relatedness (sambandha-mātratvam) : The self which is related to all things, is nevertheless simple, not composite. SB p. 24; PB p. 62.

The Siddhānta is : by composite is meant the relation of partial-total (ekadeśaikadeśi-bhāvasya vivakṣitatvāt) or as it is analysed even more clearly by Umāpati, a composite is a whole which admits of division into component members (avayavāvayavibhāva-rūpaviśeṣasya vivakṣitatvāt, PB, *Ibid*). *Māpāḍiam* which follows Umāpati here cites as examples of such discerptible wholes earth, mountains and sea; clay is 'part' of earth which *inter se* can be divided or separated by means of the operations of digging or drilling; stones likewise are separable by chiselling and water by the use of measures. p. 73.

21. The Bhāṭṭas argue that only the corporeal world is created and that the world of Primal Elements which is the 'cause' of the corporeal kingdom is itself not created or destroyed. 'na kadācid anīdṛśāṁ jagat.' Sivāgra yogin's commentary. *Supakkam* 1.8

22. 'Jagat-kāryaṁ jaḍatve sati nānāvidhatvāt jagato'sya nānāvidhatvasya kāryatvena vyāpyatvāt' SB p. 22; *Māpāḍiam* p. 73. 'anekaṃ yat jaḍaṁ vastu vastvasat tad ghaṭādivat'. PA 6.276. 'anityam āśritaṁ sāṁśam anekaṁ kāryam iṣyate.' *ibid* 6.278.

Here kārya is defined to mean what is changing and dependent (jaḍa) plus being many (aneka).

23. *Supakkam* 1.8.

24. *Ecclesiastes* III. 19.
25. *Māpāḍiam* 73.
26. PA 6-274, 275; *Māpāḍiam* pp. 73-74.
27. *Supakkam* 1.11, Sivajñāna yogin's comm., PA 6.276.
28. PA 6.276; See also Umāpati's Bhāṣya; Tattva-Saṁgraha 4 comm.; *Māpāḍiam* p. 74.
29. This criticism is repeated in the Śaivāgamas; PA 6.278. *Tattva-Prakāśika* 24, Aghora Śiva's Comm.; *Māpāḍiam* p. 74.
30. To modify the hetu as being multiple in character unassociated with the nature of being sentient (cetana-bhinna aneka-vṛttitvam) may make it easy to cite an example illustrative of the general relation of hetu and sādhya but will entail 'deviation' in the instance of 'being either māyā or mahāmāyā (māyā mahāmāyānyataratvam) which instance surely exemplifies cetana-bhinna-aneka-vṛttitvam but not kāryavṛttitvam SB p. 22; See also *Māpāḍiam* p. 74.
31. *Māpāḍiam* p. 75.
32. These demonstratives are significantly used by Meykandār : 'avanavaladu venumavai' SJB 1. See also his vārttika on it : Also *Māpāḍiam* p. 75.

    Meykaṇdār says that the world's certainty is given ostensively as the meaning of expressions like 'he', 'she' and 'it'. The world's reality is unquestioned in so far as we learn it by ostention and not by description. It may be true that some descriptive meaning too attaches to the expression by which we denote the world as 'he' 'she' and 'it'; that these are expressions primarily and avowedly ostensive in function.

    In any ontology of particulars identification of them, as Strawson points out will rest on the use of ostensive expressions with demonstrative force. Meykandār's use of expressions embodying demonstrative force suggests an awareness that identifying thought about particulars necessarily incorporates, a demonstrative element; 'he', 'she' and 'it' are expressly intended as a universally exhaustive expression.
33. '*uḷḍāich* cuṭṭappaṭṭa prapañcam'. Meykandār's vārttikam *loc. cit.*
34. 'suṭṭuṇarvāhiya prapañcam suṭṭunarviṇdri niṇdra sangārattin valiyalladu sudantaramiṇḍri nitṛalān.' *ibid* SJB 1.3.
35. Even the knowing subject—technically called sadasat is a species of asat. Vide *infra* Ch. 14.

36. *Supakkam* VI.2. Śivāgra yogin's Comm.
37. The Nyāya objection is based on its assumptions that : (*i*) all padārthas are jñeya, prameya, and abhidheya and that therefore, (*ii*) ātman too (jīvātman and paramātman) is a knowable, validly cognisable, and nameable padārtha. *Bhāṣā Paricchеda* : 2 *Muktāvalī*; *Nyāya Sūtras* 1.1.9. *Vatsyāyana Bhāṣya.*
38. 'All things produced whether by nature or by art, come from a material; for their capacity to be or not to be indicates their material nature'. Aristotle's *Metaphysics*, Book VII, 1032 A 22.
39. *Māpāḍiam* pp. 359-65.
40. Interpretation of existence in the sense of entailing the differential of guṇa is the classical counterpart couched in cosmo-psychological terms, of the contemporary concept of existence denoting of ambiguous and estranged actuality.
41. *Māpāḍiam* pp. 363-64.
42. Bhattacharya, K. C. : *Studies in Philosophy* Vol. I Progressive Publishers, Calcutta, p. 96.
43. Śaiva Siddhānta advocates anyathākhyāti-vāda. See *infra* Ch. 12.
44. *Advaita-siddhi* Nirṇaya Sāgara p. 544.
45. For a formulation of the doctrine of identity of dharma and dharmin See *Māpāḍiam* pp 228-230, also *infra* Ch. 12.
46. 'dṛśyatva' is used in non-advaita Vedānta literature as a hetu for proving the reality of the world. See the Dualist Madhva's 'Pañca-hetu' in *Vādāvali* tr. Nagaraja Rao, P. Madras 1943.
47. The speakable over-reaches the category of the presentable and is the guarantee of its own reality; the 'ungiven' sat, however, transcends even the speakable. See *infra* Ch. 7, sec. on 'God as Being'. For the distinction of the categories, *vide* Bhaṭṭacharya K. C., 'The Concept of Philosophy', *Studies in Philosophy*, vol 2, Calcutta, 1956.
48. *Ante* Ch. 1 Sec. 2.
49. 'ellām kaḷanra idame civameṇru
solläduvar kaḷanra tūyorkaḷ', *Tuhaḷaru Pōtham* 59.
50. 'nācit-cit-sannidhau' SJB, 7. See Sivāgra yogin's comments on the line SB pp. 349, 50
51. 'māyai *māmāyai* me....maruḷenil iruḷāi niṛkum ....aruḷenil aliyāy niṛkum' SVP 70. The italicised word stands for māyīya. See *Māpāḍiam* p 156

52. For the Śaivāgama doctrine of the parity of śabda and artha prapañca, *vide* PA Bindu paṭala; *Sarvajñānottara*, mantrātma-prakaraṇam; RT, Bindu parīkṣā 22-181; SB pp 201-204; *Māpāḍiam*, Jñapaka saktiyunmaī pp. 281-285
53. For the pūrvapakṣin's charge of hetvasiddhi and the Siddhāntin's vindication of the soundness of Īśvarānumāna see SB pp. 32, 41.
54. For the Mīmāṁsā arguments regarding the eternity of Śabda See *Śāstra-dīpikā* of Pārthasārathi Miśra pp. 95-96, 117.
55. For the Śaiva Siddhānta account of the evolution of the word, vide *infra* Ch. 9, sec. 1.
56. For a discussion of the hetus employed in support of the non-eternity of the world of sounds (Śabda-prapañca) See *Māpāḍiam* pp. 74-75; PA 214; PB 98; *Supakkam* 124 Śivāgra yogin's Comm.
57. The instance of the word cited here which is one in appearance only is a Tamil word. *Māpāḍiam* p. 283
58. *Supakkam* 1.20.
59. *ibid.* 9.2.
60. *ibid.* 6.1.

CHAPTER THREE

GOD AS CAUSE

From The World to the World Cause

1. 'iṇi oḍungina sangārattinalladu uṛpattiyillai' SJB 1.2. Note the use of the double-negative. This is one of the most cryptic of Meykaṇḍār's propositions summing up, as it does the purport of the entire tarkapāda of the Brahma-Sūtras.
2. This takes the form of the thesis of 'pre-existent effect' (satkārya-vāda) propounded against the asatkārya-vāda of the Buddhists. *infra* sec. The world Cause as Agent.
3. 'ulladarkkuc cheyvōnindrich cheyvinai inmaiyin' SÑP 1.2.
4. SP. 2. p. 38. The argument thus stated involves certain metaphysical assumptions about the *raison dètre* of these processes of resolution and evolution to which the world seems perpetually subject. By implication it also suggests the free nature of the Causal Agent of the world and the mode in which he may be conceived to exercise causal function, consistent with his freedom. The assumptions are : (i) karma and its 'ripening' for the sake of which there is dissolution, and (ii) āṇava and its 'ripening' for which sake there is re-evolution. These shall be discussed in chapter 5 under 'The Five-fold Cosmic Functions'.
5. Nimitta-kāraṇa is translated here in conformity with the practice of anglo-Indian writing as efficient cause. The semantic equation of *causa-efficiens* of classical and mediaeval western philosophy with nimitta-kāraṇa of the philosophical tradition of Vedānta, overlooks the exact sense in which the latter is understood, and interpreted both in Uttara-Mimāṁsā and Śaivāgama exegesis—the sense of spirit-causality, vide *infra* Ch. 4.
6. 'pupudaradi yōvara vuṇattrum oruvanai uḍaittu.' NM 57.
7. This is the method pursued in Supakkam in elucidating the concept of saṁhāra-kāraṇatva. ,The arrangement of the points of view as suggested by Śivajñāna yogin's commentary on the text is followed in the presentation.
8. The Accidentalist's position is here logically distinguished from that of the naturalist who admits a kind of 'spontaneous' causality.

Śivāgra yogin, however, treats both as same justifiably because spontaneous Creation is strictly rejection of Causation as different from mere sequence, a position reminiscential of Hume.

The animittavādin's case is : in the case of a potter's stick being a *causal* factor in relation to pot-making, neither perception nor reasoning can provide *conclusive* evidence. Even when one surely perceives the stick being utilised in fashioning of the pot, one can still doubt its instrumentality. Independent bearing on the existence or non-existence of the effect (anvaya-vyatireka) is no test. In the case of a particular observed pot, a donkey by its side may be by coincidence an invariable antecedent and so can pass the test for cause. The question of impossibility of establishing it otherwise without deviation (vyabhicārānyathā-siddhi-śaṅkā) will not also do. How does such consideration make causality secure against being assailed by doubt ? Hypothetical argument (tarka) too cannot be invoked as the remover of doubt (śaṅkā-nivarttaka). Even after repeated observation if one doubts a universal relation between the middle and the major terms, one seeks to prove it indirectly by disproving its contradictory: if 'given G is an instance of smoke G is an instance of fire' were false, then its contradictory 'there exists something such that G is an instance of smoke G is *not* an instance of fire' must be true. Admission of instances of smoke without fire to which one would be committed if one were to doubt or deny a universal relation between the two, is considered implausible only because it conflicts with the known *relation of causality* between smoke and fire. Explicit causes of universal relation are thus vindicated by the indirect method of tarka in terms of a hidden relation of causality. To remove doubt pertaining to *that* universal relation, another hypothetical reasoning will have to be invoked and so on *ad infinitum*. SB pp. 25, 26.

The Siddhānta answer is an emphatic no to the animittavādin. That there can be effect without cause cannot be a serious admission on any one's part in view of practical contradictions (svakriya-virodha) involved in the supposition. Contradictions in theory alone should not be the philosopher's concern. Life based on the premises of animitta-vāda should preclude seeking of food to appease hunger. SB p. 28.

9. For the statement of svabhāva-vāda, *Supakkam*. 1—2, 3. Also the comm. of Śivāgra yogin and Jñana prakāśa.
10. 'svabhāvato jagadbījaṁ jagat-kartṛ-hareṇa kim?
svabhāva eva vaktavyo gatvā dūram api tvayā.' MK 12.
11. *ibid*, 12. Aghora Śiva's Comm.
12. Cf. Refutation of the Sāṅkhya theory of Causation. *infra* sec. on Theory of self-Becoming.
13. 'vicitra-pariṇāmo'pi na hi svābhāvikasya tu' etc. PA 3-40. Also, 'iyalbinukku seyaladindru.' *Supakkam* 1.3.
14. 'agneḥ prakāśaḥ svābhāvye nā'prakāśo'pi tatkṛtaḥ.' PA 3-41 Also 'viruddhenaikadharmiṇi'. *ibid*. 3-40.
Also, viruddhāveka-kālasthau dharmāvekāśrayaṁ gatau itaretaranāśāt tau kuruto lopamātmanaḥ' MK 21, 22.
15. *Supakkam* 1.4. Jñānaprakāśar's Comm.
16. 'iyalvu seydi seydiyēl iyalbadindṛu.' *Supakkam* 1.3. Śivajñāna yogin's Comm.
17. 'seyal seyvāṉ oruvaṉ vēṇḍum seyaṟpaḍum asēdanattāl.' *ibid*. 1. 3. Also, 'caturṇām api bhūtānāṁ svabāvo naiva dṛśyate
iti yat kampate dhātrī kamuṣṇād grasyate kvacit,
vahnir nirvāṇamāyāti vāyurūrdhvagatiḥ kvacit
bhūteṣu hi svabhāvo na kiṁ punaḥ kāryasambhave,
sṛṣṭi-sthityanta-nāśena kāryatvenā'tra yogataḥ
jaḍatvenā' pi tadbhūtaṁ sarvataḥ kartṛpūrvakam'.
Parākhya-Āgama NVM p. 589.
18. *Supakkam* 1.4. First two lines. Śivajñāna yogin's Comm.
19. *Māpāḍiam* p. 79.
20. Mukerjee, Satkari : *Buddhist Philosophy of Universal Flux* p. 37.
21. Murti, T.R.V.—*Central Philosophy of Buddhism* p. 71. kṣaṇa and the kṣaṇika—the moment and the momentary are one. *Parapakkam* sautrantikan matam, 7 comm.
22. This is true in general of a philosophy of flux; but Buddhism being not accidentalism will admit that the fluxional nature of an entity does admit a cause; only the cause is inherent in its own constitution.

The Buddhist view of reality is not one of sheer succession but a continuum of discrete events conditioned in its flow by the causal law of dependent origination. Murti, *op. cit.* pp 72-73.
23. PB p. 441.; Parapakkam Sautrāntika mata māṟutalai, 13.

24. *Supakkam*, Jñānaprakāśar's Comm.
25. 'kṣaṇabhaṅgaṁ jagat sarvaṁ punaḥ santānato bhavet
na nāśād asadutpattis tato'nyat kāraṇaṁ bhavet
sad eva kāraṇaṁ tasmāj-jāyate sad idaṁ jagat
kāraṇasya jaḍatvena kāryakartā paraḥ śivaḥ'.
Siddha-Tantram NVM p. 594.
26. BS II 2.20. Śrikaṇṭha's Comm.
27. 'ilayitta daṇṇil layittadām,' SNP 1.2. Udāharaṇa.
28. The Buddhist too says, while agreeing with the naturalist that destruction is spontaneous (ahetuka) that origination is, however, not spontaneous but conditioned (sahetuka).
29. Pre-existence of effect is a literal rendering of Satkārya-vāda. It should not mislead one to understand the theory is a spatial sense as bodily pre-existence. Pre-existence is here used in the sense in which a whole man pre-exists in human embryo. It means the power to become, expand, evolve, manifest.
30. 'ilayitta vāruḷadā venḍum.' SÑPI.2. Udāharaṇa *Cittrurai*.
31. Meykandār enunciates the principle of satkārya-vāda but always in the key of resolution and re-emanation to mark it from the Sāṅkhya version of it; the latter has no conception of spirit as the ground of the resolution of the effect. *ibid.*
32. *The problem of causality* : Sāṁkhya-yoga view by MM. Gopinath Kaviraj (1925). Saraswati Bhavan Series, vol V.
33. *Sāṅkhya-kārika* texts, 9, 10, are cited in SB p 212; TP Srīkumara's Comm. pp 162-63; PB p. 261.
34. Ñ, v. 22. The Śakti in cause cannot come into play without its relation to what is yet to be produced. For a distinction of causal power from cause *infra* Sec. 'The world-cause as will.'
35. *Māpāḍiam* p 81; PB p 261. In both kinds of causal evolution the efficiency of a nimitta-kāraṇa consists in occasioning the re-emergence of the effect from its pre-mergence or in removing the obstruction. Contrast it with the Sāṅkhya-yoga theory.
36. 'mṛtpiṇḍādyavasthā eva āvārakatvāt' SB p. 210. *Māpāḍiam* p. 81. That it is so in the case of the latter may not be explicit but can be shown formally in the following manner: the pot 'pre-exists' in the clay prior to *becoming* overtly a pot as it becomes from thence. What does not 'pre-exist' in and as cause, from thence there can be no becoming; sands do not 'become' oil; horns do not grow

on the head of a hare. The significance of the negative vyāpti in this inference is obvious; the effect (oil) being equally non-existent in the cause, in sand as well as in the sesamum (according to the theory of pre-non-existent effect) why is oil produced from the one and *not* from the other ?

The anvaya-vyatireka-anumāna is given in identical terms in Ñ. v. 22 MA. 9-14; PB 261.

37. MM. Gopinath Kaviraj, *op. cit* p. 132.
Māyā is described as an indeterminate system of causal potency (kāraṇa-śakti-samūha). *Māpāḍiam*, p. 84. Indeterminate Matter according to Śaiva Siddhānta is rooted in the Being and will of Spirit, unlike as in Śāṅkhya-yoga.

38. 'māyā puruṣaḥ śiva ityetat tritayaṁ mahārtha-saṁhāre
avaśiṣyate punas tat pravartate pūrvavat sṛṣṭau'.
TP 69; See also Aghora Śiva's Comm.

39. Aristotle says that change cannot be between contradictories as 'is' and 'is not' but between contraries which belong to the same genus. 'From genuine contraries, like red and white there must be something which changes into the contrary state, for the contraries themselves do not change. And since the contraries pass away into each other, there must be some third thing in addition to them which persists throughout the change, this thing is the material' *Metaphysics* XII 2. (Hope's translation)

40. *Supakkam* 1.27. Śivajñāna yogin's Comm. This is not of course anekānta-vāda, because identity, either way is absolutely asserted.

41. Murti, *op. cit.* 167.

42. 'ōrinillladuvum tōndṛa duḷḷadēl udikka vēṇḍa.' *Supakkam* 1-5. No one is a better critic of 'asat utpatti' pakṣa than the Śūnyavādin. Murti. *op. cit.* pp. 170-177.

43. *Mādhyamika-Kārikā* 11.21.

44. Murti, *op. cit.* p.50

45. Das Gupta, S. N. ; *History of Indian Philosophy*, vol. II, p. 115.

46. The above is a free paraphrase of 'uḷḷadu miladu mindṛ nindṛadon tṛuḷadēl unḍām illadēl illaiyāhum tōttṛamum isaiyādāhum'. *Supakkam* 1.6. The point of this refutation is to deny the logical and semantical possibility of the dialectic by which voidity of things is sought to be established.

47. 'oruporuḷ oruvaṉiṉdṟi uḷadeladāhum.' *ibid.* 1.7.
The Jainas too, like the Buddhists accept a 'God' for the role of inculcating knowledge but not for cosmic operations. NVM p. 594.
48. *Aṣṭa-Sāhasrī* 1.
49. 'naikasmin asambhavāt.' BS II. 2.23, See Śrīkaṇṭha's Comm.
50. *Supakkam* 1.6. last two lines; Śaiva Siddhānta denies 'abhāva' as an *independent* category ; abhāva (non-existence) is a formative element in the constitution of the real which itself is existent. The distinction between 'is' and 'is not' is but a distinction within 'is'. The Jaina view that the nature of the real is *both 'is' and 'is not'* is rejected.
51. 'svayam evā'sti nā'stī'ti cā'nvayavyatirekataḥ
jagat sarvaṁ bhavet kartānā'stī'ti kathamucyate
nai' kasminnasti nā'stī'ti bhāvābhāvavirodhataḥ
kārya-kāraṇa-bhedena tathātvaṁ yujyate yadi
kāraṇasya jaḍatvena kartā'stī'ti pratīyate.'
Siddha-Tantram. NVM p. 595.
52. *Māpāḍiam* p. 83 : belief in a de facto positive effect is inconsistent with the repudiation of a positive cause, involved explicitly or otherwise in the metaphysical notions of asat, śūnya, syād etc. Not to accept categorically the 'being' nature of cause is to accept its non-being.

The World-Cause as Agent

1. MK XII
2. '*varu muṟai* vandu niṉdṟu pōvadum ādalālē *tarubavaṉ* oruvaṉ vēṇḍum.' *Supakkam* 1.1. See Śivajñāna yogin's comm. on the italicised words.
3. The Vaiśeṣika is, therefore, called a semi-nihilist. Śaṅkara's Comm. II 2.18.
4. A samavāyi-kāraṇa can have for its effect a dravya, guṇa or karma.- See, Kuppuswamy Śastri : *A Primer of Indian Logic.*
5. Bhaduri, S. : *Studies in Nyāya-Vaiśeṣika Metaphysics* 1947, p. 294.
6. The admission or the non-admission of 'stay' (sthiti) as intervening between origination and dissolution marks the difference between the asatkārya-vāda of the Buddhist and that of the Nyāya-Vaiśeṣika.
7. 'samavāyi-kāraṇasya nānātva eva tatsaṁyogātmakam asamavāyi-kāraṇaṁ labhyate.' SP p. 38.

8. It is at this point the Sāṅkhya shows itself at an advantage over the Nyāya-Vaiśeṣika and serves as the metaphysical point of departure for all Vedānta which conceives ultimate reality as the 'cause' of the world.
9. For a detailed account of the argument vide *Nyāyakandalī* of Śrīdhara, p. 31; *Nyāyamañjarī* of Jayanta Bhaṭṭa, II, pp. 72-73. Two of the arguments reported in SB pp. 166-167 alone are expanded here.
10. *Supakkam* I.11 & 12. Śivajñana yogin's Comm.
Also, 'ghaṭasya mṛd upādānaṁ dṛṣṭaṁ yad dṛśyate yathā
tathaiva paramāṇūnāṁ māyopādāna-kāraṇaṁ
māyā kāraṇam evā'hur aṇūnāṁ kāryadarśanāt.'
Cited NVM. p. 604.
11. SP p. 37; for a further discussion on this example, see SB p. 177.
12. SB p. 178.
13. *ante* Ch. 2. *God as Reality : the Central Argument*
Also, 'acetanatayā dṛṣṭā aneke paramāṇavaḥ
ghaṭavatkāryarūpās tad ghaṭopādāna-mṛd yathā
tathai'va paramāṇūnāṁ māyopādāna-kāraṇam.'
Siddha-Tantram, NVM p. 604.
14. SB p. 319; *Māpāḍiam*, p. 148
15. 'paramāṇor avayavitvābhāve dvyaṇukādi-kāryārambhakatvāyogāt avayavittvaṁ siddham. paramāṇoh saguṇatvādavayavittvaṁ ghaṭādivat saguṇatvaṁ ca sagandhādi-guṇaka-pṛthvyādīnām ārambhakatvāt' etc. NVM p. 604.
16. SB p. 178
17. SP pp.38-39. Also MA 9-7; Ñ 18, lines 21-24
18. Even the admission of adṛṣṭa to influence Creation does not make the Atom theory plausible. For there arises the problem of 'ripening' (vipāka) of adṛṣṭa, which also cannot be due to atoms or the adṛṣṭa. The operation and cessation of adṛṣṭa, like time, is an auxiliary factor in Creation and Dissolution, but the principal causal ground can only be spirit. BS II. 2.11 SKB.
19. 'aḷinṭhidum aṇurūpangaḷ ulahelām, oduṅgu mandre. *Supakkam* I. 11.
20. MM Gopinath Kaviraj, *op, cit.*
21. *ibid.*
22. *Māpāḍiam* p. 66.

23. *Sāṅkhya-Tattva-Kaumudi*, 57
24. *Māpāḍiam* p. 66
25. *Sāṅkhya-Kārikā* 21, *Sāṅkhya-Pravacana Sūtra*, II, 46
26. 'saṁghāta-parārthatvāt'—*Sāṅkhya-Kārikā*, 7.
27. 'rājas-satva-yogād asya kriyā-jñāna-śaktisambandho'pi yujyate yena jagat-kāraṇatva-siddhiḥ' Śrīkaṇṭha's comm. BS 1. 1-5
28. 'triguṇātmikāyāḥ prakṛtes tamaḥ-pārthakyena rajassatvayoga-bhāvānna ca tamasyabhibhūte rajassatvayorudreke jñāna-kriyā sambandhaḥ pradhānasye'ti vācyam. sattva-rajas-tamasāṁ sāmyāvasthā prakṛtirityaṅgīkārāt'. Śrīkaṇṭha, *ibid.*
29. The Sāṅkhya believes 'that before this world came into being, there was such a state of dissolution—a state in which the guṇa compounds had disintegrated into a state of disunion and had by their mutual opposition produced an equilibrium—the prakṛti'. Dasgupta, *op. cit*, Vol I, p 245
30. 'yatra saukṣmya-parākāṣṭhā sā māye'ti abhidhīyate' PA 3-8
31. RT 33 Comm.
32. MK 4-5
33. RT 122-123
34. 'maṇkulirṇdu vitthuṇda mūla mulaittavā tārakamam' etc. SÑP 1.2.2. See *Cittrurai.*
35. nā'naikāntikatā hetoḥ kṣīre vatsa-vivṛddhate
    cetanena gavāṁ yasmāt pravṛttaṁ vatsa-vṛddhitam,
    kṛtād dehāt pravartteta pravṛddhaś-cet svataḥ payaḥ
    na ca pravarddhate yasmāt cetanā pekṣitāt sthitāḥ PA I.81-82.
36. 'avar vinaiyāl vitthahamām.' SÑP, *op. cit.*
37. According to the Śaivāgama analysis of agency, 'the Agent' ranges over, human superhuman and even the barely animate but not inanimate objects, non-intelligent as they are. Human action, acts and activities of the more sophisticated kinds are exemplified in the simplest form of transient action which is characteristic of sentient life. Śaiva Siddhānta analysis of nimitta--kāraṇa taken along with the two implied types of cause, namely, upādāna and sahakārin, that are co--ordinate with it fits our expression and our experience.
38. Gauḍapāda says (Māṇḍūkya-Kārikā III.15) that analogies like those of clay and its transformation are purportful only as introducing the doctrine of non-difference; the non-difference,

suggested by this recurrent analogy according to Śaiva Siddhānta, where the emphasis is on the potter rather than on clay, is that of will and the willed-content.

39. MK 1-2 Comm.

40. RT 122-123 Comm.

41. 'mūlam tandiḍum sivaṇavaṇdaṇ saṇṇidi *taṇṇil niṇdrē.*' *Supakkam* 1.19. This is one of the key statements of SJS; the material and the efficient causes are, as it were, transposed in their functions : māyā evolves the world *from* Śiva-sannidhi—note the use of the ablative, with reference to efficient cause and of the nominative with reference to one Material cause.

42. Śrīkumāra states it emphatically, going even to the extent of denying technically the right of labelling upādāna as cause : 'nahyopādānādikaṁ kāraṇaṁ kartrā preritaṁ karyotpādane paryāptam iti kṣobha-siddhiriti' TP Srīkumāra's comm. p. 117.

The World-Cause as Will

1. For an analysis of spiritual life as partaking of spirit *vide infra* Ch. 14.
2. *Supakkam* 1.18; 'bindukṣobhāt pūrvaṁ śivasaṁkalpa-mātra-hetutvena tadicchā-śaktir eva sahakāri'—NVM p. 612; also, 'śaktiś-ceśvaro māyā mṛdvaccakra-kulālavat'.—*Niśvāsa, ibid.*
   'ādikaraṇaṁ mṛdrūpaṁ taccakraṁ sahakāraṇam
   kulālo'sya nimittaṁ syāt tribhirmṛdbhāṇḍa-sambhavaḥ
   tad evaṁ granthi mṛdrūpaṁ kuṇḍalī-cakra-saṁsthitam
   parameśa-kulālena kriyate tac-carācaram'. *Jñāna-Siddhi. ibid.*
   'nimittam īśvarākhyaṁ tad yad dṛṣṭaṁ sahakāraṇam.' *Parākhya Āgama*; SRS p. 24.
3. PA 6-222 to 230.
4. The Buddhist's use of the criterion of causal efficiency, to determine the meaning of what is based on the rejection of understanding isness in terms of (1) universal (sattājāti-yogitvam) (2) co-inherence in a common substratum (sattā-sāmānādhikaraṇyam) (3) indirect qualification by existence, co-inherent with it in a common substratum (sattekārtha-samavāyitvam).'sa ca arthakrīyā-kāritā rūpasattā kṣaṇikeṣveva sambhavati.' PB 439.
5. 'arthakriyākaratvaṁ tu sthāyinaṁ kramasaṁsthitam
   samarthasya sadā kārya-karatve niyamo na ca.' *ibid.* 6-227.
6. Mukerjee, S : *The Buddhist Philosophy of Universal Flux* (1936), p. 11 ff.

7. SB pp. 281-284; *Sarva-Darśana-Saṁgraha*. p. 24, from which Śivāgra yogin quotes *in extenso*.
8. 'karaṇaṁ ca na śaktyanyat śaktir nā'cetanā citaḥ viṣayā niyamād ekaṁ bodhe kṛtye ca tat tathā.' MA 3-4. 'icchai'va karaṇaṁ tasya yathā sadyogino matā.' *Kīraṇāgama* cited *ibid*. Comm. p. 124.
9. 'kālam mudaliyaṇa adaṉ vaḻittāya tuṇaikkāraṇaṅgaḷ.' *Māpāḍiam* p. 114.
10. 'agnir dāha-samartho' pi sphoṭe' ṅgulim apekṣate kramā-krama-vikalpābhyāṁ durāśā kṣaṇikatvadhīḥ.' PA 6-228.
11. 'kāriyaṅgal, kālamē taravē kāṇḍum kāraṇaṉ vidiyinukkuk kālamum kaḍavuḷ ēvalāl tuṇaik kāraṇaṅgāṉ.' *Supakkam* 1.10. Also, 'kālena jagadutpattis tat-kartā kāla eva hi
 upādānena jātena nāśenā'pi jaḍo bhavet
 tathā' pi lokasṛṣṭyādau kalo hetuś-ca karmavat
 tasmān maheśa eva syāt kālavat paripālakaḥ.' *Kīraṇa Āgama*, NVM p. 600.
12. The caramakāraṇa standing for the vyāpāra resulting in the effect is the karaṇa according to the old Nyāya school; Navya-nyāya defines karaṇa as consisting in possession of vyāpāra, not the vyāpāra itself. See for a brief discussion of their views—*infra* Ch. 11.
13. *Māpāḍiam* p. 279; SB p. 312.
14. Kumārila attacks Śūnya-vāda on the ground of its non-recognition of sahakāri-kāraṇa. The Śūnyavādin admits only vāsanā in the place of śakti which inheres (āhita) in the momentary. Why then, asks Kumārila, from the knowledge of cause the effect should not always and at all places arise ? *Śloka-Vārttika* 247-258.
15. SÑP 2-4 *Citrurai*; The Prābhākara admits śakti as an independent padārtha, identical neither with the svarūpa of a thing nor with the sahakārī. For the Naiyāyikas śakti is not different from the causal antecedents of an effect. Bhāṭṭa Mīmāṁsā, Vedānta and Śaiva Siddhānta take śakti as neither identical with nor different from the svarūpa of a thing and treat it as arthāpattigamya. ('śaktayaḥ sarvabhāvānāṁ kāryārthāpatti-gocarāḥ' *Bhaṭṭa Dīpikā*, cited Śrīkumāra's comm. TP p. 79.

 For Prābhākara, śakti is anumeya, postulated after the actual ascertainment of cause. For the other group, 'cause' (nimitta) itself is ascertained through ascertainment of sahakāri.
16. *Māpāḍiam* p. 279 ff; Srīkumāra *op. cit*. p. 79.

17. 'tadādhārāṇi kāryāṇi śakti-rūpāṇi saṁhṛtau vikṛtau vyaktirūpāṇi vyāpriyante'rthasiddhaye' MA māyālakṣanaprakaraṃ, 13.
18. As a consequence of non-recognition of śakti, the Nyāya theists (Udayana, Vācaspati etc.) assert that God's agency is nothing but will (kṛtimatva) generated by knowledge. Śaiva Siddhānta will distinguish between the will and being of the agent as between śakti and śaktimat and view the former as karaṇa and the latter as kartā.
19. Śaiva-siddhānta treatment of the concept of śakti or power of Being witnesses to the convergence of the mythological, metaphysical and physical motifs. Just as we speak of the electric, magnetic centrifugal forces of heat, gravity, cohesion, we can also speak of the power of Being as a force, possessing as it were, vibration. Śakti is the specific quality or 'virtue' latent in anything. (Cf. the meaning of the Latin *virtus*, the meaning of which is seen in such expressions as 'in virtue of'.)

    The account of śakti as karaṇa given in this section follows closely the treatment of the subject in SB p 185 ff.
20. Is not will which ultimately is adopted as the karaṇa also a psychic function and therefore only an aspect of the somatic condition ? Aghora Śiva answers this question. MK 1, 2 commentary. Like discrimination of buddhi, desire or will of manas is only a manifestation of the citśakti of the self. Discrimination or intellection is manifestation of jñāna-śakti while will is manifestation of kriyā-śakti.
21. SB p. 185.
22. 'bhāva-pratyayātmake' cchā-bodhādi-vṛtti-sahakṛttasyaiva janakatvāt anyathā kulālādis sarvadā cicchakti-rupecchādi satvena tatkāryasya ghaṭādes sadotpattyāpatteḥ.' *ibid.* p. 185.
23. 'kartṛ-vyāpāra-viṣayasyai' va karaṇatvena tadvilakṣaṇāyāś cicchakteḥ karaṇatvāyogāc ca.' *ibid.* p. 186.
24. 'kartrā vinā na kāryaṁ na tathopādāna-karaṇābhyām' TP 2, 17.
25. The being characteristic of phenomena is but the predicate of spirit. Whatever is cannot be other than spirit. For a detailed discussion of the problem of the identity of upādāna-kāraṇa and nimitta-kāraṇa see *infra* Ch. 4.
26. 'karturupādānatāprayojakasya kāryābhinnatve sati karaṇatvasya sadbhāve no'pādānatvasya sambhave'pi svādhiṣṭheyatvabhāvena karaṇatvasyānupapatteḥ.' SB p. 186.

27. 'kulālādi-samavetāyās tasyā malāvṛtatvena, aprakāśamānatayā kāryākṣamatvena viṣaya-viśeṣa-tat-prakāśārthaṁ bhāvapratyayāpekṣatve'pi sarvadā malānāvṛtāyā īśvara-śaktes tadasahakṛtāyā api janakatva-sambhavāt.' *ibid.* p. 187.

28. 'nirāvaraṇa-nirdvandva-nirupādāna-vaibhave'. RT cited *ibid.* p. 187.

29. The instance referred to is the smith's movement of raising of his hammer and lowering it with force on the anvil. SB p. 187.

30. 'śakteḥ kāryatvāpattis tu cetanatvenaikatvena cā'ṅgīkārāt acetanatvānekatvayor abhāvān-nirastā'. SB P. 187

31. 'karaṇaṁ ca na śaktyanyat....
śaktir nā'cetanā citaḥ'. MA 3, 4.

32. 'ekaivā' nekatāṁ yāti śiva-śaktir upāditā.' cited SB p. 187.
Also 'saiṣā śivāśrayā śaktir amoghā phalavardhinī
ekānaika-vibhāgeva kārya-bhedād vibhāvyate.'
RT cited and commented. *ibid.*

33. 'yā sā śaktir jagaddhetuḥ kathitā samavāyinī
icchātvaṁ tasya sā devī sisṛkṣoḥ pratipādyate
evam etad iti jñeyaṁ nānyatheti suniścitam
jñāpayanti jagad yatra jñāna-śaktir hi gadyate
evaṁ bhūtam idaṁ vastu bhavatviti yadā punaḥ
jātā tadaiva tadvastu kurvantyatra kriyocyate.'
Mālinī-vijaya III.5.9. Cited *ibid.* Also cited in PB p. 21.
The 'samavāyinī' of jagaddhātā assumes the form of desire of Him who desires to create. Learn how she becomes the manifold, though one. That by which a thing is known for certain to be 'this' and not otherwise is the jñāna-śakti in this world. When there is will to the effect 'let this thing be thus' the causal power making it so at that moment is kriyā-śakti.

34. 'jñānecchā-yatnabheda-vādināṁ tārkikādīnām api sarvadā sṛṣṭi-saṁhārādyutpatti-prasaṅga-parihārāya tattat-kāraṇa-sāhitye tattadicchādi-rūpatvam anumatam eva.' SB p. 187.

35. Though Uddyotakara (*Nyāya-Vārttika* pp. 951-52) says that God's icchā relates to all objects being eternal in nature, its manifestation has to be admitted to be contingent on time. As manifest, it cannot relate to all objects at all times.

36. *infra.* Ch. 7 Sec. on 'The Concept of Divine Will'.

CHAPTER FOUR

GOD AS THE ONLY CAUSE

God as Material Cause

1. Cf. The use and criticism which Paul Tillich makes, of the three ways of understanding the term God, namely, the supernaturalistic, naturalistic and self-transcendent or ecstatic.—*Systematic Theology*, Vol. 2 pp. 5-8.
2. Schomerus misses the significance of the concept of God in Śaiva Siddhānta when he says that matter exists 'out-side' God and God from eternity exists 'outside' matter and that therefore, God in Śaiva Siddhānta is only a demiurgas.—*Der Śaiva Siddhānta* p. 166; 170.
3. The Śvetāśvatara text 'māyāṁ tu prakṛtiṁ viddhi, māyinaṁtu maheśvaram, (IV.10) remains the scriptural norm for all shades of opinion in Śaivism. Even Śrīkaṇṭha, like those following his lead, viz. Śrīkumāra, Śivāgra yogin, clinches his discussions on the subject by appeal to the above text. Cf. Commentary on I.4.24, 27; also I.1.2.
4. upādānakāraṇatva of Brahman is common to (i) Brahma-pariṇāma-vāda, and (ii) Brahma-vivarta-vāda. Schomerus names these two theories as cosmo-pantheistic and acosmic pantheistic. *Der Śaiva Siddhānta* p. 174.
5. Taittirīya Upaniṣad III.1.1-6. Śrīkaṇṭha (I.4.24) and Śrīkumāra (TP p. 62) anchor their allegiance to Brahman's 'jagan-mūlatva' on this text. PB (p. 160) begins the pūrvapakṣa naturally with this important textual evidence.
6. '*śivāt* satya-parānanda-prakāśaika-svalakṣaṇāt
   āvirbhūtam idaṁ sarvaṁ cetanācetanātmakam'. *Sūta-Saṁhitā*, Yajñavaibhava-khaṇḍa 3-1, PB p. 84.
   'śaktiḥ prathama-sambhūtā śāntyatīta-padottarā
   tato māyā tato'vyaktaṁ *śivāc* chaktimataḥ prabhoḥ
   śaktyādi ca pṛthivyantaṁ śivatattva-samudbhavaṁ
   tenaikena ca tadvyāptaṁ mṛdā kumbhādikaṁ yathā.'
   Vāyavīya Saṁhitā, SB p. 160.

7. '*yena* sarvam idaṁ vyāptaṁ *yasmin* sarvaṁ pratiṣṭhitaṁ yasmādutpadyate sarvaṁ tam āhuḥ paramaṁ padam.' *Jñānatilakam*, PB p. 84.
8. 'ānando brahma evaitaj jāyate'smāc-carācaram.' *Acintyāgama*, *ibid.* p. 84 and identified in SB p. 160. All these citations repeat the ablative of the Taittirīya.
9. The entire discussion about the ablative case and its import by Umāpati and by Śivāgra yogin seems to bear on Śrīkaṇṭha's preamble to the Prakṛtyādhikaraṇam. I.4.23-28.
10. 'janmādyasya *yataḥ*' (BS I.1.2) literally repeats the ablative of *yato* vā imāni bhūtāni etc. *Māpāḍiam* p. 150, gives parallel citations from Śaiva hymnal literature in Tamil (*Koilnanmani malai* 24), which uses the expression '*ninnidaittondri ninnidai* odungum'.
11. 'janikartuḥ *prakṛtiḥ* (Pāṇini I.4.30) ityapādāna-saṁjñayā upādānavācino vihitāḥ' SP p. 37.

    Pāṇini gives the name apādāna to that from which a thing is born, and requires (II.3.28) the ending of the fifth case to be added to the word, which expresses apādāna. As 'yataḥ', 'therefore' refers to the material cause, and, the referent of 'yad' here in the text under discussion is Śiva, the latter is only material cause. The basis of ablation is that from which something departs.
12. 'mahābhāṣye śṛṅgāccharo jāyate gomayād vṛściko jāyate iti tasyopādānārthakatvam abhipretyo'dāhṛtam.' PB p. 84.
13. 'prakṛti-śabdasya hetvapara-paryāyatveno' pādānārthakatvāsiddheḥ' PB p. 86. Umāpati gives the following reasons for his stand : (i) the vṛttikāra illustrates the ablative ending by the suggestive example 'putr*āt* pramodo jāyate'; the word 'jāyate' agreeing with apādānam, yet, is suggestive only of efficient causality. (ii) The Nyāsakāra also says categorically that prakṛti śabda is indicative of nimitta-mātram. (iii) The Bhāṣyakāra also presumably conscious of its non-distinctness as implying upādāna-kāraṇa pleads for the deletion of the adhikaraṇa itself.

    Śivāgra yogin, (SB. pp. 167-68) while agreeing that yataḥ denotes cause in general rejects Umāpati's contention that it is indicative only of nimitta-kāraṇatva. His reasons are : (i) the Bhāṣyakāra gives the example of 'gomayād vṛściko jāyate.' (ii) The Kaiyaṭa-Bhāṣyakāra also inclines to the same view. (iii) The Kāśikā-vṛtti also does not intend to exclude upādāna-kāraṇatva.

(iv) The popular use of the ablative is only in support of material causality. (v) The example 'putrāt pramodo jāyate' must be understood poetically to mean material causality. See also SMD, p. 558. for the pūrvapakṣa, and pp. 562-63 for siddhānta.

14. *Bṛ. Up.* IV, 1.20.
15. *Muṇḍ. Up.* 1.1.7
16. koil nanmani malai; *Cit*ed in *Māpāḍiam* p. 151.
17. SN criticises the analogies of (i) gold and gold-shreds, (ii) spider and its web, (iii) tree and its leaves, flowers etc., (iv) water and its ripples, foams, waves etc. : lines 74-80. The point of objection raised against them is how the world of acit can unfold from cit : nin tarparam acittait tarumaren ? 1. line 73.
18. Śrīkaṇṭha's use of this analogy (II.1.16) and Rāmānuja's example of the rise of worms in honey are in the sense that life principle to the extent that it is *embodied*, shares something in common with the material cause. The notion of God as the material cause has a slender support from this. Cf. *Māpāḍiam* p. 151.
19. Śivajñāna yogin gives this ingenious and plausible interpretation of the Tamil text and takes this to be the intended meaning of the use of the ablative '*ninnidait* tondri' occurring in the same text. *Māpāḍiam* p. 154.
20. 'dravyopādānake guṇe dravyatvasya dugdhopādānake dadhni dugdhatvasya śṛṅgopādānake śare śṛṅgatvasya gomayopādānake vṛścike gomayatvasya cādarśanāt.' PB p. 86; *Māpāḍiam* p. 151.
21. 'upādānagatāśeṣa-viśeṣa-guṇa-sajātīya-guṇavattāyā āvaśyakatvāt tathaiva mṛdghaṭādau darśanāt'. PB. p. 89.
22. *Māpāḍiam* repeats this significant argument in other contexts, pp 106; 388.
23. *Chānd. Up.* VI.2.3.
24. *Taittirīya* II.6; also 'sṛṣṭyartham aikṣata prājñā bahusyāmi'ti śaktimān'. *Skanda-Purāṇa*, cited PB p. 85; SP p. 37.
25. 'nahi kulālasya ghaṭaḥ syāmiti saṁkalpo'sti.' PBP. 85.
26. 'uktabādhena cetanatva-śrutyā cā' ntaryāmitayā sarva-*niyāmakatvasyai'va* tadarthakatva-kalpanāt,' PB p. 88.
27. 'anyas san vyāptito'nanyaḥ.' SJB(S) II. See also SMD Vol. I, p. 558 for a discerning interpretation of the bahubhavana-saṁkalpa text : 'tadaikṣata bahu syāṁ prajāyeye' ti brahmaṇas srakṣyamāṇa-tejaḥ-prabhṛti-rūpeṇa svasya bahubhavana-janana-

viṣayaḥ saṁkalpas tu tejaḥ-prabhṛtyanupadānatvena tato bhede' pi svakīyatva-prayukta-bhedopacāra-kṛtaḥ.' But this view is later reoriented on p. 560 to suit the ubhaya-kāraṇa-vāda of Śrīkaṇṭha.

28. BS I.4.23-27. Śrīkaṇṭha's interpretation of this section bears some resemblence to Śrībhāṣya but there are striking departures as may be seen, specially when read with the help of SMD. Rāmānuja understands Brahman literally to be material cause. On the Upaniṣadic statement which declares Prakṛti to be eternal and the material cause of the world, he says (I.4.23) that Prakṛti denotes Brahman in its causal phase when names and forms are not yet differentiated. Śaiva Siddhānta criticises this view under the label of Pañcarātra. SJB I.2, Udāharaṇa Cittruari; also TS 27 Comm.

29. *ibid.* I.4.26.

30. II.7.

31. The Tamil parallels using causative verbs in apposition to the self are given, *ante* note 19.

32. *Taittirīya* II.6.

33. Tamil citations parallel to the Upaniṣadic statements, suggestive of 'nimitta-kāraṇa-pariṇāma' are given in SN 17—lines 67-85, and interpreted *ibid.* 18 lines 75-90. *Māpāḍiam* also cites and discusses similar citations under 'Brahma mudar karna vadam' pp. 150-54 :
ūn*ābi* uyir*ābi* adaṇuḷ niṇḍṛa uṇarv*ābi* piravanaittum nīye niṇṛāi. Appar 6 : 62 : 2; note the use of the participle *abi* literally, having *become*, and also *nindrai*—you do stand.

34. Appar : *Nindra Truttandakam* 1.

35. *ibid.* 6 : 94 : 5; God pervades all distinctions, that of subject and object and also of the inter-subjective. Cf. "nīyāgi nānāgi"

36. *Tiruvācakam* p. 138; *tan oruvanume* palavahi etc. chimes in with ātmānaṁ svayam akuruta of Taittirīya, *op. cit.*

37. Kāraikkālammaiyār Arbutat Tiruvandāti 20.

38. 'liṅge sarvaṁ samutpannaṁ layas tatrai'va co'cyate
liṅgaṁ śambhur iti jñeyaṁ pīṭhaṁ śaktir udāhṛtam
yoni-liṅga-prakāreṇa jagat-sṛṣṭyartha-kāraṇam
sadā saṁyoga-bhāvatvāt kāmarūpam udāhṛtam
liṅge tu jāyate tatra jagat-sthāvara-jaṅgamam
tasmāl-liṅgaṁ viśeṣeṇa-karmarūpam udāhṛtam
karmodaye tu sṛṣṭiḥ syāt karmānte saṁhṛtir bhavet

etat karmeśa-rūpam tu sṛṣṭi-sthiti-layāvaham.' etc. cited SP pp. 40-41.

39. The mantra is the blood flowing in the veins; pada is the crown; varṇa is skin; bhuvana is hair; tattva is the sevenfold components of the body (sapta-dhātu); kāla is the limbs : śāntyatīta-kalā is head; śānti-kalā face; vidyā-kalā breast; pratiṣṭha-kalā navel; nivṛtti-kalā feet. *Supakkam* I.56. Maraijñāna desikar's Comm.
40. BS I.1, 2.
41. *Chānd. Up.* 1.9.1.
42. Śrīkaṇṭha finds basis for the distinction, between akṣara (Being) and ambara (Space) respectively Śiva and Śakti in this and similar texts and also finds support for his doctrine of śakti-pariṇāma-vāda. I.3.10.
43. 'Yoniś ca hi gīyate.' BS I.4.27.
44. *Muṇḍ. Up.* I.1.6.
45. *ibid.* III.1.3; also 'umāsahāyaṁ parameśvaraṁ prabhuṁ trilocanaṁ nilakaṇṭhaṁ praśāntam. dhyātvā munir gacchati *bhūta-yonim*—Kaivalya Up. cited in Śrīkaṇṭha's comm. p. 501.
46. BS I.1.3.
47. Śrīkumāra considers the two sūtras as complementary and as conclusive evidence in support of the material causality of Śiva. TP p. 62.
48. 'yad bhūta-yoniṁ dhīmantaḥ paripaśyanti cā'tmane'—*Sūta-Saṁhitā*, cited SB p. 170; PB p. 84. Cf. Śivāgra yogin's comment: 'yoni-śabdaścopādāne pracura-prayoga-viṣayaḥ.' Also 'yoni-śabdena upādāna-vacanatvam'—*Śrībhāṣyam*, BS I.4.27.
49. While Umāpati interprets 'self becoming of God' in the light of the distinction between nimitta-kāraṇa and upādāna-kāraṇa, Śiva-jñāna yogin finds also a more natural basis for their reconciliation in the theory of advaita. *Māpāḍiam* p. 154.
50. 'āyiṇaṉ eṉba dākkiṇāṉ eṉavē.' SN 18-1. 79.
51. 'āṉāi eṉbadu anaittum avvavai
tāṉāhā maiyaic chāttridum enga.' *ibid.* lines 80-81.
52. *ibid.* lines 85-91. Umāpati here enunciates the nature of advaita relation which underlies such identifications.
53. Even Sāṅkhya which does not accept it, accepts in the empirical realm in the case of body. *Tattva-vaiśāradī* on *Yoga-vārtika I* 18, 20.

54. *Supakkam* 1.56.

55. 'ākāśas tallingāt.' BS I.1.22. Śrīkaṇṭha identifies Brahman with ākāśa; by ākāśa Śrīkaṇṭha refers to the all-pervasive, all-shining (samantāt prakāśate) cit-śakti, of which the intelligent and non-intelligent world is a manifestation, the latter rising and subsiding as bubbles do on water. Here again the issue between Śivādvaita and Śaiva Siddhānta is : does adhiṣṭhāna mean upādānatva.

56. Ākāśa is also used as a synonym for Bindu in the Śaivāgamas : "bindu...anaśvaratvenāparākāśam atiśāyikaṁ parama-vyomākhyam āgamajñāḥ prāhuḥ etc. RT. 56 commentary. See also *Śivādvaita-Nirṇaya* (Madras University), 3-183.

57. SNP 76; Supakkam I. : Śivāgra yogin's Comm. It is surprising that Śivāgra yogin who makes this pointed distinction between yoni and upādāna in these places, inclines to the view—'yoniśabdaś-co'pādāne pracura-prayoga-viṣayaḥ' in SB p. 170.

58. 'bhūtāni cā'haṁ sthirājaṅgamāni
yāvanti cā'nyānyaham eva tāni'—*Devīkalottara-Āgama,* PB p. 85.

59. SP p. 38.

60. 'jagat-sāmānādhikaraṇyaṁ śrūyate. etad apyatyantābhede satyanupapannamiti tādātmyam avagamayati,' PB p. 85.
Śivāgra yogin explains this with illustrations : 'sa ca mṛdghaṭa ityādāvupādānopādeyayor eva dṛṣṭaḥ na tvatyantabhinnayor daṇḍaghaṭayoriti.' SP p. 38.

61. 'nanu "bhūtānicā'haṁ sthirajaṅgamāni yāvanti cānyānyaham eva tāni" ityādinā' bhedo' pi sākṣāt bādhyata iti cet evam api bhede satyabhedasyopādāno'pādeyabhāva-vyāptatvena liṅgenaiva śivasyopādānatvaṁ kalpanīyaṁ tac ca liṅgam upādāna-viparyāya-nirvikāratva-śrutyā vyavasthita-nimitta-nimittitva-pratipādaka-vacanena ca bādhyata eva., PB p. 85.

62. 'yasmin suvidite sarvaṁ vijñātaṁ syād idaṁ surāḥ
tadātmakatvāt sarvasya nāstyeva prabhidā svataḥ'.
Sūta-Saṁhitā, PB p. 84; also :
'yasya śravaṇa-mātreṇa śrutam evā'śrutaṁ bhavet
amataṁ na mataṁ jñātam avijñātan-na sattamaḥ'. *ibid.* p. 85.
These repeat the sense and the expression of the *Chāndoya* text : 'uta tamādeśam aprākṣyaḥ yenā' śrutaṁ śrutaṁ bhavati, amataṁ matam avijñātaṁ vijñātam'.

63. 'prakṛtibhāveno'pādānatvavadanukūla-cikīrṣādiyogena nimittatvasyo' papatteḥ. nimitta-lakṣaṇam api prakṛtibhāvād anyādṛśopayogavattvaṁ tac ca cikīrṣādino' payogavati śive' py akṣatam iti śiva evo'pādānaṁ nimittaṁ ce' ti siddham.' SP p. 39; PB p. 84.
64. SB p. 169: 'tadeva c'opādānatvam ityeka-vijñānena sarvavijñāna-pratijñānusāreṇa upādānatva-viśeṣe tasyāḥ paryavasānam.'
65. 'rājñaḥ prādhānyāt tasmin jñāte sarveṣām amātyādīnāṁ jñāna-phalaṁ sammānādi bhavatīti prādhānya jñāpanārthaṁ vā tat jñānasya sarva-jñāna-phalakatva-khyāpanārthaṁ vā yathā loke rājñi jñāte sarve'mātyādayo jñātā bhavantītyucyate evaṁ prakṛte'pi śivasya prādhānyaṁ jñāpanārthaṁ vā tat jñānasya sarvajñāna-phalakatvaṁ jñāpanārthaṁ vaika-vijñānena sarva-jñāna-pratijñe'ti'. SB, 168. Also, PB p. 86. Also, 'talaimaiyum payanum patri anganam kuriyadu' etc. *Māpāḍiam* p. 154.
66. 'sarva-vijñāna-pratijñā-vākye idaṁ śabdānusāreṇa sarva-śabdasya jagadrūpa-kāryākārya-kārtsnya-paratvāt.' SB p. 169.
67. *Māpāḍiam* p. 155. Air is inseparable with ether, but the qualities of moistness, dryness etc. characteristic of air do not pertain to ether. The salt in sea-water does not make the sea containing the water saline. In the same manner mala is 'contained' by Śiva in so far as nothing without Him can exist but Śiva is not related to it. The two are like light and darkness, the latter subsisting in the former without being related to it. SNP 63, 64, 65. For the difficulties, in admitting 'ajanya-saṁyoga' relation between Śiva and mala, vide *infra* Ch. 10.
68. Closely following the lines of the *Chāndoyga* (VI.1.4-4) runs the *Sūta-Saṁhitā* passage :

'ekenai'va tu piṇḍena mṛttikā yā yathā surāḥ
vijñātaṁ mṛṇmayaṁ sarvaṁ mṛdabhinnatvas surāḥ
ekena lohamaṇinā sarve lohādayo yathā
vijñātās syur athai'kena nakhānāṁ kṛntanena ca
sarvaṁ kārṣṇāya saṁjñātaṁ tadabhinnatvatas surāḥ'. PB p. 86.

69. 'śrutis sanātanī sādhvī sarvamānottamottamā
prāha cā'dvaita-naiṣkalya-*nirvikāratvam ātmanaḥ*'.

Sūta-Saṁhitā,, *ibid.* p. 87.

'paravyomni śikhāntastho *niṣkalaḥ* paramaś śivaḥ'

Siddhāntāgama, *ibid.*

'sarvajñaṁ sarvakartāraṁ bodhānandamayaṁ vibhum

niṣkalaṁ svaprakāśam' etc. *ibid.*
'niṣkalaṁ niṣkriyaṁ śāntam' etc. *Śvetāś Up.* 6-19.

70. 'nirvikāratva-bodhakāgameṣu sākṣān nirvikāratva-bodhaka-padavad abheda-vacaneṣu sākṣād abheda-bodhaka-padābhāvāt eka-vijñānena sarva-vijñāna-pratijñā anyathānupapattyā ca......abhedo'-vagantavyaḥ sa ca sākṣān nirvikāra-śrutyapekṣayā durbalai' ve'tya-bheda-vacanānām evā'nyaparatvaṁ kalpyate.' PB p. 88.

71. Appayya (SMD pp. 557-58; 560-63) reconciles the pūrvapakṣa and the Siddhānta views in respect of interpretation of these texts in a manner which lends great support to the standpoint of Śaiva Śiddhānta. See *infra* Sec. on God as 'Material' cause for the considered view of Appayya on this issue.

72. 'mṛllohādi-dṛṣṭāntasya dārṣṭāntika-vacanasya cā'bhedasthale eka jñānena sarva-viṣayaka-jñāptau yādṛśaṁ phalaṁ bhavati tādṛśaṁ phalaṁ satyapi bhede ca tadvijñānāt bhavatī'tyetadartha-paratva-kalpanā-yuktā.' PB p. 87-88.

Citing Meykaṇḍār's lines to the effect that "they are possessions and we are servants" (II.4) Śivajñāna yogin says that knowledge of the possessive Owner entails knowledge of His possessions and of what is in servitude to him. *Māpāḍiam* p. 154. The definition of Pati, it may be noted, involves knowledge of Paśu and Pāśa (whose definitions are comprehended within the definition of Pati.)

God as the Subject of Existential Judgements

1. Śivāgra yogin construes this as the anumāna-pramāṇa in support of God's material causality. In 'pot is', 'cloth is' there is a syntactical identity between 'is' and what is alleged to be. Nor is this syntactic unity to be dismissed as metaphor as in 'he is a lion'. It is literal, and prima facie there is no contradiction. There are at least three ways of analysing such sentences of syntactic identity, namely, (1) as a member and class ('the pot is a thing'), (2) as quality and the qualificand ('the pot is blue') and (3) as material cause and effect ('the pot is earthen'). The statement, 'pot is' cannot be brought under (1) and (2) for obvious reasons, therefore it has to be analysed in the third way. SB p. 160.

Śrīkaṇṭha is cited in SB p. 160 as hereunder : 'san paṭas san ghaṭa iti sarva-vastuṣvanuvṛttayā sarvagatasya brahmaṇas sarvopādānatvaṁ siddhyati mṛdrūpaṁ hi ghaṭādikaṁ mṛd upādānam iṣyata iti. The original reads slightly differently :

(*a*) The order of 'san paṭaḥ', 'san ghaṭaḥ' is reversed.

(*b*) sarvavastuṣvanuvṛttayā=sarvavastuṣvanugatavṛttayā.

(*c*) sarvagatasya=sadrūpasya. BS. 1.1.2. Śrikaṇṭha's comm.

2. PB p. 86.
3. The Nyāya *tour-de-force* of 'ekārtha samaveta' (Dinakarī) in answer to an objection like whether the universal ghaṭatva has itself in turn another universal ghaṭatvatva abiding in it (Udayana's *Kīraṇāvalī*, Sec. 1 Praśastapāda's comm. on Vaiśeṣika sūtras) anticipates Price's ingenious suggestion on behalf of a philosophy of universals in reply to the demand for a universal for a universal. See his *Thinking and Experience*, Hutchinson, London 1958 Chapter 1.
4. 'sadanuviddhatayā pratīyamāno ghaṭas-sadupādānakaḥ sadanuviddhatayā pratīyamānatvāt yadyadanuviddhatayā pratīyate tattadupādānakam.' PB P. 88.
5. 'śivāt satya-parānandāt āvirbhūtam idaṁ sarvam' etc. *Sūta-Saṁhitā, op. cit.*
6. The argument of the Vedānta in support of brahmopādanatva which Śrīkaṇṭha, and following him Śīvāgra yogin adopts is endorsement of the argument of the Sāṅkhya. See *Vyāsa Bhāṣya* and *Yoga vārttika* IV. 3.
7. 'khaṇḍo gauḥ muṇḍo gauḥ ityādau gavānuviddhatayā pratīyamānakhaṇḍatvādau vyabhicārāt.' PB p. 88.
8. See also the criticism of PMNK 48 Bhaṭṭa Rāmakaṇṭha's comm.
9. 'asat śaśa-śṛṅgam asat kha-puṣpam ityādāvasad anuviddhatayā pratīyamāneṣu śṛṅgādiṣvasad upādānakatvāpatteś-ca.'PB p. 88.
10. 'tadavyaktam āha hi.' BS III.2.23.
11. *Kaṭha Up.* II.3.9, cited in SKB III.2.23. Śrīkaṇṭha thus refutes the view that existentiality characterising alth at exists is Brahman and that the negatives 'not this' 'not this' of the Śruti only negate existence *of pot*, *of cloth* etc. but affirm Existence as such which is Brahman. Still, not very consistently, he says elsewhere (I.1.2), commenting on the name of 'Bhava' ascribed to Brahman, that its denotion of Brahman is suggestive of the truth that Brahman is the material cause of all existents, whom Brahman pervades as clay pervades clay products.

12. '*hṛdā* manīṣā manasābhiklṛptaḥ', the italicised word is suggestive of Divine grace.
13. Bhaṭṭa Rāmakaṇṭha *op. cit.*
14. *ibid.*
15. 'anugata-sādṛśyatva' and not 'anugata-jātitva' is acceptable. Sādṛśya it may be noted, is identity with the thing itself and not its attribute.
16. Bhaṭṭa Rāmakaṇṭha offers the two alternatives of (i) nominalism and (ii) resemblance theory, to a philosophy of universals underlying the view of spirit as the material cause of phenomena.

Qualified Interpretations of God's Material Causality

1. 'nimittam īśvaras sākṣād upādānaṁ sa bindurāṭ' cited PB p. 85.
Also, 'śivo nimittaṁ prakṛtiḥ parāparā
kāryātmatām asya samāpnute jaḍā,' cited SP p. 39.
Also, 'nimittam īśvarākhyaṁ sahakāraṇam
upādānaṁ tu yat sūkṣmaṁ sarva kāryeṣu saṁsthitam;' PB. p. 88.
'sā tu kuṇḍalinī śaṁbhor nityādhiṣṭheya-rūpiṇī
bhogya-bhoktṛtva-sampattyai yā śarīrendriyādikam
utpādayati sā māyā khacitā'karmabhir nṛṇām', cited PB pp. 87-88.
Also the Pauṣkara text 'nā' tra śaktir upādānaṁ cidrūpatvāt-yathā śivaḥ' (2.99) in commenting which Umāpati enters into a detailed discussion of the issue of 'abhinna-nimittopādāna-kāraṇatva' ascribed to Śiva. PB pp. 84-89.
The Parākhya and the Śvetāśvatara texts which distinguish between the two causes are already referred to.
2. Cited *Māpāḍiam* pp. 151-52.
3. *ibid.* The translation of the Tiruvācakam lines is that of Dr. Pope. Also cf. *Appar* 4.64-6; 6. 54-5, for a similar suggestion.
4. The three alternatives, considered in PB p. 87 and repeated in *Māpāḍiam* p. 152, exhaust the views held in different Śivādvaitisms on the question. Cf. also, Sāyaṇa's Taittirīya-Saṁhitā Bhāṣya (Ānandāśrama, Poona) Vol. I, p. 131.
5. This may be taken to be the view represented by Śrīkumāra TP pp. 62-63 : '*paraspara-saṁsṛṣṭayor* eva māyā-maheśvarayor viśva-mūlatvena ubhayor api tadupapatteḥ. māyā tāvan na parameśvarānadhiṣṭhitā jaḍā jagadupādānaṁ bhavati. maheśvaraś-ca cetano' pi na māyāṁ vinā viśvamūlatāṁ bhajate nirvyāpārodāsīna-

mātratvād iti tayoḥ samsṛṣṭayor eva jaganmūlatvam ayaḥ-piṇḍāgnyoriva kārya-kāraṇādīti.' Also SSP p. 42.

6. This is the viśiṣṭa Śivādvaita view of Śrīkaṇṭha, outlined in brief, in the sequel.
7. Śivāgra yogin following Śrīkaṇṭha largely, also adopts this interpretation : 'māyā dvayākhya-parigraha-śakti*viśiṣṭasya* śivasyopādānatve'pi viśeṣaṇībhūta-māyayā eva vikāritvāt. vikāritve' pi kevalasya nirvikāritva-virodhāt.' SP p. 38.
8. 'sākṣāccobhayāmnāyāt' I.4.25 (BS). Śrīkaṇṭha interprets viśvādhikatva to imply nimitta-kāraṇatva and viśvākāratva to imply upādāna-kāraṇatva.
9. The concept of apūrva-pariṇāma is examined below.
10. What follows is the interpretation of Śrīkaṇṭha I.4.27.
11. *Śvetāś Up.* 4-18.
12. *Taittirīya Up.* 2.6.
13. 'idaṃ sarvaṁ asṛjata yad idaṁ kiñca.' *ibid.*
14. 'tat sṛṣṭvā tad evā'nuprāviśat.' *ibid.*
15. 'sac ca tyac cābhavat. *ibid.*
16. What is suggested, by the analogy is that childhood and youth are two viśeṣaṇas successively qualifying the same viśeṣya, viz. the individual and therefore not falling outside its unity.
17. 'māyāṁ tu prakṛtiṁ viddhi māyinaṁ tu maheśvaraṁ
tasyāvayava-bhūtaistu vyāptaṁ sarvam idaṁ jagat. *Śvetāś. Up.* 4.10.
18. Māyā and Prakṛti, it is true, are identified in this sense in the Śvetāś. Up. To take Prakṛti to mean Prakṛti-tattva an evolute of kāla will not be the right interpretation. The Śaivāgamas distinguish Māyā and Prakrti as between a cause and effect. *infra* Ch. 4.
19. 'namo'haṁ-padārtha-rūpāya' Invocatory verse SKB.
20. *Kaivalya Up. op. cit.*
21. 'viśiṣṭasyo pādānatve viśeṣyopādānatvasyā py āvaśyakatvāt. viśiṣṭasya viśeṣaṇa-viśeṣya-tatsambandhānanyatvāt. anyatve ca śivopādānatva-siddhi-prasaṅgāt.' PB p. 87; also, *Māpāḍiam* p. 152.
22. This is a part of the criticism of viśiṣṭa-śakti-pariṇāma-vāda of Śrikaṇṭha. Śivāgra yogin from whom is drawn the substance of the ensuing discussion, does not, however, mean it that way. See SB 183.
23. Śivāgra yogin discusses the soundness of, as many as four interpretations of pariṇāma: (i) avayava-*saṁyoga-mātram*, (ii) avayava-

vistāratvam, (iii) kāraṇasya pūrvarūpa-*parityāgena* tatsamāna-guṇaka-rūpāntarāprāptiḥ, and (IV) pūrva-rūpe tatsamāna-guṇaka-rūpāntar*otpattiḥ*. SB pp. 181-82. The first two smack of creationistic (*ārambha-vāda*) predilections incompatible with the advocacy of 'transformation theory'. Therefore only the remaining interpretations are taken up for discussion.

24. For the doctrine of thirty-six tattvas vide *infra* Ch. 9.
25. upādāna-kāraṇatva ascribed to Śiva in the scripture is not of course to be understood literally. See below.
26. Śivāgra yogin also lists other difficulties : (i) If spirit were material cause only for the initial evolution, all succeeding evolutes evolving from the preceding ones, this explanation will fail in the case of Aśuddha Māyā (the sixth in the order of evolution), which is not an evolute of Śuddha Vidyā (the fifth). The contingence is that spirit will have to evolve directly at least two evolutes, one Śiva-tattva and another Aśuddha Māyā, which is inconceivable on the assumption of *total* evolution of spirit. (ii) Again spirit which is Being itself is continuously present throughout the stages of evolution, as for example, even in pot, as when we say the pot *is*. This is not conceivable of a cause which only evolves the initial product. In cloth, though cotton is present, the cause of cotton-seed is not present. SB pp. 182-83.
27. Śrīkaṇṭha introduces this notion in reply to the objection : 'hanta kāraṇa-vikāra-rūpo hi pariṇāmaḥ pūrvarūpa-parityāgena rūpāntarāpattiḥ pariṇāma iti kathaṁ parameśvaro'nartha-dharmāt pariśrūyata iti cet.' SKB I. 4.27.
28. *Māpāḍiam* p. 153.
29. It is significant to note that the term pariṇāma is not used anywhere in the Upaniṣads. Commenting on the Sūtra text 'pariṇāmāt' Śrīkaṇṭha is naturally constrained to admit the concept. And yet he had to reorient the concept, as otherwise predicating pariṇāma literally of Brahman would take him into the camp of the Bhedābheda-vādin from whose view he expressly dissents. Cf. SKB. 11.1.22.
30. 'āgamasya anumānāpekṣayā prabalatvena tasyai'vānumānabādhakatvāt.' SP p. 38; Śrīkaṇṭha also tends to flout reason in favour of Śruti over this issue : 'tarkabalam apahāya śrutir-evāvalambanīye'ti' etc. SKB. 11.2.38.

31. *Māpāḍiam* p. 153.
32. Śivāgrayogin introduces Vṛtti an Āgamic notion to reconcile texts which ascribe material causality to Śiva impliedly and also, according to him, expressly, with texts declaring spirit's immutability (nirvikāra-śrutis). See the section under 'nirvikāra-śrutibādha-parihāraḥ' SB pp. 170-73.
33. See beginning of the same section.
34. These are the usual examples given. SB p. 183; Māpāḍiam p. 174; RT 49 Comm. Śrīkaṇṭha also refers to it, commenting on the Sūtra 'paṭavac ca' (II.1.19) :

    'yathā saṁkucitaḥ sūkṣmarūpaḥ paṭaḥ prasārito mahāpaṭa-kuṭīrūpeṇa kāryaṁ bhavati tathā Brahmā'pi saṁkucita-rūpaṁ kāraṇaṁ prasārita-rūpaṁ kāryaṁ bhavati'. Also 'kuṇḍalavat' III.2.26.
35. 'pūrvam api kuṭyādi-vyavahāra-prasaṅgāt'. SB p. 183.
36. Śivāgra yogin himself raises this question but answers it quite indifferently. *ibid.* pp. 183, 184.
37. It is not therefore surprising that the author of Māpāḍiam who follows the lead of Śivāgra yogin in certain respects does not endorse the theory of vṛtti. See also *Supakkam* I. 64.
38. This seems to be Śivāgra yogin's reply to the criticism of PB p. 87, viz. 'viśiṣṭasya upādānatva-viśeṣyopādānatvasyāpyā-vaśyakatvāt.' SB pp. 183-184.
39. Vṛtti, also called sūkṣma-pariṇāma is the admitted mode of 'evolution' of Śuddha Māyā, while in the case of Aśuddha Māyā it is said to be sthūla-pariṇāma. *Infra* Ch-9.
40. *Ante*, sec. on God as the Ground of Cosmic Dissolution.
41. RT rejects the applicability of vṛtti as well as pariṇāma as a mode of material causality to spirit as such : 'cetanatvād *vṛttitvāt* pariṇāmāt tatas tathā, ātmā śaktiś ca vijñeyau. 49. Vṛtti is admitted as but only sūkṣma-pariṇāma, (*Māpāḍiam* p. 175), not intrinsically different from pariṇāma : vṛtti-pariṇāmayor atyantabhedabhāvāc-ca. RT. 69 Comm.
42. The concept of vivarta is criticised below.
43. 'kevalasya kāraṇasyā' vasthāntara vaiśiṣṭya-mātram evo' pādāna-tva-prayojakaṁ guṇa-kriyopādāna-sādhāraṇam.' SB p. 184.
44. *ibid.* p. 184 ff.
45. See John Macmurray : *The Self as Agent*, p. 84 (1957).

46. Though no classical Śaiva thinker entertains this concept and interprets Śiva's material causality as vivartopādāna, it is included here for a brief notice because of its intrinsic significance as a kind of *reductio ad absurdum* of all interpretations of God's material causality. Śrīkumāra and Śivāgra yogin who advocate material causality of Śiva naturally come into conflict with vivarta-vāda, TP p. 63; SB p. 184. Śrīkaṇṭha too distinguishes his standpoint from that of vivarta-vāda : 'na vātyantābheda-vādinaḥ *śukti-rajatayor ivaikatara-mithyātvena* tat-svābhāvika-guṇa-bheda-para-śruti-virodhāt' (II.1.22).

Appayya Dikṣita, however, thinks that vivarta view is logically entailed in the doctrine of cit-śakti-pariṇāma of Śrikaṇṭha : 'tathā sakala-prapañcākārāyāḥ cicchakteḥ brahmabhedābhyupagamena viyadādi prapañcaḥ tad-*vivarta iti sidhyati*' *Śivādvaita-Nirṇaya* 3.192.

47. *Siddhānta-leśa* (2.12). The pūrva-pakṣa here is that while the function of saṁhāra may point to a material cause as the ground of world-resolution, sṛṣṭi like the creation of pot by the potter, and sthiti like governance of a kingdom by the ruler, point to an efficient cause, presumably different from the material cause.

48. Śaṅkara's Comm. *Bṛhad Up.* I.11.

49. There are three different interpretations of material causality of spirit in Vedānta, all of course subscribing to the view of effectuation as but appearance : (i) Pure Brahman alone as the material cause (Saṁkṣepa-śārīraka view), (ii) Brahman in the form of Īśvara as the material cause (the vivaraṇa view), and (iii) Jīva as the material cause (Dṛṣṭi-sṛṣṭi-vāda). *Siddhāntaleśa op. cit.* Under (ii) again there are several viewpoints : (a) Īśvara or Brahman and māyā both as the material cause (*Padārtha-tattva-nirṇaya*); (b) *Īśvara* that is qualified by māyā as the material cause (*Saṁkṣepa-śārīraka*), (c) Īśvara *as qualified by māyā* as the material cause (*Vivaraṇa, Pañcadaśī*), (d) Īśvara as being the substrate of māyā as the material cause (*Siddhānta-Muktāvalī*). *ibid.*

50. *infra* Ch. 7 Sec on God and the Absolute.

51. Murti, T.R.V : The Two Definitions of Brahman in the Advaita : *Krishna Chandra Bhattacharya Memorial Volume*, Indian Institute of Philosophy, Amalner, 1958.

52. This is argued at some length in Chapter 7, sec. on the concept of Divine will : Śakti.
53. The incompatibility of 'nirguṇa Brahman' with world-creation is the main objection against vivarta-vāda; 'palavumāna guṇam-oruvu mēkamadu venavu nīpaharin nikarilā ulakamānadanai udavumāradilai uṇarvudānumilai uṇarilē.' *Parapakkam*,. Māyāva-dimata marudalai;
54. Vide *infra*, Chapter 8.
55, PA raises the pūrva-pakṣa : 'prapañco'vastutve vastu-māyā kathaṁ bhavet?' (3.16) and replies that on valid grounds of sense and reason the world has to be taken as real : 'vastvātma-kaṁ viśvaṁ bhavet katham avastujam?' (3.25).

'tat-sādhana-phalasya brahmajñāna-nivartyatvasya prapañcasya satyatve'pi tasya jñāna-nivartyatva-vacana-sāmarthyād api sam-bhavāc ca.' SB p. 185.
56. Different theories of error are discussed in Chapter, 12. Śri-kumāra defends at great length the view that the content of error is not illusory (mithyā). TP pp. 63-64.

Umāpati raises the question of avidyā conceivable neither as (i) essentially related to spirit nor as (ii) related to spirit adventitiously (upādhivaśāt). The latter alternative may be illustrated by the example of the dark speck in a lamp-light which is not instrinsic to light but is occasioned by the adjuncts of oil, wick etc. In the same manner the world-appearance is due to the accident of Brahman's association with avidyā. But asks Umāpati, whence comes this association ? If it is 'natural' as clouds associate with ether, then its dissipation cannot be brought about by one's effort; mokṣa cannot be the end of spiritual endea-vour. If the association is not natural but is brought about, there must be some other cause to bring it about and Brahman's associa-tion with that has to be accounted. SN 4-90 to 102.
57. Schomerus, *loc.cit.* p. 173 ff.
58. SN, 3, Lines 22, 23
59. Schomerus, *op.cit* p. 174
60. 'After criticising Vivarta-vāda, Śivāgra yogin ends by saying: nā' pi tat tiraskriyate iṣṭa-vighātasyā' niṣṭa-prāpter vā' bhāvāditi. SB p. 185.

61. 'Sarvaṁ kāryaṁ mithyai'va vikalpāsahatvāt' is the argument for vivartopādanatva. SB. p. 184.
62. 'jaḍa-kārya-svabhāvānusāreṇa māyayai'va pariṇāmitvaṁ śivasya tadhiṣṭhānatayo'pādānatvam.' PB p. 87.
63. There is no clear-cut distinction to be made between the two positions : Śiva *qualified by* Māyā as the material cause and Śiva the *ground of* Māyā as the material cause, from the perspective of persons who actually held to one or the other of these positions. Śivāgra yogin, though is on the defensive about viśiṣṭādvaita and even justifies it by means of the concept of vṛtti, inclines to hold the other view as final and the more adequate from the point of view of reconciling (i) śivopādānatva and nirvikāritva of Śiva.

'sākṣād upādānībhūta-*māyādhāratayā'ṁśuvat paṭe śivasya* jagadupādānībhūta-*māyādhāratva - rūpa - paramparopādānatva-viṣayatvaṁ kalpyate* nirvikāra-pramāṇasya ca sākṣād vikārābhāva-viṣayatvaṁ kalpyate, SB p. 170.

Śrīkaṇṭha and Appayya also oscillate between the two views but seem to incline, Appayya more definitely towards the second view. See below.
64. 'evañca pati-padārtha-śivasya tadhiṣṭhita-māyāyāśca kāryabhūta-prapañcasya svadharma-sattā-sphūrti-priyādi-rūpatayā, jaḍavikārādi-rūpatayā co'bhayor upādānatvam. śivasya tu māyāyā *adhiṣṭhātṛtayā* nimittam adhikam iti viśeṣah.' SP p. 40.
65. 'tatra ca vahner iva śivasya nimittatvam iti na tadutkṛṣṭa-dharmavattvam'. *ibid.* p. 40.
66. As a theory of causation in which the parts conjoin to make for the whole is not acceptable the material cause which 'becomes' effect here in this instance, can only be fire with wet fuel. *Ibid.* p. 40.
67. 'vahni-dharma-bhūta-uṣṇyāder apy upalabhyamānatvena grāhataulyāt.' *ibid.* p. 40.
68. Śivāgra yogin gives this example in his commentary on *Supakkam* 2-1.
69. Citations from Āgama, Purāṇa, Tevaram, and Tiruvācakam are given by Śivāgra yogin of texts expressive of or implying twin causality of Śiva in the above sense, in the sequal to his commentary. *ibid.* 2-1. These have been discussed with regard to their interpretation, *ante* Sec. I of this Chapter.

70. 'nanu kartur upādānatve nāsti virodhaḥ. ūrṇanābhau darśanāt. na hi dṛṣṭe' nupapattir nāma. na ca vācyam ūrṇanābher deha eva tadupādānaṁ. sa tu kevalaṁ tantuṣviti yatho'rṇa-nābhis sṛjate gṛhṇate ce'ti śrutau tantun sraṣṭūr ūrṇa-nābher eva tallayādhāratva-pratipādanena pratyakṣa-saṁvādinā tadupādānatvasyā'pi siddheḥ. tallayādhārasya tadupādānatva-niyamāt. evaṁ ca śrutisiddhorṇa nābhi-dṛṣṭāntānusāreṇa brahmaṇo'pi jagat-kartur upādānatvaṁ kalpyate.' SMD Vol. I, p. 559.

71. Śrīkaṇṭha who advocates the viśiṣṭa-śivādvaita point of view and expounds a doctrine of unique Transformation of spirit says towards the end of janmādhikaraṇa : 'māyāṁ tu prakṛtiṁ vidyād iti māyāyāḥ *prakṛtitvam īśvarātmikayā* eva 'māyinaṁ tu maheśvaram iti vākyaśeṣāt'. At another place (1.4.10) he says commenting on the word 'ajā' of the same Upaniṣadic text : pralaya-kāle nāma-rūpe vihāyā' cid-vastu-rūpā māyā'pi sūkṣma-rūpeṇa maheśvarasya śarīratayā tiṣṭhatītyajā sṛṣṭi-samaye nāma-rūpopetā tat-kāraṇike' ti....*evaṁ prakṛter ajātveśvara-kāraṇikatvayor avirodhaḥ.*'

(Italics ours)

For a true clarification of the meaning of ubhaya-kāraṇatva attributed to God in the Śvetāśvatara text, according to Śivādvaita one has to consult SMD pp. 134-35 :

'māyopādānam iti brahmā'pyupādānam eva apṛthak-siddha-*kāryāvasthāśrayatva*-rūpaṁ hi māyāyā upādānatvaṁ samarthanīyam. tat sāmarthyamānam eva *brahmaparyantam* āyāti....māyāyāḥ brahmāpṛthak-siddhyai'va tadapṛthak-siddhāyāḥ kāryāvasthāyā api brahmāpṛthak-siddhis sidhyati. evaṁ ca yadyapi *brahmāśrayā māyā* viyadādyacetana-rūpeṇa pariṇamati brahmāśrayā tadāśraya-jīvāśrayā ca cicchaktiḥ jñānādi-rūpeṇa na tu brahma kenāpyā-kāreṇa pariṇamati. tathāpi tathā tathā pariṇāmamānānāṁ *māyādīnāṁ brahmai'vāyuta-siddhāśrayatvaparyavasāna-bhūmir iti* brahmaparyantam upādānatvam āyātī'ti bhāvaḥ. (Italics ours)

Śivajñāna yogin makes reference to this clarification of Appayya, in his estimate of the closeness of Śivādvaita and Śaiva Siddhānta over this issue, *Māpāḍiam* p. 153.

72. 'vikāritāpādakopādānatvasyai'va asmābhir niṣiddhyamānatvāt.' PB p. 87.

73. The nimitta-kāraṇa of the Śaivite is not identical with the concept bearing the same name as understood by the Nyāyā-Vaiśeṣika,

no more than his upādāna-kāraṇa is identical with the samavāyi-kāraṇa of the latter. *Ante* Sec. on the World-Cause as Agent.

74. 'tārakamai *viravi* niṇdru adittittalān.' *Māpāḍiam* p. 153. This is the demand underlying Śivādvaitin's contention that Brahman is also the upādāna-kāraṇa. Were God upādāna-kāraṇa only in the sense of being the ground of material existence without also *pervading* it, even the floor on which rests a pot may be considered the material cause of the pot.

'anyathā mṛdi ghaṭākāreṇa pariṇamamānāyāṁ tadākāreṇā' pariṇamamānaṁ bhūtalam api tadupādānaṁ kalpyeta,.' SMD p. 557 (Vol. I).

75. This kind of vyāpti is distinguished as aupaśleṣika from another variety of vyāpti called vaiṣayika where pervasion is extrinsic like ether pervading all objects of determinate form. *Supakkam* 1.1; Śivāgra yogin's Comm.

76. The karaṇa is present in the cause as moisture and also in the effect as its sap. In the same way, Śiva is the sole cause in the sense of being the ground of the world phenomena and also present pervasively in the latter through His śakti.

77. *Māpāḍiam* p. 158 ff.

78. Śiva-ñana-Siddhi therefore describes nimitta-kāraṇa as ground *par excellence* to distinguish it from the so-called 'ground' viz. material cause :
"iṛudiyil aranē ellām aṛittalāl avanāl iṇṇum
perudunām ākkam nokkam *pēradikaraṇattālē*."
Supakkam 1.55. See Śivajñana yogin's Comm.

CHAPTER FIVE

GOD AS THE LORD OF COSMIC FUNCTIONS

The Five Cosmic Functions

1. The pre-eminence of saṁhāra in relation to other cosmic functions is explained, *ante* Chapter 2, Sec. on God as the Ground of Cosmic Dissolution.
2. *Māpāḍiam* p. 112. SB 341-342
3. The expression 'reality' is used as appellation of God : 'sarvasyāpi jagataḥ kartā śiva eva, sa eva ca paratatvam iti.... tad yadi nityaṁ, svatantraṁ pradhānaṁ syāt, tat śivasya paratvāt tasyāpi paratvaṁ syāt' SB p 143. 'janmādikaṁ janmasthiti-pralaya-tirobhāvānugraha-rūpam.' SKB I.1.2. These cosmic functions are explained below. We owe the clarification of the meanings of Śiva, Śakti and Pati to the illuminating commentary of Śivajñāna yogin, *Supakkam* 2.1.
4. The three categories of prakāśa, vimarśa and maheśvara recognised in the Trikā system correspond to Śiva, Śakti and Pati of Śaiva Siddhānta.
5. These three issues constitute respectively the subject matter of the following sections of the present chapter. The order of presentation follows with slight variations the adhikaraṇas of Meykaṇḍār's SÑP sūtram 2.
6. *Māpāḍiam* p. 112.
7. Even Thomas Aquinas implies a distinction between the standpoint of the wise—the mystics who know the essence of things, and that of the layman, in his theology. "The proposition *God is* is self-evident *of itself* for the predicate is the same as the subject because God is His own being. But because *we* do not know the essence of God the proposition is not self-evident *to us* but needs to be demonstrated by things *more* known to *us*, though less known in their nature". *Summa Theologica* 1.9.2. a .1.C.
8. The taṭastha-lakṣaṇa is apprehended through pramāṇa and lakṣaṇa. Svarūpa-lakṣaṇa is apprehended through sādhana and phala. *Māpāḍiam* p. 400. Also Chapter 7 *infra.*

9. Two definitions of Brahman according to Advaita : T.R.V. Murti (1958).
10. As an illustration of their continuity may be cited the discourse of Varuṇa in Taittirīya Up. which begins with taṭastha-lakṣaṇa : 'yato vā imāni bhūtāni jāyante' etc. and ends, *in the same tenor*, with svarūpa-lakṣaṇa : 'ānandād hyeva khalvimāni bhūtāni jāyante' etc. Jagat-kāraṇatva and ānanda-guṇakatva are both indicated in the same manner as lakṣaṇas of Brahman. PB p. 9.
11. This forms the subject of the 3rd adhikaraṇa of the first sūtra of SÑP.
12. The definition of Brahman given in BS I.1.2 involves possession of the qualities mentioned above and Śrīkaṇṭha shows how these metaphysical attributes are uniquely met by the eight names indicative of Śiva—Bhava, Śarva, Rudra, Īśāna, Paśupati, Ugra, Bhīma and Mahādeva. See the comments of SMD on them, vol I, pp. 125-138.
Also 'saccidānanda-rūpī yaḥ sadasadvyakti-varjitaḥ
sa śivas sarvagaḥ sadbhir brahma-śabdena śabditaḥ'
NVM p. 416
13. This is discussed at great length in SKB and SMD 1.1.21-22; 1.2.3-8. Also SB pp. 126-135; *Māpāḍiam* pp. 86-94.
14. The distinction is Tillich's. *Systematic Theology*, Harper and Row, 1967, Vol. I pp. 225-226.
15. This section is based on the accounts given in Pañcakṛtya Prakaraṇam. MA; *Māpāḍiam* pp. 110-117; and most important on the Cindanaiurai. Verse no 18 SVP.
16. *Tiruvācakam* 33, 4 note in this verse the transition from causative verbs (marappittu, paṇṇuvittu) to non-causative verbs (arindu, kūruvadē). Ignorance, forgetting are unsconscious processess while to know 'I am ignorant' 'I had forgotten' are conscious, processes.
17. MA 6-7, 8.
18. '*pandam* vīdu pārttidin aruḷe ellām. *Supakkam* I. 37.
19. The concept of 'pāka' or 'paripāka' implies conjunction with agencies like time which bring about a termination of the potential condition of a thing. See *infra* Chapter 14. Also Ṛg *Veda* VII. 59.12 : 'May he release me like the cucumber from its stem' 'mṛtyor mukṣīya māmṛtāt'

20. 'eyum mummalangaḷ tattam toḷinai iyattra ēvum tūyavan tanatōr sakti tirodāna *kariyadu.*' *Supakkam* 2.87.

21. 'tirobhāvaḥ saṁsāri-vargasya nityasiddha-jñāna-kriyā-śaktyādyāvaraṇaṁ sakala-sāṁsārikānartha-mūla-bhūtabandhākhyam.' SMD Vol. 1 p. 109.

22. What is matured by saṁhāra is strictly the sañcita-karma. The desire for Bhoga arises in the soul in strict accord with the maturation of a part of the sañcita. BK 1, Comm.

23. 'anugrahas tato mokṣaḥ.' SMD p. 109; also TP 36, Aghora Śiva's Comm. The causal relation between (i) bhogānubhava (ii) karma-nāśa, and (iii) mokṣarūpa anugraha is the continuity between Bondage and Freedom. Śrīkumāra also gives an interesting explanation of the sense of continuity between tirodhāna and anugraha *ibid.* Comm. p. 7. See also SMD. Vol. 2. pp. 49-51.

24 'azippiḷaip pāttṛal,' *Supakkam* 1.37.
'oḍukkam iḷaippozittal,' Svp 18.
Also, 'saṁsāre khinnānāṁ sarveṣāṁ prāṇināṁ prabhuḥ *kṛpayā* kurute mahārtha-saṁhṛtiṁ eteṣām eva *viśrāntyai.*' TP 70. Also BK. 122, Comm. The TP text is cited in SMD Vol. 2, p. 50; Also, Śrīkumāra cites the following in his commentary (p. 166) :

'kāryavyāsakta-cittānāṁ viśrāntyai rajanī yathā
saṁhāraṁ bhava-khinnānāṁ kṛpayā kurute śivaḥ'

25 In saṁhāra, the physical vital and mental existence of self—the annamaya, prāṇamaya and manomaya kośas involved in a life of activity, is subject to resolution; there is consequently upa-saṁhāra for "tanu, karaṇa, bhuvana and bhoga" There is termination for the māyā-kārya (which are counter-active against mala-obstruction). In sṛṣṭi, again what is terminated is revived from their causal condition viz. māyā, which exists outliving Dissolution. *Supakkam* 1.33. Śivāgra yogin's Comm.

26. 'ākkam avvavar-kanma mellām kazittiḍal', *Supakkam* 1.37.
'karmavipācanahetoḥ paśu-*dayayā* punarapīha parameśaḥ sṛṣṭiṁ vidhāya karmāṇyevaṁ pācayati dehabhṛtām.' TP 71.

27. According to Aquinas the actual existence of a world existing solely because of God's infinitude demands necessarily that its actual existence be sustained every instant by creation on the part of the Creator. See also Tillich, P., *Systematic Theology* Vol I pp 261-270, *op. cit.*

28. 'nuhatac ceydal kāppadu.' *Supakkam loc. cit.*
29. SMD Vol I gives (p. 112) a discerning analysis of the concept of sthiti. The concept is distinguished from sṛṣṭi in the following way. It is a common place that, of two objects produced simultaneously at a time, one *lasts* for a longer duration than the other. The difference in the duration of their existence is to be traced to difference in the mode of production, ultimately again to be traced to the will of an intelligent agent to that effect. What is true of inanimate object is also true in respect of the 'stay' of animate existence. The latter is conditioned by differences in karma referrable again ultimately to the Divine will. Conservation of life and existence like their creation is therefore a cosmic function of the Lord.
"tad adṛṣṭa-dvayaṁ tajjanya-kāryagatālpādhika-kālāvasthānābhisandhimat-parameśvara-preraṇādhīna-karmānuṣṭhāna-prabhavam iti sidhai'va tayor alpādhika-kālāvasthiteḥ parameśvara-saṁkalpāpekṣā."
Also, "kiñ-ca janmavataḥ prapañcasya yāvan nāśaṁ sthiti-ruhyamāna--jalakumbhasya sthitir devadattasye'va parameśvarasya dhāraṇa-vyāpāram apekṣate sa ca vyāpāro janmavad idaṁ *yāvan nāśam itthaṁ tiṣṭhatvityājñā-rūpas tasya saṁkalpa* eva'.
A third interpretation is also given : 'kecit tu prapañcāntargata-cetanācetana-padārthānāṁ parameśvara-niyukta-svasvakārya-karaṇena maryādāyām avasthitiḥ sthitirity āhuḥ.' *ibid.* p. 112. All are different versions of the same truth of will-causality—the source of will to which conservation of existence life and value like their creation is to be traced.
30. TTN 20, Comm. Also 'tezittidal malangalellam maraippu.' *Supakkam, loc. cit.*
31. Compare 'namaḥ śaṅkarāya ca, mayaskarāya ca'
32. 'sarvajñatvena sarveṣāṁ saṁsāriṇāṁ duḥkhaṁ jānataḥ sarvaśaktikatvena sarvān api tān yugapad eva moktuṁ śaktasya parameśvarasya śiva-śaṅkarādi-nāma-khyāpitā sarvabhūtaviṣayiṇī karuṇā nirupādhiḥ paraduḥkha-prahāṇecchārūpā teṣām anādibhava-sañcita-nānāvidha-duḥkha-janaka-karmavṛnda-sāmarthyaṁ paribhūya sarvānartha-mūlāvaraṇocchedapūrvikām ātyantika-duḥkha-nivṛttiṁ teṣāṁ yugapad eva katham na kuryāt. yadi tasya tattat-karmānuvartanasvabhāvatayā teṣāṁ sakala karma-bṛnda-dāhaka-sva-

viṣayasākṣātkārodaya-paryantaṁ teṣu sahaja-karuṇonmeṣa-virodhi-tattadāvaraṇānuvṛtti-saṁkalpo na syāt. atas tathābhūtasaṁkalpāvaśyaṁbhāve tadadhinānuvṛttikasyāvaraṇasya yasmin satyagrimakṣaṇe yasya sattvaṁ yadvyatireke cā' sattvam tattajjanyam iti lakṣaṇānusāreṇa tasya tajjanyatvasiddhau parameśvara-kartṛkatvam api tasya siddhyati. kāryānukūla-saṁkalpavattvasyaiva kartṛlakṣaṇatvāt.' SMD Vol. 1 p. 110; *Māpāḍiam* pp. 115-16.

As Śivajñāna yogin observes it is because of the fact that obstruction or concealment is due to the will of the Lord that it is intelligible that self's knowledge and action are manifest sometimes and dormant at other times and also admit of a progressive ascent towards fulfilment. *Ibid.* p. 323.

33. 'tāsāṁ māheśvarī śaktis sarvānugrāhikā śivā
dharmānuvartanād eva pāśa ityupacaryate
pariṇāmayatī tāś-ca rodhāntaṁ kārkacittviṣā
yadonmīlanam ādhatte tadā'nugrāhikocyate.' MA 7-11, 12.

MA brings out the exact sense of the tirodhāna function in reply to the question how the gracious nature of the Lord is compatible with His pāśānugrahatvam. The Lord effects bondage by activising the inert bonds as only a means or occasion (upāya). One cannot attain to Freedom as long as one is under the authority of mala, Freedom being ultimately freedom from Mala. The authority of mala (malādhikāra) does not terminate without actualisation of the potential śaktis of mala, and actualisation is not accomplished of its own accord, even were mala fit to be actualised. sarvathā sarvadā 'yasmāc cit prayojyam acetanam.' Therefore there is no incompatibility between bestowing grace and activising mala into its action of binding as only a means thereto. *ibid.* 7-13 to 17. See also the illuminating comments of the *Vṛtti* and the *Dīpikā* on the passages.

34. These analogies are used in the Śaiva texts. MA 7-17; *Supakkam* 2.52.

35. It thus follows that not only the fifth of the five cosmic functions but the other four too are functions of grace.

'pōttralarum arul aruleyandri mattrup puhandravaiyum arulozíayap puhalonāde.' SVP 18, see also *Cindanaiyurai* (Samājam, 1934).

The example of fire latent in tender and dry wood respectively illustrates the presence of mala in man in an unripe and ripe condition. *Supakkam* 11. (as solar heat in any combustible material).

36. 'na cā' yaṁ paśūnāṁ patyanugrahākhyo mokṣas tāvat pravartate yāvad eṣām anādi-caitanyāvārakasya malasyādhikāro na nivartate.' SSP p. 2; also, tamaśśaktyadhikārasya nivṛttes tat-paricyutau, vyanakti dṛkriyānantyaṁ jagadbandhur aṇo śivaḥ.' MA, cited *ibid.* p. 2.

37. *Periya Purāṇam* is the account of lives marked by such abrupt disruption *ante* Chapter Sec. on the Formative Factors of Śaiva Siddhānta.

God as Non-dual

1. God's aseity is not understood in Śaiva Siddhānta as exclusive of His relatedness. Deity and absoluteness are reconciled in the concept of śakti. *infra* Ch. 7. God's aseity in Hindu theological thinking does not import any sense of necessity but means the Freedom of God which is enunciated in the concept of Śakti.
2. Chapter 3, Sec. on the world-Cause as Agent.
3. *Māpāḍim* p. 118 ff. Umāpati raises the issue of the 'telos of creative function of the Lord' as part of his critique of Śivādvaita, and as a preliminary towards an understanding of the new concept of advaita which Śaiva Siddhānta puts forward. SN 18, lines 9-17.
4. Cf. the doctrine of Aristotle that God moves the creatures *from without* as the object of their love. *Metaphysics* Book 11, op *cit.*
5. 'kuṇḍalādiṣu bhāveṣu sarvathaiva svarṇataḥ' *Śivadṛṣṭiḥ* VI. 92 athāmbudhi-vīcivat' *ibid* III. 37.
6. 'porppaṇi pol apedamum iruḷveḷipōr pedamum corporul pōl pēdāpēdamum indri.' SVP 8.
7. 'na prayojanavattvāt'. BS II. 1.32.
8. 'lokavat tu *līlākaivalyam.*' *ibid.* II. 1.33.
9. 'āṭkoṇḍaruḷum viḷayāṭṭu,' literally, the game of the redeeming grace. The reference here is to all cosmic functions whose one homogeneous purpose is redemption from the evil of mala.
10. Śivajñāna yogin's Comm. *Supakkam* 1.36; also *Māpāḍiam* p. 119. SJS suggests either of or both the alternatives of (i) līlā and (ii) fulfilment and reclamation of the bound souls, implying their mutual compatibility: 'munnavan viḷayāṭṭendru mozidalumām,

uyirkku manniya putti mutti vazangavum aruḷāl munne tunniya malangaḷ ellām tuḍaippadum cullalāme.' *ibid.*

11. 'avaiyē tānē yāy'. SÑP 2. See Śivajñāna yogin's Comm. The clue for a comprehensive interpretation of Meykandār's phrase seems to have been supplied by the lines from N : 'nilanīr tīkal veḷiyuyir yāvum/*avaiye tanavai tāne yābi*'. Also, 'unnindra sōthi *ura-nindra orudal*' TM 450.

12. 'anyas san vyāptito' nanyaḥ.' SJB (S) 2, is interpreted by Śivāgra yogin on pantheistic lines as identity between God as material cause and the world as effect. It is Śivajñāna yogin who makes a discerning distinction between 'tādātmya' and 'advaita' relations in the above manner.

13. *Chāndogya Up.* VI. 2.1. The word 'advaita' indeed occurs in several passages of the Veda. Of these 'eka eva rudro na dvitīyāya tasthe' (*Yajur Veda* I. 8.6),'eko hi rudro na dvitīyāya tasthuḥ' (*Śveta. Up.* 3.2), and the Chāndogya text are of special moment. The latter text relating to Creation is interpreted in the light of the two other texts in respect of (i) the occurrence of both ekam and advaitam used appositionally to the same subject, (ii) the use of the word advaitam which occurs in its original form 'na dvitīya' with the suggestion of conscious negation and (iii) interpretation of Being (sat) in a supra-deterministic, and not indeterministic sense, on parity with 'Rudra'. (just as the latter term has its super-personalistic connotations, *ante* Ch. 2, Sec. I, sat also has personalistic implications .

Cf. "śaktiś śivaś-ca sacchabda-prakṛti-pratyayoditau
tau brahma-sāmarasyena samastajagadātmakau".

Quoted SKB I. 1.5).

14. The Tamil word *udanādal* is the aptest, as suggestive of a bare denial of difference (vērarakkudi nitral, *Māpāḍiam* p. 122). And the word is used in the doctrinal and devotional literature of Tamil :

'ullamum tānum *uḍane* irukkinum
uḷṭam avanai uruvariyāde.' TM 431.

'vērāi *uḍanānan*'. Sambandar 1.11.2; Appar 11.2; also 4.75.3

15. Schomerus, *op. cit.* p. 81, 'Dementsprechend umschreiben die Kommentare das Wort Advaita mit *Nicht fremd sein*, *Nicht gretrennt sein* in Verbindung stehen.' (italics added)

16. *Śabda-Kalpadruma* gives six meanings of the negative particle : 'tatsādṛśyam abhāvaś ca tadanyatvaṁ tadalpatā aprāśaṣtannirodhaś ca nañarthāṣṣaṭ prakīrttitāḥ'
17. The author of *Vacanālaṅkāra Dīpam* on SJB cites the authority of *Paribhāṣenduśekhara* in support of equating anyārtha which Śaiva Siddhānta adopts, with sādṛśya : 'nañ iva yuktam anya-sadṛśādhikaraṇe tathāhyarthagatiḥ.'
18. nā'sya dvitīyaṁ vastvanantaraṁ vidyata ityadvitīyam.' Śaṅkara's Comm. *Chāndogya Up. op. cit.* Rāmānuja also interprets it monophystically : 'advitīya-padenā' dhiṣṭhātrantaranivāraṇād asyai'vā'-dhiṣṭhātṛtvam api pratipādyate. *Vedārtha-Saṁgraha* (Jour. of Annamalai Univ. Vol. VIII, p. 8).
19. Srīkumāra always interprets 'ekam' as synonymous with 'advitīyam.' TP. Comm. p. 3, 14. Contrast it with Aghora Śiva's interpretation.
20. Māpāḍiam makes this analysis in order to distinguish the interpretation which Meykandār gives of the concept of advaita from the classical interpretations of the term. The apellation 'Śuddhādvaita' is used for the Advaitism enunciated in SJB. pp. 121, 122, 392-95.
21. Cf. Marcel's distinction between the notions of co-presence and of prescience. *Being and Having* (Boston, Beacon Press 1951), pp. 80, 81.
22. The conjunctive particle 'udan' in Tamil as used in Śaiva and Vaiṣṇava hymns and focussed by Meykandār for the theological construction of Śaiva Siddhānta, is to be understood in a different context of ideas from that of the spatial relation of accompaniment (the spatial 'with'). *Being-with* does not mean X being accompanied by or being in the company of Y. It signifies an existential relation, as being freely bound up or involved with what is not itself in its existence. Such is the uniqueness about the structure of the being of spirit. Being of spirit differs from the being of objects precisely in this respect.
23. There are two ways of understanding non-existence or non-being, one in an absolute sense, which is more of the nature of a limiting concept in relation to being, and other, non-being but in a relative sense, having a dialectical relation with being. The sensitiveness and genius of Tamil language, specially that of the hymnists provides the possibility of distinguishing the second from the first;

'dialectical' non-being which affirms while also denying is called *anmai* as distinguished from *inmai* which is negation in the accepted sense of denial. The first is negation of quality while the other is negation of existence. When 'anmai' is predicated of something the suggestion is not certainly that of affirmation of its opposite, nor again a denial of it *in se*, but only denial of a quality with the implied assertion of existence compatibly with that quality.

Negation in the dialectical sense (anmai) is illustrated by reference to an old use of the term, in *Tirukkural* : 'Porul *alla*-vattraip porulendunarum marul etc.' (36.1) which defines the function of Delusion (marul) whereby men deem that the truth which *is not*. The expression 'alla' is suggestive, not of absolute non-existence but only non-existence of a quality : delusion which apprehends as value (porul) what *is not a value*.

We are certainly on surer grounds when we come to Śaiva hymns. *Appar* uses this form of negation frequently : virikadir nayir*allar* mati*yallar* vedavidi*yallar* etc. (4.8.2). Also, mann*allai*, vinn*allai*, valayam*allai*....penn*allai* an*allai* pedum*allai* pirit*allai* *ānāyum* periyay (6.45.9). Note the dialectical transition to its opposite in the last word underlined. *Sambandar* also uses it as negation preceded by affirmation:'puvi mudal aimbhut*amāyp* pulan ain*dāi* nilan ain*dāi* karanam nān*gāi* avayavaiser payanuru*vāi*' *alla-vuruvāi* (1.129.7). *Tiruvācakam* almost distinguishes between anmai and inmai in the above sense in a passage : 'onru niy*allai* andri ondr*illai*'. Thou art *not* aught in universe (and yet it is not quite literally true, for) naught (absolutely) is there save Thee. The second naught (illai) implies absolute non-being in so far as Śiva (thou) is Being itself. Also, 'niyalarp piritu matt*rinmai*, occurring in the same verse where *inmai* relates to the emptiness of absolute non-being *without* the Thou (ni); naught absolutely is, different (piridu) from Thee. The verse under study is considered the hṛdaya-śloka of *Tiruvācakam* as enunciating the supreme truth of non-duality.

The distinction is not, however, scrupulously adhered to, the two forms being used quite often interchangeably.

24. Just as a-brāhmaṇa by ceasing to be brāhamaṇa never also becomes a kṣatriya or vaiśya or śūdra, two by ceasing to be two does not also become one, numerically.

The idea of number itself, of one no less than of numbers other than one is occasioned when the complementary notions of separateness and togetherness are joined to constitute a unity.

25. Schomerus remarks that aneka means many and not not-one. Not a negation of one but affirmation of many. The term does not exclude the existence of one, because in that case aneka will mean nothing (*nichts*). *op. cit.*, p. 80.

26. Advaita relation is a variant of tādātmya relation and is to be understood like the latter neither as external relation nor as internal relation. Śivāgra yogin defines it as an identity-in-difference relation—difference as is compatible with identity : 'bheda eva mukhyaḥ abhedastu na bhedābhāvaḥ kiṁtu tādātmyarūpo vyāpti-paryāya-sāmānādhikaraṇya - vyapadeśa - nirvāhako'bhedakalpo vaiśiṣṭya-sambandha ityāha anyas-san vyāptito'nanya iti'. SB p. 144.

What is defined here as tādātmya relation is the same as Advaita; the only difference is that advaita is a non-dual relation obtaining between two entities, entiatively two, while tādātmya is a non-dual relation between two distinguishable aspects of one self-same entity. *Māpāḍiam* p. 365.

27. 'attuvidamendra collane ekamennil ekamendru suttuvadunmaiyin attuvidamendra colle anniya nattiyai unarttumayittu'. SJB 2.1, vārttikam. Meykandār's statement amounts to saying that God has not 'told us' that He is in no sense self-conscious. Instead He is described as of the nature of 'I am God'. The *Bṛ. Up.* says after stating that 'brahman indeed was this in the beginning' that 'it knew itself only as 'I am Brahman'. (tadātmānam evāvet ahaṁ brahmāsmi iti.) *Bṛ. Up.* I.4, 10. Also 'nanyad ātmano' paśyat so' ham asmi iti agre vyāharat'. *ibid* I. 4. 1.

28. Paiṅgala approaching Yājñavalkya asks for the secret of 'kaivalyam'. Yājñavalkya replies to him : 'sad eva saumye'dam agra āsīt. tan nitya-muktam, avikriyam, satya-jñānānandam, paripūrṇaṁ sanātanam, *ekam evā'dvitīyaṁ brahma.*' *Paiṅgala Up.* 2.

29. Unity (ekatva) and not 'being one' (eka) is taken to be the very essence of Brahman according to Advaita Vedānta, so that the illusion of duality can only be grounded in that unity. Ekatva is a formal concept unlike eka which is material and it constitutes the fundamental being of all beings which are predicated of it. This is the common ground between Advaita and

Viśiṣṭādvaita. For both, one thing could be many. The internal difference is that while for the latter it is sāmānādhikaraṇya, for the other it is lakṣaṇāvṛtti. Śaiva Siddhānta's criticism of it is reminiscent of Aristotle's criticism of the Pythagorean doctrine of the indeterminate one and also of Plato, who believes after Pythagoras that duality too is a being. (*Metaphysics,* Book Alpha, section 5 and 6).

30. The sense of the negative is of greatest moment for the siddhāntin in interpreting 'Advaita'. It is intended as an ambiguous reference to what is meant by a number of positive interpretations. It does not signify a constituent of the fact to which the expression as a whole might refer but indicates that the proposition is to be interpreted in a special way, that is, *negatively*. It must be interpreted as a variable with an ambiguous reference to certain positive propositions. The assertion of non-duality does not mean that something is one or two or both. None of these propositions express the meaning of negation. Nor does one assert all these propositions. The indeterminateness is an essential meaning of the expression. The negation is unspecific in reference in any ontic sense, and to make it specific is to rob it of its negativity. A negative is not merely *what is meant*. The *manner* of significance is no less constitutive of the meaning of negation than are the things it might signify. Śaiva Siddhānta on account of its interpretation of advaita in an 'unqualified' sense as meaning inseparable, non-dual existence, is called *Śuddhādvaita*. The term 'śuddha' is not understood on par with viśiṣṭa or kevala as introducing some qualification to the notion of advaita but as 'qualifying' advaita negatively as unqualified. As example of such expression is cited *Śuddha*-sattā (pure reality) as opposed to viśiṣṭa-sattā (qualified reality) of the Naiyāyika, where śuddha is not a viśeṣaṇa of sattā lest in that case it becomes non-different from viśiṣṭa-sattā. Cf. *Māpāḍiam* p. 364.

31. See Ānandagiri's gloss on *Chāndogya Up.* VI.2.1; ekam and advaitam both exclude bheda, one sajātīya-bheda and the other svagata-bheda.

32. *Vedārtha-saṁgraha, op. cit.*: 'ekam eva iti jagadupādānatāṁ pratipādya advitīya-padena adhiṣṭhātrantara-nivāraṇād asyai' vādhiṣṭhātṛtvam api pratipādyate.'

Even Śrīkaṇṭha interprets 'advaitam' to mean oneness as the material cause of phenomena : 'ekam eva ity avadhāraṇam adhiṣṭhātrantara-niṣedha-param. *advitīyam iti jagadupādānatvam ucyate.*' Śivāgra yogin who mostly follows the lead of Śrīkaṇṭha accordingly interprets SJB (S) 2 : 'anyas-san vyāptito'nanyaḥ' to define the material causality of Śiva. SB pp. 143-46.

33. Summing up the import of Śrīkaṇṭha's interpretation of the Chāndogya text 'ekam evādvitīyam', Appayya says : 'ekam evādvitīyam iti viśeṣaṇa-dvayaṁ brahmaṇaḥ sakala-jagat-kartur upādānarūpatva-pratipādanena nirvāhakatayā tasya sarvajñatvaṁ sarvaśaktikatvaṁ cā'kṣipat viśeṣāntarasyā' pi prāpakaṁ na tu kasyacid api viśeṣyasya niṣedhakam iti' etc. SMD p. 184.

34. The dvaitin too pleads justification for resorting to lakṣaṇā in interpreting identity-texts. Cf. Sharma, B.N.K., *A History of the Dvaita School of Vedanta and its Literature*; Vol. II, Bombay 1961, pp. 124-139.

35. The metaphysical compatibility of the two notions is brought out in the Section on Śakti, *infra* ch. 7.

36. *Bṛhad. Up.* I.4.10.

37. *Chāndogya Up.* VI.8.7.

38. *Māṇḍūkya Up.* 2.

39. *Aitareya Up.* III.1.3. The Mahāvākyas are representative of the four Vedas, (1) from Yajur Veda, (2) from Sāma Veda, (3) from Atharva Veda, and (4) from Ṛg Veda.

40. 'adu vennum ondrandradu' SÑP 6.2, fifth udāharaṇa.

41. *Māpāḍiam* p. 392.

42. Cf. Sūryanārāyaṇa Śāstrī's '*Akhaṇḍārtha*' in *Collected Papers of Professor S. S. Sūryanārāyaṇa Śāstrī* (Univ. of Madras, 1961).

43. The term 'tat' refers to the infinite—of the nature of Being (sadākhya) which is the infinite ground of the world (jagato mūlam), and not immediately known to be the self of all. 'Tvam' on the other hand, relates to the individual self, immediate and yet not known to be identical with the infinite ground of existence. Śaṅkara's Comm. *Chāndogya Up.* VI. 8.7.

44. According to jahadajahallakṣaṇā, the sentence is interpreted according to the supreme sense of the terms which alone is adequate to its implications. Cf. Sūryanārāyaṇa Śāstrī *op. cit.*

45. It is not a case of positing of equivalence between two different things as between substance and attribute, cause and effect etc. but assertion of unqualified identity despite the form of appositional equivalence in which the identity is expressed. For a lucid exposition and defence of the position *vide* Datta D. M., *Six Ways of Knowing* (Allen and Unwin, London.) pp. 311 f.

46. Rāmānuja enunciates the principle of objects being denoted by words denoting aspects, and extends this principle to denotation of Brahman by the word denoting jīva. Śrībhāṣyam I.1.12-19.

This is based on the theory that the forms standing in apposition in a sentence denote but one entity; one entity as qualified by the charateristics connoted by the terms of the sentence. This is the concept of co-ordinate equivalence (sāmānādhikaraṇya) of subject-term and predicate-term in a proposition. 'bhinna-pravṛtti-nimittānāṁ śabdānām *ekasmin* arthe vṛttiḥ sāmānādhikaraṇyam'. The terms of the proposition have different connotations but identical denotation, For Śaiva Siddhānta *difference* in connotation (pravṛtti-nimitta) will entail difference in denotation (artha) and *vice versa.* For elucidation of the siddhānta doctrine of non-difference of connotation (guṇa) and denotation (guṇin) see *Infra* Ch. 12.

47. The expression śabdo nityaḥ, e. g. can be split also as śabdo-anityaḥ. For Vyāsarāya's defence on the interpretation based on a new pariccheda—atattvamasi, vide Sharma B.N.K. *op. cit.* p. 132 ff.

48. The nine illustrations are those given in Sections 8 to 13, sixth chapter of the upaniṣad. See also Sarva Darśana Saṁgraha, Pūrṇa Prajñamatam.

49. The father begins his discourse in which he repeats tat tvam asi several times, significantly, by appealing to the state of sleep where the sense of egoity and independence is not apparent :

'uddālako hāruṇiḥ śvetaketuṁ putram uvāca svapnāntaṁ me saumya vijānīhī' ti yatraitat puruṣaḥ svapiti nāma satā saumya tadā sampanno bhavati svam apīto bhavati' *Chāndogya Up.* VI.8.1.

50. Other identity-texts which are unequivocal are interpreted by Madhva to imply the transcendental oneness of Brahman.

'sādṛśyācca pradhānatvāt svātantryādapi vābhidam
āhurīśena jīvasya na svarūpābhidam kvacit'

Aṇu vyākhyā cited in Sharma B.N.K. *Philosophy of Sri Madhvāchārya* (Bharatiya Vidya Bhavan, Bombay, 1962). p. 229.

51. Schomerus *op. cit.* p. 80.
52. Cf. Heschel's account of the world of separation as the world of profanity in Hebrew Kabala : *God in Search of Man* (Meridian Books, 1959), p. 341.
53. SÑP XII. 4. 1. udāharaṇa Venva
54. Nicholas Beredeav conceives a dialectic of Divine-human relation which has an 'apophatic' and a 'cataphatic' aspect corresponding to the negation and the positive complement of negation in 'advaita'. See his last work *Divine and the Human*, Geoffrey Bless, London.
55. Tillich, P. *op. cit.*, p. 63.
56. Umāpati assembles all these analogies and evaluates them in one crucial verse, SVP, 7.
57. The analogy of mind-body relation yields a metaphysic of reality in its full intension and extension. It is phenomenologically significant for we do not have to go outside our immediate experience in order to pass from the individual to the universal. In knowing our own mind we know what mind is. In knowing our own body we know what body is . The 'body' of this analogy, it may incidentally be noted, is not that of biological science with its bones, muscles, sinews joints and nerves . 'Body' is as it is given to our direct awareness and in the way it is given as the implicans of bodily-consciousness.
58. SÑP 2.1, first udāharaṇa.
59. 'porpanipol apedappirappiladai', SVP *loc. cit.*
60. 'avanulamai *allan*uma mangu,' SÑP *loc. cit.*
61. 'dyāvā-bhūmī janayan *deva ekaḥ.*' *Śvetaś.* Up. III.3.
'eko hi rudro na dvitīyāya tasthuḥ'. *ibid.* III.2.

Śrīkaṇṭha also says that 'ekam eva' does not imply negation of the co-existent souls. The latter are uncreated, though names and forms are created. The 'eva' excludes existence only of name and form. SKB II.4.17.

In the same manner 'oneness' of saṁvid (spirit) is to be interpreted not to exclude jaḍa (matter) but as a rhetorical way of affirming its eternity, ubiquity etc., RT 221, 223; also comm.

62. 'ondrendradu *ondre* kan.' SÑP 2.1.2. Also, 'oruva*ne* tevanum' Tirumandiram 2103; ondravan *tane. ibid.* 2.

63. SÑP 2.1.2. The 'difference' is summed up in the words pati and paśu in the text.
64. For points of comparison, See Schomerus *op. cit.* pp. 56-57.
65. Understanding of the visual sense as a species of light, a body having in its own right some kind of translucence is not without scientific plausibility. Retina has its own 'light'. It is impossible to do away with it. Even in a completely dark room a light of minimal intensity is perceived against a background of physiologically determined light of low intensity. See Boring, E. J., *Sensation and Perception in the History of Experimental Psychology*. 1939.
66. The three modes correspond to three types of God-language : God within, God without and God that is 'co-present' beyond the distinction of within and without. God is the indwelling ground; he is the infinite ground; and he is the creative ground. Co-presence signifies that God is the creative ground of whatever here and now always and everywhere. Being creative ground involves overcoming of the *de facto* distance between the finite things and the infinite ground. The illustration used is indicative of the truth of man and Being reaching each other in their very core. They lose the determination placed upon them by metaphysics.
67. Marcel *op. cit.*; Marcel's notion of *co-appartenance* à—a coordinate parity of function as if belonging to the same destiny brings out the precise sense of *udanātal* of Śaiva Siddhānta.
68. Meykandar's Vārttikam (2, 1) bears a clear reference to the *Bṛ. Up.* passage III. 7. 23: nānyoto'sti draṣṭā nānyoto' sti śrotā, nānyoto' sti mantā nānyoto' sti vijnātā eṣa ta ātmā antaryāmī amṛtaḥ (Cf. 'anniya nāttiyai unarttumāyittu').
69. SÑP 11, 1 udāharaṇa verse No. 3.
70. See citrurai on *ibid* 1, 3 for stipulations in interpreting the illustration.
71. Udanātal is understood in express disjunction with veṛātal Cf. *Irupā.*
72. The concept of a 'three-dimensional' relation between God and man was the formulation of *Sambandar*; Tiruveezimizalaī decade, 1.
73. *Supakkam.* 6. 8 and 9 bring out the '*theological dialectics*' forcefully thus :

    1. "*To know* God and self are identical is to know that they are not identical but different. 2. *To know* them as different again—in so far as knowledge cannot be *different* from knowledge, is to know them as non-different. 3. *To know* them as non-different, as actively co-present is again to imply what is *prior* to active co-presence, viz. being *identical*, and so on again."

Chapter Six

THE MORAL SOVEREIGNTY OF GOD

The Moral Argument for God vis-a-vis Karma

1. The Pārākhya text giving the moral argument for God is cited in SB p. 11 :
   'karma cidrahitaṁ tasmād yojakaṁ tadapekṣate
   yojakas sa maheśāno svecchayā balavān yataḥ.'
2. For an interesting discussion on the issue vide, *Indian Philosophical Annual* Vol. I, Centre of Advanced Study in Philosophy, University of Madras, 1967.
3. It is mystery in the sense in which mystery is contrasted from a problem by Marcel. It is not susceptible of objectification or reducible to external data. It involves one that attempts to grasp it being a symbolism for one's life in the hereafter. Berdyaev is wrong in thinking that karma doctrine is an attempt to rationalize human destiny or that it seeks to work out the proportion between suffering and evil. See his *Freedom and Spirit* (Geoffrey Bles, London, 1944) p. 285.
4. The parity is brought out by the way in which the two—the cosmological and the moral approaches, are distinguished in the system : one in terms of the performance of *ati-sūkṣma-pañca-kṛtya* and other of *sthūla-pañca-kṛtya.* See below.
5. 'śivasya jagat-sraṣṭṛtva-prayojanābhāvena bāla-tulyatvaṁ nyūnādhikaḥ sukha-duḥkhādikaraṇena vaiṣamya-nairghṛṇye ca syātām ityāśaṅkā-paramparāṁ dvitīya-sūtreṇa prādhānyena nirākurvan' etc. SB p. 143; Also 'vaiṣamya-nairghṛṇye na *sāpekṣatvāt* tathā hi darśayati.' BS. II. 1.34. Appaya interprets 'sāpekṣatva' in a truly Śaiva Siddhānta way : malapāka-sāpekṣatvād iti vā tatpākopayogi-svakāritakarma-sāpekṣatvād iti vā' rtho draṣṭavyaḥ.' SMD Vol. 2, p. 50.
   Also see below.

   SDS begins its account of Śaiva Darśana with the significant remark that the system following the authority of Śaivāgama *rejects* the view that the Supreme being as cause is independent of our action, on the ground of its being liable to the charge of partiality and cruelty. The distinctive view of Śaiva Darśana—which also is the view of Vedānta, is accordingly its view of God as cause as freely dependent on our actions. *ibid.*

6. "I looked out myself into the world of men" says Cardinal Newman "and there I see a sight which fills me with unspeakable distress. The world seems simply to give the lie to that great truth of which my whole being is to fill and the effect upon me is in consequence, as if it denied that I am in existence myself. If I looked into a mirror and did not see my face, I should have the sort of feeling which actually comes upon me when I look into the living busy world and see no reflection of its Creator." Cited from '*The Credibility of Divine Existence*', The Collected Papers of Norman Kempsmith, Macmillan, 1967, p. 52.

7. 'kiñca-sṛṣṭeḥ saṁhāra-pūrvakatvāt sakalaṁ yugapat saṁhārataḥ parameśvarasya nairghṛṇyaṁ ca bhavet. tad evam apuruṣārtha-sambandhāpādinyā jagat-sṛṣṭyā kiṁ parameśvarasya ?' SKB II.1.34.

   Reference to universal Dissolution is specially significant. If it is creation unpreceded by Dissolution it is understandable that inequalities are part of creation being governed by auxiliary factors like karma. But in universal Dissolution which mediates creation there are admittedly no inequalities. How then do they form part of creation following Dissolution ?

   'sade' va somye' dam agrā' sīd' iti sṛṣṭeḥ prāg ekatvāvadhāraṇena karmaṇām abhāvāvagatyā sargādi-kāle karmān apekṣyai' va prāthamika-deva-manuṣyādi-viṣama-sṛṣṭim kurvatas tasya vaiṣamya-doṣāpattyaparihārāt, kathañcidapi nairghṛṇyādi-doṣāparihārāc ca kramika-viṣama-sṛṣti-hetu-bhinna-kalā bhūyo'lpa-puṇyapāpa-rūpa karmavaiṣamyavatāṁ prāṇināṁ yugapad aviṣama-saṁsāra-hetu-karma-sāmyāsambhavena tatra karmāpekṣāyā vaktum aśakyatvāc ca karma-sāpekṣatve tasyā'nīśvara-prasaṅgāc-ca.' SMD, Vol. 2, p. 46.

8. In saṁhāra, karma is 'made fit' for fructification while in sṛṣṭi and sthiti the fructification process is accomplished as a step in the process of 'ripening' mala.

   'svāpe vipākam abhyeti tat sṛṣṭāvupayujyate.' MA 8.5. See. *infra.*

9. All the variety and diversity of creation are summed up under this concept of two-foldness and are traced to the two-fold nature of karma.

10. 'karma-viśeṣamūlaṁ jagat vaiṣamyam īśvaras tadutpattau sādhāraṇa-kāraṇaṁ yathā sasyotpattau parjanyaḥ sādhāraṇa-kāraṇaṁ tad bhūyo' lpatva-vrīhiyatvādi-vaiṣamyaṁ kṣetra-bījādi-vaiṣamyakṛtam. evañ-ca ne' śvarasya niravadyatva-hānir iti.' SMD *op. cit.* p. 46.

11. For the positive view of saṃhāra vide *ante* Ch. 5. Sec. on 'God as the Lord of Cosmic Functions.'

12. 'pralaye'grima - sṛṣṭyupayogino māyā - karmādi - pāka - vyāpārasya satvāt.' SMD *op. cit.* p. 51. This is, technically, *sūkṣma-pañcakṛtya*-in support of which is cited the following MA text 'svāpe' pyāste bodhayan bodhya-yogyān rodhyān rundhan *pācayan karmi-karmamāyā-śaktir vyakti-yogyāḥ* prakurvan paśyan sarvaṁ yad yathā vastu-jātam iti.' Cited in SMD *op. cit.* pp. 50-51; BK 122 Comm.; SRS; *Māpāḍiam* pp. 116-117.

13. SNP. 2.2, pratijñā.

14. 'ullade tōtra etc. SÑP 2.2 illustrative venba.' See below. Also SMD Vol II, pp. 34-38.

15. *Supakkam* 2.88.

16. The moral acts, it may be noted, are not determined but are only contextual to the experiences of pleasure and pain in response to which man as the moral agent is called to exert. My heredity and environment—natural and cultural are the fruits of my karma and they condition and not *account* for, my reactions thereto. I am in theory free in my reactions.

17. 'iruviṇai iṇbat tuṇbat tivvuyir piraṇdirandu
varuvadu pōvadāhum.' *Supakkam* 2.4. This sums up most comprehensively the theory of law of karma.

18. Though sukha and duḥkha the correlates of the right and the wrong according to the law of karma, are the motivating factors of the human mind—there are primordial passions (rāga and dveṣa) arising from a natural impulse e. g. the desire of punishment to our enemies, happiness to our friends, hunger, lust and other human appetites. These passions, properly speaking, produce sukha and duḥkha and proceed not from them. Underlying man's actions are his habits of likings and aversions. Śaiva Siddhānta theory of mūla-karma or kārmaṇya-mala can contain the naturalist's

interpretation of moral distinctions. For this concept vide *Māpāḍiam* p. 145.

19. For kāryaliṅgānumāṇam which argues from the perceived effect to the unperceived cause *ante*. Ch 2. Sec. on the knowledge of God's[a] Existence, note no. 17. The argument, it may be noted, though seemingly like the hypothetico-deductive method of the scientist by means of which the 'cause' is sought to be elicited, is really a species of the transcendental method throughout employed in the system.
20. Supakkam mentions these 'six' endowments of man's moral life, endowments which condition and colour man's reactions of a moral nature. 2.7 Śivajñāna yogin's Comm.
21. *Supakkam* 2.21.
22. 'tato na kutracit kiñcit svabhāvena viruddhayoḥ kāryayoḥ kāraṇaṁ tasmād viruddhaṁ kāraṇāntarāt.' PA 3.49. Also *Supakkam* 2.5.
23. *Supakkam* 2.5-6 Śivajñāna yogin's comm.
24. PA 6.31-48 refute the Sāṅkhya view.
25. PB. *ibid.* Buddhi stands for knowledge which modifies into diverse modes of experience (bhogya) for the experient self; as the receptacle for all dispositions it serves as the 'support' for all the accumulated merit and demerit of one's past deeds. Therefore it is karma which determines one's experience *vis-a-vis* one's buddhi.
26. *Supakkam* 2-7, 8.
27. 'oruvinai seyyādōrum *uḍaiyar* ivvulakattuḷḷe.' Supakkam 2.8.
28. *Ibid.* 2.11 Śivajñāna yogin's comm. The vegetative form of life is also appetitive, of the nature of 'seeking the good'. The Śaivāgama doctrine is that appetite (icchā) is an integral part of sentience as such. See *infra* ch. 11. Sec. on Nature of Knowledge.
29. *Supakkam* 2.12.
30. Sarvajñatva (omniscience) sarva-kartṛtva (omnipotence) and sarvānugrāhakatva (omni-graciousness) are the divine attributes suggested by moral governorship. *Māpāḍiam* p. 132, *Supakkam* 8.17. Justice, mercy, and freedom are alike in evidence in the divine dispensation of bhoga in accord with the law of karma. *Māpāḍiam* p. 242.
31. 'seyali nukkuk *kari* vēṇḍum. Sivan uḷan endrariye.' (*Parapakkam* 128).

32. SÑP 2.2 Illustrative venba.
33. 'irum svargam poyyar vāz narakam pūmi pundiyir kiḍantu pōndadu ?' *Supakkam* 2.19, 20.
34. *Suppakkam* 2-46, 47; *Supakkam* 180, 202 last two lines. Also *Irupā*, 14 lines 5 to 14.
35. *Supakkam*. 2.22. Śivajñāna yogin's Comm.

This brings out the finitude of self as agent of action. As subject of knowing also, self is dependent on 'eight concomitants' of knowledge and in addition an intelligent revealer of knowledge; the self has knowledge in no other way. *ibid.* 5.4, 5. The concomitants of action and knowledge are comprehended under the tattvas three-fold in kind and thirty-six in number, and the tāttvikas. See *infra* Ch. 9.

36. SVP. 64.
37. 'ezudum *kīzkaṇak* kinnambar īśanē'. Appar 5.21.8. Also, 'muttamar seyvinaikkum murseyvinaikkum chelvan *paṭṭōlai tīṭṭum* paḍi pōtṛi'. *Pōtṛi Pahrodai,* lines 41, 42.
38. 'srotāṁsi pratipuṁsi sūkṣmatanugais tattvair yadā'nekatā, māyājānyakhilātma-bhogya-bhuvanādyādhāra-tattvais tadā sthityai tāṅś-ca narān niyojayati (tair na lakṣito'dhiṣṭhitaiḥ) svārthāptyai tanu-deva-bhāva-bhuvanair bhoge śivas sādhanaiḥ.' SSV. Jñānapāda, 22.

Dissolution matures, i.e. 'makes fit' karma-mala for fructification and use which necessarily precede āṇava-mala becoming 'fit' for removal by knowledge or intuition of the transcendent (Patijñāna). See Ch. 14.

39. 'uḍanāi niṇḍru ēṇḍṛu koḷḷum mudalvan', *Māpāḍiam.* p. 495.
40. *Ante* Ch. 1. Section on the Meaning of Saiva Siddhānta.
41. For the positions of Sautrāntika, Nikhandavādin and the Ājīvika and their anti-theistic interpretation of karma, vide *Parapakkam* 2. 21-31; 3. 1-8; 4. 1-10.
42. Cf. the transmutation of the ideal of dharma into that of Mokṣa in the Prābhākara as well as the Bhāṭṭa schools in the history of Mīmāṁsā system. *Māpāḍiam.* p. 56.
43. 'aṛan vidhi aṛulatu.' *Supakkam* 2.51.
44. 'kāṇbavan seyale' etc. *Ibid.* 2.26.
45. Moral law as divine decree does not represent divine fiat in Indian religions.

46. The same metaphysical explanation for knowledge having to be revealed to man as unaided, man cannot know, accounts for the need of an omniscient and gracious God for revealing what is good for man. See *Tuhalaru podam* verse no. 39.
47. *Parapakkam*, ulakāyadan matam 9.
48. Murti T. R. V. : *Buddhism and Vedānta* (1954). Cf. 'a stone-pillar does not suffer'. *ibid.* Proceedings, Indian Philosophical Congress. 1956.
49. For the concept of identity of insight or intellectual intuition and spiritual freedom in Mādhyamika and Vijñānavāda schools of Buddhism see Murti T.R.V. *The Central Philosophy of Buddhism* op. cit. p. 223.
50. Cf. Allen E. L. *God as Gift and Prize in Forum* (World Congress of Faiths, No. 26, October 1955).

    This short paper is an admirable focus on the experience out of which the Hīnayāna originates and seeks to perpetuate, finding a parallel for it in the contemporary thinker's stress on the reticence of God.
51. A verse in Purānānūru (192) expresses the ascetic mood inspired by a consideration of the inexhorability of man's destiny :

    "Good and evil come, not caused by others
    Pain and relief are brought likewise, not by others;
    Dying is not new; nor living gave us joy;
    Misery we hated not. As in the flood,
    Caused by clouds that poured in torrents
    On a mountain top with lightning flash
    A raft goes in the direction of the stream
    So the swarm of lives move onward
    In the way of destiny. This we have discerned
    From the teachings of sages strong in wisdom
    So we admire not the great; nor scoff at the churl."

    (Pope's Translation)
52. See *infra* Ch. 15. Sec. on Recovery of Self (ātma-lābha).
53. The following verse of Tirumandiram (2048) satirizes spiritual leadership with acquired perfection as one of blind leading the blind only to fall into a pit one behind the other :

    'kuruḍarkuk kōlkāttic cellum kuruḍar
    muranum patankuei vīlvarkaḷ munpin

kuruḍarum viḷvarkaḷ munpinaṛave
kuruḍarum viḷvar kuruḍaro ḍākiye.'

54. This was precisely the point at stake between the heterodox systems of Buddhism and Jainism on the one side and Śaivism as a resurgent form of Vedic orthodoxy. See *ante* Chapter 1, Sec. on Meaning of Śaiva Siddhānta.

55. S. Sūryanārāyaṇa Śāstrī : *op. cit. Karma and Fatalism* p. 233.

56. Nanamirdam describes the 'pathos' of an exoteric understanding of the law of karma thus : so long as there is the body there is no escape from karma and so long as there is karma binding there is no escape from the wearying rounds of births and deaths. One thus feels desperate—as helpless as a deaf-mute who sinks unanswered in a wild sea in a dead of night :

"mārip pāṇāḷ ārkaḷi azundum
ariya ūman pola aḷiyan." 22

The solution that is implied in this problem is an inner understanding of the dynamics of the law : that something that in a sense tightened the bonds of karma, through that could it be snapped just as water which precipitates mire also helps to cleanse it :

"sēdakam payaṇta sezunīr sedakam
māśuka maṇṇia denna āsuka
ayantīr peyta arimati
payantōn vinai vidal viyandō anṟe'. *ibid.* 23.

Water, it may be noted is a recurring symbol of grace.

57. For the compatibility and congruence of divine justice and divine compassion. See *Supakkam* 2.15. The terms used respectively are 'muniva (literally, wrath) and 'parivu' (literally, kindly concern, compassion) Also for the homogeneity of the senses of justice, legal moral and religious see *ibid* 2.31 : 'eṅgum āṇaiye āṇaiyē kāṇ.'

58. 'Iraṅguvān *paṇi*' is the expression which Siddhiar uses to describe man's action *ibid* 2, 23.

59. 'nūnaṅgal adikam nōkki nukarvippān *vinai nōi* tīra'. *Supakkam.* 2.21'. Vinai here refers to the primordial self-willedness which is as it were the stuff of which are made man's appetitions and aversions and the consequent right and wrong, good and evil and pleasurable and painful actions.

60. In the case of the 'liberated' God with whom the liberated is consciously identified owns and 'appropriates' the latter's actions;

consequences thereby are no longer binding on the ego-less individual. See Ch. 15.

God as Inner Illuminer of Experience

1. What is expounded under this section as the metaphysical-epistemological implication of the religious concept of God as the moral sovereign (pati) is a free reconstruction of the theme of SÑP Fifth Sūtra which purports in the impressive words of Meykandār himself to inculcate the 'prevenient benevolence' (mudalupakāram) of God.
2. Śuttaṛivu, literally, determinate, discursive knowing, relates to the necessary limitation of human power of apprehension, one's inability to 'apprehend or observe everything about what one observes of which Kant speaks.' (Critique of Pure Reason A. 189. B. 243) Indeed it implies also one's inability to *think* it all at once. Thinking is necessarily discursive. In thinking of the house that I apprehend, my apprehension requires to be split up into sections, each section taking the form of a judgement making use of separate concepts. We have to think separately about its shape size and material, as well as about the separate parts and sides of the house.
3. The pattern of 'knowing as being shown' is, however, the essential characteristic (svabhāva-lakṣaṇa) of self and not an accident due to its finitude :

   Cf. 'kiñcijjñaḥ sarvato'pyātmā tato *bodhyāvabodhakaḥ*
   sarvajñaḥ sarvatas tasmād ātmānaṁ bodhayec-chivaḥ.'

   Niśvāsa cited ÑVM p. 486. Mala-obscuration is only the cause of ajñatva, not of kiñcijjñatva. See *infra*. However, 'cetanāntara-preryatva', in the sense of pāratantrya is a predicament due to mala, 'cetanasyā'pi cetanāntara-preryatve' navasthe'ti tat saṁsāri-cetanasyai' va cetanāntara-preryatvāṅgīkārān nirastam.' SB p. 329. This is the subject of debate between Śaiva Siddhānta and Śiva Samavāda. See Ch. 7.
4. The pakṣa being self in its generality no positive instance (sapakṣa) of concomitance between the middle and the major terms is possible. *Supakkam* 5.1. Śivāgra yogin's Comm.
5. 'akṣāṇi puṁsāni tāni pravartitāni jñānaṁ janayanti na tu svayam. acetanatvena svataḥ pravṛtter asambhavāt.' SB p. 325.

6. Outer senses, inner sensorium, in short the entire concatenation of auxiliaries of knowing grouped under 'ātma-tattva.' 'poṛipulan karaṇamellām purudanālaṛin dānmavai yaṛidarā.' *Supakkam* 5.1.
7. When the sense-object-contact takes place the object becomes revealed and in this, sense-perception itself remains uncognised, and is cognised by a separate mental perception. With this theory of the Nyāya, the Śaiva siddhāntin is in agreement, particularly with the doctrine that the sense organs operate unperceived. But the metaphysical basis of the theory in the two systems is different. *infra* Ch. 6, Sec. V.
8. 'anavastheṣvavasthitam. *Kaṭha Up*. I. 2. 22
9. 'asthiraś cañcalo lupyamānaḥ saspṛho vyagraś-cābhimānitvaṁ prayātā iti ahaṁ so mamedam iti evaṁ manyamāno nibadhnā-tyātmanātmānaṁ jāleneva kha-caraḥ.' *Maitri Up*. iii, 2.
10. Cf. 'parāñci khāni vyatṛṇāt svayambhūs tasmāt parāṅ paśyati nā-ntarātman.' *Kaṭha. Up*. 2.1.1.
11. That is the Tirodhāna function. Anugraha is continuous with it in the sense that God is still the revealer of infinite knowledge and 'giver' of infinite experience. Only, it is also equally God knowing Himself, coinciding with self 'knowing' God. See Ch. 15.
12. The Sāṅkhya too admits a sva-svāmibhāva relation between puruṣa and buddhi but it is a case of false identification (abheda-samāropa) bred by Ignorance. *Tattva-Vaiśāradī* 1, 3 and 4.
13. For the Sāṅkhya too, self cannot be manifested by matter. The empirical self, viz. buddhi and its evolutes cannot intuit puruṣa. *ibid*. III, 35.
14. This is in refutation of the Sāṅkhya for whom the senses do not owe their function to the will of self, the self being non-active. The senses act by themselves for the self's sake. *Sāṅkhya-Pravacana-Bhāṣya* II. 35.37.
15. This is '*mudalupakāram*' in Meykaṇḍār's Vārttikam on SÑP. 5. meaning prevenient Grace. The reference here is to Tirodhāna-śakti which is the principle of revelation at the phenomenal level.
16. For a descriptive account of how this is accomplished through evolution of tattvas, vide *infra* Ch. 9. What is to be noted here is that the divine assistance to knowledge is both from within and from without :

'*bahirantar-vibhāgena* tila-tailam iva sthitam.' *Sarvajñānottara-Āgama* 1.47. Antarniyamana and bahiḥpravarttana are the twin modes of divine assistance. But it is only the first that is apparent at the finite level. See below.

17. SB p. 329.

18. *Supakkam* (5-4) lists this characteristic disability of self as the final symptom of finitude bringing self on par with not-self. The other elements of finitude congenital to self are (*i*) knowing a thing *through* a channel of knowledge, (*ii*) forgetting what it has known, (*iii*) knowing a thing again in the above manner after having forgotten it.

19. Cf. Meykandār's expressions : tam*muḍal*, tammuṇarvin *tami*. SÑP, 5th. Sūtra.

    The eye that is illumined is initially shrouded in darkness which is later destroyed. Destruction of darkness is the function of illumination. The illuminating light itself was never shrouded in darkness. Were it also shrouded then, being itself in need of illumination, it cannot function as illuminating agent.

20. The definition of God, it may be recalled, is performing of cosmic operations which is inclusive of His function of initiating knowledge for the self. *Ante* Ch. 5.

21. *Supakkam* 5.1, Śivāgra yogin's Comm.

22. The figurative use of 'ripening' in the contexts of mala has already been explained. Karma-paripāka means karma come to be in conjunction with *all* the auxiliaries necessary for issuing in its respective fruits. Time for example is one such necessary factor. This may be seen to be the case in the illustration of the blossoming of the flower, which is also a case of the flower attaining to a condition fit for bearing fruit, which it accomplishes through a conjunction with factors like sunlight.

23. 'bōgiyayirun duyirkkup pōkattaip puridal ōrār 'etc. *Supakkam* 1.50.

24. It is, however, only the revelatory grace — kāttumupakāram, not the knowing Grace — kāṇumupakāram, that may be admitted at the level of phenomenal knowledge. The latter kind of Grace though at work is self-hidden. God is 'hid' in the self as its 'I' 'suffering' to know and enjoy as 'I know' and 'I enjoy.'

    The following verse distinguishes between 'the self that sees' and the 'self that is hidden'.

'aṇḍapiṇḍam kaṇḍālen ? aruṅkaruvi kaṇḍālen ?
kaṇḍavuyir kaṇḍālen ? karanda uyir kāṇātār.'

Cittrambalanadikal Kottu.

25. The goal and consummation of the Pañcakṛtya, viz. Anugraha was understood with reference to a condition of ripeness of mala to which condition the preceding four kṛtyas are a preparation. In the same manner, in the five stages of the rhythm of revelatory initiation of empirical knowledge the final one relates to a condition of 'ripeness' for the mala obscuring the self, when it shall be able to know in strict commensuration with revelation, becoming a transparent medium for the latter's illumination.

26. By anthropo-genetic process is meant here the emergence of the knowing man from his dogging disability of eternal oblivion. *Supakkam* 5.8. The illustration is again suggestive of the idea that God initiates experience by Himself experiencing just as embodied self participates in its bodily experience. Ati-sūkṣma-pañca-kṛtya is implicit in the sthūla and sūkṣma Pañcakṛtyas.

27. The scope of ati-sūkṣma-pañcakṛtya does not apparently extend beyond the wakeful span. Hence arises the objection. Just as wakefulness (jāgrat), dream(svapna), sleep (suṣupti), beyond the sleep (turīya) and beyond even the beyond (turīyātīta)—the five states (avasthās) of the self correspond and form the counterpart of the five cosmic operations, the five avasthās falling within the wakeful itself correspond to the five ati-sūkṣma-pañca-kṛtyas. Also called anugraha-pañcakṛtya. ÑVM p. 99.

28. *Supakkam* 5.8.

29. Through bringing about a 'balancing of karma' in one's life following a wearying round of births. *Ibid.* Śivāgra yogin's Comm. See also *infra* Ch. 14.

30. For the concept of Bhoga in a transcendental sense and its non-discursive character, see Ch. 15.

31. Combining the three-fold Pañca-kṛtyas of the Lord distinguished respectively as sūkṣma, sthūla and ati-sūkṣma, we may say that the Lord (*i*) knows in advance in a general way in preparation to what is to follow (sūkṣma); (*ii*) having known He creates investing the Self with 'body, senses, worlds and objects' (sthūla); and (*iii*) having created He initiates the knowing process from within the embodied self (ati-sūkṣma) causing 'enjoyment' for the

self launched on its career in the world with objects of enjoyment (bhogya).

Cf. 'ulahelam *aṟinda*vai*yākki* verai oruvaṉē uyirkatkellām uyirumāi *uṇartti* nirppan.' *Supakkam* 5.5. Śivajñāna yogin's Comm.

32. Schomerus : *op. cit.* p. 86.

33. 'yac ca svabhāvaṁ pacati......pācyāṅś-ca sarvān pariṇāmayed yaḥ'. *Śvet. Up.* V. 5. Śrīkaṇṭha says: 'parameśvareṇa samam eva sarveṣām anugrahe kriyamāṇe' pi ye pakva-malās te mucyanti, apakvamalāḥ kālakramād eva, yathā savitṛ-kiraṇa-sandohe samam eva santate' pi pakvānye'va padmāni vikasanti, nā' pakvāni.' B. S. 2.1.35.

34. TKP 87. Cited *Citrurai*, SÑP 5.2.1.

35. Schomerus *loc. cit.* pp. 96-97 ff.

36. Schomerus, *op. cit.* p. 87.

37. SÑP 5.2 Udāharaṇa.

38. *ibid.* Śivajñāna yogin's Comm.

39. The conception of God as Agent of activity is itself part of a doctrine of grace. Agency in respect of operations, cosmic and microcosmic, bespeak on the one hand divine perfection as omniscient and omnipotent and on the other divine grace. Śrīkaṇṭha says (2.1.35) : "tataḥ pūrṇo' pi parameśvaraḥ parārtham eva sarvāṁ pravṛttiṁ karoti". The following citation from *Vāyavīya Saṁhitā* (Uttara 12:15, ff) given in SKB (*ibid*) brings out the intimate relation of deity and grace :

'ādityena yathā hīnaṁ tamo-bhūtam idaṁ jagat
śivenā' pi vinā tadvat tamo-bhūtam idaṁ jagat
vaidyaṁ vinā nirānandāḥ kliśyante rogiṇo yathā
śivaṁ vinā nirānandaṁ kliśyate hi jagat tathā
vyādhīnāṃ bheṣajaṁ yadvat pratipakṣaṁ svabhāvataḥ
śivas saṁsāra-doṣāṇāṁ pratipakṣaḥ svabhāvataḥ
tathā' nādiḥ pravṛtto' yaṁ ghoraḥ saṁsāra-maṇḍalaḥ
tathā' nādiḥ pravṛtto' yaṁ śivas saṁsāra-mocakaḥ.'

40. These are briefly considered in the sequel to the Section on God as Will. *infra.* Ch. 7.

41. SÑP 5.2.2 Udāharaṇa. The light of the stars and other luminous bodies is but part of the light of sun is the accepted doctrine of the Veda.

Schomerus subjects this and the analogies of (i) crystal, (ii) actor impersonating roles, (iii) the lotus and the sun to unmeaning distortions; they are according to him incompatible with the eternal existence and history of other substances in whose midst God exists unaffected by relation with them. But the latter is not the view of Śaiva Siddhānta and Schomerus is quite unwarranted in thinking that the only way out of dualistic thinking is either monism of the Vedānta or as he hints acceptance of the Christian conception of an absolute Creator who takes all limitations that He has Himself created upon Himself. *op. cit.* pp. 97-100.

42. *ibid.* pp. 97 ff.

43. Everything which a corporeal self experiences, indeed, experienced, not through the body but through ātma-cit-śakti vis-a-vis the body : "Alles, was die mit ihm verbundenen Sealen erfahren, geschielt durch ihn, aber nicht direkt, sondern durch seine Śakti." *loc. cit.* p. 99. But this śakti activates everything, not by direct grasp, not by a palpable causal relation, but through will. God's exertion of causal efficiency by which He initiates knowledge for the self is analogous to 'psychic' causation. To use the words of Schomerus again, cit-śakti operates but through her 'thoughts' which introduce themselves as realities in manifestation, such that for Śiva everything remains nothing but the 'thoughts' of śakti. "Ihre Gedanken treten in den anderen Substanzen als Realitaten in Erscheinung. Für Śiva aber bleibt alles nur Gedanke seiner Śakti." Then the 'business' of the world activated through the 'thoughts' of śakti do not mean for Him a plus or more; nothing accrues to God by the human experiences which he initiates by participating through His śakti. Corporeal experience is part of matter and matter itself is so constituted that it is unable to make any impression on spirit; in spirit's presence indeed it does not exist in a specific way.

See below for a brief discussion of the problem that Schomerus raises in connection with this concept analysed by him with great discernment.

44. All objects are only comprehended (jñeya) and not 'experienced' (prameya) under God's omniscience. Anubhava in its technical sense is germane only to self. See *infra* Ch. 5, Sec. I.

45. 'sarva-bhūt*āntarātmā* na lipyeti lokaduḥkhena *bāhyaḥ*.' *Kaṭha Up.* II. 2.11.

46. Ignorance is the cause of servility (parādhīnatva) which is the source of all pain. When the self recovers its authentic freedom there is no pain.

'Tunbamām *ellam* paravasaṇāit tāṇ *tuvalil*
inbamām taṇ vasanāyē yirukkil'. TKP 49 : *viz*.

All is pain if one 'swerves' or 'strays' into the sphere of determination, and all blissful if one recovers one's authentic freedom of self-determination.

47. 'aruḷ iraivanukku *anikalam*'. *Supakkam* 5.9, Śivajñāna's Comm.

48. SÑP 5.2.2. Śivāgra yogin discusses different interpretations of the concept of sannidhi : (i) kāryotpattideśo' avasthānam, (ii) kāryaunmukhya-viśiṣṭa-śakti, and (iii) kāryotpatyanukūla-cikīrṣā-yogitvam. SB pp. 332-33. He rejects(i) and (iii) and redefines (ii) as 'kāryānukūla-sahakāri-sāhityam'.

49. *Śveta. Up.* VI. 14; *Kaṭha. Up.* II.2.15; *Muṇḍaka. Up.* II. 2.5; *Bṛhad. Up.* IV. 2.4.; IV.3.6.

50. 'tadvikāri śivaś cen na kānto' yovat sa taṁ nayet.' SJB 5. For a discussion of the concept of Vikāra, see SB *op. cit.*

51. 'sivasakti avvak kāriyaṅgaḷil uṇmukamatalākia saṅkalpam' *Māpāḍiam*. p. 349.

52. 'sonna sivan *kaṇṇā*'. Udāharaṇa, *op. cit.* 'sarva-lokasya cakṣuḥ'. *Kaṭha. Up.* II.2.11.

53. Umāpati gives a most graphic illustration with his telling insight into the nature of the problem. SVP 66 :

When the sun rises in the dawn and dispels the encircling darkness stirring people to activity, awakening them from their 'night' of invisibility, the people see only things they were longing for in silence during the night. The points suggested by the analogy of the sun are (i) that it rises not at the behest of the people but of its own accord in utter spontaneity, (2) that it pervades through its rays the objects by dispelling invisibility due to darkness, and also permeates the eyes that see so that they may be able to 'see', (3) that as it thus illumines from within and without, freely, under no pressure, the seeing man, nevertheless, experiences his own desires and (4) that it reveals with no partiality impersonally unaffected by others' desires and yet contributing to a fulfilment of their desire by conquering their night and constituting the 'day' for them making experience possible in whichever way it is freely desired.

Just as the active man never pauses to reflect that his experience, for its genesis as well as for its fulfilment, owes to the sun, but is under the delusion that his experience owes everything to his self-will. The choosing, knowing self is too self-willed to realise that its jñāṇa and kriyā manifest and articulate because of 'assistance' of divine jñāna and divine kriyā. The result of this delusion is that his pleasure-pain experiences 'attach' to him and bind him, while they do not bind the Spirit within the self.

54. The concept of Inner Revealership that is implied by Divine Sovereignty (patitva) is suggestive of the metaphysical attribute of Bliss (ānanda) as the infinite presence that makes and articulates all experience, of Omniscience (cit) as spirit that reveals like the sun and as Being (sat) as the Pure that is unsullied by anything phenomenal.

Meykaṇḍār uses 'Śiva' in all the three senses when he uses the word deliberately thrice in connection with explaining God as the Revealer of knowledge. *Māpāḍiam.* pp. 349-50.

Appayya etymologically derives 'Śiva' from the root vaś 'to will' and quotes from Mahā-Bhārata :
'śivam icchan manuṣyāṇāṁ tasmād devaḥ śivaḥ smṛtaḥ'.
SMD, Vol. I, p.2.

See also *Śivārcana-Candrikā* ((Deva Kottai) where he at length interprets the Ātma-Nivedana-mantra—śivo dātā śivo bhoktā etc. He gives many fanciful derivations of the word 'Śiva' and implies the three meanings stated above. Also *Śiva-Tattva-Viveka* (Harihara Sastri 1895), p. 3 for the three-fold interpretation. Also *Kriyākrama-dyotikā* (Deva Kottai), p. 1. *Māpāḍiam* makes reference to the last two works.

CHAPTER VII

GOD AS WILL AND BEING

The Concept of Divine Will (*Śakti*)

1. Understanding of Absolute or Being in Śaiva Siddhānta is reflected in the theological doctrine of śakti. It is not in the exclusive sense as the negative of the relative or becoming. Becoming is in being. Being is conceived in terms of a polarity of being and becoming, eternal and temporal infinite and finite. The polarity is not literal but symbolic.
2. SÑP 2-4, the pratijñā of the Vārttikam.
3. *Māpāḍiam* pp. 271-72.
4. For a discussion of the arguments and the counter-arguments see *ante* Chapter 3.
5. 'avan *ēkānekam irandu* minri etc. SÑP 2-4 hetu. 'As the sun rays are of the same essence as the sun and exist only in close connection with the sun, but yet are not identical with the sun and possess in a certain sense an independent existence, and the will of the king equals the essence of the king and can exist only with the king and not without him but yet is not identical with the king and possesses in the form of commands and laws an independent existence, so is the śakti of Śiva of the same essence with Śiva and exists only in relation with Śiva, is but yet not identical with Śiva and can be differentiated from Śiva, *Schomerus*. p. 68.
6. 'ananyānyā śivāt śaivaḥ PA, 1.39 On the Purānic citation given by Umāpati commenting on the verse runs the following: 'aikāśaktis saśaikopi śaktimān ucyate śivaḥ' PB p 37.
   Also Cf '*ēkan anēkan* iraivan aḍi vāzka'. *Tiruvācakam* 1. line 5
7. SJB 2-4, Illustrative venba.
8. 'irandennil engumuḷa' nardṛu .' *ibid.*
9. 'evattṛevaṇum aṅgaṇ avai avanaṇdṛillai.' *ibid.*
10. Pervasion (vyāpti) is defined to mean being the ground of another's origination and endurance as well as resolution. RT 120.
11. 'poṇṇoli pōl īśan.' SJB *loc. cit.* udāharaṇa.

12. The two are not mutually exclusive; they are not mutually inclusive also; in manifesting other objects it does not cease to be self-manifest, but the converse of it is not true.
13. 'parānapekṣaṁ śivasaṁjñam asya rūpaṁ parāpekṣam api śrutijñaḥ śaktyākhyam āhus tadabhinnarūpas sa dharma īśas sa dharmi-rūpaḥ.' SSV 2. *Māpāḍiam* refers to this text. p. 274.

    The following text distinguishes between the concepts of Śiva and Śakti :

    'parānapekṣaṁ rūpaṁ yad vijñānaṁ *śiva*-saṁjñitam tasya *śaktim* parāpekṣaṁ rūpam āhur vipaścitaḥ.' RT. 288.
14. 'cidviṣaye ca ātmani viṣaya-grahaṇa-rūpasya svaniṣṭhasya grahītṛsvarūpasya svasaṁvedana-siddhatvād etat siddham.' RT. 289-90 Comm.
15. *Advaita-Siddhi* Vyākhyā pp. 87-88.
16. Universality of spirit—of self and God is interpreted 'dynamically' by the classical commentators of the Śaivāgamas : 'vibhus tatra śambhupuruṣau *sarvagatāv* eva asarvagatatve vyomādivad amūrtatyena gamanāsambhavāc-chivasya sarvādhiṣṭhānam ātmanaśca deśāntara-karma-phala-bhogo no' papadyate.' TTN. 3. Comm.
17. The doctrine of Nicolaus Cusanus making use of this impressive geometrical analogy is referred to in Tillich, *Systematic Theology*. vol 1, p. 277. Harper and Row, 1967.
18. To go from the periphery to the centre we require the help of radius. We conceive the centre, not in the abstract but as 'potent' with the radius to make itself accessible to any point beyond it. The centre of the circle is, in this sense, indefinitely 'all pervasive'. It is the centre of infinite radiations.
19. The Māyāvādin also will admit that the centre being there radiation into circle is possible, but will not, therefore, identify the two. They are rather identical as the 'rope' and the 'rope-snake' are identical. Being alone is real and the process by which Being is manifested being no constituent of Being, is not real. Dynamics belong to the 'structure' of Reality but only in a negative sense; it 'belongs' to it *qua* not belonging to anything else. Śakti is a condition and not the '*cause*' of the world. For the Śaktivādin it is cause—kāraṇa, integral to kartṛ. It is not a false adjunct of spirit mysteriously attached to it but is its essence. This is plausible in so far as spirit is as such agent without its

having to become determinate and then be identified with something in order to be agent. See *infra* pp. 301-302 ff.

20. yet another significant point of distinction between Advaita Vedānta and Śaiva Siddhānta. God is both a term and a relation according to the latter. He is not only the one who relates Himself, he is the relating itself. Cf *Tiruvācakam*, *loc. cit* line 4. According to Advaita Vedānta what serves as the relation is on a different level from the terms standing in relation; it is their 'ground' or depth and is identifiable with the term only as conditioned (upahita). It is approachable as the reality of what is on the surface.

21. RT gives a succint exposition of the Advaita point of view with reference to the doctrine of Śakti. 201 ff.

22. 'svotthair nibadhyate tasmāc chaṅkā-pāśair vimūḍhadhīḥ mucyate tebhya evā' yaṁ bandhamokṣau na vastutaḥ.' RT. 210. This view is set forth as the standpoint of 'those obsessed with Advaita' to which the Śakti-vāda of the 'Siddhāntāgama' is offered as the corrective :

   'ityadvaita-grahāviṣṭāḥ pralapanto dayālubhiḥ
   gurubhiḥ pratibodhyante siddhāntāgamadāyibhiḥ.' *ibid.* 211.

23. *ibid.* 212 Commentary.

24. 'yadyadvayeyaṁ saṁvittiḥ pramāṇair vyāvahārikaiḥ
   sādhyeta taireva dṛḍhaṁ tasyāḥ syāt sadvitīyatā.' RT. 212.

25. Compare Abhinava's criticism of citing scriptural evidence for non-difference in the Advaitin's sense of the term. IPV. *Kriyādhikāra* 4.3.

26. 'kiṁ ca śabdāḥ parityajya mukhyamarthaṁ virodhataḥ
   vartamānā hi dṛśyante gauṇe'rthe lokavedayoḥ
   gaur brāhmaṇo' yamādityo yūpa ityevamādayaḥ' RT 221-22.

   Introducing the import of this verse Aghora Śiva sums it up thus : 'idānīṃ cicchaktirekaiva khalvityādīnām advaitasṛṣṭīnāṁ pramāṇāntaravirodhān mukhyārthāsambhavaṁ darśayitumāha'

27. Abhinava says : if bheda is subject to bādha (negation) in experience despite its appearance, the same thing may be said of abheda too, as bādha is but only the rise of a reverse form of knowledge. If you anchor your faith in the experience of bādha why cannot bheda for that reason be real as that too is negated in empirical experience. IPV. *loc. cit.*

28. 'api cā'nyatvam advaita-bhedayorabhyupaiti cet
bhedaḥ sidhyetānanya-bhava evaṁ ca sādhyate' RT. 228.

29. *ibid.* RT. 228. The position of Śakti-vāda with regard to the inter-relation of difference and non-difference is : Śakti implies differencea and also non-difference. *Difference* is in the following sense—Śiva signifies the dharmas of (i) kartṛtva , (ii) āśrayatva (iii) sarva-viṣayānirūpyatva, , (iv) parameśvaratva , (v) mahatva, (vi) vyāpakatva. Śakti, in contrast is : (i) karaṇatva , (ii) āśritatva, (iii) sarvaviṣaya-nirūpyatva, (iv) parmaiśvaryatva, (v) mahimārūpatva, (vi) vyāptitva . The two sets are not synonyms of each other, and hence *different*.

Translated in modern idiom, it is the (i) polarity of causal agency (kartṛtva) and causal means (karaṇatva), (2) of being the supporting ground (āśrayatva) and the supported or grounded (āśritatva), (3) of being the unproved or the unknowable (sarva-viṣayānirupyatva) and the provable or the knowable (sarva-viṣaya-nirūpyatva). The last point is significant : the argument from the world (nirūpaka) to the world cause (nirūpya) is of the dharmāt dharmi anumāna type. God combines within Him the inaccessible depth (Śivam)as well as the element of cognitive accessibility (Śakti) or the aspect of self-giving but for which it would not be possible to approach God through reason or revelation. The latter is the gift of śakti. See *Supakkam* 5; 1, 69.

The *non-difference* of Śiva and Śakti is as guṇa and guṇin; guṇa and guṇin are one. Śiva is not a mere background, *of* which or *on* which there is śakti. Śiva is śakti itself; śakti is *in* it. Guṇin and the guṇa *in it* are non-different. If śakti were to imply *only* non-difference, then śakti cannot be karaṇa. Therefore Śaiva Siddhānta defines it as a relation of *non-difference as is not exclusive of* difference. Māyā-vāda posits *exclusive* non-difference while Śaiva Siddhānta advocates *inclusive* non-difference and claims the support of parsimony. Paradoxically, the inclusive variety includes the non-inclusive also, while the converse of it is not true. SB. p. 190. The argument is reminiscential of the modern arguments of Charles Hartshorne. His 'absolute' and the 'surrelative' aspects of the Deity will correspond to the distinction of Śiva and Śakti. See his '*The Divine Relativity*' (Yale, 1948).

30. RT. 229.

31. *ibid.* Commentary.
32. The unity of spirit or self does not consist of being one substance but one subject. Unity is meaningless except as the capacity of unifying diverse elements into a continuity of consciousness. Diversifying the unity and unifying the diverse—'abhede bhedanaṁ bhede abhedanam' (IPV. 1)—this is the pattern. Spirit is not like an indivisible point 'devoid' of the dimensions of length, breadth and thickness; in the sense that the latter are potentially there in the point.
33. The Advaitin's notion of unutterable unity or identity is approached through a dialectical refutation of diversity and difference (dvaita-nirākaraṇa) See *infra* Ch. 8.
34. Jacob Boehme calls it the 'theogonic' process. It takes place in eternity and signifies not the birth of a previously non-existent God but a divine mystery-play going on in the eternal hidden life of the Deity, the perpetual birth of God out of the *Ungrund.*
35. *infra*, Ch. 9.
36. For an enumeration of its classifications and kinds, see SB. p. 202; *Māpāḍiam.* pp. 274-75.
37. 'sattitan vaḍivēdennil *taḍaiyilā ñanamāhum.*' *Supakkam.* 1.62.
38. *ibid.* Śivajñāna yogin Comm.
39. These are the Pañca-Śaktis. *ibid.*
40. *ibid.* 1.63.
41. 'ondṛinoṇḍṛāi *pavantarum*', 'navandaru bēdam' etc. *ibid.* 2.64.
42. 'navandaru bēdamēka nādanē *naḍippanandṛē.*' *ibid.*
43. Professor T.P. Mīnākṣisundaram in his Endowment Lectures on Śaiva Siddhānta at Banaras Hindu University in 1963 developed this theme as the second of his three lectures. The lectures still await publication by the Annamalai University. Annamalainagar, India.
44. This vision of a theogonic process is adequately expressible in myths and symbols. It is what explains God, assuming such forms as those of man-woman (Umā-maheśvara) life of enjoyment for the selves, of the yogi (Dakṣiṇāmūrti) signifying yogic transmutation as the means for release. The indispensability of the processes of Divine will for bhoga as well as for mokṣa is brought out in a negative manner through impressive myths. When

Umā closed the eyes of the Lord in sport the entire world was plunged in darkness. Consistent with his nature as Grace, God out of concern for the world opened the third eye of his forehead in order to restore process to life. When the Lord was lost in yogic meditation all activities of enjoyment were suspended and life of sexual love came to an end notwithstanding the fact that Māra, the God of sexual love, was alive. When Māra sought to disturb the Lord out of his meditation in order to revive sex in the world, he was burnt to ashes by the enraged Lord, who then restored all love in the world by wedding the daughter of the king of the Himalayas. Śiva is the life of the universe inspiring all activities through His self-active will. These impressive illustrations are referred to by Arulnandi Śiva in *Supakkam*. 1. 50-53.

45. Saint Appar refers to this sūkṣma-pañca-kṛtya in the words : In the state of Premieval Darkness following total Dissolution, on the stage strewn with the corpses of the creative and conserving Gods my lord shall play on the lute in order to *revive Creation again*—"*Varunkaḍan mīla* emmiṛai nalvīnal vāsikkummē" 4.112.7. Music is the significant symbol of subtle Creation (Nāda).

The Mṛgendra text relating to sūkṣma-pañca-kṛtya has already been cited. *Ante*. Ch. 6. The distinction between the sūkṣma-kṛtyas seems to be : revealing in accordance with the degree of ripeness of mala is anugraha, concealing in similar accordance is tirobhāva, bringing about 'ripeness' for sañcita is Saṁhāra, preparing māyā for the 'delivery' of the world (prasavonmukhīkaraṇa) is Sthiti, and barely knowing what exists eternally within its unity, viz. cit and acit is Sṛṣṭi. MA. *loc.cit*. Vṛtti and Dīpikā on the verse. Also SMD. *loc.cit*.

46. In Sūkṣma-laya, Śiva is Para Nāda, and Śakti Para-Bindu, and in Sthūla-laya, Śiva is A-para-Nāda, and Sakti A-para-Bindu. The four forms are Formless Forms (Niṣkala). *Māpāḍiam*. pp. 275-76.

47. Śiva in this bhogāvasthā is Sadā-śiva and is of the form of 'Form and Formlessness' (sakala-niṣkala). What is to be noted is that from now on there are no distinction in terms of *several* function between jñāna and kriyā, and therefore, no separate mention of the pairs of Śiva and Śakti.

48. *infra* Ch. 4, See. II.

49. Śiva in this adhikārāvasthā is Maheśa, of Form (sakalā), discharges the office of Sūkṣma adhikāra and brings to pass sṛṣṭi etc. of the Pure Realm. In respect of the Impure Realm Maheśa vests his office with Ananteśa-Rudra, Viṣṇu and Brahmā—selves of different degrees of spiritual ripeness and through them brings to pass Sṛṣṭi etc. The latter figure as functionaries in cosmic operation but only as bearers of the adhikāra-śakti of the Lord. *Supakkam.* 1.59; *Māpāḍiam.* p. 276.

50. The differences of Śiva, Śakti, Sadā-śiva and Maheśa are Śambhu-pakṣa while those below Maheśa, viz. Ananteśa, Rudra, Viṣṇu and Brahmā are aṇu-pakṣa. *Māpāḍiam.* p. 276. The nine forms of theogonic functions are distinguishable in terms of *specific* functions. Brahmā, Viṣṇu and Rudra have respectively, sṛṣṭi, sthiti and saṁhāra as their *specific* functions though this does not prevent interchange of functions in a non-specific sense. Maheśa and Sadā-śiva have the respective *specific* functions of tirobhāva and anugraha though in a non-specific sense they do the other functions too. Apara-nāda has the specific function of Sūkṣma-Pañca-kṛtya while Para-nāda is distinguished in terms of pure concern or awareness preceding all other functions. Ananteśa is generally included under Maheśa as the point of indistinction between Infinite will and Finite will. *Supakkam* 2.64; *Māpāḍiam.* pp. 275-77.

51. "And the cause of the flowing over into being is the wisdom of God; and the cause of the wisdom is the Trinity of the uncausable Godhead; and the cause of the Trinity is the Single unfathomable Will; and the cause of the will is the nothingness". Boehme, quoted in *Spirit and Reality* : Berdyaev, p. 130. Berdyaev who is greatly influenced by Boehme's vision gives his own interpretation of Boehme as initiating the voluntarist tradition in European thought as different from that of Aquinas. What is specially relevant in Berdyaev's re-orientation of Boehme is its implication of the impossibility of finding freedom in the objectified or natural world. There is a remarkable parallel between this and Śaiva Siddhānta.

Śaiva Siddhānta in explaining cosmic functions always talks of Creation preceded by Dissolution. Even the distinction between Pārama-Śiva and Śiva bears on universal Dissolution.

Śiva is initial 'craving' (Boehme) to terminate the state of Universal Dissolution while Parama-Śiva is even without it, one with that state. But, significantly, Śaiva Siddhānta also concedes Ādi-sṛṣṭi — First Creation as an ideal presupposition of Punas-sṛṣṭi— Creation preceded by Dissolution, in which God is conceived to create the 'archetypal' body (sūkṣmaśarīra) for the self against an uncreated freedom of which two-fold karma is proto-type. The freedom preceding karma is the *karma-mala* and is identical with the 'dialectical negativity' in God—His Freedom itself. See *infra* Ch. 4, Sec. I.

God and Absolute

1. The Śaiva Siddhānta concept of Absolute as reflected in the theological doctrine of śakti was analysed in the previous section and in the present one attention is focussed mainly over the question of *knowledge* of Absolute.

   It is not that Meykanda Śāstra literature is a stranger to the notion of Absolute. The first of the fourteen texts comprised under it namely, Tiruvundiār, a pre-Meykaṇḍa Śāstra in the first verse speaks of the Absolute :

   'akaḷamāy yārum aṛivari dapporuḷ
   sakaḷamāy vandadeṉ dṛundīpaṛa
   tāṉākat tandadeṉ dṛundīpaṛa'.

   The two features of the Śaiva Siddhānta notion of Absolute are here brought out (*i*) its unknowability (arivaridu. Cf. also Meykandār's 'aṛivaṛiyā mey' (6.2.1), and (*ii*) its Freedom or Grace (tāṉāhat tandatu) through which it becomes accessible to man.

2. jñātṛ-jñāna-jñeyetvaiśca vihīnaṁ tat paraṁ padam.' *Acintya-Viśvasādākhya MNP*, p. 125.
3. 'patiś-ca kimvidho jñeyas sādhikāra-padā sthitaḥ śivaśca kīdṛśaḥ prokto yo' adhikāra-vivarjitaḥ'. *Sarvajñānottara*. 1.3.
4. 'aprameyam anirdeśyam anaupamyam anāmayam
   sūkṣmaṁ sarvagataṁ nityaṁ dhruvam avyayam īśvaram'
   Svāyambhuva-Āgama. Cited SP. p. 29. See also the *Mataṅga-Vṛtti* citation (*ibid.*) which brings out the implied negative meaning of terms like Sūkṣma etc.

   Also, 'anubhūya ca tat sarvaṁ dvādaśānto' pi tatkṣaṇāt
   nirguṇe nirmale śūddhe vācya-vācaka-varjite

nityānandamaye sūkṣme bhāvābhāva-vivarjite
kaivalye cidgaṇe śānte śive tu paribhāvayet.

Also, śāśvataṁ turīyarahitam ānandaṁ paramaṁ padam
jñātṛ-jñāna-jñeyatvaiś-ca vihīnaṁ tat paraṁ śivam
rāgārāga-vinirmuktaṁ dvaitādvaita-vivarjitam
cintyācintya-vinirmuktaṁ vācya-vācaka-varjitam'
Acintya-Viśva. cited in MNP p. 159.

5. And, 'śivo vastuparas tasmān mantrātīto nirañjanaḥ
nirāmayo nirādhāro varṇa-rūpa-vivarjitaḥ
sarvajñas sarvagaś śāntas sarvātmā sarvatomukhaḥ
atīndriyo nirālambas sūkṣmasca śāśvato dhruvaḥ
sa eva bhagavān vyāpī hy aprameyo hy anaupamaḥ
bahir-antar-vibhāgena tile tailam iva sthitaḥ.'
Sarva-Jñānottara, I.45, 47.

Also, 'yo' sau sarvagato devas sarvātmā sarvatomukhaḥ
sarvatattvamayo' cintyas sarvasyopari samsthitaḥ
sarva-tattva-vyatītaś ca vāṅmanonāmavarjitaḥ' etc.
ibid. II.3, 4.

'nā' dyakṣaṁ nā' pi talliṅgaṁ na śabdam api śāṅkaram.'
Acintya & *Pauṣkara,* cited SB p. 335; SP p. 30.

6. 'cittinōdu aciptumallan' *Supakkam* 1.70.
7. *ibid.* 1.70; also, 'sṛṣṭi-saṁhāra-varjitaḥ'.
Sarva-jñānottara. II.8.
8. Note the expression by which the Veda is generally referred in the Śaiva hymns, viz. marai, literally, 'what conceals or hides'.
9. The Śaiva hymnists extol God's Grace over the Revelation of the Veda. The latter too is grace; in that it too is revealed by Him, but He is still beyond it. The paradox is : He cannot be known by Revelation; He cannot also be known except through Revelation.

The truth seems to be that revelation (Śruti) can only prepare for the intuition of Grace, though *only* Revelation can prepare. The real 'event 'of knowledge (jñānaccheydi) is what takes place in man's subjectivity in union, and śruti and yukti lead to it. Even the leading presupposes Grace—the 'hidden' grace. *Māpāḍiam.* p. 361. Cf. also 'marai īr riyā maraiyone.' *Tiruvācakam* 5. 89.
10. Cf. Marcel's words : 'The whole reflexive process remains within a certain assertion which *I am* rather than which I *pronounce*—an

assertion of which I am the place and not the subject.' *Being and Having* p. 171.

11. 'If I see that which is (tan) (it is indeed identity) as That encompasses the seer also. Conversely, if I see myself I become dual to myself.' *Citrambala Nādigal Veṇba*, 59, *Tiruvāduturai* Adīnam 1954. Also cited in SMKK p. 31 (Kaḷakam ed.).
12. *Supakkam* 1.68. Śivajñana yogin's com.
13. *Supakkam* 1.44.
14. Sambandar gives vivid expression to the sense of the mystery and inscrutability of God in the decad sung by him as a public demonstration of the futility and inadequacy of the heterodox Jaina way of life :

    'ārarivār avar pettriyē ?'
    'endaiyāravar evvahaiyār kolō ?'
    'ketpān puhil alavilai; kiḷakka vēndā !'

    Tiruvācakam describes God as the 'great sight whom none can see' (1, line 78) and also as 'the sight *and* the dense Darkness, whose greatness consists of His not being manifest' (1, line 72). In a well known verse (6, 97, 10) speaks of God as the one whom even analogies cannot approach (uvaman illi) and none can even paint with colours and form.

    Kāraikkāl Ammaiyār (Arpudat tiruvandāti, 61) says : *Then* also I became Thine without seeing the face even as now I do not see Thy Form. TKP (90) uses the picturesque example of sea : 'Even when the great sea makes itself accessible to one to tide over it and swim it remains the unmeasurable.'
15. *Sambandar* : 2.15.4.
16. *ibid* : 1.39.1.
17. *ibid* : 1.121.3.
18. *ibid* : 3.3.8.
19. *Tiruvācakam* : 5.15.
20. *Sambandar* : 1.8.3.
21. *ibid* : 1.110.5; 2.11.7.
22. *ibid* : 3.121.6
23. *ibid* : 1.61.6.
24. *ibid* : 2.21.3.
25. *ibid* : 2.30.3.
26. *ibid* : 3.93.5.

27. *ibid* : 2.14.9.
28. *ibid* : 1.52.6.
29. 'Veṛai uḍaṇāṇānodu' etc. 1.11.2.
30. For elucidation of the idea of God the life behind life *ante* Ch. 7 Sec. 'God as the inner illuminer of experience.'
31. Self in the sense in which it is non-identifiable with 'I' is synonymous with sat and cit; relatively even the 'I' is asat and acit. see below.
32. These are understood, of course, as implying a non-rational or supra-rational subject of which they are predicates. They are essential, and not merely accidental attributes and yet, in the happy words of Otto, *synthetic* essential attributes. "We have to predicate them of a subject which they qualify, but which in its deeper sense is not, nor indeed can be, comprehended in them; which rather requires comprehension of a quite different kind." *The Idea of the Holy* (Oxford Univ. Press), p. 2.
33. The precise meaning of the sense in which God as Bliss is the negative of empirical pleasure is brought out in *MNP*, 19 com.
34. Śaiva Siddhānta possesses these predicates in unique abundance and clarity. The 'eight predicates' of Śiva are one of the distinguishing features of the system. The *Kāmika* mentions them:
'sarvajñatvaṁ vibhutvaṁ ca jagat-kartṛtvam eva ca
nirmalatvaṁ ca nityatvaṁ sarvānugrāhakaṁ tathā
aiśvaryaṁ ca prabhutvaṁ ca śivatvāṣṭaguṇās tathā'. cited *MNP* p. 244. Also *Sarvajñānottara Agama* 2.
35. The following table is suggestive of their equivalence :

Sat	*Cit*	*Ānanda*
alupta-śakti	sarvajñatva	nitya-tṛptatva
ananta-śakti	anādi-bodha	svatantratva
viśuddha-deha	(nirāmayātmā)	

Sat is indicative of conservation, universality and 'purity' of being (described as viśuddha-deha). Cit indicates the twin notions of omniscience and unconditioned freedom from mala (described as nirāmayātmā). Ānanda is indicative of plenary perfection (described as nitya-tṛpta and its synonyms of amṛta, paripūrṇa cidākāśa etc.) and Freedom as will. For the metaphysical distinctions implied by these terms, vide *SMD*. Vol. I.

Meykandār speaks only of Sat and Cit implying that Ānanda is implicit in the two. *Māpāḍiam*.

A plausible explanation can be that while a knowledge of the svarūpa-lakṣaṇa of God as such involves transcending the mode of empirical knowing, and can only be exoterically formulated. The Ānanda aspect represents the stage utterly transcending knowing existence (jñeya) through essence (jñāna). Sat and Cit describe the stage of Yoga (Śiva-yoga) or union with śatki, while Ānanda implies going even beyond it. Meykandār throughout in the sixth Sūtra speaks of the accessibility of Absolute *through* Revelatory Grace, reserving ānanda for a phenomenological description as the culmination of spiritual life in the eleventh Sūtra. *infra* Ch. 6, pp. 679-688.

36. Cf. the distinction drawn between Śiva-yoga and Śiva-bhoga *infra*. Chapter 15.

37. 'sadbhogaṁ vāṅmano' tītaṁ svayam evā'nubhūtimat
tad eva śivabhogaś ca tad eva paramaṁ sukham.'
Vātulottara, cited *MNP*. p. 299 and also 268.

The *Saivajñānottara-Āgama* after describing the nature of the Absolute (Śiva) in negative terms raises the question of knowledge of it :

'athā' nyaṁ saṁpravakṣyāmi hy upāyaṁ tatvato guha
agrāhyasyā' pi sūkṣmasya sarvagasya tu niṣkalaṁ
yena vijñāyate samyag taṁ jñātvā tu śivo bhavet
guru-paramparāyā yat tam adṛṣṭaṁ sarvavādibhih.' (2.1-3)

And then describes the nature of non-dual intuition by which alone it is apprehensible :

'so' ham evam upāsīta nirvikalpena cetasā
yo' ham eva paro devas sarva-mantramayaś śivah. (2.5)
aham ātmā śiva hy anyaḥ paramātme' ti yaḥ smṛtaḥ
evaṁ ya upāsayen mohān na śivatvam avāpnuyāt
śivo' nyas tv aham evā' nyaḥ pṛthagbhāvaṁ vivarjayet
yaś śivas so' ham eve' ti hy advayaṁ bhāvayet sadā
advaita-bhāvanā-yuktas sarvatrā'tmani saṁsthitaḥ
sarvagaṁ sarvadehas taṁ paśyate nā' tra saṁśayaḥ. (2.12-14)

Also another Mūlāgama says :

'dāso' ham iti sammohaṁ so' ham eva paribhramam
aham eva paribhrāntiḥ svānubhūtyai mumukṣukaḥ'

cited MNP. p. 268. Also,
'śivo' ham asmī' ti siddhāntaṁ vedāntaṁ so' ham asmi tu.'
ibid. p. 269.

38. 'yad eva niṣkalaṁ jñānaṁ śāśvataṁ dhruvam avyayam
nirvikalpam anirdeśyaṁ hetu-dṛṣṭānta-varjitam
aliṅgam akṣaraṁ śāntaṁ viṣayā*tītagocaram*' etc. *Ibid.* 2.6.

39. 'ariyātatu indrām' *Supakkam* 6. 1.

40. *ibid* 6.4.

41. 'irutiran alladu' SNP, 6. Meykandar's rendering of 'śunya' is as the nought 'unmai'.

42. Even objective knowing involves union, identification; it is grasping the object into itself, into union with the subject but it is a case of subject in union with what is not itself.

43. It is acceptance of this conception of spirit as not merely the ground of the possibility of knowledge but as the ground by virtue of its knowing, also simultaneously with revealing, that introduces some distinction in the Siddhāntin's concept of aparokṣānubhūti. See *infra*.

44. The Śaiva text stating the paradox thus : 'self-knowledge involves duality; conversely to know 'that' is non-duality for where is the knowing 'I' unembraced by That ?' has already been cited *Ante* Note No. 11.

45. 'astī' ti bruvato' nyatra kathaṁ tad upalabhyate ?' *Kaṭha. Up.* II.3.12.

46, 47. These concepts are defined in Ch. 14.

48. Being is used in the sense of reality as ultra-subjective Tān literally that which is or the Itself is the Tamil expression for Being used in Meykanda literature : Cf. tan sivam used appositional to each other by Umāpati in *SUP* 13.

49. The etymology of the word as given in a citation from *SKB* (1.1.5) is :

śaktiś śivaś ca sacchabda-prakṛti-pratyayoditau
tau brahma-sāmarasyena samasta-jagadātmakau.'

It must, however, be noted that this power of resisting non-being is understood as participation in Being which is its āśraya. See SMD on the verse cited, Vol. I, p. 196. The precedence is more aesthetic than logical.

50. See Ch. 15, last section, for a discussion of the alleged endurance of mala in mokṣa 'too'.

51. The one-sidedness and the non-logical character of the precedence of śiva in relation to śakti is already expounded *Ante* Sec. 'The Concept of Divine Will'.

52. The adoption of 'Being' as an unequivocal name for God does not prevent the siddhantin from using the expression 'non-being' to refer to God : 'uṇmaiyumāy *unmaiyumāi*' *Tiruvācakam* 5, 15. Being here used as expressive of the essence of God-head is truly beyond the distinction of being and non-being so that both of them can be applied indifferently to describe its nature.

53. SÑP. 6.1 'nīrmēlezuttum nikal kaṇavum
pēyttērum ōriṇavai iṇḍrāma roppu'.
Also *Supakkam*. 6.3. The conjuror's show is a phenomenon conditioned by the circumstance of the conjuror blinding the eye of the credulous so as to make the unreal appear real. The dream is the experience through subtle body. Similarly the phenomenon of mirage is conditioned by sun's rays with which it disappears. The world phenomenon too is likewise conditioned transcendentally in repsect of its appearance and disappearance. *Māpāḍiam*. p. 394.

54. 'oliyum iruḷum orumaittu' TVP 7. 4.
See also *Ante* Ch.4 section on 'God as the Material Cause' Note 67.

55. *infra* Ch. 10 section on 'Arguments for Mala' Notes 15, 17.

56. In 'I know', the subject and the predicate both experientally certify to the 'givenness' of the knowing subject and its knowledge, even as in 'I do not know', the knowing subject and its ignorance are given. The given-ness cannot be disputed even though the *real* nature of what is given may be different from the verdict of the experience. But Being is certifiable by no empirical experience, as Being is not the given. Śivajñāna yogin evidences a deep awareness of this problem. *Māpāḍiam*. p. 356.

57. 'pandamum vīdumāya pada padārthaṅgaḷ allaṉ.' *Supakkam*. 1.44.

58. 'andamum ādi illan aḷappilan'. *ibid*.

59. 'endaitān iṇṇaṇeṇṟum, iṇṇadām innadāhi
vantiḍān eṇṟum colla vazakkodu mātṟamiṇḍṟē.' *ibid*.
Also, 'bandha-mokṣa-padārtheṣu na kaścid parameśvaraḥ
ādyanta-rahitaḥ śambhuḥ sarva-vyāpī jaganmayaḥ

tad anyaś-ca svarūpeṇa buddhi-vācām agocaraḥ'
Kālottarāgama, cited *JVM*. p. 653.

Sarvajñānottara (1.29, 30), therefore, describes Śiva as śūnya. It is śūnya and yet not quite śūnya :

'sarva-śūnyaṁ tam ābhāsam ātmānaṁ bhāvayet sadā
nai'va śūnyaṁ na cā'śūnyaṁ na śūnyaṁ śūnyam eva ca
pakṣapāta-vinirmuktam ātmānaṁ paryupāsayet.' See *infra* for a discussion of this paradox.

60. Cf. The Vedāntic distinction between vṛtti-vyāpti and phala-vyāpti in knowledge.
61. *Māpāḍiam*. p. 256.
62. The dilemma posed here is the problem in answer to which is felt the need for the distinction of śuddha avasthā from that of sakala avasthā. See *infra* Ch. 14, Sec. on 'Knowledge and Śuddha avasthā'.
63. The term Śūnya is understood in several senses. Here it is used as a synonym of alīka, the unreal. Its other meanings are (*i*) the unmanifest, (*ii*) the indeterminate, in all of which senses it is used in Śaiva Siddhānta.
64. Cf. Citsukhācārya's definition of svayaṁprakāśa as avedyatve sati aparokṣa-vyavahāra-yogyatvam. Śaiva Siddhānta will interpret avedyatva as pāśāgamyatva or vāṅmanotītatva and aparokṣatva as gocaratva, pati-jñānaikagamyatva for the difference in their account of intuition.
65. Combining the import of texts like 'pāśāgamyo maheśāno', 'nā' dhyakṣaṁ nā' pi tal-laiṅgaṁ na śabdam api śāṅkaram', 'yat sukhaṁ paramaṁ jñeyam', 'svasaṁvedyaṁ paraṁ jyotir' etc. Śivāgra yogin formulates the svarūpa-lakṣaṇa of God as : 'paśu-pāśa-jñāna-pramāṇāvedya-svaprakāśa-cid-rūpa-parānanda eva śivasya svarūpam.' *SB* p. 342.
66. 'In the case of that which is light there is no need of enlightening and in the case of that which is not light there can be no enlightening' SÑP 6, 2 hetu.
67. By spiritual effort is here meant enlightening knowledge or intuition which is occasioned by the processes of worship rite and meditation. See *Māpāḍiam* p. 366.
68. See Śaṅkara's comm. on 'sātmā savijñeya'. *Māṇḍ. Up*. 1.16.
69. 'eṇkaṇṇi uḷadeṇḍṛal ?' SÑP 6.2.1.

70. 'aṛivariyā *mey*'. *Ibid.* Meykandār's use of mey as equivalent of sat of the *Chāndogya. Up.* is noted in *Māpāḍiam.*
71. 'tam ādimadhyānta-vihīnam ekaṁ vibhuṁ cid ānandam arūpam adbhutam umāsahāyaṁ parameśvaraṁ prabhuṁ trilocanaṁ nīla-kaṇṭhaṁ praśāntam', etc. *Kaivalya Up.* 7.
72. *Supakkam.* 6.5.
73. Vinā venba 11. For the implied restatement of triputi as dṛk dṛśya and darśayitṛ see *Supakkam* 6, 6.
74. This becomes retrospectively evident in the transcendent experience of Integration with Grace and unitive life of śuddha avasthā, *infra* Ch. 15.
75. Explained *ante* in sec. on 'The Concept of Divine Will' and Ch. 5, Sec. on 'God as Non-dual'.
76. TAP 7. 10; 7. 3; 6. 10; 6. 8; SVP 80.
77. 'Tā*niraṇḍāik* kāṇān tami', *SJB* 6.2.2. Meykandār's use of the pronominal term 'tan', in line with its usage in the Tevāram to refer to the 'Being that is accessible through grace' is the aptest in this context. In Tamil it is used primarily in the third person but is also used in a quasi-figurative sense in the first person and second person. It is contrasted from nān (I) but sometimes paradoxically used for referring to 'I' specially in contexts where the 'I' is addressed in the third person. Sambandar at one place distinguishes 'tanadu' from 'enadu'—'enadurai tana duraiyāha' but at another place identifies tan (He) with tan (I) "tān tānāccheydu'. The pronoun 'tan' is, strictly, inter personal, outstretching the"It", "Thou" and "I". Meykandār makes use of the expression 'tān-tānat cheydu' in more than one place in his illustrative verses.

    In human language God's own language makes itself heard. Sambandhar's words of prayer and the miracle that they perform in the literal and metaphorical sense illustrate the theological significance of prayer: Prayer is the experience in which God is experienced, not as a psychic phenomenon but as a response in which God's word comes to expression. It is upon such experience of God understood very significantly as Personal Revelation that the theology of Śaiva Siddhānta is based. Personal Revelation is experience of Prayer as a form of union and communion where the will and therefore speech becomes 'oned'.
78. *Māpāḍiam* pp. 370 ff.

79. For the concept of Śiva-yoga see *infra* Ch. 15.
80. *Māpāḍīam* p. 372.
81. See Jñānaprakāśar, *Śiva jñāna bodha vṛtti* p. 61. SÑP 6.2.4. *citrurai,*
82. SÑP 6.2.4.
83. The following texts from *Sarva-Jñānottara* bring out the inherent absence of parity between śiva-śakti and ātma-śakti :
'avijñātaḥ paśus so hi sṛṣṭi-dharma-samāśritaḥ
vijñātaḥ śāśvataś śuddhaś śivo nā'tra tu saṁśayaḥ
tasmād ātmā sadā vedyas suvicāryo vicakṣaṇaiḥ
parāpara-vibhāgena *sthūla-sūkṣma*-vibhāgaśaḥ
paraḥ param anirvāṇo'paraḥ sṛṣṭi-vibhedakaḥ
sthūlo mantramayaḥ proktas sūkṣmo dhyānaika-gocaraḥ
sarve dharmā ātmanas tu (dharmā ātmanas santi) yam eva parikalpayet
tat tad bhavatyasandehāt so'pi tadbhāvanā-yutaḥ
ityevam ātma-vijñānaṁ kathitaṁ tu samāsataḥ
jñātvā' tmānaṁ idaṁ sarve hyātmānaṁ paryupāsate'. (2.17-23)
84. According to *citrurai* (SÑP 6. 2. 4) the *pūrvapakṣin* is the Śivādvaitin and the Śuddhaśaiva.
85. aṛiyum aṛivē śivamumām. SÑP 6.2.5.

BOOK III

Chapter Eight

INTERPRETATION OF MĀYĀ

The Concept of *Māyā*

1. For the formulation of satkārya-vāda, see Ch. 3.
2. For a treatment of Sāṅkhya-dualism as a basis of the evolution of pluralistic and absolutistic thinking in India, vide Murti : *The Central Philosophy of Buddhism* op. cit.
3. 'nimittam aprayojakaṁ prakṛtīnāṁ varaṇa-bhedastu tataḥ kṣetrikavat.' *Yoga-Sūtra* IV.3.

3.a. 'śaktimad-adhīna-sthitikatva-rūpam īśvarādhīna-sthitike bindāvapyakṣatam eva.' SB p. 186. Another significant definition of śakti which too is comprehensive to include Māyā or Bindu given by Śivāgra yogin (*ibid.* p. 186) is : 'ananya-pravartyatve satyādiśaktimad-avasthitatvaṁ śakti-lakṣaṇam.' Being activated by none other but the initialmost possessor of it.

4. Being manifest to self means for Śaiva Siddhānta two things : (i) the self to whom it is manifest is finite and unfree (paśu) and therefore, (ii) the latter cannot be the *cause* of the former's manifestness. See below.
5. Unlike as in Sāṅkhya-yoga. *Ante* Chapter 4.
6. 'śambhuḥ puruṣo māyā nityaṁ vibhu *kartṛśaktiyuktam* ca.' TTN 3. Māyā is asat but not strictly, acit, vide *ante* Schomerus makes note of this : *Der Śaiva Siddhānta* p. 179.
7. 'māyā ca kartuḥ parameśvarasya śaktyādhiṣṭhitā' etc. *ibid.* Comm.
8. For example, between a will to bring about the movement of one's hand and the movement itself, there is continuity; no line can be drawn between the two to indicate where willing ends and action begins. Action is but a concretion of will.
9. For analysis of will, in contradiction to knowledge which is here utilized for interpreting māyā the basis is Bhattacharya, K. C.: The Absolute and its Alternative Forms', *Studies in Philosophy*, Calcutta, Progressive Publishers, Vol. II, 1958.

10. Ananta is a mature soul of the group of Vijñānākalas free practically from all the malas except for what is called 'adhikāra-mala' which keeps him in his appointed role in the performance of cosmic functions. See Ñ. V. 66.
11. 'pōhia *nāma visēḍameydal* uladu.' *Ibid* lines 5-6.
12. This is what necessitates in turn a material cause for Ananta's 'body, sense, world and eṇjoyment'. See below. Also RT. 60-61.
13. Cf. SMD., Vol. II, p. 107.
14. The Śaivāgamas use such expressions as: māyāṁ *vikṣobhyati* (TP 40). Cf. Aghora Śiva's comments on the term underlined: 'prasavābhimukhīkaroti'; Śrīkumāra's note brings out the sense of the relation of will and the willed content: 'na hyupādānādikaṁ kāraṇaṁ kartṛ-preritaṁ kāryotpādane paryāptam iti kṣobha-siddhir iti.'

    The Pauṣkara text (2.13) māyādyupādānaṁ...kṣubdhaṁ kāryakaraṁ tasya kartuḥ' etc., suggests that the process suggested by the term points at one end to a (kṣobhaka) kartā and at another to its content (kṣobhya).
15. 'Śiva-śakti-kṣobhitā mahāmāyā yad yatkāryam utpādayati tatra tadadhiṣṭhātrayos śiva-śaktyoḥ kārya-bhedena sthāna-bhedeno'pacārāt tat tat saṁjñā bhavati.' *RT* 270 Com.
16. The expression is that of Schomerus *op. cit.* p. 93 : Er ist der *Stuckpunkt* der Māyā in ihrem unentwickelten Zustand. Also cf. p. 132.
17. 'da sie in—und miteinander existieren'. *ibid.* p. 93. Schomerus, however, writes inconsistently elsewhere that Siddhānta takes the existence of matter as '*outside*' God who is also from eternity '*outside*' it, and is only a demiurge. See p. 166.
18. God's knowledge of the upādāna-kāraṇa is aparokṣa-jñāna. *SB* pp. 106-107. Cf. its with Ananta's knowledge of Māyā.
19. 'als alles erfullendes.', Schomerus, *op. cit.* p. 93 ff.
20. 'muṉṉavaṉ avvasittai virittevaiyumākkum, mudanmaiyadu koḍuttadena mozindiḍāre.' SVP. Umāpati, as was indicated earlier interprets all non-causative verbs used appositionally with God, expressive of self-becoming on the part of God, in this sense. They demand to be translated into causative, transitive verbs but in the above paradoxical sense.
21. Umāpati frequently refers to the *derived* supremacy of Māyā; TVP. 3.10; 4.10; SVP. 70. Cf. also TKP. 12 ff.

22. Respectively termed 'aṛivittal' and 'asaivittal' in the terminology of *Māpāḍiam*.

23. Creation *ex nihilo* is interpreted by the Medieval Scholastics in the sense that the world was nothing before creation but only in the strict line of existence. The world in creation is produced not out of absolute nothing—absolute nothing lies only at the basis of whatever implies contradictions, but out of a possible-reality not-actually-existing. What is already there, presumably as one with Divine existence is given a further reality in the strict line of existence only. For a suggestive comparison between the Hindu and the Thomistic theory of Creation, vide De Smet's 'St. Thomas Aquinas and Medieval Scholastics', *History of Philosophy, Eastern and Western,* Vol. II, Allen & Unwin, 1952.

24. The precise sequence of ideas leading to the Advaitin's equation of māyā, a cosmological notion with 'avidyā' which is epistemological and soteriological must be kept in view : What is can never decease but knowledge causes the total decease of non-knowledge (avidyā). The phenomenal world due to māyā deceases at the attainment of release. Therefore māyā is equated with avidyā which is destroyed at the mere touch of knowledge. The siddhāntin's rejection of 'māyā-vāda' is in precise reference to such equation. Umapati devotes a long section in SN to a refutation of māyā-vāda.

25. 'na hi prapañco vastvātmā (i) pramāṇānām abhāvataḥ prameyābhāvataḥ (ii) tadvat sambandhābhāvato'pi ca.' PA 3.10. See PB. ff 125-127.

26. The Advaitins right from Bādarāyaṇa (e. g. BS 2. 1. 13-14) to Madhusūdana have reasoned out pure monism by means of a dialectical refutation of 'difference'. For a summary statement of refutation of difference in the writings of some of the important representative post-Śaṅkara Advaitins see Sundaram P. K. and Subhramanya Sastri S, *Dialectic of Difference,* The Madras University Journal Sec. A, 1957.

27. Is it the case that even perceptual evidence does not support the notion of difference ? The arguments of the Advaitin are well-known. There is strictly no knowledge of *difference* in the assertion that there is the object. 'This is pitcher' and not that it is not , say, some piece of cloth is what perception can vouch. Per-

ception strictly does not have the function of exclusion. Even if the function of perception were with regard to exclusion why may not difference be said to be perceived? Because, it is argued, difference *is* exclusion. If perception does not 'exclude', it does not also apprehend difference. Difference, in brief, cannot be formulated without the help of 'not' or its equivalents which are the semantic counterpart of exclusion. PB, *op. cit.*

28. The Vedāntic dialectic of difference is thus simplified under two headings, viz. the problem of knowledge and the problem of relation, in the Śaivāgamas and works based on them. PA 3.10-26; RT; *Māpādiam.*
29. This has been expounded under 'God as Divine will; Chapter 7.
30. 'sambandho jñāna-ghaṭayor jñāpya-jñāpaka-lakṣaṇah.' PA 3.25.
31. 'sarveṣāṁ sarvadā kumbhaḥ kumbha eve'kṣate yataḥ
nai'vam rajjuḥ kadācit tu yatas sarpāyate nṛṇām,
mālāyate tad anyeṣāṁ nai'vaṁ kumbha-ghaṭādayaḥ.' *ibid.* 3.20.
32. It is interesting exegetically that SNP does not treat māyā separately either under pramāṇa section or under the one of lakṣana. See Below note. 72. The fifth sūtra purporting to elucidate the initial aspect of Grace ('mudalupakāram') is taken to comprehend under tirodhāna-śakti both māyā and karma for obvious theological reasons. *Māpāḍiam* p. 344 ff.
33. Schomerus raises this issue and enters into a detailed 'historical appreciation' of the doctrine of Māyā, (*op. cit.* p. 164 ff.) discussing the anomaly or otherwise of labelling a positive cosmological notion by the name of māyā whose meaning has been preempted by the slant given to it by Advaitic absolutism.
34. Schomerus *op. cit.* p. 178; he lists the meanings implied by the root mā: (*i*) to measure, (*ii*) to build, to organise, to attribute, (*iii*) to develop, manifest or show, and (*iv*) to unfold; self-construction.
35. Two derivations, similar in meaning are suggested, *SP.* p. 87; *SRS* p. 44 :
    i) ***mayati, dadāti viśvam,*** what ***gives forth*** the world; *Cf.* also 'māyāty asmāj jagad viśvaṁ māyā tena samīritā', PA 3-1. Also the expression 'mūlaṁ ***tanthidum*** siva-navantan sannidi tannil nindre', ***Supakkam*** 1.19.
    ii) 'mātyāyati viśvam atreti'; literally the whence and the whither of evolution of the world. *Cf.* also 'māti yatra jagat ***suptau***

sṛṣṭvā vā yāti sā tataḥ. māyā tena samākhyātā tattvam uktaṁ guruttamaiḥ.' *ibid.* *Cf.* also Śiva-Sūtra 5: aviveko māyā sauṣuptam, which also bring out the idea of māyā as dreamless sleep.

The first is indicative of its necessary relation to spirit, while the second one is indicative its role as *causa materialis.*

36. Māyā understood as Aśuddhā Māyā alone has its deluding function. Śuddhā Māyā, also called Bindu and its sphere of Pure Realm (śuddhādhvan) are outside its sweep. *infra.* Śuddhā Māyā, like Aśuddhā Māyā, is, however, pāśa. SSP.

37. TP 39, Aghoraśiva's Comm. MA therefore describes Māyā as 'aśivaḥ' (9. 2); see Dīpikā on the word.

38. 'mayai mayakkal varaittal vinaikūttal'.—*Tuhalaru Bodham* 17. Also, commenting on the Pauṣkara text *op. cit.* giving the etymology of māyā, Umāpati interprets *mayati* to mean : 'paśu-jātaṁ mohakāt mayati muhyati tena kāraṇena māye'ti samīritā......*samasta-paśu-mohakatvam lakṣyatāvacchedakam*', though he hastens to add 'tena prakṛtyāder māyā-kāryasya yat-kiñcin mohakatve'pi na sarva-mohakatvam iti' etc. *PB* p. 119.

Also cf. 'mayai mayakk*amum* seyyumandre'.—*Supakkam* 2.53. In the tradition of Advaitic tantras too, Māyā is described as the source of a spell under which the individual passes through, constitutive of his empirical life. *Vijñāna Bhairava* describes Māyā as : māyā vimohinī nāma kalayaḥ kalanam sthitam' etc. verse 75.

39. Dean Inge is fond of quoting a passage of Plotinus dealing with the active, and yet unconscious Nature. "If any one were to demand of Nature why it produces, it would answer, if it were willing to listen and speak: You should not ask questions, but understand, keeping silence as I keep silence for I am not in the habit of talking". "What ought you to understand ? In the first place that what is produced is the work of my *silent* contemplation for being myself born of contemplation I am naturally contemplative while I contemplate I let fall as it were the lines which mark the forms of bodies". (The British Academy Lecture on Plotinus, 1929).

40. The category of jaḍa in this sense is distinguishable from the category of acit. SSUKK.

41. This is one of the profoundest syntheses of Umāpati which he makes in SVP 70; Śivajñāna yogin interprets this verse under

reference in the above manner in *Māpāḍiam* pp. 191 ff. The verse is quoted in the next note.

42. 'maruḷenil *iruḷāi* nirkum aruḷenil *oḷiyai* nirkum'. SVP *op. cit.* In Śaiva Siddhānta, freedom comes from that very ultimate source from which bondage too, in its actuality or actualised form proceeds. Freedom does not come from the material, from nature. Neither does nature therefore bind, in opposition to Sāṇkhya view.

43. This paradoxical nature of Māyā, popularly known as the aghaṭana-ghaṭana of Māyā, is technically described in Kashmir Śaiva works as 'durghaṭatva'. Abhinava calls it the aiśvarya of the Lord, the capacity to bring to pass the effects impossible to produce—ati-durghaṭa-kāritva, and rightly links it up with the svātantrya-śakti of God. IPV I.1.1.

44. Boehme's *magic* also corresponds to this notion of Māyā : "It is the mother in all the three worlds and makes each thing after the model of that thing's will. It is not the understanding, but it is a creatrix according to the understanding and lends itself to good or evil...from eternity the ground and support of all things. In sum : magic is the activity in the will-spirit.' Cited in Zimmer's Myths and Symbols p. 24.

45, 46. "*oṇḍroṇ drovvā uṇmaiyadāi*......maṇṇiyiḍum aranaruḷāl māyai-tāne". SvP 22. See *Cindanaiyurai*, *loc. cit.* on the entire verse.

47. sahakkaru mattin mihatihaz iṛaiyai/araibenna vaṇikiḷar ulaham *ērupādānam iṇdṛeṇiṇ iṇdṛudai* / nūlindrenin iṇdṛeṇa. Ñ, 21 lines 7-10.

'kartrā vinā na kāryaṁ na tatho' pādāna-kāraṇābhyām.' TP 37. Also, 'kartā' numīyate yena jagaddharmeṇa hetunā
teno' pādānam apyasti na paṭas tantubhir vinā.' MA cited SRS p. 46; SSP.

48. SB pp. 165-166.

49. This is the view of the Dialectical Absolutism of Śūnya-vāda : 'krama-yaugapadyābhyām artha-kriyā-kāritvānupapatyā sarvasyā'-pi kṣaṇikatve siddhe suṣuptikāle artha-kriyābhāve ālaya-vijñāna-santānābhāvena śūnyasyaiva jāgarādyasantānopādānatvāt.' *ibid.* p. 166.

50. Śaiva Absolutism relates to the Kāśmīra Śaiva tradition. The Śaiva absolutist like the Buddhist absolutist (Vijñānavādin)

rejects the concept of the 'object'. All arguments adduced to establish the 'objective' prove the subjectivity of the objective. IPV, Jñānādhikāra, Āh. V.8-9.

51. 'yat punar idaṁ yogināṁ icchāmātreṇa pura-senādi-vaicitrya-nirmāṇaṁ dṛṣṭaṁ tatro'pādānaṁ prasiddha-mṛtkāṣṭha-śukra-śoṇitādi-vaicitryamayaṁ na sambhavatyeva'. IPV, *op.cit.* 7 Also *Śiva Dṛṣṭi* 1, 44-45.

52. 'nanu yogi-sṛṣṭānāṁ ghaṭa-paṭādīnāṁ prasiddha-ghaṭa-paṭādyapekṣayā svarṇa-ghaṭādivad vaijātyam eva.' SB p. 166. Also, 'na ca etat prasiddhaṁ paramāṇubhya eva sthūlaṁ ghāṭādi jāyate iti' etc. IPV, *op.cit.* ff.

53. 'evaṁ jagadapi paramayogī śiva-sṛṣṭatvād anupādānakam eva. SB p. 166. Abhinava concludes from the yogin's analogy of the Kārikā that Saṁvid too, by its accredited spontaneity and unimpeded desire manifests or projects the objects of the world which are present within identical with it, as 'this' : 'yad ābhāsa-vaicitryarūpam arthajātaṁ prakāśayatīti tad asti sambhavaḥ yad saṁvid eva abhyupagatasvātantryā pratītā lakṣaṇād icchā-viśeṣavaśāt saṁvido'nādhikātmatayā'napāyād antaḥsthitam eva sadbhāvajātam idam ity evam....vitīrṇakiyanmātra-saṁvidrūpād bāhyatvenā' bhāsayati.' IPV, *op.cit.* The negative meaning of 'Ābhāsa theory' is decisive for Śaiva Siddhānta too, to the extent it suggests that the projected does not go beyond the will and that will maintains its hold on it. Also, IPK 107 'cidātmai'va hi devo'ntaḥ sthitam icchāvaśād bahiḥ yogī ca nirupādānam artha-jātaṁ prakāśayet.' This is cited in SB p. 166 and also SKB II.2.38. From the comment of SMD (infra.), the citation seems to be from a Śaivāgama, though Māpāḍiam (p. 147) considers it 'Śaiva-Purāṇa-vacana'. SB also cites another couplet in this connection: 'anupādāna-sambharam *abhittāveva tanvate*, jagac-citraṁ namas-tasmai kalāślāghyāya śūline.' This is also cited in IPV, Kriyādhikāra Āh. IV. 10.

54. Śaiva Siddhānta, however, admits change of states of consciousness (avasthās) for the non-variant subject, Impurity-ridden as the latter is and is being systematically revealed by a never-Impure consciousness from within. 'For arguments against asat-kārya-vāda, and for reduction of Śūnya vāda under asat-kārya-vāda, ante Ch. 3.

55. RT (34) appeals both to reason and scripture in support of Māyā 'utpatti-nāśau māyeya-dharmāvāha maheśvaraḥ.'
Also, 'tottramum nilaiyum irum mayaiyin toziladendre sattridum *ulakam*', *Supakkam* 1.14. The *word in italics*, according to Śiva-jñana yogin refers to the Vedic testimony, to the Śvetāśvatara text about Māyā.

56. *Spanda Nirṇaya* (p. 19), a Kāśmīra Śaiva work raises the question how if spirit (Śiva) were the upādāna-kāraṇa of the world, spirit is not concealed in its effect being rendered unmanifest *qua* effect 'even as a lump of clay is concealed in the pot'. The reply given is as follows : The world supposed to obstruct consciousness is either self-manifest or not. If self-manifest it is identical with spirit; if not it is *non-est*. Whatever shines is of the nature of spirit, the Light. The entire phenomena in the form of knower, knowledge and the known find their existence in spirit and have their being manifest by its light. Instead of the world obstructing or concealing it loses itself in Śiva's manifestation. One's nature is not hidden in one's wakeful and dream states, which are voluntary conditions. As freely owned states they, on the other hand, serve to manifest one's nature as freedom.

Śaiva Siddhānta is in substantial agreement with this position, except for terminological difference; Māyā is the material cause of the world in producing from which Śiva does not indeed produce from a causal material outside His unity. Māyā as the śakti, does not infringe but manifest the freedom of Śiva.

57. K.C. Bhattacharya : 'The Absolute and its Alternative Forms'. *op.cit.* p. 142.

58. Śaiva Siddhānta is therefore non alignable with Trika philosophy despite the commonness of terms and concepts. Its rejection of pan-psychism is cognate with its rejection of the pantheism of Viśiṣṭādvaita Vaiṣṇavism and Śivādvaita Śaivism and of the acasmistic pan-en-theism of Advaita Vedāntism.

59. *Spanda-Nirṇaya*, *op.cit.*

60. 'In order that a work of art should be created, the prospective artist must have in him certain unexpressed emotions' Collingwood : The Principles of Art, P. 130 (Oxford, 1938). Collingwood exposes the unsoundness of a literal interpretation of

'creation of the world out of nothing' in a section entitled 'Making and Creating'. *ibid.* pp. 128-30.

61. Śaiva Siddhānta also uses this analogy but to bring out the un-involved nature of spirit in creating the world. *Supakkam* 1. 31.

62. Abhinava himself concedes the plausibility of such interpretation at least in these cases : iha tāvat svapnasmaraṇa-manorājya-saṁkalpādiṣu nīlādyābhāsa-vaicitryaṁ bāhya-samarpaka-hetu-vyatirekeṇai'va nirbhāsate iti yadyapi asti sambhavas-tathā'-pi....pūrṇānubhava-*saṁskārajatva*-sambhāvanād avastu iti śaṅkyet.' IPV Jñānādhikāra, Āh. 5.7. But if so why may it not be conceded in the case of the yogin's creation too?

63. 'yogisṛṣṭau-ghaṭādiṣu prasiddha ghaṭādyapekṣayā vaijātya-kalpanena tatra mṛdādeḥ kāraṇatvenā' kalpanatvāt *SB* p. 176.

64. 'na cā'trā'pi jagati prasiddha-ghaṭādi-kārya-vaijātyakalpanaṁ pramāṇābhāvāt.' *ibid.*

65. Utpala's plea that 'yogi-nirmāṇatābhāve pramāṇāntara-niścite kārya-hetuḥ' (IP, Kriyādhikāra, IV. 11), therefore sounds question-begging, from this point of view.

66. 'jagadupādānam eva ne' ti tacchivasya jagadupādānatva-sādhanāt sāmanyato nirākṛtam eva viśiṣṭyā'pi nirākriyate.' *SB* p. 176.

67. 'yogināṁ api mṛdbīje vinaivecchāvaśena tad ghaṭādi jāyate *tat tat sthirasvārtha-kriyākaram.*' IP. Kārikā *op.cit.* Āh. IV. 10. See Abhinava's comments on the words in italics.

68. *Ante*, foot-note no. 53.

69. *Māpāḍiam* p. 147. *Cf.* also Appaya's interpretation of the verse in question : 'āgamāntara-śloke antaḥ-sthitam ityasya svātmani *sūkṣma-rūpeṇa sthitam* ityarthaḥ. atha tasyopādānatve prāmāṇya-siddhiḥ. evam āgamānāṁ śivasyo'pādānatve'pi tātparyasadbhāvāt.' SMD, Vol. II, p. 111. In another context (I.2.9.) citing this very text, Śrīkaṇṭha says in equivocal terms : 'sarga-kāle svasaṁkalpa-matreṇa *samavāyikāraṇa-nirapekṣaṁ eva* svasmāt prathama-śakti-parisphuraṇa-pūrvakaṁ....sakalaṁ cidacid arthajātaṁ sṛjati prakāśayati tathā....cidātmaiva hi' etc. Appaya's comments on these lines, however, introduce clarity : 'sṛjatī'tyetat *satkārya-vādaṁ anusṛṣtya* vyācaṣṭe-prakāsayati'ti....nirupādānamity etat *svapṛthaksiddhopādāna-nairapekṣyaparaṁ*....' SMD Vol. I, p. 341. That Appaya's clarification is in harmony with Śrīkaṇṭha's own views in this

respect may be seen from what Śrīkaṇṭha says in the same sequel : 'yathā ghaṭaniṣpattau kulālasya svaśarīra-pṛthaktvena mṛtpiṇḍa upādānaṁ dṛśyate, tathā na parameśvarāt pṛthak siddhaṁ māyādyupādānaṁ māyādi-rūpāt parameśvarāj jagadutpateḥ. ato na virodhaḥ. tataḥ svarūpapṛthag-avasthāna-sūkṣma-māyā puruṣaḥ parameśvara eva svayam upādānam apī'tyucyate.' *ibid.*p. 341.

70. The yogin is also a finite agent and his creations too are governed by the conditions of space-time-causality; his powers too are 'natural'; for bringing to pass anything as well as for assuming any corporeal form the yogin is dependent on Māyā in precisely the same sense in which God is not dependent on a material cause. *Supakkam* 1, 40-41. Also, *TS* 46-47 Comm.

71. *Māpādiam* (p. 147) suggests very plausible interpretations of the text of Tiruvācakam. Seedling (vicchu) may be taken to mean either the generality of cause, or specifically, *causa materialis.* In the former sense again the text affirming creation (of the world) without a seedling may mean either of two things : the world etc. is created *initially* without the pre-requisite of the twin karmas of the souls, the reference here being to Ādi-sṛṣṭi (Primeval Creation) in which the original matrix from which alike proceed the karma-series and the series of embodiments for the souls, viz. sūkṣma-śarīra is created. That this refers to initial-most creation may be seen from the next line in the same verse which speaks of creation preceded by Dissolution ; *vaicchu vāṅguvāy.* Or, creative activity without the help of a cause may relate to God's assuming a form and personality freely of his own śakti, and not as in the case of the mortal from something which exists before Him—in other words, from a cause. What lends plausibility to this interpretation is that the term seed is sometimes used as a synonym of karma (*Cf.* 'karmāṇi....bījadṛṣṭa-sahakāryādibhiḥ *paryāyair* udīryante.' SSP p. 31. Also, cf. 'uṇakkilatator *vittu* mēl viḷaiyāmal eṇviṇai ottapiṇ'. *Tiruvācakam*, where the underlined stands for karma.)

According to the second meaning where seedling is a synonym for material cause, God's creation without a material cause will mean God performing the cosmic function without the pre-requisite of a material cause *such as is required by a finite agent.* The worldly seedling is not always at the disposal of the cultivator, but has to be acquired; it is particular and local and different from the agent. The material cause from which God creates the world is eternal, omnipresent real, willed into eternal existence (ādheya) by the eternal omnipresent spirit (ādhāra): it has no being *other than* the being of its ground with which it stands nondifferent under the form of eternity. It is not so much *śaktimat* but śaktimad-adhīna, i.e. *Śakti.*

It may be seen from the above note that it is in the same sense Śaiva Siddhānta asserts, and Śaiva Absolutism denies that God creates the world from a material cause. This offers a close parallel to the issue between Creation theory and Emanation theory in Christian Theology.

72. This is in answer to the suspicion that SÑP does not explicitly mention Māyā as the material cause of the world. In the enunciation of twin karmas as instrumental factors conditioning birth and resolution reference to māyā is evident though not explicit. *Māpāḍiam*. p. 344.

73. Karma is of the stuff of being experienced (bhogya-rūpa); as of the form of latent impressions it is unseen (adṛṣṭa) but as self-manifest pratyayas of the form of pleasure, pain etc., it is perceptible. Either way the bhogya is inalienable with the feature of being objective (jaḍa) and therefore cannot *inhere* in the locus of self which is spirit. SSP p. 30.

For the Naiyāyikas, karma (unseen destiny) operates as a causal factor by being connected with objects but inheres in self. Karma inhering in the locus of self is connected with all objects as the all-pervasive soul is connected with all objects. The Naiyāyikas in fact derive an all-pervasive self from the all-pervasiveness of the adṛṣṭa; the moral cause and its operation is universal and the substrate of this unseen moral cause (adṛṣṭavad ātman) also must therefore be universal. *Nyāya-Vārttika*. 1.1.5.

74. Does not karma inhere in buddhi as buddhiguṇa, and if so, how can māyā be said to be the supporting locus of karma ? Māyā by the implied sense here stands for its evolute, viz. buddhi : 'tathā ca tanmadhyāvayava-bhūtasya sarvārtha-pratibimbādhāratvena sukhādi-rūpatvena ca bhogyatvāpannasya buddhi-tattvasyai'va dharmādyaṣṭa-guṇavattvaṁ ghaṭate. tathā'pi tallakṣaṇayā tanniṣṭhasya tat-sajātīya-tattva-samaṣṭiniṣṭhatvam abhyupagamya karmaṇo māyāśrayatvam uktam.' SSP. p. 31.

IX

THE DOCTRINE OF THIRTY-SIX TATTVAS

The Concept of Bindu

1. 'tatrā' kṣubdhe bhaved bhogo bindāvānandarūpiṇi
kṣubdhe' dhikāro devasya layo'tikrāntabindukaḥ.' RT. 179.

2. Such are souls of the Vijñānākala group—those that have crossed the ocean of Māyā and unhinged the bolt of karma and are at the gate of Mokṣa : 'uttīrṇamāyāṁ-budhayo bhagnakarma-mahārgalāḥ. aprāpta-śiva-dhāmānas-tridhā vijñānakevalāḥ.' *ibid.* 23.

Unlike as in Mīmāṁsā, Vedānta, Sāṅkhya, Nyāya and other schools, Śaivism believes in a hierarchical personalism of souls, ranging from those with the kalās of māyā, and therefore implying also mala and karma, viz. sakalās at one end of the scale, to those without such kalās—those that have been divested of them through their vijñāna, and have consequently outgrown the shackles of māyā and karma but not mala, at the other.

Bindu is required as a universe of experience not for the Vijñānākala as such but for the most 'mature' of the groups of Pralayākalas as well as the Vijñānākalas in whom, the original Impurity of Mala has attained to a condition of ripeness, and their māyā and karma have consequently been set at nought by divine grace. Such souls are still left with the lingering taints of adhikāra-mala. *Māpāḍiam.* p. 164.

3. RT (24-29) recognises again in this kind a hierarchy—the Vidyās, the Vidyeśvaras and the Anusadāśivas typifying successive stages of spiritual perfection. The lowest of them—the Vidyās or the Mantras as they are also called are 'agents' only of the fifth of the Five-fold cosmic functions being deputies in the service of the Vidyeśvaras. The latter because of their higher perfection are 'agents' in respect of performance of all the five functions. Śuddha-vidyā is the sphere of the Vidyās, the universe of their planes of residence and stuff of which their bodies, senses etc. are made. The dawn of divine wisdom consequent to the bestowal of Grace, the fifth cosmic operation, is to all the souls, through

the agency of the Vidyās is the origin of the tattva called Śuddha-Vidyā. Above it lies Iśvara-tattva, the sphere of the Vidyeśvaras also called Mantreśvaras, and above it again Sadā-Śiva for the Anusadāśivas or as they are also known as Mantra-Maheśvaras. The difference between the last two kinds is that the latter are nearer the goal of Anugraha on receiving which they transcend the Śuddhādhvan. The two Vidyeśvaras and the Mantreśvaras too have their tanu, karaṇa, bhuvana and bhoga made of the substance of pure materiality which are their physical analogues of their spiritual perfection. The cosmic agency of all these souls, it may be remembered is agency that is delegated (prayojya-kartṛtva) and not agency that delegates (prayojaka-kartṛtva).

4. The sphere of Bindu by contrast may be understood as inert but not impure, a source of pleasure (sukha) unmixed with pain etc. above the scope of triple malas, object only of transcendental experience (śuddha-bhoga) and is free from the hazards of change in consequence of its 'precedence' over time. Now difference in the nature of the material naturally calls for differences in agencies of will that stir them into action. RT 41-42.commentary:

   'śuddhe'dhvani śivaḥ kartā prokto'nanto'srite prabhuḥ' *Kiraṇāgama* cited *ibid.*

5. The agent of the pure realm is to be understood by contrast as free, i.e., self-commanding, incorporeal, of indeterminate knowledge, and 'one' with the material cause.

6. *RT* 43-44.

7. 'Words' constitute the determinancy of knowledge but they are not the sounds—the products or manifestations of ākāśa, which is a distant evolute of Māyā and is non-existant at the commencement of Impure creation. See below.

8. 'ito' pi lakṣyate bindur-aṇu-vaiṣamya-darśanāt.' RT 49.

   The vaiṣamya is in respect of knowledge : 'dṛśyante pudgalāḥ kecid alpajñānāḥ kriyānvitāḥ. tebhyo'dhikāḥ pare'nye tu sarvajña-balaśālinaḥ.' *ibid.* 50.

9. The argument is similar to the one used for Mala. *infra* Ch. 10. Mala is posited presumptively as the cause of the factual non-omniscience (asarvajñatā) of the self while nāda is here presumed as the condition accounting for the factual variety of knowledge.

10. 'abhidyeya-buddhi-bīja'. SB p. 191.

11. This is in consistency with the view that Bindu never obscures but only reveals. However it must not be forgotten that Bindu too is metaphysically a limitation. See below.
12. Nāda is the first tattva, Bindu in its stirred state. Bindu as such has no relation with the individual self but as Nāda it underlies it as the apriori condition of knowledge.
13. *Māpāḍiam*. p. 164 ff.
14. Therefore the cause of overt sound, viz. ākāśa an evolute in turn of śabda-tanmātrā (see below) cannot also be the cause of varṇātmaka-śakti, i.e. nāda. As determinate knowledge has to be suffused, with word in this sense, those residing in the worlds beyond ākāśa cannot have determinate knowledge, were word too like sound produced by ākāśa. Even for those residing in buddhi-tattva which is the sphere of determination (niścaya) in so far as determination or decision is another name for deter minate knowledge Nāda is the source of knowledge. 'What gives to buddhi the subtle implicit speech by means of which it determinately grasps the object reflected in buddhi is nāda. NK. 8. Comm.
15. Varṇa is ushered into action by implicit movements involved in the ideational process and is, therefore, implicit speech while dhvani which manifests the inner 'sound' is ushered into action by overt articulations. *ibid.* p. 165.
16. For the arguments, see below.
17. So much so their function is likened to that of spirit, notwithstanding their inertness. The śuddha-tattvas are called caitanya (*Supakkam*. 2.61.), while śabda in its causal form as parā vāc is termed śabda-brahman. See below.
18. *Māpāḍiam*; SB.
19. 'sthūlaṁ śabda iti proktaṁ sūkṣmaṁ cintāmayaṁ bhavet cintayā rahitaṁ yat tu tat paraṁ parikīrtitam'. *Kālottara-Āgama*, cited RT 22 Comm.
20. As different from Para-nāda the cause thereof, viz. Pure Śabda (Bindu), Sūkṣma-nāda is Para-nāda *in its quickened form* and is, therefore, interchangeable with it.
21. Also called Apara-Bindu as different from Para-Bindu.

    The latter is a synonym of Anāhata-Bindu or Para-nāda all standing for Mahā-Māyā or Kuṇḍalinī.

22. The Kālottara text cited above is a classification of speech in respect of overtness and subtleness. The present classification of levels is in respect of the relation of speech and the spoken.
23. This again, of course proceeds from differences in the nature of bondage. See *Māpāḍiam* p. 439.
24. *Supakkam*. 1. 26.
25. Degrees of bondage imply also degrees of liberation, but such liberation is penultimate liberation (apara-mukti). In the ultimate Liberation which is reached through transcending of nāda there are no degrees. See *Māpāḍiam* p. 7 : TTN 23, 24, 25.
26. See below.
27. NK. 11 Commentary.
28. *Supakkam* 140 See Comms. of Śivajñāna yogin and Śivāgra yogin: SVP 38.
29. Madhyamā vāc is defined in all Śaiva Śiddhānta writings by being distinguished from Vaikharī in the above manner. RT. 74; PA 2.22; PB pp. 100-101; *Supakkam* 1.21; SVP 38.

    Madurai Sivapirakasar commenting on the last work, however, mistakes the comparison for that between Sūkṣmā and Madhyamā and says wrongly that prāṇa-vāyu functions in the case of Maddyamā vāc. *Ibid.* 38 Com. (Samajam, 1940). Scope for differences of view is not, however, ruled out. See '*Philosophy of Word and Meaning*' : Gaurinath Śastri, Calcutta 1959, p. 71.
30. RT; Also the Kālottara text cited, ante note no. 19.
31. Other instances where this principle is used in the account of evolution of tattvas are : (i) the five bhūtas with their differentiated qualities arise from the Bhūtādi-Ahaṁkāra but as mediated by the five tanmātrās where the qualities are actual and yet unmanifest; (ii) guṇa-tattva with its differentiated structure in terms of sukha, duḥkha and moha is derived from kalā-tattva but *via* prakṛti-tattva which is the stage prior to concretisation potently containing the differentiated structure 'concealedly within' it. *Māpāḍiam*. p. 198.
32. References may profitably be made to Dr. K.C. Pande's discerning analysis of the differences between Śaiva Siddhānta and the Philosophy of Grammar according to Bhartṛhari. *Bhāskarī*, Vol. III, pp. xcvi. xcviii.

Somānanda in his *Śiva Dṛṣṭi* criticises the Vaiyākaraṇika standpoint for its non-recognition of Parā vāc as different from Paśyantī. Dr. Gaurinath Sastri suspects Śaiva influence on the later grammarians who make mention of Parā vāc. *Philosophy of Word and Meaning* (Cal. 1959), Ch. IV. Pratyabhijñā system, however, while distinguishing Parā from Paśyantī, would identify it with Parama Śiva. *Śiva-Dṛṣṭi*, op. cit. p. 37. This is but part of the Ābhāsa Theory of Evolution *ex nihilo* already considered. *Ante* Ch. V. In *Mahārtha-Mañjarī* another Kāshmira Śaiva work, we get a useful hint (pp. 128-29). The classification of the vāc in terms of its different levels is linked up with the different forms of cit-śakti. Vaikharī typifies kriyā-śakti, Madhyamā jñāna-śakti, Paśyantī icchā-śakti and Sūkṣmā involving a unification of the three vācs, typifies the state preceding differentiation of śakti-forms. Gaurinath Śastri, *op.cit.*, p. 76. The hint is quite significant as the evolution of the speech- and spoken-worlds is to be understood as 'exteriorisations' of the triple Śakti.

33. It is comparable to the Platonic 'essence' which is eternal in the sense of being completely independent of existence. A thing is essentially *what* it is whether or not it actually is. Essence and sense are identical. Knowledge of reality is knowledge of the sense of the signification of things. The sense of things, their signification, is not to be found in a contingent world of things existing independently of consciousness. It is to be found precisely in consciousness itself where signification is concentrated *a priori*. This is in a broad sense what Kant also said namely, that the sense of things is precisely contributed to them by the consciousness which a subject has of them....
34. *Supakkam*. 1.43—'uḷḷōr sōdiyāy'.
35. *RT* 79, Comm.
36. *Supakkam*. 1.43.
37. 'buddhyasmitāmanobhyo vidyat rāgataḥ kalāyāś-ca
 māyāpuṁśaktibhyo nādo'nyo dṛśyato dhvanibhyo' pi.' *NK*. 1.
38. The essence of a thing is known simply by knowing the concept of that which is known. Only, the 'intelligibility' of things is not limited to what can be *conceptualised*, conceptualisation itself pointing to a pre-conceptual insight. Nāda's function underlies the sphere of the pre-positional as well and is therefore even more

basic than Kant's categories. Cf 'āgopālāṅganā-bālā mlecchāḥ prākṛta-bhāṣiṇaḥ *antarjalagatāssatvās-to'pi* nityaṁ bruvanti te'· NK Commentary, 15.

39. NK. 2-7.

40. "pūrva-varṇaja-saṁskārayukto'ntyo'rṇo'bhidhāyakaḥ". *ibid.* 12. Comm.

41. The problem about the sequence of letters in a word in the role of conveying of meaning in the Indian philosophies of language raises issues which are not without significance for the modern mind. Do the isolated letters (varṇa) convey meaning individually or in a combinatorial sense ? Either alternative is unplausible. Against the latter one the objection is : the letters conceivably come into existence in consciousness one after another and they can never be perceived together as a whole. For the Naiyāyika śabda, jñāna and kriyā each comes into existence in the first instant, stays for an instant and perishes in the third instant, so that the question of the letters *together* denoting sense does not arise. There cannot be a single instant when all the letters of a word are sensed together. But the other alternative, namely, that letters in their monadic isolation convey sense also is absurd. If each letter in isolation in its own right can denote something, the initial letter of a word itself must suffice to denote what is intended by the word. The utterance of succeeding letters will be a superfluity.

The advocates of varṇa theory suggest a way-out of this *impasse*, which resembles the ingenious explanations of nineteenth century empiricist psychologists in answer to the problem of the perception of spatial series. Each letter indeed appears in consciousness upon the subsidence of the previous one but it can well be that it leaves impression behind, so that when we come to the last letter the apprehension of it with the aid of the accumulated impressions of the previous letters suffices for the purpose of denoting. Cf. the Pārākhya text cited *ante* note 40.

For a clear and precise statement of rival theories, Brough, John, '*Some Indian Theories of Meaning*' (Transactions of the Philological Society, Oxford, 1953) is still classical.

42. *Māpāḍiam.* p. 284.

43. For a dialectical refutation of Sphoṭa-vāda, see Aghora Śiva's Commentary. NK. 7; *Māpāḍiam.* pp. 282-85.

44. 'sattappirama vadi mata marudalai', *Parapakkam* 8 ff.

45. In the list of the factors mentioned as 'facilitating' self's knowledge, viz. the thing the sense, psyche and the 'hidden' śakti (Tirodhāna) that reveals śabda does not find a separate mention; it is the presupposition of the thing. A thing is not a thing except as intelligible and this implies speech (nāda). What is here argued is that admission of this is not equal to admitting the *priority* of the factor of intelligibilty over what is made intelligible. The latter includes the former.

46. 'poruḷāvadu sol *nalam*'. Sattappiramavadi matam 1.

47. *ibid.* 2.

48. *Tolkappyam.*

49. RT. 77; *Supakkam,* 1.24.

50. *Parapakkam.* Maṛudalai *op. cit.* 1.

51. The grammarian's philosophy of Śabda-Brahman has been variously interpreted as absolutism implying vivarta-vāda and as monism with a theory of pariṇāma. *Cf.* Vācaspati's statement : 'ye punar abhinnasya śabdabrahmaṇo vivartaṁ vā pariṇāmaṁ vā'-rtham ācakṣate.' *Nyāya-kaṇikā* (p. 293). Cited Gaurinath Sastri, *op. cit.* Arulnandi Śiva's refutation is evidence of his acquaintance with the two-fold interpretation of the philosophy.

52. *Supakkam op. cit.*

53. *ibid.* 4.

54. *ibid.* 5.

55. 'muṇkaṇ ḍaporuḷ peyarā taliṅāl
piṇkaṇ ḍapazam puṇarum peyarāl
naṇkaṇ ḍaporut kōruna vāmatiṇḍṛu. *ibid.* 6.

56. 'sākṣāt paramparayā'bhāvābhogadāyakam āpralayāvasthāyi ca yat tat tattvam ityuktam.' TP. 73, Aghora Śiva's Comm. They are noumenal in the sense that they transcend the phenomenal limitations of space and time so that, 'a body or a pot', a pillar or a pitcher may not be called tattva :

"tatatvāt santatatvāc-ca tattvānī'ti tato viduḥ
tatatvaṁ deśato vyāptiḥ santatatvaṁ ca kālataḥ
lakṣādi-yojana-vyāpi tattvam ā pralayāt sthitam
anyathā stambha-kumbhādir-api tattvaṁ prasajyate"

cited in Śrīkumāra's Comm. *ibid.* p. 174.

57. For their enumeration in the order of their resolution, see Aghora Śiva's Com., TP. 73; *Supakkam* 2.72.
58. Bhoga is another name for upalabdhi : 'bhogas tu vedanā puṁsaḥ sukha-duḥkhādi-lakṣaṇā', cited Comm., BK. 73.
59. Infra Ch. 11 sec. on Nature of knowledge.
60. For the metaphysical assumptions underlying the mechanics of manifestation of knowledge, see below.
61. SVP 40 : 'irai sakti udanāi nindre'.
62. The *raison d'etre* of a tattva consists of its exclusive capacity to exercise a *specific* function. Admission of one identical function being subserved by two tattvas amounts to a rejection of the very principle underlying the enumeration of tattvas. Nevertheless the functions are all congruent with each other as all serve the same purpose ultimately and we may accordingly group them in terms of relative similarities. The tattvas are, ultimately, distinct only numerically while cit-śakti which activates them is different from them qualitatively.
63. Ratna-Traya is the Śaiva work having for its subject the three jewels of knowledge and being.
64. Śiva is nimitta-kāraṇa directly in the Pure realm and indirectly in the Impure realm. Śakti is sahakāri-kāraṇa but functions in the Pure and the Impure realms through sub-accessories like kāla, karma etc. In the Pure realm also there is śuddha-kāla and śuddha-karma. Bindu is the upādāna-kāraṇa for the Pure realm, and Māyā, its impure counterpart, is the upādāna-kāraṇa for the Impure realm. Bindu may be looked upon as the upādāna-kāraṇa of the Impure realm too but *vis-a-vis* kalā.
65. The order of ascent must be from the 'lower' to the higher. Our account of their enumeration, however, follows the reverse order in conformity with the speculative, exoteric approach to the issues adopted.
66. This is the Transcendent Śiva—*Parama-Śiva,* to be distinguished from Śiva or Laya-Śiva who stands as jñāna-śakti *per se.*
67. That is why while tattvas grade as Pure as well as Impure— those resulting from being immediately quickened by Will being Pure, and those quickened mediately through finite wills being Impure, kalās form part of Pure realm (Śuddha-prapañca).

68. The synonyms of Bindu, each significant of its nature as the ultimate Material cause, are given in RT. 70 :

'śabdatattvam aghoṣā vāg brahmā kuṇḍalinī dhruvam
vidyā śaktiḥ parā nādo mahāmāye'ti deśikaih.'

69. As it is so in the case of the emergence of Nāda too. Śiva-tattva has other appellations each again indicative of the nature and function as the first tattva : (*i*) Laya-tattva, as it still retains the character of inaction notwithstanding its awakening, relatively to its activities yet to follow, (*ii*) Niṣkala, as it is devoid of forms, (*iii*) Śaktimat, as still only potent and not active, (*iv*) Nāda (apara-nāda), as the support or stay for sūkṣmā vāc (nāda). The presiding divinity of this tattva is named in these ways.

70. It is śakti-tattva because it is presided over by Śiva called by the name of Śakti, (*i*) Sthūla-laya-tattva and sthūla-niṣkala, in relation to Śiva-tattva, (*ii*) Bindu as the support of Paśyantī vāc. The distinction between Śiva and Śakti tattvas is a distinction within the phase of laya.

71. Presided over by Śiva named Sadā-Śiva and having the synonyms of (*i*) udyukta, (*ii*) bhoga, (*iii*) sakala-niṣkala-tattva (having forms of śakti and being without the forms of māyā). Sadā-Śiva is the nodal Śiva-tattva, the nexus between pravṛtti and nivṛtti.

72. Presided over by Śiva named Maheśa; synonyms are (*i*) sūkṣma-adhikāra, (*ii*) sūkṣma-pravṛtti, (*iii*) sūkṣma-sakala etc.

73. Presided over by Śiva who is the source of all vidyā. Synonyms : sthūla-īśvara, sthūla-adhikāra; sthūla-pravṛtti,sthūla-sakala. Distinction of Maheśvara and Śuddha-vidyā is distinction within the phase of adhikāra.

74. This is transcendent bhoga (Śuddha-bhoga) its difference from empirical experience being that (*i*) it is unmixed with the elements of duḥkha and moha arising from the delusive effects of māyā, and (*ii*) it is experienced in unhampered consonance with one's desire showing its freedom from karma. The propriety of talking of transcendental bhoga in a sphere transcending time process may not be questioned. PA duplicates all the tattvas time inclusive, in the Pure realm too and understands them as archetypal processes. *Māpāḍiam.* p. 171.

75. This includes the Vedas for which it is another name. SKB. II. 1. Quoted in Ch. 1.

76. SB. pp. 132; *Māpāḍiam*. pp. 173.
77. From māyā being the ultimate cause it follows that it is beginningless and from its beginninglessness again it follows that it undergoes only *partial* evolution.
'anādi parama-kāraṇatvāt. yac-cā'nādi na tat sarvātmanā pariṇamate, kintu śaktyātmanā' vasthitāyās-tasyā ekadeśato māyātmakād-utpadyate vyaktim āsādayati. yeṣāṁ sarvātmanā jagad-bījaṁ pariṇamate teṣāṁ tad anityam ityanādi-padena ekadeśa-pariṇāma-siddhiḥ.' SRS pp. 48, 49.
Umāpati, therefore, rejects the following for their non-implication of ekadeśa-pariṇāma : (*i*) paṭakuṭivan-nyāya(Śivādvaita), (*ii*) dadhi-kṣīra-nyāya (Sāṅkhya), (*iii*) bījāntarāṅkura-nyāya(Bauddha), and (*iv*) śukti-rajata-nyāya (Māyā-vāda). *ibid.* p. 48.
78. *Māpāḍiam* p. 285.

Māyīya : **Evolution of *Vidyā* and *Ātma* Tattvas**

1. *Supakkam* 2. 87 what in effect renders finite the infinite 'knowledge desire and action' of self is mayiya or the māyākārya. The commentator notes the difference between māyā and māyīya and in respect of binding comparable to the distinction in function between parāśakti and tirodhāna-śakti which is also spoken of as a species of mala. *ibid* Siva ñana yogin's comm.
2. The Pure and the Impure tattvas may be compared with the Infinite and Finite modes of Spinoza. 'The endless succession of finite modes each related to the next as transitive cause, is as necessary and effect of God's nature as are the infinite modes which are eternal'. *Ethics* 1. prop. XXVIII and its scholium. The modes are realities in and through which God's nature expresses itself; and they have an 'essence' the idea of which is eternally in God's mind. In their determination of one another to action God determines them. The hidden teleology in Spinozism bears some resemblance to the theory of tattvas.
3. *Ante*. Ch. VIII.
4. Cf. the Advaita vedānta distinction of māyā and avidyā as respectively the adjuncts of Iśvara and Jīva. *Pañcadaśī* 1. 16.
5. *Supakkam* 2.50; the ablation in 'vindu*vin* mayạiyāki' is the issue. Also SVP 10.
6. RT, 153 ff.

7. Ajñāna as a disposition of buddhi means viparīta-jñāna. See *Māpāḍiam* p. 208.
8. Here finitude is used to mean not only paśutva but also paśutva-vāsanā like adhikāra-mala, etc.
9. Ratna-Traya clarifies the position by implying this suggestion, negatively. See, 153 and 164 for the two *prima facie* points of view. This solution is also in accord with the position that Māyā, Śuddhā as well as Aśuddhā, is Pāśa : *vartamānā paśuṣveva pāśatvena vyavasthitā* *RT*. 167.. Bindu, when not discriminated from kriyā-śakti,spells repeated births and when discriminated causes cessation of births for the paśus. Bindu causes bhoga (Śuddha) and also mokṣa as a contributory cause. Māyā causes only bhoga, being 'sarvadā paśūn mohayati' *ibid.*168. comm.
10. This is suggested when it is said that Śuddha-tattvas can be sahakārin in respect of the creation of the Aśuddha sphere (e. g., Śuddha-kalā as the basis of the emergence of Aśuddha-kalā) but the converse is not admissible. Time (of Aśuddha sphere) cannot condition the emergence and subsidence of Śuddha-tattvas.
11. The 'varying' function of the Śiva-tattvas activating from above accounts for the variations of the avasthās. See below.
12. This is what distinguishes the sakala self from the Pralayākala self. The latter is never the Puruṣa. See *MA* 6, 2-3.
13. *TS* 25, 26 Aghora Siva's comm.
14. 'etaśca tattva-dvayam kalādyapekṣayā bahiraṅgatvād'. *ibid.*
15. 'tato niyati-saṃśleṣāt viniyamyate kālena kāla-saṅkhyāna-kārya-bhoga-vimohitaḥ' *Kiraṇa Āgama,* vidyāpāda, paśupaṭala, 18.
16. This accounts for the precedence of Kāla and Niyati over Kalā etc. *SB*. p. 171.
17. *Māpāḍiam* pp. 177-78.
18. We can also understand the distinction of śuddha kāla and a-śuddha kāla even more plausibly as the distinction of *sacred* time and the time of the de-sacralised existence that is characteristic of 'earthy' individual selves (sakala), the *profane* time. In Śaiva Siddhānta theology the 'sacred' sphere (śudhādhvan) is the mythic region primordial and non-temporal where 'events' take place not in a continuous irreversible temporal succession but in an 'instant'. which is durationless and therefore non-metricised. It is Great Time unsullied by the adjuncts of karma annd māyā of the profane kinds.

19. Kalayitri śakti assumes the form of time for Śiva's functions.
20. The argument for time, reminiscent of Aristotle namely that if nothing depended on time for its realisation everything would have already happened, is given in *Mṛgendra Vṛtti Dīpikā*, p. 266. *Māpāḍiam* p. 177; *SB*, pp. 222, 223; *PB* pp. 328, 329.
21. *PB* p. 328.
22. This is one of the chief points of difference between Advaita Vedānta and Theistic Vedānta like Śaiva Siddhānta. The former derives the world experienced as well as the experiencing subject from Ignorance. The states of the self do not really pertain to it. The self does not *really* pass through the avasthās. But for the Śaivite, Paśu is pañcāvasthita. The concept of avasthā of a subject 'having' states (avasthita) involves time relation. A reference to object is implicit in the notion of avasthā. A reference not to one homogeneous object but to a diversity of objects experienced, diverse not only spatially but temporally. The self can have states and is subject thereto implies the reality of time. See for a full-fledged discussion of the alternative solution of Advaita Vedānta.
23. Karma-pāka, mala-paripāka, ātma-pakva—all imply the reality of time. The novelty of the future, the strength of the present and the limitations of the past are the significance of time for man, according to Umāpati. *SVP*. 40.
24. Time and change are held to be necessarily perpetual by Aristotle. His argument is of a 'back-to-front' kind : there must be imperishable substances lest otherwise time and change shall have beginning and end which is impossible. But if ever there were no changeable things there was then no change and no time. It is therefore quite conceivable that time and motion are non-perpetual. See Aristotle's *Physics* V. 1; *Metaphysics* XI, 11.
25. Time is brought into connection with movement either because we explain movement in the light of original successiveness of time or because on the contrary we suppose that movement from the before to the after forms moments which in their succession constitute time. Saiva Siddhanta, like Kant, adopts the first approach and rejects an empirical approach like that of the Nyāya Vaiśeṣika. *Māpādiam* p. 182.
26. PA 5. 43-64; *Māpāḍiam* pp. 181-184.

27. 'niyati-saṁśleṣāt svārjite viniyamyate' *Kiraṇa Āgama op. cit.* 18.
28. 'avibhogeṣvaniścintā niyojayati sā balāt svārjiteṣveva ne'hā'-nyair-arjiteṣu kadācana.' PA 5.83.
29. The law of karma does not stress so much individual responsibility as impersonal responsibility. It is niyati which 'individualises' it :

    'karmaṇāṁ tu phala-sampādakatvam eva kevalaṁ na tu kartṛgata-phala-sampādakatvam api iti bhāvaḥ' *PB* p. 475.

    By karma, in the law of karma, in Śaiva Siddhānta, is not meant *respective* karmas of persons causing *respective* bhoga. It is simpler to assume a causal relationship between karma *qua* karma (karmatvena), not *qua one's* karma (svakṛta-karmatvena) and bhoga. Karma as such is kāraṇatāvacchedaka and bhoga is kāryatāvacchedaka. *infra* Ch. X, sec. on 'Arguments for Mala'.

    For experience of bhoga, karma is the upādāna kāraṇa; the sahakāri-kāraṇa or karaṇa is *Māyā* which contributes śakti to the experience through Niyati and other tattvas by 'tieing' the self to bhoga. The nimitta-kāraṇa which transcendentally secures the bhoktṛtva for the self is mala. *Cf.* analogy of 'tuṣa-kambukavad jñeyaṁ māyā vāpāṅkurasya tat'. *Svāyambhuva,* cited *SRS.* p. 36.
30. The notion, like that of time, has its cosmic as well as existential horizons of meaning. Niyati is the principle of cosmic justice which enforces the right of the agent to his experience of the fruit of his actions both negatively and positively. Niyati is equated with justice in the specific sense of enforcement against nature. The natural disposition being always in the direction of avoidance as such of the unpleasant and the painful and welcome as such what is pleasant and rewarding, the function of cosmic determination *perforce* metes out due fruits of deeds to the doer despite the doer's unwillingness to 'enjoy' the unwholesome consequences of what after all are his own evil deeds. Likewise, it *perforce* provides against the doer's appropriation of the pleasant experiences which are consequential to other's deeds. Basic to the understanding of this tattva is the law of deed and consequence of deed. The cosmic law of karma cannot be conceived to articulate but for the specificity with reference to *one's* experience. Experience conceivably can be structured according to the requirement of the law of karma if and only if such experience is also *my* experience as distinct from *yours* and also *vice versa.* Karma is niyati-sāpekṣa.

The Tamil concept 'ul' (Tirukkural devotes an entire chapter to its analysis.) is a composite of the two notions of karma and niyati.

31. A. G. Hogg : '*The Christian Message to the Hindu*', p. 74.
32. The example of a maṇi or mantra or auṣadha whose presence serves as the neutralizing agent counteracting against experience of heat-sensation is frequently used in Śaiva Siddhānta texts. *Māpāḍiam* p. 186. Also infra Ch. 15.
33. *Māpāḍiam* p. 188.
34. MA gives the root sense of kalā: kala ityeṣa yo dhātus-saṁkhyāne preraṇe ca saḥ protsāraṇaṁ preraṇaṁ sā kurvati tamasaḥ kalā. Nārāyaṇa kaṇṭha clarifies the two senses thus : kalāyāḥ kṣepārtha-vṛtti-prakṛti-bhutaḥ prathamaḥ dvitīyastu saṁkhyānārta-vṛttiḥ kalanādiyattayā niyamanāt kalāśabdāpara-paryāyāśca niyateḥ. (10.6) Cf also the descriptions 'kalā bandham' (*PA* 5, 7); 'kalā malam' (*TP* 3, 6).
35. 'lakṣanaṁ tu kartṛ-śakti-prakāśakatvam' SB p. 213. What does manifestation of the power of agency mean ? It cannot mean modification, intelligent as the power of agency is. Nor does it seem plausible to conceive it as cessation of obstruction (āccādaka-nivṛtti). For the unclarity of the notion of cessation is obvious : is cessation total or partial ? If latter, is it enduring or non-enduring ? Sivāgra Yogin's explanation of 'cessation of obstruction' is : without of course the agent causing obstruction deceasing, the obstructing power of the agent is 'de-obstructed' and consequently, to the extent self's obstruction has deceased to that extent is effected cessation of obstruction : 'malasya svarūpeṇa anivṛttāvapi ācchādana-hetu-śaktyabhibhave tadupahitatva-rūpācchādaka-tvābhāvena ācchādaka-nivṛtter vaktum śakyatvāt'. *ibid* p. 214.
36. 'malān sarvātmanā bhitvā caitanya-prasarātmanaḥ
caitanya-vyañjakā hyatra kalā mala-nivartanāt' *PA* 5-2.
'sarvātmanā kalanaitat caitanyaṁ vyañjyatyaṇoḥ
kintu karmānusāreṇa kalāvṛttyekadeśataḥ'. *ibid* 5-4.
37. *Mataṅga Āgama* (cited in *Śrīkumāra* p. 121) gives another picturesque illustration of a similar nature :
'yathāgni-tapta-mṛtpātram jatunāliṅgane kṣamam
tathāṇūm kalayā viddham bhogaḥ śaknoti vāsitum
bhogapātrī kalā jñeyā tadādhārāś-ca pudgalāḥ' *Kalā Tattva paṭalam*, 28.

38. 'karmānusāreṇa kalāvṛtyekadeśataḥ' PA 54. Karma defines the scope of every Vidyā tattva. Just as a rock flung at a mossy surface clears the moss at its point of contact for a second, kalā effects a partial removal of mala-obscuration 'on its surface' and its rhythm of action punctuated by intervals of re-obscuration is governed by the requirements of karma.

39. Kalā is the tattva that typifies finitude; by associating therewith ensues bhoga and by dissociation mokṣa. BK, 1.
Also 'bhogānāmapi nānyo'sti kalāṁ tyaktvā samāśrayaḥ
tato'yaṁ niyamas spaṣṭaḥ saṁsāro'tiduruttaraḥ'
Mataṅga Āgama, kalātattvapaṭala. 33. Cited also *Śrikumāra*, p. 121.

40. The tattvas of the bhoga-kāṇḍa are therefore also termed ātma-tattva. See below. Cf. this with the Sāṅkhya orientation to tattvas.

Kalā's function of de-obscuring mala and re-activating the stalled power of action (kriyā-śakti) of self cannot also be usurped by karma. The latter is, technically, the agency that accounts for experience as such (bhoga-janaka). The material cause of bhoga is karma, instrumental cause māyā and efficient cause mala. Cf. 'tuṣa-kambukavad jñeyaṁ mayā vāpāṅkurasya tat' *Svāyambhuva* Āgama cited in SRS p. 36. Sivāgra Yogin would class karma along with body that is evolved from māyā as instrumental in effecting a 'general' manifestation of the kartṛ-śakti of the self, but being themselves 'non-luminous' (a-taijasa) do not contribute to the process of de-obstructing the obstructive darkness-like effect of mala. Against this need for a 'specific' manifestor stands kalā; The viśeṣānumāna is :
'kartṛ-śaktyāvārakasya tamorūpasya malasya nivṛttis-taïjasa-padārthāyattā tamo nivṛttitvāt sammatavad iti'. *SB.* p. 214.

One other interesting point about kalā tattva is : because it *lets* self's power of agency manifest itself and thus contributes to being agent of action, it lends itself to be classed as agenct rather than as instrument; being 'identical' with the agent-self : 'ubhayaṁ vipra sambhūyā'nanyavat sthitam' MA 10, 7. Cf. also the remarks of SB p 214 : 'idaṁ ca kalātattvam kartṛśakti-abhivyañjakatvena tat prayojakatayā hetu-kartṛtvena kartṛ-kāraka-koṭi-niviṣṭam ata eva 'prayoktyādi mahi prānta' ityatra prayokti-śabdena kalā nirdiṣṭā.' PA 5-6, 7 explains this fusion of agency and instrumentality in the function of kalā somewhat more picturesquely: kalā bandha is the initialmost bond coinciding with the first or the nominative in the sense that without it the nominative agent-self would be devoid of manifest consciousness and consequently on par with nothing. Quoting *Parākhya* Āgama text 'kalā samāyukto bhoge' ṇuḥ kartṛ-kārakaḥ', Aghora Śiva clarifies the distinction of the roles of kalā and aṇu as agents thus : 'tatas-sā prayojikā hetuḥ kartrī bhaṇyate sa cā' ṇuh...kartṛ-kārakam ucyate' : As one that *lets* like a lamp the power of agency of aṇu manifest from being enveloped in darkness, it is agent in the causative sense, while the aṇu itself as thus assisted by kalā is agent in the transitive sense. BK, 99 Commentary.

41. *PB* p. 310; *Māpāḍiam* p. 187.

42. The śuddha tattvas activate aśuddha tattvas, and also in relation to classes of individual selves who are freed from the thraldom of paśutva as 'manifestors'. *Tukalaru Pōdam* and *Tattuva Pirakāśam* following it, of the post-Meykanda literature explain the mode of activation of the vidyā tattvas by śuddha tattvas. Kāla, niyati and kalā are activated by śakti-tattva, vidyā by śuddha vidyā (also called sad-vidyā) rāga by maheśvara, māyā by Śiva-tattva and puruṣa by sadā-śiva. The following table brings out the plausibility of the explanation :

kāla niyati kalā	kartṛ-śakti-prakāśaka	→	śakti tattva (kriyā-mātra)
vidyā →	jñātṛ-śakti-prakāśaka	→	śuddha-vidyā (jñānaśaktirudrikta kriyāśaktinikṛṣṭa maheśvara)
rāga →	icchā-śakti abhivyañjaka	→	kriyaśaktirudrikta jñānaśaktinikṛṣṭa
māyā →		→	śiva tattva (jñāna-mātra)
puruṣa→		→	sadāśiva (jñāna-kriyā-śakti-sāmya)

Māyā as the vidyā-tattva is aśuddha-māyā which comes under the immediate stress of will and commences evolution. The function of will which stirs it into action, therefore presupposes activation by śiva-tattva which is jñānamātra. Puruṣa-tattva likewise implies accomplishment of jñātṛtva-kartṛ-śakti-prakāṣa and, therefore, presupposes activation by sadā-śiva-tattva.

The author of *Tukalaru pōdam* explains variations in the states to which the self submits in its empirical life as due to permutations and combinations of the five-fold śiva-tattva which functions non-synchronously so as to cause diversified experiences for the individual selves in accord with their karma. The work also appeals to the sequence of five-fold kāryāvasthas within the wakeful open to phenomenological inspection as providing an inward knowledge of the working of śiva-tattvas. See *Kattalaik Kalitthurai* verse 37.

For the correlation of bhogajayitri or bhoga-kāṇḍa and the bhogya-kāṇḍa see *NVM* p. 811. The table suggested is :

māyā	⟶	PrakṛtI
kāla	⟶	All the tattvas
kalā	⟶	ahaṁkāra
niyati	⟶	citta
vidyā	⟶	buddhi
rāga	⟶	manas
puruṣa	⟶	indriyas

(indriya-grahaṇāvasthā purusa-tattvamucyate; Also *SVP* 41) *NVM* p. 814.

43. 'kalāyāḥ kartṛbhūtasya buddhilakṣana-karmaṇah alokane yat kāranaṁ sa vidyā sivaśāsane' *PA* 5-9. SB citation (p. 216) reads 'kartṛyuktasya'.

44. 'bhoga-svīkaraṇe vidyā saṁvidaḥ karaṇaṁ tataḥ' *Ibid* 5-20.

The same verse, it may also be noted, explains the need for reckoning vidyā in addition to kalā tattva : 'kalāvṛttim vinā tasya nānayoḥ kārya-saṁkaraḥ'. PB clarifies the distinction thus : 'yadyapi kalāyā malanivṛttau jñatva-śaktirapyabhivyaktā tathāpi *viṣaya-grahaṇa-kṣamatvarūpa malanirāsane* vidyayā apekṣitatvād itI bhāvaḥ.' p. 315. SB defines vidyā-tattva, likewise, in terms of what either helps manifest the power of knowing (dṛkśakti-vyañjaka) or is the indispensable means of apprehending (buddhi-grahaṇakaraṇam) in its modification as pleasure-pain experiences. p. 215.

The apprehending buddhi itself (buddhi-grahaṇa-karaṇa) specially in respect of its overtones of pleasantness and unpleasantness.

45. They are sākṣi-vṛttis for the Advaitin. *infra* Chap. 5, sec. II. Śaiva Siddhānta concept of cit-śakti and the Advaitin's śakti are similar and yet metaphysically different. See *infra* Sec. IV.
46. Icchā is jñāna-viśeṣa and therefore the manifestor of Icchā is an evolute of the manifestor of jñāṇa-śakti. For differences of opinion on this, see *PB.* p. 301.
47. One general objection to the admission of rāga, and also *a propos* to admitting vidyā and kalā tattvas is that buddhi can fill the bill : Attachment, e. g. which is one of the 'dispositions' of buddhi can itself, and indeed must alone, must manifest the icchā-śakti of the self as otherwise a manifestation of the specific contents which are discursively grasped by the intellect (buddhi) will not be accounted for. Admission of a general manifestation prior to intellect's determination before which all contents would be alike will fail to account for specific determination as to the 'what' of content (niyāmaka). For the same reason vidyā-tattva also is dispensable. Vidyā like rāga is neutral in relation to the given so that a determination of the given in respect of its specific nature isnot achieved by it. Buddhi-vṛtti accomplishes the task. Likewise kalā-tattva also with its function of a general arousal of the cognitive potential of the self cannot meet the requirement of discursiveness. In answer to it is available ahaṁkāra-tattva whose function is expressly one of dfferentiation (saṁrambha) in terms of a subjective resolve.

The answer to this objection coming from those who do not concede the legitimacy of counting more tattvas than the twenty-four of the Sāṇkhya is : abhilāsa, bodhavṛtti and saṁrambha necessary as indeed these are for activating the conative and practical power of the self, are not however sufficient. Without a general arousal or manifestation, specific orientation to objects is not possible. Differentiations in the effect cannot derive without obtaining implicitly or undifferentiatedly in the cause.

Moreover the basic question is one of distinction of what manifests and what is manifested. Bodha-vṛttis are the vyañjakas. Like in the case of sense their functions are made possible because of the individual self of the nature of spirit. As the latter however is be-clouded by mala which renders it *in effect* inert and inane, manifestors are needed to counteract its inanity and restore its original nature of being the living and knowing presence which grounds the psychic and somatic functions. *SB* pp. 217, 218.

48. *TP*. 11. Aghora Śiva's Comm. Also TS 12; BK 91 c. The whole discussion is a plea against looking upon soul as pure sentience, without 'attachment for bhoga'.

49. 'asya viṣayāvabhāsena vinā puruṣa-pravṛtti-hetutvāt.' *TP*, Śrīkumāra's Comm. p. 124.

50. If attachment were due to Rāga-tattva, Rāga being one of the permanent fixtures of man will it not mean again the same absurdity of man being in perpetual attachment ? The answer is : Rāga is of two forms (*i*) jñāna-rūpa, and (*ii*) vāsanā-rūpa. Attachment in the form of impressions persist in the self while that in the form of perception is what functions as the disposition of Buddhi. The latter rise and perish while the impressions endure. *PA*. 5. 44-45.

51. The agent of action (kartṛ) is also a concomitant of action (kāraka) though rightly accorded the leading place in the order of enumeration. Kartṛ-kāraka is explained thus by Aghora Śiva : 'pravṛttau ca nivṛttau ca kārakāṇāṁ ya īśvaraḥ apravṛttaḥ pravṛttau vā sa kartā nāma kārakaḥ.' BK, 98c com. He is agentconcomitant who causally controls activity as well as cessation of activity no matter whether he is himself active thus or otherwise. What lets him be 'active' unconstrained by obstruction as contributory to the role of agent-concomitance is also by transference called 'agent'.

See also *Ante* Ch. 6, sec. The 'Moral Argument for God *vis-a-vis* Karma' Note 35, 36.

52. 'tattuva varṇa *rūpaṇ*'. SVP. 64.

The propriety of including the intelligent self in the list of tattvas has been questioned. Pusuṣa-tattva is aptly described in Supakkam as 'cidacit' (2.66) which contains the answer to this question. It is cit in essence and yet acit in form.

53. It is this bhogonmukhatva (described in Tamil works as pokattirkolkai) that makes puruṣa typical of sakalāvasthā. The Pralayakevalins and Vijñāna-kevalins do not have empirical bhoga (Sakalāvasthā). It is the 'cleansing' of the cause of this impulsion to bhoga caused by Puṁstva-mala that constitutes Śuddhi for Puruṣa-tattva. *Māpāḍiam*. p. 196.

54. The pañca klēṣas which constitute the pumstva-mala is the 'occasion' for the kañcukas : 'kalādi pañcakasyaiva yadi puṁstve nimittāḥ'. PA, 6. 4. The very limitations of the finite agent constitute the elements of finite experiencership (bhoktṛtva). In this precise sense classes of selves other than the sakala are devoid of finite experience. See also *PB* p.352.

55. *Māpāḍiam*. p. 198.

56. Guṇa is not, strictly, an evolute but an extension (vṛtti) of Prakṛti, differing in this respect from Kalā-tattva which is evolved from Māyā.

57. The correlation of the three categories of pati, paśu and pāśa with the three guṇas of prakṛti, with the conative cognitive and practical powers of the self and with Being Intelligence and Bliss aspects of God is a suggestive interpretation given by one of the commentators of SVP .*Cindanaiyurai*, p. 794 ff. (samājam, 1940).

58. They are more appropriately translated as constitutive elements than as qualities. For a lengthy treatment of the topic consult *Māpāḍiam* pp. 228 ff, PB pp. 454-460. Cf. also Suryanarayana Sastri S. S., *Substance and Attribute in Saiva Siddhānta*. Collected Papers, University of Madras 1961. See *Infra* Ch. 12, sec. 'Affinities and Differences with Realism'. The general upshot of the doctrine in the present context of evolution of the subjective and objective world *vis-a-vis* guṇas is that the 'substance' apart from its modes is nothing but the substance that is its cause : Cf. the equivocation in the use of the term guṇa in applying it to tanmātrās and also to the attributes of bhūtas.

59. SVP. 24, first two lines.

60. BK. 48.

61. *Māpāḍiam*. p. 202.

62. 'indiriyam pulaṇgaḷ tāmnuharum aḷaviladil *mundiyuṛum*'. SVP. 43.

63. This is not, however, literally true. Puruṣa is the only nominative though Kalā and after it Ahaṁkāra, because of the inwardness of their function, may be said to be nominative by way of eulogy. *PA* Comm.

64. In the Sāṅkhya system Sāttvīka is called Vaikṛta and the Rājasa is called Taijasa.

65. Rājasa is, for the Sāṅkhya, only an auxiliary to Sāttvika and Tāmasa so that jñānendriyas as well as karmendriyas are derived from Sāttvika only.

66. Citta is the avasthā-viśeṣa of manas with a distinguishable function.
67. Prāpyakāri view of sense function accepted by the generality of Hindu orthodox systems—the Nyāya, Mīmāṁsaka and the Vedānta systems is the basis for the more specific Śaivāgama doctrine of 'pervasion' of object by sense. See *Māpāḍiam* p. 399.
68. *ibid.* pp. 220-21.
69. The 'karma' in karmendriya relates to kriyā-śakti. *ibid.* p. 224.
70. The 'mātrā' in 'tanmātrā' means guṇarūpamātrā. *ibid.* p. 228. See also *ante* Note 58.
71. PA. 6. 246-250. See also Umāpati's commentary; *Māpāḍiam.* pp. 228-30. See *infra* Ch. 5, Sec. III, for explanation.

CHAPTER TEN

THE DOCTRINE OF MALA

Ignoance and the Problem of Evidence.

1. See SÑP, 4.2 for the distinction of sahaja and āgantuka malas.
2. 'iruḷoḷira irunda mohamāy.' SVP 20. For the true significance of this comparison with the darkness, see below. What is suggested by this paradoxical expression is that there is no perceptibility of mala. It is pre-eminently part of the function of mala that it covers itself as well as it covers or veils the knowledge of the self. For a detailed comparison in this regard with the 'avidyā' of the Advaitin, see below.
3. SB p. 297 ff.
4. The concepts bear a close homology to each other but are nevertheless significantly different. Their difference epitomises the differences between the orientation of Advāita Vedānta and Śaiva Siddhānta.
5. The Advaitin's *ajñāna* is explicated epistemologically while for the Śaiva Siddāntin the issue does not originate as an epistemological problem. It is only in the defensive that he enters the arena.

6,7. Murti T.R.V., Ajñāna, Luzac. p. 141 ff.

8. For Saiva Siddhānta, self's states only provide a negative evidence for mala. See below.
9. Contrast the analysis of the nature of paśu *qua* subject to states. infra Ch. 11 sec. on 'The self, its existence and states'.
10. kaṉavu kaṉaveṇḍṟu kāṉparidam kāṉil
    naṉavil avai siridum naṉṉā......
    yān avattai kāṉumāṟen ? *Vina Venba* 4. Also *Parapakkam* 53. The Śaiva solution is in terms of the continuously present but *hidden* cit-śakti.
11. *Perception and its Object* : T.R.V. Murti (Philosophical Quarterly, Vol. X).
12. Śaiva Siddhānta in adopting this line of explanation rejects by implication perceptibility for Mala. The Advaitin's point of view in this regard is critically expounded first and latter criticised. The

Pūrvapakṣa and the Siddhānta throw useful sidelight on the unique features of the Śaiva Siddhānta concept of Mala. The treatment follows closely Śivāgra yogin's exposition and criticism, freely reconstructing the arguments. What the Advaitin admits in the case of defining avidyā viz. that it does not stand scrutiny, the Saiva Siddhāntin applies the same to mala in respect of perceptual evidence for it.

13. The sense of nañ in 'aham *aj*ñaḥ' 'mām anyaṁ ca *na* jānāmi' is that of absence (abhāva).

14. Śaiva Siddhānta is apparently in the company of the Nyāya-Vaiśeṣika who advocates 'privation' view (abhāva) of ignorance in such judgments. What is not to be ignored in this alliance is that while for the latter there is no concept of a knowing self which is spirit, for Śaiva Siddhānta Mala-obscured spirit (Paśu) is basic for knowledge.

15. 'pratiyogi*jñānājñānābhyāṁ* tadanupapatteḥ.' *SB.* pp. 298-99.

16. 'aham ajña iti jñāna-sāmānyābhāvasya yāvad-viśeṣābhāvasya vā pratītir-ityevā'bhāvaviṣayakatva-vādinā'ṅgīkartavyatvena yatkiñcij-jñānasatve'pi tadgrahāsambhavāt.' *SB.* p. 300.

17,18. anyathā' jānato' pi viśeṣābhāvasatve nā' ham ajña iti pratītyāpatteḥ. *SB.* p. 299.

19. Not mere pratiyogi-jñāna but pratiyogitāvacchedaka-viśiṣṭa-pratiyogi-jñāna, and again, saprakāraka-pratiyogi-jñāna. *ibid.* pp. 299-300.

20. The alternative modifications in the meaning of abhāva in *aj*ñāna considered so far are :
    i. jñānatvāvaccinābhāvaḥ
    ii. ghaṭajñānatvāvaccinnābhāvaḥ
    iii. ghaṭādigocara-pratyakṣānumititvādyavaccinābhāvaḥ
    iv. purovarti-viśeṣyaka-ghaṭatvaprakāraka-jñāna-smṛtes tathāvidhatvābhāvaḥ

21. The negative particle 'nañ' in ajñāna is understood in the sense of opposition (virodha) according to this alternative.

22. 'jñānaparyudāse ajñānam iti gṛhyate.' Vivarṇam, quoted in *SB.*

23. To be ignorant of the' pitcher is to be aware of its opposition to a knowledge, the determinant of which is pitcher; therefore, ignorance of pitcher on this theory too presupposes a prior knowledge of pitcher.

24. That is why it is denied that sākṣi-jñāna is a species of pratyakṣa; the latter are occurrences while sākṣi-jñāna is primary intuition (anubhūti-rūpa) eternal and unoriginated. Sākṣi-jñāna is not, technically, pramāṇa. Compare Śaiva Siddhānta concept of Pramāṇa in this respect. infra Ch. 5 sec. 11.
25. Abhāva-jñāna is dharmi-pratiyogi-jñāna-sāpekṣa while sākṣi-jñāna is nirvikalpaka-jñāna.
26,27. *SB.* p. 302 ff.
28. Sākṣi is akartṛtve sati bodhyatvam. Pāṇini derives sākṣi from sākṣāt from yat sākṣāt aparokṣāt. *Chānd. Up.*
29. The 'witness-self' in the system figures even initially as veiled by the impurity of Mala and is, technically, the Puruṣa—the five-coated individual, in association with Prakṛti, an evolute from Māyā through Kalā-tattva and experiencing Avidyā, the first of the five kleśas as a prelude or precondition of experiencing the empirical world in the wakeful life.
30. *SB.* p. 302 ff.
31. The hetu is not known to exist in the pakṣa before the inference is made. See *SB* p. 303.
32. The conjunction of manas with puritat nāḍī is the Nyāya explanation given for accounting for unconscionsness during sleep. *SB. ibid.*
33. The above is a free reconstruction of the point of view of Advaita summarised with great clarity in *SB.* pp. 303-05.
34. 'ajñānasya sva-nivartakatvābhimata-jñānaviśeṣābhāva-vyāpyatvena suṣuptikāle pratiyogismṛtyāder virahasyāsiddheś-ca tasmāt suṣuptikāle jñānābhāvāsiddhir ubhaya-samādheyā. *SB.* pp. 305-6.
35. 'ādara-pratyaya-viṣayasya vastu-viśeṣādes tatkālānubhava-janya-smaraṇābhāve nā'nubhavābhāve'numite, tena kāraṇāntara-sattva-sahakṛte ne'ndriyavyāpārābhāve pariśiṣyeṇa niścite tenā'pekṣaṇīyagocara-jñānābhāvasyā'pi siddhir aviruddhe' ti. *ibid.* p. 306.
36. For a similar critical notice being taken of inferential basis for ajñāna, see Ramanuja's *Śrī Bhaṣya's* pramāṇānupapatti BS 1, 1, 1. What is subject to criticism there is the Vivaraṇānumāna.
37. An explanatory example of the nature of a familiar instance which is known to possess the probandum by virtue of the probative reason which it possesses in common with the minor term is not

possible in the case of demonstrating (supersensuous objects) something transcending experience.

38. Śivāgra yogin gives the anumāna for Avidyā evidently from Tattva-Pradīpikā, pp. 50-51. The anumāna is: 'caitrapramā caitragata-pramā-prāgbhāvātiriktānādinivartikā, pramātvāt, yajñadatta-pramāvat.' *SB.* p. 306.

39,40. 'caitragatatvasyā'nādiviśeṣaṇatve dṛṣṭāntasya sādhya-vaikalyāt prāgbhāva-viśeṣaṇatve caitra-bhramas tadicchā vā tadgatābhāvā-tiriktānādinivartikā ityādivad aprayojakatvāt. pramāprāk-padayor vaiyarthāc-ca tadvinākṛte sādhye caitrāsamavedatvasyo'-pādhitvād yajñādatta-pramāyā api tadgatābhāva-nivṛttirūpatayā nivartakatvābhāvena sādhyāprasiddheś-ca.' *ibid.* p. 306.

41. Umāpati's significant remark about mala suggesting the 'existential' nature of awareness of mala :
"oruporuḷum kāttādiruḷuruvam kāttum
iruporuḷum kātta didu". *TPN.* 3.3. See *ante* Note 2.

42. 'sudaral irultedac connān' *Satamaṇikkovai*

43. PA uses other kinds of anumāna for mala; see below.

Arguments for Mala

1. *Māpāḍiam* gives a comprehensive account of a series of inter-connected considerations for arguing to the existence of mala, following the lead of PB. The account given in this section follows however Śivāgrayogin's account for obvious reasons.
2. 'ātmā malāvṛtas sarvajñatve kiñcijjñatā yataḥ
na kiñcijjñatus yas so'yaṁ malenā'pi na saṁvṛtaḥ.
yathā śivas tathā cā' yaṁ malenai" va samāvṛtaḥ.' *PA.* 4-125.
3. Man being athirst for knowledge which Aristotle takes to be natural is taken here as providing a negative evidence for mala. See below.
4. PA 4-126. Also BK 3 comm.
5. Cf. the uses of 'bhoga-mokṣa', 'bhukti-mukti' as terms of contrast.
6. *ibid.* 4. 127-128.
7. 'baddha-mukta-vibhāgānyathānupapattyā mala-siddhiḥ *SB.* p. 307.
8. The implication is that mala is precisely the point of distinction between bondage and liberation.
9. Vṛtti-jñāna is dissolved in pralaya while Svarūpa-jñāna endures in the mokṣa state also. *ibid.* p. 307.

10. For Śaiva Siddhānta as it is for the Śāṅkhya and the Vedānta, dharma etc. are buddhi-gata,. Only for the Vaiśeṣika they are ātma-guṇas. Ante Sec. III; BK 4.8 Comm.
11. See ante Ch. 9, Sec. on vidyā-tattvas.
12,13. *ibid.* p. 308. It is useful to recall the differences between the functions of māyā and mala. Māyā is constructive, mala is obstructive; māyā projects and builds, mala veils and arrests; māyā facilitates, mala inhibits; māyā illumines, mala is darkness. Freedom from mala should imply, the latter *terminating* (apagamana). Śaiva Siddhānta faces the problem by positing *terminable* śaktis for mala.
14. *ibid.* p. 308. This is another demand on mala that its persistence even as a potentiality in mokṣa is incompatible.
15. 'anāder anavacchinnānandānubhavāvarakasya malasyā'pagamenai'-va vimuktatva -vyapadeśo vācya iti malo'bhyupeya iti.' SB. p. 308. Mokṣa has, of course, positive meaning also. See Ch. 6.
16. Śivāgra yogin defines Pāśa neatly as : 'pāśatvaṁ nāma śivānandābhivyaki-virodhitvam.' SP. p. 73.
17. The theory of a plurality of śaktis for mala is in answer to plurality of selves.
18. *SB.* p. 308.
19. svarūpa-prakāśa-viraha (1).
20. svarūpa-prakāśāvasthā-viśeṣa (2).
21. viṣaya-sambandha-viśleṣa (3).
22. tamas-sambandha (4).
23. tadviṣayaka-vṛtti-prakāśa-viccheda (5).
24. 'saṁsāra-daśāyām api ānumānika-śabdādi-nivṛtti-sattvāt.' SB. p. 309; 'nivṛtti' in this citation can be misprint for vṛtti. It may be noted that for Śaiva Siddhānta even perception of feeling is a species of judgment (vṛtti-jñāna). But as this may be objected to, as for example, by the Advaitin for whom it is direct intuition (sākṣi-jñāna), instances of ānumānika and śabdikā vṛttis are given here; these are admitted on all hands to be vṛttis.
25. 26. *ibid.* p. 309.
27. 'tasya svarūpa-prakāśa-virodhitve prakāśasya nityatva-prasaṅgād avirodhitve'prakāśa-padasya tatra pāribhāṣikatvāpatteḥ.' *ibid.* p. 309.
28. SB. p. 309.

29. That bliss-experience is available as the chief feature of mokṣa is explained in Chapter 15.
30. The critic's objection was that the vyāpti between utpattitva and vināśitva will be excepted in the case of mokṣa itself which has utpatti but, admittedly, no vināśitva. The reply is mokṣa itself being nothing more than manifestation of the previously non-manifest bliss presents no separate problem besides the issue of manifestness and non-manifestness of bliss under discussion. *SB.* p. 310.
31. 'aprakāśaś-cāvaraṇābhāva-viśiṣṭa-cicchaktyabhāvaḥ.' *SB.* p. 310.
32. 'taddhetutvaṁ tu viśeṣaṇābhāvarupasyā'varaṇasya tat-prayojakatvam.' *ibid.* p. 310.
33. 'viśiṣṭābhāva is the prayukta of viśeṣaṇābhāva or what is same, viśeṣaṇābhāva is the prayojaka of viśiṣṭābhāva.
34. The viśeṣaṇa is āvaraṇābhāva; viśeṣaṇābhāva will be āvaraṇābhāvābhāva or more simply, āvaraṇa.
35. 'nā' sti na prakāśata iti vyavahāreṇa sāmānyato' numitasyā' prakāśasya viśeṣyābhāvamātrarūpatva-sambhavena viśiṣṭabhāvatva-niścaye tatprayojakatayā viśeṣaṇābhāvarūpāvaraṇa-kalpanopa patteḥ.' *ibid.* p. 310. Mala is known as (i) the general implication of the expression nā' sti na prakāśate and more specifically as (ii) what pertains to self as its adjunct.
36. The dilemma is : 'svarūpa-prakāśa-virodhitvāvirodhitvābhyāṁ sāmānyato bandhanam.' *Ante* .
37. 'viśeṣyāvirodhitve' pi viśiṣṭavirodhasya sadbhāvāt.' *ibid.* p. 310
38. For the precise nature of this 'embodiment' See below.
39. 'māyāyā eva prapañca-sūkṣmāvasthā-rūpatayā śaktitvena tadvināśānupapatteḥ.' *ibid.* p. 310.
40. According to sat-kārya-vāda (ante Ch. 3) Śakti *is* the causal form which becomes the effect (vyakti); śakti is prefigurence of effect *as* cause. Māyā is thus a name for a system of causal śaktis (kāraṇa-śakti-samūha). Contrast this with the *satkāraṇa-vāda* of the Advaitin according to which the effect is in the cause, rooted in it and the cause itself is the unmodified ground of effect-appearance. Māyā or avidyā itself performs the dual function of (i) veiling and (ii) creating or projecting, while, for Śaiva Siddhānta they belong respectively to (i) mala and (ii) māyā.

41. The argument is : ātmaprakāśo na tamasāvṛtaḥ prakāśatvād ālokavat.' *SB.* p. 309.
42. 'Tamas' is one of the synonyms used for mala. *MA.* 4; RT. 255.
43. The pakṣa and the dṛṣṭānta must have identical hetu. The critic's argument is on par with : pṛthvī śṛṅgavatī gotvatvāt apparently because 'go' means both earth and cow.
44. Either way there will be hetvasiddhi-sādhana-vaikalya in dṛṣṭānta or svarūpa-siddhi with respect to pakṣa. *ibid.* p. 309.
45. In a dharmi-grāhakānumāna by the same evidence by which the dharmin is apprehended its other dharmas are also apprehended, e.g., Īśvarānumāna. Where by the self-same reason not only God but His omniscience, unity etc. are also apprehended. *Ante* .
46. Mala is known to exist, as what by its existence conditions and constitutes bondage and by its *ceasing to exist* causes and constitutes mokṣa. So from the very arthāpatti-pramāṇa by which mala's existence is derived its non-eternity also is derived.
47. Vyāpyāropapūrvaka-vyāpakāropasvarūpa is the accepted interpretation of *tarka* according to Navya-Nyāya School (Tattva-Cintāmaṇi, Anumānà, p. 210). According to this, what constitutes the merit of *tarka* is the demonstration of the erroneousness of the proposed hetu (viparya-paryavasānam) and the defect of the *tarka* will be its failure to so demonstrate (viparyāparyavasānam). Here in the above instance there is such failure.
45. SB. p. 311.
49. 'jaḍenā' jaḍarūpasya tiraskāro na yujyate
āvṛttiś-ca na yuktā' sya vyāpakatvena hetunā.
anādikālasaṁrūḍhān malākhyād vāsitād aṇo
ajaḍā'pi tirobhūtā' śaktir nityā jaḍātmanā.
kiñ-ca jaḍaṁ jadenai'va bādhyate nā'jaḍena tu
svajātīyatvato hetor aṇūnām īśvaro yathā
yathā' bhibhūtagandhasya nimbatvak candanasya tu
kiñ-cā'jaḍamajaḍān no cet bādhyam tat kena bādhyate
ajaḍaṁ tu jaḍaṁ vā' pi dvayaṁ vastu viniścitam
ātmanā' tmā' ntarād bādhyo vināśād bādhakātmanā
tannāśam antarā yasmān muktir na syāc cidātmanaḥ
jaḍenaivā'jaḍaṁ tasmād bādhyam abhyupagamyatam'.
PA. 4. 148-153; also *SB.* p. 309.

50. *PB* p. 295-296.
51. *SB.* (pp. 311-12) enters into a detailed analysis of the concept of śakti and vindicates its legitimacy as a valid concept.
52. This valuable distinction is made in PA. 4. 169, in answer to the objection that all knowledge being content-defined,—reference to the content being the *proprium* of knowledge, it is inconceivable that knowledge is intact but without its apprehension of content.
53. *ibid.* 4. 173.

BOOK IV

CHAPTER ELEVEN

THE SELF AND ITS KNOWLEDGE

The Self : Its Existence and States.

1. The other terms used for self in the Śaivāgama are 'pudgala' (Kiraṇa, Mataṅga, Kāmika) cit, citta, jīva, puruṣa (for the self of the Sakala class) and ātman itself in the minimal sense of the all-pervading (and again in the specific epistemological sense of cognitive pervasion in which sense alone it is descriptive of selfhood and not in the sense characteristic of Spirit: cf. 'asittaṛu vyāpakam pōt vyāpakam aruvam indrāi vasittida varum vyāpi enum vazak kudaiyanāki' *Supakkam* 4. 20). Umāpati speaks of paśu as different from cit : 'cid-vilakṣaṇatayā paśu-svarūpam' etc. SRS p. 32. Terms expressive of the 'middle' position occupied by the self are : (i) Cidacit, in the epistemological relation of subject and object where the self as a knowing subject at the same time is identified with the known object and becomes one 'object' among objects. (ii) Sadasat in the ontological sense of what is Sat relatively to Asat though compared to Sat itself it is indeed Asat. See *infra* Ch. 14. Sec 'Self-understanding of Self.'
2. cf. SÑP Sūtra 3, See that Meykaṇḍar in his vārttikam on sūtras 3 and 4 describes them as alike expressive of 'ānma pirakāsam.'
3. For an elaborate explanation See Bhattacharya, K.C. *Studies in Philosophy op. cit.* Vol. 1, appendix.
4. *Māpāḍiam*, p. 261. f.
5. 'kiṁ cidḍhi paramārtham ālṁabya aparamārthaḥ pratisiddhyate yathā rajjvādiṣu sarpādayaḥ tucchapariśiṣyamaṇe kasmin cidbhāvo'-vakalpate'-, Śaṅkara's comm. BS III. 2. 22.
6. The real adhiṣṭhāna in 'this is rajata' is not śukti but śukti-avacchinna-caitanya or to use the terminology of SB 'śuktivṛttyu-paruddhā cicchaktiḥ'. For the generality of ātma-vāda (in contradistinction with anātma-vāda) in all cognitive experience it is consciousness in the substantive sense (caitanya or cit-śakti).

directly or as circumscribed by some adjunct that serves as the adhiṣṭhāna. See below Sec. 'General Conception of Means of Knowledge.'

7. 'pratyutārdhajaratī yā yāritum ayuktatvād draṣtur abhyabhāvaḥ.' SB. p. 268.

8. This argument of Śaiva Siddhānta reminds one of the well known steps by which Descartes would advance from a position of universal skepticism. However much the thinking which we think away is under suspicion, the thinking which thinks it away remains. Descartes thinks that this is the one judgement regarding real *existence* which is indubitable. The *cogito* enables us "to distinguish between mind and body more distinctly than hitherto." "to define the nature of the self in its distinction from all that is corporeal" "By the light of this torch" says Descartes referring to the principle *dubito, cogito ergo sum*" "I see more accurately in myself what is not visible to the eyes and I am more persuaded that I possess what cannot be touched than I ever have been of possessing a body......I can affirm that as soon as I commenced to doubt I commenced to know with certainty. But my doubt and my certainty did not relate to the same object, my doubt regarded only things which existed outside me, my certainty concerned me and my doubt."

The aforementioned comparison may not however be taken to imply a vindication of approaching the problem of the *existence* of self in the spirit of rational psychology. In saying that the 'I' stands self-evidenced in the very denial of the nihilist, it is not held that one can know self as a direct object of knowledge. I cannot know the 'I' but only the 'me' or rather 'mine'. The transcendental 'I' is beyond the reach of intuition and understanding. See for the distinction that Śaiva Siddhānta makes between ātma-rūpa, ātma-darśana and ātma-śuddhi on the one side and ātma-lābha on the other. *infra* Ch. 14.

9. *Supakkam* 3, 2. SÑP 3, 2, udāharaṇa.

10. SÑP 3.3. adhikaraṇa, citrurai.

11. The case for vitalism rests *inter alia* on the semantic consideration that ātman is the name of prāṇa (Ṛgveda, X. 163). The Tamil word 'uyir' likewise denotes self or soul as well as the vital air. See also *supakkam* 3.3.

Nature of Knowledge

1. 2. For the epistemological and linguistic significance of nāda. See *ante* Ch. 9 Sec. on 'The Concept of Bindu'.

3. Cf. the grounds for rejection of indriyātma-vāda *ante* Sec. 'The Self, its Existence and States.'

4. jñātṛtva belongs according to Vedānta, to caitanya but as upahita. For Śaiva Siddhānta, while subjectivity in respect of knowing is inherent to self, its epistemological counterpart, viz. objectivity (prameyatva) is due to the condition of mala-obscuration. *PA*. 5. 109-113.

5. Cf. Srikaṇṭha's comm. BS 2.3.30.

6. *PA* 4.101.

7. Murti, T. R. V., Perception and its Object, Proceedings of Indian Philosophical Quarterly 1933-34.

8. 'anubhava' is not originated in the self by mind-sense-object con-tact as it is for the Naiyāyika but is inherent in self.

9. The pūrvapakṣa here is the vijñāna-vāda. Śaiva Siddhānta as a Vedāntic system shares the epistemological realism of the Vedānta.

10. *Māpāḍiam* p. 387.

11. Knowledge is a case of self's 'immersion' in the flow of empirical experience. Contrary to the thesis that it is the senses or the internal psyche that immerses itself Śaiva Siddhānta holds that it is the self itself that immerses in experience self is spirit whose mode of knowledge is experiential where by experience is meant precisely 'immersing' in the objective data of experience. Not standing aloof as witness in knowledge but as an agent that involves itself in that which is known.

12. *SSP*. p. 3.

13. *Māpāḍiam*. p. 396.

14. *NVM*. p. 447.

15. And yet the absoluteness of the distinction is the basis on which senses, buddhi etc., are discountenanced as the pramāṇa. See below.

16. Śivajñāna yogin makes out this discerning distinction in his refutation of the Śivasama-vāda commentary on Supakkam.

17. The factor of acquaintance cannot be gainsaid in valid memory as otherwise valid memory and non-valid memory or imagination cannot be distinguished.

18. The spuriousness of the distinction between memory and perception in terms of the presence and the non-presence of images is brought out in the writings of contemporary epistemologists. Broad, Price, Woozley and others.
19. *Māpāḍiam* p. 397.
20. Viśiṣṭa-jñāna arises logically from viśeṣaṇa-jñāna; nirvikalpaka-jñāna is, therefore, immediate knowledge of the viśeṣaṇa. SB. p. 109.
21. *Māpāḍiam* p. 397.
22. Nāda persists as long as there is even a modicum of mala-obscuration. Even the most exalted of the category of selves like mantra, mantra-maheśvara etc. are not free from condition of individuation, viz. nāda; they are not free because of the vestige of mala still left in them (adhikāra-mala); they are, therefore, only non-ultimately liberated. *Ante* Ch. 4, Sec. II.

General Conception of Means of Knowledge

1. The Tamil word 'aḷavai' used in N, 21; *Supakkam*, Aḷavai 1, as the equivalent of pramāṇa brings out this sense.
2. The same expression *alavai* is used to mean measurement in all these instances : nīttal alavai, literally, the measure of length; muhattal alḷavai, literally, the measure of the volume; niruttal aḷavai lit. the measure of weighing. Measuring knowledge is called more simply as 'alavai' as it is measure *par excellence.*
3. 'Porulin uṇmaikku aḷavukūruvān todangi'etc. Śivajñāna yogin's Com. *Supakkam* 7.
4. 'kaṇṇillārkkillāk kaviffpoffdrum' etc. from another verse quoted in Maraiñāna deśikar's Comm. *ibid.*; also 'irāha mariyār iśaippayan tānariyār'. The parity is clearly brought out in these two verses quoted in the commentaries of *Supakkam.*
5. 'sataś-ca sadbhāvo' sataś-cāsadbhāvaḥ' *Nyāya bhāṣyam,* 1. 1. 1. See also *Nyāya Vārtika* for the interesting but commonplace stipulation almost the nature of what is (tattva)
6. 'pramīyate anene'ti pramāṇam.' *Nyāya-Bhāṣyam* 1.1.3.
   Śaiva Siddhānta which does not advocate the 'instrument' view of pramāṇa will derive it, not according to the karaṇārtha, but bhāvārtha (without the lyuṭ pratyaya : pramīyate iti pramāṇaḥ). Pramāṇa is constitutive of and not the instrument of knowledge;

knowledge itself is understood *as what is*, and not as what is produced by some means : bhāva-vyutpanna-jñānapadena etc. *PB* p. 520.

7. *SB* p. 95.
8. 'nanu naśyāt kuto mānaṁ yattatpramiti-sādhanaṁ. tanna dīpadṛgādīnāṁ pramāṇatva-prasangataḥ.' PA cited *ibid.*

Objection to cit-sakti as pramana

1. *SB* p..96.

2., 3. 'kevalā cicchaktir-na pramitiḥ kintu tattadviṣayāvacchinā sā ca viṣayāvacchedasya janyatayā janyeti na tat-sādhanāsambhavaḥ.' *ibid.* p. 96.

4. 'cakṣurādyasannikarṣe'pi viṣayotpattyanantaram eva cicchakter viṣayāvaccheda-sadbhāvena tatra cakṣurāder ajanakatvāt saṁśaya-viparyāsāder-api tattadvisayāvacchinna-cicchakti-rūpatvena tat-karaṇe'tivyāpteś-ca.' *SB* p. 96.

Some Definitions of Karana

1. The procedure which PB and after it SB follow herein is of course based on the tradition associated with Kaṇāda (Vaiśeṣika sūtras 9. 2. 12) that pramāṇa sāmānya lakṣaṇa should be based on the consideration that the karaṇa of pramā must be 'pure'—karaṇa-siddhi-mūlaka.
2. 'phalāyoga-vyavacchinnam' *SB*, p. 98. This is the Navya Nyāya view.
3. Raghunātha Śiromaṇi gives the positive version as phalopahitatvam 'instrumental cause as immediately preceding the result'. *Ingalls*, p. 31 f.
4. Śivāditya gives another example : anumāna as the karaṇa of anumiti is anumiti-pramāyoga-vyavacchinnam—distinguishable from causes not immediately connected with anumiti-pramā (phala). *ibid.* p. 31.
5. Happiness etc. are called 'existents invariably associated with experience' (jñātṛ-sattākam); unlike objective existents these internal objects never exist unknown or unfelt. Feeling pleasure and pleasure are invariable co-existents.
6. This is the view of the Old Nyāya School.

7. For the one the vyāpāra itself is the karaṇa while for the other that in which vyāpāra inheres, is karaṇa. The distinction is between the old and the new schools of Nyāya.
8. For example vyāpti-jñāna associated with parāmarśa will be karaṇa according to this definition, constitutive of vyāpāravatvam, of which anumiti is the phala.
9. Parāmarśa being itself the intermediary vyāpāra is not the possessor of vyāpāra (vyāpāravatvam) and will, therefore, not be karaṇa according to the definition. Cf. vyāpti-jñānaṃ karaṇam, parāmarśo vyāpāraḥ. *Tattva-cintāmani*, II, p. 550, quoted in *Ingalls*, p. 32.
10. *SB* p. 96.
11. *ibid.*
12. Cf. The etymological sense of the root 'pac' in pacati.
13. The grammarians' definition. *ibid.* p. 96.
14. 'śarīrādyativyāpteḥ parāmarśādyavyāpteś-ca' etc. *ibid.*
15. The issue against the grammarians' view is that it fails to distinguish karaṇa and kartṛ. Chapter 3, Section on 'God as Will'.
16. *SB* p. 97.
16a. As examples of the causal factors which combinedly eventuate in the production of perceptual cognition we may cite (i) the Sautrāntika theory of ālambana pratyaya, samanāntara-pratyaya, sahakāri-pratyaya and adhipati-pratyaya combinedly condition knowledge, and (*ii*) the Nyāya theory of the complex of all specific physical and mental conditions of knowledge (bodhābodha-svabhāva-sāmagrī) as constituting pramāṇa.

    The unity between potential subject and potential object lead to further questions of ambiguity. In the above illustrations non-distinction between subjective and objective factors in the formula of causation. Pratītya samutpāda represents an intermixture of psychological subjective and material-objective causes which are equally effective to product the texture of existential forms.
17. The vyāpti and the udāharaṇa are : 'yad yato' vyatiriktaṁ tattato bhinnaṁ svarūpavat.' PA 7-22. 'yathā vastu-svarūpaṁ svāpekṣayā vyatiriktatyena dṛśyamānaṁ svasmād abhinnam eva.' *PB* p. 527.
18. SB p. 97; also PB p. 527. 'ayaṁ pramātā idaṁ pramāṇam idaṁ sahakārītyādi vivikta-vyavahāra-lobhaḥ.
19. 'sādhana-sāmagryādīnāṁ meyatvena mānatvasyāyuktatvāc ca.' *SB* p. 97.

20. 'yan meyaṁ nahi tanmānaṁ yato māne na mīyate'. PA cited SB *ibid.*
21. A detailed estimate of this approach is in order because of its uncritical adoption by many internal schools of Śaivism, with the refutation of which Śaiva Siddhānta is immediately concerned. Extracts of these views classified under 'Nyāya ekādeśī mata' are given in NVM pp. 432--34. The pūrva-pakṣa in the discussion of pramāṇa in PA may be identified with the obscure standpoints of some of these Śaiva schools. Also *ibid.* pp. 434-40.
22. *SB* p. 97; PA 7-18.
23. 'iti buddhi-prakāśo' yaṁ bhāvaḥ pratyaya-lakṣaṇaḥ bodha iti ucyate bodha-vyakti-bhūmitayā paśor-iti.' *Mṛgendra*, cited in *SB* p. 98
24. *SB* p. 97; *PA* 7.18-19.

Cit-sakti as Pramana

1. 'karaṇaṁ ca na śaktyanyat.' MA, cited SB p. 186.
2. 'tattadviṣayāvacchinna-cicchaktis-tattadarthe pramā śaiva-pramāṇam api,' *ibid.* p. 97.
3. Cit-śakti is unlike dharma-bhūta-jñāna of Viśiṣṭādvaita. Māpāḍiam p.· 321.
4. 'yathārthānubhūtirūpa-buddhivṛttyupārūḍhatvaṁ-viṣayasya cicchaktyā sambandha iti kadācid eva viṣayāvacchedāt kādācitka-prakāśa-sambhavaḥ.' *SB* p. 98.

   Two similar views are expressed in Advaita treatises about the role of vṛtti in the relation of self to the object in knowledge : āvaraṇa-nivarttaka or āvaraṇābhibhavārtha-vṛtti, and citsambandhārtha vṛtti. *Siddhāntaleśa*, Chapter 1, 5.1.
5. *SB* p. 97.
6. This point is raised in anticipation of an objection which the editor of Śivāgra Bhāṣyam voices in a footnote on p. 97 against Śivāgra yogin's interpretation of the Pauṣkara text : 'saṁśayādi-vinirmuktā cicchaktir mānam ucyate.'
7. 'saṁśayādi-vihīnā tu cicchaktir mānam iṣyate'. PA 7-21. 'saṁśayādi-vinirmuktā cicchaktir mānam ucyate.' *ibid.* 7-5. Śivāgra yogin's interpretation of these lines is a model of exegetical writing served with a rare philosophical discernment. This is cited also in the Comm. of SNP p. 21.
8. Cf. Sūryanārāyaṇa Sāstri, *Truth in Saiva Siddhānta, in collected Papers of S. S. Sūryanārāyaṇa Sāstri,* University of Madras, 1969.
9. See infra Ch. 12 Sec. on Non-valid Knowledge.

CHAPTER TWELVE

VALID AND NON-VALID KNOWLEDGE

The Nature of True or Valid knowledge

1. SB p. 98.
2. Cf. the definition given of Indriya-pratyakṣa as a mode of awareness unmediated by error and vikalpas, *Supakkam,* Aḷavai 4. Error too can be implicitly present in it. See below.
3. SB, p. 97, 98.
4. This is not however, literally true. For even in nirvikalpa-jñāna *qua* the preceding source of savikalpaka-jñāna, the that-what structure must be implicit. However, epistemically, there is only the viśeṣaṇa without the viśeṣya.
5. For stipulations see below.

Some Definitions of Validity

1. Cf. Sivaraman K. *Truth and Correspondence.* An Analysis in Indian Thought, *Language and Reality,* Centre of Advanced Study in Philosophy, Banaras Hindu University, 1967.
2. artha-sadṛśatva (1), SB p. 98. Umāpati considers various definitions of validity and subjects them to the twin tests of (i) adequacy to cover all known cases under the proposed definition, unexceptionally, and (ii) exclusiveness in its application so as not to apply to an instance known to fall outside the limits of the definition. PB pp. 511-12. They are elaborated and interpreted in this sub-section in the order of presentation followed by Śivāgra yogin (SB pp. 98, 99) who repeats them in a less laconic form.
3. 'samartha-kriyā-janakatvam' (2), *SB* p. 98.
4. The two, viz. fruitful activity and validity are distinguishable as the 'limitor' (avacchedaka) and what is 'limited' (avacchedya), 'describer' (niyāmaka) and what is 'described' (niyāmya), and intention (prayojaka) and the intended (prayukta); one cannot be the definition of the other. SB *ibid.*
5. *Citsukhī* (p. 218) gives the example of a mistaken knowledge of the lustre of a gem for the gem itself, as an instance of erroneous

knowledge proving useful. Śaiva Siddhānta like Vedānta accepts usefulness neither as the meaning of truth nor as a criterion for testing truth, the truth being self evidently apperceived (*infra*, Ch. 13) according to it.

6. Arthāvyabhicāritattvam (3). *ibid.* p. 98. The use of the abstracts even when referring to percepts, here as well as in the definitions about to be considered, is suggestive of the truth that even a so-called percept really stands for a judgment. Even a proper name like Devadatta is equivalent to an object possessing the characteristic of being Devadatta (Devadattatva-prakārakam). All knowledge analysed in logic is determinate knowledge. Also it is suggested by the use of abstracts that what is understood here by concept or judgment standing for the concept or the sentence expressive of the same not individual inscuption but classes of inscuptions of similar form not individual things but classes of things.
7. On the first meaning of avyabhicāritva, the relation of invariable concomitance as constitutive of validity will under-pervade the instance of the relation of buddhi and buddhi-vṛtti between which there is invariable concomittance. While on the second meaning it will over-pervade doubt and error. PB p. 511.
8. 'viśeṣyaniṣṭha-bhāvpratiyogi-dharma-prakārakatvam' (4). *ibid.* p. 98.
9. 'Viśeṣyaniṣṭhā'tyantābhāvāpratiyogi-dharma-prakārakatvam' (5). *ibid.* p. 98.
10. *ibid.*
11. This objection is valid only according to the old school of Nyāya. The notion that there is no redness in a cherry which is not yet red or has ceased to be red means respectively prior absence of red and posterior absence of red but not constant absence of red. In the substratum of the prior or posterior absence there can be no constant absence, because the first is the contradictory of the second. The new school of Nyāya, however, questions this and inclines to hold that constant absence is present even at the time of creation or destruction of absence. *Bhāṣā Pariccheda* 12, *Muktāvalī.*
12. 'viśeṣyaniṣṭha-saṁsargābhāvāpratiyogi-prakārakatvam' (6)
13. 'sva-viṣaya-kālāvacchedena viśeṣyaniṣṭha-saṁsargābhāva-pratiyogi-prakārakatvam' (7). *ibid.* p. 98.

14. The Nyāya view is that moment is time under the limiting of adjuncts of action by reference to which alone time is called the moment. *Bhāṣā Paricchedа* 46, Muktāvalī.
15. Four moments shall be required minimally to constitute gross time. For example in the case of cherries turning red having been blue, the disjunction of blue or the conjunction of red will each involve a minimum time-interval of four moments associated with-(i) the previous absence of the disjunction, (ii) disjunction determined by the antecedent conjuction, (iii) previous absence of that conjunction and (iv) subsequent conjuction—four distinguishable actions measured in time-sca'e, each as one moment. *ibid.* Muktāvalī.
16. See foot-note of the Editor *SB.* p. 98.
17. The above account is an elucidation of the crisp statement; 'sthūla-kālāvagāhinī kālānavagāhinī ca tasmin jñāne'vyāpteḥ.' *ibid.* pp. 98-99.
18. 'samūhālambana-jñāna. Here flower is the counter-correlate of the relational absence of vase, and *vice versa—both simultaneously.*
19. Cognition of pot and cognition of cloth are both valid cognition as constituents of a valid cognition and yet if the definition of validity proposed in terms of anyonyābhāva (with or without reference to time) were true, they will *by turn become non-valid.*
20. 'viśeṣya-vṛtti-prakārakatvam' (8). *ibid.* p. 99.
21. 'vahniguñjāpuñjayor-imau vahnī imau guñjāpuñja-vahnī' ti jñāne cā' tivyāpteḥ.' *ibid.*
22. 'prakārāśraya-viṣayakatvam' (9). *ibid.*
23. 'prakārāśraya-viśeṣyatvam' (10). *ibid.* p. 99.
24. 'prakārānāśrayāviśeṣyakatvam' (11). *ibid.*

Truth as Correspondence between Judgement and Fact

1. 'tattadviśeṣyakatve sati tatprakārakatvam' (12). *ibid.* tadvad viśeṣyakatve sati etc.
2. In 'atra ghaṭatvam' the universal 'ghaṭatvam' is the qualificand (viśeṣya) while ghaṭa, the particular in which usually the universal inheres, is the predicate (prakāra); the reversal of the grammatical subject and predicate is permissible as consistent with the intention of the speaker.
3. 'sva-virodhi-dharmā' navacchedena' etc. PB p. 512.

Though dharmas constitute the dharmin, only non-discrepant dharmas can be constitutive of the dharmin of a valid knowledge.

4. A negative way of stating the case, viz. that the assertum must not be determined, by a nature incompatible with its own, instead of a positive stipulation to the effect that it must be determined but by its own nature has also its advantage.
5. The distinction is between saṁyukta-samavāya and samavāya.
6. 'ullikhyamāne'ti viśeṣaṇena *sākṣāt sambandhavad* viśeṣyakatvaprayuktā' tivyāptir nirastā.' *SB.* p. 99. Also see editorial foot-note.
7. The example 'ghaṭavad ghaṭatvam'—'pot-possessing (is) potness' which erroneously attributes pot to potness, may claim validity if tatprakārakatvam were to be interpreted as tat-sambandhavat prakārakatvam; under the category of relation, even predicates known to be errroneous may be brought. To this the reply is that the judgment is false, not because of the absence of relation but because a particular relation is asserted which is not there. *SB* p. *100.*
8. It is mis-relation and a consequent failure of correspondence that constitutes error; Śaiva Siddhānta advocates anyathākhyāti-vāda. *infra* Sec. on Non-valid Knowledge.
9. SB p. 100.
10. The above is an elaboration of the stipulations summed up by Umāpati and Śivāgra yogin as hereunder :
'sva - virodhi - dharmānavacchedeno'llikhyamāna - tattad - prakāra-tattat-sambandhavad-viśeṣyakatvā'vacchedena tattat-prakārakatvaṁ yathārthatvam.' *ibid.* p. 100.
11. 'Truth in Śaiva Siddhānta' : Collected Papers; S. S. Śūryanārāyaṇa Śāstri (1931) *op. cit.* This valuable article was throughout consulted in this section. Some of these critical remarks are discussed in the next sub-section.

Affinities and Differences with Realism.

1. The difference between the Nyāya and Śaiva Siddhānta deserves to be kept in view specially under the circumstance that Umāpati in his PB freely employs the Nyāya categories and concepts.
2. See below Truth and the Doctrine of the Guṇa and Guṇin.

Truth and the doctrine of the relation of *guṇa* and *guṇin*.

3. The late Prof. Sūryanārāyaṇa Śāstrī was intrigued by his discorvery of this doctrine of Śaiva Siddhānta as may be seen from

his 'Substance and Attribute in Śaiva Siddhānta' (1931). But it is surprising that he could not see the supreme relevance of this doctrine to Śaiva Siddhānta theory of truth. In his 'Truth in Śaiva Siddhānta' (*op. cit*) where he raises the issue of coherence theory in connection with siddhāntin's account of truth, he does not refer to this doctrine.

4. *Māpāḍīam* 229.
5. 'sarvaṁ jñānaṁ dharmiṇyabhrāntaṁ prakāre tu viparyayaḥ.' *Sapta-Padārthī*. p. 25. Comm.
6. *The Theory of Judgment in the Indian Systems*, Murti, T.R.V. Indian Philosophical Quarterly, 1936.
7. Difference of things is really difference of predicates; an identical predicate belonging to different subjects is not admissible. *Māpādiam op. cit.*
8. Infra Ch.-13
9. "Perceptual assurance is an ultimate form of consciousness, autonomous and self-correcting which can neither be overthrown nor justified by any other form of consciousness". Price, H. H., *Perception*, Methuen & Co Ltd. 1950 p. 192 ff.
10. This is the eommon ground of Vedānta, Nyāya and Mimāṁsā realistic systems and Śaiva Siddhānta.

Non-valid Knowledge : Forms and Theories

1. For other sources of doubt see infra.
   Only the Jainas consider smṛti to be pramāṇa (parokṣa pramāṇa).
2. PB p. 520; The contrast of the words śruti and smṛti in this context is quite significant. The vogue of excluding smṛti from pramāṇa seems to have originated from the theological-logical issue about the validity of Smṛti in relation to Śruti (Vedas), the validity of what is only remembered derives from the validity of what is directly perceived, heard.
3. *Supakkam*, P. 125; Śivāgra yogin's Comm. When the author does not, significantly, mention 'memory' Śivāgra yogin reads it as implied; Śivajñāna yogin rejects this. *ibid.* p. 128. (Aruvarurai ed. Vol I)
4. The typical example given of memory in the Āgamas (kāmukaś-cakṣuṣā viśvaṁ kāminīmayam īkṣate) to which the commentators refer as erroneous memory, is suggestive that all memory

tends to be imaginative and therefore erroneous. By its very structure memory cannot be pure representation but suffused with imagination. *ibid.* p. 125; *NVM* p. 463.

5. This means the paradox that memory of past erroneous cognition also can be valid memory provided it is a faithful recollection.
6. Umāpati adopts the Nyāya solution to the problem of dhārāvāhika-jñāna. Though like smṛti it takes cognizance of what has already been cognised, unlike smṛti it is pramāṇa. Memory is exclusively a case of impression of past experience; it rests on past experience for its validity. In dhārāvāhika-jñāna knowledge of the second and succeeding moments are not saṁskāra-janya, but generated by the very objective conditions which occasion that initial knowledge; they stand by their own right and claim validity as does the first moment. *PB.* p. 520.
7. Should not 'tarka' also be discussed under non-valid distinct knowledge ? *NVM* (pp. 467-68) thinks tarka, like smṛti, also is a form of non-valid knowledge. PA, however , does not mention it in its list of non-valid knowledge (7-4 to 7). *PB* gives reason for the non-inclusion; a hypothetical argument is a species of erroneous knowledge (viparyaya-viśeṣa). *ibid.* p. 520.
8. PB 521.
9. 'saṁśayo nāma sādhāraṇa-dharma-darśanāt koṭidvayā'valambinī *buddhi*....viparyayas-tu atasmiṅs-tad-*buddhiḥ*.' *SP* p. 2
10. 'ihdu yadovena ondrittruṇivu piravādārāyum ñama sakti siyam enappadum' Śivajñāna yogin's Comm. *Supakkam*, Alavai 3.
11. In PB p. 517, both these interpretations are hinted. This shows that according to the system saṁśaya as a form of cognition is expressly taken as alternating between valid and non-valid cognition.
12. *PB* p. 517. Also *Māpāḍiam* p. 312. Śrīkumāra, however, objects to this and, therefore, to anyathākhyāti itself. His grounds are that were the illusory silver the one seen in the shop and remembered now, there would be recognition of silver and not perception of it. *TP* p. 60.
13. Attention is confined only to four or five theories discussed in *PB* pp. 518-20.

Rival Theories of Error and the Perspective of Siddhanta

1. This unconventional grouping of khyāti-vāda is inspired by the treatment of the subject in *PB* pp. 517-20.

2. PA 6-237; Sākāra-Vijñāna-vāda is the logical basis for the denial of external reality.
3. That all knowledge is erroneous with regard to its object is the common implication of (i) ātma-khyāti of the Yogācāra, (ii) the asat-khyāti of the Śūnyavādin, and also (iii) of the anirvacanīya-khyāti of the Advaitin, and knowledge is, therefore, for them, rooted in Ignorance. For Śaiva Siddhānta all determinate knowledge-error is also part of determinate knowledge, is a function of buddhi an evolute of māyā (māyeya) in partial contravention of ignorance due to Āṇava mala. While māyā distorts, it reveals nevertheless.
4. Śaiva Siddhānta, Bengal Vaiṣṇavaism advocate anyathā-khyāti, while Rāmānuja advocates sat-khyāti.

   The realist's concern is as with Plato, (Sophist 162-3) to distinguish the notion of falsehood from that of unreality. A false belief is not simply an unreal belief i.e. no belief at all. It involves a mental putting together of real elements which are in-fact apart or a mental putting apart of real elements which are in fact together. The character is misplaced or put in the place of another.
5. 'mayai mayakkamum seyyumaṇḍṛe,' *Supakkam* 2. 261; that is why māyā while being an abhivyañjaka is also said to be mala. while bhoga and bhoktṛtva are due to the respective upādhis of karma and āṇava, bandhana is due to māyā. *Ante.* Ch-10.
6. Smṛti is (i) knowledge of the *past*, and also (ii) knowledge *as* of the past. It is the latter feature which constitutes 'memoriness.' In the cognition of nacre as silver what is said to happen is there is a revival or retention of past experience of silver but a failure to understand such retention as an effect of past experience (smṛti-pramoṣa). This is what accounts for the apposition usage of idam (perception) and rajatam (memory).
7. 'rajatatva-prakāraka-śuktiviśeṣyaka-pravṛttir-eva svasamāna-prakāraka-jñānaṁ sāḍhayati'. *PB* p. 517.
8. Śrīkumāra who rejects anyathā-khyāti also thinks that a mere non-distinction between two types of real leads to activity : athālaukika-rajatāvabodhe laukika-rajatārthinas tatra pravṛttyabhāva-prasaṅga it cen na alaukikasyāpi laukika-bhedāgrahaṇena pravṛttyupapatteḥ.' TD p. 63.

9. *PB* pp. 517-18.
10. *ibid* p. 518.
11. According to Śrīkumāra, TP p. 63, the error-content is 'alaukika sat' : *laukikaṁ valaya-karaṇādi-samartham*; *alaukikam atra pratibhāsamānaṁ tad asamartham*. Alaukika or laukika, it is of course real, not 'illusory' : *paramārthatvān-na mithyātvam*; nedaṁ rajatam' merely serves to differentiate the 'alaukika' from the 'laukika' reality of the physical silver. The typical error experience prior to cancellation is accountable according to him because of not grasping the distinction between laukika and alaukika sat.
12. *PB* p. 519.
13. jñāna-lakṣaṇa-sannikarṣasya doṣa-viśeṣarūpa-sannikarṣasya vā kalpanāt.' *ibid.* p. 519.
14. The Saṁkṣepa Śārīrika view (viṣaya-karaṇa-doṣān na samvid) is referred to approvingly in *PB*. p. 519. Also *Māpāḍiam* p. 301.
15. *PB* p. 518.
16. The terminology is that of Hull. Woodworth, Robert S., *Contemporary Schools of Psychology*,
17. 'rajata-raṅgayor ime raṅga-rajate iti samūhālambana-bhramasthale aikaikatra yugapat pravṛtti-nivṛttyāpatteḥ.' *PB* p. 518.
18. 'anyathā anyātmanā viṣayīkurvat jñānam anyathā khyātiḥ' is the definition given by Madhva, for which reason his thory is also called abhinava anyathākhyāti (see Nagaraja Rao's Article JOR. Vol. XI, pp. 302-303).
19. And also of 'sat' as 'asat' 'asataḥ sattva-pratītiḥ sato asattva-pratītir ityanyathā-pratītir-eva bhrāntitvāt.' *Nyāyasudhā* p. 47 (quoted *ibid.* JOR).
20. PB p. 519 : 'trikāla-sarvadeśīya-niṣedha-pratiyogitā' *Nyāyāmṛta* quoted *ibid*. This text has given headache to scholars in matter of fixing the date of Pauṣkara Bhāṣya. See for a very interesting defence B.N. Krishnamurti Sharma's article in Poona Orientalist, 'Vol. III, p. 145.
21. *Nyāyasudhā*, p. 48.
22. *PB* p. 519.
23. The difference between 'asatkhyāti-vāda' of the Buddhist and that of the Madhvites seems to be that while for the latter only the representative factor is asat and the presentative thing—idam—is

sat, for the Buddhist Śūnyavādin idam and rajatam are asat; as mutually implicatory neither can be real.

24. sat-khyāti in a wider sense would include, as observed before, every theory of error other than the asat-khyāti, and in a narrower sense refers to the theories of error offered in the Schools of Mīmāṁsā and Viśiṣṭādvaita. The term has a special significance, when applied to the Viśiṣṭādvaitin's theory of error as suggesting that in error no less than in truth there is *literally* no deviation from reality.
25. Dasgupta, History of Indian Philosophy Vol 3.
26. 'pratinidhi-śrutyanusāreṇa.' PB P. 520.
27. 'nedaṁ rajatam iti bādhānupapatteḥ' etc. *PB* p. 520.
28. For the Viśiṣṭādvaitin, there is really no bādha but only abhi-bhūta (supersension).
29. PB *op. cit.*, p. 520. *Māpāḍiam* (p. 311) commenting on dehātma-bhrama says that it is doṣa that leads to the perception of resemblance where there is no basis for it.
30. 'pratinidhi-śrutistu tad-avayavādi-sadṛśāvayava-tatparā na tu tadavayavānusyūtiparā tathātve pūttikādāvapi somalatotpatti-prasaṅgād iti.' PB p. 520.
31. Ante Sec. on Truth and the Doctrine of the Relation of Guṇa and Guṇin.
32. 'akhyāti-saṁvalita-yathārtha-khyāti' is the description of Vedānta Deśikā : cited in Hiriyanna—*Indian Philosophical Studies*, p. 60, foot-note.
33. rajatam *idaṃ* na; negation (na) is in respect only of the idaṁtva (thisness); rajatam is outside the sweep of negation; it is real as idea.
34. *Śloka-vārttikam*, p. 245, st. 116. This is the classical argument of realism which every non-idealist repeats.
35. 'na samvid arthena bhidyate tayā' pi saḥ tadbhedako na ced arthaḥ samvid-bhedaḥ kathaṁ bhavet ?' *PA* 6-238.
36. "yad yena saha niyamena pramīyate tattad abhinnaṁ yathā jñānena sahopalabhyamāna ātmā" vijñānena sahopalabhyante ca nīlādayaḥ ataḥ vijñānābhinnāḥ.' etc. *PB* p. 450.
37. 'nīla-jñānaṁ pīta-jñānam ityādiṣu jñānasyānuvṛttyanubhavāt nīlādīnāṁ viṣayāṇāṁ vyāvṛttyanubhavāt yasmin anuvartamāne yad vyāvartate tat tato bhinnaṁ yathā kusumebhyas sūtram.' *PB* p. 452.

38. 'anuvartamānatva-vyāvartamānatva-viruddha-dharma- sambandhāt jñāna-jñeyayor-bhedas siddha iti.' *ibid.* p. 452.
39. anyathānupattyā śuktau pratīyamānaṁ rajataṁ sadasad-vilakṣaṇam eve ' ti.' *ibid.* p.520.
40. "paraspara-virodhe hi na prakārāntara-sthitiḥ" iti nyāyena satvāsatvayor anyatara-bādhe anyatarasyā' vaśyakatvena ubhaya-vailakṣaṇyāsiddheḥ.' *PB* p. 520.
41. The Advaitin considers the possibilities of contradiction here under three headings and finds none of them tenable :
    (*a*) paraspara-viraha-rūpatayā, involving mutual negation,
    (*b*) paraspara-viraha-vyāpakatayā, involving mutual pervasion, and
    (*c*) paraspara-viraha-vyāpyatayā, involving its converse. *Advaita-Siddhi-Vyākhyā* pp. 92-94.
42. Śrīkumāra criticises the view of the false as not existing during the time of illusion. TP Comm. ; his distinction between laukika-sat and alaukika-sat as a plausible alternative to 'neither sat nor asat' is already referred to. According to Abhinava Gupta (īśvara-pratyabhijñā-vimarśinī) illusion arises because of an incomplete knowledge of the real (svarūpākhyāti); non-cognition which is endemic to all phenomenal knowledge, renders our perception incomplete. In a complete vision the difference between the laukika-sat and the alaukika-sat, the perceived and the remembered, the 'false' and the real will not be lost sight of, and hence paradoxically no error.
43. Śaiva Siddhānta rejects the two postulates of (*i*) bhāvarūpa-ajñāna, and (*ii*) sākti-caitanya on which rest the cogency of anirvacanīya-khyāti-vāda, and puts forward in their place the concept of a consciousness obscured by a congenital impurity (malāvṛta-citśakti).
44. '*Appearance and Reality*', p. 166; Bradley of course distinguishes error from truth as a distinction within appearance, within the phenomenon of 'a what loosened from its that'; every appearance involves a divorce between quality and being. Error is only hardening of this looseness into a 'fracture'. Saiva Siddhānta, in agreement with the general tenor of all 'orthodox' systems of philosophy starts from the opposite assumption : all knowledge is a qualification of reality, ascribes a content to existence where existence has a content 'colliding within itself' the relation of this 'what' is error.

CHAPTER THIRTEEN

SELF-VALIDITY OF KNOWLEDGE AND REVELATION

Theory of Self-Apprehension of Validity

1. For the secondary implication of 'prāmāṇyaṁ svataḥ' see infra. Secs. Theory of Extrinsic Generation of Validity of Knowledge and Extrinsic Apprehension of Invalidity of Knowledge.
2 *SB* pp. 99, 100.
3. Ryle : G, The *Concept of Mind*, Barnes and Noble, 1959, p. 151.
4. These are suggested negatively by 'svāśraya-grāhaka-grāhyam' which is the correct interpretation of svataḥ grāhyatvam.
5. The assertion p, and the assertion, '*p is true*' are not identical, since their constituents are different; they of course express *equivalent* propositions. Modern symbolic logic uses the same symbol, viz p for the assertion p or '*p is true*'.
6. This view may be identified with that of Vedānta-Paribhāṣā (I. 51) : 'vṛtter vṛttyantara-viṣayatve'pi sva-viṣayatvābhyupagamena' etc. Śaiva Siddhānta rejects this view.
7. *SB. op. cit.* p. 100.
8. Cf. the definition of cit as sva-para-prakāśa. Self illumination is uniquely descriptive of cit while buddhi etc. are distinguished from it as *a-cit* on ground that the latter is only para-prakāśa. *SJB* 4-1. Citrurai.

The Concept of Cognition of Cognition

1. See note no. 6 of previous section.
2. The terminology of 'contact' is that of the Nyāya; for Śaiva Siddhānta with its category of cit-śakti, contact is really 'pervasion', 'grasp', 'comprehension'. Sannikarṣa and its types are admitted after the fashion of the Nyāya (*PA* 7-32) but always against the background of an 'un-self-manifest' cit-śakti.
3. PA 7-8.
4. *Śāstra Dīpikā*, p. 157; by kāraṇāt kāryānumāna cognition is inferentially known by means of the middle term 'cognisedness'.
5. Prābhākara also says that jñāna is inferred from phalasaṁvṛtti; between Kumārila and Prabhākara, the difference is that while the

former admits jñāna is the bhāvārtha, the latter understands it like the Nyāya, in the kāraṇārtha, meaning by it jaḍa-sāmagrī; for the latter after-cognition is of the form of inference from the effect of the knowledge-phenomenon (saṁvid-rūpa-phala) to the causal agregate (sannikarṣādi-jaḍa-sāmagrī)which is jñāna-guṇa-janaka. *Prakaraṇa Pañcikā*, p. 63.

6. Cf. the famous statement sarvaṁ citta-caittānām ātma-samvedanam, of Dharmakīrti. Also apratyakṣopalambhasya nā'rthadṛṣṭiḥ prasiddhyati, quoted in Satkari Mukerjee (1935), p. 325. svaprakāśa and para-prakāśa are interchangeable according to this view.
7. *Vedānta-Paribhāṣā* 1.51.
8. *Tattva-Cintāmaṇi* : Anuvyavasāya-vāda. It may be noted, however, that the full implications of the recognition of a permanent knowing self, for knowledge are not drawn out; jñānatva is treated as an accident and not the essence of self.
9. 'avaśyaṁ jñeyatvenābhyupagamān-nā'navasthād', quoted in PB p. 523.
10. Śaiva Siddhānta itself raises these questions against the Nyāya in a different key. See below.

Statement of the Theory

1. SB p. 99-100.
2. 'bādhā'navatāra-kālīna-svāśrayagocara-yāvallaukika - pratyakṣagrāhyatvaṁ paratastva-vādinaṁ pratisādhanīyam.' *ibid* p. 100. This crisp statement like most that follow, is adopted by Śivāgra yogin from PB almost verbatim.
3. *ibid* p. 100.
4. Validity of a judgment ceases to be perceived subsequent to knowing the *absence* of the relation between its 'that' and 'what' (tadvattvābhāvopasthiti); the latter is contradictory knowledge and when that arises the original apprehension of validity is suspended. Doubt originates only from tadvattvābhāvopasthiti and therefore the paratastva-vādin's charge that doubt cannot arise at all on svastva-pakṣa is born of ignorance of this condition pertaining to svatastvam. See below.
5. 'yāvallaukika-pratyakṣa-grāhyatvam' etc.
6. 'svavṛtti-vartamāna-jñāna-gocaram eva laukikaṁ pratyakṣam'. *ibid.* p. 101.

The Chief Argument for Self-Apprehension of Validity

1. kim atra pramāṇam iti cet sāmagrye've'ti brūmah. *ibid.* p. 101.
2. For the Naiyāyika anuvyavasāya is included under jñāna-lakṣanā-pratyāsatti. In anuvyavasāya there is (1) jñānāṁśa (with respect to which it is laukika-pratyakṣa) and (2) viśeṣyasya tadvatāṁśaḥ (with respect to which anuvyavasāya is a-laukika pratyakṣa).

   The two stages are :

   (1) bhūtalaṁ ghaṭavat (vyavasāya-jñāna)

   (2) ghaṭavat-bhutala-jñānavānaham (anuvyavasāya-jñāna)

   The 'truth' of (1), which may be said to consist in the 'thatness characterised by its what' (viśeṣya-tadvattvam), is present implictly (upanīta) in (2) as 'ghaṭatva-bhūtala-viṣayatvam.

   Śaiva Siddhānta will include anuvyavasāya comprehensively under mānasa-pratyakṣa without necessarily committing itself to the Nyāya concept of extra-ordinary perception. See *Supakkam,* alavai 6, com. of Śivajñāna yogin and Śivāgra yogin.
3. This objection seems to echo modern objections to self-evidence based on a distinction between knowledge and belief. Russell : *Analysis of Mind*, p. 269. The modern terminology is deliberately introduced even at the risk of some over-simplification.
4. 'mūla-jñāna-viṣayatayā grahaṇe'pi svātantryeṇāgrahaṇān-na prāmāṇya-graha iti.' SB p. 101.
5. 'svātantryeṇa grahaṇasyānirvacanāt.' *ibid.* p. 101; Śivāgra yogin (SB p. 101) elaborates this discussion in a refreshingly original manner taking his cue, of course, from PB p. 314.
6. 'jñāna-viṣayatvenā' grahaṇe grahaṇam'. *ibid.* p. 101.
7. PB. p. 515.
8. See for a further discussion of the issues involved here, *ibid* pp. 101-102.
9. *ibid.* p. 102.
10. The difference between modern thinkers like Russell and the Nyāya in respect of this issue is that for the former primary belief is likely to be false even though seeming to be indubitable, while logical certainty free from error is reached through a logical process of reasoning. *Analysis of Mind*, pp. 262, 263. For the Nyāya the reverse seems to be true. It is primary intuition (mūla-jñānam) to which the subject of knowledge is wholly, and once for all, given, that is 'independent apprehension', while introspection implies

a fall from logical certainty to mere psychological belief. Śaiva Siddhāntin's only plea is that if this be so, even reasoning will be only belief and no certain knowledge; if, however, certainty is claimed for reasoning, why may it not be claimed for introspective knowledge too ?

11. SB p. 102; also, 'pramātvaṁ na svatogrāhyaṁ saṁśayānupapattiḥ.' *Bhāṣā Pariccheda* 137. Also 'prāmāṇyasya svato' grāhye'nābhyāsa-daśotpanna-jñāne tatsaṁśayo na syāt.' *Tattva Cintāmaṇi*, Prāmāṇyavāda, 22.

12. 'jñānasyāgrahe dharmijñānābhāvād grahe ca prāmāṇyāgrahe sva-tastvabhaṅgāpatteḥ prāmāṇya-grahasya satvād.' *ibid.* p. 102.

13. The argument here is that it is only decision, determination (niścaya) and not its impressions (niścaya-saṁskāra) that is inimical to the rise of doubt; impression is, relatively, weaker (durbala) and can coexist with doubt or denial.

14. The counter argument is that just as niścaya is pratibandhaka to saṁśaya, apramuṣṭa-saṁskāra of niścaya also is pratibandhaka.

15. 'aprāmāṇya-saṁśaya-samādhānaṁ tu doṣa-janyatva-saṁśayān-niścite'pyarthe jñānasya doṣa-janyatva-saṁśayena saṁśayadarśa-nāt.' SB p. 102.

16. 'dharmi-jñānāsya-janakatve mānābhāvena saṁśaya-rūpasyai'va dharmi-jñānasya niṣpatti-sambhavāc-ca.' *ibid.* p. 102.
What is suggested here is that saṁśaya-rūpa-dharmi-jñāna is part of dharmi-jñāna and the latter is preceded by dharma-jñāna.

17. 'dharmi-jñāna-niyāmakasyai'va saṁśaya-niyāmakatva-sambhavāt. *ibid.* p. 103.

18. *SB* p. 103; *PB* p. 514.

Examination of Extrinsic Apprehension of Validity

1. SB p. 103. The infinite regress brings home to us the fact that the intelligibility that philosopher is seeking is not to be had along the path he has begun to tread. Having failed to achieve it by introducing a single form into the situation, he is not going to do any better by introducing still more forms.

2. In vyatireka-vyāpti, there is no sādhyāpasiddhi but only sādhyā-bhāva-prasiddhi; for the latter there is no dearth of dṛṣṭānta.

3. 'sādhya-prasidhyabhāvenā'navatārāt.' *SB* p. 104.

4. The dilemma before the paratastva-vādin is : a positive concomitance is not possible in the absence of an instance; a negative concomitance is not possible with the non-establishment of the major term.
5. Refer to *Tattva Cintāmani* prāmāṇya-vāda pp. 165-188. *Mohanty* for Nyāya attempts to meet the charge of sādhyāprasiddhi.
6. *PB* p. 515.

Extrinsic Apprehension of Invalidity of Knowledge

1. 'pramāṇatvāpramāṇatve svataḥ sāṅkhyaḥ samāśritaḥ.' *SDS* p. 279.
2. 'tadabhāvavattvasya vyavasāyā' nupanītatvenā' nuvyavasāyena grahaṇāsambhavāt.' *SB* p. 104.
3. 'bādhopanīte tadabhāvavattve manasā tad-graha-sambhavāt. na cai' vam anuvyavasāyenā' pi tad-grahaṇaṁ yuktaṁ tadabhāvattvasya vyavasāyānupanītatvābhidhānāt'. *ibid.* p. 104. Śivāgra yogin makes this ingenious suggestion in anticipation of the objection from the critic, that in an inference about apramātva there will be dṛṣṭāntānupapatti. The words of SB are identical with those of *PB* p. 515.

Theory of Extrinsic Generation of Validity of Knowledge

1. Specially from the standpoint of acknowledging a metempirical source of valid knowledge, viz. Āgama-pramāṇa, See below. Plato makes a similar discerning distinction between the question of origin and the question of truth (*Phaedrus,* 275 B.C.)
2. Śaiva Siddhānta departs from the Mīmāṁsā-Vedānta tradition in upholding paratastvam in respect of the ***origination*** or ***constitution*** of validity. 'utpattau tu prāmāṇyasya paratastvam eva.' PB p. 515; *SB* p. 106. It is interesting to note that Śivāgra yogin who adopts and extends the arguments of PB in this regard, holds to an opposite thesis in his SP p. 26, where he defends the view: 'prāmāṇyaṁ svata eva gṛhyate utpattau ca' (*ibid.* pp. 25-26) and gives the usual argument for utpattau svatastvam : 'yāvat svāśraya-jñāna-janaka-sāmagrī-janyatvam, jñāna-sāmagrī-janyatve sati tadatirikta-hetvajanyatvaṁ pramāyāḥ svatastvam iti.' The anomaly cannot be explained.
3. 'paratastvaṁ tu apramā-vyāvṛtta-kāraṇa-nirūpita-kāryatā'vacchedakatvam.' *PB* p. 515; *SB* p. 105.
4. The formulation in the terminology of Navya-Nyāya used in PB p. 515, and repeated and elucidated in SB p. 105 ff. and the tenor of

the entire discussion that ensues is evidence of the influence of Gaṅgeśa's *Tattva-Cintāmaṇi*, pp. 286-91. Vide also Nīlakaṇṭha on Tattva Cintāmaṇi, Prāmāṇya-vāda, pp. 186-88 for terminological resemblances. It is useful, however, to remember that the author of PB and SB after him, rejects the view that we come to apprehend with certainty knowledge's validity only when knowledge leads to successful activity prompted by it, which is the view of *Tattva-Cintāmaṇi*, 1. pp. 189 ff; 401 ff.

Argument for Extrinsic Generation of Validity

1. Navya Nyāya uses words in their general meaning. Employing them referentially to mean directly the objects has the disadvantage of suggesting that the meaning of a word is the object to which it may refer on the different occasions of its use. For a competent discussion of the Navya Nyāya theory of relational abstracts vide Daniel Ingall's *Materials*, pp. 44, 45 ff.
2. This is called anyūnātirikta-vṛtti, *Avacchedakatva Nirukti*, p. 2. A characteristic of smaller and wider extension cannot be a determinant e.g. the avacchedaka of an inherent cause of conjunction or disjunction is substance-universal (dravyatva).
3. When it is said that ghaṭatva is kāryatāvacchedaka, what is suggested is 'ghaṭatva' itself being a jāti, is not kārya, but is determinant of effectness as all individual pots which are 'only and always' effect of a cause. So with pramātva also.
4 SB p. 105, f.; Knowledge neither valid nor non-valid is hypothetical; actually knowledge is always either valid because of the presence of the guṇa, or non-valid because of the presence of doṣa.
5. The relation is not a tautology, like 'what is effect is effect' but a significant general proposition of which the terms are : (i) being only effect (p), and (ii) being effect of a uniquely 'describing' cause (q). The suggested inference is of the valid form p implies q, p, ∴ q and p implies q—q, ∴ -P, viz. *modus ponens* and *modus tollens*.

Some Objections Considered

1. *SB* pp. 106, 107.
2. According to the Navya-Naiyāyika, śuddha-sattā and viśiṣṭa-sattā are logically equivalent though either cannot be substituted for the other. See *Ingalls*, pp. 69-70 ff.

A cognition of pot will not even be kārya-mātra-vṛtti-dharma if it is taken as God's cognition of pot which is eternal, unoriginated. Therefore is selected as example a non-eternal cognition of pot.

3. In the case of the 'blue pot' etc., there is kārya-mātra-vṛtti-dharmatva but no kāraṇatāvacchedakatva. Why ? No *special* cause is necessary to give rise to the perception of 'blue pot'; sense-object conjunction, and inherence in what the sense is in conjunction with, together account for the perception of a blue pot.
4. 'pramātvāvacchinnaṁ pratyanugata-kāraṇa-sambhave na bādhāc-ca.' *SB* p. 105.
5. 'nīla-ghaṭatvavad viśeṣyakatvāvacchinna - kāraṇāt tat prakārakād vā'vacchinna - kāraṇāc - cā'rtha-samāja - mahimnopapatteś-ca.' *ibid.* p. 105.
6. This is the main plank of paratastva in respect of pramātva : 'pramākaraṇa-vijātīya-kāraṇājanyatve pramāyās tadvijātitvan-na syāt.' *ibid.* p. 105.
7. 'nīlaghaṭa-paṭa-jñānādeḥ pītaghaṭa—paṭa-jñānādi-kāraṇa-vijātīya-kāraṇa-janyatvābhāve'pi tadvaijātya-darśanāt. tatra tadvijātīya-tvenā' janakatve' pi vijātīya-kāraṇa-janyatvam astī'ti yadi tad ihā'-pi vijātīyatvena janakatvaṁ na sidhyet tasmān-na pramātvasya. kāryatāvacchedakatvam iti.' *ibid.* p. 105.
8. 'pramātvaṁ kāryatāvacchedakaṁ......*bādhakābhāve sati* kāryamātra-vṛttitvād ghaṭatvavat.' *ibid.* p. 106.
9. Given something having the character of being 'only' effect and subject to the proviso that it is not being contradicted by cases known to the contrary, it is determinant of effectness.
10. 'avacchedakāntaropapanna-kāryatvādhikaraṇakatvam', is one of the forms of bādha sought to be excluded. The other form of bādha is given, *infra*.
'tattad-viśeṣyakatve sati tat-prakārakatvasya samūhālambana-bhramasādhāraṇaṣyā'rtha-samāja-mahimno' papannatve'pi tattad-viśeṣyakat*vāvacchinna* - tat - prakārakatvasyā'vacchedakāntaropapanna-kāryatvādhikaraṇatvābhāvāt.' *ibid.* p. 106.

Extrinsic Conditions of Validity

1. The svataḥprāmāṇya-vādin's (utpattau ca) very first attack is on this score. 'na tu adhikaguṇam apekṣate pramāṇa-mātre'nugataguṇābhāvāt'. *Vedānta-Paribhāṣā* VII. 1.

2. 'apramāyām apyanugatasya doṣasyā'bhāvena pittādi-tattad-doṣa-janyatvenai'va paratastvāṅgīkārāt.' *SB* p. 108.
3. SB p. 108, considers the suggestion of a common 'excellence' as the generator of validity formulated as hereunder : 'pramā-mātre viśeṣya-vṛtti-viśeṣaṇa-jñānaṁ guṇa ityāhuḥ'. Śivāgra yogin, however, turns it down as over-simplification; conjunct invalid cognition also can claim validity in the name of the guṇa thus stated. *ibid.* p. 108.
   Gaṅgeśa, it may here be noted, does not admit the possibility of a generic effect that is not accompanied by specific characteristic : viśeṣavinākṛta-sāmānya-kāryābhāvāt *Prāmāṇya vāda*, Mohanty. *op. cit.*
4. SB p. 106.
5. Lack of maximal sense object contact is one of the factors of perceptual illusion, vide *ante* Ch. 12.
6. *Vedānta-Paribhāṣa*, 7-2; SB p. 106; PB p. 515.
7. Sūryanārāyaṇa Śāstri, *Truth in Śaiva Siddhānta op. cit.* para 34.
8. 'jñānākaraṇakaṁ jñānaṁ pratyakṣam' : *Siddhānta-Muktāvalī*, p. 237.
9. PB, p. 515 ff.
10. A qualificant (viśeṣya) which is expressed by the subject of an assertion, has qualities (viśeṣaṇa) the chief of which is expressed in the predicate, and is distinguished as the 'chief qualifier' (prakāra). The generative 'excellence' of valid inference is knowledge of the qualificand having also the actual possession of sādhya among its qualities, while its chief qualifier is possession of hetu. The English terminology adopted here, as at other places throughout the chapter is that of *Ingalls*.
11. Instead of formulating it simply as 'sādhyavad viśeṣyakaṁ hetu-prakārakam', it may be reformulated as : 'anumiti-pramātvāva-cchinnaṁ prati sādhyavad viśeṣyakatvāvacchedena hetu-prakāra-kaṁ jñānaṁ guṇaḥ.' *SB* p. 106; PB p. 516.
12. 'yathārtha-parāmarśo guṇaḥ.' *PB* p. 516.
13. *SB* p. 106.
14. '*yathārtha-parāmarśo guṇaḥ*' is the Nyāya view which is being examined here in the light of other Nyāya presuppositions.
15. 'īśvarasya yathārtha-parāmarśas tatrā'pyasti.' *ibid.* p. 106.
16. Unlike the ayathārtha-parāmarśa of the form of dhūli-paṭala-gocara-dhūma-bhrama.

17. 'klipta-hetu-bhāvasyai'va tadīyasya parāmarśasya guṇatva-sambhave'*vyadhikaraṇasya tat* kalpanāyogāt.' *ibid.* pp. 106-107.
    The expression *apyatikaraṇasya* found in the printed text is a clear misprint and the editorial foot-note seems misguided.
18. 'abādhitatva-pramā guṇaḥ' : this view finds favour with *PB* p. 516; but SB rejects it for very cogent reasons stated below.
19. 'sādhya-niścayasyābhāve abādhitatva-pramā na sambhavati bhāve tu siddha-sādhanān-nānumityudayas syād iti vācyam.' *ibid.* p. 107.
20. 'śabda-pramāyāṁ tu vaktṛ-vākyārtha-yathārtha-jñānaṁ guṇaḥ'. *PB* p. 516.
21. 'tatrā' pi (i. e., in the case of the Veda) guṇa-janyatvānusāreṇa īśvarasya vaktṛtva-kalpanenā' vaktṛtvā' siddheḥ.' *ibid.* p. 107.
22. 'yogyatāyās tat pramāyā vā guṇatva-sambhavāt.' *ibid.* p. 107.
23. 'ananya-niścaya-viraha.' *ibid.* p. 107.
24. saṁsarga-rūpatvam. *SB* pp. 107-108.
25. 'atītānāgatādi-rūpatvena janakatvāyogāt.' *ibid.* p. 108.
26. 'eka-padārtha - saṁsarge'para- padārtha - niṣṭhā'tyantābhāva - pratiyogitva-pramā-viśeṣyatvābhāva-rūpatvam.' *ibid.* p. 108.
27. Except for this change of the negative into the positive form, the definition merely restates the first view replacing 'niścaya' with 'pramā' with a view to exclude error.
28. 'anīśvara-vādi-mate bādhābhāva-paryavasānatayā bādhābhāvadaśotpanna-bādhitārthaka-vākya-janya-sādhāraṇatayā guṇatvāsambhavāt. *ibid.* p. 108.
29. This then is the clinching argument of *PB* against the Mīmāṁsā-Vedānta thesis of 'svataḥ prāmāṇyam utpattau ca' *PB*. 516.
30. 'pakṣīya-saṁśayasya niyamagrahāvirodhitvād anaythā-vahnyāder-api dhūmādi-pūrva-vṛttitva-niyamo na siddhyet parvatādau tatsaṁśayāt.' *ibid.* p. 108.
31. The Buddhist standpoint is represented to be the inverse of prāmāṇyaṁ svataḥ : saugataś-caramaṁ svataḥ, SDS p. 279. This has, however, been questioned. Buddhism accepts no regulation (niyamita) in this : 'na hi bauddhair eṣāṁ caturṇām ekātamo'-pi pakṣo'bhīṣṭo'niyama-pakṣasye'ṣṭatvāt. Tathā hi ubhayam apyetat kiñcit svataḥ kiñcit parataḥ iti pūrvam upavarṇitam. ata eva pakṣa-catuṣṭayopanyāso'pyayuktaḥ; *pañcamasyāpyaniyama-pakṣasya sambhavāt. Tattva Saṅgraha Pañjikā*, V. 3123. So has

it been claimed on behalf of Jainism too : tat prāmāṇyaṁ svataḥ parataś-ce'ti...*Parīkṣāmukha* 1.13. Also 'tadubhayam utpattau parata eva jñaptau tu svataḥ parataś-ce'ti.' *Pramāṇanaya-Tattvāloka*, 1.21. But even to the extent they do not accept regulation in the matter of validity, they deny self evidence and advocate epistemological skepticism. Citations given here are taken from Sukhlalji's *Advanced Studies in Indian Logic and Metaphysics* (1961).

BOOK V

CHAPTER FOURTEEN

SPIRITUAL LIFE AS MEANS : SĀDHANA

1. *Supakkam* 8. 18. The 'jñanāvaraṇa' tradition of Siddhānta Śaiva sets itself on contra-distinction with the karmāvaraṇa siddhānta. See below. See also *ante* Ch. 1. Sec. 'Śaiva Siddhānta Literature.'
2. jñanāt tveva kaivalyam. See *infra* for discussion. Cf. jñānenaiva tu kaivalyaprāptis-tatra na saṁśayaḥ" *Suprabheda Āgama*, jñāna pāda, Śiva-sṛṣṭi-vidhi-paṭalaḥ 5. Also, 'māna-sādhyodhikāro hi muktiś-ca vyaktir-īsvaraḥ'. PA 1.5.

   Sivāgra yogin cites the evidences of śruti and yukti in support of the thesis 'through knowledge *alone* is mokṣa' : 'samuccaya-nirāsāvasare udāhariṣyamāṇair *jñānād eva tu kaivalya*-prāptis tatra na saṁśaya ityādibhir jñānasya mokṣa-sādhanatā-pratipādaka-vacanair jñāna*syaiva* mokṣa-hetutvāt.' SB. p. 368. Also commenting on the unequivocalness that is implied by the 'alone' he continues : 'jñānasya mokṣa-sādhanatā-pratipādaka-vacanānurodhena tasya sādhya-vyāpakatva-niścayāt yadyapi jñānasyaiva dikṣāyā api sādhanatva-pratipādakam vacanamasti tathā'pi jñānādevetyādā*vevakā*reṇa anya-yoga-vyavacchedena jñāna-sādhanābhava-pratipādanād dīkṣā-viṣayaṁ vacanaṁ paramparā-sādhanatvaparam.' *ibid* p. 369.
3. *Supakkam* 4, 2.
4. Ante Ch. 5. Sec. on God as the Lord of Cosmic Functions.
5. *Māpāḍiam* p. 452.
6. *Supakkam* 8.28 ff.
7. *ibid* 8.230.
8. Ante Ch. 1. Sec. on 'The Point of View.'
9. *Māpāḍiam* p. 453. Also umapati's *Unnaineṛiviḷakkam.*
10. Rūpa is synonymous with the logical notion of lakṣaṇa whose function is to differentiate and designate : vyāvṛttir vyavahāro vā lakṣaṇasya prayojanam is the Nyāya dictum.

11. Tattva-jñāna is metaphysical knowledge and knowledge of *more* tattvās is taken to signify greater comprehension in theory and better control in practice .
12. Cf. interpretation of tattva-darśana, ātma-*darśana* and Śiva-darśanam in all of which the knowledge or insight *precedes* union and therefore implies 'abstraction'.
13. *Māpāḍiam* p. 504.
14. The theme of daśakārāyāṇi is the central topic of post Meykenda Śaiva Siddhānta literature. Cf. Tiruvāduturai Adeena Publication No. 132 : Pandāra Sattiram, *tasakariyangal,* 1959.
15. While there can be 'Śuddhi' in the context of Tattva and Ātma there is no Śiva-śuddhi but only Śiva-yoga in its place. The reasons are obvious.
16. *Infra* Ch. 15, last section.
17. *Māpāḍiam* p. 503.
18. *Supakkam* describes the 'Phala' in the Sādhana section itself (8th Sūtra).
19. Supakkam compares the jñānī to jīvan-mukta. 8.29.
20. In the terminology of rūpa-darśana-śuddhi, the stages that are involved in the process of self gaining reality are (1) through tattva darśana arises ātma-rūpa, (2) through śiva-rūpa, ātma-darśana and (3) through śiva-darśana, ātma-śuddhi. See *infra.*

Self-understanding of Self

1. Ātma-darśana is the portal to a phenomenology of spiritual life Meykandār formulates it at the beginning of the section on sādhana SÑP, VII, third adhikaraṇa.
2. Discussion here presupposes the distinction between sat and asa already made. *Ante* Ch. 2, 8.
3. SÑP 7.1. This is the approach of Śivādvaita.
4. Śivādvaita oscillates between monism and absolutism. The ontological status of paśu in relation to Śiva is the decisive point at issue between Śivādvaita and Śaiva Siddhānta.
5. Śrīkumāra cites the following verse of *Śivarahasya* : 'anubhavati hi paśu-bhāvaṁ śiva evāṇava-tirohitātmā, guṇaḥ so'pi malo yaḥ kaścana śaktilāvaḥ sarvathā sārvaḥ.' TP p. 24. Also Cf. 'What experiences 'nothingness' in deep sleep is the finite

knower—the śūnya pramātṛ under limitation. When freed of limitation he is Śiva Himself' :

'śunya-pramātuścā' pavedya suṣuptatvaṁ na kiñcid rūpa-parimita-pramātṛ-rūpatvāt aparimita-bhāve tvasyaiva śivatvam.'

Bhāskarī Vol. 1, p. 322.

6. *Paramārtha Sāra* 7, Meykaṇḍār uses this example to illustrate ātmaśuddhi. See below.
7. SÑP, 7, 2. This is the view of Śivasaṁkrānta-vāda.
8. 'jñātvā devaṁ mucyate sarva-pāśaiḥ'. *Śvetāś'. Up.* VI. 13. 'tathā' pi mucyate dehī patiṁ vijñāya nirmalam', quoted SB. p. 342. Also, 'pāsattaip pasukkal viṭṭup patiyaṇai aḍaiya mutthi', *Parapakkam*, 295.
9. Schomerus calls it the 'deistic ground statement' (deistischer Grundsatz) which stands apparently in contradiction with theistic statements like that God is the pati of other realities. *Schomerus*. p. 67. How the two statements are reconciled by means of the concept of śakti is explained with great insight by him elsewhere *ibid* p. 94.
10. The mediating as Schomerus would say, must be homogeneous with the mediated : "das Vermittelnde muss dem zu Vermittel inden homogen sein," *ibid* p. 334.
11. In mokṣa it is acceptable both for Śivādvaita and Śaiva Siddhānta that the freed self does not have discursive knowledge. Meykaṇḍār asks how this is conceivable except on the presumption that the supreme that the self is in union with is only pure, non-discursive consciousness. SÑP 7.1 vārttikam.
12. *ibid* 7, 1, udāharaṇa.
13. *Supakkam* 7, 1.
14. 'tanaikkodon drunardalānum tānasat tunaranande.' *ibid.*
15. The māyīya comprising the sphere of the tattvas constitute the accessory to knowledge of every kind, the common correlates of experience for selves of all grades and the specific correlates of experience unique for each self. *Infra* Ch. 9 Section 'Māyīya : Evolution of Vidyā and Ātma tattvas.'
16. *Supakkam* 2. 69.
17. The intuitive light of self even in its limited manifestation serves as the factor of illumination for the contrast implied by darśana. Ātma-rūpa entailed by tattva darśana is therefore the nexus between natural knowledge and the advent of Revelation.

18. SÑP, 7. 2. 1.

19. The categories and forms of objective experience (bhogya) the 'generators (bhojayitṛ) and even the transcendental functions of activation (preraka) of experience—all are evolutes and extension of Matter. *Ante* Ch. 9.

20. 'aṛiporuḷ acittāi *vēām*', *Supakkam*. 6.6.

21. The locus of light, viz., wick is also called by the name of light. Cf. the Tamil work Tattuva Pirakāsem.
Cf. the Tamil work Tattuva Pirakāsam.

22. SÑP. 7.3 vārttika and Citrurai ff.

Cf. also 'now the self is the bridge, the separating boundary for keeping these worlds apart. *Chānd. Up* VIII. 4.1.; 'the person in the embrace of the intelligent self knows nothing without or within', (implying there is something 'anya-tattvam' different from the intelligent self) *Bṛhad. Up*. IV. 3. 21.

23. *Supakkam* 7.2.

24. The significance of the concept of sadasat is the acknowledgement of the necessity of understanding the being of man, such that ignorance and alienation can be a possible way of being for him.' 'Sundering of soul from spirit' in the words of Paul is a possibility theologically speaking before which we always stand. Not only on the materialistic and mechanistic view of man but on an abstractly spiritual view of man too, according to which man is spirit as such, this would be an illusion. For the Advaitin illusion itself is illusory, a highly paradoxical notion which rightly comes in for criticism at the hands of religious philosophers. What is imported by the notion of sadasat concerning the religious knowledge of man is that man knows himself and grasps his point of selfhood from outside himself. The phenomenon 'man' can only be understood with the help of a dimension which is 'without' man, be it biophysical, or theo-spiritual. Only in the case of the second, what is infinitely 'without' is also paradoxically infinitely 'within.' One other point to be noted about 'sadasat' is that its admission in addition to sat and asat may seem like a cross-division : sat-asat division is dichotomous, and if something cannot be neither as the siddhāntin himself urges in refutation of anirvacanīya-khyāti something cannot also be both. The truth is that even 'sadasat' falls under the category of asat (*ante* chapter 7, section on 'God and

Absolute'). This becomes evident not at the level of ātma-rūpam and ātma-darśanam but at the level of ātma-śuddhi. See below.

25. 'sarve dharmā ātmanas tu (dharmā ātmanas santi) yam eva parikalpayet
tat tad bhavatyasandehāt so' pi tadbhāvanāyutaḥ
ity evam ātmavijñānaṁ kathitaṁ tu samāsataḥ,
jñātvā'tmānam idaṁ sarve hyātmānaṁ paryupāsate.' *Sarva-Jñānottara-Āgama* 2.21.
'vijñānam evaṁ samupāsya vidvān viśatyakāyaṁ satataṁ niyuktaḥ sa sarvāgāmī bhavatī' ha muktas *taddharmadharmī* bahir-antas-saṁsthaḥ.' *ibid.* 1.55.

26. Ante Ch. 5. Sec. on God as Non-dual.

27. In the terminology of Śaiva Siddhānta, what makes for the possibility of *śuddha* avasthā for self on parity with its empirical life of avasthās but implying a new horizon of understanding insight and integration, is metaphysically, is self being of the nature of sadasat.

Self-Insight

1. By self-insight is here meant ātma-darśana which is concomitant with Śiva-rūpa and tattva-śuddhi. For explanation, see below.
2. *Supakkam*. 8. 23-27.
3. *Māpāḍiam*. p. 420.
4. *ibid.* pp. 419-20.
5. SVP. 10.
6. *Supakkam*. 8. 27 'aññānattāl uruvatutān pantam'. Also SSV Jñāna-pāda 8 Comm.
7. Śaṅkara's Comm. *Bṛh. Up.* II.1.20; *Śrī Bhāṣyam* 1.1.4.
8. SÑP 8 *Citrurai*.
9. The preceptor's presence symbolic of awakening to the dimension of sat is hailed by the pupil as a case of divine love limitless and unconditional appearing under the condition of a limited finite existence, as a case of the divine appearing in flesh. See how Umāpati hails the presence of his teacher in NT, lines 82-90. Also Mānickavācagar refers to the Lord as the 'Gracious one that left the heavens, entered this earth and made men this own 'Tiruvācakam, kuyil Decad, 4.
10. Darśana is vision entailing contrast, and always implies a revelatory source from within or without. The vision is not the product

of an inherent dynamism of thought, a moment in its interior dialectic, but a new outcome through illumination. See *ante* Sec. I.

11. As Darśana means illumination, Śuddhi implies freedom. See in the case of Ātma-śuddhi, See below.
12. The evil of phenomenal life is described significantly as one of 'languishing in the company of the senses' (SÑP. 8.1) to show that the redeeming knowledge which lifts it out of the prison-house of its sense cannot be itself sense-dependent knowledge.
13. Self-knowledge to use a Platonic term the equivalent of paśu-jñāna must imply self's knowledge of itself as otherwise it will be non-distinct from sense-knowledge (pāśa-jñāna). See SÑP 4 citrurai *Māpāḍiam* p. 306. Sense-knowledge is luminous but not self-luminous, while self-knowledge is self-luminous.

Are there Alternative Sádhanas ?

1. Aghora Śiva, Bhaṭṭa Rāmakaṇṭha and others that follow their lead, notable among them Ñānaprakāśar, a commentator of Supakkam. The distinction between the standpoints of Jñānāvaraṇa and Karmāvaraṇa is important. See *ante* Ch. 1, Sec. on Literature on Śaiva Siddhānta.
2. TTN. 8; TS. 29, Aghora Śiva's Comm.
3. MK. 47-52.
4. *ibid*, See Bhaṭṭa Rāmakaṇṭha's Comm.
5. Ñānaprakāsar's Comm. *Supakkam*. 8.27.

5a. TS. 29, 39, Aghora Śiva's Comm.

6. The suggested inference is : 'malo jñāna-nivartyo bhavati. ātmakaraṇācchādakatvāt. timiravat, paramārtho malaḥ. malinīkaraṇārthakriyākāritvāt. yathā kāca-timirātmako malo bhramotpādakaḥ.' RT. 236-37 Comm.
7. Ñānaprakāsar's Comm. *op. cit.* p. 2166.
8. Caryā, kriyā, yoga as well as jñāna are alike alleged to be the 'aṅga' of Dīkṣā. *Māpāḍiam*. p. 418.
9. Ñānaprakāsar, *op. cit.* p. 2162 ff.
10. *ibid.* p. 2165.
11. Quoted in Aghora Śiva's Comm. TS. 29.

Dīkṣā is the sixth of the six padārthas recognised in the PA under the title of kāraka : 'bhukti-mukti-vyakti-phalā kriyā *dīkṣā* vyāpāra-ṣaṣṭho'bhidhīyate' 1, 14.

12. SSV, Kriyāpāda, 30, 31. Trilocana Śambhu's Comm.
13. 'poruvil nirvāṇam. aruvahaiyum oruvi ṉinaivaritām parapadattul uyir vṟṟavappāyiṟṟumaṉṟē'. SVP 9.
14. Refutation of Śiva-Samavāda Commentary, p. 155.
15. *Supakkam*, 8.32.
16. *Devīkalottara-Āgama* (Jaffna), verses 14-16.
17. Refutation *loc. cit.*
18. *ibid.* p. 156.
19. *Ante* Ch. 11 Sec. on 'General Conception of Pramāṇa.'
20. "kriyayā hetubhūtatvāt kriyāśaktiś-cid eva yat". RT. 138.
21. Refutation *loc. cit.*
22. For the nature of darkness as substantial, see *Māpāḍiam*. pp. 220-22. Also infra Ch. 15, last section.
23. MK. 70-71, Bhaṭṭa Rāmakaṇṭha is not very specific in his interpretation of netra-paṭala analogy.
24. 'dīyate vimalaṁ jñānaṁ kṣīyate karma-vāsanā tena dīkṣe'ti proktā', see SB. p. 369.
25. *Māpāḍiam*. pp. 28, 29.
26. *ibid.* p. 29.
27. SNP. p. 179.
28. *Supakkam*. 8.10. Śivajñāna Comm.
29. *Māpāḍiam*. p. 30.
30. RT. 236.
31. 'kriyaienamaruvum avai yāvum jñānam kiḍaittarkku *nimittam*'. SVP. 10.
32. All advocates of 'bhakti' specially within the fold of Vedānta argue that jñāna is either the *aṅga* of or only (synonym) for bhakti. See *Śrī-Bhāṣyam*, I.1.1.

    Refer also to SSM 1.4.5. Śivaliṅga Bhūpati's Comm. where a case is made on metaphysical grounds for the primacy of upāsanā over karma and jñāna on grounds that upāsanā overlaps with karma and jñāna but not *vice versa*.
33. See references of Śivadharmottara in *Suppakkam* 8.23 Comm.
34. *ibid.* 8.26, Śivajñāna Comm.
35. TKP. 15.
36. SÑP 11.2. varttikam.
37. This is based on the acceptance of Meykeṇḍār's twelfth sūtra, SÑP as interpreted by Śivajñāna yogin, Periapurāṇam,

incidentally is the twelfth of the 'divine collection' of sacred texts, *Tirumurai.*

38. *Supakkam* 8.26. *op. cit.*
39. The concept of 'tandar' embodies the combination of jñānī and bhakta.
40. *Supakkam* verse 4.
41. 'There is no calling or pursuit which is a private road to the deity.' Bradley, F. H., '*Appearance and Reality*,' Introduction.
42. PA. 1. 7. Also *Muṇḍaka Up.* 1, 1. 4-5 for a similar distinction of para and a-para vidyā.
43. 3.7. Also referred to in Śivajñāna Comm. *Supakkam.* 8.23.
44. The yajñas are (1) Karma-yajña, (2) Tapa-yajña, (3) Japa-yajña, (4) Dhyāna-yajña and (5) Jñāna-yajña, the first four leading to bhoga and the last one leading to mokṣa. *ibid.*
45. The first three too although among the necessary preliminaries for the preceptor-given knowledge, viz. the fourth are useless without it.
46. Cf. how Śivajñāna yogin interprets the instance of the life of the child saint Jñānasambandar. *Māpāḍiam* p. 417.
47. SÑP. 11. Citrurai.

Preliminaries and Accessories to Knowledge

1. By ethical 'discipline' we mean karmas done 'with skill' which makes it yoga (yogaḥ karmasu kauśalam, Gītā. 2.50) leading to *Karma-Sāmya*, and by religious discipline what are called Śiva Puṇyas. See below.
2. The concept of Śaktinipāta provides the key for comprehending the subject of preliminaries of Jñāna.
3. This is understood in a technical sense implying achievement of egolessness, analogous to the egolessness of the jīvan-mukta. See below.
4. The paradox is expressed in the eloquent form of a question by Arunandi to his preceptor Meykeṇḍār, and the answer is also implied by the form of the question : Irupa, 2, lines 19-33.
5. Bhattacharya K. C. : '*Studies in Philosophy*', *op. cit.*, p. 140.
6. *Māpāḍiam* p. 420.
7. For the ontological identity of tirodhāna and anugraha-śakti. See comm. on TP, kārikā pp. 45-46; see also Dasgupta *op. cit.* Vol. V, p. 162.

8. *Māpāḍiam* p. 440.
9. SÑP, 8.1.2.
10. Ñ.25. *Māpāḍiam* p. 424.
11. *Māpāḍiam*, p. 423.
12. Cf. Meykaṇḍār's '*irappil* tavam', SÑP. *op. cit.*
13. *Māpāḍiam*, *op. cit.*
14. Although there is some element of Śiva-puṇya in it unintentionally (abuddhipūrva).
15. The Śaiva saint Sundarar's statement about God feeding him with the admixture of the sweet sugarcane and the bitter neem is cited in *Māpāḍiam* p. 425.
16. See for a classical statement of this thesis, *Bṛhad Up.* passages with the refrain of ātmanas-tu kāmāya II. 4.5.
17. Sambandar implies this distinction between ascesis in the sense of austerity as understood in Jainism or Buddhism and ascesis in the sense of devotion to the Lord (1. 2. 10). To adopt a scheme of fortuons self-discipline is not tapas. What one does spontaneously must itself be transmuted into ascesis. Life itself must be one sustained consecration (3.3.10) Judged by this norm the 'heretics' are unfortunate men being deprived of enjoyment here and the hereafter (1.116.1).
18. *Supakkam* 8.18, 19. See the comms. of Sivajñāna yogin and Sivāgra yogin.
19. *ibid* 8.20.
20. *ibid* 8.21.
21. The difference between tirodhāna śakti and anugraha-śakti is : the first is *progressive revelation*, implying a correspondingly regressive obstruction (revelation being another name for de-obstruction or unveiling); the second one is Revelation as accomplished andfinal implying complete de-obstruction of obstruction *Ante.* Ch. 5.
22. The point to be noted here is : justification of symbolic meaning and of its metaphysical interpretation by the theology which looks upon caryā, kriyā, yoga and jñāna alike as a spectrum of worship. While all of them exemplify the use of religious symbols as evocative in the act worship which is symbolic of praise of the epiphany of the Holy; they are at the same time in the impressive words of Urban 'invocative' calling upon the Divine as a reality

beyond human consciousness Urban, W. H. *Humanity and Deity*, Allen & Unwin London, 1939, third chapter.

23. These are denoted as Pada-mukti, the difference between it and Para-mukti being that it involves a return to the world again (*Supakkam*. 8.25), while in the latter there is no return. Allied with the latter there is another grade of Mukti from which also there is no return, viz. Apara-mukti, the goal of men divested of the three malas but not of the mala-vāsanā.

24. *Māpāḍiam*, p. 422.

The beatitude of love is the exemplar of all joys, because it involves surrender of the objective attitude (or forgetting of objects) Cf. *Bṛhad. Up.* IV. 3.21.

25. The author of ÑVM classifies the internal schools of Śaivism in relation to Śaiva Siddhānta on the basis of the distinction in terms of those accepting padamukti Schools assigned under caryā in yoga, kriyā in yoga and yoga in yoga are distinguished from those assigned under jñāna in yoga. The author reserves the title Śaiva-sāṅkhya-siddhānta-bheda to the latter. The terms karmāvaraṇa and jñānāvaraṇa siddhānta are used to refer to schools assigned under caryā in jñāna, kriyā in jñāna, yoga in jñāna and jñāna in jñāna. The lead for this classification seems to be from *Jñānasiddhi* Āgama from which the author quotes profusely. ÑVM pp. 289 ft.

Karma-sāmya, malaparipāka and Śakti-nipata

1. The ideal of complete detachment from the effects of praise or blame figures in the history of mysticism as a *sine qua non* of mystical illumination. The Spanish Kabbabish Issac of Acre says : "He who is vouchasafed the entry into the mystery of adhesion to God, *devakuth* attains to the mystery of equanimity." Scholer, *Major Trends in Jewish Mysticism* (Schocken Books, New York) p. 96. The following Kabbabstie or sufie anecdote reported by Scholem (p. 97) indicates the significance of the mystery of equanimity "Once upon a time a lover of secret lore came to an anchorite and asked to be admitted as a pupil. Then he said to him : 'my son, your purpose is admirable, but do you possess equanimity or not ? He replied : indeed I feel satisfaction at praise and pain at insult but I am not revengeful and I bear no grudge. Then the master said to him : "my son go back to your home, for as long

as you have no equanimity and can still feel the sting of insult you have not attained to the state where you can connect your thought with God."

2. The Śuddha Śaivas—an internal variety of Śaivism, gives a naive interpretation of the doctrine to which SN. refers and criticises. Among the Śaiva writers themselves Śivāgra yogin holds a view similar to that of the Śuddha Śaiva. SNP. v. 144 Comm.

   PA (4.22-36) gives two main interpretations of this doctrine which Śivajñāna yogin adopts in his Māpāḍiam. pp. 431-32. Aghora Śiva's interpretation (RT.311 Com.), although little different from the Siddhāntins finds dis-favour with Velliambala Tambiran (MNP.).

   The real clue to the interpretation of karma-sāmya comes from our understanding of jīvanmukta in relation to karma. The difference between the sādhaka and the jīvanmukta is only a difference of degree in respect of śaktinipāta.

3. Cf. *Bhagavad-Gītā* XI, 12-19.
4. RT. 311 Aghora Śivas' Comm.
5. *Māpāḍiam* p. 432; see also SÑP pp. 135-136, also SVP, 48 comm. of Madurai Śivappirakasar.
6. The 'two karmās' (iru vinai) in the Meykanda śāstra literature unless otherwise specified refer to mūla karma, or karma understood not as action itself but the accusative of action.
7. *Periapurāṇam* is a collection of biographies of men living in the finite but in virtue of a God-relationship. Ante Ch. 1, Sec. 'Formative Factors'.
8. The function of mala is as the nimitta-kāraṇa of bhoktṛtva. Ante Ch. 10.
9. The impulse to objectification spear-headed by the 'sprout' of karma and strengthened and reinforced by the intervention of māyā constitutes the core of bondage which as it were envelops the self as husk covers the kernel from the very inception. *Ante* Ch. 10 Sec. on 'Arguments for Mala'.
10. Maturation or ripening process is understood on the biological model, of a fruit's transition from its green to ripe condition SB. pp. 365 ff. Stated in mechanical terms the same phenomenon may be explained as a transition from a state which was one of imperviousness to the factors which eventually 'neutralise' the

latent power to a state of yielding to or freely conjoining with them submitting to their influence. *Māpāḍiam* p. 431.

11. The difference that is marked by karma-sāmya in the otherwise even tenor of the Karmic life of self is the abeyance of mala karman allowing no further scope for karma saṁskāras and rendering them ready for final dissipation.

12. The upasarga *ni* brings out the sense of descent or fall appropriate to the cataclysmic nature of its incidence in the even tenor of man's life. Cf. the illustration of stir or excitement that is created by the throw of rocks on an assembly of men. Ñ 69 lines 16-22.

13. The blessedness of Śiva's *manifest* Grace to the 'liberated' is described in picturesque language by Mānikka vācakar in one decad 49, *Tiruvācakam* Cf. 'The perturbations all from blindness spring shall cease—shall it not be' *ibid* 5 line 3, Also Cf. his manner of describing the incidence of śakti-nipāta as the refrain of each verse in the language of conditional :

'If He that cast the net—the woodman come in grace *made manifest to me*'; (1, line 8). 'If He that hath the bull, my Lord whose I am within me shall *entering come*; (2, line 8). 'If God, my own loving Lord *in presence encounter me here*' (3 line 8). 'If Perumān that hath me, the Gracious Lord *come* (or *give this Gracious Presence*)' to (4, line 8).

14. Also 'bhaktiś-ca śivabhakteṣu śraddhācchāsake vidhau anenānumitiś śiṣṭa-hetoḥ sthūla-dhiyāmapi' MA, 5.

Umāpati speaks of spontaneous devoutness and love toward the Lord's devotees as the symptom of the approaching saving event : pp. lines 56, 57.

Knowledge and *Śuddha avasthā*

1. Kevala avasthā is not a state of unrelieved solitude. Admission of sakala and śuddha avasthāṣ as modes of relief shows that absolute solitude is not the ineluctable destiny of the self. 'Revelation' of Śiva from out of His concealment implies the availability of His presence as the priori even during kevala, and its transforming effect on the self, *Māpāḍiam* p. 434.
2. *ibid* p. 388.
3. 'meyññānam *tane* valaiyum.' *Supakkam*. 8.2.1.
4. Āvirbhāva and not avatāra is the mode divine descent, theologically admitted in Śaivism. The hagiologies are theologically speaking

of different genre from the 'histories' (itihāsa) narrating the birth, activities and the *end* of incarnations.

5. SÑP. 8.2, Vārttika and Citrurai. Also *Tiruvācakam* 1. line 46.
5. *ibid.* 8.3.1.
7. Cf. *Bhagavad-Gītā* II. 79.
8. Cf. the distinction that citrurai makes between a state when mala serves as the supporting basis and the one when instead, Śiva serves as the supporting base. Citrurai 8.4 : Hetu : 'when the swing rope is snapped, the ground becomes the mother.'
9. SÑP. 8.4.1.; *Māpāḍiam.* p. 446. The mala-self relation is *sama-vyāpti,* while Śiva-self relation is *vyāpaka-vyāpti.* Dissociation or alienation is possible only with respect to the first relation and not the second.
10. *Supakkam.* 8.38.
11. *Parapakkam*, Pañcuratra-mata-marutaḷai 23.
12. *Māpāḍiam.* p. 448. The knowledge imparted is of the nature of a retrospective awareness of the kevala-sakala complex, on the one side and on the other, the Śuddha, which is a present fact of experience. PP lines 87-89.
13. *Supakkam* 9.2.
14. 'To him who is without He is without; to him who is not without, He is not without. *Irupā* 20 line 2. Arunaudi's reference is to the words of Sambandar, Tiruvālavāi Decad 2 : 'ulakin iyarkai oziṭṭittu *attravarkkatra* Sivan.' The 'worldly-nature' impugned here refers to the attitude of self-assertiveness.
15. *Māpāḍiam.* p. 456.
16. SMKK (Kazakam ed. 1934) p. 102.

Self-Purification (atma-suddhi)

1. *Supakkam.* 8.39; SNP. 9.1, '*ūname*llām oḍa'.
2. SÑP. 9.2, Vārttika ff.
3. 'veṛum *poy*yeṇa', SNP. 9.6.
4. *ibid.* Śiva-jñāna Comm.
5. SÑP. 9.2, the second reading of the Vārttika.
6. *ibid.* 9.2.3; *Srikaṇṭha's Comm.* BS IV. 1.3.
7. *Supakkam.* 9.7; *Srikaṇṭha's Comm.* III. 2.24.
8. Garuḍa in Garuḍa-bhāvanā is only an upalakṣaṇa for all species of life, every form of which according to *Sarvajñānottara Āgama* is a

bearer of divine power that presides over it and is invokable as presence in mantra-śāstra. Even inanimate thing can be the media of divine power :

'sa devāsura-yakṣāṇāṁ kinnarāpsara-rakṣasāṁ pitṛ-mātṛ-gaṇānāṁ tu siddha-vidyādharādiṣu nāga-gandharva-tiryakṣu piśācānāṁ tu mānuṣām śivādau sarva-tattvānāṁ mantra vindanti śāśvataḥ.'

Sarvajñānottara, mantrātma prakaraṇa, 2, 3 Umāpati cites the instance of nakula-bhāvanā meditation of identity with mangoose for the same end in view. TPN, 47.

9. All existence has three levels of being, viz., ādhyātmika, ādhibhautika and ādhidaivika. In the example cited, Garuḍa the bird will be the ādhibhautika Garuḍa, the inspiring deity thereof the form of Garuda-mantra adhidaivika Garuḍa, while the indwelling Śiva-śakti standing 'along side' of the mantra and meting out its results to the māntrika will be ādhyātimika Garuḍa. *Māpādiam*. pp. 462-63.

10. *Supakkam*. 9.7, Śivajñāna yogin's Comm. Pati is 'vyāpaka', Paśu 'vyāpya' and Pāśa 'vyāpti' so that what is logically conceivable is dissociation between Paśu and Pāsa and *not between* Paśu and Pati.

11. *Śruti-Sūkti-Mālā*, v. 135. See Śivaliṅga bhūpati's comm. also.

11a. 'pandai maraihalum adu nāṇānenṛenṛu pāvikkaccholuvathu ippāvakattaik kāṇe'. *Supakkam*. 9.7.

12. *Māpāḍiam*. p. 463.

13. *Supakkam* 9, 8 Sivajñāna yogin's comm.

14. 'nokkitṛai *nokki* niṛkumākalin'. SJB. 9.3.

15. 'anjezuttāl *ānmāvai aranuḍaiya parisum aranuruvum* anjeluttāl *aranudamaiyum* aṛindiṭṭu etc. *Supakkam*. 9.8. See Śivajñāna yogin's alternate interpretation, which is here adopted as being in accord with the accounts given in SVP, and TPN.

16. *Pañcākṣarap pahrodai* (Tiruvaduturai), lines 12, 13.

17. SÑP 9.3. Udāharaṇa, venbas 1 and 2. See citrurai, See below.

18. TVP. 9.4-7. The form in which the mantra is more popularly recited—the one beginning with nakāra, viz., na-maḥ-śi-vā-ya does not have this significance and is therefore meant for a lower stage of sādhana. Śivapāda Sundaram makes out that this form is meant to lead one from worldly to unworldly life and not from unworldliness to Godliness as the mukti-pañcākṣara does. See his '*An Outline of Śiva-jñāna Bodham*' (1951), pp. 45, 46.

19. *Supakkam* 9.8. Śiva-jñāna Comm.
20. TVP. 9.3.
21. 'ma na mihutiyate vāsiyil āsaiyinrikkaruvaliceralālum. SVP. 91; *Supakkam*. 11.88.
21a. 'na mel olittin arulonkum'. SVP. 92.
22. *Supakkam*. 9.8; SÑP. 9.3 udāharaṇa; Kodikkav 4.
23. TVP. 9.7.
24. SÑP *op. cit.* Citrurai on '*kotaṇḍam sāṇikkiīl*'.
25. *Tirumandiram*, v. 2387, 2394, 2403.
26. SÑP. *Pāyiram* 'perumpeyark kaḍavul'. See Citrurai.
27. Śivapāda Sundaram *loc. cit.* pp. 45, 46.
28. 'Yea, closer until all of me worn to an atom, worn to be *no longer I*, was *one* with Thee'—*Tiruvācakam* 22.7.
29. *ibid* 11.18.
30. Cf. Appar's words : '*embirān ennapip pinnaittannuīe karakkumentṛāīl* etc.
31. St. Pattinattar. Tiruvekamba mālai, 10.
32. 'anjezuttāl *ullam aranuḍaimai kaṇḍu*'. SÑP. 9.3.1.
33. 'mattṛatu patṛa utṛu angu īsaṇil ēkamāhum'. SvP. 92.
34. SÑP 9, 3, 2nd. Udāharaṇa.
35. *ibid*, 1st Udaharaṇa : 'anḍanām seḍanām angu.'
36. *Švetāś. Up.* I. 15.
37. *Suppakkam*. 9.10. ff.
38. The meaning of vyāpaka-vyāpya relation is explained in terms of sthāna and sthānī. *Māpāḍiam* p. 155.
39. ulahuḍai nāyanār (11th Tirumurai), cited in *Māpāḍiam* p. 468.
40. For other interpretations of the hṛt-puṇḍarīka and its parts, vide *Māpāḍiam*. pp. 468-69.
41. Uṇmaiviḷakkam, v. 34.
42. For the correlation between pañca-kṛtya symbolised as dance and the recital of pañcākṣara, See *ibid* v. 36 39.

CHAPTER FIFTEEN

SPIRITUAL LIFE AS END : MOKṢA

Recorery of Self : Integration with Siva (Siva-yoga)

1. Meykardari's vārttika. SÑP. 10.
2. *Supakkam* 8, 10; Also SvP 31 : Mikudi sorum.'
3. Ñ 68, line 3.
4. *Tiruvācakam* 1, line 13.
5. The Śaivāgama makes nse of the analogy of rope-snake illusion. *Suprabheda*, Yogapāda-nāḍicakra-vidhi-paṭala. Also PB. p. 519.
6. This underlies Umāpau's preference for the more reverant thou. I, relation of Mukti-pañcākṣara in lieu of the I-Thou relation of the classical pañcākṣara. TPM Sec. 9.
7. *Māpāḍiam* p. 473.
8. 'nānavan endrenninarkku nādumulam undātal tanena ondrin driye tānaduvāi'. SÑP 10, 1, udāharaṇa.
9. For elaboration of the points see Citrurai, SÑP 10, 1.
10. 'Trai paṇi naiṛka' SÑP 10.
11. Umāpati's formulation of this is 'taṇ paṇiyai nīttal', SvP. 84.
12. Ñ 18 lines 37-38.
13. By karma is here meant the taints of āgāmi-karma, sañcita having been destroyed by Dīkṣā and Prārabdha-vāsanā remaining to be 'lived out'. See Cindarai urai, SVP 31.
14. Schomerus, *op. cit.* p. 430.
15. MA 7.4 : pāratantryam bandhatvam.
16. For a discussion of the meaning of 'svātantrya' See, SB 325 ff; SSUM p. 119.
17. SSUM, *ibid*, 120.
18. Sambandar brings out this distinction between the freedom of karma which binds and freedom from karma which liberates. 1.116.1.
19. This question arises because Śiva-yoga implies attainment of Freedom (mokṣa).
20. SÑP. 10.2.1.
21. SRS. p. 18, Umāpati's interpretation of 'Śānta' as rāgadveṣa-rahita brings out this sense.

22. St. Appar asks in the agony of his stomach-pain—which marked his mystical conversion : 'tannai aḍaindār viṇṇai tīrppadandrō talayāyavartam kaḍanā vadu' ?
23. Ante Ch. 5.
24. *Supakkam* 10.2, 4.
25. SÑP. 10.2.3.
26. Meykaṇḍār's phrase. *ibid.*
26a. *ibid.* 10.2.4.
27. Ante Ch. 7, Sec. on God and Absolute.
28. SÑP, 10.2.5.

Recovery of Self : Transcendent Enjoyment of Śiva (Siva-bhoga)

1. The author of *Māpāḍiam* makes this valuable distinction in the context of answering the objection arising from an apparent lack of parity between SÑP nand the Sanskrit version, especially in respect of the 11th sūtra. The issue of non-parity apart, the distinction is in itself valuable and is adopted here.

   Śiva-bhoga in the sense of supernal experience ensues as a consequence and a culmination, union (yoga) typifying complete transparency and total self-giving of the medium in which the supernal principle reveals itself. The ambiguity of the expressions 'siva-yoga' and 'siva-bhoga' without clarity about the senses of the genitive is inherent to the situation. In fact in the cases of 'Śiva-jñāna', 'śiva-yoga' and 'śiva-bhoga', thẹ compound is appositional not genital, as in 'puruṣasya caitanyam', 'Rahu's head'.
2. Cf TVP 8, 2 for the implied distinction.
3. Ante, Ch. 5, Sec. on God as Non-dual.
4. 'arivoli pol' SVP, 7
5. It is in this sense that self figures as the eighth in the eight mūrtis of Śiva (aṣṭamūrti)
6. Śaiva Siddhānta in thus defining the mukti relation between Śiva and self disagrees with systems which conceive it as identity, qualified identity, similarity, simple conjunction etc. The Advaita concept is distinguished from as many as fifteen kinds of identity :
   i. Identity without qualification (nirūpacaritaikya) as between bimba and pratibimba
   ii. Identity through negation (bādhitaikya) as between pillar or port and a person (sthāṇu & puruṣa).

iii. Identity through transformation (pariṇāmaikya) as between gold and its ornaments.

iv. Inseparable identity as between guṇa and guṇin (samavāyaikya), as between nīla and utpala.

v. Identity through combination of complementary characteristics (anyonya-dharmaikya) as between fire and iron.

vi. Identity through conjunction (saṃyogaikya) as between stream and sea.

vii. Identity through beginningless conjunction (anādisaṃyogaikya as between oil and seasamum.

viii. Identity through contemplation of oneness (tādātmyaikya) as between māntrika and garuḍa.

ix. Identity through dissolution (layaikya) as between water and red-hot iron.

x. Identity through 'possession' (āveśaikya) as between a 'possessed' and the spirit possessing.

xi. Identity through non-manifestation (anabhivyaktayaikya as between friction-stick and fire.

xii. Identity through eclipse of śakti (abhibhavaikya) as between a lamp-light and sun-light.

xiii. Identity through common experience of bliss (ānandaikya) as between the beloved and the paramour.

xiv. Identity through mutual *tele* (snehaikya) as between two companions.

xv. Identity through resemblance (sādṛśyaikya) as between 'go' and 'gavaya'. MNP. pp. 77-78; Also *Māpāḍiam*. pp. 471-2.

7. SÑP. 11.1 Vārttika.

8. This aspect of mokṣa experience is unique to Meykaṇḍār's formulation and is brought out most adequately by *Māpāḍiam* pp. 504 ff.

9. Maṛakkiṟppaṇe etc., Appar, Tirukkuṟuntokar 5.93.

10. All these, it must be remembered are features of *para-mukti*. The cognitive active and ecstatic functions are those of spirit and are the components of experience, empirical and transcendental. Their being mediated by psychic functions of buddhi etc., is accidental to the condition of bondage.

The only difference between para-mukti and jīvanmukti in respect of the exercise of the functions—as beautifully described in the 12th Sūtra of SÑP, is : the free self which is embodied is cognitively alert (jñāna) against possibilities of relapse to the condition of bondage through prārabdha-vāsanā, is ecstatic in desiring to mix in the company of the Śiva-bhaktas and is worshipful (kriyā), of Śiva's temple of the bhaktas' outward forms etc. as Śiva Himself. SÑP. 12. 1, 2, 3.

11. The *karaṇa* is also the same in both, viz. śakti. In empirical experience the karaṇa operates 'hidden' while in unitive experience it operates manifest. Only in the latter case the karaṇa becomes merged with the content. In the transition from the sakala to śuddha state of existence, the empirical content is raised to the level of the condition of divine will and in the culminating place of śuddha avasthā the will is merged in being.

12. It may be observed here that this constitutive element of Bliss, viz., self 'knowing' Śiva as the knower of its knowledge, is hidden in bondage and manifest in mokṣa. In fact its hiddenness is itself the bondage and its manifestation is mokṣa. Mala is the principle involved in both. Positively it obstructs Bliss-manifestation and contributes to and constitutes bondage. Negatively, by withdrawal of its screening śakti, it contributes to and constitutes Freedom. See below.

13. Cf. Meykaṇḍār's 'taṇnilalam pati' (9) 'cemmalar nondrāḷ' (12) of SÑP.

14. This is very similar to the concept of receiving revelation in Christian theology which it derives from the doctrine of spirit in the Fourth Gospel. For an analysis of the concept see Tillich, Paul : *Systematic Theology*, Vol. I Harper & Row 1967, pp. 128-129.

15. For this distinctive interpretation of Advaita ante Ch. 5.

16. For the symbolic meaning of experience understood in the context of Spirit , ante Ch. 7, God and Absolute.

17. The term ānanda is therefore understood in the sense of experience of happiness (āhlāda) due to union. The root meaning of the word is : a (prefix)—ṭunadi=nand (root)+ghañ (suffix). Happiness, joy, delight, felicity, bliss is the meaning. Śaiva Siddhānta distinguishes this meaning of the term from two other senses : an intrinsic quality of self like jñāna etc. (Ātmānanda-vāda); a name for the jñāna and icchā of self in their fully manifest form—jñāna-kriyā-samṛddhi (Śivasama-vāda). MNP. p. 70.

18. Sat-cit-ānanda is the definition of Śiva (Saccidānanda-*rūpī* yaḥ, *Kāmikāgama*, cited MNP. p. 85). The term sat though common to pati, paśu and pāśa denotes pāśa as implying the characteristic of mere subsistance; similarly, Sat and Cit though common to paśu and pati denote paśu as implying subsistance and sentience; Sat, Cit *and ānanda* define exclusively pati. *ibid.* p. 74.
19. '*Uṇmai Viḷakkam*', v. 29; the Tamil word used is *viḷaivittal*—causative verb. In the Bound state also mala-function is chatacteristically indicated by causative verb (anniyamanavai *unartti,* literally *causing* objective experience—SVP 24) Bondage too, Mala constitutes, by being the occasioner (nimitta) of 'bhoktṛtva' The latter is what sustains phenomenal life constituting its core, while at the same time being only an external shell of self which is cit. Cf. the example of husk in relation to rice. In Mokṣa too Mala may be conceived in an inverse sense the extraneous 'occasioner' of Experience.
20. Cf. Ch. VI Sec. on God as the inner Illuminer of Experience, note no. 48.
21. That mala is an immutable (kūṭastha) of the nature analogous to that of spirit is the Śaivagama doctrine TS 28, Comm.
22. For the understanding of mala as the implied presupposition of the distinction between bondage and liberation, ante Ch. 10 Sec. on Argument for Mala.
23. *Supakkam* 11.5 .
24. This is a problem for all those who admit a plurality of individual selves.
25. TVP. 2.1.
26. *Ante* Ch. 9 Sec. on Māyīya. Evolution of Vidyā and Ātma-tattvas.
27. *Māpāḍiam*, p. 390.
28. For a systematic approach to this problem, along the lines developed here, See *Siddhānta-nicchayam* of Tirunavukkarasm-desika; ed. Muthuttandavarāya Pillai, 1928.
29. Umāpati's illustration of light and darkness expressly bears this significance PP lines 77-78; SVP 88, 89; Also *Supakkam* 11, 4.
30. *Siddhānta-nicchayam*, *op. cit.* v. 53-57.
31. *ibid.* v. 95. 'abhibhava' (as in āvaraṇ*ābhibhavā*rtta-vṛtti) is making nothing rather than destroying or doing away with; nihilation rather than annihilation. The corresponding usage in Tamil of

the negative is not without its foundation in the language e.g. to *be* nothing ('indrāi') or 'is not'; allavāi (to be not is to be other than), reminscential of the contemporary existentialist's notion of nichtet (Heidegger) and neantise (Sartre).

32. The paradox of 'eternal newness' is expressed in a variety of ways in the Śaiva hymns. The citation given below stated in the language of untranslatable sexual ecstasy is typical :

 puṇarndārp puṇarumtorum perumbogam *pīnnum puditāy*
 maṇantāz alkul pōla *valarhindrade Tirukkovaiyār*, 9.

 The sense of the paradox which, incidentally, is a striking feature of mystical experience, can be understood with the help of Kierkegaards 'repetition' as what is recollected forwards in contradistinction to Plato's 'recollection'. The latter view is that ontologically but there is no novelty but is essentially the old and the pre-existing, obscured momentarily by forgetfulness but essentially present to the exclusion of real novelty. In 'repetition' there is an element of the pre-existing but there is also an eqally present element of the new, the creative and the spontaneous.

 Cf. also Kierkegaard's remarks about 'persistent striving' and 'Systematic finality'. He says that the ideal of a persistent striving is the only view of life that does not carry with it an inevitable disillusionment. 'Even if a man has attained to the highest, the repetition by which life receives it content will again constitute a persistent striving because here again finality is moved further on and postponed. It is with this view of life as it is with the Platonic interpretation of love as a want and the principle that not only he is in want who desires something he does not have but also he who desires the continued possession of what he has'.

 Cf. also Augustine's comments on the Psalm "Seek His face evermore" and "And thus he who is loved is sought even when present, while there is constant charity, which busies itself that he never become absent......" The meaning is that finding should not end that seeking by which love is testified, but with the increase of love the seeking of the found one should increase.' *Enarrationes in Psalmos* in PS CIV, 3.

33. Cf. Tiruvācakam 1, line 44 : 'More subtle than fragrance.'

34. *ante* Note No. 32.

GLOSSARY OF TECHNICAL TERMS

abādhita-jñāna, non-contradicted knowledge.

abādhitatva-pramā, uncontradicted true knowledge.

abhavat, became.

abhāva, privation, non-existence, negation.

abhāva-jñāna, the knowledge of absence.

abhāva-kūṭa, conjunction of specific absences.

abhāvārtha, privative or negative sense.

abheda, identity, non-difference.

abheda-graha, apprehension of non-difference.

abheda-śruti, identity text of the Veda.

abhidhya, volition.

abhilāpa, expression, name, label.

abhinna-nimittopādāna-kāraṇa, material-cum-efficient cause.

abhiniveśa, identification.

abhivyakti, manifestation.

abrāhmaṇaḥ, the brahmin-like but different from the brahmin.

acetana, non-intelligent, non-conscious.

acintyatva, incomprehensibility.

acit, non-intelligent, non-spirit.

ādhāra, ground, base.

a-dharma, opposite of value, dis-value, the negative ought.

adharma, a disposition of intellect implying towards demerit due to preponderance of dense nature.

ādheya, the grounded, the consequent.

adhikāra, competence, office, assuming of office.

adhikāra-muktas, The liberated who still have the limitation of office.

adhikaraṇa, ground.

adhiṣṭhāna, the ground, the indwelling intelligence.

adhiṣṭheya, that which is grounded, the consequent.

adhiṣṭhita, 'activated or founded.

adhomāyā, aśuddha-māyā.

adhvamūrti, of the form of the adhvan.

adhvan, pathways.

adhva-śuddhi, ritualistic purification of adhva.

ahita, the wrong.

adhyāsa, false superimposition, illusion.

ādi-śakti, ādya-śakti, the prevenient śakti or power presupposed in any exercise of śakti.

adṛṣṭa, the unseen potency, the supersensible disposition.

adṛśya, not perceived or cognised.

advaita, nonduality, secondless.

advitīya, the non-dual, or secondless.

Āgama, Scripture, Special Revelation.

Āgama-mīmāṁsā, hermeneutics or exegesis of the Āgama.

āgamānumāna, scriptural inference.

āgama-pramāṇa, Testimony as the means of knowledge.

āgāmi-karma, the on-coming deed, karma that is being earned for future experience, the prospective karma.

āgāmi-vāsanā, traces of the freshly eked out karma arising on the wake of the lingering of the already begun karma (prārabdha vāsanā, rendered infructuous in the face of the dawning of saving knowledge.

āgantuka, adventitious, the non-intrinsic, conditioned.

āgantuka-malas, 'consequential' bonds, (māyā and karma).

āgantutatva, adventitiousness conditionedness.

agraha, non-perception.

aham, the I or the me.

aham ajñaḥ, 'I am ignorant', 'I do not know'.

ahaṁ brahmāsmi, 'I am Brahman'.

ahaṁ jānāmi, 'I know'.

ahaṁkāra, ego-sense entailing subjective resolve; the 'I' that is asserted in all assertions.

ahaṁ-padārtha-rūpa, of the form and substance of I.

ahaṁ sukhī, I am happy.

aikṣata, having the insight, willing.

aikya, identity, union.

aikya-vāda-śaiva, Internal sect of Saivism advocating union in mukti.

aindrika, of the sense.

aiśvarya, a disposition of intellect implying plenitude due to the preponderance of luminous nature.

aja, uncaused, unborn.

ajaḍa, non-material.

ajña, command or will.
ajñāna, non-knowledge, Ignorance.
akala, formless.
ākāśa, ether.

akhaṇḍa, impartite, infinite.
akhaṇḍārthavākya, identity-judgements of the Veda.
akhyāti, non-knowledge, no-erroneous-knowledge.
akhyāti-vāda, the theory of non-knowledge of 'error'.
akṣara, the immutable, alphabet.
akṣara-bindu or bindu, intermediary form of (pure) speech.
alaukika-pratyakṣa, extra-ordinary perception.
āma, green, unripe, immature.
anādi-bodha, eternally omniscient, the unconditionally intelligent.
anaiśvarya, a disposition of intellect implying impoverishment due to the preponderance of dense or dark nature.
ānanda, Bliss, perfection.
ānanda-prakāśatva, non-manifestness of bliss.
ānanda-rūpa, Being of the nature of Bliss (rather than having or experiencing bliss).
Ananta, the representative agent of cosmic functions, a nature soul of the class which is free from all but the bond of office.
ananya-sākṣātkāra, non-dual intuition, non-separate immediacy.
ananya-tādātmya, inseparable relation of identity.
ananyatva, non-difference, identity.
anaśva, 'non-horse', the mule.
āṇava-mala, the spiritual impurity, the monadising Dirt.
aṇḍa, macroscosm, cosmos.
aneka, multiple, the non-one, the non-single.
anekānta, the non-unitary or manifold nature, diverse.
anekānta pakṣa, Non-absolutism, Relativism.
anekatva, plurality or not being an unity.
aṅga, part, auxilary.
aṅgī, whole.

animitta, uncaused, the unoccasioned.
animitta-vāda, Accidentalism.
anirvacanīya, the indeterminable, indefinable.
anirvacanīya-khyāti, theory of error as the indeterminable.
antaryāga-pūjā, internal worship, where the ritual is interiorized.

anubhava, personal or individual experience, participative experience.

anubhava-*jñāna*, knowledge by being, knowing by participation or union, experimental knowledge.

anubandha, what accompanies, the bond of karma.

anubhayātmaka, neither as cause nor as an effect.

anugraha, Grace.

anugraha-śakti, the power of revelatory Grace.

anumiti, inferential cognition.

anupalabdhi, non-cognition.

anusyūta, indwelling, the underlying.

anuvyavasāya, second order cognition, knowledge of knowledge.

anuvyavasāya-jñāna, cognition of cognition.

anuyogī, locus of negation.

anuyogitva, correlateness of negation.

anya, the other, different.

anyathā-khyāti-vāda, theory of knowledge of error as mis-relation.

anyathāsiddhatva, nonestablishment otherwise.

anyonyābhāva, mutual absence, reciprocal negation, difference.

apara-jñāna, penultimate knowledge, 'mediate' knowledge.

apara-mukta, the non-ultimately liberated.

apariṇāmī, immutable, the non-transformable.

aparokṣa, immediate.

apavarga, emancipation.

aprakāśa, non-luminous, opaque.

aprakāśatva, non-manifestness.

aprakāśīkaraṇa, condition of non-illumination.

apramā, non-valid knowledge.

apramātva, erroneousness, the non-trueness of non-true knowledge.

aprāmāṇyābhāva, absence of invalidity.

aprāmāṇyasya parato grāhyam, non-validity of non-valid knowledge is apprehended 'extrinsically'.

apratigata-svecchā, unrestrained will unobstructed or unthwarted volition.

apratigata-svecchānuvartitva, freedom, conformity with one's own unrestrained will, free unhindered compliance with one's own will.

apūrva-pariṇāma, transformation of a unique kind.

ārambha, beginning, creation, construction, origination.

ārambha-vāda, theory of new creation, or construction.

āropita, imagined, feigned.

artha, sense, meaning.

arthāpatti, implication, presumptic proof.

artha-prapañca, the 'spoken' world, the world of meaning intended by intelligence.

asādhāraṇa-dharma, the non-generic, or specific character, the differentia.

asad-vyāvṛtti, negation of non-being.

asahāya, unsupported, unaided.

āṣakti, desire, craving.

asambhava, error of impossibility.

asaṁvidātmaka, the non-intelligent, of the nature of non-conscious.

aśarīri, bodiless, incorporeal.

asat, object, unreal, non-existent, non-being, phenomenal, objective existent.

asatkārya-vāda, theory of previous non-existence of effect.

asat-khyāti, perception of the non-real.

asatsamāna, non-existent.

asi, you are.

asmi, I am.

asmitā' I-amness, egoity.

āśrayā' siddhi, the fallacy of uncertainty about subject (minor term).

asti, Being.

āstika, one who affirms,the believer, orthodox Hindu systems of Philosophy.

aśuddha, the impure.

aśuddhādhvan, the Impure adhvan or stratum of cosmos.

aśuddha-māyā, material cause of the impure order of creation.

aśvamedha, horse-sacrifice.

asvatantra, unfree.

atadrūpa-pratiṣṭhita, perceiving a thing as what it is not.

atiśaya, supplementation.

atisūkṣma-karma, primordial appetitive and averse predispositions by whose dynamics one in the course of experiencing the fruits of previous karma comes to acquire a fresh stream of karma. Synonymous with mūla karma.

ativyāpti, over pervasion, the fallacy of too wide a definition.

ātma-cit-śākti, The conscious power of the self; the means and method of knowledge.

ātma-darśana, self-insight.
ātma-guṇas, the qualities intrinsic to self.
ātma-khyāti, theory of error as knowledge of the other.
ātmakṛteḥ, self's activity, action predicated in apposition to self.
ātma-lābha, recovery of authentic self.
ātman, spirit, self.
ātma-rūpa, self-understanding.
ātma-tattva, the principle of self.
atra ghaṭatvam, here is the pot-universal.
attā, eater.
atyantābhāva, absence which is constant, the total negation.
atyantābheda-vāda, the theory of absolute non-difference.
atyanta-bheda-vada, theory of absolute difference.
avacchedaka, determinant, limitor.
avacchedakatā, the quality of 'defining characteristics' of being the limitor.
avacchedaka-sambandha, determining relation, the relation of limitor-limiting.
avacchinna, determined, the limited.
avadhāraṇa-varjita, lacking in decision, unconclusive.
avairāgya, a disposition of intellect toward attachment.
avāntara-pralaya, periodic dissolution intermediary deluge.
āvaraṇa, veil, screen, obstruction, arrest.
avasthā, state of consciousness.
avasthā-viśeṣa, change of form of state without change of substance.
avayava, part, organ, limb.
avayavī, composite, whole, organism.
avidyā, non-knowledge, ignorance.
avinābhāva, inseparable existence.
avināśī, non-terminable.
avyabhicāritva, non-presence of the one without the other, literally absence of promiscuity.
avyāpya-vṛtti-saṁyoga, partial conjunction.
ayam, this (third person).
ayathārtha-smṛti, erroneous memory.
bādha, cancellation, contradiction.
bādha-jñāna, contradictory knowledge.
bādhaka, obstruction.
bādhakābhāva, absence of contradiction, the unobstructed.

bādha-pratyakṣa, perception of contradiction.

bhakta, devotee.

bhakti, devotion.

bhakti-mārga, path of love.

bhautika, the elemental, of the material elements.

bhāva, existence, affirmation being, a positive factor.

Bhava, Being, a descriptive epithet of God.

bhāvanā, mediation, contemplation.

bhāvas, dispositions (of intellect).

bhāva-kārya, positive effect.

bhāva-rūpa-ajñāna, a positive Ignorance.

bheda, difference.

bhedābheda, identity in difference.

bhedāgraha, non-apprehension of difference.

bhoga, enjoyment, enjoyment and suffering experience, empirical experience.

bhogya, the acculature of the experience of pleasure and pain phenomena, object of experience.

bhogya-bhoktṛ-bhāva, enjoyer-enjoyed relationship.

bhogya-khaṇḍa, the group of reals, representing in general the sphere of the objective.

bhojaka, determinant of experience, what lets experience to take place.

bhoktṛ, bhoktā, the experiencing self, the experient self.

bhojayitṛ, what is generative of experience for the self, the generating principles underlying sentient and cognitive experience.

bhojayitṛ-khaṇḍa, experience-generating group.

bhoktṛtva, experiencership, sense of mine.

bhrānti-vasanā, impression of delusion.

bhūtādi, a variety of ego-sense.

bhūta-yoni, birth-place of the elements.

bhuvanas, the worlds.

bindu, root matter, the pure counterpart of māyā, latent essence. The point devoid of dimensions.

bodha, knowledge, consciousness, exegetic evaluation.

brahman, spirit.

brahma-pariṇāma-vāda, theory of transformation of Brahman.

brahma-yoni, birth place of the creator of the world-soul.

buddhi, intellect.

buddhi-guṇa, quality of intellect.

buddhi-tattva, the principle of intellect.

buddhi-vṛtti, intellect, mode of the intellect, the knowing act.

caitanya, spirit. intelligence, knowledge, consciousness.

caryā, external worship.

cidantarāpekṣā, requiring the help of another spirit.

cid-rūpa, form of knowledge.

cit, consciousness per se, spirit,

cit-karma, intelligent, action.

cit-śakti, conscious power, Grace intelligent will, dynamic self's consciousness, intellect consciousness.

dāna, gift.

daṇḍa, stick.

daṇḍin, one with the stick.

darśana, discriminative insight.

daśa-kārya, ten acts or deeds, the ten stages of knowledge.

darśana, discriminatory wisdom, self's insight or vision quickened by a sense of contrast.

dehātma-bhrama, the illusion of viewing body as the soul.

dehi-paśu, spirit dwelling within the gross body is paśu.

dhārāvāhika-jñāna, persistent or non-discret cognition.

dharma, a disposition of intellect toward merit due to preponderance of luminous nature, form, attribute, quality, essence, value (conceivable) predicate property, good predicative element, dutiful.

dharmin, subject of predicate, substance, substrate, thing, qualificand.

dharmi-jñāna, cognition of 'that'.

dhvani, overt sound, the audible sound.

dīkṣā, initiation.

doṣa, defect.

dravya, substance.

dravyatva, substantiality substanceness.

dṛkkriyā-śakti, the power of knowledge and action (inherent to the nature of self as spirit).

dṛṣṭānta, illustrative instance.

dṛṣṭa-sādhanā, pertaining to the seen or the seeable.

dṛśya, cognised, the seen objective.

duḥkha, pain, sorrow.

dveṣa, aversion.

dvitvābhāva, two-less-ness.

ekadeśa, partial, finite.

ekākṣara, one-letter mantra form of pañcākṣara.

ekam, the one, secondless Being.

ekam eva, one only, absolute unity.

ekārtha-samaveta, qualified by existence.

ekātma-vāda, monistic theory.

guṇa-tattva, the principle of material constituent.

hetu, reason; the middle term of an inference.

hṛt-puṇḍarīka, the heart-lotus; one's heart contemplated as the sanctum for invoking the presence of the deity.

jaḍa, non-intelligent, inert, inane, material, objective.

jaḍatva, inertness, materiality or not being spirit.

jagad-bīja, the world's-seed, the embryoonic form of the cosmos.

jīvanmukta, the one who is liberated while living.

jñāna, knowledge, consciousness, any cognitive function like remembrance, recognition and even volition.

jñānābhāva, negation or absence of knowledge.

jñāna-kriyātmaka, cognitive as well as conative, of the nature of knowledge and action.

jñāna-mārga, path of knowledge, discipline of the gnostic.

jñāna-mātra, Intuition *per se*.

jñāna-naṭana, dance of wisdom, dance symbolising inculcation of knowledge.

jñāna-pāda, knowledge-section of the Śaivāgama.

jñāna-pūjā, worship by knowledge; knowledge itself imaged as an act of worship.

jñāna-śakti, power of intelligence, the intelligence-potential of the intelligent.

jñānāvaraṇa, the knowledge tradition.

jñānaviṣayatvena grahaṇam, knowing expressly as not the content of a cognition.

jñāna-viṣayatvena grahaṇe grahaṇam, what is not apprehended as the content of cognition.

jñāna-viśeṣābhava, absence of some knowledge.

jñāna-yajña, the sacrificial act of knowledge; knowledge itself conceived as a ritualistic act.

jñānendriyas, sense organs, the sensorium.

jñānī, one possessing true knowledge.

jñāpaka-hetu, cause cognoscendi, cause of one's knowledge of things.

jñāpaka-śaktis, informative causal potencies, powers causative of knowledge of things.

jñāpanā, revelation of knowledge, what facilitates knowledge of the knower.

jñapti, intuition, immediate knowledge.

jñātā, knowing subject, self which intuits.

jñātam, 'belief'.

jñātatā, knownness in the knowledge of the knower.

jñātṛtva, knowership.

jñeya, the known, the accusative of intuition.

ñeyam, (Tamil, negam), the Given in Intuition, what is non-discursively revealed.

ñeya-viśeṣa, species of what is known.

kādācitkatva, the occurrent character, contingency.

kaivalya, emancipation.

kāla-kāla, Death of death itself, the end of that that ends all things.

kāla-tattva, the principle of time.

kāla, particle, the principle (tattva) that is generative of finite experience, one of the six strata (adhvan) of cosmos, structured as five-fold comprehending the sphere of tattvas from pṛthvī to Śiva.

kāma, desire.

kāmya-karma, optional duty.

kañcuka, permanent vesture, invariable vesture.

karaṇa, special cause, specific means, chief means, operative cause.

kāraṇa, cause, causal entity, causal function or power, operative condition, condition.

karaṇa-liṅgānumāna, (inference) from the perceived cause to the imperceived effect.

kāraṇatā, cause-ness, character of being cause.

kāraṇatva, instrumentality, causal condition.

karaṇa-doṣa, causal defect.

karaṇa-guṇa, specific excellence, causal condition.

kariṣyāmi, let me create or create.

karman, accusative, the action.

karma, moral law, pleasure-pain-torpid experiences agency.

karma-śaktis, productive causal potencies.

karma-sāmya, the ever balancing meritorious and unmeritorious karma.

karmendriyas, the motorium, motor organs.

kartṛ, *kartā*, agent, causal agent, agent of actions, subject, the nominative, a kāraka.

kartṛ-preryatva, being controlled by some agency.

kartavya-śakti, the power of action or agency (cognate with the power of knowledge).

kartṛtva, causal agenthood, agency,sense of I, in relation to 'I do'.

kārya, effect, product.

kārya-liṅgānumāna, (inference) from the perceived effect to the unperceived cause.

kārya-mātra-vṛtti-dharma, the property of being 'only effect'.

kārya-pravartana, action of self.

kāryatā, effecthood, effectness, nāture or character of effect.

kāryatāvācchedaka, limitor or determinant of being effect.

kāryatāvacchedakatva, being determinant of effectness.

kārya-vṛttitva, originatedness.

kāryonmukha, orientation toward the effect.

kevala, being alone, solitude, isolation.

kevalādvaita, rigorous unity, pure monism, nonduality of pure Being.

kevala-avasthā, pre-biographical or pre-transmigratory state of isolation, state of consciousness characterised by ignorance due to impurity and a consequent aloofness or solitude.

kevala-nimitta, mere efficient causality.

kleśas, hindrances, impurities.

kriyā, action, act.

kriyā-pāda, ritual section of the Āgama.

kriyā-śaiva, activist.

kriyā-śakti, *kartṛ-śakti*, creative power, the active potential of spirit.

kṣaṇika-vāda, theory of momentariness.

kṣaya, loss, destruction.

kṣobha, stirring in the equilibrium.

kṣobhya, the stirred, the accusative of the act of stirring.

lāghava, parsimony, occam's razor.

lakṣanā, definition, defining characteristic.
laya, identity, resolution, absorption.
layādhiṣṭhāna, the ground of resolution.
liṅga, sign.
mahābhūtas, gross elements.
mahāgrāsa, the Great Devourer.
mahā-suṣupti, cosmic night.
maheśvara, primarily the name of one of the functional aspects of the Agent and also the name of one of the śiva-tattvas which are 'evolutes' of Bindu.
mala, impurity *per se*, fallenness, impurity of spirit, bond.
mala-paripāka, ripening of impurities in readiness for dissipation.
mala-śakti, power of veiling multiple in kind in answer to multiple number of individual selves.
manana, reflection, cogitation.
manas, mind.
mānasa-jñana, mental cognition.
mantra, incantation, the mystic formula that is recited.
mantra-śakti, the power due to the inspiring divinity of the syllables recited to invoke it.
māntrika, recitor, the person who incants.
mātṛ, the knower or knowing subject.
māyā, the material substratum of the cosmos existing as the accusative of the willing agent, the deluding medium.
māyā-vāda, A cosmistic pantheism, the theory according to which the world is illusion.
māyeya, material locus, phenomena, not-self.
māyika, of material nature.
māyīya, the evolutes of māyā; the sphere of the tattvas.
meya, the known object, object of knowledge.
miśrādhavan, the cosmic sphere showing an admixture of impurity of Bonds and purity of freedom from Bonds.
mithyā, appearance, the false, the unreal with pretensions to reality.
moha, illusion, delusion, affective insensibility.
mokṣa, transcending of bonds, liberation, freedom.
mokṣa-sādhanā, disciplines preparatory for the attainment of liberation.
mukhya, the chief, primary.
mukta, the liberated man.

mūrtatva, possessing magnitude.
nāda, evolute of Bindu, the primordial speech.
nāma, name, appellation.
nañ, negative particle, with a spectrum of senses ranging from the wholly negative to the wholly positive.
nāsti, 'it is not'.
nāsti na prakāśate, it is not and it is not manifest.
nāstika, one who says 'no', the unbeliever, the heretic or the heterodox.
nedaṁ rajatam, this is not silver or this is non-silver.
netra-paṭala, cataract in the eye.
nidbidhyāsana, contemplation, intuitive realization.
nimitta, the occasioning factor.
nimitta-kāraṇa, efficient cause, ground.
nimitta-kāraṇatva, efficient causality, will causality.
nimittakāraṇa-vāda, theory acknowledging an efficient cause.
niradhikaraṇa-dīkṣā, Initiation rite performed with no accessory or ritualistic medium.
nirdharmaka, devoid of qualities.
nirūpaka, the determinant, or describer.
nirūpita, determinate, described.
nirvāṇa, transcendent freedom.
nirvāṇa-dīkṣā, highest kind of initiation, symbolic of the inculcation of saving knowledge.
nirvikalpaka-jñāna, indeterminate knowledge.
nirvikāra, unchanging, immutable.
nirvikāra-śruti, texts affirming immutability of spirit.
nirviśeṣa, devoid of character relationless.
nirviśeṣa-brahman, Pure Being.
niṣkala, non-visible, formless.
nitya, eternal.
nitya-karma, daily duty.
nitya-tṛptatva, plenitude and perfection aseity.
nivṛtti, removal, cessation, recoil from exertion, 'orient' activity towards the non-desired.
niyamana, to manifest it into being.
niyata-pūrva-vṛttitva, invariable precedence.
niyati, the principle of determination of karma.

odana, food.

pāka, ripeness.

pakṣa, The subject or position, also the minor term of an inference.

pakṣa-dharmatā-jñāna, knowledge of an occurrence in the minor term.

pañca-kṛtya, the five cosmic functions of God.

pañcākṣara, the incantation of five letters for meditation and knowledge of God.

pañcīkaraṇa, the quintuplication of the different elements.

paṅkaja, lotus.

pāpa, demerit.

para-jñāna, ultimate knowledge.

paramādhāra, the transcendent ground.

paramaṁ jñeyam, the supreme object, the Given.

paramāṇus, Primal Atoms.

parāmarśa, reflexion.

parāmarśa-jñāna, knowledge of the middle term.

parama-sukha, Supreme Bliss.

paramātman, Supreme Self.

parameśvara, Great Lord.

parā mukti, ultimate release, not a mere state, but beyond all states.

parānapekṣatva, independence of will; non-dependence on the other.

parāpreryatva, uncontrolled by another.

parā-śakti, Knowledge per se, Revelation per se.

para-śarīra, inmost body.

parataḥ prāmāṇya, extrinsic apprehension of truth.

parataḥ prāmāṇya-vāda, advocacy of non self-evidential theory of Knowledge.

paratastva, extrinsicality.

parā vāc, transcendental speech, ultimate source of the denoting capacity of speech.

pravṛttana, to sustain its function.

pāribhāṣika, terminological.

parigraha-śakti, the assumptive power.

pariṇāma, evolution, transformation.

pariṇāma, change, transformation.

pariṇāma-tāratamya, configuration of minuteness.

pariṇāma-vāda, transformation theory, theory of self-becoming.

paripāka, maturing.

parokṣa, non-perceptible.

parvata-niṣṭhādhikaraṇatā, the locus resident in mountain.

paryāya, change.

pāśa, bondage, the world, known object, primary Bond.

pāśa-jñāna, empirical knowledge, knowledge that is due to the mediation by the not-self, knowledge which is motor-ridden.

pāśa-kṣaya, wearing out or destruction of pāśa.

paśu, creature, finite creature self, finite man or self, knowing subject.

paśu-bhāvana, condition of paśu.

paśu-jñāna, self-knowledge, the knowledge that is intrinsic to self.

paśu-pati, Lord of the Bound, Lord of the Creature.

paśu-puṇya, acts of merit directed towards a finite self.

paśutva, man's finitude.

paśyantī vāc, the speech-form with the impulsion to concretise into the overt and the empirical, looking for (literally).

paṭala, film.

pati, Lord, Sovereign Spirit of Being. ruler, God, moral governor.

pati-jñāna, knowledge of spirit, saving knowledge, divine knowledge.

patitva, Lordship, sovereignty.

phala, fruit, consequences, spiritual Fruit, object.

phala-niyata-vyāpāra, a function leading invariably to a result, a function issuing necessarily in a result.

phalopadāyaka, causative.

piṇḍa, microcosm.

pradhāna, pre-eminent.

prādhānya-jñāpanārtha, suggestion of pre-eminence.

prajñānaṁ brahma, Intelligence is Brahman.

prakāra, mode, 'what'.

prakārin, substance.

prakāśa, manifestness.

prakāśātmaka, manifestness.

prakāśatva, luminosity.

prākaṭya, manifestedness.

prakṛti, material cause, unmanifest nature, the object.

prakṛti-tattva, the principle of material nature.

pralaya, dissolution.

pralayākala, classes of selves in whose case the material manifestors of experience have been destroyed during world-dissolution.

pramā, valid knowledge.

pramātā, perceiver of valid knowledge.

pramāṇa, validation, the acknowledged means of valid knowledge, means of knowledge, means of valid knowledge.

prāmāṇya, validity.

prāmāṇyaṁ svataḥ, validity is self-apprehended.

prāmāṇyaṁ svato grahyam, self-apprehension of validity.

pramātva, validity.

prameya, object of knowledge, world experientially known, object.

pramiti, valid knowledge, right knowledge.

pramiti-sādhana, the avenue of valid knowledge.

pramuṣṭa-tattāka-smaraṇa, a case of memory not aware of itself as memory.

prāṇa-vāyu, vital-air.

prāpyakāri, sensory function as pervasion of the object sensed.

prārabdha-karma, karma, which has already begun to bear fruit.

prārabdhānubhava, experience due to the deed that has already begun to bear fruit.

pratibandha, obstruction.

pratibandhaka, counteracting, counteracting factor.

prātibhāsika, illusory.

pratīti, 'givenness'.

pratiyogin, the thing negated, the absent, counter-correlate.

pratiyogi-jñāna, knowledge of the presence.

pratyakṣa, perceptual knowledge.

pratyaya, determination.

pravṛtti, affirmation, exertion, 'adient' activity in respect of the desired, activity

prayojaka-prayukta, intention-intended.

preraka, initiator.

preraka-khaṇḍa, activating group, the directing complex of tattvas.

prerya, directed.

priya, endearing.

pṛthvī, earth element.

pūjā-sthāna, sanctum of worship.

puṁstva-mala, human impurity.

punas-sṛṣṭi, re-creation.

puṇya, merit.
puruṣa, world-soul, agent-self, the experient self, agent of experience
pūrvapakṣa, first view.
puryāṣṭaka, incorporeal body.
puryāṣṭaka-deha, the individual 'physical' vehicle of experience.
puttika, plant.
rāga, the principle of attachment or set for experience, desire, attachment.
rāga-tattva, the principle of attraction.
rajas, a quality of drive underlying quickness and immediacy of comprehension, and a sense of appropriation typifies the quality of dynamist in personality.
śabda, word, speech, word-form.
śabda-bodha, verbal knowledge.
śabda-pramā, valid verbal knowledge.
śabda-pramāṇa, verbal testimony.
śabda-prapañca, world of speech.
sac ca tyac ca abhavat, It became both the visible (actual) and the non-visible (beyond).
sad-asat, being and non-being.
sadāśiva, primarily the name of one of the functional aspects of the Agent and also the name of one of the five siva-tattvas which are 'evolutes' of Bindu.
sādhaka, the aspirant for salvation who is on way to realization of the goal.
sādhakatama, par excellence.
sādhana, means.
sādhanā, spiritual discipline.
sādhana-bhakti, devotion characteristic of those who are on the path towards the goal.
sādhana-sāmagrī, the causal assemblage.
sādhya, major term.
sādhya-bhakti, devotion characteristic of those who have attained the goal.
sahája-mala, primordial bond.
sahakārin, instrument, auxilary, necessary condition.
sahakāri-kāraṇa, instrumental cause.
śāivāgama, revelation.

sajātīya-dvitīya-vastu-rahita, no second to Him or His class.
sakala, visible form.
sakala-avasthā, active life,
sakala-niṣkala, visible cum non-visible form.
sākṣāt-kartṛtva, direct agency.
sākṣāt sambandha, direct relation.
sākṣin, transcendental consciousness.
sākṣi-caitanya, witness-consciousness.
sākṣi-grāhya, what which is apprehended by witness-consciousness.
sākṣi-jñāna, transcendental consciousness, transcendental intuition.
śakti, Divine Will, power, Divine Function, primarily the name of one of the functional aspects of the Agent and also the name of one of the five śiva-tattvas which are 'evolutes' of Bindu, immutable will, faculty, potency.
śaktimat, the possessor of śakti.
śaktimattantratvam, ontological dependence on spirit.
śakti-nipāta, descent of Divine Power marking the advent of the instructive phase of Grace.
śakti-saṁkalpa, function of will.
sālokya, a state of liberation marked by entry into the world of God.
samādhi, total absorption.
sāmānādhikaraṇya, co-ordinate equivalence.
sāmānādhikaraṇya-nirdeśa, language of co-ordinate equivalence.
samanidhatva, coincidence, concurrence.
sāmānya, universal.
sāmānyābhāva, generic absence.
sāmānyato-dṛstānumāna, 'analogical' inference, inference based on the observation of the universal.
sāmānyato-dṛṣta-sādhana, what is unseen and yet may be conceived on similarity.
samatva, equality.
samavāya, co-inherence, inherence.
samavāyi-kāraṇa, inhering cause.
samavedya, co-inherence, identity.
samaveta, integral.
samayogācāryas, founders of Śaivism.
sambandha, relation.
saṁhāra, dissolution , world dissolution.

sāmīpya, a state of liberation marked by an attainment of the proximity to God.
saṁkalpa, will.
saṁkoca, retraction or inwardisation,
saṁkrānta, transmutation.
saṁsargābhāva, relational absence.
saṁsargārthaka, relational judgements.
saṁśaya, doubt.
saṁskāra, residual impressions.
saṁskāra-janya-jñāna, knowledge generated by past impressions.
saṁskāra-janya, generation by impression.
samudāya, combination.
samudāya-vāda, the theory according to which a thing is a complex of particulars like a heap of grains.
samudāyī, the conjunct elements.
saṁvid, universal consciousness.
saṁyoga, conjunction.
sañcita, stored up, consequences of an unseen nature.
sanmārga, right path, true path.
sannidhi, benign presence.
sannikarṣa, relation.
śarīra, body.
sārūpya, a state of liberation marked by an attainment of the likeness of God.
sarvam, all things.
sarva-saṁhāra-kartā, the universal Destroyer.
sarvātmaka, being everywhere.
śāstra-yoni, the source of the world of speech.
sat, Being, spirit, reality.
satkārya, the ever conserving pre-existent matter.
satkārya-vāda, doctrine of self-becoming, theory of the pre-existence of effect.
sat-khyāti, theory of knowledge according to which only what is real is known.
sattā-gata-tādātmya, co-inherence in universal existence.
sattva, quality of illumination.
sattvākārānugata-pratīti, perceptual knowledge of the identical and abiding.

savikalpaka-jñāna, determinate, differentiated knowledge.
savikalpaka-pratyakṣa, determinate perception.
saviśeṣa-brahman, qualified being.
śeṣa, that which serves, the remainder in relation to a principal.
śeṣa-śeṣi-bhāva, attitude of ontological dependence.
śeṣin, that which is served, the complementing principal in relation to the part.
siddhānta, final view.
siddhāntin, the one who holds the conclusive view.
siddhi, achievement, realisation, attainment.
Śiva, Divine Being, the auspicious, spirit, also the name of one of the functional aspects of God as agent and also first of the five śiva-tattvas which are 'evolutes' of Bindu.
śiva-bhakta, devotee of Śiva.
śiva-bhoga, transcendent enjoyment or experience of Śiva.
śiva-jñānin, the gnostic, the knower of Śiva.
śivānandānubhavecchā, the spontaneity toward an experience or enjoyment of the Bliss of Śiva, the will to unitive Experience.
śivānubhava, transcendent experience.
śiva-puṇya, acts of merit directed towards the Infinite.
śivasya vyāpārātmaka-śaktiḥ, exteriorisation or manifestation of the power of Śiva.
śiva-yoga, integration with Śiva.
śivo'ham asmi, I am Śiva.
so'ham, He is I.
spandana, vibration.
sparśatva, tactility.
sphūrti, intelligible.
śravaṇa, listening to the word.
Śrīkaṇṭha Rudra, the agent of intermediary world-dissolution, a mature soul, belonging to the class whose bonds are shaped at the time of ultimate world-dissolution.
sṛṣṭi, world creation.
sṛṣṭi-kartā, agent of world creation.
śruti, the Veda and the Āgama.
sthānin, the installed.
sthānin and sthāna, the grounded and the ground.
sthiti, conservation, creative function, world preserveration.

sthiti-kartā, agent of world preservation.
sthūla, manifest.
sthūla-cit, gross spirit.
sthūla-deha, corporeal body.
sthūla-laya, gross self-absorbtion.
sthūla-nāda, gross sound.
sthūlatara, the grossest.
śuḍdha, pure.
śuddha-adhvan, pure realm.
śuddha-avasthās, states of consciousness characterized by freedom from Impurity, pure state of spiritual realisation.
śuddha-bhoga, transcendent experience.
śuddha-kāla, transcendental time.
śuddha-vidyā, primarily the name of one of the functional aspects of the Agent and also the name of one of the five śiva-tattvas which are 'evolutes' of Bindu.
sukha, happiness.
sukha, duḥkha & *moha*, three modes of bhoga.
sukha-prabha, fore-taste of Bliss
sūkṣma, subtle, latent condition.
sūkṣma-laya, subtle self-absorbtion.
sūkṣma-nāda, Pure speech in relation to its externalised forms.
sūkṣma vāc or nāda, ultimate source of the denoting capacity of speech
śūnya, void, non-existent, unreal, nought.
Śunya-vāda, the Śunya-theorist.
suṣupti, state of serene sleep, sleep-state.
sūtra, aphorism.
svabhāva, natural, nature, persisting nature.
svabhāvavādin, naturalist.
svābhāvika, natural.
svābhāvikatva, naturalness.
svādhiṣṭheya-karaṇa, auxiliary dependent on a kartā.
svajātīyd, homogeneous nature.
svakṛta-karma, one's karma.
svalakṣanas, unique particulars.
svaniṣṭha, in itself.
svānubhūti, self-realisation.

svarūpa-jñapti, direct intuition.

svarūpa-lakṣanā, ultimate essence or nature, knowledge of essence, ultimate nature, uniqueness of the thing.

svarūpa-prakāśa, essential manifestness, self-illuminating, self-evident.

svarūpa-sambhandha, selfrelation.

svarūpa-sattva, Sui generis existence.

svarūpa-yogyatā, potentiality.

svataḥ grāhya, self apprehended.

svataḥ prāmāṇya-vāda, theory of 'self evidence'.

svatantrādhiṣṭhāna, Free Forms.

svātantrya, freedom.

svātantryeṇa grahaṇam, independent apprehension.

svatastva, self evidence.

śvetaketo tat tvam asi, O Śvetaketu ! that thou art.

tadabhāvavattvam, 'being not that'.

tadātmānaṁ svayam akuruta, ātman transformed itself into its own self.

tādātmya, identity, identical relation, evidence of identity, identity as between substance and attribute, identity relation Divine unity.

tatprakarakatva, whatness.

tadrūpa, perceiving a thing as what it really is.

tadubhayor-asaṁsargāgrahaḥ, non-apprehension of an absence of sense-relation between 'this' and 'what'.

tadvattvam, 'being that'.

tadvattvābhāvopasthiti, apprehension of the absence of relation.

taijasa, the luminous, a variety of ego-sense.

tajjanyaḥ tajjanyajanakaś ca vyāpāraḥ, the intermediate factor which a cause causes which in its turn contributes towards producing the effect is called vyāpāra.

tamas, the quality of inertia and denseness, of indetermination and antipathy, darkness, non-manifest.

tanmātras, subtle elements.

tāratamya, variation.

tarka, *reductio ad absurdum*.

tat, that, infinite.

taṭastha-lakṣana, general definition, 'general' knowledge, general feature.

tattva, fundamental principles of existence.

tattvātīta, transcending all principles of existence.

tirobhāva, concealment.
tirodhāna, initial phase of operation.
tirodhāna-śakti, concealing śakti.
tryasareṇu, the smallest visible particles.
trimūrti, trinity.
tryaṇuka, molecule.
tuccha, nought.
turīya, the fourth state beyond the wakeful, dream and sleep.
turīyātīta, transcendental state of the self, beyond even the fourth (turīya).
tvam, thou, immediate you (second person form).
udbodhaka, the cue.
ūna-naṭana, the cosmic dance : divine activity symbolizing the cosmic process.
upacāra, symbolic.
upādāna-kāraṇa, the material cause, first cause.
upādāna-kāraṇatva, material causality.
upādāna-upādeya-bhāva, material cause and effect relation.
upadeśa, inculcation, instruction.
upadeśa-śāstra, treatise of inculcation.
upadeṣṭā, revelatory.
upādhi, adjunct, condition.
upasecana, condiment or sauce.
utpatti, origin.
uttejaka, reactuating.
vācaka-jñāna, to know God verbally.
vahni-nirūpita, 'described' by fire.
vaikharī, overt speech form ; word used as the articulate symbol.
vairāgya, a disposition of intellect toward detachment.
vāṅmanotīta, beyond the sphere of word and meaning.
vāsanā-mala, lingering taints of Impurity.
varṇa, equating word, word part, gross form of (Pure) speech.
vastu, thing.
vibhu, infinite.
vigamana, termination.
vijātīya-bheda, reality of species belonging to different classes.

vijñāna-kaivalya, the state of liberation from the bonds of mala and karma achieved by means of knowledge.

vijñānākala, classes of selves in whose case material manifestors of knowledge are dissolved by knowledge.

vijñana-vāda, subjective sense.

vikāra, change, modification, alteration.

vikāsa, expansion or exteriorisation.

viparyaya, error.

virodha, opposite.

virodhādvaita, the opposite of monism.

viṣaya, the known content.

viśeṣana, attribute, qualification, determinant, determinant part, bare predicate.

viśeṣanābhāva, absence of the predicative element.

viśeṣana-jñāna, knowledge of the predicate.

viśeṣana-sannikarṣa, sense-relation to the 'what'.

viśeṣana-viśeṣya-yoga-sannikarṣa, sense-relation to the 'this-what'.

viśeṣya, 'that', cit-śakti per se, what is defined, the substance, determinate object.

viśeṣyatva, the substrate of predication.

viśiṣṭa, unity, qualified, the determinate whole, qua defined.

viśiṣṭa-advaita, rich unity, monism with qualification, non-duality of Being but with qualification.

viśiṣṭa-jñāna, determinate cognition, determinate perception.

viśiṣta-kārya, complex.

viśrānti, rest.

viśvādhika, transcendent.

viśvādhikatva, world-transcendence.

viśvākara, immanent.

viśva-kāraṇatva, world-causality.

visvāntaryāmitva, world-controllership.

viśva-rūpatva, world-form.

vivarta, illusory appearence.

vṛtti, modal change, change of state evolution or simple extension mode, understanding.

vṛtti-dharma, 'occurring in'.

vṛtti-jñāna, the connected factors of the mind, judgmental cognition

vyakti, actuality.

vyaṅgya, manifested.

vyañjaka, manifestor.

vyapadeśa, specific points of view.

vyāpaka and vyāpya, the depending and the depended.

vyāpaka, infinite, omnipresent will.

vyāpāra, intermediate function.

vyāpāravattva, possession of some active function through which the effect is produced.

vyāpti, universal relation concomitance.

vyāpti-viśiṣṭa-jñāna, knowledge qualified by pervasion of middle and the major.

vyāpya, 'determinate' content.

vyāpyatāvacchedaka, concomitanthood.

vyavasāya-jñāna, initial cognition.

yad, whom.

yadṛcchā, accidence or chance.

yaj, to worship.

yathārtha, truth.

yathārthānubhūtyuparūḍha-vṛtti, the mode of the intellect of the nature of valid experience.

yathārtha-smṛti, valid memory.

yena, whereby.

yoga, mystical union, integration.

yogyatā, compatibility or mutual fitness of words.

yogyatā-pramā, valid knowledge of compatibility.

yoni, birth place.

yukti, specutation, reason.

BIBLIOGRAPHY

A. Śaivāgamas and works relating to them (Published and unpublished manuscripts, in Grantha, Nāgarī, Kannaḍa and Telugu scripts) :

Kāmikāgamam : Pradiṣṭādyutsavānta (Kriyāpāda) Grantha ed., with Tamil Translation.
Sadyojyoti Śivācārya, 1916, 45 Paṭalas, 1330 ślokas.

Kāmikāgamam : Pūrva-bhāga (Kriyāpāda) Gr.* ed. with Tamil Tr. Alagappa Mudaliar, Madras. Four Sections : Āgamotpatti, Nityāṅga-Grahālaya-Vidhi, Ātmārtha-Parārtha-Pūjā, Pratiṣṭhā-vidhi.

Kāmikāgamam : Uttara-bhāga (Kriyāpāda). Gr. ed. Shanmuga SundaraMudaliar, 5001 Kali. Nine sections : Pūjā-vidhi, Utsavavidhi, Dīkṣā, Utasva-Pratiṣṭhā, Śrāddha, Prāyaścitta, Jīrṇoddhāraṇa Śānti and Dāna. 98 paṭala, 6477 ślokas.

Pūrva-Karaṇāgamam : First Part (Kriyāpāda). Gr. ed. Alagappa Mudaliar, Madras. Four sections, Karṣaṇa, Pratiṣṭhā, Utsava and Prāyaścitta. 147 paṭalas, 10,528 ślokas.

Suprabhedāgamam : (Kriyā, Caryā, Yoga and Jñāna Pādas). Gr. ed. Alagappa Mudaliar, Madras, 5030 Kali, Kriyāpāda, 56 paṭalas — Caryāpāda, 12 paṭalas—Yogapāda, 3 paṭalas and Jñānapāda, 3 paṭalas.

Kiraṇāgamam : Gr. ed. Devakottai, Śivāgama-Siddhānta-Paripālana, 1932 (Vidyāpāda, Kriyāpāda, Caryāpāda and Jñānapāda), 64 paṭalas, 1990 ślokas.

Kiraṇa-Tantram (Mss) : Darbar Library Catalogue, 11, pp. xxiv P. 99.

Vātula-Śuddhyākhyā : jñānapāda with vyākhyāna. Gr. Ed. Alagappa Mudaliar, Madras. 5013 Kali, 10 paṭalas and 782 ślokas.

Vātula-Tantram : with Vyākhyāna (Mss), Adyar Library Manuscript.

Vātulāgamam : with Vyākhyāna. Oriental Res. Inst., Mysore (contains more verses in the 10th paṭala in which Vīraśaiva doctrine is extolled.

---

*Gr. =Grantha

Ajita-āgama : Vol. 1 (1964), Vol. 2(1967), Institute Francais D'indologie, Pondicherry.

—— : Mss. Madras Oriental Manuscript Library.

Pārameśvara-Tantram : Mss. Darbar Library Catalogue 11, pp. xxi, p. 46.

Pārameśvara-Tantram : Kannaḍa script. 22 patalas, 2235 ślokas (Tantra Saṅgraha, Sankarappa Achappa Topigi, Mysore, 1914).

Jñāna-Siddhyāgamam : Mss. Mysore Manuscript Library, No. 3726.

Rauravāgama : Vol. I. Les Agama Civaites par Jean Filliozat (L'institut Francais D'indologie Pondichery, 1961).

Yamala-Tantram : Mss. Nepal Darbar Library copied in 1012 A. D. (Bagchi 'Studies in the Tantras', p. 7).

Niśvāsa-Tattva-Saṁhitā. Mss. Gupta script. Nepal Darbar Library (Bagchi, *op. cit.* p. 11).

Mataṅga-Pārameśvara-Āgamam : (Vidyāpāda) Nāgarī ed. 1924, Text only. Devakottai Śivāgama Saṅgha Paripālana, 26 paṭalas, 3500 slokas.

—— : With Bhaṭṭa Rāmakaṇṭha's Vṛtti (Mss.) Tiruvaṇṇāmalai Adīnam, Kunrakkuḍi. Also, Library Govt. Sanskrit College, Calcutta.

Mṛgendra-Āgamam : Vidyāpāda. Gr. ed. with Tamil notes. Alagappa Mudaliar, 13 paṭalas, 445 ślokas.

—— : Kriyāpāda et caryāpāda avecle commentarie de Bhaṭṭa Nārāyaṇakaṇṭha, ed Institut Francais D'indologie Pondicherry, 1962.

Mṛgendra-Tantram : Vidyāpāda and Yogapāda with Narāyaṇa-kaṇṭha's Tīkā (Nāgārī ed.), Kashmir series, Text and Studies, 1930.

—— : Vidyāpāda and Yogapāda (Nāgārī) with Nārāyaṇakaṇṭha's vṛtti and Aghora Śiva's Dīpikā. Devakottai Śivāgama Saṅgha Paripālana, 1928.

—— : Vidyāpāda, Text (Nāgarī) with Tamil Tr. in verse of Velliambalavana Tambiran, 6 paṭalas only, Dharmapura Adīnam, 1946.

—— : Vidyāpāda, Text (Nāgarī) with English Tr. and notes by Nārāyaṇaswāmi Iyer (11 paṭalas only), Siddhānta Dīpikā, Vols. IV, V & VI, 1904-06.

Pauṣkara-Āgamam : (Jñānapāda) with the Bhāṣya of Umāpati Śivācārya, Gr. ed. with Tamil introduction by Ambalavana Navalar, 8 paṭalas 972 ślokas, 1925.

—— : Gr. ed. with Tamil translation. Shanmuga Sundaıa Mudaliar, 4992 Kali, 8 Paṭalas, 977 ślokas.

—— : Jñānapāda (Mss.), Oriental Manuscript Library, Madras (with Jñānaprakāśar's Vṛtti).

Sarvajñānottarāgamam : Gr. ed. Text with Tamil rendering in verse. Notes by Muthaiya Pillai, 1923. 240 ślokas.

Devīkālottarāgamam : Gr. ed. with Tīkā by Kailāsa Pillai. (Jaffna).

—— : Tamil rendering in verse and notes. Muthaiya Pillai, 1923.

—— : Text only (Kannada script), 83 ślokas (Tantra-Saṅgraha, Sankarappa Acchappa Topigi, Mysore, 1914.

Śiva-Dharmottarāgamam : Tamil rendering in verse and notes by Maraijnana Desikar, 1938 ed.

Sakalāgama-Sāra-Saṅgrahaḥ : Gr. ed. Shanmuga Sundara Mudaliar, 1898, Madras.

Siddhānta-Sārāvalī : Gr. ed. with Tamil notes from Trilochana Sambu's Com.

—— : (Kannaḍa script). Text, 10 paṭalas, Devaśikhāmaṇi Rāmānujācārya (Kāśīnātha Grantha-mālā 7, Mysore).

Sūkṣma-Tantram : (Kannaḍa script) Text, 10 paṭalas, 807 ślokas (TantraSaṅgraha, Sankarappa Acchappa Topigi, Mysore, 1914).

Vātula-Śuddhyākhya-Tantram : (Kannaḍa script), 10 paṭalas, 664 ślokas (Tantra-saṅgraha, *op. cit.*).

Bhogarāga, *Tattva-Prakāśikā* with Aghora Śiva's Com. (Nāgarī) Devakottai Śaivāgama-Saṅgha-Paripālana, 1926).

——, with Śrīkumāra's Com. (Nāgarī), Travancore Sanskrit Series, 1921.

Sadyojyoti, *Tattva-Saṅgrahaḥ*, with Aghora Śiva's Com. Devakottai *op. cit.*, 1926.

——, *Tattva-Traya-Nirṇayam*, with Aghora Śiva's Com. Devakottai *op. cit.*, 1926.

Śrīkaṇṭhācārya, *Ratna-Trayam* with Aghora Śiva's Com. (Nāgarī) Devakottai *op. cit.*, 1926.

Sadyojyoti, *Bhoga-Kārikā*, with Aghora Śiva's Com.(Nāgarī), Devakottai *op. cit.*, 1926.

——, *Mokṣa-Kārikā*, with Bhaṭṭa Rāmakaṇṭha's Com. (Nāgarī), Devakottai *op. cit.*, 1926.

Bhaṭṭa Rāmakaṇṭha, *Nāda-Kārikā*, with Aghora Śiva's Com. (Nāgarī) Devakottai *op. cit.*, 1926.

Sadyojyoti, *Paramokṣa-Nirāsa-Kārikā*, with Bhaṭṭa Rāmakaṇṭha's Com. (Nāgarī), Devakottai, 1926.

——, *Nareśvara-Parīkṣā*, with Bhaṭṭa Rāmakaṇṭha's Com. (Kashmir Series Texts and Studies, 1921).

Aghora Śiva's Commentary on *Paśu-Pati-Pāśa-Prakaraṇa*, (Nāgarī) Mss. Mysore Manuscript Library.

Śivāgrayogin, Bhāṣya on *Śivajñāna-Bodham*, Gr. ed., 1920, Madras.

——, Laghu Tīkā on *Śivajñāna Bodham*, Kāśī, 1908, (Nāgarī).

Sadāśivācārya, Vyākhyā on *Śivajñāna Bodham*, Gr. ed. Azagappa Mudaliar, Madras. No date.

Jñāna Prakāśar, *Śiva jñāna bodha Vṛtti*, Gr. ed. Kailāsa Pillai, Jaffna 1927.

Śivāgra yogin, *Śaiva-Paribhāṣā* (Nāgarī), Oriental Res. Inst. Publication, Mysore, 1950.

Sri Sūrya Śiva, *Śaiva-Siddhānta-Paribhāṣā* (Nāgarī), Devakottai, 1928.

Umāpati Śviācārya, *Śataratna-Saṁgraha*, with Śataratnollekhinī of Umāpati. Avlon Tantric Texts, Vol. XXII, 1943.

Tiru jñāna Sambandam, *Śataratna Saṁgraha*, English tr. in *Śaiva Siddhānta*, Vols. 2-6, 1967-71.

Sarvātma Śambhu, *Siddhānta-Prakāśikā*, (Mss., Nāgarī). Tiruvaduturai Ādīnam.

——, Tamil translation with notes. Tiruvaduturai Ādīnam. 1949.

Jñāna-parkāśar, *Siddhānta-Śikhāmaṇi* (Gr. ed.) Jaffna. date not given.

——, *Śivayogaratnam* and *Śivayogasāram*, (Gr. ed.) date not given.

Somaśambhu, *Kriyākhaṇḍa-Kramāvalī*, (Gr. ed.) Devakottai, *op. cit.* 1934.

Aghora Śiva, Paddhati of Aghora Śiva called *Nirmalamaṇi* (Gr. ed.) Cidambaram, 1927.

Śaiva-Bhūṣaṇam, with Tamil notes, Devakottai, op. cit.

Śivāgrayogin, *Śaiva-Sanyāsa-Paddhati*, (Gr. ed.), 1921.

Appaya Dīkṣita, *Śivārcanā-Candrikā*, (Gr. ed.), Devakottai, op. cit.

Arunachalam, M, The Śaiva Paddhatis in *Śaiva Siddhānta*, Vol. 2, Nos. 3 & 4, 1967.

Ramana Sastrin, V. V., *The Psychology of Shaḍadvā*, Siddhānta Dīpikā, 1909.

——, *A Synopsis of the Lectures on the Śaivāgamas*, Siddhānta Dīpikā, 1909.

B. Vedas, Upaniṣads, Purāṇas, Brahma-Sūtra, etc.

The Hymns of the Ṛgveda ed. Max Muller, 2 vols London, 1877.

Śrī Rudra Bhāṣyam of Abhinava Śaṅkarācārya.

The Veda of the Black Yajus School (*Taittirīya Saṁhitā*) A, B. Keith, 2 vols., Harvard, 1914.

Atharva Veda Saṁhitā, Whitney and Lanman, Harvard, 1905.

Pañca Rudrīyam, Collection of sections on Rudra from the four Vedas with Tamil translation of Śivānanda Munivar, Madras, 1921.

Vēnkataramanyya, N, *Rudra-Śiva*, University of Madras, 1941.

Upaniṣads, Texts and Translations and notes, Advaita Āshrama Editions, Calcutta, 1955-67.

Radhakrishnan, S, *The Principal Upaniṣads*, London, 1953.

Anonymous (A Science Graduate) *A Study in Śvetāśvatara Upaniṣad*, Jaffna, 1949.

——, *Vedānta Moola Sāram* (Study of Nine Major Upaniṣads on Śaiva Siddhānta lines), Jaffna, 1949.

Śaivopaniṣads, Theosophical Publishing House Adyar, 1950.

Śaivopaniṣads, English Tr., Theosophical Publishing House, Adyar, 1953.

Śvetāśvatara Upaniṣad, Text in Gr., with Tamil and notes by Śrīnivāsa Dīkṣitar, Madras, 1902, (Upaniṣad Vidyā).

Atharvaśikhā Upaniṣad, Text in Gr., with Tamil tr. and notes by Śrīnivāsa Dīkṣitar, Madras, 1903 (Upaniṣad Vidyā).

Śiva Mahāpurāṇam, Kāśī Ed.

——, 4 vols., English Tr. by a Board of translators, Motilal Banarsidass, Delhi, 1972.

Vāyu Sangithai (Tamil), Verse tr. of *Vāyavīya Saṁhitā* by Ativiīrarāma Pāndiyan, Madras, 1901.

Skānda Mahāpurāṇam, Madras, 1892.

Upadeśakāṇḍam, Gr. Ed., Madras, 1909.

Sūta Saṁhitā with Tātparya Dīpikā of Mādhavācārya, Balamanorama Press, Madras, 1932.

Narayaṇaswāmi Iyer M, 'The Sūtasaṁhitā on the Śaivāgamas' *Siddhānta Dīpikā*, Vol. IV, 1901.

Kacchiyappa Śivachārya, *Kanda Purāṇam* (Tamil) Kasi-mutt, Tiruppanandal, 1968.

Sūtasangithai in Tamil verses, by Valloor Devarāja Pillai, 1900.

Śivarahasyam, Tamil tr. by Maruvur Ganesa Śāstrī, Madras.

Īśvara Gītā, P. E. Dumont, Baltimore and Paris, 1933.

Brahma Sūtra with Śrīkaṇṭha's Bhāṣya and Śivārkamaṇi Dīpikā of Appaya Dīkṣita, 2 vols., Nirnayasagar Press, 1908.

Brahma Sūtra Śivādvaita Śaiva Bhāṣyam Tamil tr. by Kāśivāsi Sendilnatha Iyer Tirumangalam, 1907.

Śrikaṇṭha Bhāṣya, Free English tr. by Mrs. Romā Chaudhuri, '*Doctrine of Śrikaṇṭha*', 2 vols., Calcutta, 1959.

——, English tr. Mahādeva Śāstrī *Siddhānta Dīpikā* vols. 1-7.

Brahma Sūtra Bhāṣyam in Gr. and Tamil summarising Śaṅkara, Rāmānuja and Madhva and Śrīkaṇṭha Bhāṣyas, Madras, Author anonymous.

Radhakrishnan, S, *The Brahma Sūtra*, The Philosophy of Spiritual Life, Allen and Unwin, London, 1960.

Suryanarayana Sastri S. S., *The Śivādvaita of Śrīkaṇṭha*, University of Madras, 1930.

——, *Śivādvaita Nirṇaya* of Appaya Dīkṣita, with text and tr., University of Madras, 1939.

Subramania Pillai, K, *Tirunanmarai Vilakkam in Sentamiẓ Selvi,* 1931.

Sambasadasivam Pillai V, *Tirunan-marai Vilakka araicchi,* Madras, 1932.

C. Śaiva Siddhānta Texts and Commentaries.

I. Canonical Literature (Tirumuṛai).

Sambandar *Tēvāram First Tirumuṛai,* with notes, Dharmapura Ādīnam, 1953.

—— *Second Tirumurai,* with notes, Dharmapura Ādīnam, 1954.

—— *Third Tirumuṛai,* with notes, Dharmapura Ādīnam, 1955.

Appar Tēvāram *Fourth Tirumuṛai,* with notes, Dharmapura Ādinam, 1957.

—— *Fifth Tirumuṛai,* with notes, Dharmapura Ādīnam, 1961.

—— *Sixth Tirumuṛai* with notes, Dharmapura Ādīnam, 1963.

Sundarar *Tēvāram Seventh Tirumuṛai* with notes, Dharmapura Ādīnam, 1964.

Durairangaswami, M. A., *The Religion and Philosophy of Tēvāram,* 2 vols, University of Madras, 1959.

Māṇikkavācagar *Tiruvācakam* and *Tirukkovai* (Eighth Tirumuṛai) with notes, Dharmapura Ādīnam, 1969.

—— The *Tiruvācakam,* text with tr. by G. U. Pope, Oxford, 1900.

—— The *Tiruvācakam,* N. Kantasami Pillai ed. with alternate readings, Annamalai University, 1964.

—— *Tirukkōvaiyār uṇmai,* vidwan Daṇḍapāṇi deśikar, Tiruvāduturai Ādīnam, 1965.

Maraimalai adigal, *Māṇikkavācakar varalāṛum kāla ārāicchiyum,* 2 vols., Kazakam, Madras, 1957.

Navaratnam, Ratna, *A New Approach to Tiruvācakam,* Annamalai University, 1951.

—— *Tiruvācakam, The Hindu Testament of Love,* Bharatiya Vidya Bhavan Bombay, 1963.

Schomerus, Hilko Wiardo, *Meister Eckehart und manikkavacagar,* Mystik auf deutschern und Indischem Boden, Verlag C, Bertelsmann, 1936.

Kellar, Carl A., L'Homme Interieur Chez Manikkavacagar, Poet et Mystique Tamoul, Asiatische Studien, 1970.

Sendanār and Others, *Tiruviśaippa* and *Tiruppallāṇḍu Ninth Tirumuṛai* with notes, Dharmapura Ādīnam, 1971.

Tirumūlar, *Tirumandiram, Tenth Tirumuṛai,* V. V. Ramana Sastrin's ed., Madras, 1909.

——, *Tirumandiram* with commentary by Ramanatha Pillai, P, Kāzakam, Madras, 1969, 2 vols.

Daṇḍapāṇi Deśikar S, *Introduction to Tirumandiram,* Tiruvaduturai Ādīnam, 1956.

Tirumandirak Kaṭṭuraikal, 6 vols., Tiruvāduturai, Ādīnam, 1960-1969.

Paṭṭiṇattār and Others, *Eleventh Tirumuṛai* Samājam, Madras, 1941.

Kāraikkal Ammaiyār *Arputat Tiruvantāti,* with notes by Tiru V. Ka., Madras, 1946.

—— *Arputat Tiruvantāti,* ed. Karavelane, Institut Francais d'indologie, Pondicherry, 1956.

Śekkizār, *Periyapurāṇam, Twelfth Tirumuṛai,* Nāvalar Ed. with valuable notes (Kolu), Madras, 1928.

Sekkizār, *Periyapurāṇam,* with commentary by C. K. Subrahmaṇia Mudaliār, Ten Vols., Madras, 1931-50.

Rājamāṇikkam, M. *Periyapurāṇa ārāycchi,* Madras, 1960.

Subrahmaṇia Mudaliār C. K., *Sekkiẓār* (Madras University Lectures) Madras, 1933.

Nallaswāmi Pillai, J. N., *Periyapurāṇam,* The Lives of Śaiva Saints, Madras, 1924.

Sendilnāda Iyer, Kāśivāsi, *Tevāram vedasāram,* 1911.

Senkalvarāya Pillai, V. S., *Tevāra Oḷineṛi,* (Glossary) 6 vols., Kazakam, Madras, 1950-66.

—— *Tiruvācak Oḷineṛi,* (Glossary) Kazakam, Madras, 1971.

Doraiswami Pillai, Avvai, *A History of Tamil Literature* (Śaiva Literature) in Tamil, Annamalai University, 1958.

Vellai Vāraṇar, K., *Panniru Tirumuṛai Varalāṛu*, (History of Śaiva Tirumuṛai), Vol. 1, Annamalai University, 1957.

—— *Panniru Tirumuṛai Varalāru*, (History of Śaiva Tirumuṛai), Vol. 2, Annamalai University, 1970.

Kingsbury F. and Philips, G. E., *Hymns of the Tamil Śaiva Saints*, Calcutta, 1921.

II. Doctrinal Literature (Śāttiram)

Vāgiśa Munivar, *Ñanāmirdam*, with old commentary, Ed. by Avvai Doraiswami Pillai, with notes. Annamalai University, 1954.

Uyyavanda Tēvar, Tiruviyalur, *Tiruvundiār* with old commentary, Samājam, 1940.

—— *Tiruvundiār* with modern commentary by K. Vajjiravelu Mudlaiar, Madras, 1969.

Uyyavanda Tēvar, Tirukkaḍavūr, *Tirukkalitruppadiār* with old commentary, Samājam, 1940.

Kulasabaratnam, *Tiruvundiār*, English tr., *Siddhānta Dīpikā*, Vol. iii. 1907.

Meykaṇḍār, *Śiva ñāna podam* with Citrurai of Śiva ñāna yogin, Samājaṃ, 1934.

—— *Śiva ñāna poda Māpāḍiam* of Śiva ñāna yogin, Kazakam, 1936.

—— *Śiva ñāna podam* with *Pāṇḍipperumāl vṛtti*, Tiruvāduturai Ādinam, 1961.

Nallaswāmi Pillai, J. N., *Śiva ñāna pōdam*, English tr., Dharmapura Ādīnam, 1949.

Hoisington, H. R., *Śiva jñāna potham*, English tr. *Journal of the American Oriental Society*, IV, 1853-54.

Sivapāda Sundaram S., *An outline of Śiva jñāna Bodham*, Jaffna, 1951.

Navamoney David Nadar, *Saint Meykaṇḍa Deva Nayanār's Sivajñāna Botham*, English tr. Tiruchirapalli, 1927.

Mathews, Gordon, *Siva-jñāna-Bodham*, A Manual of Śaiva Religious Doctrine, English tr. Oxford, 1948.

Sendilnāda Iyer Kāśivāsi, *Śiva ñāna boda vacanālaṁkāra Dīpam*, Madras, 1929.

Rangaswami Pillai, S., *Meykaṇḍār varalāṛu*, viruddacalam, 1958.

Aruḷnandi Śivāchārya, *Śiva ñāna siddhiār Supakkam,* with Śiva ñāna yogin's commentary, Samājam, 1940.

—— *Śiva ñāna siddhiār Supakkam,* with six commentaries, 4 vols., Madras, 1904.

Velliambalavāṇar, *Nānāvaraṇa viḷakka māpāḍiam,* Dharamapura Ādīnam, 2 vols., 1957.

Arunandi Śivāchārya, *Śiva ñāna siddhi Parapakkam,* with old commentary, Samājam, 1940.

Nallaswami Pillai, J. N., *Śiva ñāna siddhi supakkam and Parapakkam* English tr., Madras, 1927.

Śivarāman, K., *Śiva ñāna siddhi Supakkam,* English tr. with text, Kasimutt, Tiruppanandal, 1950.

Arunandi Śivāchārya, *Irupā Irupahdu* with old commentary Samājam, 1940.

Nallaswāmi Pillai, J. N., *Irupā Irupahdu,* with English tr., Dharmapura Ādīnam, 1950.

Manavācakam Kadantār, *Uṇmai Viḷakkam,* with modern commentary by K. Vajjira velu Mudaliār, Dharampura Ādīnam, 1954.

Nallaswāmi Pillai, J. N., *Uṇmai viḷakkam,* with English tr., Madras, 1929.

Umāpati Śivāchārya, *Śivappirakāśam,* with the commentary of Madurai Sivappirakasar, Samājam, 1940.

—— *Śivappirakāśam* with Cindanai Urai of Nallasiva Devar. Samājam, 1934.

Subramanya Pillai, K., *Śivappirakāśam,* with English tr., Dharmapura Ādīnam, 1949.

Hoisington, H. R., *Siva Pirakāśam* English tr., *Journal of the American Oriental Society,* IV, 1853-54.

Umāpati Śivāchārya, *Saṁkalpa Nirākaraṇam,* with old commentary, Samājam, 1940.

Murukeśa Mudaliar, N', *Saṁkalpa Nirākaraṇam,* English tr. Śaiva Siddhānta, Vols. 2-4, (1968-72).

Umāpati Śivāchārya, *Tiruvaruṭpayan* with the commentaries of Niramba azakia Desikar and Cinndanai Urai, Samājam, 1934 and 1940.

Nallaswāmi Pillai, J. N., *Tiruvaruṭpayan,* with English tr. Dharmapura Ādīnam, 1945.

Umāpati Śivāchārya, *Tiruvaruṭpayan,* with the commentary of S. Sivapādasundaram, jaffna, 1918.

Umāpati Śivāchārya, *Tiruvaruṭpayan,* with the commentary and textual revision by K. Vajjiravelu Mudaliar, jaffna, 1969.

Pope, G. U., *Tiruvaruṭpayan,* English tr. with notes in the Tiruvācakam, Oxford, 1900.

Umāpati Śivācharya, *Nenjuvidu Toodu,* with old commentary, Samājam, 1940.

——, *Pottrippahṛoḍai,* with old commentary, Samājam, 1940.

——, *Koḍikkavi, Vināveṇbā* and *Uṇmaineri Viḷakkam,* Samājam, 1940.

Nallaswāmi Pillai, J. N., *Siddhānta Trayam,* English tr. Dharmapura, Ādīnam, 1946.

Citrambala Nadikal, *Tukalaru pōdam,* with commentary Tiruvāduturai Ādīnam, 1952.

——, *Kalitturai,* and other works Tiruvāduturai Ādīnam, 1954.

Tattuvappirakāśar, *Tattuvappirakasam,* with commentary, ed. with notes by M. Arunachalam, Samājam, 1966.

Meenākṣisundaram Pillai, T. S., ed. *Śatamaṇikkovai,* Tiruvāduturai Ādīnam, 1949.

Paṇḍāra Śāttirangal, *Śivabhogasāram* and other works with modern commentary and English tr., Dharmapura Ādīnam, 1947.

Paṇḍāra Sāttiram, Tiruvāduturai Ādīnam, with Introduction by K. Subramanya Pillai, 1931.

Paṇḍāra Śāttiram, Daśakāryangal with commentary by Daṇḍapāṇi Deśikar, Tiruvāduturai Ādīnam, 1959.

Śivāgra yogin, *Śiva nerippirakāśam,* with old commentary Tiruvāduturai Ādīnam, 1969.

Tambyah, Isaac, *Psalms of a Śaiva Saint,* London, 1925.

D. Modern Works on Śaiva Siddhānta

Ramanathan, P., *The mystery of Godliness,* New York, 1895.

——, *The Culture of the Soul among western Nations,* Putnam's Sons, New York and London, 1906.

——, *The Spirit of the East* Contrasted with the spirit of the west, Brooklyn Institute of Art and Sciences, 1905-1906.

Schomerus, Hilko Wiardo, *Der Caiva Siddhānta,* Eine Mystik Indians Leipzig, 1912.

Nallaswāmi Pillai, J. N., *Studies in Śaiva Siddhānta,* Madras, 1910, reprinted Dharmapura, Ādīnam, 1962.

Paranjoti, V., *Śaiva Siddhānta,* Second and Revised Ed., Luzac, London, 1954.

Ponniah, V., *Śaiva Siddhānta Theory of Knowledge,* Annamalai University, 1952.

Piet, H. J., *A Logical Presentation of Śaiva Siddhānta Philosophy,* Madras, 1952.

Śivapāda Sundaram, S., *The Śaiva School of Hinduism,* Allen and Unwin, London, 1934.

Maraimalai Adigal, *The Śaiva Siddhānta as Philosophy of Practical Knowledge,* 1941, Reprinted Kazakam, Madras, 1966.

Kāntimatinātha Pillai, *The Cult of Śiva* or Lessons in Sivajñānabodham, Kazakam, Madras, 1961.

Dasgupta, S. N., *A History of Indian Philosophy*, Vol. 5, Cambridge, 1957.

Devasenapati, V. A., *Śaiva Siddhānta,* The University of Madras, 1958.

——, *Of Human Bondage and Divine Grace,* Annamalai University, 1963.

Arokiasamy, A. P., *The Doctrine of Grace in Śaiva Siddhānta,* Trichinopoly, 1935.

Dhavamony Mariasusai, *Love of God According to Śaiva Siddhānta*, Oxford, 1971.

Mahādevan, T. M. P., 'Religion and Philosophy of Śaivism' (*articles*) in *The History and Culture of the Indian People,* Bhāratīya Vidyā Bhavan, Bombay, 1960.

——, *The Idea of God in Śaiva Siddhānta,* Annamalai University, 1955.

——, '*Śaiva Siddhānta*' in Philosophy Eastern and Western, Allen and Unwin, London, 1952.

Sūryanārāyaṇa Śāstri, S. S., *Substance and Attribute in Śaiva Siddhānta,* reprinted in *Collected Papers of Professor S. S. Sūryanārāyaṇa Śāstri,* University of Madras, 1961.

——, *Śaivism and Tamil genuis,* reprinted *ibid.*

——, *The Philosophy of Śaivism,* reprinted. *ibid.*

——, *Truth in Śaiva Siddhānta,* reprinted *ibid.*

Bālasubramaṇiam, K. M., *Special Lectures on Śaiva Siddhānta,* Annamalai University, 1959,

Murugeśamudaliār, N., *The Relevence of Śaiva Siddhānta Philosophy*, Annamalai University, 1968.

Vajjiravelu Mudaliār, K., *Lectures on Śaiva Siddhānta,* Annamalai University, 1953.

Nārāyaṇa Iyer, C. V., *Origin and Early History of Śaivism in South India,* University of Madras, 1936.

Nīlakaṇṭha Śāstri, K. A., 'A Historical Introduction to Śaivism' (article) in *The Cultural Heritage of India,* Vol. IV, Calcutta, 1956.

Subramaṇia Pillai, K., *The Metaphysics of Śaiva Siddhānta System,* reprinted by Kazakam, Madras, 1958.

Jesudoss, D. I., 'The Concept of Āṇava in Śaiva Siddhānta', *Tamil Culture,* iii, 1954.

Śeshādri, K., 'Saiva Siddhānta as Religion and Philosophy', *Tamil Culture,* VIII, 1959.

INDEX OF ENGLISH WORDS

INDEX OF SONSKRIT WORDS